The Handbook of Global Corporate Treasury

Founded in 1807, John Wiley & Sons is the oldest independent publishing company in the United States. With offices in North America, Europe, Asia, and Australia, Wiley is globally committed to developing and marketing print and electronic products and services for our customers' professional and personal knowledge and understanding.

The Wiley Corporate F&A series provides information, tools, and insights to corporate professionals responsible for issues affecting the profitability of their company, from accounting and finance to internal controls and performance management.

The Handbook of Global Corporate Treasury

RAJIV RAJENDRA

WILEY

Published by John Wiley & Sons Singapore Pte. Ltd.
1 Fusionopolis Walk, #07–01, Solaris South Tower, Singapore 138628

Other Wiley Editorial Offices

John Wiley & Sons, 111 River Street, Hoboken, NJ 07030, USA
John Wiley & Sons, The Atrium, Southern Gate, Chichester, West Sussex, P019 8SQ, United Kingdom
John Wiley & Sons (Canada) Ltd., 5353 Dundas Street West, Suite 400, Toronto, Ontario, M9B 6HB, Canada
John Wiley & Sons Australia Ltd., 42 McDougall Street, Milton, Queensland 4064, Australia
Wiley-VCH, Boschstrasse 12, D-69469 Weinheim, Germany

ISBN 978-1-118-12283-9 (Cloth)
ISBN 978-1-118-12282-2 (ePDF)
ISBN 978-1-118-12281-5 (Mobi)
ISBN 978-1-118-12734-6 (ePub)

Typeset in 10/13 pt. Photina Regular by MPS Ltd., Chennai, India.
Printed and bound by CPI Group (UK) Ltd, Croydon, CR0 4YY.

C9781118122839_190324

To my parents,
Indrani and Kashinath Rajendra,
The best textbooks in the world:
No book can match the learning that you have provided us.

Contents

Foreword xiii

Preface xv

Acknowledgments xix

PART ONE: THE WORLD OF CORPORATE TREASURY 1

Chapter 1: Role of Treasury in a Global Corporation 3

Introducing Treasury Leadership 4
Organisation Structure and Responsibilities 6
Treasury Functions and Responsibilities 10
KPIs and Deliverables 15
A Day at the Office—What Does the Treasurer Do? 17
Summary 19

Chapter 2: Treasury Design 21

Key Elements of Treasury Design 22
Introducing Centralisation 24
Evolution of Treasury Models 25
Summary 36

Chapter 3: Treasury Culture 37

Qualities 38
General Skills 40
Technical and Work-Related Skills 41
The Many Hats of the Treasurer 43
Summary 44

Chapter 4: Importance of Operations and Control Efficiency 45

Tools 45
Different Offices: Front, Middle, and Back 48
Summary 54

PART TWO: TRANSACTIONS AND CASH MANAGEMENT 55

Chapter 5: Account Management and Structure 57

Putting an Account Structure in Place 58
Account Operation and Approaches 62
Rationalising Account Structures 65
Examples of Account Structures Across Sectors 68
Summary 69

Chapter 6: The Movement of Money 71

Money Transfer Mechanisms 71
Domestic Clearing and Settlement Systems 75
Cross-Border Payments and Collections 83
Summary 94

Chapter 7: Netting 95

Introduction and Concepts 95
Netting Implementation 101
Benefits and Caveats of a Good Netting Solution 106
Summary 107

Chapter 8: Liquidity Management Introduction and Float 109

Introducing Liquidity Management 109
Pooling as a Concept 111
Float and Its Causes 111
Summary 121

Chapter 9: Cash Pooling and Efficiency 123

Cash Concentration Structures 123
Pooling Structures 127
Implementation Aspects of Concentration Structures 130
Summary 134

Chapter 10: Cash Flow Forecasting 135

Forecasting in the Context of Liquidity Management 135
Forecasting Methods 139
Summary 143

PART THREE: BALANCE SHEET AND LIQUIDITY MANAGEMENT 145

Chapter 11: Liquidity and Working Capital 147

Working Capital in the Operating Cycle 148
Cash Conversion Cycle 149
Financial Supply Chain and Its Potential Pain Points 158
Summary 168

Chapter 12: Financial Strength and Linkages with Liquidity **169**
Importance of Company Financials 169
Key Financial Ratios 171
Summary 194

Chapter 13: Sources of Capital **195**
Capital Markets 195
Capital Structure 197
Factors in the Capital Decision 199
Debt Capital Markets 203
Equity Capital Markets 205
Summary 211

Chapter 14: Financing the Supply Chain **213**
Physical and Financial Supply Chains 213
Different Financing Solutions 215
Summary 225

Chapter 15: Managing Operating Cash and Investments **227**
Different Elements of Cash 227
Managing Operating Cash 228
Surplus Cash and Investments 230
Considerations and Aspects of Investment Decisions 230
Investment Process 237
Summary 237

Chapter 16: Credit Ratings and Bank Credit Assessment **239**
Credit Ratings 239
Credit Rating Methodology 243
Bank Credit Assessment Process 247
Important Focus Areas and Discussion Points with Banks During Credit Reviews 252
Summary 253

PART FOUR: MARKETS AND RISK MANAGEMENT **255**

Chapter 17: Art and Science of Risk Management **257**
Kinds of Risk 257
Classical Definitions 258
Why Manage Financial Risk? 266
Styles of Risk Management 269
Factors Impacting Risk 270
What Does Risk Management Do? 273
Objective of Risk Management 276
Summary 278

Chapter 18: Markets and Risk Aspects of Each Market **279**
World of Markets 279
Movement of Markets 287
Summary 289

Chapter 19: Risk Management in Practice: Ensuring the Right IMAGE© **291**
IMAGE© Methodology 291
Risk Identification 292
Risk Measurement 293
Risk Accounting and Reporting 314
Risk Governance 315
Risk Management Evaluation 320
Summary 321

Chapter 20: Products for Managing Risk **323**
Forwards Family 324
Options Family 333
Swaps Family 346
Credit Family 351
Summary 353

Chapter 21: Combining the Products to Manage Risk: Risk Governance **355**
Devising Risk Strategy Using Products 356
Using Products to Manage Risk 358
Credit Risk 362
Liquidity Risk: Balance Sheet and Asset-Liability Management 363
Use of Analysis 364
Operations and Technology Risk 367
Legal and Compliance Risk 367
Summary 374

Chapter 22: Risk Management Governance Strategies **375**
Key Elements of the Governance Strategy 375
Sample Strategy A 377
Sample Strategy B 378
Sample Strategy C 381
Summary 386

Chapter 23: Operational Aspects: Documentation and Execution **387**
Documentation 387
ISDA Framework of Documents 388
Execution 392
Summary 394

PART FIVE: THE TOOLKIT 395

Chapter 24: Treasury Policy 397

Framework 397
Aspects of Policy Implementation That Need Closer Scrutiny 398
Review 399
Implementational Aspects 400
Summary 401

Chapter 25: Treasury Systems 403

Treasury Management System Background 403
Some System-Related Questions 410
TMS Establishment Process 411
Developments and Standards 417
Summary 423

Chapter 26: Centralisation 425

Rationale for Centralisation 425
Basic Model Design 427
Post-Model Design Stage 429
Barriers to Centralisation 429
Summary 430

Chapter 27: Key Performance Metrics for a Treasury 431

Introducing Performance Metrics 431
Some Criteria for Deciding Performance Metrics 432
Performance Metrics 434
Some Caveats on Metrics and Evaluation 437
Sample Treasury Performance Metrics 438
Treasury Fitness 441
Summary 441

Chapter 28: Banks and Service Relationships 443

Sample Bank Organisation Structure 443
Banking Services and Products for a Corporate Treasury 446
Bank Selection and RFP Process 449
Review Process 449
Service and Relationship Management 454
Summary 456

Chapter 29: Operations and Control Checklist 457

List of Processes 457
Right Control at Treasury 458
Control Checks and Reviews 459
Some Common Causes for Error and Control Lapses 461
Summary 468

Chapter 30: Outsourcing **469**
Selection Stage 469
Pre-Implementation 471
Implementation 471
Post-Implementation 473
Summary 478

Chapter 31: Building and Sustaining a Treasury Culture **479**
Evaluation 484
Summary 485

Chapter 32: Managing Treasury in Uncertain Times **487**
Uncertainty and Its Impact on Treasury Management 487
Triggers and Events 490
Simple Method to Manage Treasury During Times of Uncertainty 491
Summary 493

Glossary **495**

Further Reading **505**

About the Author **507**

About the Website **509**

Index **511**

Foreword

OVER THE PAST SEVERAL decades, globalisation has had a profound impact on business and in the scope of responsibility for corporate Treasury departments. While treasurers have long been responsible for managing cash—which now reaches into the trillions of dollars for corporate cash balances—Treasurers are now being drawn further into the strategic framework of organisations, and this framework is increasingly global.

As companies reevaluate how they manage their internal resources and external business relationships around the world for maximum efficiency, excellence within their Treasury department is critical for success. Treasury evaluates when and how a company invests its assets. Treasury is the department responsible for ensuring that a company has enough cash on hand to fund its very operations. From liquidity management to risk management, Treasury now sits at the intersection of many critical decisions.

Repeatedly, we have seen that successful companies are the ones with the most knowledgeable and well-trained Treasury departments. It is our belief that ongoing education and training in the evolving discipline of global Treasury management can help corporate Treasury practitioners lead their companies to better business decisions. *The Handbook of Global Corporate Treasury* represents an important commitment by Rajiv Rajendra to advance the conceptual knowledge of the profession, bolstered by the type of real-world examples and casework that will help readers apply this knowledge within their functional roles almost immediately. We support global Treasury professionals around the world in meeting their business challenges ahead.

Jim Kaitz
President and CEO, Association
for Financial Professionals (AFP)

Preface

IN THE CONTEXT OF TODAY'S business world and volatile markets, be it the efficient management of money, managing the financial risks for the firm, or raising and running capital and the balance sheet, the treasurer's function has become a critical cog in the wheel of an enterprise's smooth functioning.

This book is a ready reference for anyone interested in the nuances and practicalities of the large world of corporate Treasury. It is designed to be a bottom-up building block for readers interested in knowing more about corporate Treasury, very similar to the training programmes that we at Aktrea run for our clients, across basic, intermediate, and advanced levels. In the book, I cover cases from our existing case database and also pick up experiences from corporate and banking experts touching on challenges and solutions across the world.

To borrow a soccer term, the concept of *total football*, where every player is expected to take on the roles of defender, midfielder, or forward when required, is applicable to most global treasurers. The reality for corporate treasurers is that they are expected to be all-rounders, and for employees in Treasury, their functional knowledge across all aspects of Treasury increases their mobility within, and outside, the firm. In short, treasurers cannot afford to have one technical strong point. They are expected to have multiple strengths, given the demands of their role.

In this context, a book that covers the entire corporate Treasury space should be a welcome offering for its target market, where readers can pick off one book, an all-rounder, covering all themes relevant and applicable for managing a successful and efficient corporate Treasury.

For CEOs, CFOs, and treasurers looking to re-align their treasuries with the growth of the global firm, bankers who seek to increase their dialogue and value created for their corporate clients, Treasury and finance employees and students requiring a more holistic perspective on the corporate Treasury function in the context of their roles, or aspirants into corporate Treasury, this book provides an easy-to-read, simple-to-assimilate approach to this exciting and increasingly complex world.

The Toolkit provided also gives practitioners an available reference point that they can adapt immediately for use in their firms, thereby also providing a low-cost, high-efficiency advisory solution hitherto not easily available.

FOR WHOM IS THIS BOOK INTENDED?

Managing or working in a successful corporate Treasury assumes a basic learning, awareness, and understanding of key aspects and themes and then the ability to put these to practice where required.

This management starts with developing a deeper understanding of various aspects:

- The transactional element of the cash and liquidity of the group
- The balance sheet and sources of capital and liquidity of the group
- The various financial risks for the group

It also involves implementing and driving key firm and group elements, such as policy, systems, and structure and managing people.

The Handbook of Global Corporate Treasury, in its current version, aims to logically construct, using a unique bottom-up approach, the building blocks for learning and follows this through with a Toolkit that practitioners can pick up and customize for their own corporate use.

The book is intended as much as a medium for learning as it is for a useful starting point to create a robust Treasury model. I use my experience of having advised and trained corporates across countries, especially multinational firms, to generate a single and powerful point of reference that is as informative as it is educational.

Through this book, I am hoping to provide:

- A reliable and available knowledge base for CEOs, CFOs, and treasurers of firms that are looking to redesign or reengineer their Treasury and funding activities
- A practical go-to source for treasurers and CFOs of companies that are increasing their footprint across countries or becoming more global
- A ready-made perspective on their roles within a larger framework for employees within corporate Treasury and for other employees who interface with or handoff to Treasury
- A reference for bankers covering corporate treasuries to engage in more meaningful conversations with CFOs and treasurers as well as look for opportunities to add value for their clients
- A guide to the world of Treasury for those who aspire to corporate Treasury roles
- An introduction to the world of corporate Treasury for postgraduate students who are exploring career alternatives or doing course work in institutions-related themes
- Quick education material for service providers including consultants, auditors, lawyers, system vendors, processing agents, and others who interface with or are about to commence services for the Treasury of a company

FEATURES OF THE BOOK

The flow of this book has been created to ensure maximum readability and to facilitate quicker grasp of concepts and practical aspects. Throughout the book, illustrations, boxes, snippets, and diagrams help to articulate concepts and thought processes for a stronger understanding. Cases, examples, and experiences from a diverse set of experts with deep and varied experiences helps to provide different perspectives to round up the learning. For readers interested in numbers and the number aspect, many examples have been provided.

The Toolkit from the Website provides ready-to-use templates that the readers can customize, adapt, enhance, and use for their operations. The tools provided are generic; care must be taken to review applicability and add elements that the reader's firm or clients will need to suit their own specific company and regulatory and other environments.

We are also in the process of bringing a mobile app for the *Handbook*—the app is expected to have multiple new features and be an interactive tool for the buyers of the book and the author.

Support will be available to a degree on the Website and the planned app for further explanations and examples. The blog at the Website is also expected to be a useful source of market updates and regular features from contributors and readers.

Updates to the *Handbook*, as relevant, in between versions, will be available from time to time on the Website—so do please check www.wiley.com/go/treasury handbook for the same.

HOW THE BOOK IS STRUCTURED

The structure of the book is similar to how we run our rigorous but fun training programmes and courses at Aktrea: First I introduce concepts, the basic building blocks, across each of the themes: cash, liquidity, financial supply chain, working capital, trade, balance sheet, funding, markets and risk. I then cover key tools that readers can adapt to their organizations and contexts.

My aim for the book is that it serves not only as a learning tool but also becomes, for practitioners, an advisory manual as they work on improving their treasuries. This goal is in line with our consulting/advisory work.

Our collective learning has been embedded into this book. The material on which this book is based comes from years of working with treasuries across the world for multinational companies, developing and advising on products and solutions, as well as training employees of these firms and the bankers who service them.

All the themes are relevant and form a bulk of discussions that we at Aktrea have with CEOs, CFOs, and treasurers of firms around the world.

HOW CAN YOU READ THIS BOOK?

This book can be read in many ways. The first, and most obvious, one is to pick up the book and go step by step, chapter by chapter, operationally and organically. The book uses a spiral method of teaching, where elements are referred to initially in context, explained further, and inserted into the wider context of Treasury operations.

You also can start with any area of the book and work through it—each section and each module stands alone in its concept of explanation, building fundamentals, and practical casework. References are made to other sections and chapters for continuity and context, and readers can refer to these areas immediately for a complete contextual understanding of each module.

MAY THE BOOK BEGIN

Writing a book in the field of one's work is an honour. Putting into words one's learning and experiences augmented by experts' views in their own words, with the objective of sharing and letting others benefit from one's knowledge (or the lack of it!), is the privilege that few attain in their lifetime.

And so it is with me. With these words, dear reader, I hand you over to the book, for it shares with you its contents and takes you on your path to more knowledge.

It has been my most sincere effort to be factually, conceptually, and philosophically accurate in my rendition of experience and fundamentals. In case there are any errors or aspects that you might disagree with, I offer my humble apologies.

I would love to hear your feedback and keep improving this text over the years. One of the most critical components to do that would be to get your input, perspectives, and comments on what you liked and where you think this book can be improved. I have embarked on this journey, and I know now that I am not alone, for you, dear reader, have joined me in it. I need your support to continue, and continue well. Thanks in advance for your feedback and comments.

May the light and happiness of knowledge shine upon you.

Rajiv Rajendra
Singapore
October 2012

Acknowledgments

THIS BOOK IS ONE of the milestones of my journey. Many people have helped shape my learning, thought process and experiences along the way. To all of them, my thanks and deepest gratitude. They include:

- My parents, who were so excited that I was writing a textbook that they encouraged, pushed, and stayed awake into the wee hours of the morning as I worked through the manuscript.
- My wife, Suman, who patiently bore my long absences with cheer, enthusiasm, and encouragement.
- Our first born Tara, who emerged into the world during the copyediting, lighting up the house in general.
- My friend Gourang Shah, one of the finest brains to have graced the financial sector and a gem of a human being. As he transitioned from being a client to a colleague to dear friend and go-to guy, Gourang's clear thinking, solution orientation, and broad vision have greatly helped my own thinking and learning. Indeed, I'm not sure if I would have written this book without his expertise and moral support.
- My colleagues at my former employer, Citi, who provided the excitement and bonding in our common journeys. They included bosses, mentors, team members, and colleagues around the world: V. Srikanth, Sim Lim, Tushar Gundecha, B. V. Krishnan, Vikram Sud, Amol Gupte, Kumar Ramachandran, Umang Moondra, Anand Chopra, Rahul Singh, Akshaya Bhargava, John Gilson, Okan Pekin, Petr Roegner, Fahmi Sami, V. H. Suresh, Puneet Singhvi, H. N. Patil, V. Sankaran, N. A. Dorai, Sankara Subramoni, N. Mahalakshmi, S. Narayanan, and the team at the old branch in Chennai, Adam Gilmour, Rodrigo Zorilla, Paco Ybarra, Nadir Mahmud, Vipul Chandra, Manish Bhai, Malay Ghatak, Saneth Gamage, Jackque Diasz, Nirupan Wijeyanathan, Kapila Jayawardene, Thivanka Atukorala, Ravin Basnayake, Pushkaraj Gumaste, Priya Taori, David Rosa, Sanjay Nayar, Dennis Hussey, Ravikumar Balasubramaniam, Ananth Doraswamy, Vijayan Subramani, and others.
- My professors at my alma mater, XLRI: Dr H. K. Pradhan, Dr Madhukar Shukla, Dr Sharad Sarin, Dr R. K. Premarajan, and Dr T.A.S. Vijayaraghavan.

- Associates who have helped shape Aktrea to what it is today: Dr Dayanath Jayasuriya, Arvind Mathur, Charana Jayasuriya, Avancka Herath, Dr G. Balasubramanian (IFMR Chennai), and Mukund Santhanam.
- Many denizens of the corporate world. For want of space I must restrict the list: Suresh Senapaty, Lan Lakshminarayana and R. Sivakumar (Wipro), V. Balakrishnan (Infosys), and Piyush Gupta (DBS).
- My fantastic contributors—a big thank you for your perspectives and inputs to make this book more meaningful: Gourang Shah (Citi), Dr Hong Zhang and Anne Yang (INSEAD), Dr Jeevan Perera (NASA), Damian Glenndinning (Lenovo), Dean Sharrar and Derek Phillip (Bancorp), Mick Lopez (Aricent), Kelvin Hayes (SGS), Suresh Senapaty and Shankar Jagannathan (Wipro), Rakesh Dhamani (Times Group), and Carlo Palmers and David Dobbing (SWIFT).
- Jim Kaitz of the Association of Finance Professionals for very kindly agreeing to write a foreword for the book, and Steven M. Bragg, Sim S. Lim, V. Srikanth, and Yasantha Dissanayake for their readings and endorsements. It means a lot to me, and thank you.
- My adorable and incredibly patient and sweet publisher Nick Melchior, for all the support and ease with which he took everything end to end. Nick, it's been an absolute pleasure to work with you.
- The other support personnel at John Wiley & Sons: Gemma Rosey for sifting through the technological basis of formatting and providing amazing team spirit, Jules Yap for coordination, and Stefan Skeen for his responsiveness, patience, and value-add through the process (which included bravely risk-managing Hurricane Sandy).
- Thomson Reuters for assistance in providing, for research and data in the book, access to Thomson Reuters Eikon for Corporate Treasury, a popular tool with market information, news, analytics, and trading capabilities for corporates. Special thanks to Prabodh Shetty, Fiona Shaw, and Oliver Otto from Thomson Reuters.
- Our tech-man, P. Manikandan, for his work on the app and topping up the site.
- My assistant Mukesh Sharma, who assisted with all the formatting and sometimes research, keeping the administrative and Website hearth burning while I was working on the book.

The Handbook of Global Corporate Treasury

PART ONE

The World of Corporate Treasury

THE TREASURY OF A CORPORATION is often called its lifeblood, and with good reason. Treasury is responsible for the money of the organisation and its flow, reaching funds where and when it is needed, in the right form.

The term *treasury* has been used for centuries, with the first noted use of the word from the term *tresorie*, which means "room for treasure." Those treasures have since been replaced with money and assets that companies own and use to generate value for stakeholders—shareholders, customers, employees, and partners.

Money and assets exist in different forms, and move around, sometimes exceedingly quickly and sometimes very slowly. In an increasingly global and connected world, the Treasurer, who has direct responsibility for the Treasury, is faced with the numerous challenges of handling the funds, assets, liabilities, and cash flows of the firm across locations, each of which has different regulatory and market environments, optimising the use of these resources and ensuring availability to support the business.

Over time, with increasing complexity in business environments, the Treasurer's role has increased, with chief financial officers (CFOs) also taking on additional responsibility for the function. With complexity, however, comes the need to simplify the support and financial structure to ensure that the firm's functioning is smooth and the environment to encourage business growth is built.

This book aims to do precisely that: decipher the complexity of the treasury world and today's environment, and simplify them for practitioners, so that they have a strong foundation of key treasury activities and functions.

Treasurers are the core of a company's management, and on the way toward achieving business leadership, the firm needs to ensure that it has achieved treasury leadership, which will pave the way and set the stage for financial outperformance. The treasuries of all of the world's leading organisations are cases in point—each one of them has built, achieved, and maintained treasury leadership.

Part One of this book answers some of the questions associated with treasury functions and responsibilities:

- What does a treasury look like—what do the employees in a treasury function do?
- What do a chief executive officer and a CFO expect of their Treasurer?
- What does a Treasurer consider his or her primary responsibility?
- What does a typical day in the treasury department of a global firm look like?
- What is treasury culture?
- What are the core attributes of a good treasury design?
- Why are operations, processes, and control so critical to a firm's work?

We begin by looking at treasury in an organisational context.

CHAPTER ONE

Role of Treasury in a Global Corporation

AS BUSINESSES GROW AND BECOME more complex and competitive, and markets become closer and more interrelated, the dimensions that need the attention of a transnational corporation's board and management increase dramatically.

While the core business and operations themselves require direct attention, the money that needs to flow through the veins and arteries of the organisation as well as its various dimensions require detailed expertise and focus, a team that understands the working of money and markets, from both a tactical and a strategic standpoint.

That is where the Treasury team puts up its hand to support the chief executive officer (CEO), chief financial officer (CFO), the board, and the business units in ensuring that the business side of the company works unhindered, by setting a broad monetary platform for businesses to grow and outperform.

INTRODUCING TREASURY LEADERSHIP

We first introduce the concept of Treasury Leadership, wherein Treasury positively influences the performance of the firm and drives the organisation toward industry and segment leadership. Treasury Leadership creates an environment that fosters excellence of capital building, execution, and support across all aspects of Treasury and works with the business to produce outperformance.

Treasury Leadership is hence translated into being a path-breaking and cutting-edge Treasury comprised of:

- Best practices in Treasury management
- Most efficient turnaround times
- Highest degree of control
- Most motivated and skilled employees with a great work–life balance
- Zero defects or errors on processing
- Optimum cash and liquidity
- Highest visibility of firm-wide cash flows
- Ability of the business to set newer standards for industry performance
- Firm's outperformance over competition through well-managed Treasury processes, funding, and risk management
- Most stable and environment-proof risk management
- Great partnership with other group functions to increase firm value
- Treasury seen as an attractive function to work in

The three components of Treasury Leadership (depicted in Figure 1.1) are:

1. **Treasury Design.** Creating the right processes, structures, and approaches at the right place with the right infrastructure and the right people
2. **Treasury Culture.** Enabling an atmosphere of knowledge and positive teamwork to ensure highest work and motivational standards

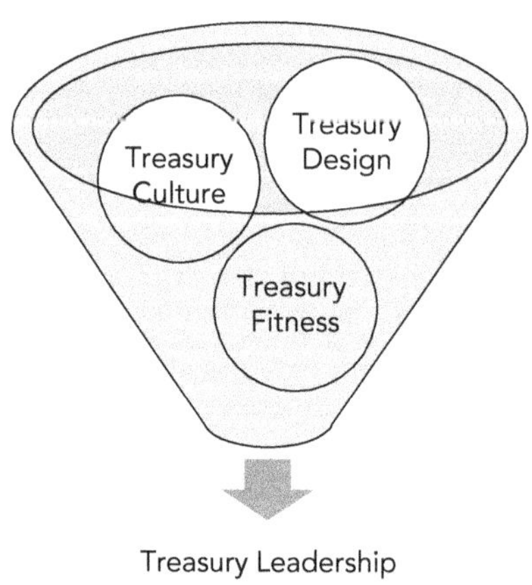

FIGURE 1.1 Components of Treasury Leadership

3. **Treasury Fitness.** Assessing the functioning of the Treasury, similar to a fitness test for the human body, to identify potential pain points and to prevent any significant potential breakdown

We cover the concept of Treasury Design and Treasury Culture in Part One and introduce Treasury Fitness in the online content.

The world of Treasury deals with the flow of money—the flow of money through the balance sheet, from sources of capital to its financial uses. The idea that Treasury will be the storehouse of money or capital for the firm is extended here: Treasury flows work in tandem with the business of the firm, through the supply chain. Suppliers provide raw materials that are held as inventory, converted to finished products through the manufacturing and production process, and finally sold and delivered to the customer. The flow of money is in the opposite direction to the flow of goods or services, and forms the basis of the financial supply chain flows, or commercial flows, of the organisation. Money due to the supplier becomes an accounts payable, which finally gets paid out. Money owed to the firm by the customer becomes an accounts receivable, until it gets realised and money is paid into the firm's account. Many of these terms will be further elucidated in later chapters.

The funding and movement of money associated with these commercial flows is done through Treasury. Figure 1.2 shows the essence of Treasury flows and their linkages with those of the financial supply chain.

The entire process requires capital in order to run. Until the customer pays the firm, the inventory, operations and supplies need to be funded. Proceeds from sales received across locations need to collected and deposited, so that payments can be

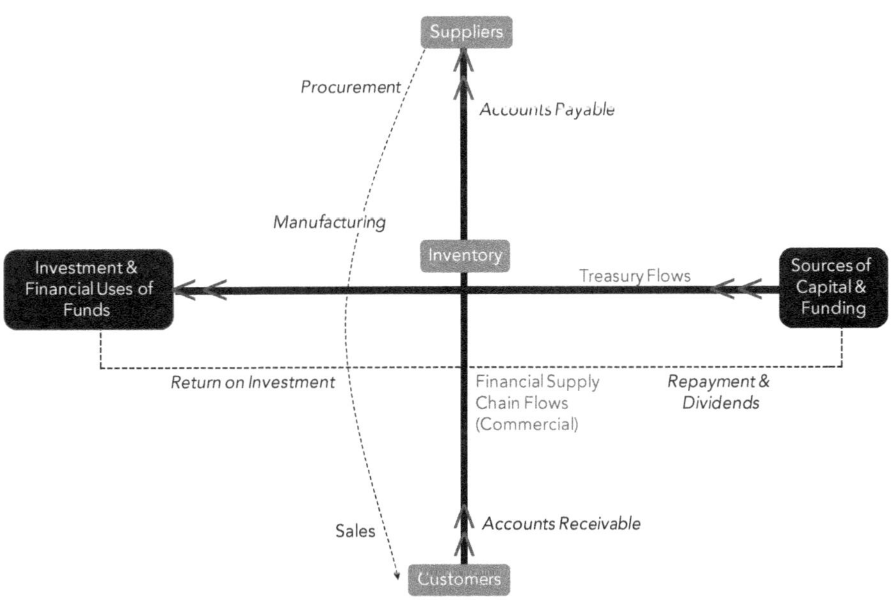

FIGURE 1.2 Treasury and Financial Supply Chain Flows: A Context

made from those or other locations for purposes of running the business. Accounts need to be maintained in these locations, perhaps in different currencies, and these accounts need to be managed. Trade transactions need to be funded, and documents must be prepared and used. The entire aspect needs to be planned and executed, and this forms the basis of one of treasury's key roles, which is to handle transactions as part of cash management, managing the cash and funds of the organisation.

It is preferable to use the firm's own money to make these payments, and hence the monies need to be moved efficiently from one location to another, making them available where they are needed. Where it is not possible to use the firm's own cash, alternative arrangements need to be made—for example, borrowing from a local bank. Even if access to these funds becomes difficult, the firm still has to keep running—ensuring that there is money available when required ensures liquidity for the firm. Excess cash needs to be invested securely to generate return for the firm until such time that the cash is needed. Long-term projects require capital—this needs to be arranged at the least possible cost and putting least pressure on the firm's cash flows. The organisation needs to be creditworthy, and the financials of the firm have to be aligned to ensure that the performance is consistent with or better than expectations in order to sustain and improve the creditworthiness of the firm and hence its ability to generate liquidity and lower its cost of funding. This calls for managing the balance sheet efficiently, and with the right structure. This entire set of activities, the second of treasury's key roles, covers managing the balance sheet and the firm's liquidity (which is another aspect of cash management).

As the firm moves across borders, sells or buys from another country, or exposes itself to other counterparties and undertakes financial transactions, it exposes itself to risk or uncertainty that the business and financial objectives will not be met because of a change in some factors—perhaps market movements, defaults of trade partners or banks, or internal errors. The management of these risks forms the third of treasury's primary roles.

How do the Treasurer and his or her team at Treasury achieve these goals? What do they have to do to make sure that their job is done and the support provided to the firm and to business and other functions is robust? How do they fit into the global context of the organisation?

We answer some of these questions in the book.

ORGANISATION STRUCTURE AND RESPONSIBILITIES

Prior to describing the treasurer's fit in the organisation, it would be useful to refresh our understanding of a common multinational organisation and its structure. Figure 1.3 provides a snapshot of the roles in typical in-country operations and the linkages with cash and goods/services flows. This is also explained in detail in the section on the financial supply chain in Chapter 14.

In the country or subsidiary operations, the procurement team would place the order and obtain the goods from the supplier. Credit terms, primarily credit period

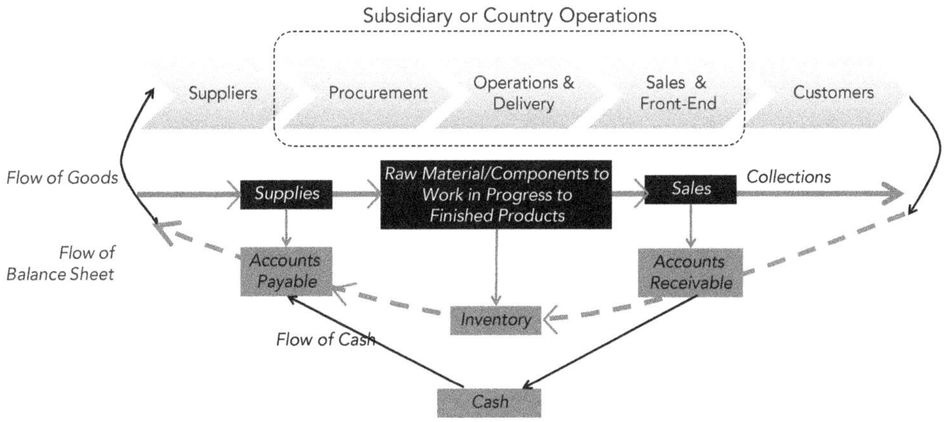

FIGURE 1.3 Roles and Organisational Flows

extended by the supplier at the agreed price, or a discounted price if the payment is made earlier, are agreed. On the balance sheet, if the payment is to be made later, a payable is booked. The raw material and components are then warehoused, and the production process creates the final product that is sold by the sales and front-end team to the customer, based on certain credit terms. If the payment is not being made immediately by the customer, a receivable is booked in the accounts. The payment is made to the supplier on or before the due date, removing the payable from the books. The collections team is responsible for obtaining the payment, which, when received in cash into the account, liquidates the receivable on the balance sheet. The cash received from the customers is used to pay the suppliers, pay off any loans taken, or procure fresh supplies.

Figure 1.4 presents a simple Treasury and control structure in a firm.

The Treasurer, along with the financial controller, typically reports to the chief financial officer or finance director. The controller looks after the accounts payable and receivable, managing collections and disbursements and focusing on the accounting and balance sheet aspects of the cash management. The responsibility of managing the days sales outstanding (DSO) and days payables outstanding (DPO) usually rests with the controller. The country and subsidiary operations continue to manage the procurement, sales, and collections processes at their end. The Treasurer then becomes responsible for the liquidity aspects of cash management, working with banks and other parties to provide funding, managing the balance sheet and financials, and managing risk. Increasingly, the Treasurer in many firms is playing a consultative role in the management of the accounts payable (AP) and accounts receivable (AR), monitoring the DSO and DPO (since they form a core part of the firm's financial ratios and assessment), and providing inputs to various entities on the credit and financial impact of their decision making. The last section of this chapter provides a window to a day in the life of a Treasurer, while Chapter 3 sheds more light on each of treasury's key themes and how they all fit in together.

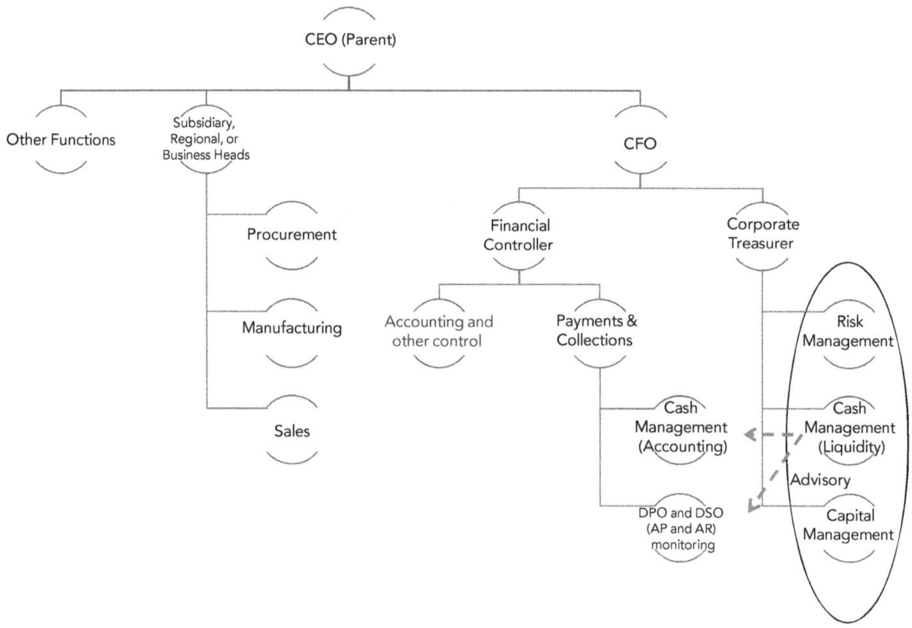

FIGURE 1.4 Treasurer in the Organisational Context

The role requires the Treasurer to have varied skills and an approach that fosters teamwork with a solution-centric approach. The concept of a Treasury Culture is elucidated in Chapter 3.

The Treasurer and the Treasury team have to interface with, on a regular basis, entities from outside as well as in-company functions. Figure 1.5 illustrates some of these contact points for a corporate Treasury.

Some of the external interfaces of the Treasury team are:

- **Regulators**. The regulatory aspect of capital and fund flow, apart from market operations, makes Treasury a critical contact point for regulators. Compliance with local regulations and law is paramount. Areas for which Treasury is directly responsible—the movement of money and the participation in local markets for various reasons, such as investment, risk management, foreign currency requirements, trade flows, collections and payments—are areas where such regulations and laws could be contravened, because of process lapses, operational error, fraud, or other reasons. Hence, central banks, securities and exchange commissions and regulators, registrars of companies, and ministries in relevant departments are some of the important regulators with whom an interface is required.
- **Exchanges**. If the entity is listed on the exchange, the Treasurer, as the key interface for execution of capital, would be in contact for compliance and reporting purposes
- **Banks**. The Treasurer is usually the key contact point for banking relationships for both the bank and the company. The Treasury puts together the various

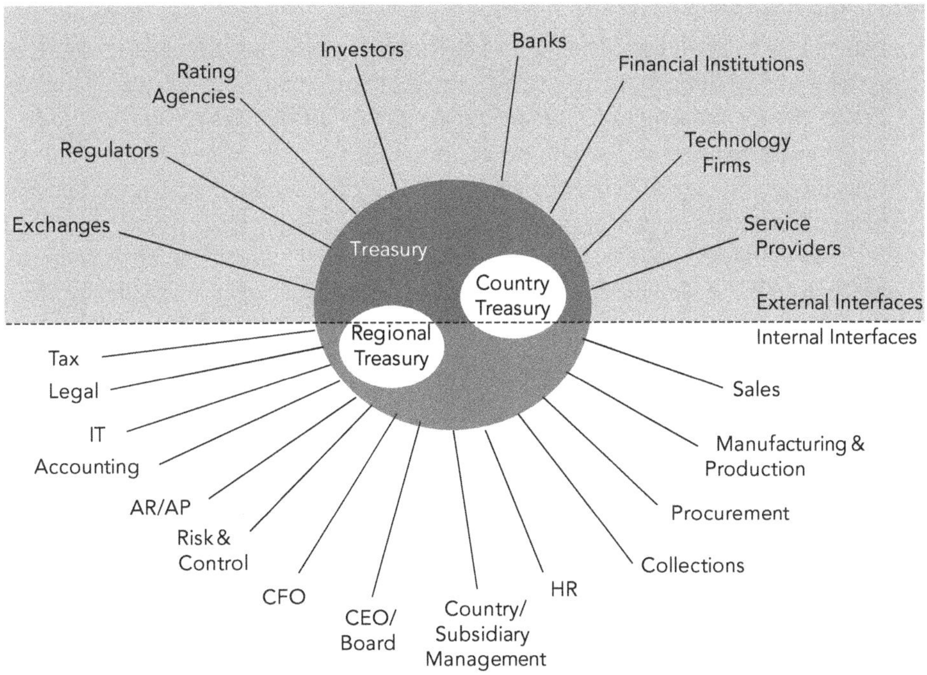

FIGURE 1.5 Treasury Linkages

geographical, operational, funding-based, cash management, trade, hedging, markets, and account operations that are the key ingredients of the banking potpourri. Also, for longer-term capital market transactions, the Treasurer remains the key driver and hence the main contact point for the bank.

- **Investors**. As the company goes out to acquire diversified and alternative sources of capital, the Treasurer, being in charge of capital raising and also having the most visibility on the firm's balance sheet, financials, and cash flows, would be the key resource for investors to have a discussion with to gain a broader understanding of the firm's financial position and hence their return expectation. In many organisations, the Treasurer is also given the responsibility of managing investor relations. This is a logical additional responsibility given to the Treasurer but is not technically a Treasury function.
- **Rating agencies**. The Treasurer is responsible for the credit rating of the firm and for achieving the optimal credit rating. Hence the interface with the rating agencies (and sometimes analysts) is driven by the Treasurer.
- **Financial institutions**. In many countries, financial institutions (nonbanking finance companies, funds, money market players) remain a source of capital as well as originators of useful investment products and channels (funds, investment banks, etc.). In line with the duties of Treasury, the interaction with financial institutions for both origination and investment is driven by Treasury.

- **Technology firms.** Modern-day Treasury uses technology and systems as a critical tool to drive the function and day-to-day operations. Specialised Treasury systems and ancillary systems, such as market information systems (e.g., Thomson Reuters Extra), risk engines, and forecasting and reporting tools are playing leading roles in determining productivity and performance of treasuries. Regular interface with the technology service provider/vendor for maintenance, upgrades, and feature enhancement is an important access point for Treasury.
- **Service providers.** Many activities and functions of Treasury can be outsourced, and many service providers offer efficient, scalable, and highly controlled levels of service across different levels. Netting, collections, lockbox, and reconciliation are only some of the services that Treasurers choose to outsource.

Within the organisation, the Treasury team interacts with most functions on a regular basis. The nature and content of these interactions will become clearer in other chapters book. To summarise, these functions are:

- CEO and board of directors
- CFO
- Accounts receivable/accounts payable (AR/AP) teams
- Risk and control
- Controller
- Accounting
- Tax
- Legal
- Information technology/systems
- Human resources
- Country or subsidiary management teams
- Procurement
- Production and delivery
- Sales
- Collections

TREASURY FUNCTIONS AND RESPONSIBILITIES

Earlier we mentioned that the Treasurer is the provider of liquidity, responsible for the liquidity aspect of cash management and the manager of risk, funding, and investment for the firm. In this section, we delve deeper into the various activities and functions that make up the Treasury department. We also discuss the infrastructure required for the Treasury team members to outperform in their roles.

Treasury Functions

Treasury's core functioning can be classified across the management of three main themes illustrated in Figure 1.6.

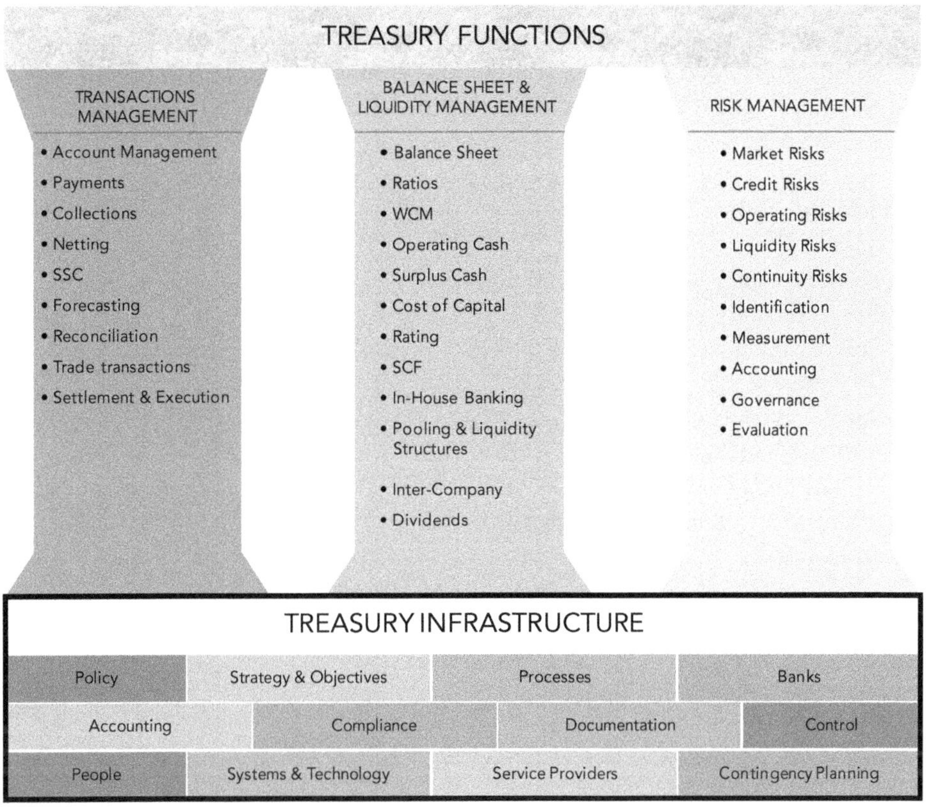

FIGURE 1.6 Treasury Functions and Responsibilities

Transactions

The transactional and operational element of cash management and the movement of money is the first of the three functions. This includes:

- Managing accounts
- Monitoring and enabling payments and managing the payment process and timing
- Monitoring the collections process and facilitating the concentration and movement of funds received
- Coordinating the process of consolidating and netting payments for increased efficiency
- Supporting financial control in the creation of a shared service centre to optimise the AR and AP processes
- Establishing an appropriate forecasting process for cash flows to enable better planning and management, and coordinating with various business units and functions
- Reconciliation of accounts and cash flows
- Execution of trade-related transactions, such as letters of credit and bank guarantees
- Settlement and execution of cash flow and cross-border transactions

Balance Sheet and Liquidity

The balance sheet and financials and liquidity element of the organisation's money and assets and how it funds these assets is the second of the functions. This involves the management of:

- Balance sheet
- Ratios
- Working capital management (WCM)
- Operating and surplus cash
- Cost of capital
- Credit rating
- Supply chain finance (SCF)
- In-house banking
- Pooling and liquidity structures
- Intercompany financing and capital
- Dividends

I often get asked the difference between cash management and liquidity management. The following note articulates the same.

What Is the Difference between Cash Management and Liquidity Management?

Liquidity management for a company is a part of cash management. The overall ambit of cash management is the movement of money from where it is sourced to where it is needed. Liquidity management is a subset of that—ensuring that funding is available at a location in a currency required, when it is required, and optimally utilising the cash—if the money is not needed in one location, it could yield better returns used elsewhere.

Risk

The element of managing the various financial risks because of market movements, credit deterioration, operational issues, market liquidity, and contingency situations is the third of the functions. This involves the management of:

- Market risk (such as foreign exchange, interest rates, commodity, etc.)
- Credit risk (includes counterparty and cross-border risk)
- Liquidity risk
- Operational risk
- Contingency risk

This management can be accomplished using many methods with various elements of rigour and flow. This book covers the use of Aktrea's Set IMAGE© methodology, which involves a simple continuous five-stage process.

1. Identification of risk
2. Measurement of risk
3. Accounting and reporting of risk
4. Governance of risk
5. Evaluation of the risk management process

Treasury Infrastructure

Managing and working with the resources that the Treasury team needs to perform their functions and fulfill their responsibilities form a core part of the Treasury function's activities. The various elements that make up the infrastructure for Treasury Functions are discussed next. Guidelines for some of these elements are included in the Toolkit in Part Five.

Policy

Policies are the core of a treasury's functioning. It is important to have a thought-out but simple policy approved at the board level and reviewed periodically. The Treasury policy will set out all aspects of the treasury's functioning, including transactions, balance sheet and liquidity, and risk management, and also the reporting and review methodology for these functions. A sample policy is provided in the online appendices.

Strategy and Objective

It is essential to define treasury's objectives and strategies as well as how to measure its performance. Whether Treasury is a cost centre or a profit centre, whether it needs to be an active Treasury or a passive one, are all aspects that have to be identified up front and the objectives must be set accordingly. Chapter 27 has a detailed set of key performance indicators (KPIs) that can be a starting point for goal setting and performance measurement.

Contingency Planning

For treasuries that work across countries, regions, and continents, having a continuity-of-operations plan in place is critical. The more centralised the operations, the more important the need for a well-planned, tested, and robust contingency plan.

Processes

Processes and their management can differentiate treasuries. Smooth and efficient processes result in quick turnaround and service levels, which in turn reduce operating and financial costs and increase employee motivation. The importance of operations is discussed in Chapter 5 and in the Toolkit (Part Five).

Control

Given the linkages with money flows of the firm, Treasury needs the highest standard of control to prevent losses owing to operational, compliance, regulatory, and fraud reasons. Part Five covers the importance of some aspects of operations and control and contains an operations and control checklist that can be built on to create a robust control environment for an organisation.

Compliance

For a multinational organisation with a presence and operations across countries, local regulations and laws have to be complied with at all costs, and processes, systems, reporting, and other statutory aspects have to be aligned accordingly. In some cases, the local regulations could determine the course of operations as well.

Documentation

With the background of cash and money flows, watertight and properly executed documentation becomes one of the backbones of a robust Treasury.

Accounting

Different accounting norms across locations make it imperative for Treasury to be aligned with the accounting process. Since the Treasurer is responsible for the balance sheet and the capital structure, the accounting methods, translation, and recognition of revenues and expenses make a difference to the firm's profitability and financial position. Some transactions may have an economic benefit but could be unfriendly from an accounting standpoint. Mark-to-market values on hedges and investments could also create volatility in the financials. Market moves could change the values of assets, liabilities, and cash flows. Given the Treasurer's responsibility to manage uncertainty, which includes the variability of the balance sheet, the Treasurer's linkages with the accounting systems and the financial controller become paramount in the smooth functioning and performance parameters of Treasury.

Systems and Technology

Always enablers, systems have become an integral part of the modern Treasury, linking every part of the globe to increase visibility of cash flows, managing risks, and deploying cash where and when it is needed. The advent of great banking platforms and outsourced solutions has also dramatically increased the ability to leverage systems and technology.

Service Providers

The use of various service providers for activities such as such as systems, integration, netting, reconciliation, system maintenance, and the like is becoming more and more popular, to ensure greater degree of specialisation, scalability, and control. Outsourced treasuries, covered in more detail in Chapter 30, are also returning in popularity.

Banks

Banks form the infrastructure of treasury's architecture. No Treasury is complete without a banking partner. Whether the Treasury is a simple one with operations only in one country or a complex group-wide, in-house bank acting as a bank for all group companies, an efficient suite of banking services and solutions is paramount to delivering value to the business. Throughout our discussions, the roles and offerings of banks will be discussed. In the Toolkit, we also provide a note on how to go about picking the right banking partner.

People

Systems and process define a Treasury, but the people run it. Having the right people at the right places with the right approach and motivation is a necessity for a great Treasury. The roles in Treasury offer empowerment, opportunity, learning, and perspective and are a great breeding ground for finance and business leaders of tomorrow. In Chapter 3, we introduce the concept of a Treasury Culture, an empowering approach for a stronger dynamic in building a cutting-edge Treasury.

Treasury infrastructure, while being the nonglamorous part that does not hit the headlines when times are good, plays one of the most pivotal roles in the successful functioning of a Treasury.

KPIs AND DELIVERABLES

Now that we have explored the role that Treasury plays in the organisation and the context of its operation, it is important to explore the value that Treasury creates, its objectives and goals defined adequately and transparently.

Given the linkages that Treasury has with other functions, and the interdependence of other functions and extraneous factors, such as markets, regulations, liquidity, and the banking system, quantifying and measuring treasury's direct contribution to the organisation becomes a complex task. It is compounded by the nature of the Treasury desk, which is also a service unit in many firms, intended to provide robust support to business and operations around the world to ensure smooth running of the company globally. A disruption to operations or the financial supply chain because of an absence of funding, or high volatility in the markets, will impact the organisation as a whole adversely.

Thus we make an effort to identify specific parameters of treasury's performance—its contribution to the financial indicators of the firm—and to directly link the output of Treasury with the overall organisational performance. A detailed set of sample metrics is provided in Chapter 27.

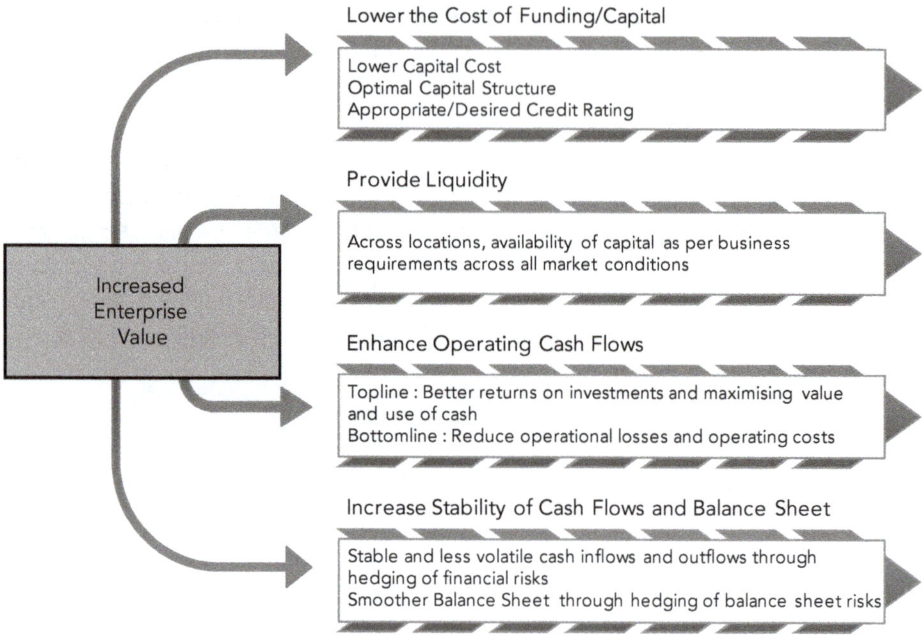

FIGURE 1.7 Treasury Performance Indicators

Figure 1.7 summarises the performance indicators of Treasury. If we define the core objective of Treasury as supporting the business to increase enterprise value, we can identify four distinct but related objectives with which Treasury can contribute:

1. Lowering the cost of funding and the cost of capital
2. Providing liquidity to the firm
3. Enhancing operating cash flows
4. Increasing the stability of cash flows and the balance sheet

Lowering the Cost of Funding and the Cost of Capital

This is achieved by looking for the right capital sources and achieving an appropriate capital structure, targeting and achieving an appropriate credit rating and maintaining or improving it, and looking for opportunities to lower the existing cost of capital through the use of lesser external capital and other means.

Providing Liquidity to the Firm

This is achieved by identifying the right sources of liquidity, preferably internal, and reducing dependence on market and external sources, providing the firm with the ability to move cash, increasing visibility of the firm's money, and finally providing money where it is required, when it is required, and for the amount and currency in which it is required and the time period for which it is required.

Enhancing Operating Cash Flows

This is done through prudent and active management of resources including managing and improving the top line through investing surplus cash (without compromising liquidity or increasing levels of risk), optimising the use of capital investments and balance sheet, and extracting maximum value on those investments and balance sheet. Bottom-line improvements will come by reducing costs through process efficiencies and use of technology and appropriate models, relevant banking and account structures, and available and customised products and services to improve efficiency and reduce resources required internally. Higher productivity per employee will also result in a smaller human resource requirement.

Increasing the Stability of Cash Flows and the Balance Sheet

This can be achieved through optimal hedging and risk management, and cash management to reduce volatility and increase visibility.

We now visit a Treasurer's office and take a sneak peek at what a typical day looks like.

A DAY AT THE OFFICE—WHAT DOES THE TREASURER DO?

A typical Treasurer's day is depicted pictorially in Figure 1.8. We have assumed in this example a reasonably centralised Treasury with a fair degree of automation.

The day gets off to a start with an overview of the previous day's bank balances, pooled and concentrated, through bank statements. The cash position is analysed and reconciled with the expected numbers from the previous day's forecasts. Large exceptions that result in a significant shortfall (urgent alternative funding sources could be required) or surplus (funds from another day's expected numbers could have come in, or funds expected to have been debited have not gone out, and hence need to be utilised accordingly) are examined and confirmation of the same is received. Short or excess payments made or received are also identified, and the new cash position is obtained after the relevant corrections and expectations. The next day's forecast is also factored in to the expected liquidity and cash position. Overnight moves in markets are looked at, and risk limits and positions are reviewed. Clarifications are sought on any large amounts or variances.

Foreign exchange transactions for the day's payments are made, and any maturing forwards, swaps, and options factored in before executing the trades with the bank.

Interruptions to the schedule on urgent queries or transactional follow-up are to be expected; the Treasury team does well to prioritise the time critical queries for resolution immediately.

Based on the revised cash position, the balance sheet and liquidity position is reviewed, and any arrangements for the day's funding requirements are planned for through incremental borrowing, drawdown, or deposit cancellation. Sometimes risk management transactions with positive mark-to-market values may also be delivered early or unwound if the risk management objectives for the trade have been achieved.

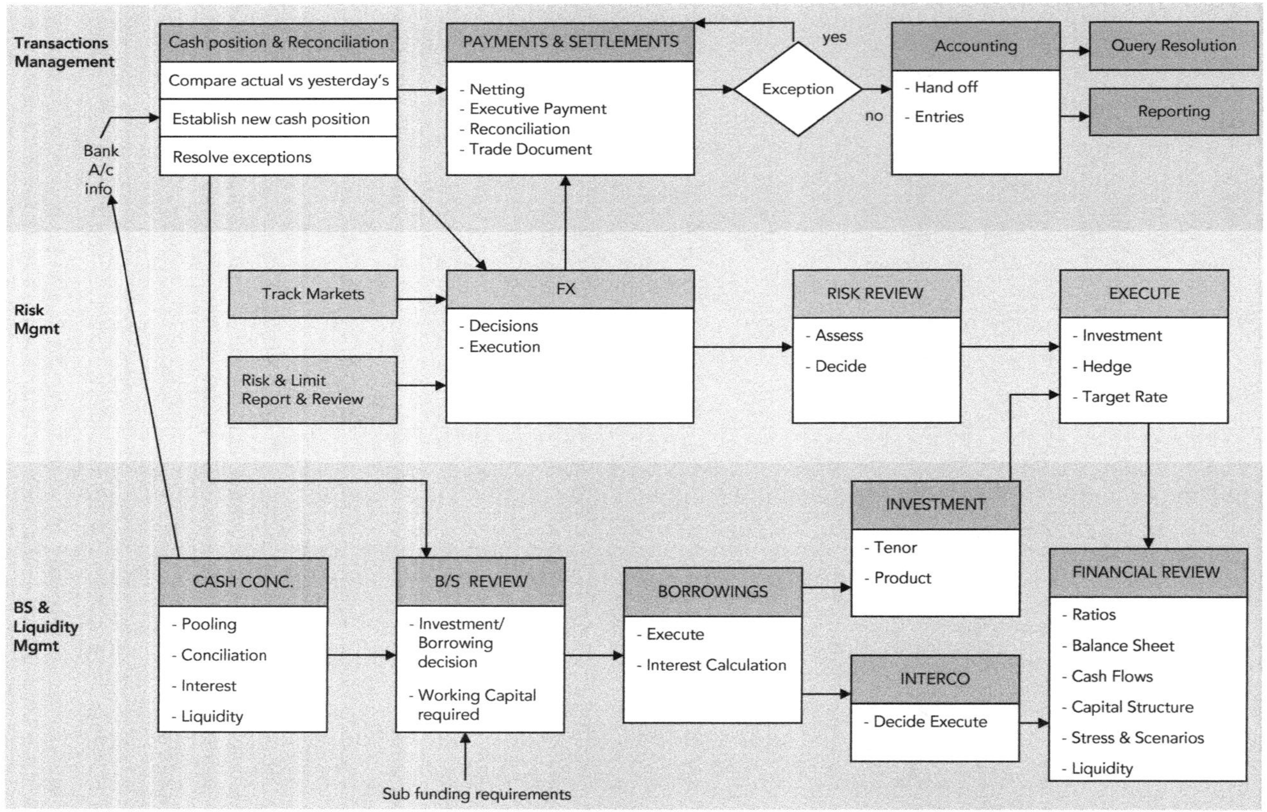

FIGURE 1.8 A Day in the Treasurer's Hot Seat

Payments are made and executed. These include trade-related payments and documentation and netting payments, if applicable. Post-payment reconciliation is done to ensure that all proposed payments have gone through.

If there are payments still pending, these are referred back and resolved.

Meanwhile, incremental borrowings are executed, and the money inflows are recognised.

After a well-earned lunch, the Treasurer is back at his or her desk reviewing the risk management aspect, looking at the overall risk positions and taking stock of any incremental hedges that need to be put out. Corrective actions on any limit excesses are also planned at this time. Discussions with bankers and economists on general market views reinforce some of the views and decisions to be made.

On the balance sheet side, investment decisions are made. Intercompany loans and money movements are identified and executed.

Risk management and investment transactions are then executed with banks and professional counterparties, and the deals are booked in the system.

On the transactions side, the Treasury ensures that the handoff entries to the general ledger system or enterprise resource planning are posted and accounting entries are passed into the back end. Any reconciliation issues with the books of the firm and Treasury systems are also reconciled, and reverse handoffs are posted.

Queries coming in from the field are resolved after this. (Very critical queries are likely to have been resolved earlier in the day.)

All reporting activities are also finalised and circulated before the day ends.

The final piece of the daily puzzle is filled in when the Treasurer reviews the financials of the firm. Any large material changes or expectation of changes based on forecasts are also explored. Results of stress and scenario analyses may also be examined at this time, and discussions may take place on possible resolutions.

SUMMARY

In this chapter, we went through the context of the Treasurer's role in the organisation, along with key responsibilities and functions in Treasury. We discussed the important aspects of Treasury infrastructure that help make a Treasury more robust. We concluded with a look at some of the KPIs for a Treasury and went through a typical Treasurer's day, across various themes of transactions management, balance sheet and liquidity management, and risk management, starting off with time-critical morning activities and ending with reviews and matters of strategic importance.

CHAPTER TWO

Treasury Design

THE CONCEPT OF TREASURY DESIGN is simple: to organise the Treasury function, its people and processes, working toward efficiency, elegance, and utility.

The starting point for Treasury Design is a study of the key performance indicators (KPIs), since the existence of Treasury and its structure has the eventual goal of achieving these performance goals. These KPIs were mentioned briefly in Chapter 1 and are further elucidated in the Toolkit in Part Five.

Since it is possible to have more than one route and model to achieve similar goals, other considerations come into play in designing an appropriately organised Treasury for the organisation. These considerations are:

- Lower cost
- Lower turnaround times for decision making and resolution
- Higher degrees of control and wider net for control
- Lower cost of capital and increased availability and diversity of capital
- Legal environment of various locations
- Accounting practices followed by the firm and accounting environment of the geographies in which the business is being done

- Tax aspects
- Automation required
- Existing and future volumes
- Growth and increase in business and geographies
- Expectation of turbulence of competitor and industry landscapes

The three Treasury themes or functions—the management of transactions, balance sheet and liquidity, and risk—are the foundation for these KPIs and considerations.

Figure 2.1 shows the development of the Treasury Design process.

KEY ELEMENTS OF TREASURY DESIGN

Next we run through the key elements of Treasury Design and then explore some models and how they can be made to work.

System Design

The importance of systems and technology and their role in Treasury was introduced earlier. Systems must be designed with various aspects and considerations in mind. The Toolkit in Part Five contains a detailed overview of the Treasury system selection, implementation, and integration process.

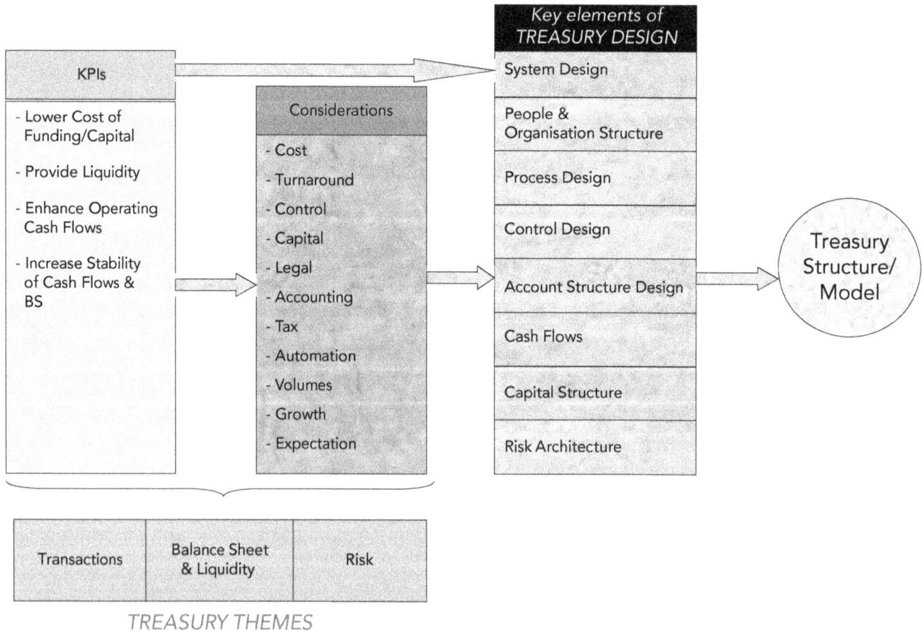

FIGURE 2.1 Treasury Design

People and Organisational Structure Design

This people and organisational structure design entails identifying the right people, equipping them with the right skills, and putting them in the right jobs with the right reporting line. It is also linked to the decision of the degree of centralisation and outsourcing.

Process Design

Based on creating watertight processes with controlled and measurable handoffs, the process design forms the bulwark of the Treasury function.

Control Design

A strong control element is a safeguard against potential hazards and situations around implementation and execution. Even if the rest of the Treasury Design elements are put in place, a weak control design element will not help sustain the strength of the implemented Treasury Design and processes. We explore the control element through the various chapters and end with a detailed overview in the Toolkit in Part Five.

Account Structure Design

Covered in more detail in Part Two of this book, designing the right account structure is an often-underrated element. Ad hoc account creation can result in increased cost, lower control, and poor visibility and utilisation of cash. In some countries, regulatory conditions could also force the decision on which account structure to go with.

Cash Flow Design

Cash flows can occur across locations, in various forms and currencies at different times. Consolidating and concentrating these flows creates greater efficiencies through reduced cost, increased control, and better visibility of flows.

Capital Structure

One of the Treasurer's key areas of delivery is ensuring that the firm is adequately capitalised and that the price the firm pays for the capital is the lowest in the circumstances. Capital structure also has a bearing on the firm's credit rating and financial perception and performance, making it one of the critical areas evaluated by potential investors and lenders.

Risk Architecture

The last, but one of the most critical, components of Treasury Design, covered in detail in Part Four, is that of risk management and its architecture.

We now explore the evolution of Treasury models, with snapshots of various models, and discuss some of their benefits and concerns.

INTRODUCING CENTRALISATION

Centralisation as a topic has been one of the larger areas of focus of Treasurers over the past few years. Growing businesses, increasing geographies, evolving technologies and emerging markets have necessitated fresher approaches to managing cash and risk more efficiently.

Centralisation itself can cover a wide gamut and array of themes. The concept itself evolved to achieve three key objectives:

1. Increase efficiency
2. Reduce cost
3. Achieve deeper and wider control

What are we actually centralising? Centralisation involves concentrating aspects into one physical location. The factors going into the choice of these locations vary by company and situation and are described in detail in the Toolkit in Part Five. The aspects that can be centralised may be broadly classified into the following:

- **Accounts and financial activity**. Moving the actual venue of where the accounts and financial activity, such as capital raising, cash concentration, risk management, and investments, are situated is one of the aspects. The drivers of these will be location specific, such as availability and cost of capital, cost of maintaining accounts, accounting status, tax friendliness, any potential financial benefits on offer, and the like.
- **Systems and infrastructure**. Cost, control, backup, access, and service providers, among other aspects, determine the location of centralised systems and infrastructure.
- **People (processing, execution, and decision making)**. Location of the people actually performing these roles could be different from the locations of the accounts and systems. For example, a centralised Treasury with accounts in Singapore could be operated by people based in London with the databases and systems located in Hong Kong.

With these objectives and areas in mind, we explore the context and themes of centralisation, depicted in Figure 2.2.

The idea is to move from multiple systems, nonuniform processes, different legal entities having different degrees of control in different locations, various service providers, numerous bank accounts in various currencies, and varied degrees of support, toward an operation that minimises all of these; the end result is close to having uniform systems and processes to support various entities from one location, with a rationed set of service providers, minimal bank accounts, and consistent service levels.

Various benefits accrue from these that tie into the three key objectives discussed earlier.

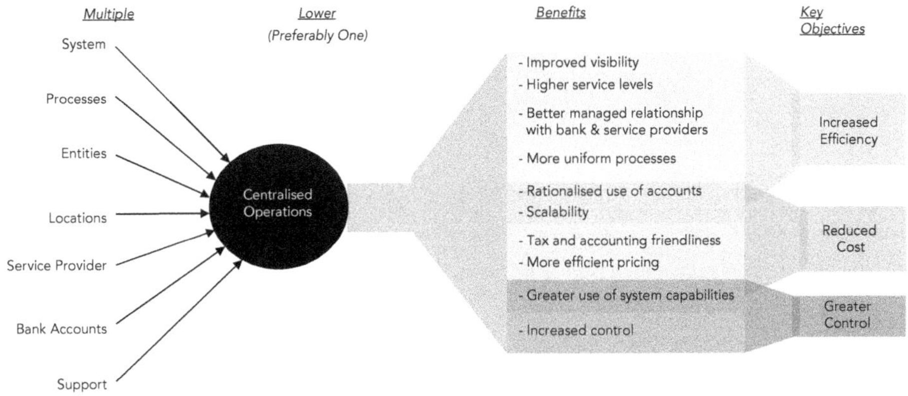

FIGURE 2.2 Centralisation Themes

EVOLUTION OF TREASURY MODELS

We now explore the various models of Treasury and what they mean across various parameters.

Figure 2.3 (not to scale) summarises the value added across various stages of centralisation.

The definitions here are only indicative, and different companies follow different models of implementation and achieve varied degrees of success and benefits from these models. Some companies do not follow a progressive, stage-by-stage route but prefer to implement entire structures at one go.

Decentralised Treasury

The decentralised Treasury is the basic model, where many companies start off. Decision making across various criteria is decentralised at a subsidiary or country level, with headquarters (depicted as HQ in Figure 2.4 and subsequent figures) only consolidating the numbers and framing the overall group policy. This is more in vogue in younger firms where business leaders in each country run the businesses more or less independently with an entrepreneurial and sometimes unstructured approach. The dependencies and control then depend very much on the people running them, and consistency of results and value is not guaranteed.

As can be seen in Figure 2.4, the bulk of activities in the boxes are being done by the local teams on the ground. Aspects such as systems, reporting line, and performance measurement can be done centrally at headquarters or locally, or a hybrid model can be developed.

The benefits of this model are increased flexibility and speed of operations. Control, economies of scale, and lack of synergy could contribute to increased costs, potential losses, and larger degrees of exposure and risk to the firm's financials.

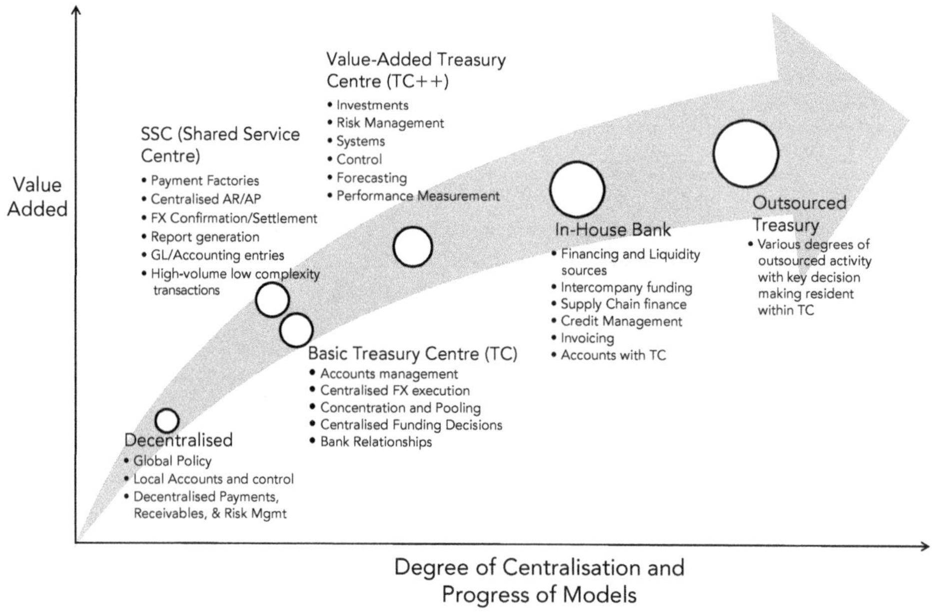

FIGURE 2.3 Evolution of Treasury Models

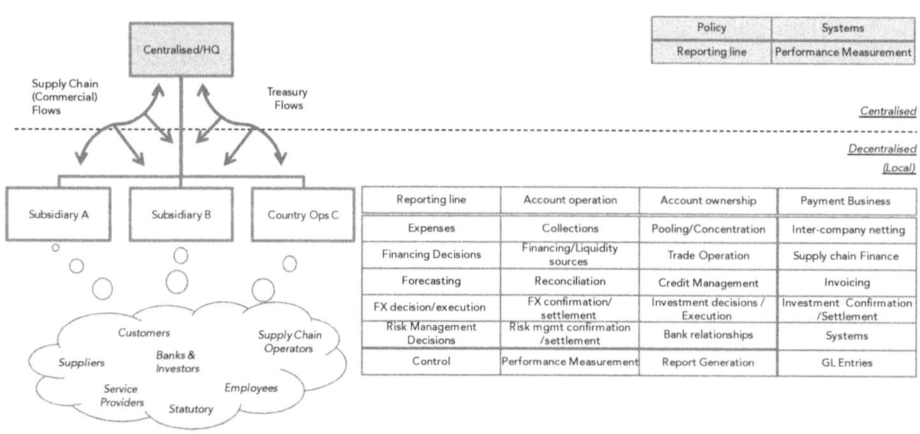

FIGURE 2.4 Decentralised Treasury Model

Shared Service Centre

A shared service centre (SSC) utilises the concept of centralised processing of high-volume and low-complexity activities, achieving economies of scale by concentrating activities and control in one location through the use of systems, communication, and interfaces with banking and service provider technology.

Processes such as payments and disbursements, accounts receivable (AR) and accounts payable (AP) management, reconciliation, expense processing,

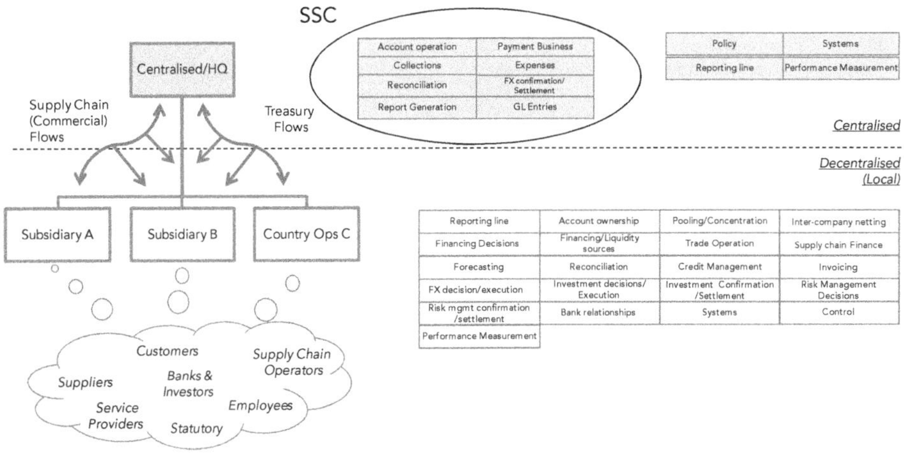

FIGURE 2.5 Shared Service Centre Model

payroll, general ledger (GL)/enterprise resource planning entries, and report generation are typically handled by the SSC, sometimes referred to as a payments factory (an accurate but incomplete description). More evolved SSCs also perform confirmation and settlement of foreign exchange (FX), risk management, and investment transactions.

The SSC technically covers areas that report to the financial controller. While it retains very close linkages to the functioning of the Treasury, it can be distinct from an organisational standpoint. Given the closeness and proximity, transactionally and conceptually, to Treasury activities and process and the interconnectedness of the two, we have included these areas in the scope of this discussion. Figure 2.5 shows the activities typically housed in an SSC.

Basic Treasury Centre

The basic Treasury centre (TC) model (see Figure 2.6) adds value in parallel to an SSC. Here, more complicated activities are taken up, and the TC comes under the direct ambit of the Treasurer.

Cash concentration, trade operations, netting, centralised bank relationship management, financing decisions, and FX decisions are made in the basic TC. In addition, account ownership may reside with the TC. What is the key difference between an SSC and a TC? The answer is quite simple: complexity and core functions. The SSC is a typically high-volume, low-complexity shop with lesser decision making and a high process and task orientation. The TC is a typically high-complexity, lower-volume shop that is more oriented towards decision making and policy. Figure 2.7 highlights some of the activities occurring between the two centres.

Various aspects of TCs and SSCs, including structure and location decisions, are covered in detail in the Toolkit in Part Five.

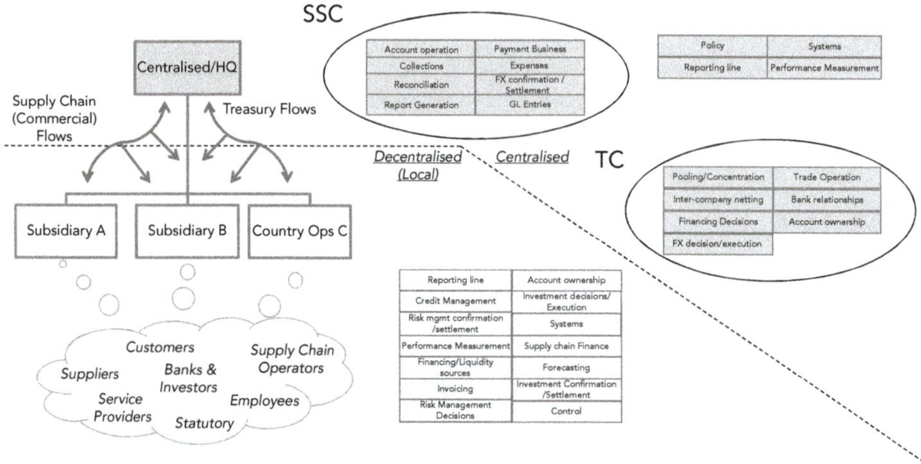

FIGURE 2.6 Basic Treasury Centre Model (with SSC)

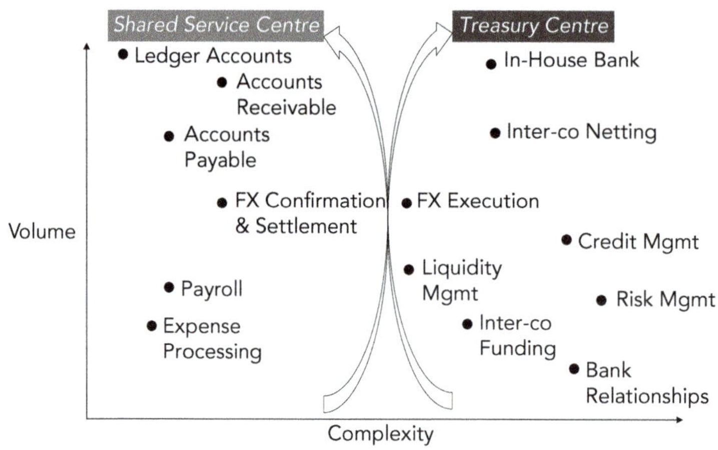

FIGURE 2.7 Division of Activities Between SSC and TC

Picture courtesy of Gourang Shah

Value-Added Treasury Centre

The value-added Treasury centre (TC++) concept takes off from the basic TC, with activities of forecasting, risk management decision making, investment decisions, funding and liquidity sourcing and intercompany funding, systems, control, and reporting all moving to a centralised location. Likewise, the confirmation and settlement of the risk management and investment transactions could move into the SSC or the TC. Now we have reached a stage where the entire Treasury operations are now centralised, with very little activity residual within the subsidiaries or country operations (see Figure 2.8). There may be some variations on this format, depending on regulations regarding outsourcing and ownership.

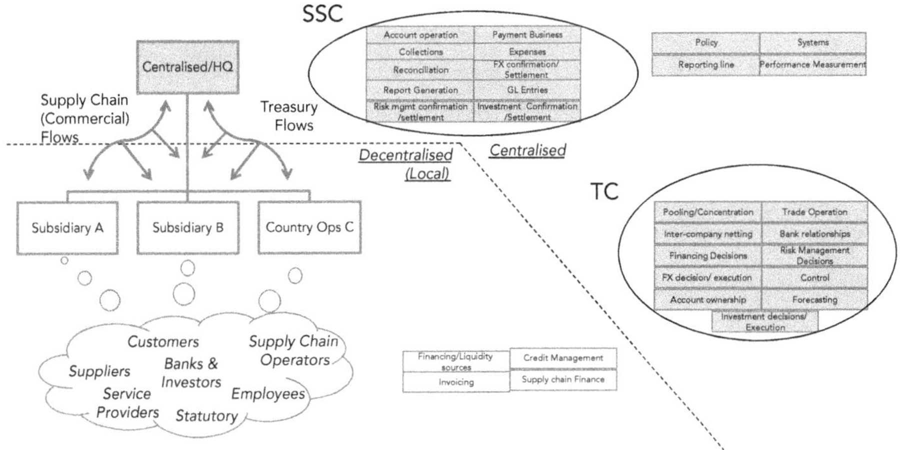

FIGURE 2.8 TC++ Model (with SSC)

In-House Bank

The next stage in the evolution is the concept of the in-house bank, typically as part of the TC (see Figure 2.9) Value-added services such as invoicing (or re-invoicing), credit management, and supply chain financing are taken up here. Most important, however, the TC acts as a bank for all subsidiaries and countries that come under the ambit of the in-house bank. The TC behaves as a banking service company, providing account management, funding, funds transfer, investments, and risk management solutions to the entities. In turn, the TC interfaces with banks and professional market counterparties to execute consolidated transactions on behalf of the entire group.

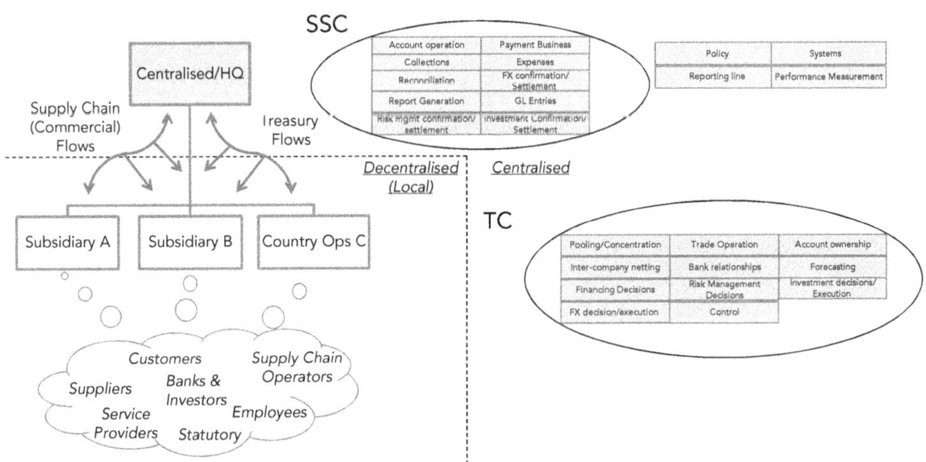

FIGURE 2.9 In-House Bank Model

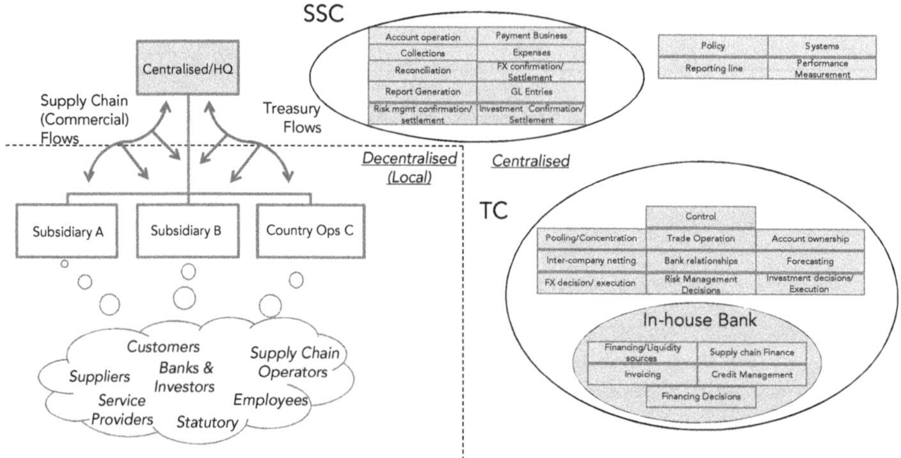

FIGURE 2.10 Outsourced Model

An in-house bank requires a very high degree of expertise and a high process orientation. The scales of the operations and financial transactions of the group must also justify the investment and maintenance cost of the in-house bank.

Outsourced Model

The outsourced model of Treasury works in a rather simple way: Outsource the process-focused or non–decision-making activities and keep the decision making, review, and ownership in house (see Figure 2.10).

> ### Caveats of Outsourcing Jobs and Data
>
> With increasing pressure on employment, many countries are looking adversely at outsourcing value-adding jobs. Also, data protection laws are becoming stringent about keeping confidential financial and strategic data housed in servers resident overseas. These aspects have reduced the speed of the outsourcing bandwagon, and companies would do well to assess the impact of outsourcing across each geography and market prior to embarking on an activity that is effort intensive to put together and expensive to roll back.

The Toolkit in Part Five covers outsourcing in some detail with a checklist on essential aspects of outsourcing.

Figure 2.11 summarises the various processes and centralisation aspects across these sample models. This is only an indicative list. Companies must thoroughly analyse their requirements and situation prior to embarking on this exciting but involved journey.

Progress by Activity

Aspect	Function	Decentralised	SSC	Basic TC	TC ++	In-House Bank	Outsourced
Policy	TC	Central					→
Reporting Line	TC	Local & Central		→	Central		→
Account Ownership	TC	Local	→	Central	→	With TC	→
Account Operation	TC/SSC	Local	Central			- - - →	Outsourced
Payments - Business	SSC	Local	Central			- - - →	Outsourced
Expense (Incl Payroll & other Internal)	SSC	Local	Central			- - - →	Outsourced
Collections	SSC	Local	Central			- - - →	Outsourced
Pooling/Concentration	TC	Local	→	Central		→	Outsourced
Intercompany Netting	TC	Local	→	Central		→	Outsourced
Financing Decisions	In-House Bank	Local	→	Central			→
Financing/Liquidity Sources	In-House Bank	Local			→	Central	→
Trade Operations	TC	Local	→	Central		→	Outsourced
Supply Chain Finance	In-House Bank	Local			→	Central	→
Forecasting	TC	Local		→	Central	→	Outsourced
Reconciliation	SSC	Local	Central			- - - →	Outsourced
Credit Management	In-House Bank	Local			→	Central	→
Invoicing	In-House Bank	Local			→	Central	Outsourced
FX Decision/Execution	TC	Local	→	Central			→
FX Confirmation/Settlement	SSC	Local	Central			- - - →	Outsourced
Investment Decision/Execution	TC	Local		→	Central		→
Investment Confirmation/Settlement	SSC	Local		→	Central	- - - →	Outsourced
Risk Mgmt Decisions	TC	Local		→	Central		→
Risk Mgmt Confirmation/Settlement	SSC	Local		→	Central	- - - →	Outsourced
Bank Relationships	TC	Local	→	Central			→
Systems	TC	Local or Central		→	Central	→	Outsourced
Control	TC	Local		→	Central	→	Outsourced
Performance Measurement	TC	Local & Central		→	Central		→
Report Generation	SSC	Local	Central			- - - →	Outsourced
GL Entries	SSC	Local	Central			- - - →	Outsourced

FIGURE 2.11 Detailed Processes Across Various Sample Models

Hybrid models can also be structured as a combination of these models, where some activities are done in-country or in the subsidiary and the remaining activities done centrally at the SSC or TC.

We now go through a case of Treasury Design for a global company in the growth stage.

CASE STUDY: TREASURY DESIGN FOR A GROWING GLOBAL COMPANY

Any company that thinks globally and has started growing in that direction needs to start thinking in the same way.

Sample company Global Growing Group (GGG) has increased its presence to over 50 countries now and is continuing to grow (Figure 2.12).

The company's unchannelised growth had made decision making complex, involving various people at headquarters, region, and on the ground in the various countries. In some locations, two different businesses in the same country would work independently even though both were 100% subsidiaries of the parent company.

(Continued)

- Acquisition–based inorganic growth
- Hugely diversified operations
- Little control at parent level
- Original parent processes and policy complicating on-the-ground situation across businesses and support functions

FIGURE 2.12 Treasury Reengineering Case

Year on year, the massive increase in revenue was driving up margins, but the expense side continued to balloon. With a recession around the corner anytime now, and the resultant prospect of a slowdown in sales looming large, the management of the firm got together in the hotbed of activity: Asia.

Forced by increasing costs and an inability to bridge the people, processes, business, and financial gaps with the current structure, the chief executive and his team decided to focus the current year on reassembling the moving parts and integrate the company to increase efficiency, drive down cost, and achieve a higher and more aggressive profitability target.

The Treasurer was faced with the unenviable task of kick-starting the process at his end. The chief financial officer (CFO) provided full support, allowing the Treasurer to explore functions directly outside his domain if it meant ringing in positive news on the expense front. Also, the Treasurer had been complaining for a while about the need to streamline funding and intercompany lending, since each acquired firm had insisted on running with their existing bankers and funding arrangements. Despite having proven that this course of funding was suboptimal, the Treasurer's pleas had fallen on deaf ears, since the skyrocketing sales figures had drowned out the relative financial importance of any other situations.

Now things had changed, and the Treasurer redid his exercise, confirming her earlier assumptions and updating his available spreadsheets with the latest numbers. Table 2.1 summarises some of the transitions and shifts.

There are a huge number of challenges and resolutions in a long project. Representing this in a two-dimensional matrix is simple enough, but in many cases, creating such a meaningful matrix is a result of months of hard work, negotiation, implementation, and cost. The cost angle needs to be explored thoroughly, and the gains achieved through such projects have to be quantified, since the focus is to drive efficiency and sustain profitability.

The other challenges were:

- **Regulatory** (capital control, outsourcing, and data). It is important to speak to the regulators and sensitise them to the developments. Any concerns highlighted are to be mitigated through concrete action. Possible concessions may also be obtained in some cases, so it is better to look for these opportunities and speak with the regulator.
- **Systems integration**. Especially with different legacy systems and culture, integrating requires effort. Single turnkey project responsibility with the vendor is one approach that can be adopted.

TABLE 2.1 Treasury Reengineering

Theme	Starting Point	End State
Location of Treasury Ops	Decentralised	TC++ model.
Location of AR and AP Ops	Decentralised	Integrated with TC++ model (SSC).
Banks	Locally decided and mandated	Centrally decided and managed, moved down to few global relationships and local ones only where required.
Systems	Parent and 2 subsidiaries using systems	Centralisation necessitating increased use of systems. Integration with global banking and local banking systems.
Accounts	Multiple. More inactive accounts than active ones. Some subsidiaries have one active account per stock-keeping unit (product item)	Accounts rationalised and moved to one per subsidiary as much as possible. Intelligence in the reconciliation built into the transaction reference number and easy to track through integration of systems mentioned above.
Cost	Distributed and multiple operations	Headcount saved through removal of redundant activities and reaching economies of scale (redeployment of resources). Banking costs rationalised and saved—potentially over 50% saved. Uniform pricing from global banks and local banks.
Service and Relationship Management	Multiple relationship management and service levels	Location of Treasury operations centralised to another location with one person located at head office reporting to Treasurer to manage banks' relationships centrally. Banks' service side managed by Treasury operations with identified points of contact from the banks' side.

- **Professional services support.** Accounting, tax, and legal across countries have to be deeply involved in the process. HR and related aspects will also have to be considered.

Some of the challenges are captured in the next case.

In summary, growing companies may not always have the management bandwidth to implement centralised operations right away, but smooth process management and integrating policies and systems when acquisitions are being done helps to reduce the effort to centralise considerably, when the time comes.

The next case study, contributed by one of my favourite Treasurers from his own experience and observations in the industry, articulates some of the important but unwritten situations that companies could face.

CASE STUDY: OVERCOMING HURDLES IN IMPLEMENTING CENTRALISED CASH MANAGEMENT

Every Treasurer—and every company—understands the benefits of centralised cash management. They are:

- Using cash available in some legal entities to avoid borrowing in others, thereby avoiding the bid/offer spread.
- As a result, reducing pressure on funding lines for the borrowing and counterparty limits for the deposits.
- Reducing the number of banking relationships and rationalising them. This results in greater bargaining power and more customer attention from the cash management banks which are retained.
- Ability to offset currency positions, to reduce the amount of hedging required
- Enhanced visibility of the cash position and balances, reducing the need for cash buffers across the company
- Improvements in cash forecasting—or, at least, a reduced dependency on accurate forecasting, as errors in individual legal entities will tend to offset each other, and emergency cover can always be provided from the central Treasury.
- Enhanced Controls
  - There is no longer a need to monitor the activities of multiple local Treasury teams to ensure compliance with policies.
  - Enhanced separation of duties—often the finance or Treasury teams in subsidiaries are not big enough to ensure this.
  - The central Treasury team can also invest in skill levels not necessarily available—or desirable—in smaller subsidiaries.
- Last, and not least, a reduction in the overall number of Treasury headcount.

These benefits can be even further enhanced by the implementation of a re-invoicing centre. This can have the benefit of providing funding via a goods (or services) current account, thereby eliminating the need for intercompany loan agreements and the associated issues with arm's-length pricing and potential withholding taxes. It can even simplify items like HQ funding and internal royalties, by building them into the price of the goods or services. The resulting elimination of intercompany billing between subsidiaries can be a significant saving.

If these benefits are so significant, why isn't every company in the world operating this way?

First, many companies have moved some way towards this approach. While true, 100% centralised treasuries are still rare, it is equally unusual to find a group in which each subsidiary is entirely free to raise and invest its cash as it sees fit. At the very least, there is usually some form of regional Treasury centre, even if this sometimes operates as a centre of expertise and advice rather than as an operational Treasury centre executing transactions.

The main reason many companies hesitate to centralise fully often lies in psychology and internal politics. Control over funding and payments is a key element of power and autonomy. As long as they control their cash and their funding, the general manager and CFO of each company feel they have the ultimate control over their own destinies. To transfer this responsibility to someone else is to give up an essential aspect of being a separate company.

Naturally, the objections are never expressed in these terms—the immediate answer would be that they are part of a larger group, not an autonomous entity. Instead, these arguments are usually heard:

- The central Treasury operation will not be able to make urgent payments in time. This will mean that essential items, such as taxes and payroll, will be paid late.
- Payroll has to be paid via a local bank. Employees cannot be made to open accounts with an international cash management bank, which usually will not have enough branches in the country.
- Customers will not agree to pay cash directly into an account with a foreign bank.
- It is difficult to close the relationship with the local banks that have provided support to the company over the years.
- The international cash management bank will not provide the same level of service as the local bank.
- The local Treasury team can get better rates by trading—and timing—in the local market.
- The central team "just don't understand" the local environment.

Not included in the list—but nonetheless often a factor—is that the CFO and the general manager will no longer be invited to lunches or golf days organised by the local bank.

How can you combat these arguments?

A lot will depend on the company's structure, and the relative internal political forces. A strong finance function, with a strong CFO who is convinced of the business case, will be able to push this through. But even then, it will be a tough struggle—every glitch in the operations, no matter how temporary or how it was caused, will be brought forward as evidence that the approach does not work.

Of course, it is preferable to implement this kind of project by convincing the business of the merits and getting everyone's buy-in. It is indispensable to build a good business case and to communicate the benefits of the new approach to all members of the business's senior management, especially line management, who normally tend to side with the objections brought through the country line management team.

At the same time, it is necessary to develop a convincing technical answer to all the points brought forward by the local teams.

Some of the items in the list do not merit serious consideration. But some are real issues that have to be addressed.

- **Payroll** is often a real problem. Employees often choose to have their personal accounts with a local bank rather than with one of the recognised international cash management banks. It is important to have a payment process that interfaces with the local clearing system. This can be surprisingly difficult—especially in Europe and Latin America. If worst comes to worst, an account can be maintained with a local bank, just for payroll—the bank can often be incented to provide good service by giving it the opportunity to access the personal banking requirements of the company's personnel.

(Continued)

- **Confidentiality** is also a major issue with payroll. The best modern banking interfaces provide a summary debit to the account for accounting and reconciliation purposes, so the Treasury and accounting teams do not see all the details of the payments. Again, the availability of this facility can be uneven, but it can be a determining factor in deciding on a local versus an international bank.
- The **local service levels** are a problem. Even the best international cash management banks can find it difficult to provide top-quality service to the smaller local entities, which often are not big enough to be serious clients for their local teams. In awarding international cash management mandates, it is essential to make sure the bank can always give top-quality service, even to the smaller entities that do not represent a significant business opportunity for the local branch. The effectiveness of this process often depends on the internal incentive and management systems of the bank; do not be afraid to ask how these operate for international mandates.
- **Funding** is essential. In negotiating a cross-border cash management mandate, it is important to make sure that sufficient local liquidity lines are available. This can be a significant challenge—not all international cash management banks have cheap access to local funding in all countries.
- At the same time, it can be very helpful to call in references from other companies that have implemented these solutions, to demonstrate that they can work.

During the implementation phase, it is essential to make sure that full communication is maintained and that all issues are addressed openly and in a timely manner. Experience says that once a centralised process is up and running, most local CFOs will actually appreciate the fact that it makes their lives easier. But it is essential to do everything to win the hearts and minds of the doubters until the implementation phase is over.

Even once the project has been completed, it is important to guard against complacency. The banks that have lost out as a result of the centralisation will continue to campaign and apply pressure. It is important to make sure that the banks that win the central cash management mandates do not become complacent and let their service levels drop. And finally, the choice of location to centralise to will always be the subject of some internal politics.

In summary, the benefits of a centralised cash management structure are clear. But, as with all centralisation projects, it is possible to make this happen only by removing autonomy and independence from the local operating units.

Getting full buy-in for this is a real challenge, and requires an exceptional level of communication and enthusiasm by the central Treasury team. It also requires flawless execution: The smallest failing will be used as a reason for turning the clock back.

The savings are real—but so are the challenges.

Contributed by Damian Glendinning, vice president and Treasurer, Lenovo; president, Association of Corporate Treasurers (Singapore)

SUMMARY

In this chapter, we explored the concept of Treasury Design, dwelling on the key themes of a good Treasury Design, and evaluated some Treasury models that could be adopted by global firms, with the use of shared service centres, Treasury centres, in-house banks, and outsourcing many process-oriented activities.

CHAPTER THREE

Treasury Culture

THE CONCEPT OF TREASURY CULTURE as introduced in this book is a thought and action process essential to the path of Treasury Leadership. It involves creating the right mind-set and environment for the employees of the Treasury function to work together and with other functions to produce best possible results and service standards. Practically, doing this includes equipping the employees with the right knowledge, skills, tools, empowerment, atmosphere, and attitude to generate best results.

A good Treasury Culture can explain the difference between two high-performance treasuries: one, a high-speed, cutting-edge, and efficient Treasury where motivated employees make everything appear smooth and well-oiled, with zero defects, prompt service and turnarounds to other functions, and a fun environment at work, where a Treasury role is sought after; the other, a good well-organised Treasury where employees are stretched and work overtime under intense pressure to deliver the same results, where Treasury is perceived to be a silo support function that burns the midnight oil.

Qualities	General Skills	Technical and Work-Related Skills
• Proactiveness • Control • Teamwork—internal and external • Transparency	• Relationship building • General knowledge • Technology • Process orientation • Written communication	• Business • Financial and markets awareness • Accounting • Regulatory

FIGURE 3.1 Components of Treasury Culture

The steps to initiate and develop a Treasury Culture are relatively simple, and a few key qualities and skills inculcated into the Treasury team over the course of the development process. This is done through example, top down, through the actions and the approach of the Treasurer him- or herself, and through training, simulation, and coaching. Figure 3.1 summarises the different elements of a Treasury Culture.

It is important to note that these elements of Treasury Culture are enablers that work along with professional/job competence and skills to increase the effectiveness of the individuals and the team within Treasury.

QUALITIES

Certain generic qualities are required in any employee of any organisation. Of these, those critical in the Treasury function are mentioned here.

Proactiveness

The proactive nature of Treasury personnel comes into play when dealing with the dynamic situations and potential areas of problems and disconnects that occur on a day-to-day basis. Proactive resolution of issues and potential problem areas, as well as stepping up to preempt liquidity or situations for the internal clients, will increase the fluidity of business operations.

Control

A control orientation is critical, given the nature of work in a Treasury and access to funds. Owing to opportunities for errors, and for fraudulent misappropriation of company money internally and externally, Treasury staff members need to be trained and, more important, cognizant of these opportunities for losses and perform their duties accordingly.

An interesting case study of "the Insider" is one of the many possible situations where employees have chosen to go down the wrong path.

CASE STUDY: THE INSIDER

The use of company funds for social ends as part of the firm's social responsibility is a given in today's corporate world. Ever since the corporate world began, some employees have benefited from their company's largesse apart from their official compensation. We're talking about internal fraud, with or without complicity.

Many companies that issue dividend payments have a long list of investors or shareholders who do not redeem their warrants. The monies for this purpose are usually held in a separate escrow and remain there for a period of time. Typically, banks are instructed to flag any transactions on such accounts immediately as exceptions. As M, an employee of a company's centralised Treasury who had direct responsibility for account management, had figured out, the dividend account of a few years' past had not been monitored apart from his sign-offs on the bank accounts.

A test transaction followed—a forged funds transfer instruction from a particular dividend account was flagged in the bank's system, but the bank's operations manager called M, since he always handled all account-related clarifications. On M's assurances that the transaction was genuine, the operations manager released the small payment. Since no one else in the organisation tracked these balances and since the amount was not large, the next audit thereafter caught no specific transaction.

Then the funds outflow took shape. Over the next 15 months, M transferred over USD 400,000, all in small amounts, to accounts with other banks, from where the money was siphoned off to further accounts in the names of A's relatives.

Since the quarterly impact was not significant as a percentage of the company's operations and the reconciliation process was not being followed for this account in the absence of reporting, the transfers did not set off any of the other control triggers.

When M was promoted to a more senior role, he insisted on retaining responsibility for account management, which his managers took to indicate his extreme dedication.

When his lifestyle began to improve quite a bit over time, another employee, Q, thought it fit to red flag the situation. Doing her utmost to review the process, she did a few quick investigations into M's lifestyle and found that it was rather lavish—quite a change from when he had joined the firm.

When flagged, the report went through to the human resources (HR) head. When confronted with questions around recent developments in his life, M took offense and threatened to quit and also to show documents from his inheritance from a dead uncle. M promised to place some of the money in an escrow account with the company for the duration of his employment. The HR head was moved and went along, failing to call M's bluff.

Another employee, F, had moved to the middle office and, oblivious to the goings-on, intercepted account statements sent by the bank to M's attention. F became curious. A few investigations revealed that the accounts in question were not part of the recon process.

F, unclear of the company's whistleblower policy, shot off two parallel sets of letters—one went to the chief financial officer (CFO) and Treasurer, and the other went to members of the board of directors. Both sides promptly raised this with

(Continued)

the chief executive officer (CEO), who was then asked by the board to be involved in the ensuing investigations. M, who had become aware of the investigation when a bank staffer asked him for information required for the investigation, had made plans to leave the country and was caught at an immigration checkpoint.

The company's control processes were strengthened after that, but the sense of control displayed by two employees showed that the individuals' sense of responsibility, more than the company's control culture, ultimately saved the day. The moral of the case is that while our instincts sometimes tell us what facts will later prove, the presence of a control culture can reduce instances of financial losses to a degree. The adage "trust, but verify" is certainly applicable in this context.

Teamwork

Earlier we discussed the various linkages and partnerships that Treasury needs to develop in order to add value to the business. Treasury will not be able to add value without a requisite amount of teamwork. Organisationally, joint cross-functional team goals in employee and team appraisals also enforces teamwork.

Transparency

The cost of capital and operations of Treasury get passed on to the business or operational units in many firms, since Treasury is mainly a support function. Given the cost of capital, returns on investment, gains or losses on marked-to-market (MTM) positions on hedging and targeted rates, apart from cost of operations and account maintenance, the cost and return parameters of Treasury will likely have an impact on the financial performance of various business units. Transparency with numbers, operations, and turnaround times will go a long way in reinforcing other units' faith in the Treasury group.

GENERAL SKILLS

General skills involve interpersonal and basic technical skills that the treasurers have to look at from a development and training perspective.

Relationship Building

Treasury team members need good interpersonal skills given their dual responsibility of managing the Treasury and being service managers to support the business. Their interpersonal skill, specifically in relationship management, is key, given the various interfaces that Treasury has with external and internal entities. (See Figure 1.4 in Chapter 1 for a snapshot of these linkages.)

Culture Knowledge

Since interactions with people from different backgrounds, countries/nationalities and culture is a way of life in the Treasury function, being able to understand and appreciate other cultures would assist in smooth interactions and in gaining the most from meetings, conversations, and discussions with the other party. Working in a cross-cultural, multinational environment also requires an appreciation of the backgrounds, markets, and environments of the various team members. Team contributions and performance depends a great deal on how well the team members work together to create solid and efficient output.

Technology

Members of Treasury teams do not need very technical skills but definitely have to be very good users of technology. Those involved in system decision making and implementation/integration need a good, well-rounded understanding of system architecture and usage so they have the tools to make decisions on which systems to use.

Process Orientation

Tightness of processes and zero tolerance for errors help make a Treasury perform beyond expectations. Along with a control mind-set, process orientation of Treasury employees creates respect within Treasury for the sanctity of well-laid out processes, which in turn ensures that other functions and external service providers also participate to make the end-to-end financial supply chain work seamlessly and efficiently.

Written Communication

A global Treasury has a lot of interfaces with entities through email and, where required, letters and notifications. Given the increasing dependence on email for most forms of communication, and the corresponding increase in the volume of emails, Treasury emails need to be crisp and articulated well enough for readers to immediately grasp the situation and respond should immediate action be required. Information-related emails should be clear and unambiguous, ensuring that there is no further follow-up that could waste precious time for both parties. There is a corresponding danger of overcommunication—in order to reduce reverse queries, some information emails contain an overload and excess of information. In these cases, the receiver could well come back to Treasury asking for where the information could actually be found and how to read the mountain of data that was sent.

TECHNICAL AND WORK-RELATED SKILLS

The final category of Treasury Culture involves finance and job-specific items that are core to the functioning of a well-rounded Treasury team.

Business

Basic business skills and the understanding of the company's business model, supply chain, dynamics, and industry and competitor backgrounds will serve in good stead to help Treasury employees understand the context of their roles. Many Treasury employees, especially at the junior level, struggle to understand the impact of their roles and how they are actually helping the organisation. Every Treasury role is critical, and the Treasurer and CFO would do well to ensure that each and every employee within the function has a good business understanding that will in turn help them add value to their roles instead of simply performing and executing tasks automatically.

Financial and Markets Awareness

Awareness of the global environment, especially the political and economic situations of the world around and its impact on markets, including the ones in which the company is present or likely to enter, is an important aspect for a global Treasury. It is important for Treasury members to be generally aware of key market factors, how they work, and general market trends and levels. Reading economic and industry reports regularly will also help to hone this knowledge base. Basic understanding of economics and balance sheet is also required.

Accounting

Given the impact of treasury's actions on the balance sheet through the accounting process, employees of Treasury must have at least a rudimentary knowledge of accounting and, more important, the basic accounting practices of the firm across its key locations. In particular, aspects of the cash conversion cycle (explained in Part Three), mark-to-markets or valuation of risk management transactions (explained in Part Four), and impact of translation of the balance sheet and related aspects should be well understood.

Regulatory

Treasury interfaces regularly with central banks, exchange commissions, foreign exchange regulators, and other regulatory and statutory bodies. The nature of Treasury work, especially cross-border and capital-related transactions, can sometimes create ambiguities around contravening regulations. It is critical to ensure that all activities and transactions follow appropriate regulations. In case of doubt, the compliance officer in charge must take the call, and unresolved or sensitive situations must be escalated to country or global management. While it is not in the realm of the Treasury employee to take the final regulatory call in sensitive or unclear situations, he or she must know the regulations well enough to recognise ambiguity or potential contravention.

An interesting example in the regulatory context is given below.

EXAMPLE: A PARALLEL CURRENCY

The nondeliverable forward market (NDF) is an often sensitive topic—the market exists, and certain central banks are concerned with trading on their currency outside of their purview, in locations where the notes are not legal tender.

We cover the NDF market in more detail in Part Four. Here we consider an example of a Treasurer who threw caution to the winds and decided to hedge a Latin American currency that was largely restricted on hedging, through the NDF market. The rationale was the time spent in getting approvals or documentation ready for onshore hedges. The local Treasurer would undertake these hedges with global banks outside the country, booking the deals on the parent's books. The Treasurer then worked out a method to "reimburse" the local company through internal accounting adjustments.

When the local subsidiary suffered large losses owing to massive currency movement, the regulator was unimpressed. The parent had reported good figures, including profitable numbers from the local company. The disconnect was obviously the hedging of the local exposure through the NDF process. Furthermore, email communication from the local entity to overseas banks on the NDF transactions solidified the evidence.

The Treasurer and the local CEO were called in, and a few sensitive conversations later, the process was changed to hedge only onshore, with all efforts being made to ensure compliance on approvals and documentation.

In contrast, the regulator of another country who kept receiving annual request for approvals for overseas parent companies to hedge their capital onshore studied the market. A group of treasurers had gotten together to present the case to the central bank. Once aware that many other firms were instead routing their hedges through the NDF market and recognising the genuine need for such transactions, the central bank refused to provide case-by-case approvals. Sometime later, the entire transaction category itself was included under the heading of "Hedgeable Risks" that overseas entities could perform onshore with minimal documentation and no prior approval. This brought even the NDF flows into the country. Proactiveness is best when it is two way.

THE MANY HATS OF THE TREASURER

The Treasurer wears many hats to fulfill and excel in his or her duty. This is a part of Treasury Culture, to inculcate a multidimensional "DNA" among senior Treasury personnel and wear these hats to assist the Treasurer and CFO, and to create a second-line to replace the Treasurer when the time comes for the current incumbent to move on.

Some hats of the Treasurer, illustrated in Figure 3.2, are listed next.

- Marketer
- Astute observer and analyst
- Fund manager (securing the firm's money)
- Gatekeeper
- Systems specialist
- Innovator
- Consultant and trusted advisor
- Lobbyist and regulatory interface
- Trainer
- Process engineer
- Economist and market expert

As we move through the various functions of Treasury, the relevance and applicability of these hats, and when the Treasurer wears them, will become more evident.

FIGURE 3.2 The Many Hats of the Treasurer

Putting in place a Treasury Culture is a process—it takes time to establish and requires effort to sustain. The effort will be worth every cent of time and money invested. History has proved it.

SUMMARY

In this chapter, we observed the importance of the Treasury Culture and how a Treasurer can, over time, create and sustain the culture that is an important determinant to achieving Treasury Leadership. We looked at the various hats that the Treasurer needs to wear, and aspects that would help the next generation of Treasury managers to try out and prepare for higher responsibility and empowerment.

CHAPTER FOUR

4

Importance of Operations and Control Efficiency

PROCESSES FORM THE CORE of the Treasury function, with systems and technology being enablers to implement and achieve efficient processing. Unfortunately, processes are also some of the most ignored aspects of many a Treasury, relegated to the shadows away from the glamour and spotlight of investor relations, mergers and acquisitions, capital planning, exotic concentration solutions, and risk management.

This chapter highlights the importance of processes—their operations and control—and some of the tools required to put processes in place. The Toolkit in Part Five discusses some of these tools in detail.

TOOLS

There are many tools available in the Treasurer's armoury. The following tools (Figure 4.1) are especially critical from an operations and control standpoint.

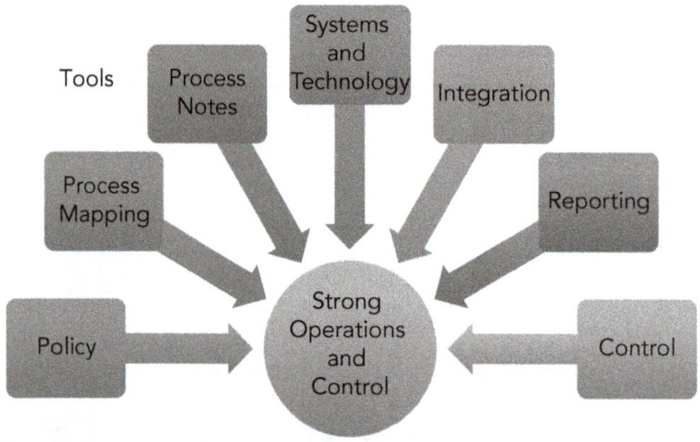

FIGURE 4.1 Tools for Strong Operations and Control

Policy

A Treasury policy, a sample of which is provided in Part Five, is a starting point in the Treasury operations and control journey. Key elements, activities, risks, and mitigants are identified; roles and responsibilities are allocated; and limits and functioning parameters are defined. Processes and procedures have to work in tandem with the policy.

Process Mapping

Process maps lay a strong foundation for watertight process notes. There are different styles and standards of process mapping. I favour maps where the process is mapped out by role and each handoff point from one role to the other is clearly demarcated. A separate role for system inputs and handoffs and the activity performed by the system segregates the human element from the technological one. The handoffs are one of the key differentiators that maps bring to the table. Opportunities for errors creep in when there are handoffs. It is important to document handoffs appropriately and try to minimise their frequency and number. Figure 4.1 shows an illustrative process map for Treasury risk management.

Process Notes

Process notes, which are referred to by many other names, such as standard operating procedures, are detailed documentation, by activity and role, of each Treasury process. Some of the advantages of standardised process notes in uniform formats are that they:

- Improve efficiency and effectiveness of operations.
- Provide a ready reference tool for new employees to start performing their roles immediately and a refresher for existing employees backing up or ascertaining process-related aspects in situations of ambiguity.
- Enable auditors, reviewers, and regulators to understand the process end to end and hence lower the opportunities for miscommunication.
- With greater transparency, show up opportunities for error and improvement, thereby increasing control and process watertightness.

- Improve employee motivation, awareness, and morale.
- Reduce cost.
- Provide a pan-company, cross-location standard for cutting-edge Treasury Design.

Systems and Technology

The advent of systems and technology across the spectrum has vastly increased the efficiency of Treasury processes. Irrespective of the nature of the business and industry, and for a business in any stage of maturity, size, and growth, Treasury is one unit that certainly benefits from automation and systems. Increasingly proactive banking systems, payment gateways, and vendor automation have greatly added to the bulwark of a robust Treasury process. Two key questions arise, which are addressed below. We subsequently revisit the Systems discussion in Part Five.

1. Is it better to align processes around a good system or to align systems around existing efficient processes?

   One of the reasons for procuring a new system is to improve processes. With the assumption that a robust system that has been tried and tested will make the whole process more efficient, it is more practical to use the opportunity to enhance existing processes with the system as enablers, without having to change the system and retain existing processes.
2. Is it better to have good use of excellent technology or excellent use of good technology?

   It is said that a system is only as good as its usage. It is always better to use a system in an excellent manner to extract the most from its capabilities than to invest in a state-of-the-art system but use it only partially and not leverage its complete capability. Of course, any system must fulfil the criteria for which it has been procured and must have the desired capabilities.

Integration

Integration of systems, processes, accounting, and control with the entire firm's architecture increases process coordination and reduces the need for duplication and rework.

Reporting

A good reporting mechanism utilises little human time and effort, is timely and appropriate, and optimises level of detail for each level of management. Overreporting can waste time and lower the perceived level of importance of information or require more effort to identify the meaningful and necessary information from an ocean of data. Under- or inadequate reporting has its own obvious consequences.

Control

Regular review and control of processes ensures that there are few surprises and operating or other losses incurred as a result of inadequate or inadequately followed procedures. A detailed overview of the control process is given in Part Five.

DIFFERENT OFFICES: FRONT, MIDDLE, AND BACK

The delineation of duties across the front, middle, and back offices is increasingly gaining popularity. Of the many innovations and thought processes that the banking sector has lent to the world, one of the most crucial is the middle-office function. This function monitors and works closely with both the front and back offices, reporting independently and ensuring that management receives regular updates regarding activities of the two other cogs in the Treasury wheel.

- **Front office**. Focuses on planning, transacting or dealing, funding, investment, risk management, interacting with banks, and owning the accounts. This is the front end with the key decision making and transacting. This function reports directly to the Treasurer.
- **Back office**. Focuses on confirmation, settlement, processing the transactions, basic reconciliation, and passing the entries into the enterprise resource planning (ERP) or general ledger (GL) accounting system. This is the back end with key execution and operations responsibilities. If the Treasurer is also a transactor or dealer who regularly executes transactions, the back-office reporting should be independent, preferably the responsibility of the controller.
- **Middle office**. Focuses on control, valuation, reconciliation between front and back offices, performance evaluation, model validations, risk reporting, and limit monitoring. This area is appropriately called the middle office because its function has oversight of both front and back ends, with key control and reporting responsibility. The middle office always reports independently of front and back offices, either to the controller (if the Treasurer does not have a transactional role) or to the chief financial officer (CFO) or risk head (if the controller has oversight of the back office).

Figure 4.2 provides a snapshot of the various responsibilities across these three arms of Treasury activities.

In many situations, the lack of role clarity could result in items falling in between tables and having no ownership. The case study below illustrates such a situation.

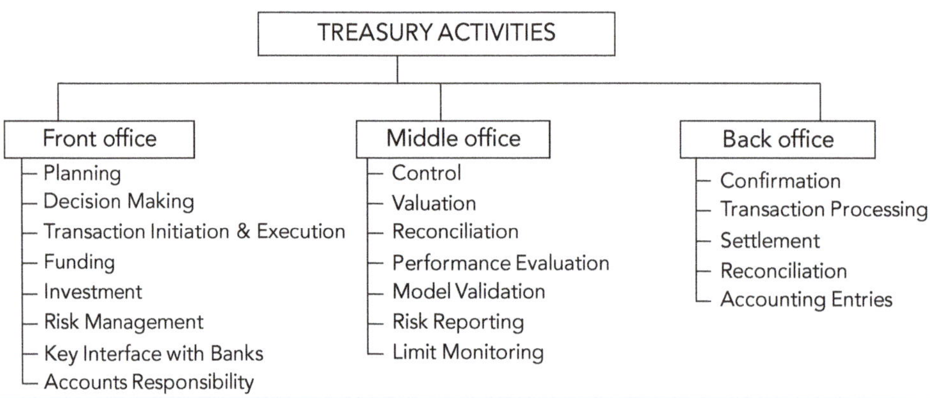

FIGURE 4.2 Sample Segregation of Duties Across Front Office, Middle Office, and Back Office

CASE STUDY: WHICH DESK SHOULD LOOK AFTER THIS ISSUE?

The CFO of a European technology company was in a quandary. The books in the control system and the Treasury system were showing different numbers. The Treasurer, who had claimed a massive savings as a result of his hedges, had resigned when the controller reported that the hedging process over the past two years had actually lost the firm a lot of money and that the objectives of achieving stability and visibility of financials were not being met. The week after the Treasurer had quit, one of the dealers came to the CFO with a problem: A hedge transaction that the Treasurer had done earlier in the month as part of the hedging programme that had also been reported in the GL system (ERP) had come up for maturity, but the bank had no records of the supposed transaction. Similarly, a payment that was supposed to have gone for an earlier hedge settlement through the electronic system had shown a confirmation, while the bank was still asking for the payment to be made.

The Treasury team was responsible for the transactions and interface with banks and for accounts and liquidity management. Any entries to be passed were done so by the controller's team based on reports issued by Treasury. The control team members were not experts on Treasury decisions and products; they left decisions to the expertise of the Treasury team, agreeing in the spirit of teamwork to help pass the entries in the back end. Implementation of a state-of-the-art Treasury system had assisted the process. Entries were now mostly automated except for a few processes, where the front end or dealers still handed over reports and the transaction entries in the ERP were then be passed by control based on these inputs.

The CFO immediately requested an independent review, and after two weeks, he received the report. Sifting through the points, there was one thread that was common: the differences between the various elements, systems, or desks on their evaluations, numbers, and balances. The reconciliation process had gone awry. The ERP (GL system) and the state-of-the-art Treasury system that the company had invested in on the treasurer's recommendation were showing completely different numbers on account balances and hedging transactions. Transactions reported on the Treasury system and whose mark-to-markets were being correctly reflected in the accounting books were not present in the banks' reports. Limit excesses by traders had been checked (the checklists had been ticked) but not reported, since the checks had been done by the traders themselves—system and banking reports would come in to the dealers who would perform the verification to the best of their ability.

The CFO called the controller and the senior members of the Treasury team. All of them had done their day-to-day operational jobs to the best of their abilities, but when the time came to discuss reconciliation, the answers were ambiguous. Owing to direct system handoffs between the Treasury system and the ERP, no one had felt that there was a need for reconciliation. The banks' offer to integrate their systems with the Treasury system had been rejected owing to incremental implementation costs. Hence the activity had remained with the Treasurer and his team. Limit checks were designated a noncritical activity by the dealers and hence were not factored into reviews on automated system reports—where they had

(Continued)

been built, the recipient e-mail addresses listed the dealers themselves, and post-migration, the addresses had not been changed. The inbox of the Treasury team members was thus flooded with over 100 reports that kept being flushed to the "Unread reports" folder and purged whenever the mailbox exceeded its limit.

The solution again was simple: The reconciliation process had to be done, regularly. The question was, by whom?

Would it be done by the front office, giving it access to the back-end systems as well? Or was it a back-end task, reconciling tasks after the entries had been passed? Or was it worthwhile to invest in a middle office, which would be responsible for all the reporting and the reconciliation, independent of the activities of deal origination, decision making, and booking in the firm's ledgers?

The next case discusses a real-life case of the National Aeronautical and Space Administration (NASA) and shows how a situation for a control and information security risk was resolved.

CASE STUDY: IMPORTANCE OF MANAGING INFORMATION TECHNOLOGY SECURITY RISK IN OUTSOURCING CONTRACTS

Information technology (IT) security has become a main area of focus with increasing interconnectivity of systems and networks around the world and scattered information and data storage through the use of various service providers. When activities are outsourced, the criticality of building in adequate measure of information security (IS), especially sensitive financial and balance sheet information that Treasury possesses and uses, is escalated. This case study explores how NASA builds in IS risk into its outsourcing contracts and how it addressed and resolved a situation of noncompliance.

Background: Importance of IS

IT security and safety of information and details are critical for any firm. When your firm runs the largest and most advanced space programme in the world, the risk is possible at the highest level, which could result in human fatalities.

Incomplete IS aspects and classification for any project could lead to a number of potential issues. NASA takes its IS risks very seriously, especially in the background of the consequences shown in Figure 4.3.

Information classification must be unambiguous and easy to interpret, since the use of the classification and the data protection around each classification or category of information will be different. Each data item must be identified and classified beforehand to avoid rework and reduce chances of error and risk. NASA uses the classification provided in Figure 4.4.

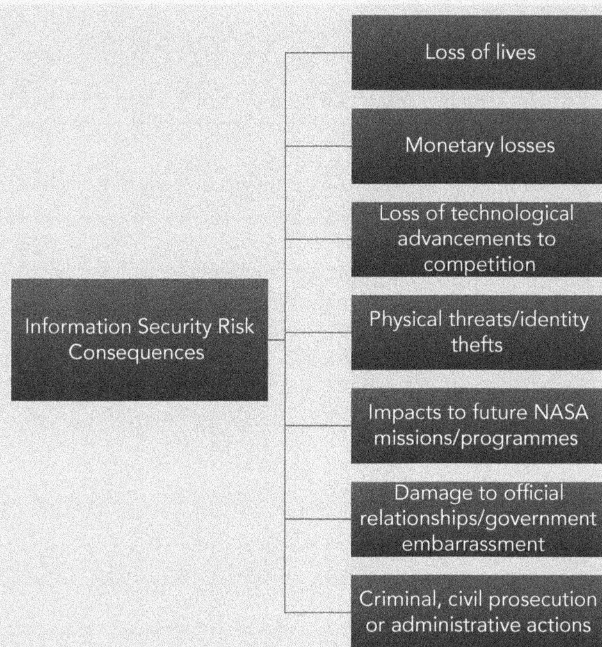

FIGURE 4.3 Consequences of Information Security Risk Issues

Information Security Risk-Classified National Security Information

Unclassified but Sensitive or Restricted Information (SBU)

- information, regardless of its form, the release of which could cause harm to programmes or operations essential to NASA's missions or the safeguarding of our national interests, adversely impact non-governmental firms or institutions, or damage a person's privacy interests or economic or physical welfare
- Other types of protected data including export controlled

Other (vast majority of the information NASA deals with)

- Other types of NASA information are not per se automatically releasable for non-business purposes.

FIGURE 4.4 NASA Information Classification

(Continued)

Situation: Contract Built In But No Compliance with IT Security

The Orion project is an advanced spacecraft programme in the implementation stage. Also known as the Multi-Purpose Crew Vehicle (MPCV), it is being built to explore farther into our solar system, including potentially returning to the moon, visiting an asteroid, and/or mounting a hugely complex and risky mission to Mars. The first manned mission is expected to take place after 2020. Each Orion spacecraft is projected to carry a crew of four astronauts. Most of the Orion project activities have been outsourced to selected prime contractors.

During a review, NASA discovered that appropriate security clauses around sensitive but unclassified (SBU) information had not been incorporated appropriately into the vendor contract.

NASA had redefined the responsibilities for information as part of establishing its security protocols (see Figure 4.5). However, the details of the requirements were not established until after contract award.

When the vendor was requested to assess the contract cost impacts of incorporating the new security protocols, the cost was more than NASA could bear. NASA now had two options:

1. Seek a waiver from NASA headquarters (HQ) and governing security agencies regarding levying the new security protocols on the Orion contract.
2. Negotiate between the Orion prime contractor and the owner of the security requirements (NASA HQ) to meet the intent of the levied security protocols to ensure the protection of sensitive information while maintaining the cost impacts within budgetary constraints.

On examination, it was evident that a waiver would have an irreparable impact and leave much sensitive information vulnerable to theft or misuse. The vendor was a long-standing partner of NASA; hence from a relationship perspective, it should be possible to work with it to find a solution.

It was decided to renegotiate the requirements with the prime contractor and HQ. However, there would be a price to pay, and the team at NASA recognised that. The way forward was to work closely to identify the security requirements and reduce risk to the largest extent, and also identify how these requirements could

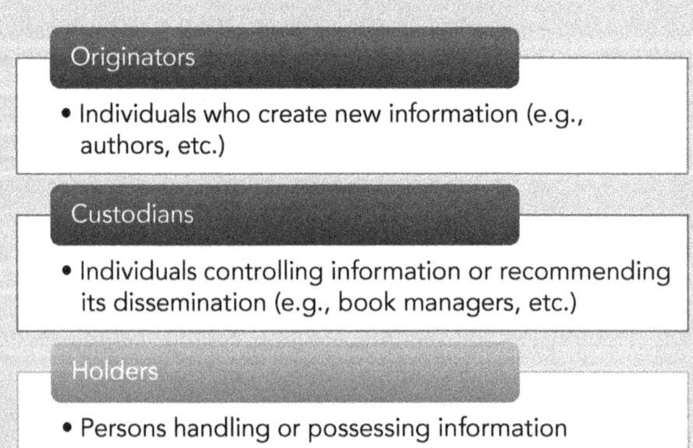

FIGURE 4.5 Responsibilities for Information

be levied on the prime contractor with minimal cost impact from wording or process changes (see Figure 4.6).

One of the key elements was training the team at the vendor side, so that they could fully understand and implement the new security protocols. The training would involve:

- Proper identification and categorisation of information (in this case, sensitive but unclassified)
- Proper marking of information
- Proper handling of sensitive but unclassified information
- Storage requirements
- Transmission requirements
- Decontrolling information

The consequences of noncompliance or failure to identify information as such could result in:

- Increased risk to programmes or operations essential to the mission
- Damage to a person's privacy interests or economic or physical welfare
- Possible administrative action and criminal prosecution
- Competition having access to the information

Once the vendor came back with estimates and the plan, the team at NASA worked with the vendor team to finalise the revisions and negotiate on the cost, for a win-win situation in the context of the information security gap.

Contributed by Jeevan Perera, PhD, JD, Johnson Space Center, NASA

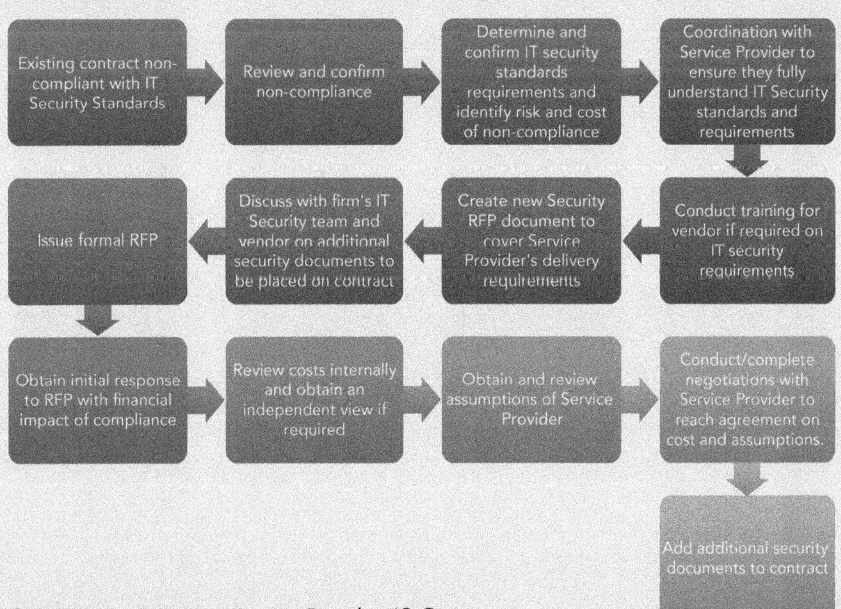

FIGURE 4.6 Process Map to Resolve IS Gap

(Continued)

Learnings

IT security is critical to the organisation, especially information on bank accounts, financials, risk management, and investments that Treasury is privy to and owns. IT security needs to be built in to outsourcing contracts to reduce operational risks.

If such clauses have not been factored into existing contracts, it would be worthwhile, as we saw in the case of NASA, to subsequently incorporate these clauses into the contracts and rationalise the incremental cost structure by working with the vendor or outsourcing partner.

SUMMARY

In this chapter, we looked at some of the important elements of Treasury processes, operations, and control. The importance of process mapping and other tools were highlighted. Finally, the delineation of Treasury activities and responsibilities across front, middle, and back offices and the growing importance and context of the middle office were discussed.

PART TWO

Transactions and Cash Management

IN THE NEXT THREE PARTS, we go through the key treasury functions in detail: transactions management, balance sheet and liquidity management, and risk management. In Part Five, we provide a Toolkit for use across various important elements of the treasury function.

Part Two introduces the importance of managing transactions and accounts that ensure fund and document flows while minimising cost and inefficiencies. We also introduce the concept of the financial supply chain and its management.

In this part, we answer some of the questions related to the management of accounts, cash, and cash flows and related transactions, such as:

- How can we derive the optimal account structure for a global group of companies?
- What are the methods to transfer money from one location or account to another?
- How is float and its management critical to the lifeline of a company?

- When do liquidity management solutions deliver maximum value to the firm?
- Why is netting becoming such a popular tool for Treasurers?
- What are the various elements in cash flow forecasting and how can these be used by Treasurers to improve the working of their function?

We begin with a look at account structures across various contexts.

CHAPTER FIVE

5

Account Management and Structure

THE ACCOUNT STRUCTURE is a critical part of Treasury Design and depends on many factors. These factors include business operating model, type of transactions, cash flows, currencies, Treasury structure and staffing, culture, control elements, and budgets. Some of the decisions to be made in structuring accounts are given diagrammatically in Figure 5.1.

Account structures are linked with the people operating them and systems. Systems make the entire design and setup of accounts quite sticky—once implemented and tested, these systems would be geared up to support a certain kind of structure. More often than not, even a small change in the way accounts are managed results in significant costs and effort involved to change the entire process, since the account structure is one of the bases for the company's financial operations.

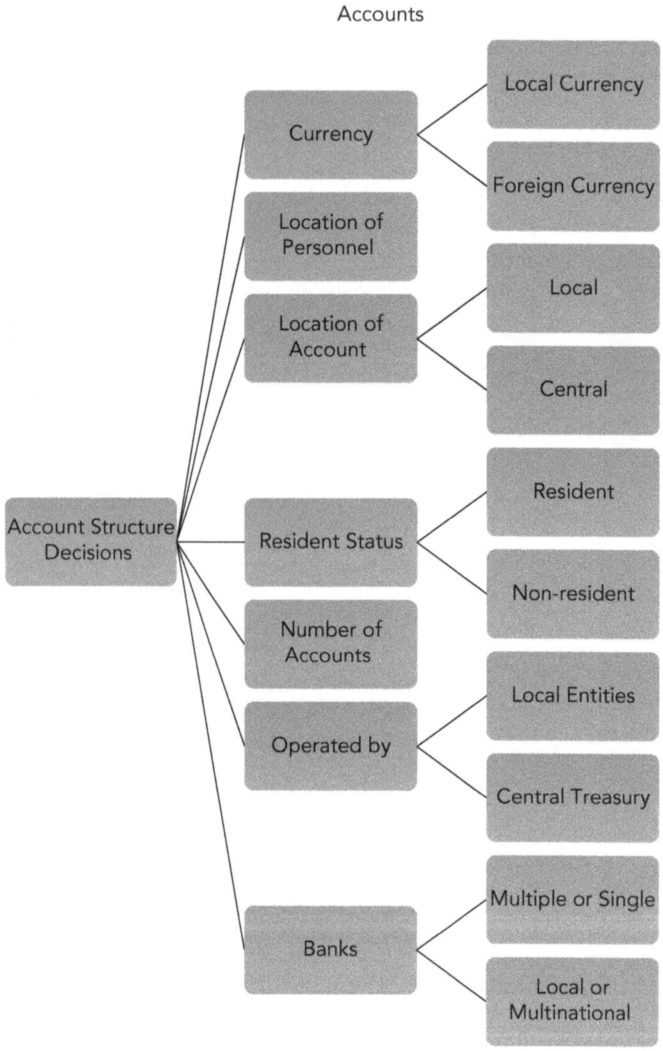

FIGURE 5.1 Decisions for Account Structure

PUTTING AN ACCOUNT STRUCTURE IN PLACE

We now look at some of the considerations for account structures as well as the need and ways to use different kinds of accounts across currencies, resident statuses, and locations. The steps involved in designing, setting up, and maintaining an account structure are given in Figure 5.2.

In the first stage, consideration is given to various aspects, and the needs are discussed and documented. In the second stage, the banking partners are decided on and finalised. In the final stage, the implementation and integration is done.

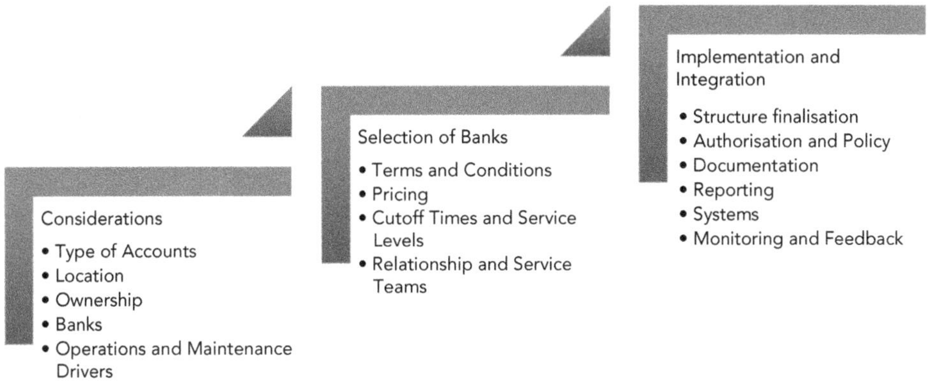

FIGURE 5.2 Account Structure Design and Implementation

General Considerations for Account Structures

Some of the considerations for account structures are listed next:

- Organisational structure and business flows: While separate accounts will be needed for separate legal entities, some business units, client segments, or regional operations might warrant separate accounts
- Business processes: risk management settlements, payables, receivables
- Different banks for different services
- Network or reach of the banks
- Special-purpose accounts, such as dividends or escrow
- Special local processes
- Segregation of customers' funds
- Trust accounts
- Transaction volumes
- Complexity of operations
- Recycling foreign exchange inflows and outflows
- Decentralised management culture
- Location of invoicing and Treasury centres
- Tax advantages
  - Sales tax: Impacts selling and invoicing decisions
  - Withholding tax: Depends on countries of origination and destination, also impacts nonresident payments and borrowing/investment decisions
  - Income tax
  - Tax benefits: Especially for decisions on financial centres/Treasury centres

As part of the Treasury Design spoken of earlier, these elements have to be considered at the time of setup or review. The Treasury policy can also contain the account structure to be used and followed.

Considerations for Multiple Currency Accounts

Any multinational firm needs to deal in different currencies, given a global client, supplier, investor, or service provider base. Hence, operations and cash flows in foreign currencies are inevitable. The question then arises as to whether accounts must be maintained in foreign currency, and if so, where they will be maintained and by whom will they be operated.

Some of the considerations for opening and maintaining foreign currency accounts are listed next:

- Regulatory requirements: With different legal entities in different locations, there could be a mandate to open accounts in the currency of the local entity (in the country)
- Suppliers' invoicing currency (procurement/supplies in different currencies)
- Products and supplies in the same currency
- Timing of products and supplies payments
- Cost of opening and maintaining foreign currency accounts
- Current and future foreign exchange and rate risks
- Possibility of creating intercompany loans
- Method of foreign currency payments
  - Inflows are used to fund outflows
  - Bought from bank or centralised Treasury
  - Conversion done at local bank

Also, where these accounts should physically reside—whether in-country, at the Treasury centre, or at the home location of the currency (e.g., SGD account in Singapore and GBP accounts in London)—also must be considered, as must be the decision as to whether to use a local bank (in-country), a relationship bank in-country, or centralise with Treasury.

Table 5.1 provides an overview of location and bank alternatives for the design of account structures

Considerations for Nonresident Accounts

A nonresident account is the locally or domestically based account of an overseas entity that has been legally incorporated or domiciled elsewhere and does not have a legal resident status in that country.

The resident status of an entity can generally be determined through any of these criteria:

- Location of incorporation
- Legal status of local entity: branch of parent or a permanent establishment
- Registration with local industry bodies
- Registration or status with domestic tax authorities
- Duration of presence in that country

TABLE 5.1 Location and Bank Alternatives for Account Structure Design

Aspect	Relationship Bank (Centralised Treasury)	Domestic Bank (Local)	Relationship Bank (Local)
Banking	Same bank with all accounts More issues on cheque acceptability Commission/charges	Lower cost and hence commission Issues on cheque acceptability Closer to local subsidiaries and customers Requires use of different banks	Lower use of correspondent banks Cost and hence commission Fewer issues on cheque acceptability Closer to local subsidiaries & customers
Funds transfer	Easier transfer funds/cheques to local currency (LCY) account Longer credits and clearing times No domestic payment or collection instruments (automated clearinghouse [ACH]) Funds transfers are cross-border payments	Funds transfers are domestic Quicker clearing and credits Slower advices	Funds transfers are domestic Domestic instruments for collections Quicker clearing and credits Advices through electronic banking (EB)
Operations	Easier interface with fewer language/communications issues Easier reporting Easier delivery of payment instructions More restricted cutoff times	Payments initiated remotely Less restricted cutoff times More restrictions possible Need for lockboxes Slower reporting language and communication problems, including documentation Delays in signatories and transaction initiation	Payments initiated remotely (EB) Quicker cutoff times Reporting communication and fewer language issues and delays on documentation Standardised documentation and pricing
Registration/tax	No significant tax issues in many cases	Potential tax situations?	Withholding tax–related concerns?

Nonresident accounts usually are in either the domestic currency or the currency of the parent entity.

However, in many countries, the treatment of nonresident accounts from the perspectives of usage, interest, overdraft or lending, and repatriation are generally different from those of locally domiciled entities. In this context, taxes, banking charges, regulatory norms and approvals, concentration structures (pooling), and restrictions on the usage of the money for specific purposes will be different and hence should be considered during process setup.

Regulatory approvals might be required just once or on a case-by-case basis. It becomes the responsibility of the locally based entities (such as the bank or the branch office) to fulfil the regulatory conditions, such are reporting and transaction use. The importance of the banking partner here becomes even more critical: Banks that have good relationships with the regulators have had past history of dealing with such cases. Banks that play the role of trusted advisor to the firm, assist in the process of obtaining relevant regulatory and other approvals, and clarify ambiguity in new situations are likely to be a priority bank for the enterprise (to be discussed in further detail in Chapter 28).

Considerations for Account Ownership

Who owns and operates each account is a matter that needs to be determined during the design of the account structure. Depending on the legal status of each entity and the nature of the operation, ownership can be:

- Single ownership of the operation or legal entity
- Joint ownership
- Centralised ownership

Other aspects to consider prior to deciding ownership are:

- Local regulations and reporting
- Resident status
- Tax status
- Domestic (in-country or local) clearing requirements
- Credit facilities
- Pooling regulations
- Netting capability and regulations

ACCOUNT OPERATION AND APPROACHES

Operating bank accounts is a task that sounds easier than it is. When one combines the operational element of multiple accounts across territories, jurisdictions, time zones, languages, service levels, and cutoff times with managing balances, investments, concentration, the currency element, and unpredictability of flows in a highly controlled environment, the complexity increases manifold.

Maintenance of foreign currency accounts has many angles; some of these include:

- Operations and technology aspects (process)
- Maintenance cost
- Interest-related costs
- Currency-related aspects
- Balance requirements

These aspects are highlighted in Figure 5.3.

Drivers of Account Structure

While other considerations for the account structure are being determined, treasury's priority will be a key driver for selection of account structure: Does Treasury want to achieve more efficient flows, or does it want to achieve more efficient liquidity? While efficiency of flows is always important in an overall context, a Treasury's priority tends to slide toward liquidity in times of crisis.

Since the middle path between liquidity and flows cannot be taken easily, one of the two paths would have to wait a little more than the other.

Table 5.2 provides an outline of various aspects of account structure set-up with either path (flows or liquidity) as priority.

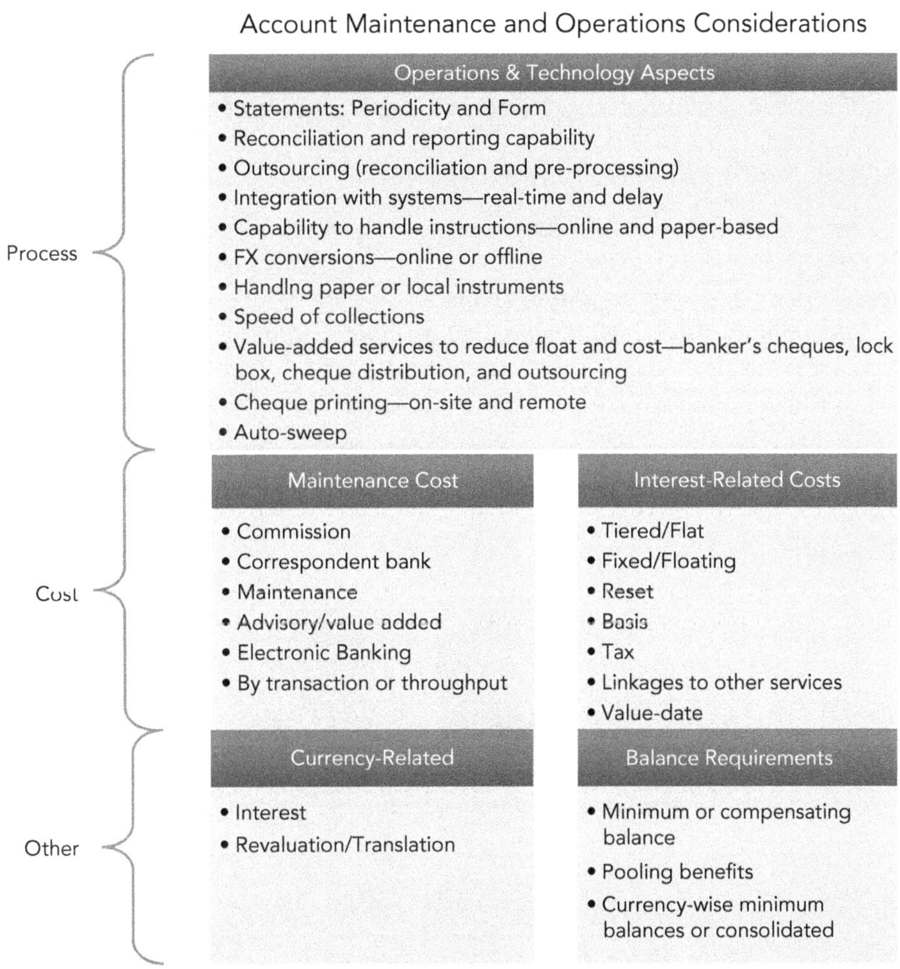

FIGURE 5.3 Account Maintenance Aspects

TABLE 5.2 Drivers of Account Structure

Aspect	Effective Flows Management	Efficient Liquidity Management
Banks	Domestic banks providing reach and service	Fewer banks
Location of accounts	On-site for easy management locally	Centralised at treasury centre
Number of accounts	One for each purpose for easier tracking and handling and easier business processes	As few as possible
Currencies of accounts	Multiple, in local currencies of payment	Single

Implementation of account structures is an involved process and generally is difficult to roll back or unwind without material cost and disruption to Treasury operations. Hence, the need to get it right at the start is extremely high.

Introducing Simple Account Structures

We now look at some simple structures based on control, location, and the ability to pool money together (see Figure 5.4). The aspect of liquidity and pooling is also introduced here and is covered in detail in Chapters 8 and 9.

Two primary aspects of the account structure—control and location of the accounts—form the basis of these sample structures. Accounts can be controlled locally or by a centralised Treasury. Similarly, accounts can be located in-country or

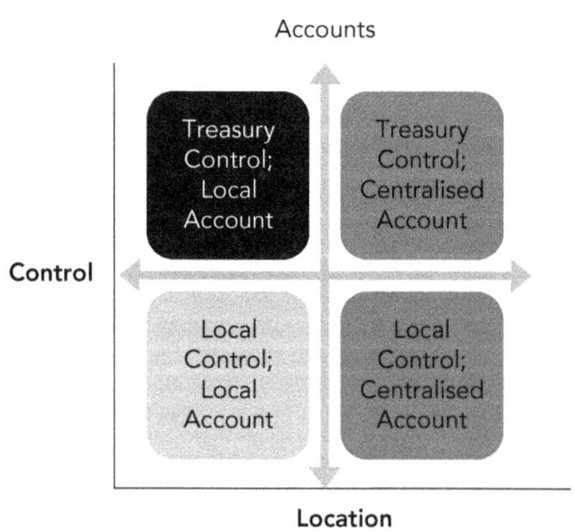

FIGURE 5.4 Simple Account Structure Classification

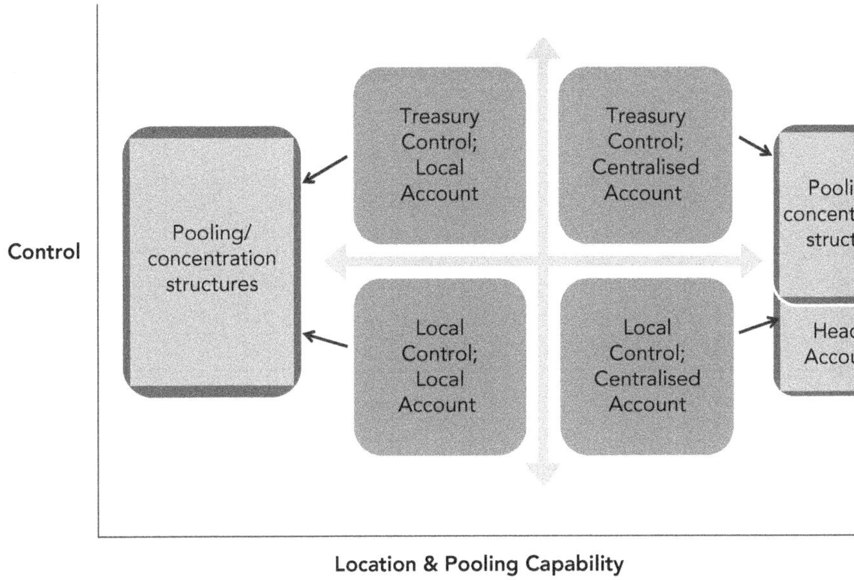

FIGURE 5.5 Account Structure with Pooling Capability

at a central location. The central location can be the currency of the country or the centralised Treasury.

Next we discuss the bases of some of the account structures. When we cover the more advanced themes of pooling and concentration, we superimpose these account structures and explore how the account structure design can be further reinforced through the use of intelligent liquidity tools. Figure 5.5 provides a snapshot of the account structure design with the variation of pooling structures thrown in.

Next we turn to simple account structures and their advantages and disadvantages.

RATIONALISING ACCOUNT STRUCTURES

Regulations of many countries do not allow for either the account location or its control to be outside of the borders of the country. Hence, such regulations may necessitate the single approach of having local accounts managed locally. Treasurers must review the regulations and laws of the countries specifically to determine the applicability of account structures.

Depending on the needs and the nature of payments, it is possible that no one structure will meet all requirements, and a mix of structures can be developed to suit the needs of the group.

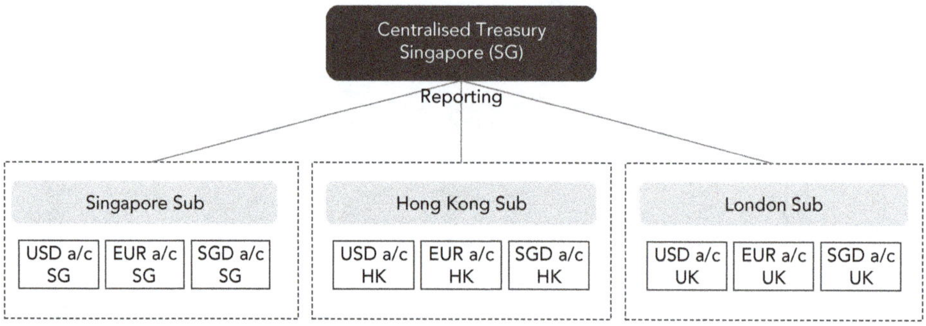

FIGURE 5.6 Local Accounts with Local Control

Local In-Country Accounts with Local Control

Local in-country accounts with local control make up the basic form of account structure prevalent in many companies. The local subsidiaries have their own accounts and operate them independently, with the numbers and transactions being reported back to centralised Treasury. The policy and authority/limits are governed as per global mandates, but ownership and operation are locally done. Bank decisions are made on the ground or in consultation with headquarters. In the case of requests for proposals (RFPs), global or relationship banks will be awarded the accounts. A sample structure of a centralised Treasury in Singapore (SG), with subsidiaries in Singapore, Hong Kong (HK), and London (UK) is elucidated in Figure 5.6.

This structure provides flexibility and control to the teams on the ground. A good working equation is developed, and service issues and reporting are settled locally. The centralised Treasury is involved from a distance and provides policy support. Control, information flow, and liquidity (use of funds) are aspects in which this structure falls short.

Centralised Accounts with Local Control

Two variants of centralised accounts with local control are discussed. In the first, depicted in Figure 5.7, the accounts of each entity across currencies are domiciled at the location of the currency. Hence, in the example, all USD accounts are held in New York (NY), all Singapore dollar accounts are in Singapore, and all euro accounts are in London. While this increases complexity to a degree by creating another location, one potential benefit is the simple use of header accounts or overlay structures, along with availability of liquidity and funding in that currency.

With the advent of Treasury centres and liquidity across major currencies in different centres, along with seamless funds transfers and banking partner support, there are simpler and more efficient measures by which to attain benefits similar to those provided by this structure.

The second variant is to keep all accounts at central Treasury or the in-house bank, irrespective of currency (see Figure 5.8). The operation is still in the hands of the local team, but the money is concentrated in one location. Cash pooling and concentration structures, discussed later, including using header accounts, could create similar benefits.

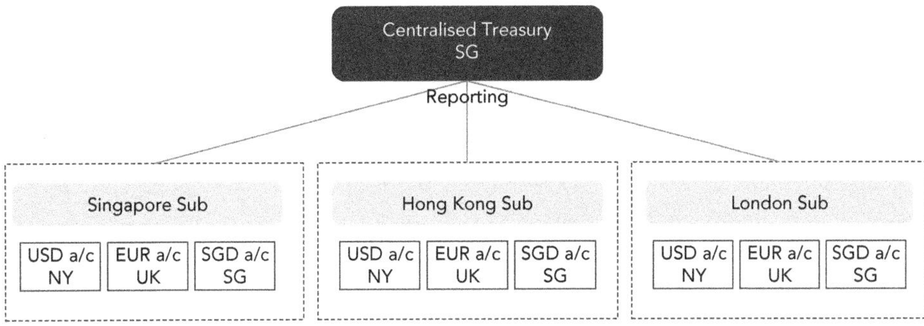

FIGURE 5.7 Accounts Centralised in Country of Currency with Local Control

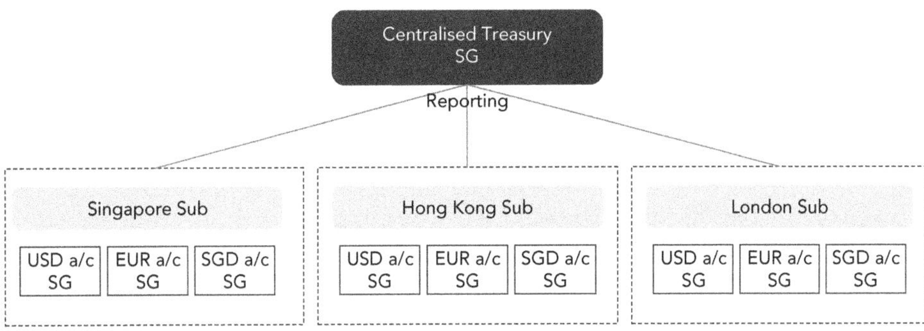

FIGURE 5.8 Local Control with Accounts at Centralised Treasury

Treasury Controlling a Local Account

As depicted in Figure 5.9, accounts located in respective countries can be operated by a centralised Treasury. This provides economies of scale on operations and makes liquidity management easier. Variants of this structure include using a single

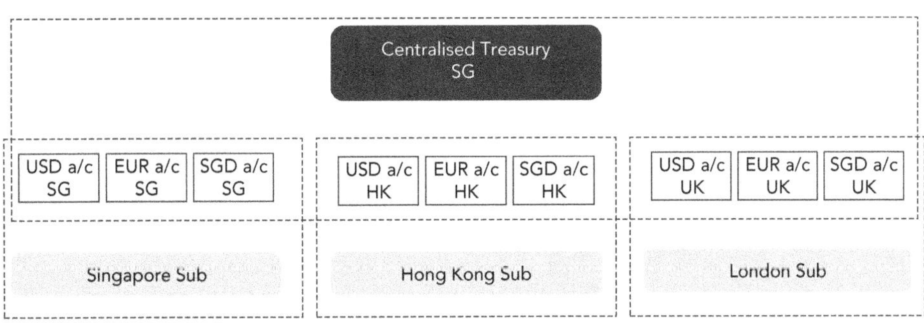

FIGURE 5.9 Local Account Controlled by Treasury

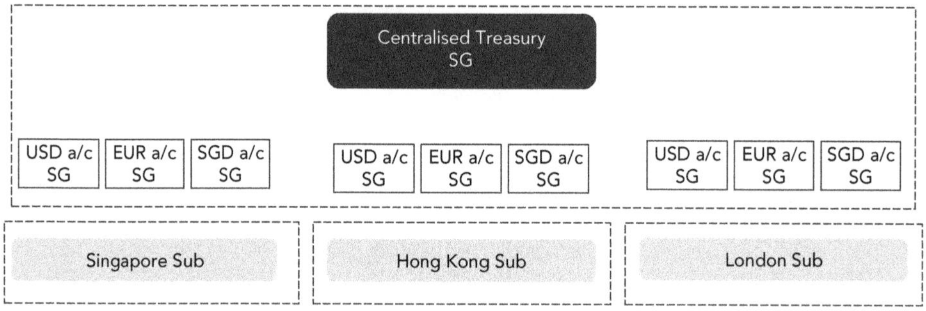

FIGURE 5.10 Treasury-Controlled Centralised Accounts

concentration bank in each country for pooling of funds, and the use of overlay structures and nonresident accounts.

Some concerns with this structure involve language (especially for interface with remote branches of domestic banks), cutoff times, and coordinating paper-based banking documentation.

Treasury Controlling Centralised Accounts

The final simple structure (see Figure 5.10) is a completely centralised one, where Treasury controls the accounts, which are also located centrally. This method can be achieved directly or through pooling structures with cross-border concentration. This method provides synergies of human resources, systems, and, most important, liquidity and is one of the end states of a completely centralised Treasury operations unit.

The hurdles of a centralisation implementation (see the case study on centralisation in Part One) apply here as well, but organisational performance, especially when linked with local subsidiary management goals, can benefit greatly in this context.

EXAMPLES OF ACCOUNT STRUCTURES ACROSS SECTORS

We conclude this chapter with a glance across some sectors and what structures might work for them.

Manufacturing

Given that large sourcing and disbursements are required for plant and supplies, many manufacturing businesses are quite payment intensive and locally operation intensive. Hence, for local procurement and payments, a local control structure with locally based accounts could be more efficient. For global orders, invoicing, and procurement, centralised control and accounts in Treasury might benefit.

Also, liquidity planning for working capital across subsidiaries is generally a strong area of focus; in such cases, additional pooling and concentration features would be implemented.

Technology and Information Technology–Enabled Services

Technology services companies generally have centralised invoicing with hubs for development and information processing. Local payments are usually required only for purposes of local expenses, such as payroll and local procurement. Hence, this operation is relatively easier to control from the centralised Treasury. A centralised structure would create large efficiencies in this context.

Retail

With largely local collections and global procurement and manufacturing, firms in the retail industry could have local accounts managed centrally for collections, with payments and invoicing done centrally. Concentration structures could be used to pool the funds centrally where possible, and local operations of accounts for purposes of payroll and the like could be established; depending on the nature of centralisation, however, a consolidated account management and set of accounts could be beneficial.

Transportation

Transportations companies, especially airlines, operate out of many locations using a single legal entity. Hence, such companies should maintain nonresident accounts that allow repatriability of collections (net of local payment) and proceeds into a central account held at the headquarters or Treasury centre. Since capital is raised centrally, and local payments are limited to fuel, airport-related charges, and salaries in local currencies, with collections being ticketing revenue, a centralised setup with nonresident accounts in the countries could be efficient.

Next we discuss the various payment systems in more depth before delving into float and liquidity and methods to manage them.

SUMMARY

In this chapter, we reviewed the key ingredients of account structure, which is one of the primary drivers of a treasury's functioning. A flawed account structure could seriously impair the smooth delivery of the monies of a company and cause a serious drag on its resources and efficiency. A well thought out and executed account structure could, however, lay the foundation for a fluid and strong Treasury. We evaluated various accounts and considerations for starting and managing them, as well as different kinds of controls and implementations, discussing relative merits and demerits. Finally, we considered a few sectors in particular with possible account structures that could work well in them.

CHAPTER SIX

The Movement of Money

IN THIS CHAPTER, we look at the various forms of money and the methods in which money can be moved within a city, country, and internationally. We review some of the global payment systems in vogue and explore China as a case study of great improvement in the payments space.

MONEY TRANSFER MECHANISMS

Various methods have been used to move money over time, and different countries, depending on their state of evolution, use combinations of methods. Figure 6.1 shows some of these mechanisms for money transfer. These are:

- Currency notes and coins
- Cheques and drafts
- Cards
- Bills and negotiable instruments
- Electronic funds transfer

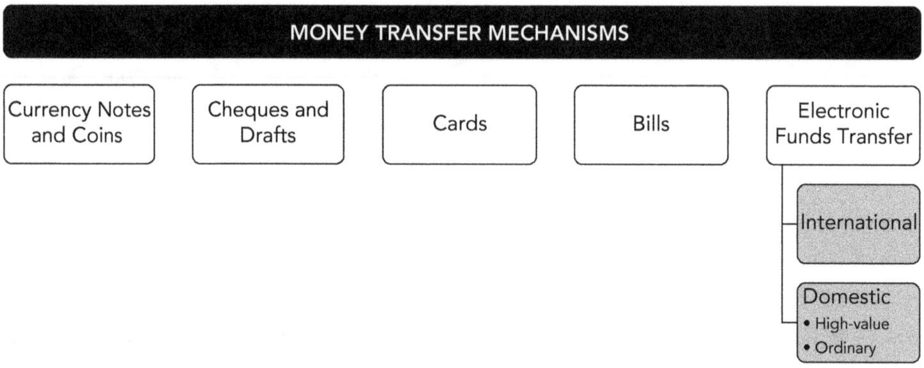

FIGURE 6.1 Mechanisms of Money Transfer

Bills are covered in more detail in Chapter 14. The other mechanisms are covered here.

Currency Notes and Coins

One of the earliest forms of exchange of value, currency notes and coins are still used for corporate transactions in many parts of the world. One of the benefits of using cash is that credit risk is eliminated, as is possible float—the cash is available in physical form and can be used immediately. However, some of the reasons for the reduced popularity of physical currency and hence for its being replaced as a transfer mechanism are:

- Loss of value (interest)
- Incremental operational issues
- Movement across a geography
- Only used for local currency settlements
- Storage
- Reconciliation/counting
- Security while in transit and in storage

Cheques and Drafts

Cheques and drafts, issued in paper form, are one of the most common forms of payment. These need to be presented physically and in most cases need to travel physically to the location where they go through a presentation or clearing process for purposes of settlement.

Different types of cheques are depicted in Figure 6.2. Cheques may be distinguished by the paying entity—the payer of the funds, the payer's bank, or a third party, which could be the correspondent bank of the payer's bank, generally a participant in clearing in the currency or location where payment is desired. Cheques can also be distinguished by location of payment; either they can be presented in a specific location, or they can be payable at par across locations. Finally, cheques may be distinguished

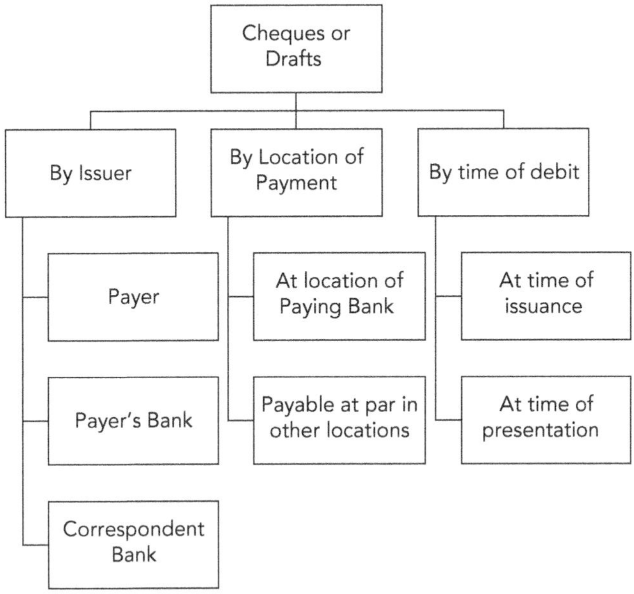

FIGURE 6.2 Types of Cheques

by the time at which the payer's account is actually debited—at the time of instrument issuance (usually the case when the payer of the draft is the bank) or at the time of instrument presentation and clearing, as is the case with most ordinary cheques.

Figure 6.3 shows the typical process for clearing of ordinary cheques through the banking system and clearinghouse, which in most cases is run by the central bank or a nominated bank usually from the public sector.

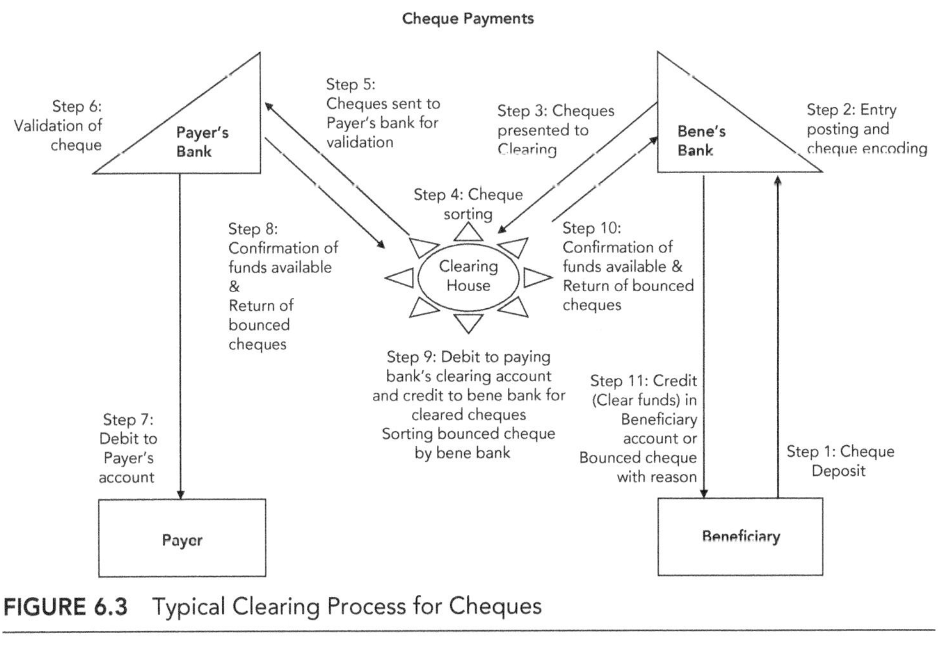

FIGURE 6.3 Typical Clearing Process for Cheques

Cards

Cards (electronic charge, debit, or credit) are finding increasing use in the corporate world. Cards are virtual or physical devices that involve the use of a specific card number along with a verification tag for authenticity. The verification tag could be:

- Physical (chip or magnetic strip)
- Data, such as a verification code printed on the card
- Signature and photograph, as established on the card itself
- Password, which could be generated at the time of the transaction or a standard

Credit cards are those in which the card issuer takes on a specific credit risk of the card holder, which allows the card holder to transact or purchase goods or services at a merchant site (either online or physically), and make the payment to the card issuer at a later time. Credit cards also allow for delayed payment of card dues, subject to some minimum servicing, on which interest is levied.

Debit cards are cards that provide, like an automated teller machine (ATM) card, debit access to the card holder's account at the time of the transaction, reducing credit risk for the issuing bank and potentially cost for the card holder while reducing opportunity of using the funds for an extended period.

Charge cards are typically like credit cards, except that the credit period is fixed (within the month), and late payments are treated similar to a default, resulting in severe late fees and restrictions on card use.

Figure 6.4 shows a sample settlement process where the card issuer and the merchant's acquirer (acquiring bank) are both banks, and the cards are issued for networks provided by corporations such as Visa or MasterCard.

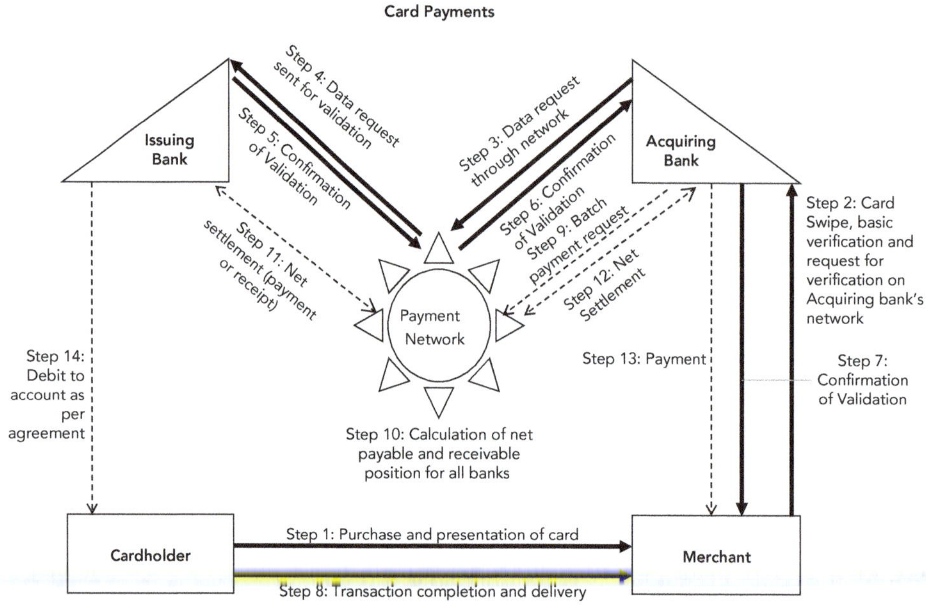

FIGURE 6.4 Typical Card Settlement Process

TABLE 6.1 Snapshot of Common Payment Mechanisms

	Push/ Pull	Possible Benefits	Key Concerns	Remarks
Cash	Push	Immediate recognition and no credit risk for payee	Operations issues Control, security, and reconciliation	Can be used in retail or low-access areas, also to reduce credit or clearing risk
Bank draft	Pull	Lower credit risk for payee	Up-front debit and charges for payer	Emergence of corporate cheques issued by bank but debit happens only on presentation
Corporate-issued cheque	Pull	Payer receives float benefit	Higher credit and float risk for payee, especially in widely dispersed geographies	Signatories; can be inefficient for high volumes and large clearing times
Cards	Pull	Immediate settlement for merchant	Transaction costs on low volumes	
Real-time gross settlement	Push	Speed of settlement	Systems have to be robust to make full use	Large-value payments
Electronic funds Transfer	Push	Efficient and cost effective	Speed (batch processing) and reconciliation effort	
Direct debit	Pull	Efficient and cost effective	Reconciliation and control effort	Used for periodic payments

Electronic Funds Transfer

Electronic funds transfers, both domestic and international, are important aspects of any corporate's funding and operations. These transfers may be either domestic, which involves payments and settlements in the same country, or international, which requires flows of money across borders.

The next part of this chapter describes some of the elements of domestic payments, followed by the international payments aspects. Table 6.1 summarises the various benefits and disadvantages of common payment mechanisms. Here, *Push* refers to the payment being initiated by the entity making the payment, pushing the payment to the beneficiary. *Pull* refers to the act of initiation by the beneficiary.

DOMESTIC CLEARING AND SETTLEMENT SYSTEMS

Domestic electronic funds transfers cater to quick and efficient payments usually in the local currency. These transfers typically are divided into two processes in most locations, based on the size of each transaction: high-value transfers and ordinary-value payments.

In this section, we discuss the mechanics of both types of payments and run through some of the systems across various countries.

I get asked this question: "What is the difference between clearing and settlement?" Indeed these terms are generally used (incorrectly) interchangeably or together. The note below provides a brief answer to this question.

Difference between Clearing and Settlement

While the terms *clearing* and *settlement* may be used together and often are used interchangeably (an incorrect usage), they are technically two distinct parts of the same process.

Clearing refers to the entire end-to-end process of receipt, transmission, reconciliation and confirmation of requests or orders for payment, and determination of the final amounts for settlement. In some cases, the clearing process includes netting of instructions.

Settlement is the provisional or final completion or discharging of payment obligations for transfer of funds from one party to another. Settlements are usually on real-time gross basis or periodic net basis.

High-Value Payments

High-value payments use the same real-time gross settlement (RTGS) concept across various countries. Each of the characteristics of the RTGS systems is important. The payments are real time, which means that they come into effect as soon as they are processed, not in batches but immediately. The settlement happens in a gross manner (not in a net or consolidated manner). This means that if A has to pay B 100, and B has to pay A 60, two separate settlements (100 from A to B and 60 from B to A) happen, instead of a single net payment of 40 from A to B.

In most instances of RTGS implementation, the central bank acts as the principal host for operations (see the note titled "Role of the Central Bank in Clearing"). Figure 6.5 shows the typical operations for an RTGS system.

Bilateral settlement occurs instantaneously through the settlements account with the clearing agent, usually the central bank. Intraday positions are covered by banks through credit facilities with the central bank that are typically collateralised.

Role of the Central Bank in Clearing

The central bank is the pivot in most clearing operations. It has an operational role by holding all the designated bank accounts and administering or overseeing the payments and settlements based on instructions. It plays a regulatory role by ensuring that infrastructure and legal mechanisms are in place for critical fund flow activities. But the most critical activity done by the central bank (and the primary reason why central banks continue to execute RTGS activity) is the provision of liquidity. The central bank fulfils its role as liquidity provider of last resort and can come in immediately to fill in a breach, should a default by any market participant cause a liquidity issue for any of the recipient banks. The central bank has its own backup to individually settle intraday risk issues with each participant—it provides credit limits that could be backed up by collateral.

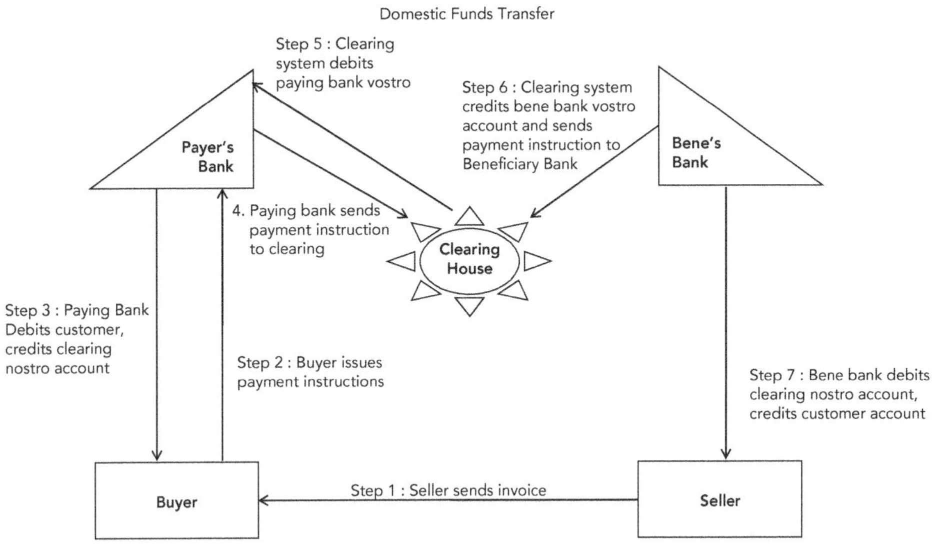

FIGURE 6.5 Typical RTGS Operation

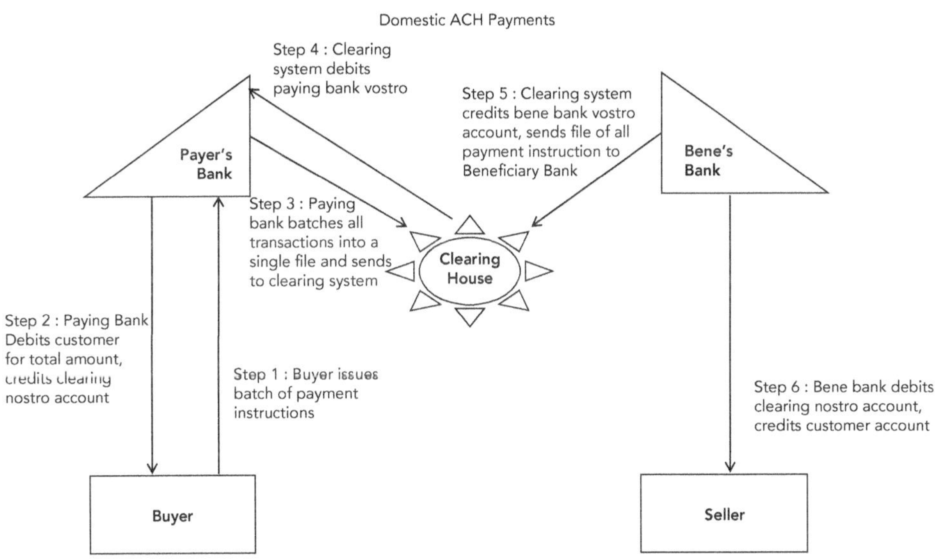

FIGURE 6.6 Ordinary Value Payments (ACH Model)

Ordinary (Low-Value) Payments

Ordinary or low-value payment systems are used for high-volume payments of identical nature that require bulk processing, such as retail payments. Low-value payments usually run off the backbone of RTGS for interbank settlements and are processed in batches to enable more efficient time windows and consolidation of payments. Figure 6.6 shows a typical operation for ordinary payments. The payment system in

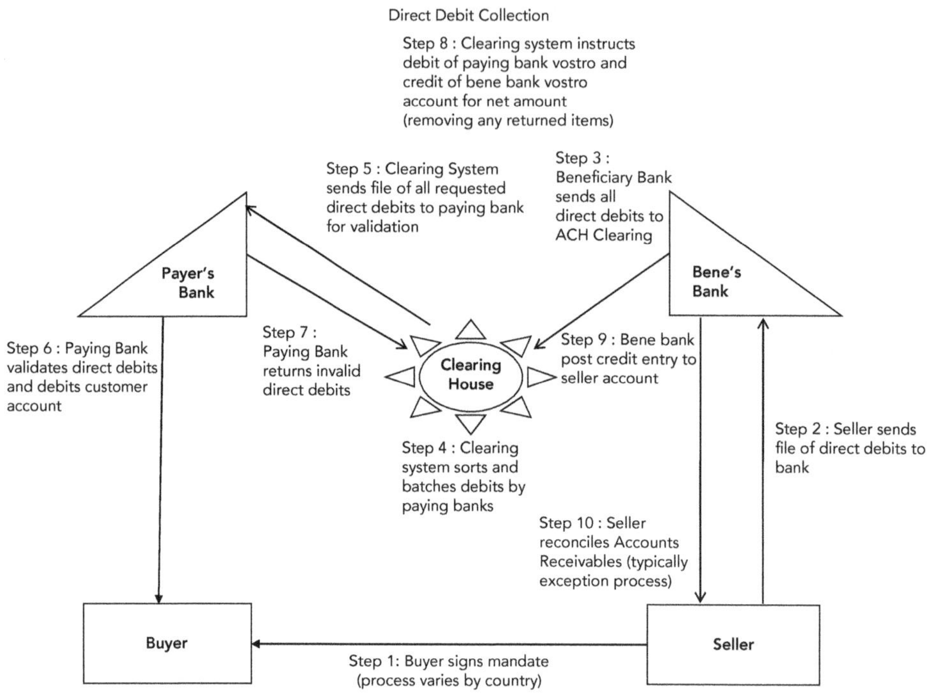

FIGURE 6.7 Direct Debit Mechanism (ACH Model)

the United States, referred to as an automated clearinghouse (ACH), has set the trend that many other clearinghouses follow.

Low-value payment systems can be used, depending on the country of operation, for ATM and retail settlements and also direct debits, which are payee-initiated pull transactions with prior authorisation by the payer (see Figure 6.7).

The ACH or ordinary payments model is a more-cost effective solution than RTGS since the transaction cost is divided across multiple payments.

We now provide a short note on key operational aspects of payments that should be kept in mind.

Important Operational Aspects to Remember for Payments

Some important aspects have to be borne in mind for the payments process.

Daylight Overdraft Limits

The daylight overdraft (DLOD) is an intraday (hence daylight) overdraft limit that the clearinghouse provides to a bank and that a bank may in turn provide to creditworthy customers (with or without collateral). Banks need these limits with the clearing entity in order to make good payment obligations while arranging for funds to be transferred to their account ("nostro") with the clearinghouse. The bank's corporate customers require these limits to cover any large payments that may be due before cutoff times while awaiting funds to bring back the balance in their accounts above the threshold.

Cutoff Times for the Bank and the Clearinghouse

As processes get more automated, the relevance of cutoff times for systems to process transactions, either at the clearinghouse or at the bank's end, will become higher. The benefit of automation for the corporate with the bank that enable straight-through processing (STP) is that the manual processes that necessitated earlier cutoffs are now replaced with systems that bring the cutoff times for banks with their customers very close to the cutoff times of clearinghouses with the banks.

Dating

The "dating" concept in clearing and settlement has to do, a little boringly, with the value date provided for the credit to the beneficiary. This date is used to determine interest calculations at all ends and availability of funds to the beneficiary, irrespective of the date of actual passing or posting of entries.

Appendix C, available on this book's companion website, shows some of the clearing and settlement systems available around the world.

The note below introduces the core principles for payment systems, an interesting concept that is bound to evolve as payment systems and mechanisms themselves undergo transformation.

Core Principles for Systemically Important Payment Systems

The Committee on Payment and Settlement Systems (CPSS) of the central banks of the Group of Ten countries established a task force on payment system principles and practices in May 1998 to consider what principles should govern the design and operation of payment systems in all countries. The task force developed an international consensus on such principles with comments, suggestions, contributions, and partnership with stakeholders and participants around the world. Subsequently the Bank for International Settlements published the Core Principles to help durability and applicability across all countries. Without being a blueprint for the design or operation of any individual system, the Core Principles suggest key attributes or properties that should be present in systemically important payment systems (SIPS).

Public policy objectives, the 10 core principles and the responsibility of central banks in applying the core principles are available for reference online on the Website of the Bank for International Settlements (www.bis.org).

We now explore the advent of state-of-the-art payment infrastructure in one of the largest economies in the world: China.

CASE STUDY: PAYMENTS IN CHINA

China has made much progress in developing its payments and settlement systems. The People's Bank of China (PBOC) and other regulators and market participants have made some fantastic progress in the development of payment mechanisms in a nation of extreme geographic dispersion and technological and communication disparity. While currency notes are still common for local payments, and paper-based instruments are still in wide use, the PBOC's efforts to increase electronic and paperless forms of payments have increased quite dramatically.

What make this progress even more inspiring are the pace and the scale of their development and operations. The opening up and creation of payments infrastructure is a model for any large country seeking to increase efficiencies and scales of their payment systems.

Figure 6.8 shows the current state of the payments systems in the People's Republic.

The PBOC has carried out significant reform of the China National Payments System (CNPS). Some of the components of the CNPS are:

- China National Advanced Payment System (CNAPS)
- Automated clearinghouses
- China Union Pay (CUP)
- Cheque imaging systems (CIS)
- Foreign currency clearing and settlement systems

CNAPS

CNAPS is a nationwide electronic clearing system set up for both intracity and cross-city RMB payment clearing and is administrated by PBOC. It provides payment clearing services for commercial banks, clearing organisations, and other Treasury or financial institutions. Settlements amongst participants are done through their accounts with PBOC. CNAPS comprises of the High-Value Payment System (HVPS) for large-value transactions and the Bulk Electronic Payment System (BEPS) for ordinary clearing.

High Value Payment System

The HVPS is the RTGS module of CNAPS primarily for large-value or higher time efficient RMB interbank funds transfers. It uses message-based payment instruction for instantaneous and irrevocable settlements.

The HVPS currently operates in a tiered way with multiple entry points for participants either directly or indirectly, backed by a central national processing centre (NPC) and 32 distributed local processing centres (LCPs). The HVPS is connected to other trading, payments, and securities settlement systems to enable automated settlements for central bank transfers. The HVPS has become the backbone of the national payments system in China.

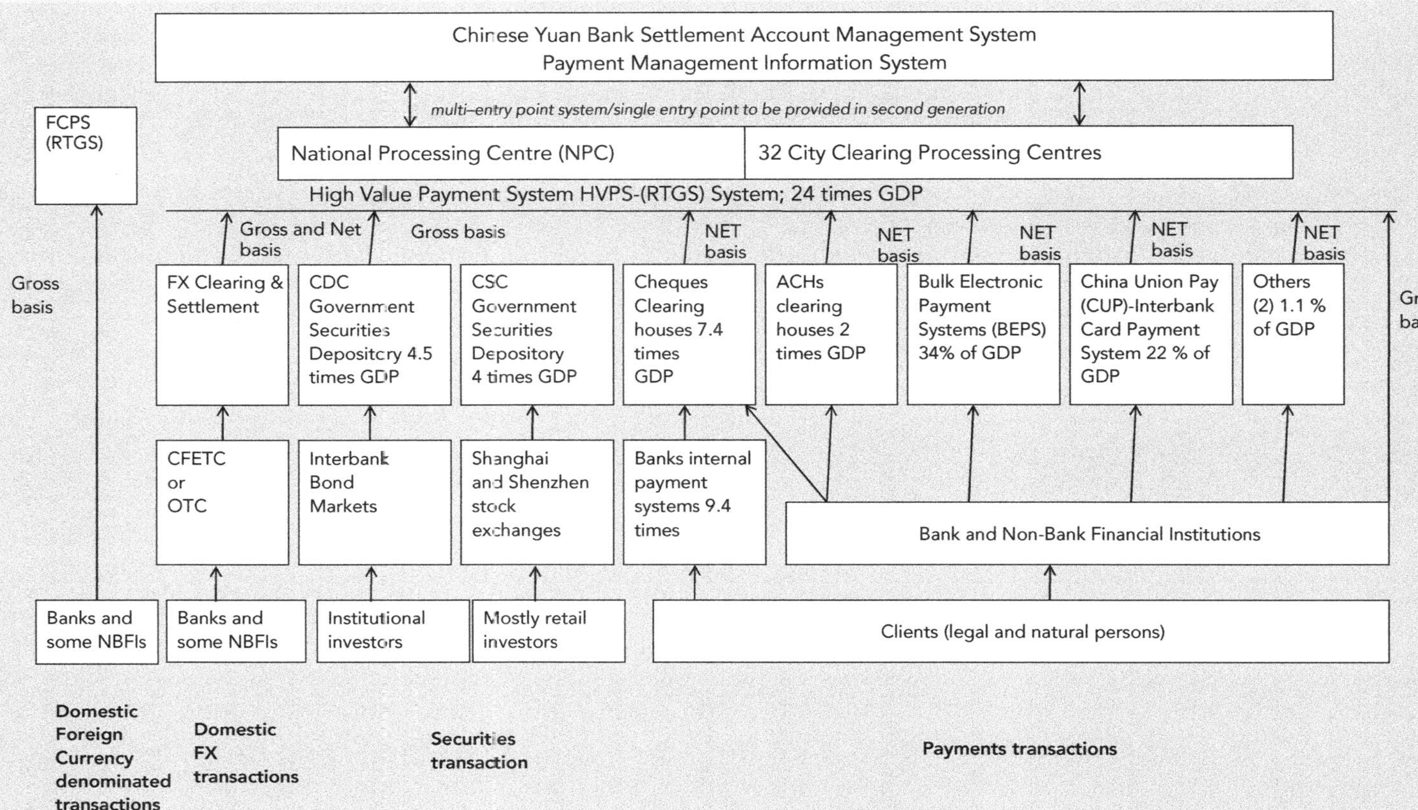

FIGURE 6.8 Payments Systems in China

Source: International Monetary Fund Country Report 12/81 (April 2012)

Bulk Electronic Payment System

The BEPS is the netting settlement module of CNAPS used primarily for cost-efficient, high-volume interbank small-value credit and paperless debits. BEPS offers 24/7 batch-based transaction processing for market participants, supporting all payment instruments.

One of the highlights of the BEPS is the credit and liquidity risk management measures adopted:

- Access is provided only to institutions that meet the targeted risk profiles and specific requirements.
- The BEPS works off the HVPS framework; hence participants use their HVPS settlement accounts and have access to HVPS liquidity facilities.
- There is a fully collateralised net debit limit for direct participants.
- Participants are can adjust their debit limit by managing their funds or collateral provided.
- Multilateral offsetting mechanisms add to the efficiency of the clearing process.

The BEPS uses a queuing system and exercises adequate control over payment orders executed by participants, managing liquidity dynamically.

China Union Pay

CUP handles the clearing and settlement of card transactions whose balances are settled in the HVPS. The key components and processes are:

- Transmission of transaction authorisation orders
- Clearing infrastructure
- Rules and norms
- Pricing implementation
- Role of counterparty for all transactions in the settlement cycle

The member banks, which act as both acquirers and issuers, use internal payment card acquiring and issuing systems that are connected to the CUP's own system. In some cases, CUP acts as an acquirer. Settlements happen on a multilateral net settlement basis in the HVPS system itself, on a T+1 basis. Participating banks either have settlement accounts with the PBOC directly or use a correspondent banking services of a bank that has such a settlement account. Importantly, the CUP provides settlement guarantees for all the transactions cleared through its system. To enable these guarantees, it operates a settlement reserve fund funded contributions from participants.

Cheque Imaging System (CIS)

The nationwide CIS system enables electronic exchange of cheque images, automated clearing of the exchange "paper" instruments, and multilateral net settlement of exchange instruments at the HVPS. Institutions that do not have direct access to the CIS (including rural financial institutions) can use bureau services offered by PBOC and many of the local clearinghouses and financial institutions.

The CIS is used primarily to clear and settle cross-region cheques and to support the 1,200+ local clearinghouses operating in China in handling local cheque clearing and settlement.

Foreign Currency Transactions

Many foreign exchange (FX) transactions are executed domestically at the China Foreign Exchange Trade Centre (CFETC). While most participants settle their transactions bilaterally, others use a net clearing model where the CFETC acts as the central counterparty. Settlement of the local currency leg occurs through the HVPS while the domestic settlement banks (which house participants' FX accounts) handle the foreign currency leg.

The Foreign Currency Payment System (FCPS), an RTGS system, was created to handle clearing and settlement of domestic transactions in various foreign currencies.

CROSS-BORDER PAYMENTS AND COLLECTIONS

In this section, we cover some of the key aspects of cross-border payments. We discuss the issues with electronic payments and communication, how they were resolved with the emergence of the SWIFT network, and conclude with an overview of how the continuous link system clearing system for foreign currency instruments increases efficiency and reduces risk.

Background: A Foreign Currency Remittance

A foreign currency remittance between buyers and sellers in different countries with the possible invoice and settlement in a currency different from that of either country can be a complex and time-consuming affair (see Figure 6.9).

There are two critical aspects of such a transaction:

1. **The security aspect of the transaction**. Are the instructions authentic and executed by responsible and genuine officers of the bank sending this instruction?
2. **The credit aspect of the transaction**. Will the bank that is expected to pay make good the funds when they are due?

A few decades ago, telex messages with test words or test keys (Tested Telexes [TTs]) were transmitted that would reduce the first risk. There were not too many ways in which the second was reduced—hence banks would wait to sight the funds in their account prior to making the onward remittance. With time zones and manual processing, the delay in sending through the next leg of each remittance was fairly large, sometimes impacting the underlying trade transaction itself.

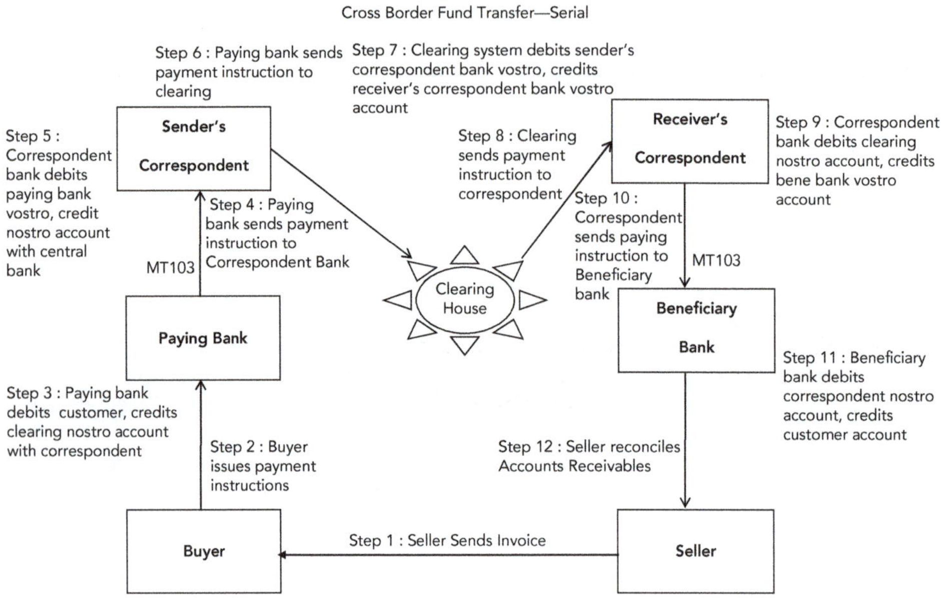

FIGURE 6.9 Foreign Currency Payment

SWIFT

The advent of the Society for Worldwide Interbank Funds Transfer (SWIFT), a worldwide cooperative of the financial industry, changed the playing field. SWIFT put in place a secure, standardised messaging services network with interface software to connect banking systems.

The SWIFT network, which became operational in the 1970s, made three big differences in financial transfers:

1. **Authenticity**. SWIFT enabled the immediate transfer of quick and authentic messages without the hassle of manually decoding any test keys. The operational efficiency of message transmission changed dramatically, and with the increased linkages to bank systems over time, SWIFT continued to increase efficiency by enabling STP. Encryption of user data within the system both in transit and on system storage devices increased the security aspect. Messages were validated on receipt, which increased authenticity.
2. **Integrity**. SWIFT enabled immediate handling of credit risk. The SWIFT messages effectively became cheques or letters signed by the parties. Receivers of the messages could act on the strength of the SWIFT message itself with the confidence that the sender could not renege on the secure communication.
3. **Confidentiality**. The high security aspect of the network ensured that access control for each message was only with the institution sending the message and the institution receiving the message.

Figure 6.10 shows how the SWIFT messaging network could reduce potential delay in the funds transfer process.

The SWIFT community today includes banks, broker-dealers, investment companies, and even corporates that are hopping on to the network. The market participant infrastructure covers:

- Payments
- Securities
- Trades
- Treasury
- Account information

Each member entity has a SWIFT code, and each of its branches or departments could have its own SWIFT code. This makes it easy for us to identify, say, the London Strand branch of Citibank or the Pudong commercial branch of the Overseas China Banking Corporation. The SWIFT code for the institution or entity is comprised of an alphanumeric code of 8 to 11 characters (with the last three characters being made up of X's in case the length is under 11). Any SWIFT code can be represented by:

$$\underbrace{\text{BBBB}}_{\text{Bank}}\quad\underbrace{\text{CC}}_{\text{Country}}\quad\underbrace{\text{RRRRR}}_{\text{Branch/Department}}$$

For example, CITIUSNY33 or CITIUSNY33XXX depicts Citibank (CITI, which is common to all branches of Citibank), in the United States (US is the standard ISO two-letter mnemonic for the United States; every country has a two-letter mnemonic), New York branch 33 (NY33 for the specific code for Citibank New York).

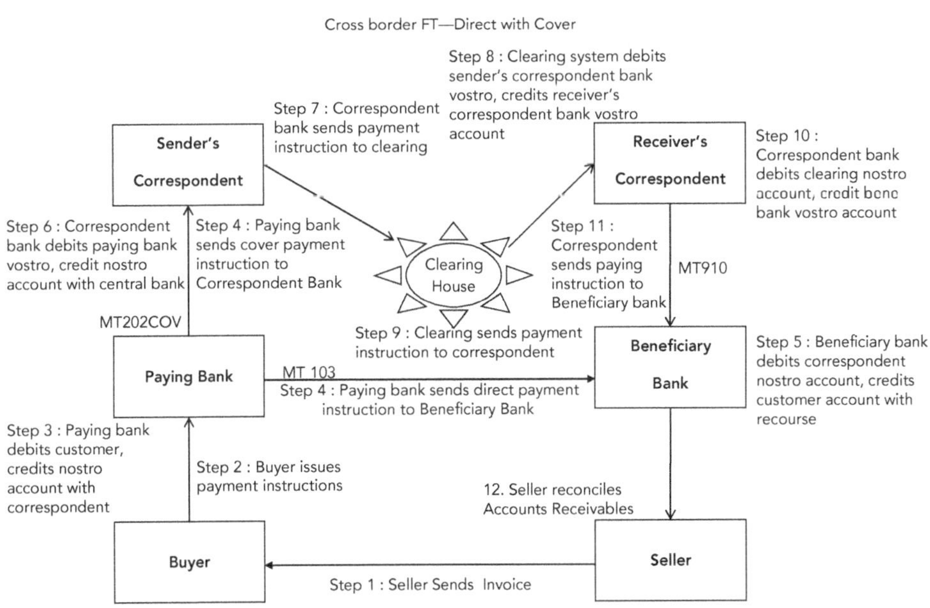

FIGURE 6.10 Simple Funds Transfer Using SWIFT

The SWIFT network allows for transmitting different types of messages (Message Type [MT]) with each message type having its own purpose. The nomenclature format for the Message Types is MT$##, where $ is the number denoting the broad category (see Table 6.2) and ## is the two-digit number indicating the type of message within that category. Each message is structured with headers, message body text, and trailers that are standardised across the financial world.

Another variation, SWIFT Net File Act, was introduced to enable users to send files containing many financial messages and large reports in standard formats with local language capabilities; it enables high-volume automated processing. SWIFT has also developed a next-generation standard called MX that uses an Extended Markup Language (XML) format based on the International Organization for Standardization (ISO) standard 20022.

Overview of SWIFT Message Types[1]

Table 6.2 provides the broad categories of SWIFT MT messages. For example, category 1 (MT1##) represents any customer payment messages, MT7## represent trade and documentary credit or guarantee-related messages.

TABLE 6.2 SWIFT Message Categories

Name Category	Description
1	Customer payments and cheques
2	Financial institution transfers
3	Treasury markets: foreign exchange, money markets, and derivatives
4	Collection and cash letters
5	Securities markets
6	Treasury markets: precious metals and syndications
7	Documentary credits and guarantees
8	Travellers' cheques
9	Cash management and customer status

Source: SWIFT

[1]The standards provided in this section are based on SWIFT Standards information, the permitted use of which is governed by the SWIFT Standards intellectual property rights (IPR) policy in effect at the time, available on www.swift.com/about_swift/legal/swiftstandards_ipr_policy.page

Table 6.3 describes many Category 1 (customer payment) MTs.

TABLE 6.3 SWIFT Message Types: Customer Payments

Type	Name	Purpose
MT101	Request for transfer	Debit a customer's account held at another institution
MT102/102+	Multiple customer credit transfer	Conveys multiple payment instructions between institutions
MT103/103+	Single customer credit transfer	Instructs a funds transfer
MT104	Direct debit	Conveys direct debit instructions and requests for direct debits between institutions
MT110	Advice of cheque(s)	Advises or confirms the issuance of a cheque to the drawee bank
MT111	Request for stop payment of a cheque	Requests the drawee bank to stop payment of a cheque

Source: SWIFT

Table 6.4 shows the format or structure of a typical MT103 message. As can be seen, each field tag has a specific purpose, and the automation is assisted by reading the tag of the field, immediately using the ensuing data items to mean the items referred to in the field tag. Each tag is preceded by a colon (:) to enable easy identification.

TABLE 6.4 MT103: Message Format or Structure

Field Tag	Field Name
:20	Transaction reference number
:23B	Bank operation code
:32A	Value date/currency/interbank settled amount
:33B	Currency/original ordered amount
:50A or :50K	Ordering customer
:52A	Ordering institution
:53B	Sender's correspondent (where there are multiple account relationships in the currency of the transaction between the sender and the receiver, and one such account is to be used for reimbursement)
:56A	Intermediary (must include the SWIFT code of the head office of the "Account with Institution") described below
:57A	Account with institution (the financial institution at which the ordering party requests the beneficiary to be paid)
:57B or :57D	Account with institution (used only for branches of receiver; includes name and address of receiving branch)

(Continued)

TABLE 6.4 *(Continued)*

Field Tag	Field Name
:59 or :59A	Beneficiary (party designated by the ordering party as the ultimate recipient of the funds)
:70	Remittance information (information from the ordering party to the beneficiary customer, about the reason for the payment)
:71A	Details of charges (BEN/OUR/SHA) *BEN* indicates that the beneficiary will be responsible for the payment of banks and related charges, *OUR* indicates that the sender or remitter will pay the charges, and SHA indicates that the charges will be shared
:71F or :71G	Senders' or receivers' charges F: currency and amount of transaction charges deducted by the sender and by previous banks in the transaction chain; G: currency and amount of transaction charges due to the receiver
:72	Sender-to-receiver information

Source: SWIFT

MT9 is used for cash management and status messages. Various MT9 items are provided in Table 6.5.

TABLE 6.5 SWIFT MT9: Cash Management/Status

MT	MT Name	Purpose
MT900	Confirmation of debit	Advises an account owner of a debit to its account
MT910	Confirmation of credit	Advises an account owner of a credit to its account
MT935	Rate change advice	Advises the receiver of general rate change(s) and/or rate change(s) that apply to a specific account other than a call/ notice loan/deposit account
MT940	Customer statement message	Provides balance and transaction details of an account to a financial institution on behalf of the account owner
MT941	Balance report	Provides balance information of an account to a financial institution on behalf of the account owner
MT986	Status report	Provides business related information about a customer or institution

Source: SWIFT

Finally, we look at the various elements of a 90 series of MT message. The 90 series of MTs—for example, MT191, MT 799—have a specific purpose within each category, usually for advices or queries. Table 6.6 shows the relevant purpose of each 90 type of message. The letter *n* before each number in the message type is the message category—for example, for advice of charges for customer payments, the MT190 message will be used.

TABLE 6.6 SWIFT Message Types: Category MTn9#

MT	MT Name	Purpose
n90	Advice of charges, interest and other adjustments	Advises an account owner of charges, interest, or other adjustments to its account
n91	Request for payment of charges, interest and other expenses	Requests payment of charges, interest or other expenses
n92	Request for cancellation	Requests the receiver to consider cancellation of the message identified in the request
n95	Queries	Requests information relating to a previous message or amendment to a previous message
n96	Answers	Responds to an MT n95 query or MT n92 Request for Cancellation or other messages where no specific message type has been provided for response
n98	Proprietary message	Contains formats defined and agreed to between users and for those messages not yet live
n99	Free format message	Contains information for which no other message type has been defined

Source: SWIFT

The use of SWIFT has now become universal—yet, the degree of automation implies that incorrect or inadequate information might lead to delay in processing. The following note explains why.

Why Should You Fill in All Possible Fields When Requesting a Funds Transfer?

Imagine a bank in New York acting as your correspondent bank for USD payments. This bank has an automated SWIFT messaging system interface that enables STP for all messages, incoming and outgoing. Hence, messages with full information, such as the bank's SWIFT code, beneficiary account number, correspondent bank details, and so on, are processed with no manual intervention.

When the information is unavailable or incorrect—for example, the SWIFT code does not exist or the beneficiary's account number is not mentioned—the transaction goes into a manual or repair queue. Say the bank receives 10,000 instructions a day; even if just 10% go into the manual queue, it means 1,000 transactions. If it takes an operator 30 minutes to resolve a query manually on average, each operator typically would resolve 16 transactions in a normal working day. This implies that this bank would have to employ 60 staff just to resolve manual transactions on any given day. The cost associated with this processing gets charged to the sender ("OUR") or to the beneficiary ("BENE"), as indicated in the message at the time of transmission.

The moral of this story is that you should fill in as many relevant payment details as you have about the beneficiary, including SWIFT codes, account numbers, and correspondent banks, to reduce the chances of the transaction not being automatically processed and to increase efficiency and processing speed and lower transaction cost and opportunity loss of funds.

SWIFT Corporate: Standardised Gateway

SWIFT Corporate Solutions offers corporates the opportunity to achieve a single standardised gateway of payments. Historically, owing to the costs involved of setting up SWIFT and being a member-participant, and the scales of corporate compared to banks, corporates used the bank route to send SWIFT messages, outsourcing this activity to the banks.

With increasing efficiency and thereby lower cost of automation, and payment scales for large global companies increasing with geographical diversity and depth, as well as increased globalisation of suppliers, operations, and customers, corporates are increasingly joining the SWIFT platform.

Next we present a brief note on the corporate programme of SWIFT and some of its aspects.

SWIFT for Corporates

SWIFT expanded its community in 1998 for corporations. SWIFT for Corporates is an industry solution that extends SWIFT from its original space between its members and their market infrastructures, toward the space between its members and their end-user corporate community.

While the early adapters included large corporates, SWIFT for Corporates continues to g ain acceptance by mid-cap corporates. These seek to utilise standardised file formats (e.g., XML-based ISO 20022 and consistent usage of FIN) to promote straight-through processing and ease integration with Enterprise Resource Planning (ERP) systems and Treasury Workstation(s).

The current economic situation urges corporates to reconsider their cash management operations and focus on more efficiency and STP, cost reduction, risk spreading (rather than account consolidation), immediate visibility, and more accurate forecasting of their cash positions. The changing banking environment requires a corporate to better manage its banking relationships and integrate with new and/or other banking applications quickly and easily.

By giving corporations access to SWIFT, banks offer them the means to achieve these goals. Testimonials of the first corporates that joined prove that all their expectations are met.

The value of SWIFT for corporate treasuries is summarised in Figure 6.11.

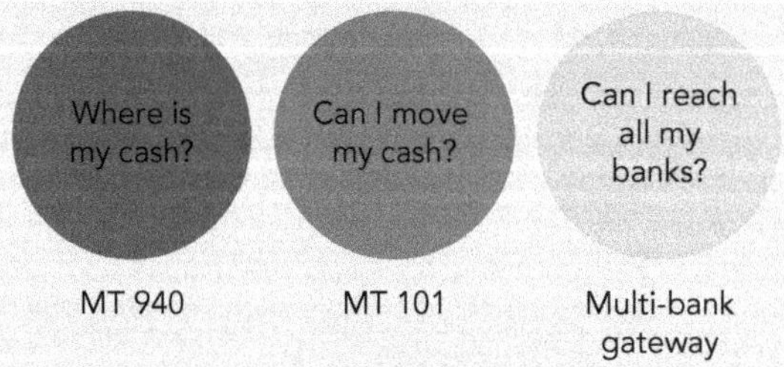

FIGURE 6.11 Value of SWIFT and Priority on Treasury Projects

SWIFT's Messaging Services

SWIFTNet offers different data transfer mechanisms, called messaging services, which define how the information is exchanged between two parties, for example, a corporate and a financial institution as shown in Figure 6.12.

- FIN: a message transfer–based store-and-forward system. FIN is the main messaging mechanism used today on SWIFTNet and is used by corporates for liquidity and risk management purposes. For example, corporates can:
  - send Treasury payments, such as MT 101
  - receive intraday/end of day statements and credit/debit advices, such as MT 940
  - exchange FX/interest rate/money market deal confirmations, such as MT 300
  - exchange trade data on letters of credit and guarantees with an MT 798
  - send instructions to deliver/receive securities, and receive statements of holdings
- FileAct: a secure, reliable, and flexible file transfer system. It is suitable for batched messages or large reports and is typically used to send mass payments, such as disbursements, collections, and payroll, irrespective of the format and/or syntax (XML, EDIFACT, domestic, proprietary, JPEG, PDF,...).
- InterAct: a secure, reliable, query/response-based messaging application, oriented to straight through processing, using new Standards XML messages. Suitable for single messages and short reports such as Exceptions & Investigations.

At this stage, FIN and FileAct are the two main messaging services used by financial institutions to deliver their services to their corporate customers.

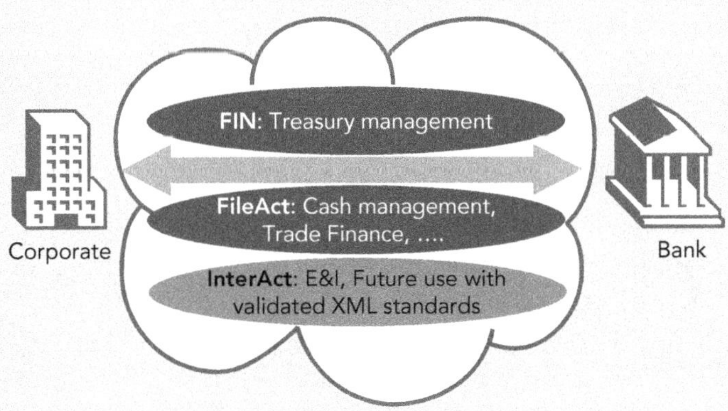

FIGURE 6.12 Corporate-Bank Interface

(Continued)

SWIFT's Connectivity Models

In addition to providing banking services over SWIFT, banks may offer support in connecting to SWIFTNet. There are several options in terms of technical setup:

- **Alliance Lite** offers connectivity to clients with lower volumes. Lite is aimed to realise a quick time-to-market for SWIFT message types.
- In a **Shared Infrastructure** model, a third party offers an infrastructure that corporations share with other users, to indirectly connect to SWIFT. Banks may in that case provide a complete package, including connectivity, registration and administration, billing, etc....
- A corporate may also acquire and operate its own infrastructure to connect to the SWIFT network and to exchange data with its financial institutions ("direct connectivity").

Connecting via SWIFT

SWIFT offers corporations three access model(s): SCORE (Standardised Corporate Environment), TRCO (Treasury Counterparty), or MA-CUG (Member Administered Closed User Group).

A SCORE member has access to all financial institutions that are registered in SCORE, a standardised, SWIFT administered environment with a limited set of well-defined messages (Figure 6.13).

A Treasury Counterparty can exchange all FIN Category 3 messages (i.e. Treasury deal confirmations), and only these messages, with any financial institution on the SWIFT network.

Alternatively, a corporate may subscribe to one or more of its banks' MA-CUGs. That allows it to communicate with these bank(s), and only these banks, under the rules that are set by the bank for its MA-CUG (Figure 6.14).

In any of the models, traffic between banks and corporates is allowed. Traffic between corporates is never allowed.

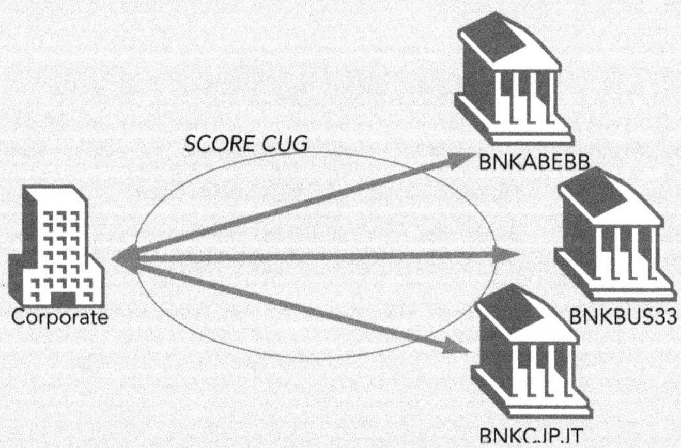

FIGURE 6.13 SCORE Model for Corporate Messaging

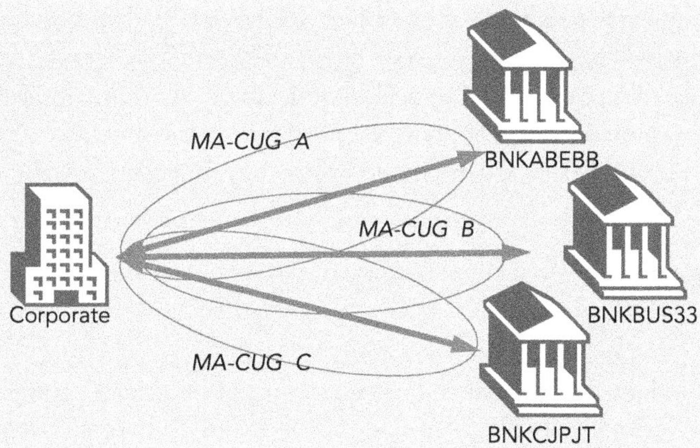

FIGURE 6.14 MA-CUG Model for Corporate Messaging

Standardising Banking Services with SWIFT

Financial instructions are exchanged over SWIFTNet in a standardised format. It allows any SWIFT participant to automate its services and build applications that communicate without manual intervention, i.e., full STP.

Contributed by Carlo Palmers, Corporate Market Solution manager, SWIFT

Local FX Clearing

If a cheque payable in a foreign currency is presented in another country, the usual process is for the cheque to be couriered physically to the country of issue by the payee's bank, handled by the correspondent bank of the payee's bank, and cleared, with funds credited to the account of the payee bank in the clearing currency (foreign currency for the payee bank). Only on sight of the funds does the payee's bank credit the payee's account. Because this process could take weeks, some countries, such as Singapore and Hong Kong, have put in place processes to clear foreign currency (USD) transactions locally (i.e., within the respective cities).

Continuous Link System

The continuous link system (CLS) is the process by which many of the world's largest financial institutions settle FX between themselves. The process is managed by the CLS Group and its subsidiaries including CLS Bank International, which is regulated by the Federal Reserve Bank. The CLS system uses a payment versus payment (PvP) process that eliminates settlement risk and matches FX trades across 17 currencies around the world. Settlement generally takes place during a five-hour time window when most international RTGS systems are operational and hence able to make and receive payments. One of the biggest advantages of the CLS system is the reduced settlement risk owing to the parties facing the CLS system directly instead of each other.

The CLS system provides the incremental flexibility of multilateral netting of all obligations per value date and provides support across instruments: FX spot, deliverable and nondeliverable forwards, options, swaps, and credit derivatives.

SUMMARY

In this chapter, we looked at various methods of moving money within a country and around the world. Local payment systems were examined in detail, and payments systems in China were explored as a case study of successful evolution of systems. We also explored the advent of SWIFT and CLS and how increased security and authentication is enabling the seamless and more efficient delivery of payments around the world.

CHAPTER SEVEN

Netting

NETTING HAS BECOME A WAY of life for many large corporations around the world. Conceptually, it appears to be a simple enough task for the planning and execution teams. However, most finance professionals who have been through a netting implementation would vouch for the discipline, process, and complete end-to-end understanding and coordination required to ensure that the project adds value to the smooth day-to-day operations of the organisation.

INTRODUCTION AND CONCEPTS

Netting of payments, commonly referred to as netting, is the periodic net settlement of specific outstanding payments between different entities or units. This is different from gross settlement, whereby each payment is made individually. Netting simply reduces the total set of payments to a smaller set of payments, where the net amounts are paid or received, thereby greatly lowering the transactional workload and foreign exchange conversions, potentially saving significant costs for the organisation.

Figure 7.1 shows a sample netting structure wherein payments from entities across the globe can be simplified into a single set of payments from a single location, the netting centre.

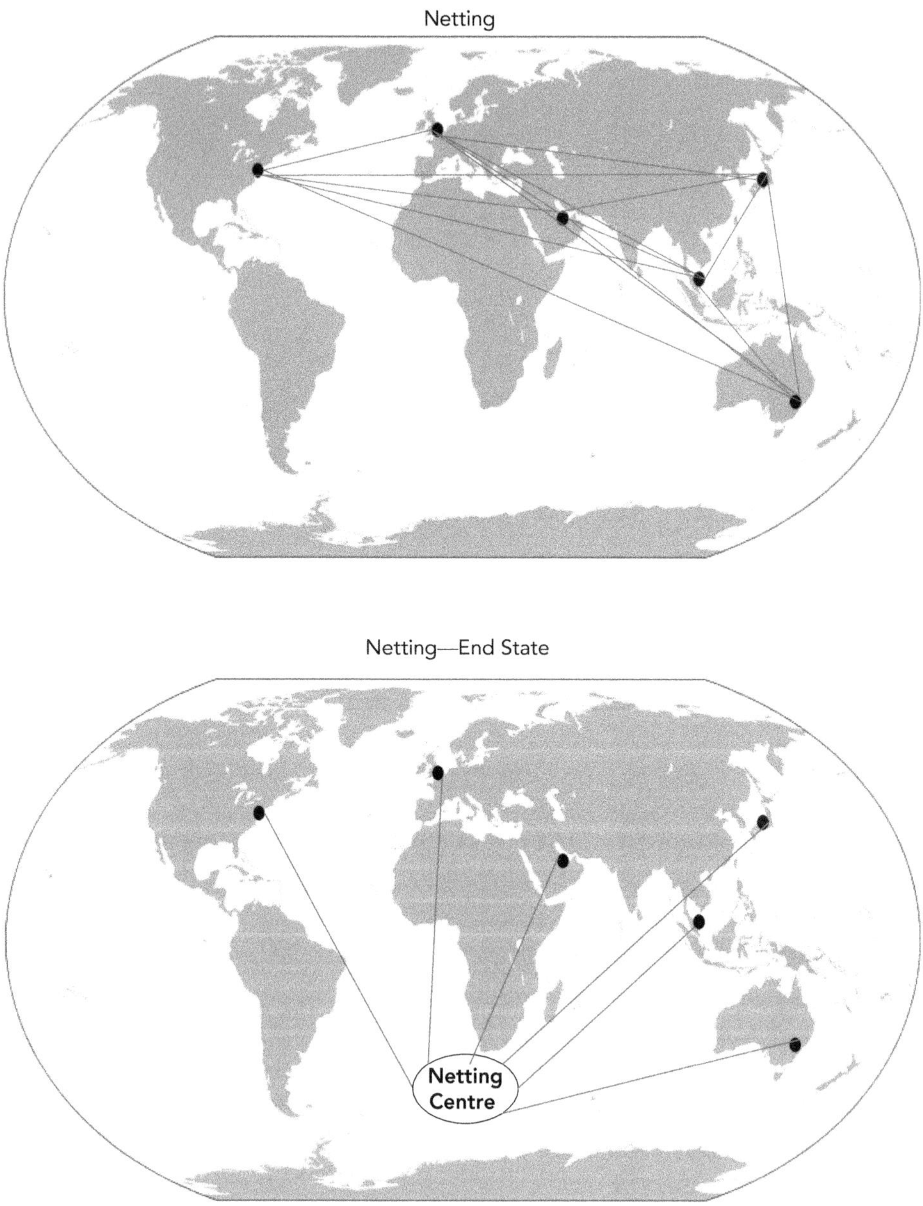

FIGURE 7.1 Sample Netting Structure

Types of Payments That Can Be Included in Netting

Different payments can be included in the netting process. These are:

- Trade (supplies, sales, logistics)
- Intercompany funding
- Debt servicing (interest payments and principal repayments)
- Investments
- Hedging or risk management contracts (internal or external)
- Service, advisory, or professional payments
- Management fees
- Royalty or license payments
- Third-party payments
- Dividends
- Surplus or contingency cash requirements

Some of the payments that usually are not included in the netting cycle are:

- Payroll (salaries, etc.)
- Tax payments
- Statutory payments
- Where payments have to be grossed up (cannot be netted off or clubbed) for regulatory or exchange control reasons

Different Types of Netting

Netting can be categorised across different themes. For example, netting across different parties can be:

- Unilateral, for different entities of the same company
- Multilateral, for different legal entities including third parties across countries

Netting across different currencies can be:

- Single currency
- Multiple currency

Figure 7.2 shows a simple single-currency netting payment. Netting is a periodic process and can happen across various frequencies (also called a netting cycle), including even daily settlements if the transaction volumes and urgencies so warrant. The payments can be variable, and in some cases there may be no payments from either party or even from both parties in a netting cycle.

In the example, Entity R needs to make a payment of USD 300,000 to Entity S. Entity S needs to make a payment of USD 450,000 to Entity R. A net payment comprises of a single payment of USD 150,000 (the difference between USD 450,000 and USD 300,000) from Entity S to Entity R. This activity would typically reduce the

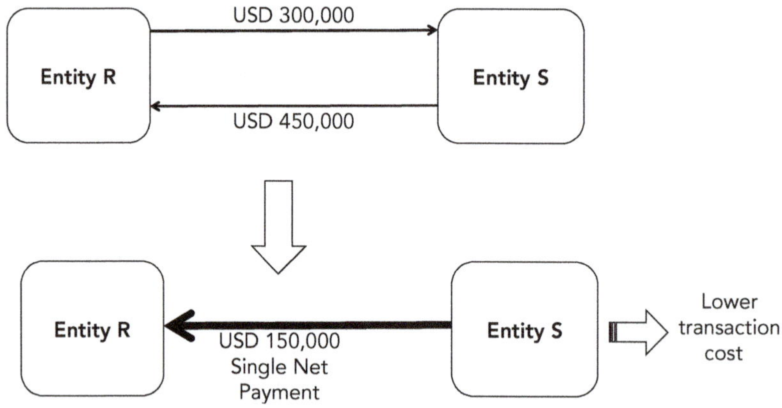

FIGURE 7.2 Single-Currency Netting

number of transactions by half and hence potentially save on resources and direct transaction cost.

Figure 7.3 continues the same theme with one additional complexity: What if both entities were euro based and hence had to convert currencies every time they had to make payments in USD?

In this case, without netting, there might have been two separate conversions and total purchase of USD 750,000 from euros (EUR). The netting reduces the foreign exchange (FX) purchased to only USD 150,000, thereby creating more process and cost efficiency.

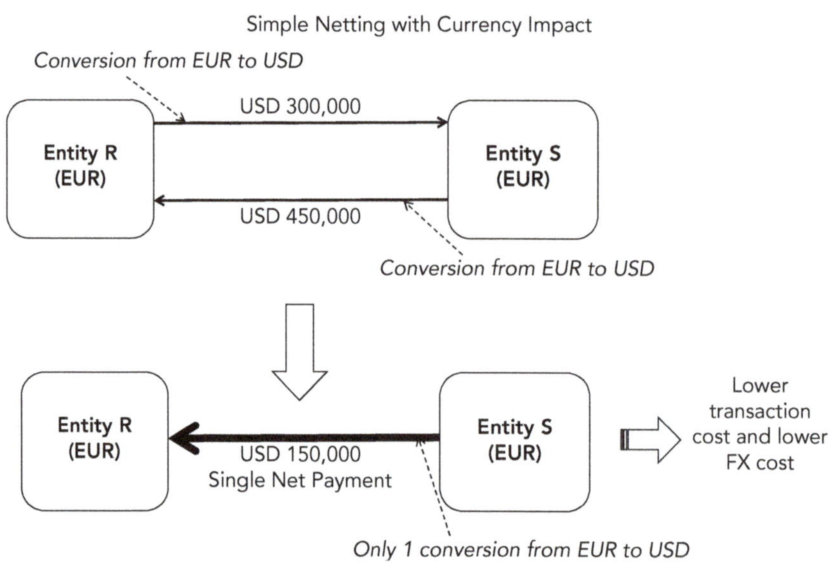

FIGURE 7.3 Netting with Foreign Exchange Conversion

Similarly, there could be cases where there are conversions on opposite sides; for example, one entity could be buying EUR and selling USD, while another entity could be selling EUR and buying USD. Netting reduces the need to have transactions on both sides, and the net resultant purchase of foreign exchange reduces not only the number of transactions but also the net purchase or sale of any currency. Later in the chapter, we cover an example on determining the benefits of netting.

Netting also can be characterised by line item:

- At an individual line item level, where line-by-line payments are considered
- At an invoice level, where payments are netted at an invoice level

In addition, netting can be characterised by payables or receivables. The premise of the netting process is to consider either:

- All payments to be made by all entities in the netting process, *or*
- All receivables due to all entities in the netting process.

Since the sum of payables across all entities is equal to the sum of receivables across the same entities, either approach must be used, but not both, since using both will result in duplication: A payable of one entity is the receivable of another, and the sum of payables less receivables is zero—it is a zero-sum game.

Example of a Simple Netting Process

Figure 7.4 depicts a sample scenario of payments across regions. In this scenario, there are a total of 14 payments across regions daily with average volumes or throughputs across currencies as depicted. There are multiple currency conversions, sometimes across opposite currencies. For example, Europe operations would have to purchase Japanese yen (JPY) and sell EUR to remit JPY to Asia. Conversely, Asia would have to buy EUR and sell JPY to remit EUR to Europe. A netting process based from a

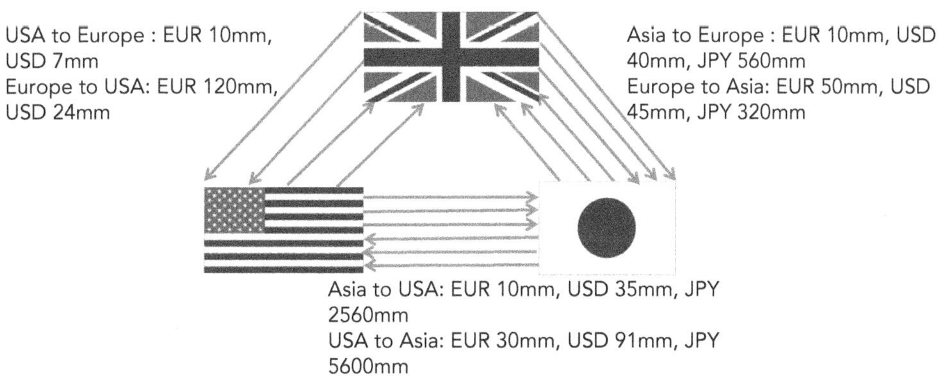

FIGURE 7.4 Payments Across Regions (Pre-Netting)

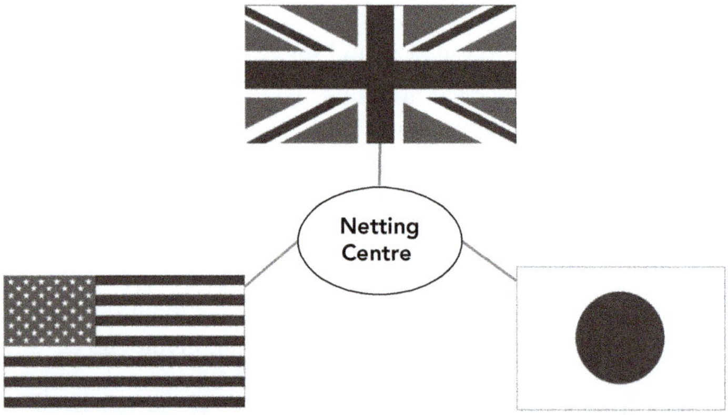

FIGURE 7.5 Netting Centre Reduces the Payments to One Only

netting centre (see Figure 7.5) could dramatically reduce the scope of FX conversions by creating efficiency through essential conversions only.

If the FX rate for the day (assuming mid-rates for convenience) was EUR USD at 1.3000 and USD JPY at 80.00, the regions would have had to pay and receive FX (all in USD) as shown in Table 7.1.

Consider this example for the receivables for Asia from Europe:

Receivable in EUR = 50 million (mm) EUR = 65mm USD (converted at 1.3000)
Receivable in USD = 45mm USD
Receivable in JPY = 3,200mm JPY = 40mm USD (converted at 80.00)
Total Receivable from Europe = 150mm USD

Hence, the receivables from each entity to the other can be plotted as shown in Table 7.1.

TABLE 7.1 Consolidated Netting Position

Region	Asia	Europe	United States	Receivable
Asia		150	200	350
Europe	60		20	80
United States	80	180		260
Payable	140	330	220	

For Asia, the receivable amount comes to USD 350mm, and the payable is USD 140mm. The net payable amount to Asia becomes USD 210mm, which is the single payment made from the netting centre. Similarly, the net payment due from Europe is USD 250mm, and the net payment due to the U.S. region is USD 40mm. As can be seen from Figure 7.6, the net sum of receivables and payables is zero.

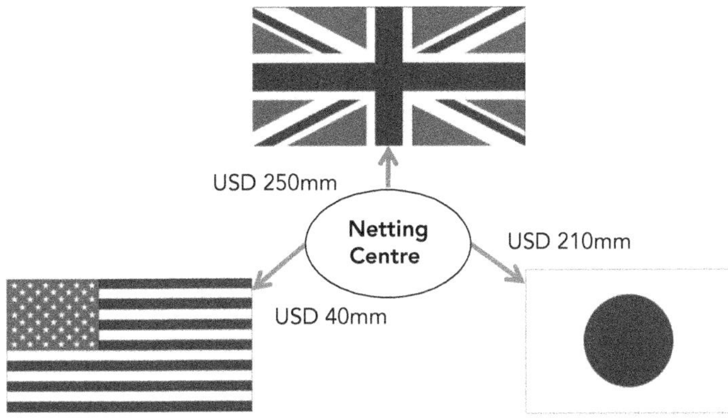

FIGURE 7.6 Net Sum of Receivables and Payables

Table 7.2 indicates the efficiency or reduction of actual throughput flows as a percentage of the total flows—a good criterion for volume-based cost estimates.

TABLE 7.2 Efficiency of Throughputs of Flows on Account of Netting

	Payments	Receipts	Net Flows	Efficiency as a % of Non-Netted Flows
Asia	140	350	210	57.14%
Europe	330	80	250	39.02%
United States	220	260	40	91.67%
TOTAL	3590	3590	250	86.07%

Table 7.3 shows the number of transactions required—hence a reduction of effort or resources that can provide an estimate of resource saved because of netting.

This simple example shows how benefits can be calculated through simplistic means. FX process efficiency and resource saving may be derived from these numbers.

TABLE 7.3 Efficiency of Volume of Transactions as Result of Netting

	Payments	Receipts	Net Transactions	Efficiency %
Asia	6	6	1	91.67%
Europe	5	5	1	90.00%
United States	5	5	1	90.00%
TOTAL	16	16	3	90.63%

NETTING IMPLEMENTATION

Implementation of netting is a simple yet lengthy process that requires rigour for setup and implementation as well to run on a regular basis. Next we discuss the various alternatives available for implementing a netting solution and cover a basic netting cycle—the process and tasks involved in running netting on a regular basis.

Netting Solution Implementation

The system and operations are two key considerations for deciding how to implement netting. The three solutions generally available are:

1. **In-house solutions.** Systems developed in-house with own operations
2. **Hybrid solutions.** Systems procured from a third party but operations managed in-house
3. **Outsourced solutions.** A third party vendor (could also be a bank) runs the entire systems and operational process required for netting

The benefits and issues associated with each are elucidated in Table 7.4.

Depending on scales and availability of vendors, the appropriate alternative may be chosen for each organisation.

TABLE 7.4 Implementation Alternatives for Netting Solutions

Alternative	Systems	Processes	Concerns	Benefits
In-house	Netting system developed in-house Netting accounts maintained in Treasury system	Run by Treasury centre FX can be done with any bank	Resource intensive to develop and set up Firm responsible for maintenance and backup for systems and staffing	High degree of flexibility on value dating, exception processing, and inclusion/change of entities Best FX rates owing to ability to choose FX bank
Hybrid	Netting system procured from vendors (could be add-on module of existing Treasury management system) Netting accounts maintained with system owner	Usually done at Treasury (netting) centre, which becomes the end user	Cost could be higher depending on features Firm is responsible for backup staffing Less system flexibility	Vendor is responsible for system maintenance Best FX rates owing to ability to choose FX bank
Outsourced	Systems and interface outsourced Netting accounts owned by vendor	Vendor does all processing and payments All entities including third parties interact with the vendor	Costs could be higher for low-scale operations but decrease as scale increases FX rates determined by bank if bank is also the netting vendor Lesser system and process flexibility	Vendor responsible for system and human resources Most efficient if scales are large

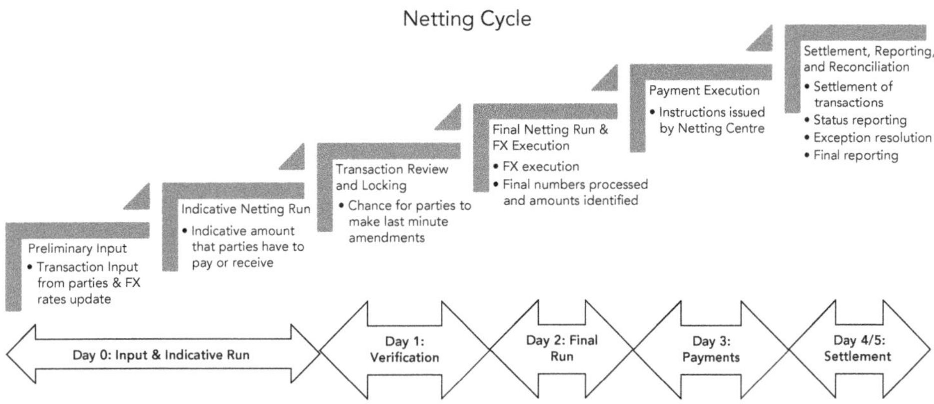

FIGURE 7.7 Sample Netting System with Timelines

Netting Cycle

The netting cycle comprises the entire end-to-end process for operationalising netting for the organisation. Figure 7.7 shows a sample netting system with timelines. Timelines may vary from firm to firm depending on the nature of the operations and implementation.

The entities are allowed to enter their transactions through direct entry or upload (or verify the transactions if the entire receivables and payables are already on the system). An indicative netting run with sample FX rates is done, and the entities are given a big-picture idea of the monies due to or from them. An opportunity is then provided for the entities to make any changes (large changes—inclusions or omissions—might have to be pre-cleared by the Treasurer for funding purposes). The final netting run and FX deals are then executed. The payment instructions are then made, and settlements are tracked by entities and reported back to the netting centre. If account management is centralised, the netting centre can track this on its own. Reporting is done, and exceptions are reconciled and resolved.

For hybrid or fully outsourced models, the service-level agreement (discussed in detail in Chapter 30) has to be well executed.

Considerations for Implementation

The elements discussed next should be part of a good implementation solution.

Quality (Accuracy and Timeliness) of Inputs

No process is well managed if the inputs into it are not accurate. The same applies for the netting process. Accuracy of inputs from the netting entities is critical, as is timeliness. Regarding accuracy, the entities have a chance to make minor adjustments to achieve 100% accuracy; regarding timeliness—not submitting the estimates or number in time—this area impacts not only their own cash position but also that of the other parties. Hence, it is imperative to keep a tab on the accuracy of these numbers and report large variances or adjustments on a regular basis.

Quality (Accuracy and Timeliness) of Execution

Accuracy and timeliness of the payments execution process is also important, not only to ensure smooth operations from a cash flow perspective but also to maintain the reputation of the company, especially where third parties are involved. Errors and exception history must be tracked, and repetitions must be acted on. This is an area that has a high degree of operational risk and opportunities for losses owing to poor operations and controls. Hence, a high degree of accuracy, monitoring, and control is called for.

Costs

Since costs are a key driver for implementing a netting solution, it is important to assess not only the setup costs but also the implementation costs on an ongoing basis. These costs include costs of operational errors and exception resolution.

Tax

Tax treatment and impact of netting-related flows have to be considered and clear counsel obtained prior to implementation. Certain tax jurisdictions might levy withholding and other taxes on payments, while some payments that need to have taxes charged could be a part of the netting process. Hence, the tax aspects have to be very clearly articulated and documented prior to execution.

Regulations and Exchange Controls

Regulations and exchange controls form a key determinant to the netting process. The different kinds of netting jurisdictions include:

- **Gross payments or net payments**. Some jurisdictions allow gross-in and gross-out in the foreign currency—that is, they allow all inflows to be clubbed together and outflows to be clubbed together. Fully developed markets without capital controls, such as New York, London, and Singapore, allow net settlement with no specific restrictions.
- **Local currency or foreign currency**. Some jurisdictions may allow only the local currency payment to be netted, while some may allow only foreign currency payments to be netted.

It is important to get a good regulatory opinion on the applicable type of netting prior to implementation.

Number of Netting Cycles per Month

The number of netting cycles per month depends on the urgency of payments and the volume. Firms use monthly, fortnightly, weekly, and sometimes even daily payment cycles. The system selected and related processes should have the flexibility to include or exclude parties from a cycle and also to have in place an exception process for these changes.

Credit Limits

Credit limits with banks, especially for daylight overdraft and contingency liquidity requirements (for payments not going through owing to exigencies), have to be set up and tested.

Infrastructural Inefficiencies

Disruptions of payments, such as acts of God or sudden public holidays, and contingency situations in the location of the netting centre, the system hosting, or any of the paying entities ought to be factored into contingency plans and thoroughly tested.

Bank Holidays

For different payment entities across regions, bank holidays across locations must be taken into account during the netting cycle. It is also possible to drop a particular location or entity from a specific cycle.

Culture

The organisation's culture (mentioned earlier in Part One) is an in important determinant in the success of a netting implementation. Senior management buy-in through demonstration of cost savings and increased efficiency and turnarounds is a must prior to implementation, as is the buy-in from all stakeholders. Another aspect for management to decide is to whether to make participation from each entity mandatory or voluntary. I personally believe that uniform processes across the organisation deliver most value, and the same rule and yardstick must be applied across all entities.

Resistance From Existing Banks

A logical resistance from existing banks (remember, the transaction costs and FX costs for the firm are direct revenue for the bank!) can be overcome by distributing other businesses to these banks. A long-term relationship bank can be rewarded by awarding them with the netting mandate. Most global banks nowadays have good and robust netting solutions, and the relationship can be sustained by routing all the flows through them. There remains only one winner among the banks, though, and some banks that do not get the mandate for netting are bound to feel left out of the company's operations.

Good Telecommunications for File Upload Integrity

File uploads for data inputs, especially for remote locations, is made more efficient through the use of good telecommunications. Poor network quality could result in file integrity issues and either non-upload or erroneous upload of payment data that could have disastrous consequences for the firm. Hence, when the bandwidth or related network speed or quality is suspect, it is better to put in incremental layers of checks and controls to ensure data integrity.

Alignment With Intercompany Payment Terms and Processes

The netting processes should be aligned with the organisation's intercompany and account policies and practices. It is good practice to have the process vetted by financial control and other applicable functions.

Stage-Wise Implementation With Parallel Test Runs

Stage-wise implementation with parallel test run is a well-recommended practice that can reduce the probability of teething issues once the entire operations go live.

Documentation

Documentation to implement netting can be time-consuming and onerous, covering many aspects. It is important to spend time and effort to complete the one-time documentation exercise in order to reduce chances of complications later on. Agreements, outsourcing and service contracts, process notes, accounting and tax reporting, and clearance and regulatory documentation (one-time and transaction-wise) need to be in place and regularly reviewed.

BENEFITS AND CAVEATS OF A GOOD NETTING SOLUTION

While there are many direct and indirect benefits of a netting solution, these come attached with caveats. There is no certainty of benefit unless some basic factors are addressed and implemented.

Benefits

Some benefits of netting have been mentioned earlier. These are highlighted in detail here.

- Higher profitability driven by lower operational expense
  - **Lower transaction cost owing to reduced number of transactions**. The vastly reduced transactional effort results directly in fewer resources being utilised for the same. Including the cost of setting up the netting system and process, the overall gains should be achieved in a reasonable time frame.
  - **Increased leverage of centralised operations**. The scale of payments will fit in easily with centralised shared service centre operations and adds to the scalability and utilisation of centralised resources.
  - **Greater control and visibility of operating cash flow**. Owing to the discipline that the netting process brings in, including accuracy and timeliness of information and financial information, the visibility of flows improves. The automated and centralised nature of the process also adds a great degree of control on a potentially high-operational risk process.

- Higher profitability driven by lower FX conversion cost
  - **Save on bid-offer spreads.** When converting across currencies, centralised FX booking for a single currency pair at one location allows for one single conversion per currency and obviates the need to have multiple conversions across sides.
  - **Lower volume of FX conversions.** The vastly reduced FX transaction volume also lowers cost.
  - **Consistency and uniformity of pricing.** Centralisation and banking at one location allows for consistency and uniformity of pricing.

Caveats

Netting certainly brings with it some gains, but there are also some caveats to bear in mind.

- In anticipation of netting payments to be made, some entities try to retain more cash than is required. This results in reduced cash visibility and utilisation of cash and also a higher degree of opportunity loss of the cash and volatility of cash. Hence, netting entities must be educated as to the benefits of adequate and optimal cash retention.
- Netting reduces the amount and extent of FX conversion and in most cases does not change the risk profile per se of the group of entities that are part of the netting cycle.

SUMMARY

Netting in many forms has become almost a way of life for companies around the world. In this chapter, we looked at some key aspects and benefits of netting. We also went through the entire netting cycle in detail with an overview of processes and explored different solutions with their related drawbacks and benefits.

CHAPTER EIGHT

Liquidity Management Introduction and Float

IN THIS CHAPTER, WE INTRODUCE the concept of liquidity management and pooling and go into detail on one of its main areas of focus: reducing float. Part Three provides further discussions on liquidity and its management.

INTRODUCING LIQUIDITY MANAGEMENT

Managing liquidity involves increasing cash visibility, efficiency, and usage; extracting value from cash; and reducing the level of working capital or external debt required for the firm. Using the firm's own cash dramatically enhances financial ratios and return on capital (see Figure 8.1).

There are many areas that the Treasurer can look at to proactively manage the firm's liquidity and improve its cash efficiency. Earlier we discussed different account structures. Concentration and pooling structures work on top of account structures and are used to consolidate cash positions around the world and

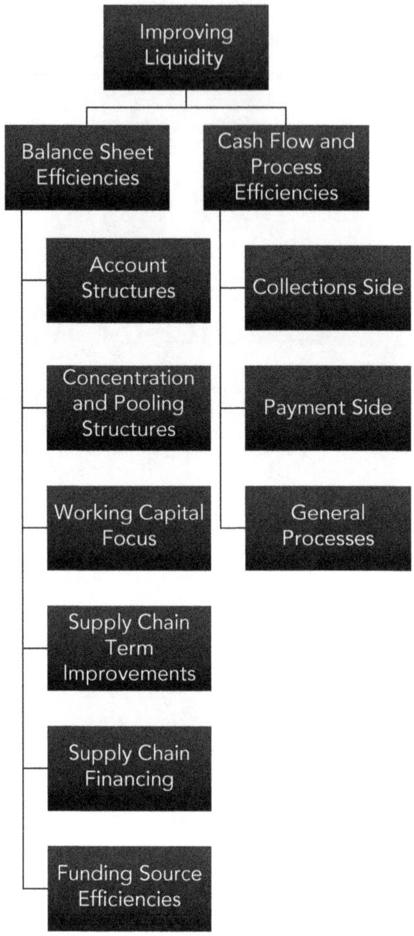

FIGURE 8.1 Liquidity Management

distribute liquidity where needed across a regional or global network. Managing working capital and reducing the requirement of working capital is a core area of focus. Structuring the financial supply chain and utilising opportunities in the supply chain are areas where Treasury is increasingly becoming involved as a trusted advisor. Finally, finding diverse, deep, and reliable funding sources at an optimal cost that can tide the firm through times of liquidity shortage (management of liquidity risk) is one of the key challenges faced by treasurers today. All of these areas are covered in later chapters.

This chapter focuses on float and achieving cash flow–related efficiencies. Efficient liquidity management and the leveraging the power of a centralised Treasury structure minimises idle balances and liquidity, enables the company to pay outstanding debt and lower its interest expense, using intercompany funding where possible, and increases yield through centralising all cash for scale and efficiencies.

POOLING AS A CONCEPT

Pooling can be defined as the reduction in a company's operating cash by combining its various fungible cash resources and thereby lowering collective volatility of its operations. The benefits of pooling come through (1) lower cash required to run the business and correspondingly (2) increased profitability through reduced borrowing costs or higher returns on larger pools of cash.

Pooling is sometimes perceived to provide benefits primarily by diverting funds from surplus locations to borrowing ones, thereby saving overdraft or interest expense. This is one reason why Treasurers of largely surplus organisations do not explore pooling more seriously.

However, one of the core benefits of pooling that can be applicable to net surplus or borrowing groups is that it creates less cash volatility at a firm level and hence higher visibility and the ability to plan for liquidity. Most important, it reduces the overall cash required to run operations.

FLOAT AND ITS CAUSES

Float can be defined as the nonavailability of funds for use to a firm owing to transit, systemic, or procedural delays (either intentional or unintentional). Float typically reduces available liquidity and interest earnings or savings owing to the use of the company's own money. There could also be an opportunity loss of the funds. Float is a common problem for companies across their various operations and has been an increasing area of focus since the liquidity issues of 2008.

An important aspect to consider, given the zero-sum nature of interest, is that someone in the system could be earning the interest on the monies that should, in ideal circumstances, be with the firm. Float loss is one of the reasons for tight liquidity situations for companies around the world. Some of the causes are depicted in Figure 8.2.

Various Kinds of Float Across the Supply Chain

Figure 8.2 provides a snapshot of the various kinds of float through the supply chain.

Float Across the Order-to-Cash Cycle

The order-to-cash cycle (see Figure 8.3), as the name suggests, is the set of activities and time taken for the money payable by a client or customer to be available to the company from the time the order actually is placed. This cycle is further elucidated as we explore the financial supply chain in subsequent chapters.

Table 8.1 depicts the various legs and the float times across each leg.

Ways to Reduce Float (Cash Flow and Process Efficiencies)

Treasury can add value in reducing float by using more efficient collection methods and more efficient balance sheet methods. We discuss balance sheet methods in Part

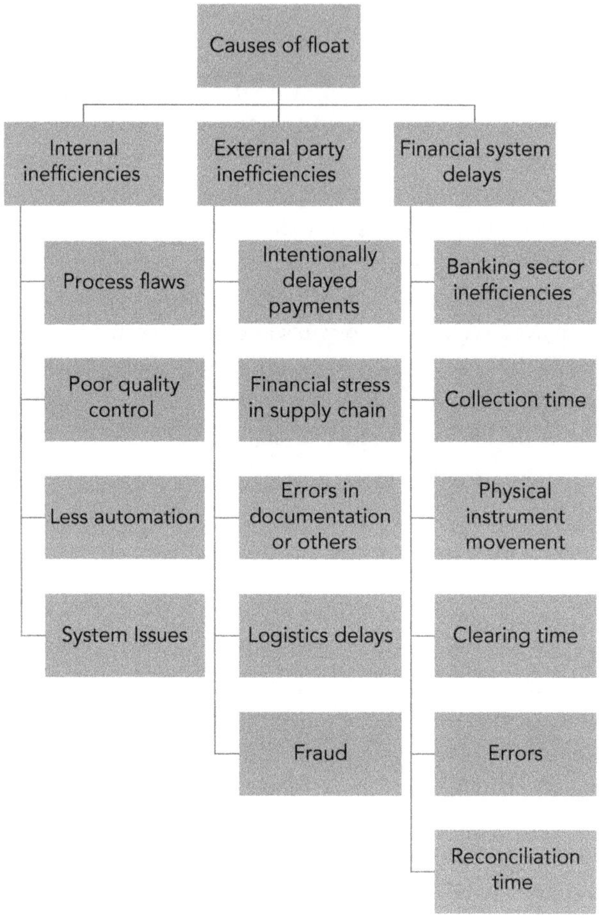

FIGURE 8.2 Causes of Float

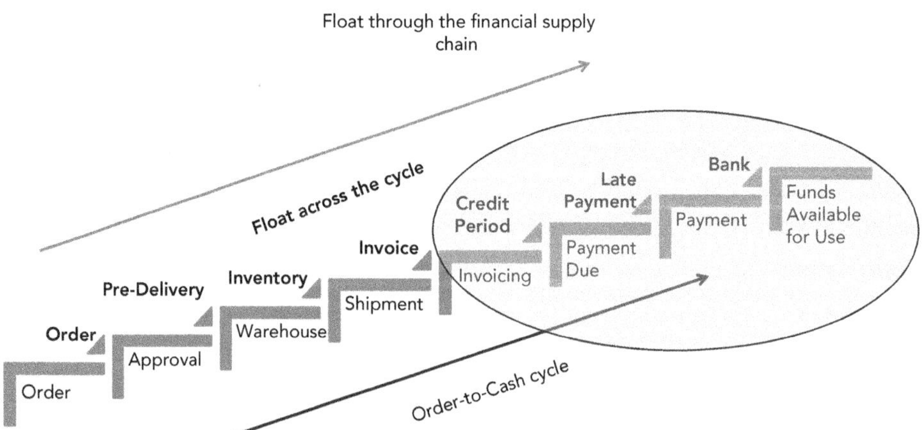

FIGURE 8.3 Float Across Different Points in the Order-to-Cash Cycle

TABLE 8.1 Different Points of Float

Float	Start Point	End Point
Order float	Order	Approval of order
Pre-delivery	Approval of order	Warehouse
Inventory float	Order	Shipping
Invoicing float	Shipping	Invoicing
Credit terms	Invoicing	Payment due date
Late payment float	Payment due date	Actual payment date
Bank credit float	Actual payment date	Money in account

Three. Methods to reduce float through cash flows and process efficiencies are discussed here.

Where Treasury Can Influence Float Times Treasury influences some of the decisions on process and financing efficiency; these elements are circled in Figure 8.3 and have a shaded background in Table 8.1.

While sales owns the process to negotiate credit terms, and collections and the accounts receivable (AR) management team own the rest of the collections process, Treasurers are playing an increasingly important role in managing the entire float process.

Figure 8.4 shows some of the various methods on reduction of float through increased efficiencies in cash flow and processes.

Collections Side The search for an efficient collections solution has been an eternal one, especially in economies that are geographically dispersed and use physical paper. The challenge is compounded by the need to have information immediately into systems and cash soonest into accounts.

Lockboxes The lockbox concept works on outsourcing the activity of cheque collection or pickup, processing, and reconciliation to an external agency, especially in remote locations. The agency or vendor collects the cheques or paper instruments, either from a customer site or from predesignated collection points/courier centres. The items are then pre-processed—sorted by bank and entity and recorded through coding their magnetic ink character recognition (MICR) bands—and images are recorded.

Data entry, if not automated, is done, and the files are processed for uploading into the firm's system.

In many cases, the vendor also provides clearing support—ensuring that the items are sent for clearing and tracking for returns and credits. Reconciliation reports with adequate controls are also built in, as are processes for exception resolution.

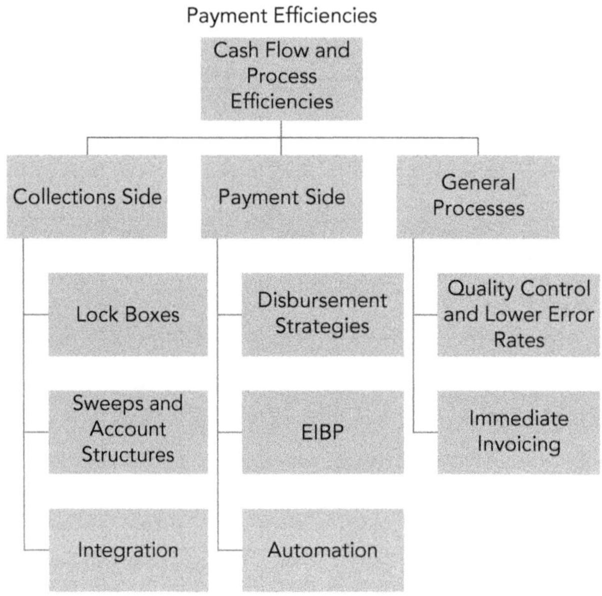

FIGURE 8.4 Reduced Float Through Increased Efficiency of Cash Flow and Process Efficiency

Lockboxes generally cut down transit (mail) time and collection float. AR collections and clearing time is also cut down, and there is quicker information flow and reconciliation. Image scanning and storage also provides for stronger data backup and matching. Lockboxes also increase visibility of cash flows by providing, in many cases, same-day collection information. Savings may also be generated through imaging, reducing transit costs of instruments as well as ease of access for other functions (see Figure 8.5).

Sweeps and Account Structures Other facilities, such as auto-sweep facilities (described in the section on pooling in Chapter 9), and account structures such as intervention accounts may be used to reduce float times.

Any incoming credits through electronic means, such as card payments, can be reconciled on a daily basis (and sometimes many times a day). Using a single banking corporation for easier access to funds across accounts is also one way to reduce float.

Integration The use of paperless receivables through an integrated system increases efficiency of collection and posting entries. The concept of against-the-sun sweeps (see the next note) enables movement of funds across time zones.

Finally, negotiating better pricing and turnaround times with the banks and integrating with banking systems reduces cost and processing time respectively, and hence directly provides savings for the firm.

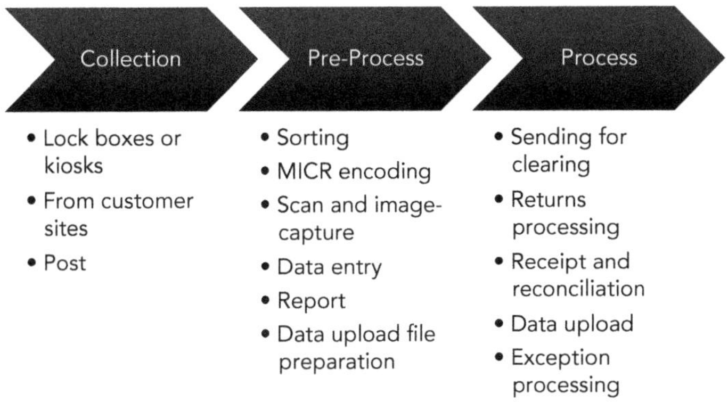

FIGURE 8.5 Lockbox Mechanism

Against-the-Sun Sweeps: West to East

Some global banks provide an against-the-sun sweep facility (see Figure 8.6) that moves cash balances from the United States into Europe and then into Asia, a practice hitherto thought impossible. When an Asian regional Treasury of a global firm located in Singapore requires funds, it calls for the same from the global account in Europe or the United States, at the end of the business day in Asia, with funds value-dated on the same day. This provides a just-in-time equivalent of managing cash and liquidity and optimises the firm's use of borrowing.

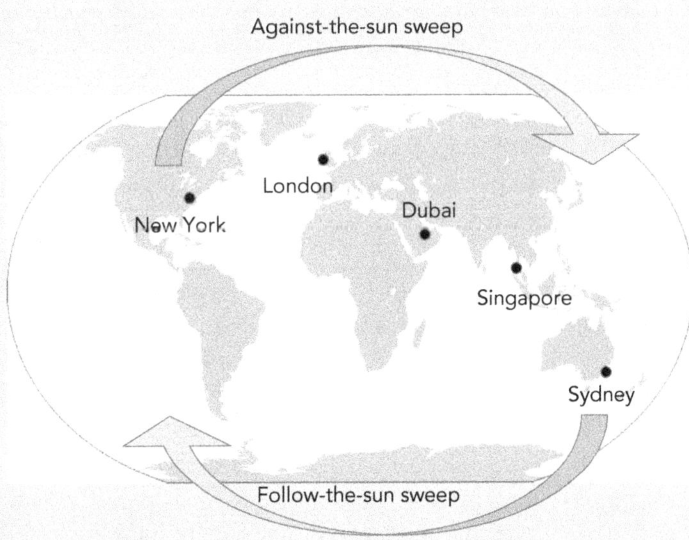

FIGURE 8.6 Against-the-Sun Sweep

Payments Side On the payments side, interesting developments have increased efficiency to reduce float on the processing side.

Disbursement Strategies Disbursement processes must be designed carefully to delay the debit and value date on which the firm's money leaves the account as much as possible, while still ensuring timely payment to beneficiaries. Various disbursement strategies are discussed next.

- **Controlled disbursement (banker's cheques).** Drafts issued by a bank are usually prefunded (i.e., the bank debits the account at the time of issuance). Presentation for payment can happen many days later. Controlled disbursement or banker's cheques are akin to drafts except, like cheques, the debit happens only on presentation.
- **Positive pay.** This method is used especially in environments prone to fraud or for cheques above a threshold. It provides cheque imaging with the customer's cheque issued file to allow the clearing process to go through. The firm itself can override exceptions or discrepancies.
- **Corporate cards.** These cards, which work off the corporate account, eliminate the need for paper, especially for reimbursement claims. Controls, limits, preapprovals, and dates can be built in, hence using automatic verification and checks that save human resources and lower cost dramatically.
- **Payroll or salary disbursements.** Moving all employee accounts to one bank enables the firm to fund accounts for salary payments only on the due date, since transactions within the same bank can be automated easily. The banks can provide incentives for employees to move their accounts, such as add-on facilities, waiver of charges on certain transactions, loans, and electronic banking, that make it easier for individuals to use the bank and allow the company to reduce its funding float. Of course, this process must be implemented with the full support and cooperation of the partners in the human resources team, and Treasury would add value only in negotiating the best deals for employees.

Electronic Invoice and Bill Payment Electronic invoice and bill payment (EIBP) is an emerging concept of combining suppliers and customers in the same marketplace for sourcing, invoicing, and payments. It is offered as an outsourced service by banks and other providers like Ariba, Alibaba, and I2. Similar services are also offered by large companies on their own using in-house solutions. The basic EIBP process is shown in Figure 8.7.

The increased efficiency allows for less wastage or float in the system, paving the way for potentially larger discounts and more efficient liquidity for all parties. In many cases, the use of EIBP has reduced the float time from over two weeks to under a week.

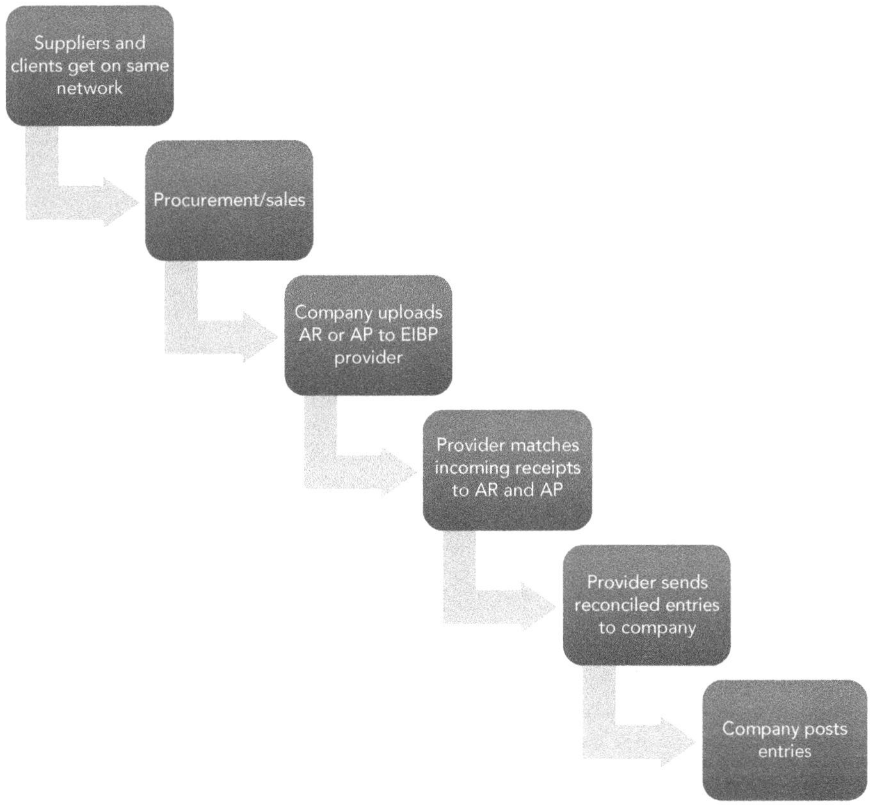

FIGURE 8.7 EIBP Process

Automation Using more electronic payments and reducing paper instruments increases the efficiency of cash flows and days that funds can remain within the corporation.

We now move to a case study that discusses an improvement of the cash management at a global firm.

CASE STUDY: OPTIMISING CASH MANAGEMENT IN A GLOBAL FIRM

Cash management is comprised of the policy, processes and practices involved in dealing with cash within an organisation. It starts with realising customer collections and other receipts, moves to making payments to vendors, employees and other stakeholders and ends with using the cash held by the business productively.

(Continued)

Wipro Limited is a company listed in the New York Stock Exchange, USA and the National Stock Exchange and Mumbai Stock Exchange in India. It operates through 80 subsidiary companies in four distinct lines of businesses—IT Services, IT Products, Consumer Care & Lighting and Infrastructure Engineering. All the four businesses have a multi-country presence and are among the leading global players in their industry segment.

The First Challenge

"How do we get global customer collections from their bank accounts to ours at the least cost and in the shortest possible time?"

This in brief is the first of the cash management challenges addressed by the Wipro Treasury team. Conceptually, a simple task of transferring money from point A to point B in the least possible time, incurring the least cost, is complicated by four hurdles—different countries with their unique regulatory environments, multiple currencies involving currency conversion cost, multiple subsidiaries restricting free transferability of funds and the challenge of a large, widely dispersed customer base. Table 8.2 details the magnitude of this challenge.

Wipro's global cash management system is built on three basic principles described here.

- First, regulatory compliance and simplicity is accorded the highest priority by ensuring that intercompany transactions are kept to the minimum.
- Subject to this hygiene standard, cash management is optimised for cost-benefit analysis. In this analysis potential investment returns obtained from holding cash is set-off against transaction and currency conversion costs to compute net benefit. While optimising sterile cash holdings, the limitations of using cash across countries and subsidiaries are factored in. The objective of minimising intercompany and trans-national fund flows is to reduce inter-company interest payments and currency conversion costs.
- The final factor targets transactional efficiency by limiting the number of banks involved in the cash management operations.

TABLE 8.2 Magnitude of the Cash Management Challenge

Business Segments	Revenue for 2010–11 Rs.mn	# of Countries	# of Currencies	# of Parties Billed To	# of Subsidiaries#
IT Services	23,760	50+	≈20	≈700	36
IT Products	36,995	10+	≈10	≈1200	15
Consumer Care & Lighting	28,436	10+	≈10	≈1000	19
Wipro Infrastructure Engineering	**	5+	≈5	≈40	4

#Most of the subsidiaries have their operations restricted to a single country
**Not separately reported

TABLE 8.3 Geographical Clustering Across Businesses

Business	Cluster of Geographies			
	First Cluster	**Second Cluster**	**Third Cluster**	**Fourth Cluster**
IT Services	India	Americas	Europe	Japan & APAC
IT Products		APAC	Middle East	
Consumer Care & Lighting		Country specific for each of the countries it operates in*		
Infrastructure Engineering		Sweden	Rest of the World	

*This is the only business that deals in consumer products and end consumers through a network of distributors, wholesalers and retailers requiring extensive distribution presence.

Based on the above set of principles, cash management is organised into geographical clusters for each of the four businesses. These clusters are formed considering the organisational structures, regulatory feasibility and ease of feasibility of fund transfers. The grouping of clusters is described in Table 8.3.

India is the first cluster for all Wipro businesses. Wipro does not directly deal with any individual consumer or customer. All its customers are business entities. They range from the largest corporate to medium sized partnership firms who deal in and distribute their wide product range covering from soaps to Laptops and truck tippers spares. Geographically, Wipro's customers are located across the length and breadth of India. Its wide distribution network ensures that its customer cheques come in from most of the 1138 Clearing Houses in the Indian banking system spread across the country. This results in Wipro offices having to deal with both the outstation cheques and local cheques.

Considering the presence of outstation cheques, Wipro has centralised all its cheque collections with a leading Indian bank that has presence in most of the locations where its customers are present, either directly or through their correspondent banks. Wipro obtain credit for all their collections on T+1 basis, i.e. money is available for use in their bank account on the next working day following the day in which they hand over the customer cheques to the bank. The bank in turn charges a fixed fee per month, which depends on the volume of transactions and other aspects of banking relationship. Wipro evaluates the bank charges based on the period for which the bank is out of funds, which is mutually agreed upon. The fixed fee ensures that the bank benefits from reducing the collection cycle as it cannot pass on additional cost due to extended collection cycles. In addition to capping the collection cost, Wipro benefits from reduced credit risk due to dishonored cheques, as the collection cycle time is minimised.

While the case and experience is India-based, the principle and execution can be practiced in many other markets where geographic spread is high and use of paper-based instruments is prevalent.

For each of the clusters outside India, Wipro has a designated pooling bank account where customer collections are consolidated. Based on the expense forecast for each of the cluster pool account, funds are retained to meet the immediate needs and the surplus transferred to a set of central pooling account in India. For almost all the accounts where money is retained for expenses, the funds are parked in overnight accounts that earn some interest.

(Continued)

The Second Challenge

"How do we minimise transit time and float?"

Wipro's payment system is designed with the objective of minimising if not eliminating the transit time and costs involved in floats arising from payments. Leveraging the technology that is embedded in the Indian Banking Payment System most of the vendor payments are made using electronic fund transfer systems, where the vendor account is credited simultaneously when Wipro's bank account is debited, thereby eliminating any manual handling of cheques and its physical movement. As soon as the payment is effected, a payment advice is generated by the bank and sent to the vendor's registered email account. This system of electronic transfer is yet to be implemented in two businesses where the volumes are comparatively lower. In these two businesses, cheques are issued to the vendors.

A prominent feature of Wipro's IT business is its large employee base. Wipro as of March 31, 2011 had 120,000 plus employees. A unique feature of Wipro's payment system is in the complete elimination of all cash transactions. All employees when they join Wipro are provided with an ATM card for a specially designated bank account titled Employee Reimbursement Account or ERA account. This bank account is different from their salary account. All employee reimbursement claims are processed centrally and the authorised amount is credited to the employees ERA account. Concurrent with the credit, an email is generated to inform the employee of the credit to his bank account. The employee at his pleasure can draw the amount from the ERA account through any conveniently located ATM. The ERA account cannot be used for any other purpose. Neither can the employee make any deposits into this account nor are cheques permitted to be drawn on it. The bank for providing this service free of cost is entitled to use the float on this account. Hence, no interest is paid on the balance retained in the ERA account.

The Third Challenge

"How do we productively use surplus cash?"

The third cash management challenge addressed by Wipro Treasury is to productively use the surplus cash to enhance the organisation's profits. Given the scale of operations, ascertaining the quantum of surplus cash in time for investments each day is itself is a challenging task. Wipro uses Treasury Vision, the web-based software that picks up the feed from all the designated bank accounts and presents a single screen view of the company position. The bank balances across banks and accounts are updated daily through an end of day SWIFT message which flows to a central SWIFT address from where balances and statements are populated into this software. Treasury Vision provides a customised view of geography level, bank level, business unit level aggregation that can be customised as per the organisation needs for optimal cash management

Wipro's Treasury's investment policy is based on prioritising the three competing claims in descending order of importance—Safety, liquidity and return. Wipro's management acknowledges that Treasury operations are ancillary and complement its main business. Consequently the focus is on safety first. Subject to safety, returns are maximised by a judicious mix of investments in instruments having different tenors. Wipro invests in a range of instruments covering fixed deposits and Certificate of Deposits of banks, Money market mutual funds, Commercial Papers and Non-Convertible Debentures. Wipro evaluates its return on a post-tax basis. For instance pre-tax returns are converted to post-tax returns at the marginal tax rate and compared with investments that yield post-tax returns like dividend from the Mutual Funds.

As of March 2011, Wipro had an investment of nearly USD 2 billion. This amount excludes cash held in current accounts, cash and cheques on hand for routine operational needs.

Conclusion

For a large and growing multi-national, multi-business enterprise, cash management is a continuous challenge. Wide spread adoption of technology is the main contributor for its continuing progress. However, measures of progress in this sphere are quantifiable and reasonably constant, and include among others the number of bank accounts operated, sterile cash holding, payment float i.e. quantum of cheques issued but not presented and return on investments compared to the benchmark rate used.

Contributed by Shankar Jagannathan, Wipro Ltd

SUMMARY

Liquidity is one of the most critical elements of the Treasury manager's domain, and ensuring liquidity through as many internal means as possible is one of the biggest challenges, and wins, for the Treasurer and chief financial officer. This chapter explored some of the tools to reduce float, which is one of the potential sources of liquidity that firms can tap without resorting to external capital sources. A case study on optimising cash in a global firm was also discussed.

CHAPTER NINE

Cash Pooling and Efficiency

ONE OF THE TOPICS OF MOST discussion in recent financial and corporate times is the pooling of cash and the processes that make the availability of cash and its use a lot tighter. The liquidity events of 2008 highlighted the use of cash, as we will see in Part Three of this book. In this chapter, we focus on the cash concentration aspects of transactions management, looking at the implementation of various structures that would help to pool cash in together.

CASH CONCENTRATION STRUCTURES

The ability to concentrate cash into one location and preferably in one currency has been a challenge for Treasurers ever since company operations became physically dispersed. Concentration structures can be one of two broad methods—notional pooling and physical pooling—or combinations of these (see Figure 9.1).

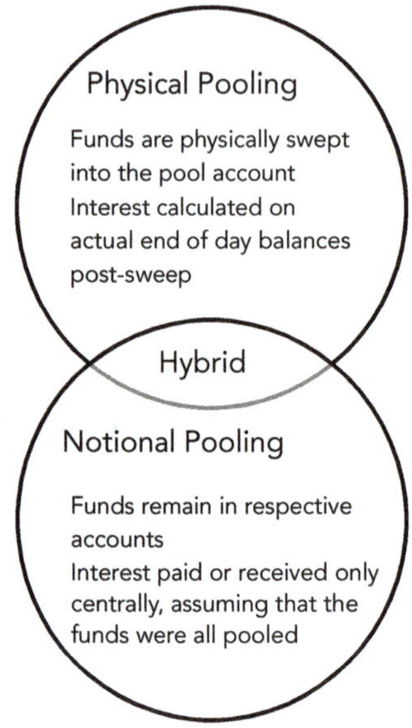

FIGURE 9.1 Concentration Structure Types

Physical Pooling

Physical pooling is the simplest method to appreciate: Cash is moved from one account to the other through a physical transfer and then moved back in the morning if required. The actual transfer happens to a master "concentration" account, and the net position is managed centrally.

Physical pooling can be:

- Cross-border
- Cross-regional
- Cross-bank
- Zero balance in each of the pooling accounts, or a targeted minimum balance

The more automated the environment is, the easier it is to achieve efficiencies with physical pooling.

Zero-Balance Account Pooling

Let us assume, for simplicity's sake, the end of day balances in accounts A, B, and C to be USD +120,000, –150,000, and +90,000 respectively (see Figure 9.2).

If the deposit rates in each location were, say, 2% and the overdraft rate were 6%, the effective interest receivable (payable) in each location is around USD 13.33 payable (see Table 9.1).

In a scenario with a zero-balance account (ZBA), where all the funds are pooled into a central concentration account (see Figure 9.3), the effective interest rate receivable (payable) in each location A, B, and C is zero, owing to all the balances (both positive and negative) being pulled away.

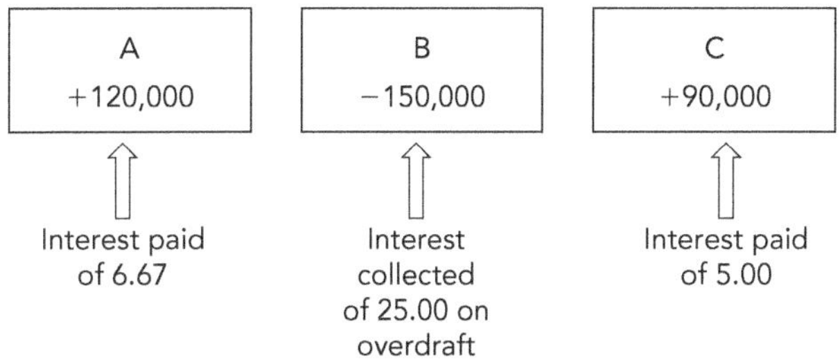

FIGURE 9.2 End-of-Day Scenario Without Pooling

The effective interest receivable (payable) at each location is shown in Table 9.2.

As can be seen in Figure 9.4, when operations begin the next day, the funds are swept back.

A target balance account (TBA) is similar to a zero-balance account, except that there is a specifically predecided amount that is left behind as an end-of-day balance in each of the designated accounts. These target balances are arrived at based on different factors such as regulatory need, banking covenants, management comfort, and contingency cushion for unexpected withdrawals.

Apart from the optimisation on interest cost and potential savings on overdraft fees that could be avoided, the benefits of physical pooling are that the cash can be used centrally for investment or funding purposes and entities not at the centre need not focus on managing their cash optimally. Pooling enables all possible benefits of cash centralisation.

TABLE 9.1 Effective Interest Receivable (Payable) in Each Location

Location	Interest Rate Receivable (Payable)	Balance (USD)	Interest Receivable (Payable) (USD)
A	2%	+120,000	6.67
B	(6%)	−150,000	(25.00)
C	2%	+90,000	5
TOTAL			(13.33)

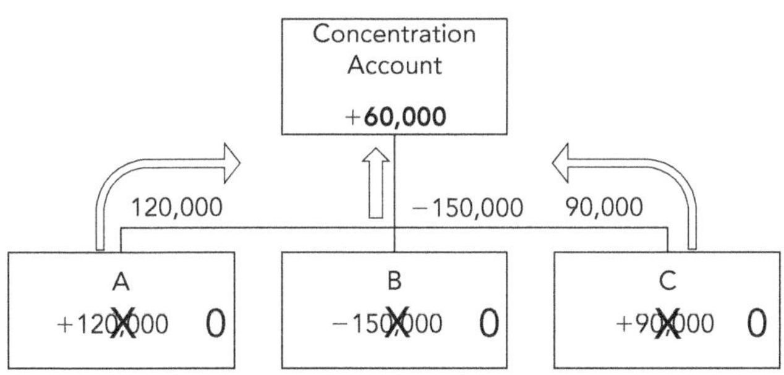

FIGURE 9.3 End-of-Day Scenario with ZBA Pooling

TABLE 9.2 Effective Interest Receivable (Payable) in the ZBA Structure

Location	Interest Rate Receivable (Payable)	Balance (USD)	Interest Receivable (Payable) (USD)
A	—	—	0
B	—	—	0
C	—	—	—
Centralised Account	2%	+60,000	3.33
TOTAL			3.33

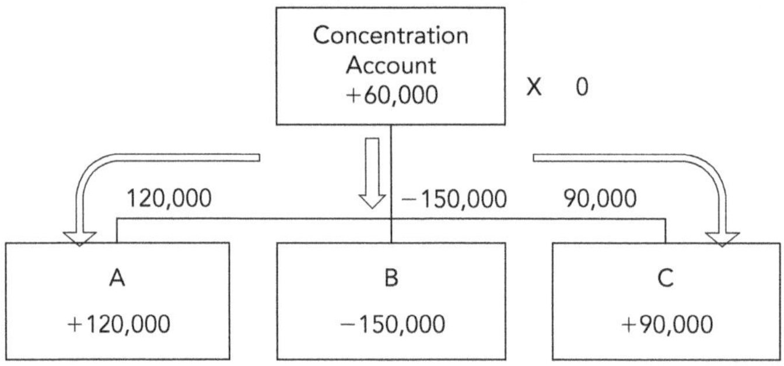

FIGURE 9.4 Beginning-of-Next-Working-Day Scenario When ZBA Funds Are Swept Back

From a regulatory point of view, regulators in some emerging market countries do not view pooling activity favourably, ostensibly because it takes away liquidity from local markets, especially if foreign currency resources are scarce and the potential conversion of local currency to foreign currency could impact currency rates. Also, since this process can be deemed to be a capital account conversion and the capital account is the one most scrutinised, easing restrictions on pooling transactions could force relaxations of far more important transactions as well.

Notional Pooling

Notional pooling, as mentioned earlier, retains the requisite balances in the respective accounts, while paying out (or debiting in case of overdrafts) the actual interest payable at the concentration centre. Notional pooling provides the interest benefit of the pooling exercise without providing the liquidity at the concentration account (see Figure 9.5). As can be seen, compared to the separate interests paid or charged in Figure 9.2 (base case), the net interest as payable in the physical pooling case (Table 9.2) is paid out centrally.

Notional pooling can also be:

- Cross-border
- Single entity
- Multi-entity

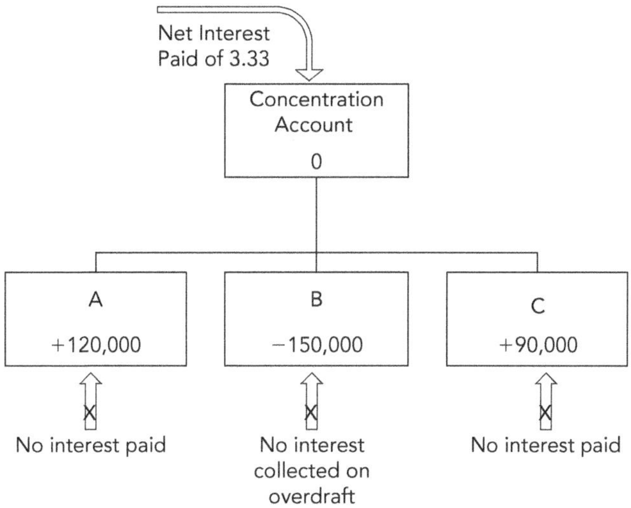

FIGURE 9.5 Notional Pooling

The "pool benefit" is the difference between the aggregate account level interest and the interest calculated on the notional pool balance. Since the operation is system intensive, the bank that does the notional pooling should have its entire systems piece well in place. Moreover, it is almost mandatory to have all accounts with the same banking entity in order to centralise the interest payment. Operationally, however, this becomes more convenient since the fewer physical transactions there are, the less chance of error there is.

From a government's perspective, the disadvantage of notional pooling could be the lack of income being shown by the bank or the customer in the jurisdiction of the subsidiaries; in the example, no income is shown by the entities A and C and no income is shown by the bank in the case of overdraft payments of B.

Hybrid Structures

Hybrid structures, as the name suggests, combine physical and notional pooling across currencies and countries to create packaged solutions. For most companies with complex operations companies located across jurisdictions, the hybrid solution could be a good fit.

POOLING STRUCTURES

Next we explore some pooling structures that could be applied to a company's cash management operations.

Single-Entity Pooling

Single-entity pooling is one of the simplest concentration techniques, where different accounts across subsidiaries, locations, or countries may be owned by the same

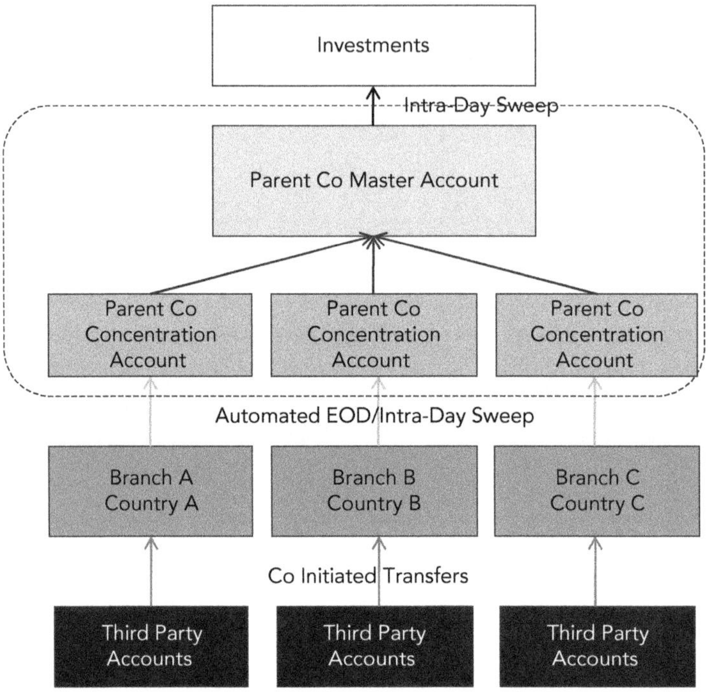

FIGURE 9.6 Single-Entity Pooling

legal entity. The bank effectively provides the company with an opportunity to use the funds without specific movement of funds within the central pool (see Figure 9.6). An end-of-day sweep keeps the money in the central pool, and any funds required by the other locations are sent through in the form of an intercompany loan. This effectively keeps interest payments within the group rather than to a bank. In some cases, the accounting view could also allow for setoff to prevent balance sheet bloating. This method also provides the Treasurer with clear visibility on the balances of each entity.

One drawback of this structure is potential thin capitalisation issues in some locations. Also, while third-party payments can also be captured, the physical nature of the transfer process ensures that third-party payments have to be made well in advance.

In some circumstances, issues and consequences of thin capitalisation may arise. Physical transfers in the case of third-party accounts have to be done well before the actual deadline to facilitate ease of payments.

Multiple-Entity Pooling

Multiple-entity pooling structures provide a concentration account for each subsidiary at the concentration centre; these accounts are then pooled notionally with the main parent concentration account (see Figure 9.7).

This method removes the need to have intercompany loans and allows for easy passing of entries to each account. Visibility is also high, as in the single-entity pooling case. However, owing to the lack of physical movement of cash to the concentration

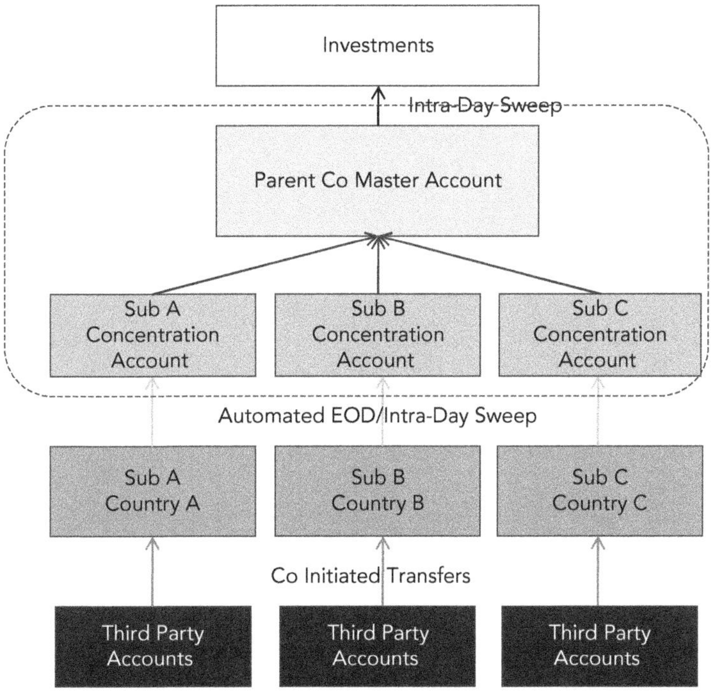

FIGURE 9.7 Multiple-Entity Pooling

account, this method is unlikely to receive setoff treatment from an accounting standpoint. Tax and documentation aspects could also be cumbersome.

Multi-Currency Notional Pooling

Multi-currency notional pooling (see Figure 9.8) uses one concentration account (either single or multiple entity) across currencies for seamless pooling benefits. The amounts for each entity are swept into a specific concentration account in the centralised location; however, these accounts are denominated in the currency (CCY) of the original amounts. At the centralised location, the bank allows for these amounts to be transferred notionally to the parent concentration account in a currency of choice, which could be totally different from any of the other currencies in which a balance has been hitherto maintained. A notional buy-sell swap is done (to convert the currencies to the master account currency and then convert it back the next day). There is no physical foreign exchange transaction, only an economic calculation by the bank.

The benefits are obvious: Multi-currency notional pooling allows for effective use of funds in the location (albeit in different currencies) while still providing the economic interest benefit of notional pooling. It potentially saves a lot of Treasury employee time due to the ease of using of process and automation. This method does, however, require a lot of documentation and exploration from the tax perspectives, plus from stringent reporting and control norms.

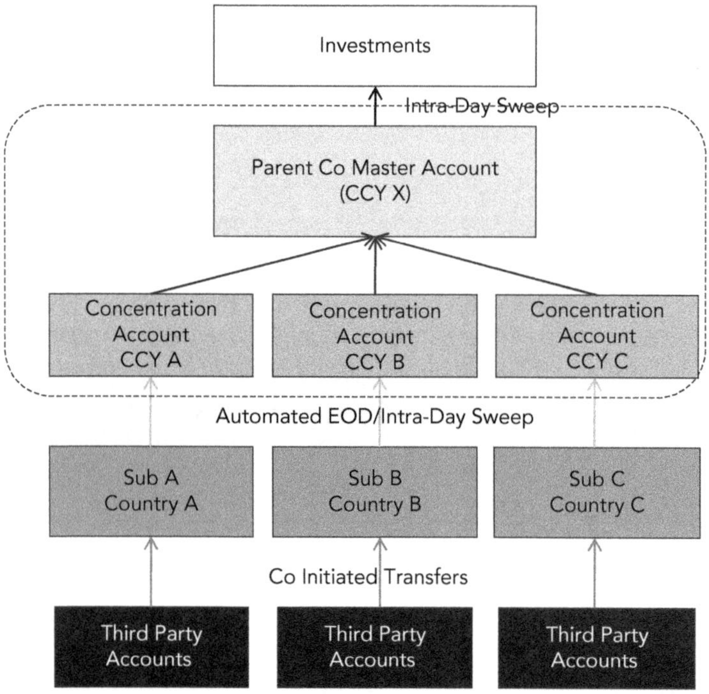

FIGURE 9.8 Multi-Currency Notional Pooling

IMPLEMENTATION ASPECTS OF CONCENTRATION STRUCTURES

It is widely acknowledged that speaking about or describing pooling structures in two-dimensional box flow diagrams is the easy part that ignores the actual nitty-gritty of transacting and setup for pooling. We now explore some of the aspects of implementation, rolling up our sleeves and getting our hands dirty as we explore the practical aspects of the pooling setup and implementation.

Locational Considerations

The decision of the location of pooling or concentration is very different from the decision on the location of the Treasury centre or the shared service centre. The employees could be located anywhere, but the location of the concentration accounts is what matters from a tax, cost, banking, investment, capital treatment, and hence profitability perspective.

These elements play a key role in determining the location of concentration:

- Tax treatment of pooling flows including notional pooling
- Tax treaties with countries from where flows are expected

- Regulatory environment
- Financial investment opportunities
- Accessibility of liquidity and banking solutions
- Business and economic climate and environment
- Account restrictions (especially nonresident accounts)
- Any statutory requirements on funds stored in accounts
- Reporting requirements
- Access to liquidity and banking services
- Banking support across all time zones
- Any incentives from the local government
- Documentation requirements, both local and banking

Of these, the tax and documentation aspect could be potentially the most involved and also the most complicated. For that reason, we discuss these aspects in more detail next.

Tax Aspects

The primary issue with increasing intercompany flows is the possible treatment as dividend. Pricing, especially for interest and capital, has to be at arm's length, and there has to be a justified business purpose or economic substance for the flow. As mentioned earlier as well, any incremental, such as withholding tax or other taxes, could be a detriment to potential benefits of implementation.

Tax authorities in all countries are fairly cognisant of the pitfalls of pooling and hence keep a wary eye out for issues that could be sensitive from a regulatory standpoint. Attractive though concentration may sound, it is always a safe practice to get a seasoned tax opinion prior to starting the implementation.

Documentation Aspects

There are many documents required (apart from any specific local requirements) for purposes of executing cash concentration. Some of these are:

- General accounting documentation
- Intercompany agreements
- Pooling agreement
- Sweep agreement
- Cross guarantees or indemnities
- Legal right of setoff
- Tax indemnities if required
- Tax opinions
- International Swaps and Derivatives Association (ISDA) membership, if required

The example below shows one way to quantify the effects of a pooling solution.

EXAMPLE: QUANTIFYING THE BENEFITS OF POOLING: A FOUR-STEP PROCESS

While exercises to implement pooling or concentration might sound very good on paper and a boasting point to peers and management, without true financial benefits, pooling might be of no use. What must be done is simple: quantify the reduction in external borrowing for working capital because of the concentration of cash.

Consider a hypothetical company with operations across various countries and daily requirements for funds (working capital [WC]) given in Table 9.3.

The Treasurer looks at this global operations list and considers how pooling and concentration will help the company. A simple four-step procedure will help.

Step 1. Calculate the WC requirement in each region for all countries that have a pooling restriction. Totaling this, we get the numbers in Table 9.4. Hence, this amount needs to be raised within the respective country.

Hence, a total of USD 44 million needs to be raised across these countries. This is the bare minimum WC borrowing requirement. Let us explore how to tackle the remaining USD 112 million.

TABLE 9.3 Working Capital Across Locations

Region	Country	Daily WC Requirement (USD million)	Pooling Restrictions
Asia	China	23	Yes
Asia	Singapore	5	No
Asia	Japan	16	No
Asia	Australia	4	No
Asia	India	14	Yes
Europe	Czech Republic	4	Yes
Europe	Germany	22	No
Europe	United Kingdom	10	No
America	United States	30	No
America	Canada	25	No
America	Mexico	3	Yes
TOTAL		156	

TABLE 9.4 WC That Needs to Be Raised in Countries That Cannot Benefit from Pooling

Region	Countries with Pooling Restriction	WC Requirement Total Where Pooling Cannot Be Used (USD million)
Asia	China + India	37
Europe	Czech Republic	4
America	Mexico	3
TOTAL		44

Step 2. Calculate the requirement in each region that can benefit from pooling, as shown in Table 9.5.

This means that each zone can rely on the amount of WC shown in Table 9.5 that can be raised from any source, apart from the minimum amount shown in Table 9.4.

Step 3. Superimpose the two requirements to show the minimum that each zone needs. Table 9.6 shows the minimum and poolable WC amounts in each zone.

The three rows for each region in column 3 have not been separated because they denote the poolable resources.

Step 4. Evaluate the benefits of concentration. Provided that the bank offering the pooling solution (and for these large amounts, more than one bank must be eager to offer their services) can move funds from one zone to other, with daylight overdraft limits in each zone that can be liquidated by monies coming in from the region in the previous time zone (e.g., overdrafts in Europe can be made good by monies being swept in from Asia when Asia closes). In that case, the amount that can be sent over from one region to the other can be raised in the region that requires the most—that is, America. If USD 55 million were raised as WC borrowings in that zone, then the same money can travel to other parts of the world through physical sweeps, and hence the funding requirements of all locations can be met (see Tables 9.7, 9.8, and 9.9). Table 9.7 depicts the status in Asia when the other regions are closed.

Hence, the total borrowing requirement moves to USD 92 million from USD 156 million, a reduction of USD 64 million in borrowing. Applying the relevant interest rates in the countries where the borrowing is not happening, the total savings can be determined after reducing the cost aspect of implementation.

TABLE 9.5 WC in Countries That Can Benefit from Pooling

Region	Countries Without Pooling Restriction	WC Requirement Total Where Pooling Can Be Used (USD million)
Asia	Singapore + Japan + Australia	25
Europe	Germany + United Kingdom	32
America	United States + Canada	55
TOTAL		112

TABLE 9.6 WC for Each Zone

Region	WC Requirement Total Where Pooling Cannot Be Used (USD million)	WC Requirement Total Where Pooling Can Be Used (USD million)	Total (USD million)
Asia	37	25	62
Europe	4	32	36
America	3	55	58
TOTAL	44	?	??

(Continued)

TABLE 9.7 Borrowings in Asia Time

Region	WC Requirement Total Where Pooling Cannot Be Used (USD million)	WC Requirement Total Where Pooling Can Be Used (USD million)	Total (USD million)
Asia	37	25 (swept from U.S.)	62
Europe	—	—	—
America	—	(55 less 25) surplus 30	Surplus 30
TOTAL	37	55	92

TABLE 9.8 Borrowings in Europe Time

Region	WC Requirement Total Where Pooling Cannot Be Used (USD million)	WC Requirement Total Where Pooling Can Be Used (USD million)	Total (USD million)
Asia	—	—	—
Europe	4	32 (25 swept from Asia and 7 swept from U.S.)	36
America	—	(30 less 7) surplus 23	Surplus 23
TOTAL	4	55	59

TABLE 9.9 Borrowings in America Time

Region	WC Requirement Total Where Pooling Cannot Be Used (USD million)	WC Requirement Total Where Pooling Can Be Used (USD million)	Total (USD million)
Asia	—	—	—
Europe	—	—	—
America	3	55 (32 swept from Europe + surplus 23)	58 (no surplus)
TOTAL	3	55	58

SUMMARY

This chapter introduced many concepts and practices relevant for the next part of the book (balance sheet and liquidity management) and some basic concepts of physical and notional pooling. Three different pooling structures were discussed with their benefits and potential issues. Implementation aspects of pooling were examined, and the chapter concluded with a simple example on calculating the benefits of implementation of a simple global concentration structure.

CHAPTER TEN

10 Cash Flow Forecasting

FORECASTING OF CASH FLOWS is one of the most underrated yet critical aspects of a company's operations, and the Treasurer is the vortex of the entire process.

FORECASTING IN THE CONTEXT OF LIQUIDITY MANAGEMENT

The goal of the cash flow forecasting (referred to in this chapter as forecasting) exercise is primarily to increase visibility of the cash and liquidity position of the firm by determining the timing, amount, currency, and location of cash inflows and outflows in advance.

The eventual objective is to determine funding requirements and liquidity usage and planning to ensure minimal borrowings and maximum utilisation of the firm's cash. This would reduce cost of capital and hence expenses and would increase returns on excess cash.

Strong forecasting also enables a robust risk management process. The core aspect of management of a firm's risk is to manage its future or expected cash flows and balance sheet positions, which is effectively the forecasted financial value of the firm.

Figure 10.1 depicts the basic forecasting process and its role in liquidity management. The inputs and influencers in the forecasting process are derived from various entities around the world, including business units, procurement units, finance, manufacturing, human resources, and the like. It is very important to keep the teamwork going and to ensure seamless cooperation across these functions.

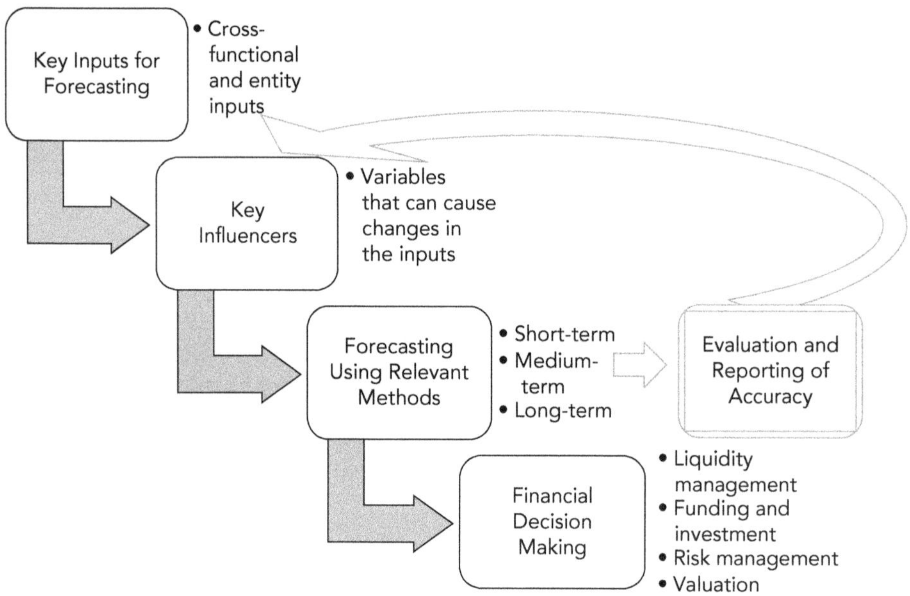

FIGURE 10.1 Basic Forecasting Process

Figure 10.2 shows the typical inputs and influencers into the forecasting process.

Various methods are used in forecasting, which are discussed later in the chapter.

Measurement of forecasting accuracy is a critical aspect (see the next note). Feedback of accuracy is passed on for business units to track to keep improving on quality of inputs.

Finally, decisions are made on the basis of these forecasts—decisions concerning liquidity, financing, investment, and risk management. Firm valuation using the discounted cash flow method also uses cash flows, and capital and corporate action decisions are taken using these critical numbers.

The following note depicts a common scenario in companies, and a possible solution.

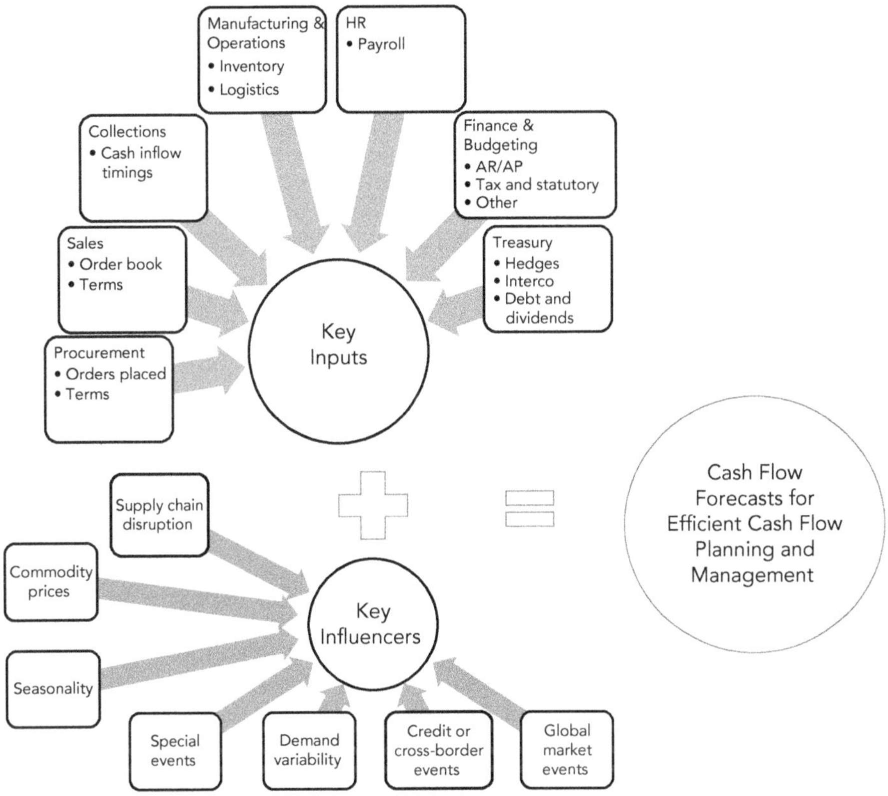

FIGURE 10.2 Typical Inputs and Influencers in the Forecasting Process

Getting Organisational Participation and Buy-in for Cash Flow Forecasting

Many Treasurer friends of mine complain that business units, subsidiaries, country management, and other partner functions view Treasury as that painful function that follows up every week for that Excel sheet. That Excel sheet happens to be the weekly cash forecast report, which is a critical input for management of liquidity and risk. What happens if the cash flow forecast is not accurate? The answer is very obvious. There are bound to be liquidity issues—cash not available where it is required, surplus cash stuck in a location where it is not needed, and borrowing where internal funds would have been enough. Risk management suffers—hedges could have been put out for cash flows that are delayed or come in earlier, and with different amounts. The cost of inappropriate liquidity and risk management is too high to be quantified, and the potential risk to the firm's operations is extremely high.

The problem lies not with the partner units themselves but with the fact that cash flows in general tend to be unpredictable. Accurately predicting the timing of cash flows for a unit is difficult. From a centralised Treasury perspective, the

(Continued)

unpredictability gets compounded with uncertainty on location, currency, and amounts. Volatile foreign exchange rates, time zone differences, and holidays add to the confusion. This is where the expertise of the teams on the ground helps. Based on history, and with some intelligence and observation, trends, seasonality, unknown factors, and client behaviour can be determined to some degree, at least for the material flows.

However, if successful forecasting can be done, why do many firms not achieve this? And how do many successful firms manage to reach a certain degree of accuracy in forecasting their cash flows? The answer could well be organisational. If partner units view cash flow forecasting as part of their mainstream job functions, and with some portion of their appraisal and key performance indicators dependent on accurately predicting the cash flows of their function, the challenges may become collective instead of being viewed as useless administrative exercises to send Excel sheets to a centralised Treasury. Changes have to be driven from the top down—the chief executive officer (CEO) has to be brought on board first; then the idea can percolate down and be implemented throughout the organisation.

There need be no tolerance for very short term (i.e., one week) forecasts, with one month forecasts needing to be very close to actual values. As the tenor of the forecast increases, the expectation for accuracy owing to the time horizon can be relaxed.

For those subsidiary or country operations that claim that the forecasting activity is resource intensive and ask for more headcount, a situation that a client of ours once faced, the CEO had one response: The subsidiary needs to, as a matter of business, have a handle on the cash flows expected. This is not a Treasury-specific activity; it is an operations-critical one.

For skeptics, this approach will never work. Those who try might be pleasantly surprised with the results.

Process Changes to Increase Forecast Accuracy

Several process improvements can increase the visibility of cash flows and hence contribute to more accurate firm financial results. These include:

- **Invoicing as per schedule**. Invoicing delays can cause incremental delays and unpredictability in client cash flows. Being in control and invoicing at a set time can significantly improve certainty of due dates and hence incoming flows.
- **Payment as per schedule**. Paying as per due date or netting cycle date increases the visibility of firm's cash outflows.
- **Attractive on-time payment terms**. Treasury can work with sales to try to incentivise customers to pay on time or at an earlier prespecified date (see the section on the financial supply chain in Chapter 14).
- **Efficient collection process**. A collections team that is in control of its receivables management and works to receive expected cash flows on due dates coordinated with Treasury, especially for materially large inflows, adds tremendous value to the firm.
- **Early-warning mechanisms**. Events that could cause disruptions to the payment environment, such as liquidity situations, cross-border or credit events, supply chain disruptions, or payment disruptions, are best prepared for in advance. In

some cases, events are triggered at too short a notice and unexpectedly. In many cases, however, early-warning signs can be felt through strong sensors on the ground. Treasury needs the complete buy-in of the teams on the ground to support it by warning of situations that are getting worse. In this manner, should the event occur, Treasury should have had sufficient time to prepare for the exigency.

FORECASTING METHODS

There are several methods for cash flow forecasting, some of which are mentioned here, along with the fundamental philosophy behind the method. Actual implementations vary depending on the firm's actual needs. Figure 10.3 shows the two classical types of forecasting, direct and indirect.

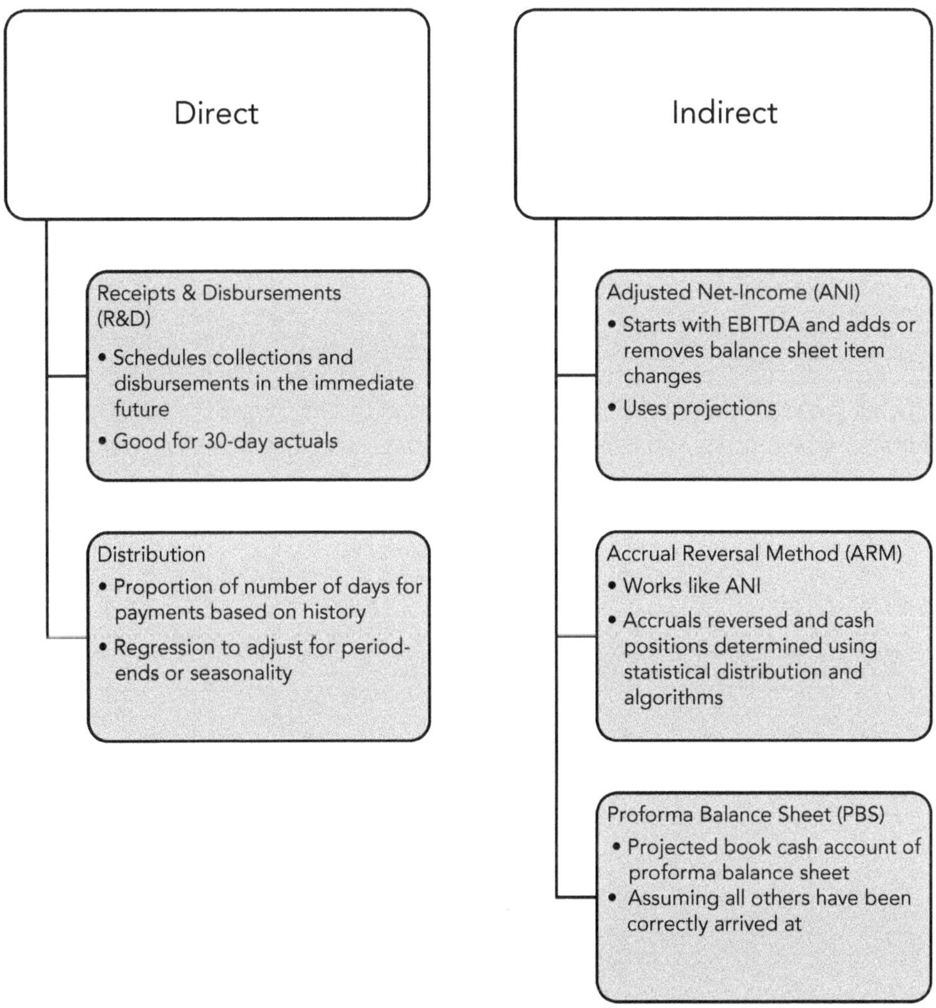

FIGURE 10.3 Classical Types of Forecasting

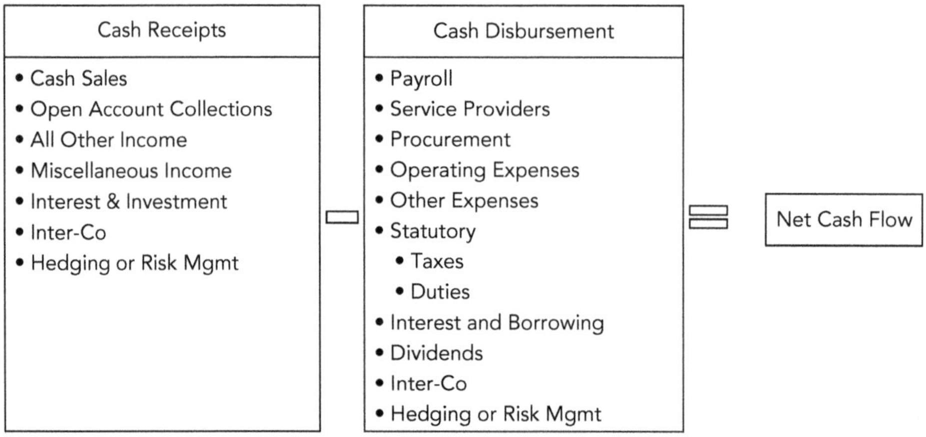

FIGURE 10.4 R&D Method

Direct methods build a bottoms-up approach to forecasting and are more likely to be used for short-term horizons. These methods are used more to generate definitive and tangible cash flows rather than to predict the future.

Indirect methods use a top-down approach that rationalises cash flows from medium- to long-term projections and arrives at estimated cash flows.

Receipts and Disbursement Method

The receipts and disbursement (R&D) method remains, across its various forms, one of the most commonly used methods for forecasting short-term cash flows. This is not as much a predictive technique but an information-gathering process of actual expected flows on which there is maximum visibility—in a sense, this is the determination of actual expected cash flow (see Figure 10.4). In effect, the R&D method seeks to schedule the receipts and disbursements of the company's cash by time period.

This is further illustrated in the following example.

EXAMPLE: R&D METHOD

This example shows how the R&D method can be used to determine cash flows on a weekly basis.

Sales		Disbursement
Week 1: 2,300,000	–	Week 1: 1,000,000
Week 2: 2,500,000	–	Week 2: 1,200,000
Week 3: 1,300,000	–	Week 3: 1,200,000
Week 4: 2,700,000	–	Week 4: 4,000,000
Week 5: 2,250,000	–	Week 5: 1,000,000

All figures in USD unless stated otherwise.

Receipts		Disbursement
30% Cash	–	50% Cash
20% 1 week credit	–	20% 2 week credit
20% 2 week credit	–	30% 3 week credit
30% 3 week credit		

All figures in USD unless stated otherwise.

In this context, if we had to estimate the cash flow for Week 4, we can work out the numbers easily as shown next.

Inflow

Cash of Week 4: 30% of 2,700,000 = 810,000
1 week credit from Week 3: 20% of 1,300,000 = 260,000
2 week credit from Week 2: 20% of 2,500,000 = 500,000
3 week credit from Week 1: 30% of 2,300,000 = 690,000
Total expected inflow for Week 4: 2,260,000

Outflow

Similarly, cash disbursement of Week 4: 50% of 4,000,000 = 2,000,000
2 week credit from Week 2: 20% of 1,200,000 = 240,000
3 week credit from Week 1: 30% of 1,000,000 = 300,000
Total expected outflow for Week 4: 2,540,000
Total net outflow for Week 4: 280,000

Distribution Method

Distribution method is often used for cheque clearing estimation, based on earlier statistically analysed distribution of the number of days it typically takes to clear cheques. Hence, a day-wise assessment of cheque clearances may be made, for example:

Business Days	Expected % of Value Cleared
1	20%
2	34%
3	36%
4	5%
5	5%

To augment the above expected value, weekly patterns may be added depending on payee tendency to bank instruments around weekdays.

Day of Week	Adjustment for Payee Behavior
Monday	−3 %
Tuesday	−1 %
Wednesday	+5 %
Thursday	0 %
Friday	−1 %

In addition, statistically backed-up month-end additions may be used based on number of days to go for month-end, since payees tend to bank cheques closer to the end of the month in some markets. Other factors such as seasonality, payroll dates and capital expenditures can also be factored in.

Adjusted Net Income Method

The adjusted net income (ANI) method uses an indirect but simple technique, starting with earnings before interest, taxes, depreciation, and amortisation (EBITDA), and gradually reducing or adding on forecasted changes to balance sheet items, such as inventory, accounts receivable, accounts payable, assets, and others. It is a good top-down method. When used scientifically, it is a reasonably good estimate for medium- to long-term cash flow forecasting.

Accrual Reversal Method

The accrual reversal method (ARM) works similar to the ANI method—starting with the EBITDA and working the forecast down by adding or removing expected changes to the balance sheet, expected accruals are reversed and expected cash increases are removed. The difference from the ANI is that with the ARM, statistical, rather than user-defined, estimates are used. The ARM is one of the more complex methods used, but if backed up by strong regression and analytics, it can be a useful tool.

Pro Forma Balance Sheet Method

A simpler method used for medium-term forecasting, the pro forma balance sheet (PBS) method uses the pro forma balance sheet of the company with projected financials. The method assumes sanctity and integrity of all non-cash items on the balance sheet, and hence takes the cash element to be correct based on the estimation of all other inputs being verified and accurate. (Though differences between the cash projections and actual bank balances need to be accounted for.)

Figure 10.5 shows a list of different time horizons and methods that can be used.

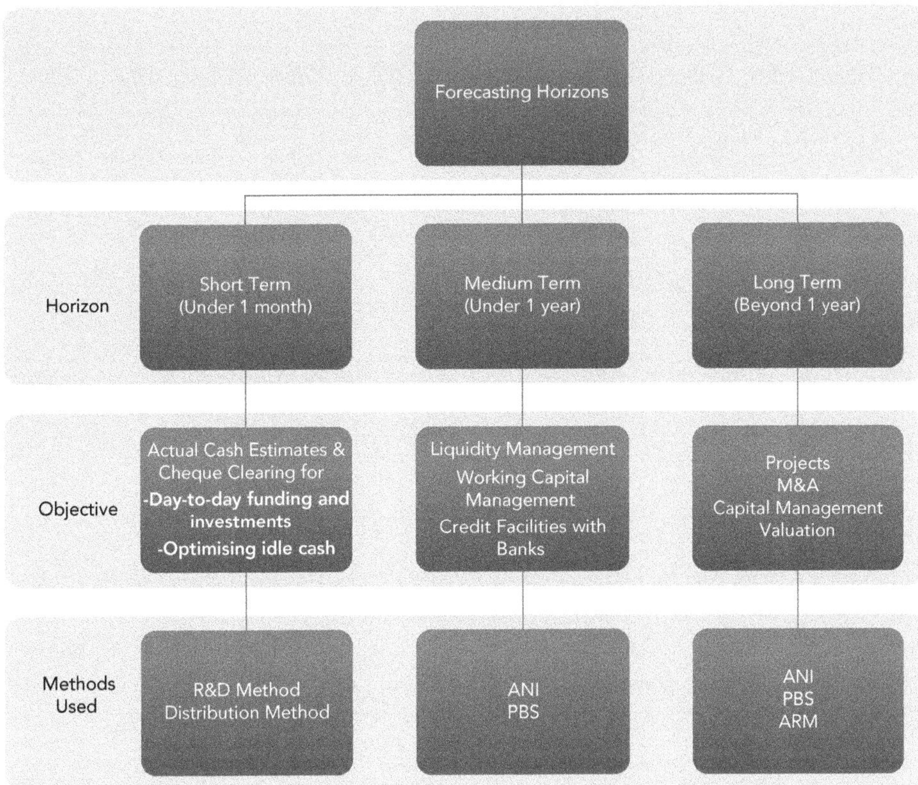

FIGURE 10.5 Snapshot of Methods of Forecasting Across Time Horizons

SUMMARY

Efficient forecasting of cash flows remains one of the determinants of a company's well-oiled financial machinery, since the accuracy and timeliness of the forecasting process determines visibility and hence ability to better manage the company's cash flows, borrowings, investments, and balance sheet. This chapter explored the context and processes for forecasting and evaluated some methods of forecasting cash flows.

PART THREE

Balance Sheet and Liquidity Management

THE FIRM'S BALANCE SHEET and managing its capital are key areas under the Treasurer's ambit. The efficient management of the supply chain and the various components that fund each stage of it, especially working capital and supply-chain financing, has become a critical aspect of managing global corporations. This part covers these important and exciting areas, plus emerging areas of opportunity and focus.

We begin by looking at the management of cash flows and the need for working capital and reducing the external sources required to fund it. We then zoom out in the larger context of the balance sheet, dwelling on some of the ratios other than working capital while exploring a real-life case study on handling a liquidity crisis. We also look at cost of capital and various sources of funding, including supply chain finance alternatives. This is followed by a look at the use of cash—how to manage operating cash and strategic cash along with investment objectives and alternatives. We conclude with a look at credit ratings with an example methodology.

This part answers important questions such as:

- How relevant is the cash conversion cycle to a firm's operations and creditworthiness?
- What can a global company do to improve its liquidity position?
- What are the determinants of a CFO's choice of capital structure for the enterprise?
- Why is the smooth functioning of the financial supply chain critical to the survival of a company?
- What are the various elements of a firm's cash and how are they managed?
- How does a typical credit assessment process work and what are the main points for a company's management to bear in mind to retain and improve the company's credit rating?

We begin with a look at the liquidity of a firm in the context of its working capital.

CHAPTER ELEVEN

Liquidity and Working Capital

IN THIS CHAPTER, WE LOOK at working capital, one of the key drivers for liquidity needs, and how companies can appreciate, measure, and reduce the need for working capital and hence external dependence on liquidity sources.

Pressure on the Treasurer to find in-house solutions for funding increases as more and more cheaper sources of liquidity dry up. There is an increasing view that many of the reasons for cash flow inefficiencies are internal, but companies sometimes tend to look at outside sources first before looking internally. Many performance measures and metrics of business and procurement units have targets and incentives based on the top or bottom line, while focus on cash flow tends to be the baby of the Treasurer and chief financial officer (CFO).

This chapter focuses on these points, and how the modern company is managing to work on them to address larger issues and find concerted solutions.

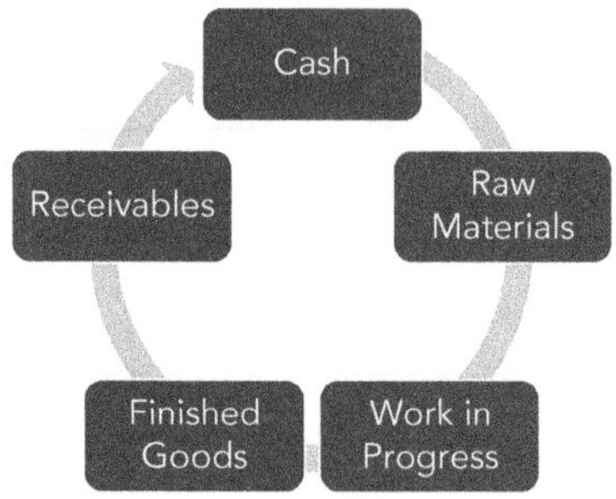

FIGURE 11.1 Operating Cycle

WORKING CAPITAL IN THE OPERATING CYCLE

The Treasurer with support from the CFO works on reducing costs through process efficiency (centralisation, dematerialisation, consolidation, and in-house banking) while adding value through balance sheet efforts (supply chain finance and working on ratios) and process automation (straight-through processing to increase control and efficiency and reduce headcount).

The operating cycle (Figure 11.1) is the chain that starts with cash and moves on to procuring raw materials, manufacturing and storing the inventory, selling the finished product, and finally recognising cash from the customer to whom the end-product has been sold. The funding of the entire process or operations on a day-to-day basis, in a nutshell, is the working capital of the firm.

From a balance sheet point of view, working capital is used for the short term (see Figure 11.2).

Working capital, which is one of the main components of capital utilised by the firm, determines the denominator of the return on invested capital, a key ratio for shareholders and debtors to assess the firm's performance. Other aspects driven by operations, such as profitability, determine the numerator.

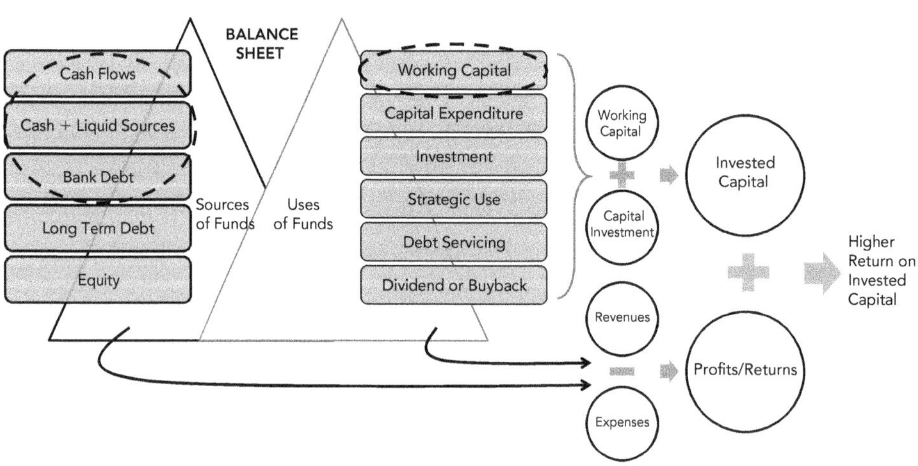

FIGURE 11.2 Working Capital in the Context of Balance Sheet and Return on Invested Capital

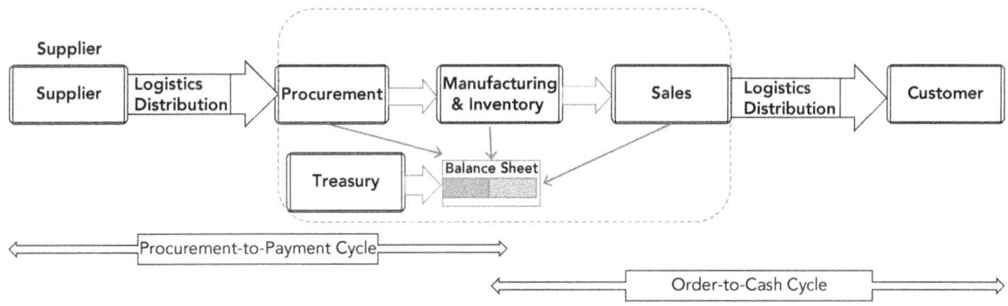

FIGURE 11.3 Supply Chain with Two Critical Cycles

Focusing back on the balance sheet, the cash flow (and hence cash) and short-term debt components work toward funding short-term resources, primarily working capital for the purposes of running day-to-day operations.

CASH CONVERSION CYCLE

Figure 11.3 depicts the supply chain with its two critical cycles, the procurement-to-payment cycle and the order-to-cash cycle.

Part II discussed these cycles in terms of their float or delays and discussed the transactions (i.e., collections or payments) aspect of these cycles and delays. This chapter focuses on the balance sheet impact of the tenor of these cycles and how improving them affects the bottom line.

The cash conversion cycle (see Figure 11.4) is rough measure (in number of days) of how long a company must finance its cash outflows for operations before it receives cash inflows from sales. The cycle can be measured by the formula:

$$CCC = DSO - DPO + DIO$$

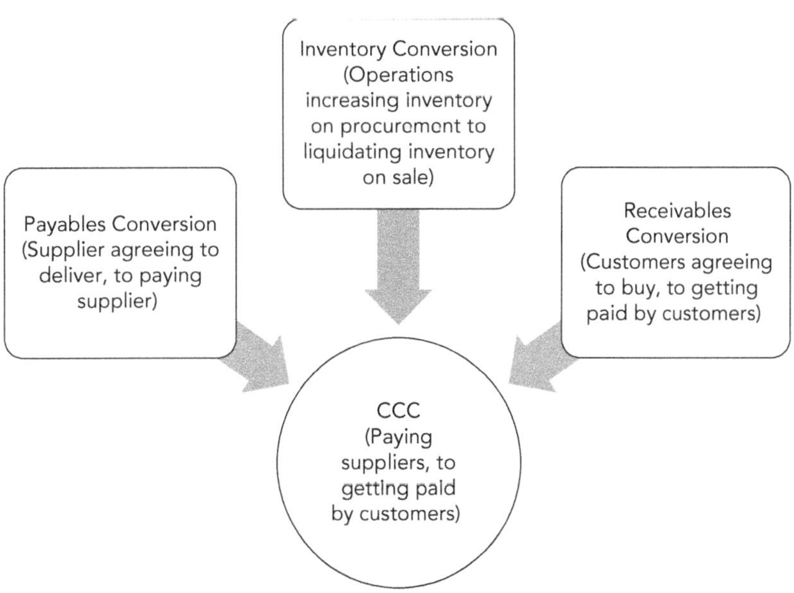

FIGURE 11.4 Cash Conversion Cycle

where:

CCC = cash conversion cycle, in days
DSO = days sales outstanding
DPO = days payable outstanding
DIO = days inventory outstanding

This means that the number of days it takes to convert cash is approximately equal to the number of days of receivable and inventory that needs to be funded, less the number of payable days (i.e., in effect, the supplier funding the firm).

The higher the CCC, possibly higher will be the cost of capital and lower the financial performance of the firm, owing to:

- Higher cost of funding owing to longer borrowing periods
- Possible supply disruption because of delays in funding purchases from suppliers
- Lower sales because of impaired ability to provide good credit periods or discounts
- Potential penalties because of late payments

The lower the CCC, the more efficient are the firm's financial operations, since the number of days of operations to be funded, and hence the working capital requirement, is lower.

Table 11.1 compares the CCC of two different companies based in Germany.

TABLE 11.1 CCC Comparison (in Days)

Component	Company Z	Company Y
DSO	75	14
DPO	35	60
DIO	15	46
CCC	55	0

The cash conversion cycle of Company Z is 55 days; it has 75 days of sales and 15 days of inventory outstanding as assets, while it has to pay 35 days' worth of payables. Hence, it needs to fund around 55 days of its operations and can quantify the amount of working capital that it required.

Company Y has a high inventory level but relatively lower receivables, which means that its customers generally pay earlier. It also makes its payments later (DPO at 60 days) on an average, and its CCC is zero days, which means that the company is just about neutral on its working capital requirements.

Procurement-to-Payment Cycle

The procurement-to-payment cycle is simply the period from the issuing of the purchase order (formalisation of the procurement) until the time the money is actually

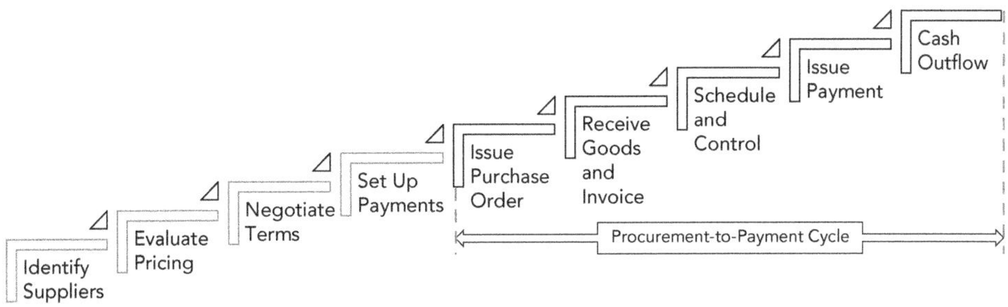

FIGURE 11.5 Procurement-to-Payment Cycle in the Context of Procurement Process

paid out to the supplier. Figure 11.5 shows procurement-to-payment the cycle in context of the processes on the procurement side.

During the procurement-to-payment cycle, the purchase order is delivered, the shipment is made, the invoice is issued, the payment is executed, and instrument or instructions are sent out. The moment the debit appears on the accounts of the firm, the accounts payable on the balance sheet is liquidated, and the procurement-to-payment cycle comes to an end for that purchase.

Days Payable Outstanding (DPO)

For an aggregate set of payments at any point of time, the DPO denotes the number of days of purchases that have been recognised but are yet to be paid. The later the payment, the longer the company has to use the money, and hence the lesser is the need to look elsewhere for working capital sources. This time period is also called payment conversion period.

The payment date or number of days of the credit period is one of the critical terms negotiated between the seller or supplier and the buyer or customer. The DPO effectively becomes a measure of the efficiency of the payments mechanism and supplier management process for the group.

$$\text{DPO} = \frac{\text{AP} \times 365}{\text{COGS}}$$

where:

AP = accounts payable
COGS = cost of goods sold

As can be seen, DPO numerically measures the AP in terms of the cost of supplies procured (COGS) and converts it to a percentage of the year or number of days.

The higher the DPO is, the longer the period allowed to make the payment and hence the greater the use of cash. Some companies take an improving DPO project to be license to delay payments to suppliers. This is not a good practice. The AP for a company is the accounts receivable (AR) for its supplier. If the payment needs to be delayed, the terms have to be agreed on up front at the time of negotiation.

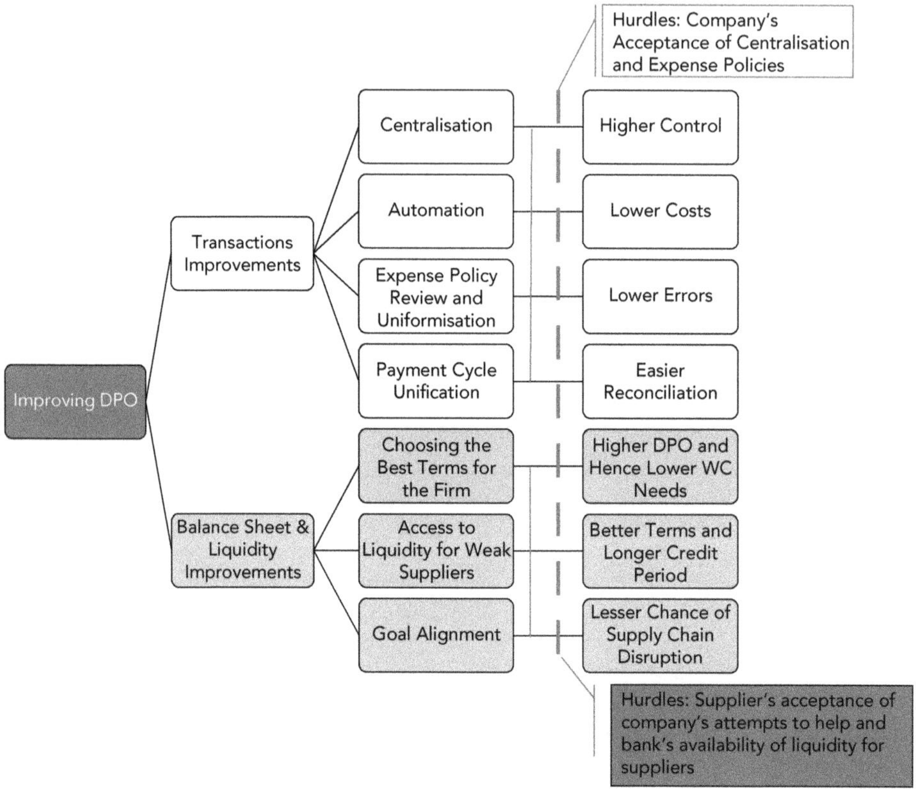

FIGURE 11.6 Generating Value in the Procurement-to-Payment Cycle

What exactly does the improving DPO project contain? Figure 11.6 describes some of the simple processes in detail.

Centralisation of processes into a shared service centre and the increased automation that it will require generally do a lot to increase efficiency on the processing and operations side. Uniformity of vendor and expense policies and aligning with global expense policy may reduce the chances of disparity, especially for a geographically distributed procurement function. Finally, keeping one or two payment dates per month generally increases efficiency on the payments process.

Related benefits of improvements in the transactions side include lower processing and vendor costs, higher degree of control, lower opportunities for error, and easier and quicker reconciliation.

Potential hurdles for these improvements are general firm-wide resistance to centralisation and expense policy changes; these can be overcome to some extent by prudent senior management and linking employee goals to the firm's performance.

On the balance sheet and liquidity side of the procurement-to-payment cycle, the supplier's choosing optimal terms, providing liquidity to weak suppliers, and aligning goals of the procurement team are the three key methods. These are explained further in the case study later in the chapter.

The main wins for these methods are to increase the DPO and hence liquidity for the firm. Indirect benefits include better terms from the vendor and reduced chances of failure or outage anywhere in the supply chain.

Certain hurdles can block balance sheet improvements, not the least of which is suppliers' willingness to admit to poor management and financial stress and to allow the larger company access to its own financials for purposes of assistance. Given the liquidity environment at that point of time, banks also may not be able to provide funding for weak suppliers, owing to prioritisation of their funds available for lending.

Calculation of DPO

Table 11.2 shows the DPO calculation for the same two European firms discussed earlier.

TABLE 11.2 Computation of DPO

Component	Company Z	Company Y
Accounts Payable (EUR)	750,000,000	1,970,000,000
Cost of Goods Sold (EUR)	7,820,000,000	12,000,000,000
DPO Calculation (AP/COGS) × 365	750 / 7,820 × 365	1,970 / 12,000 × 365
DPO (Days)	35	60

Order-to-Cash Cycle

The order-to-cash cycle (described in the earlier section in the context of float) is the period from the sale being made until the time the cash flows into the account (see Figure 11.7).

The cycle involves the booking of the sale in the company's books (creating the AR), issuing the invoice receiving or collecting the instrument or instructions on the due date, and finally receiving the credit into the account on a clear basis. The

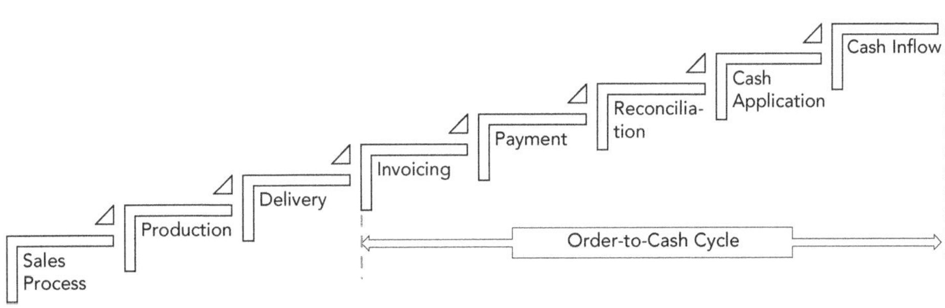

FIGURE 11.7 Order-to-Cash Cycle in the Procurement Process

moment the credit appears on the firm's account, the AR on the balance sheet is liquidated, and the order-to-cash cycle comes to an end for that sale.

Days Sales Outstanding (DSO)

For an aggregate set of receivables at any point of time, the DSO denotes the number of days of sales that have been made but for which the payment has not been received. The earlier the payment, the more use the money has to the company, and hence the lower its need to look elsewhere for working capital sources. This is also called the receivables conversion period.

The payment date or number of days in the credit period is one of the critical terms negotiated between the customer or buyer and the company salesperson. The DSO is not usually an accurate stand-alone measure of the efficiency of the group's collections mechanism and client management process. (It can be used along with overall sales, improvement in collection times after due date, and reduction in external float.) The primary use of the DSO number is to weigh the negotiation and process improvements (if any) on the customer side; in addition, it is a critical component used in measuring the CCC and hence the company's working capital requirements.

$$\text{DSO} = \frac{\text{Accounts Receivable} \times 365}{\text{Credit Sales}}$$

As can be seen, the DSO numerically measures the AR in terms of the sales made by the company and hence converts it as a percentage of the year or number of days. The lower the DSO is, the shorter the collections period and hence the greater the use of the cash. How can DSO be brought down?

The improving DSO project can be done through some of the simple process explored in Figure 11.8.

Centralisation of collection management, working on reducing float, and automation of information and interfacing with bank collections systems bring increased efficiency and controls on the processing and operations side. Goal congruence and getting partner unit (especially sales and planning) buy-in on the criticality of forecasting generates sufficient synergies in management of cash and liquidity.

Related benefits include lower processing and collection costs, higher control, lower opportunities for error, and finally easier and quicker reconciliation.

On the balance sheet and liquidity side of the order-to-cash cycle, quoting optimal terms to the customer, providing access to liquidity to financially weaker customers, better credit risk management, watching for early warning signals, and aligning goals of the sales team with that of the firm's overall financials constitute some of the key areas for change.

The main wins for these methods are to lower the DSO and hence improve liquidity for the firm. Indirect benefits include better financial condition for

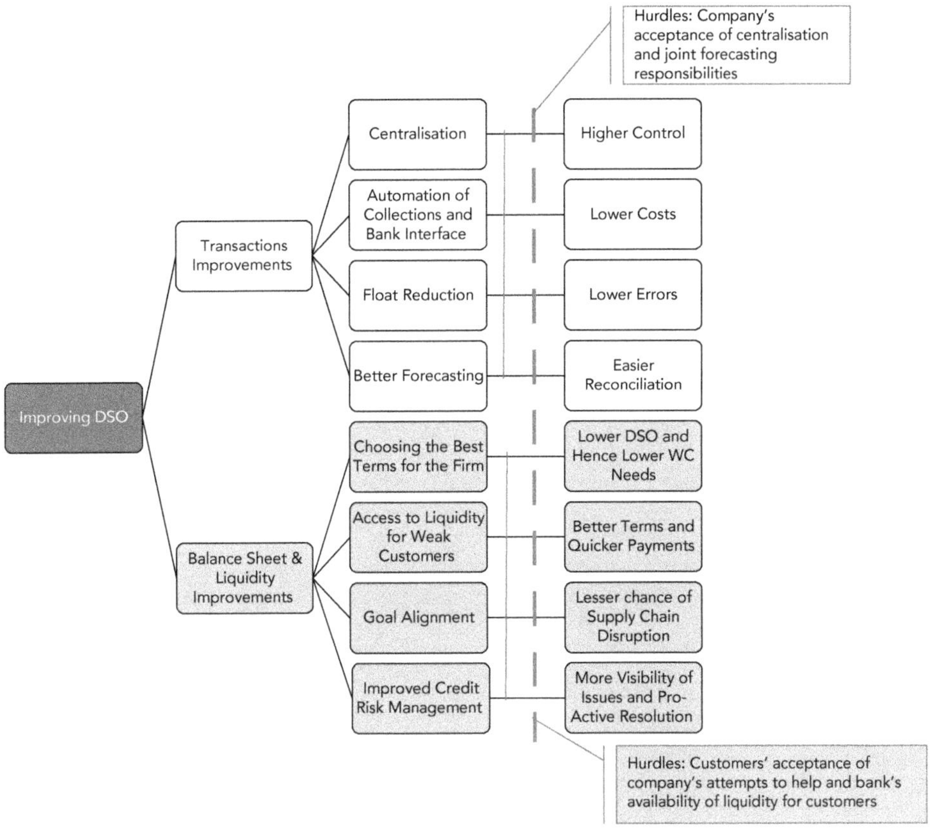

FIGURE 11.8 Generating Value in the Order-to-Cash Cycle

customers, and hence greater customer satisfaction and lower opportunities for disruption of sales.

Calculation of DSO

Table 11.3 shows the DSO calculation for the same two European firms discussed earlier.

TABLE 11.3 COMPUTATION OF DSO

Component	Company Z	Company Y
Accounts Receivable (EUR)	3,221,000,000	690,000,000
Credit Sales (EUR)	15,675,000,000	18,000,000,000
DSO Calculation (AR / Sales) × 365	3,221 / 15,675 × 365	690 / 18,000 × 365
DSO (Days)	75	14

Financial Benefits of Working Capital Requirement Improvement

We now look at how we can assess the improvements on the cost of capital to the firm when there is an improvement in the cash conversion cycle. Figure 11.9 depicts the three cycles. The aim is to increase the DPO through more efficient terms and payments while reducing the DSO through better terms and efficient collections float reduction techniques.

Let us say that the process improvement has moved the DSO down by 10 days and the DPO up by 10 days, which means that the company is collecting cash sooner by 10 days and delaying its payments by 10 days more.

In effect, the average receivables have been brought down to EUR 2.791 billion and the average payables have moved up to EUR 964 million. Table 11.4 summarises this move.

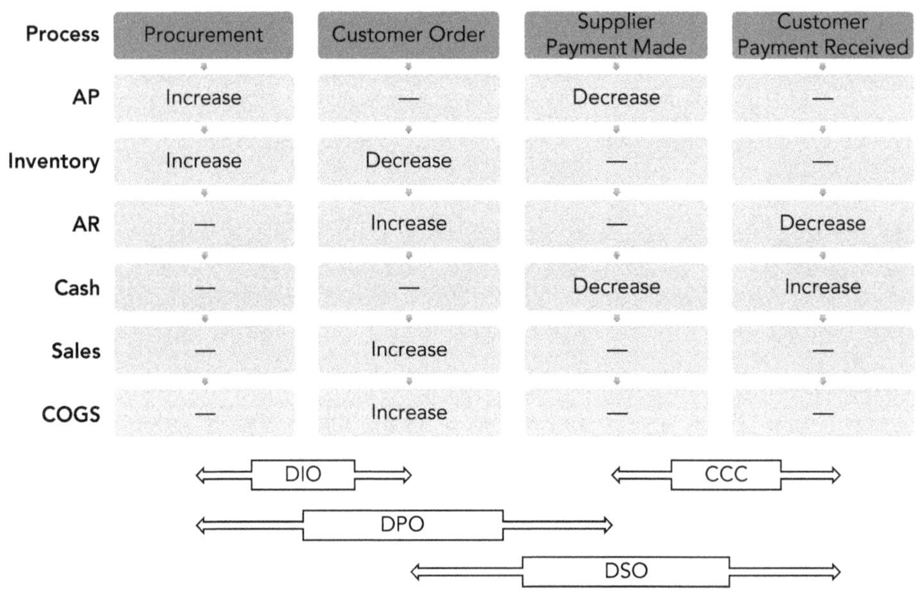

FIGURE 11.9 Impact on Financials

TABLE 11.4 Computation of CCC for Company Z

CCC Component (Days)	Before	After
DSO	75	65
DPO	35	45
DIO	15	15
CCC	55	35

⇔

Balance Sheet Item (EUR mm)	Before	After
AR	3,221	2,791
AP	750	964
Inventory	322	322
WC Requirement	2,793	2,149

Assuming that the credit sales, inventory, and COGS have not changed, the CCC has been brought down to 35 days from 55 days, resulting in working capital reduction from EUR 2,793 billion to EUR 2,149 billion or a reduced borrowing of EUR 644 million.

Assuming a borrowing cost of 5% per annum for a two-month period, the reduction in interest costs would amount to a whopping EUR 5.4 million.

Impact of CCC on Financials

How does the tracking and management of the CCC impact decisions made by the company on its negotiations on terms with suppliers or customers? What is the benefit of coordinating with Treasury on these issues?

Generally, the procurement and sales teams of most companies are equipped to handle discussions on pricing and credit periods. Incentives, performance parameters, and evaluation tend to be in terms of the price—the lower the price of procurement, the higher the price of the sale.

In cases where liquidity is tight or interest rates are high, the value or discount provided by the credit period of the supplier or the early payment for the customer could be worth more for the company in actual cash terms (interest cost).

Let us consider an example on the procurement side. The supplier offers these terms: 1–10 net 60 (i.e., 1% discount if paid within 10 days); if the company pays within 60 days, there is no discount.

What should the buyer do?

1. Buy the product at 99 (with a 1% discount) since it is better for the bottom line, especially when cost cutting is in fashion?
2. Or pay 100 on the 60th day?

Buyers will not be faulted for going with alternative 1—after all, the lower the cost, the better their performance will appear to be. Yet, from the company's perspective, the best decision will be the one that provides lower cash flow on an overall basis and perhaps more liquidity.

To answer the question, we need more information on the availability of credit and its price. Let us assume that working capital lines are available to the firm at 10% per annum for the borrowing period. To compare alternatives 1 and 2, we can assume that the company has enough liquidity to pay 100 on the 60th day. Hence, to pay earlier, the cost of borrowing 99, the amount to be paid on the earlier payment date (i.e., after 10 days), has to be considered. If the net cost is less than 100, alternative 1 is better.

$$\begin{aligned}\text{Cost of borrowing 99 for 50 days at 10\% per annum} &= 99 \times 50/360 \times 10\% \\ &= 1.375\end{aligned}$$

The total cash outflow for the firm is 99 + 1.375 = 100.375. Thus, it is better for the firm to take the 60-day credit period, which is worth paying the normal undiscounted price.

If the interest rate is 4% per annum, however, the situation could be different. In this case, the value of the discount is 99 × 50/360 × 4% = 0.55, and hence the total outflow is 99.55, which is less than the full price of 100 paid on the 60th day. In this case (and we assume liquidity is quite good since rates have dropped to 4% from 10%), it might be more effective to take the discount.

A similar approach on the sales side will also be useful—deciding the credit period and incentivising the customer to pay earlier in times of tight liquidity and higher interest rates.

FINANCIAL SUPPLY CHAIN AND ITS POTENTIAL PAIN POINTS

We conclude this chapter with a review of the financial supply chain and its various pain points, along with a case study of how a global company facing supply chain issues in 2008 put in place some measures to reduce such instances in the future. This discussion leads into supply chain financing in Chapter 14.

Pain Points in the Supply Chain

Figure 11.10 shows the supply chain with potential pain points marked with upward-pointing arrows.

The balance sheet is the focus, since any issues with the movement of cash in the financial supply chain will negatively impact the balance sheet. Decisions made by the procurement team (buyers), manufacturing, and sales have a direct impact on inventory, cash, receivables, and payables. Disruption along any part of the supply chain could result in an adverse impact and hence a liquidity issue for the company. Potential areas of pain in the supply chain include the dependence on external elements, such as the financial soundness of the supplier (and hence the longevity and reliability of supplies); operations and efficiency of the logistics (transportation, distribution, and warehousing) companies; and the customer's ability to pay on time. Some of these risks may be reduced through diversification, but not all companies have the ability, scale, and bargaining power to lower their dependencies on external sources of pain.

Interestingly, suppliers could face similar problems (where the corporation is the supplier's customer), as could the logistics companies or the end customers themselves. Each of these companies has its own supply chain, and the corporation is either the customer or supplier in those related supply chains.

Figure 11.11 delves a little deeper into the various external entities and the possible sources of their pain points.

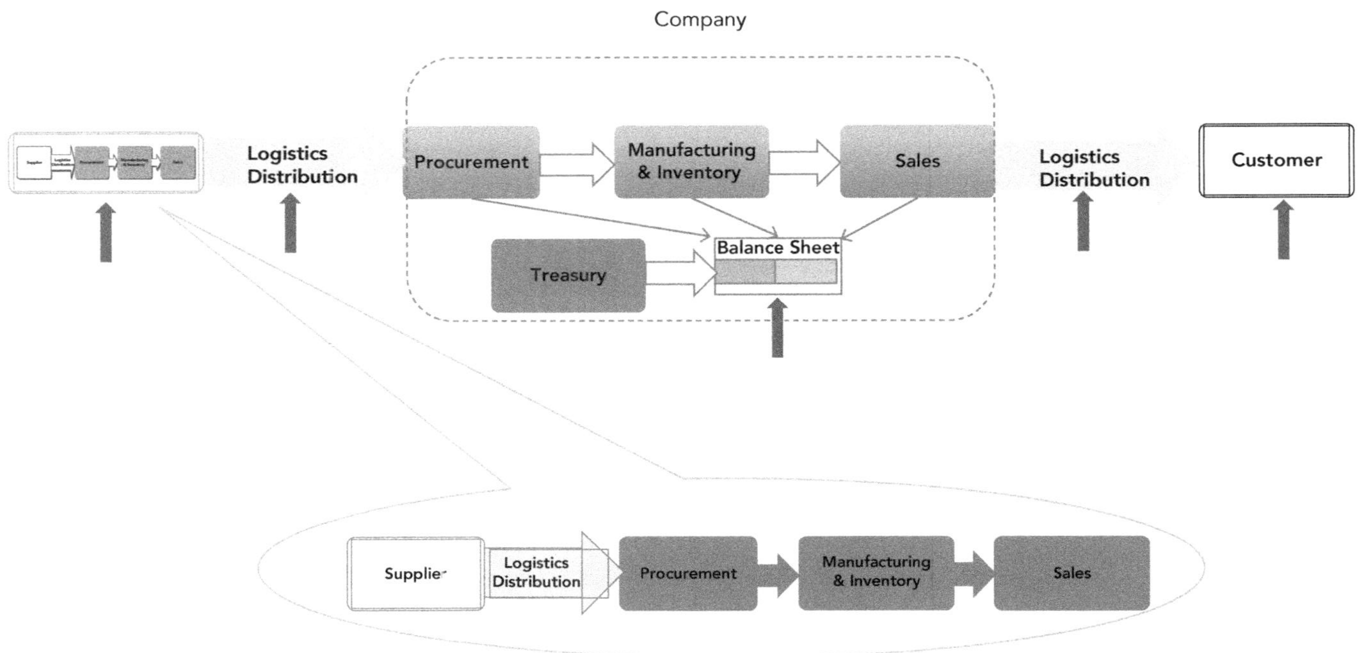

FIGURE 11.10 Pain Points in the Supply Chain

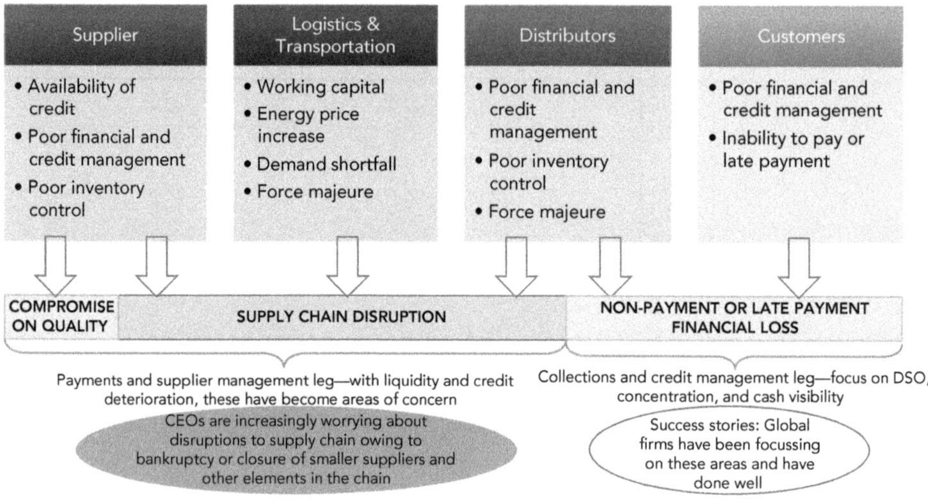

FIGURE 11.11 Causes and Impact of External Pressure Points

Each external leg of the supply chain has its own set of potential areas of distress. These could disrupt the firm's supply chain or directly result in nonrealisation of receivables.

For the supplier, a credit squeeze and poor management of finance, its own credit, receivables, and inventory could strap it for cash and liquidity. Potential compromises on quality might ensue, resulting in delayed or nondelivery of goods.

For logistics and transportation companies, the risks are a little different. In many cases, dependence on global fuel prices and relative inelasticity of pricing, coupled with variations in end customer demand, working capital management, and potential disasters (natural or man-made) directly impact their functioning.

For distribution firms, poor management and inability to address credit, inventory, and funding issues coupled with risk of natural disasters create an environment where insurance can compensate for only some immediate short-term financial value but not all, and not medium- or long-term situations. Late shipment or arrival of goods could cause issues in the supply chain, including an avalanche impact to customers' value chains.

Finally, the customer's inability to pay due to financial stress and liquidity issues at its end directly impacts the credit and receivables for the firm, delaying the availability of cash and putting added pressure on the Treasurer to sustain the operations while waiting for the funds to come in.

Over the last few years, especially after the 2008 crisis, there have been several success stories regarding managing receivables and improving the collections and cash concentration processes. Many firms have focused on the DSO aspect and have brought down their receivables and speeded up the collection process, seeing dramatic results on their working capital efficiency and hence cost of capital.

But disruptions to the supply chain through other legs have been a worry in the back of the minds of chief executive officers (CEOs) and chief financial officers (CFOs), and few firms have put thought, effort, and resources in that direction. I hope we do not need another crisis to teach us that lesson.

With simple and intuitive tools and focused efforts, firms can tap into internal available resources to help understand, develop, and reinforce the financial strength of all elements in the supply chain whose credit and financial position is weaker than their own. Doing so will enable the chain and its financial flows to work smoothly and lower the chance of disruption.

The next case study presents a different approach to supplier management. Solutions using a similar approach can be built for other partners in the supply chain.

CASE STUDY: AN INNOVATIVE APPROACH TO SUPPLIER MANAGEMENT

This case explores an alternative method to managing supplier-related issues. We explore how the Treasurer can add value to traditional methods of approaching suppliers for products and how Treasury expertise can benefit the relationships with suppliers and translate into financial improvement for the company.

Traditional Approach to Supplier Interface

Historically, procurement teams have been the main points of contact, discussing and negotiating supply terms after understanding the supplier's product/material, operations, and supply chain (see Figure 11.12).

The buyer or procurement officer is the key point of interface, keeping the scope of discussions with the supplier on the quality of the product, terms, and condition of the sale and delivery. The payments and AP management teams provide the necessary payments on due date. The finance and Treasury teams at the supplier's end maintain an independent existence, interfacing with their own bankers and service providers.

The coming of age of the Treasurer and the recognition of the Treasury team's skill sets and influence has helped to improve on these methods.

In Part I, we discussed the role of the Treasurer and some of the various hats that he or she wears. Two of these hats (see Figure 11.13) stand out with respect to the situation with suppliers: one is as trusted advisor and internal consultant and expert on credit, and the other is as trainer.

Now we explore how these Treasurer skills can be put to use in reengineering the interaction and relationship with suppliers (see Figure 11.14).

(*Continued*)

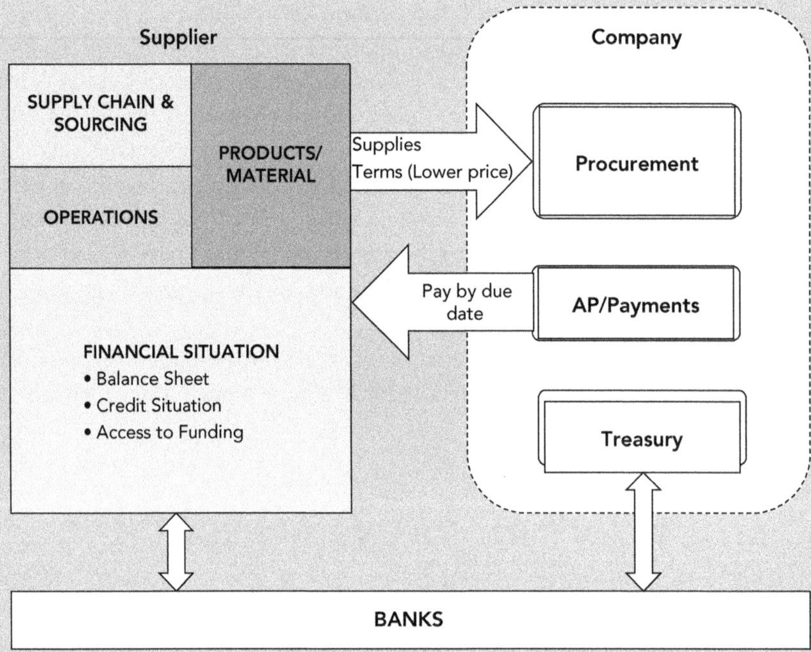

FIGURE 11.12 Traditional Approach to Supplier Interface

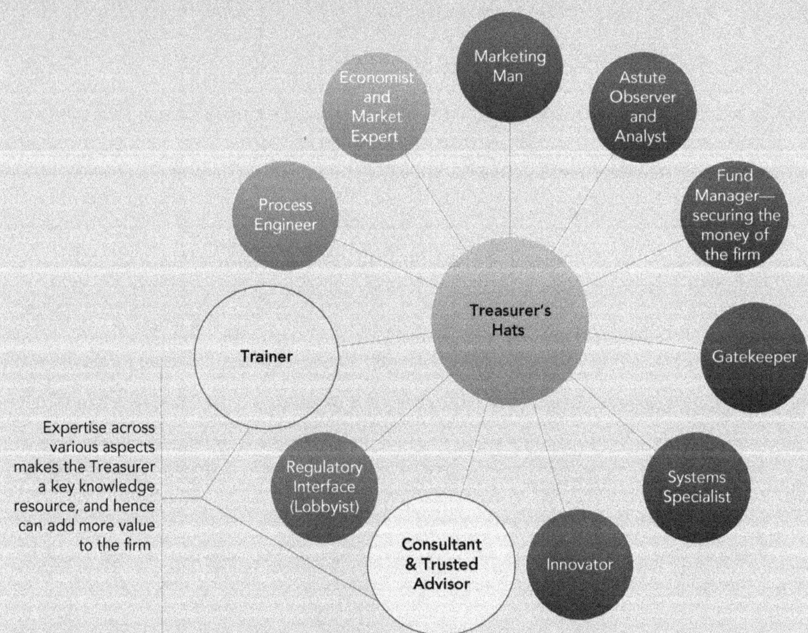

FIGURE 11.13 Treasurer's Place in the Context of Supplier Interface

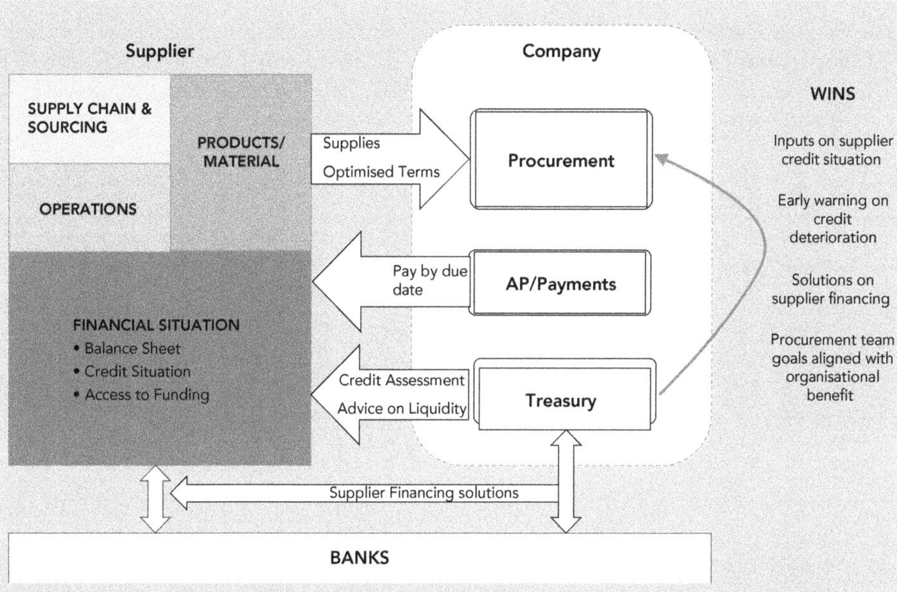

FIGURE 11.14 Improved Interface with Supplier

The difference from the traditional approach is the involvement of Treasury. The Treasurer, by his or her job description, is the person in the group who understands credit and its various aspects the best, being responsible for the credit rating and creditworthiness of the group, and is the main point of contact with the largest providers of liquidity to the corporate sector: the banks. Hence, the Treasurer can add value by providing on-the-ground support to the procurement team and the supplier in these ways:

- Assess the supplier's financials and advise on how the supplier can improve its financials
- Provide the firm and the buyers with an early-warning mechanism on potential supplier failure
- Interface with banks to provide solutions in supplier financing
- Help buyers choose the right payment terms in line with the firm's cash flow requirements and needs

The resultant liquidity, advice, and confidence add to the supplier's own liquidity position and hence profitability. In most cases these improvements result in increased partnership from the supplier's end backed by improved terms that improve profitability consistently in the medium term.

This activity is not a bottom-up one but has to be enforced top down.

A couple of bottlenecks could arise at this stage:

- For a company with a varied supplier base, this task would be suboptimal for every supplier. Hence, the bottom-rated materially important supplier (i.e., whose failure could cause an impediment to the supply chain) could be the first to target, as it is both the low-hanging fruit and the supplier that would have a maximum impact on de-risking. The company can follow up with other suppliers later.

(Continued)

- The supplier's sales team, used to dealing with company buyers and having discussions focused on product, pricing, and delivery, may not be appreciative or welcoming of what they might deem to be interference on the part of the customer. Two activities can help to change that attitude:
  1. Train the buyers to understand the core concepts of liquidity and credit, and speak the language that the customer would understand in terms.
  2. Appeal to suppliers' requirements enough to convince management at the supplier's end to be involved and also get the finance management engaged in the process.

Once the firm's finance management has enough confidence in the solution-centric approach, the Treasurer as expert can be brought in. The treasurer's core skills and knowledge can be what brings suppliers into the mainstream and empowers them with increased liquidity and reduced chances of failure (see Figure 11.15).

These Treasury team skills and networks will serve them in good stead as they work with suppliers for:

- Understanding of credit
- Appreciation of balance sheet and management
- Access to banks
- Knowledge of financing solutions
- Tools to determine financial impact of purchasing decisions and evaluating the best credit terms
- Market presence and awareness

European Firm

A European firm with a presence across all continents and a large customer base was facing serious issues and disruptions on the supply side, which were only getting worse (see Figure 11.16).

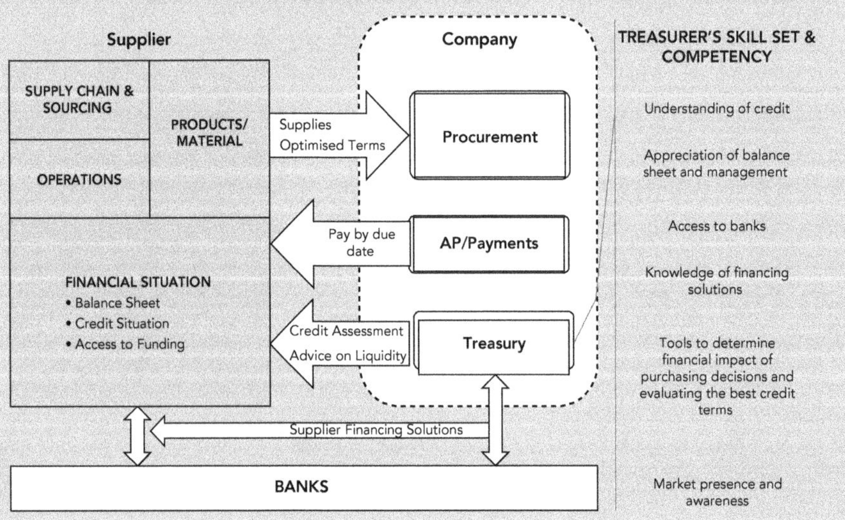

FIGURE 11.15 Treasurer's Skill and Network Set

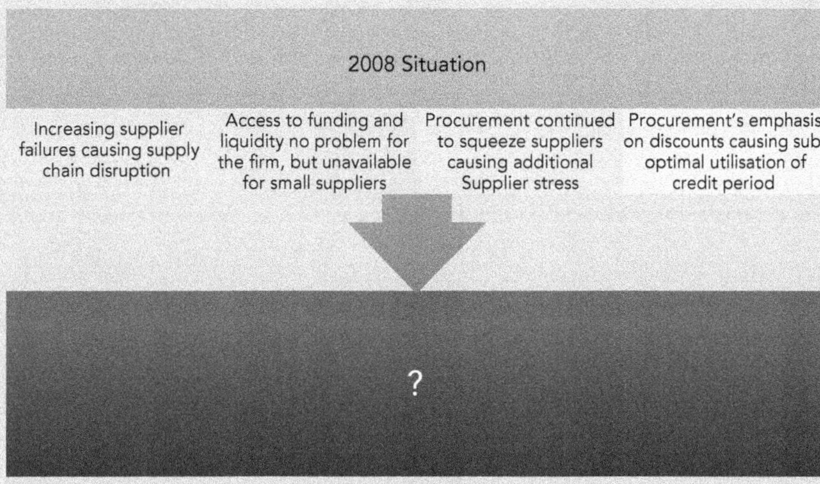

FIGURE 11.16 Company's Situation in 2008–2009

The company's suppliers were becoming financially unsound, and a few failures had caused minor disruptions in the procurement chain. Potential defaults were looming large, but some were also coming as shocks to the buyers who were interacting with the suppliers on a daily basis. While the firm itself had had no concerns about its own liquidity, across different parts of the world, bank liquidity was being tightened and the smaller suppliers were feeling the impact, being squeezed by their customers for reduced prices and heavy discounts (and longer credit periods in some cases), adding to stress on their receivables and product quality. The procurement team's emphasis on discounts was also causing suboptimal utilisation of the suppliers' credit period.

After much discussion, brainstorming, and planning with numerous stakeholders across functions, it was decided to embark on a three-pronged approach to resolve this problem (see Figure 11.17).

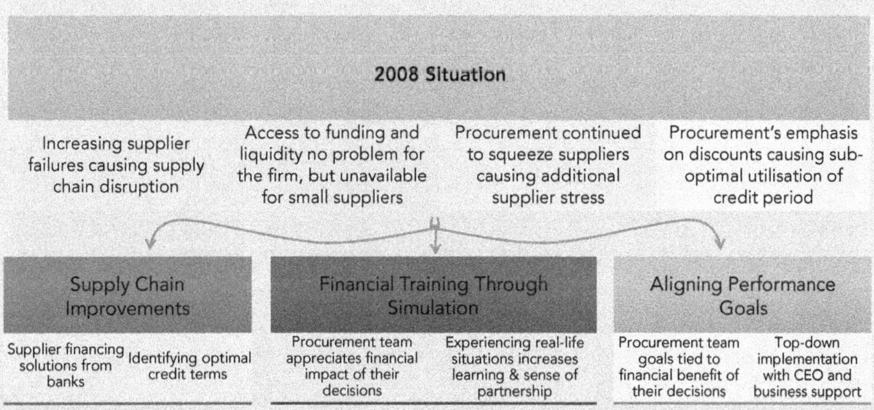

FIGURE 11.17 Three-Pronged Approach

(Continued)

The three areas of action and their action items resulted in overall better performance for the firm through a smoother supply chain, translating into better terms, higher DPO, and low working capital.

The first area of improvement, supply chain improvements, involved identifying supplier financing solutions from banks and identifying optimal credit terms. The Treasurer became involved on advice of the CEO and the CFO, working with the key lower-rated suppliers with declared liquidity issues and connecting them with banks to help find risk-mitigated funding solutions.

The second, financial training through simulation, was conducted by Treasury and rolled out globally to every procurement officer around the world. It enabled the procurement team to appreciate the financial impact of its decisions. Experiencing real-life situations increased learning and provided a sense of partnership and ownership toward the financials of the group.

The final prong, aligning performance goals of the procurement team, would not have been possible without the direct support and appreciation of the criticality of cash flow by the CEO and the board. The goals of the procurement team were tied to financial benefit from its decisions, and this enabled more rationalised thinking on the decisions and negotiations of terms with suppliers. Benefits of this approach are highlighted in Figure 11.18.

While this led to a smoother supply chain over the short term after implementation (see Figure 11.19), largely owing to better liquidity and access to credit for weaker suppliers, the firm also gained more medium-term benefits of better financial performance. These included:

- Better terms and higher DPO resulting from cheaper financing for suppliers
- Procurement team evaluating the financial benefit of the credit period versus the value of discounts
- Increased liquidity for firm and reduced need for working capital, lowering overall cost of capital

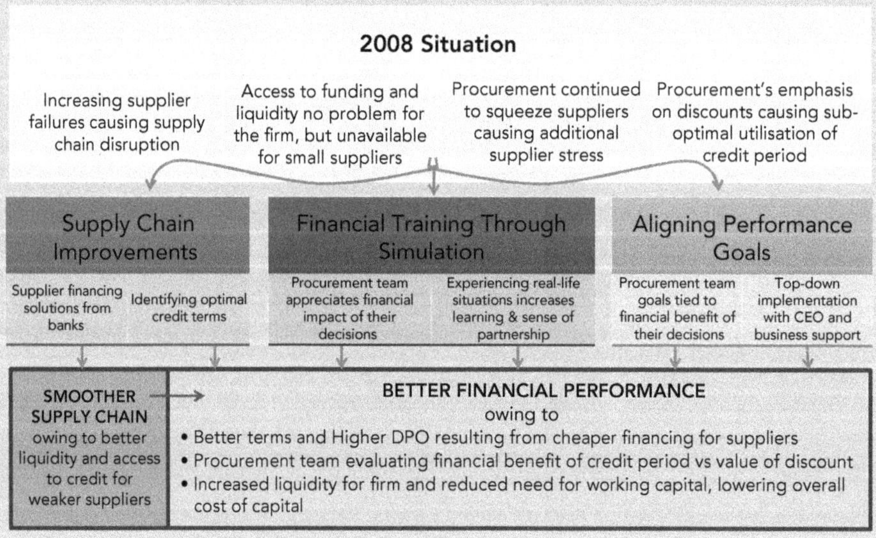

FIGURE 11.18 Benefits of the Approach

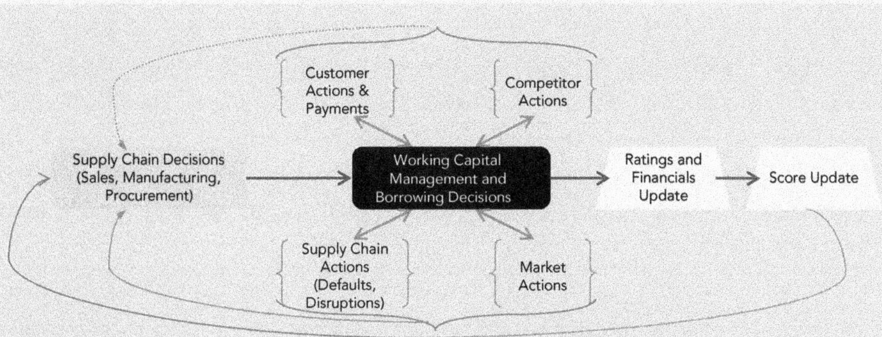

FIGURE 11.19 Simulation-Based Training to Enhance Financial Knowledge for Non-Finance Function Partners

The training conducted (see Figure 11.19) was a simulation-based effort developed for the firm, focusing on:

- Appreciating the impact of business (procurement and sales) decisions on the financials of the firm and its credit ratings
- Evaluating credit ratings of stakeholders in the supply chain
- Looking for early warning signs of distress
- Making decisions of using credit period versus using discounts
- Understanding the impact of competitor best practices on the firm's financials
- Fostering a sense of teamwork and working with Treasury to improve organisational performance

While the training and entire effort in this case was for the partners in the procurement team, the same training and partnership to achieve desired results can be used for other functions. We dwell on benefits of simulation-based training in the Toolkit section of this book (Part Five).

Key Learnings from the Company's Experience

The company learned three key things from this experience that are worthy of sharing. These are:

1. Focus on credit.
   - Understand credit of key partners in the supply chain.
   - Identify the financially weakest suppliers.
   - Identify the financially strongest customers whose credit can be harnessed.
   - Put in place a process to evaluate financial impact of credit versus discounts.
2. Implement strong training modules.
   - Train both procurement and sales.
   - Help them understand the impact of their decisions on the firm.
   - Partner with Treasury to make the best decisions.
   - Use simulation, an increasingly strong and cost-effective method that provides real-life feel and hence deeper and immediate learning impact.
3. Align organisational goals.
   - Set goals based on financial impact, and not necessarily on lower procurement price or higher sales price.

SUMMARY

In this chapter, we looked at various aspects of the balance sheet linked with working capital and at the role of the cash conversion cycle. We explored how the financial supply chain can be diagnosed for pain points and saw how financial pain on the supplier side can be reduced. We now move to a more holistic look at the balance sheet and financials and at the ratios used to assess the health of the company and its liquidity and other risk aspects.

CHAPTER TWELVE

Financial Strength and Linkages with Liquidity

THIS CHAPTER ZOOMS OUT FROM the focused discussion on working capital and liquidity and looks at these aspects in the context of the enterprise's financial strength. We review the key areas of the firm's financials, highlight some of the important ratios, and finally look at a case study that shows a practical instance of Treasury restructuring in the context of a crisis in liquidity and financial strength.

IMPORTANCE OF COMPANY FINANCIALS

The balance sheet and sources of capital and liquidity, and thus the current and expected financial strength of an organisation, form a core part of the Treasurer's responsibilities. Here we review the universe of a firm's financial statements (see Figure 12.1) and their utility for different users.

The balance sheet, profit and loss statement, and cash flow statement form the core of the firm's financial statements. The balance sheet contains the Liabilities, or the sources of funds, and the value of assets, the utilisation of these funds. The profit

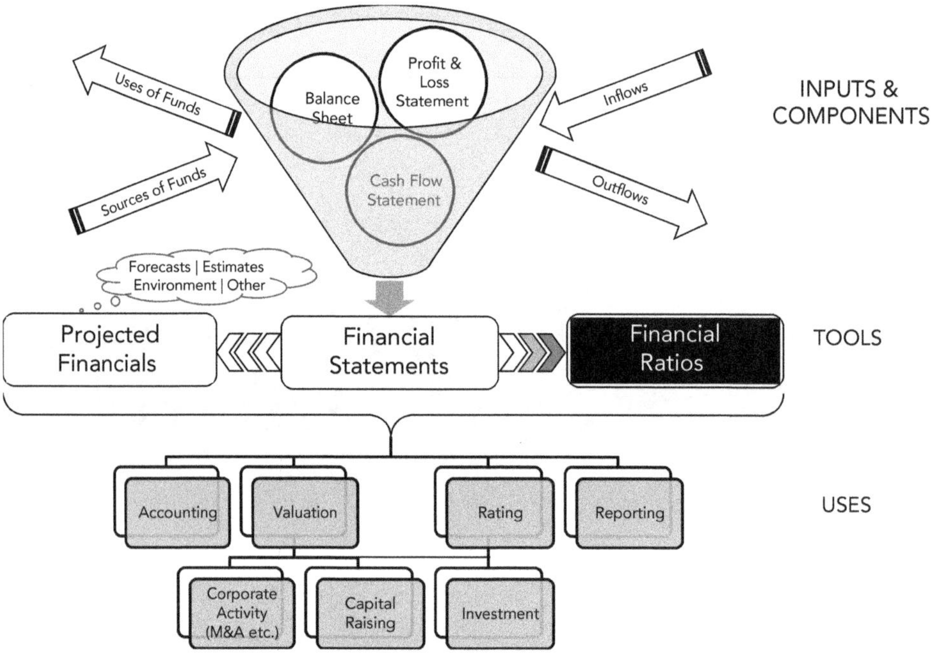

FIGURE 12.1 Role of Financial Statements

and loss or income statements show the income and expenditure elements by category, while the cash flow statements highlight the firm's inflows and outflows. Coupled with estimates and forecasts of how the business and relevant expenses are expected to perform, the financials of the enterprise are projected to determine its future financial strength. Financial ratios are also determined to provide objective assessment parameters to determine the relative and absolute performance of a firm. Since different firms have different kinds of numbers, the ratios provide a benchmark for assessment. We discuss ratios in detail later in the chapter.

Apart from being a barometer of the strength and performance of the company's management and board, financials serve as indicators to potential and current investors (directly or through research, rating, and advisory firms) of the relative attractiveness of different securities or liabilities of a company. Regulators, stock exchanges, governments, and industry use the data to assess the performance of the firm individually and in the context of the industry and the country's economy.

From an accounting standpoint, the reporting and filing of returns that the companies and subsidiaries perform in each location or jurisdiction where they are present provides an interesting challenge and pits the accounting financials against the value that the business actually believes it has generated. These are subjects of long discussions and are well covered by many esteemed authors.

We now focus our attention on some of the ratios that also serve as yardsticks to measure the company's strength across different aspects of its business, management, and operations.

KEY FINANCIAL RATIOS

Some of the key ratios and determinants of financial strength are discussed here (see Figure 12.2).

Profit and Loss (or Income) Statement Ratios

Taken from the profit and loss (P&L) or income statement of the company, these give a quick overview of the profitability of the firm at different levels.

Gross Margin

Gross margin is the first level of profitability. It depicts the direct impact of the revenue generated and the expense incurred to generate the revenue (i.e., the gross profit).

$$\text{Gross Margin} = \frac{\text{Sales} - \text{Cost of Goods Sold}}{\text{Sales}}$$

Operating Margin

Operating margin is the second level of profitability. It shows the overall operating income as a percentage of sales. Note that operating income is derived after the deduction of selling, general and administrative expenses, and depreciation from the gross profit.

$$\text{Operating Margin} = \frac{\text{Operating Income}}{\text{Sales}}$$

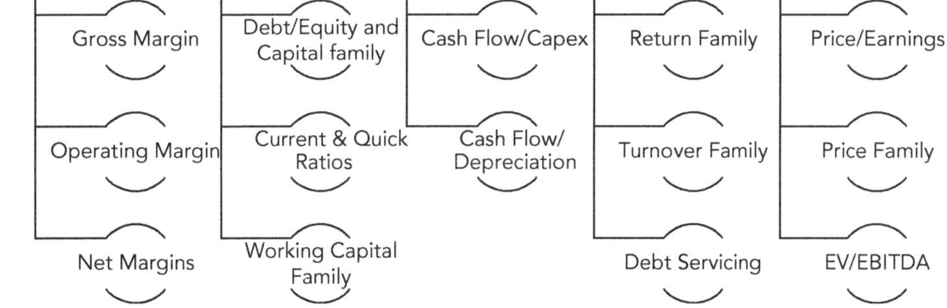

FIGURE 12.2 Key Financial Ratios

Net Margin

Net margin is the third level of profitability. It shows the net income as a percentage of sales. Note that net income is the operating income less interest expense and provisions for taxes.

$$\text{Net Margin} = \frac{\text{Net Income}}{\text{Sales}}$$

Balance Sheet Ratios

Derived directly from the balance sheet, the balance sheet ratios indicate the performance levels and nature of capitalisation of the sources of funds and their utilisation. Given the relevance and importance of the balance sheet and its contribution to the firm's strength, as well as the very wide scope and nature of different assets and liabilities, balance sheet ratios provide in-depth perspectives of a company's financial management.

Debt/Equity Family of Ratios

The structure of the firm's capital can be conveyed in many ways. The degree of indebtedness is indicated by the debt/equity (D/E) family of ratios provides in addition the dependence and hence capacity of the firm to take on more debt; e.g., a company with a lower D/E ratio will have more ability to take on debt than a similar company with a higher D/E ratio, all other things being equal.

The simple debt/equity ratio is one of the most prominent and commonly used indicators.

$$\text{Debt/Equity Ratio} = \frac{\text{Total Debt}}{\text{Total Equity}}$$

The general level of indebtedness can also be expressed in terms of the total capital, which includes the debt, equity, and minority interest.

$$\text{Debt/Capital Ratio} = \frac{\text{Total Debt}}{\text{Total Capital}}$$

The overall total assets to liabilities ratio provides an indication of the degree of asset protection, since the total liabilities can be represented by the total assets less the equity of the firm.

$$\text{Assets/Liabilities Ratio} = \frac{\text{Total Assets}}{\text{Total Liabilities}}$$

Current and Quick Ratios

The current and quick ratios provide a good picture of the firm's liquidity in case of a general shortage of cash flows. They show, for different sets of assets, the extent to which the assets can be liquidated in case of a limitation in access to liabilities to fund those assets.

The current ratio is a reflection of the current cash payable (or that which will need to be paid in the very short term) to make the payments due with cash currently available (or that which will be available in the very short term). The ability to do this can be estimated by the ratio of current assets (assets already in cash or to be converted to cash during the current operating cycle) over the current liabilities (dues that the company will need to pay during the current operating cycle).

$$\text{Quick Ratio} = \frac{\text{Quick Assets}}{\text{Current Liabilities}}$$

The quick ratio (also referred to as acid test) refers to assets that can be liquidated faster (quick assets), taking into consideration only the cash and very liquid assets, such as receivables and securities that can be sold or liquidated immediately. The quick ratio hence is a more stringent measure of immediate liquidity than the current ratio.

Working Capital Family

Working capital and its related ratios were discussed in detail in Chapter 11. The ratios provide a good estimate of the amount of working capital required for the firm to operate on a day-to-day basis. Along with the cash conversion cycle (a hybrid since it also uses elements from the balance sheet and the P&L statement), the working capital family provides an idea of the firm's ability to fund itself through internal sources.

Cash Flow Statement Ratios

The cash flow statement on its own provides a basic snapshot of the simplest financial performance, with a focus on the firm's ability to service liabilities (especially debt) through its cash flows and on the degree of flexibility and reliance on external capital sources for funding its operations.

Cash Flow/Capex Ratio

The cash flow/capital exchange (capex) ratio is one of the key elements for industries or firms with large capital expenditure items.

$$\text{Cash Flow/Capex Ratio} = \frac{\text{Net Operating Cash Flow}}{\text{Capital Expenditure Outflow}}$$

Depreciation Coverage

The firm's depreciation will provide a good indicator of future estimated cash outflows, given the certainty of this item in the cash flow projections.

$$\text{Depreciation Coverage Ratio} = \frac{\text{Depreciation}}{\text{Net Operating Cash Flow}}$$

Hybrid Ratios

Hybrid ratios are those derived across components of the company's financials. There are different kinds of hybrid ratios; here we focus on three different families.

Return Family

The return family provides an idea of the effectiveness of the utilisation of investors' capital, or how the returns from the company's financial performance fare compared to the funding that the operations use. The simplest return ratio is the return on equity, which depicts the net income of the company as a ratio of the equity of the firm.

$$\text{Return of Equity} = \frac{\text{Net Income}}{\text{Common Stock} + \text{Preferred Stock}}$$

One of the drawbacks of this ratio, and indeed of a few hybrid ratios that combine elements from P&L statements and the balance sheet, is that net income is a cumulative number across the financial year, but the equity number can be a snapshot number at a point of time (typically the year-end).

To overcome this problem, some firms use average equity, which is the average of the equity number over a period of time.

$$\text{Return on Average Equity} = \frac{\text{Net Income}}{\text{Average Equity}}$$

Throwing debt into the mix to obtain an estimate of the return on total capital, net income is augmented by two elements that are impacted by debt: the tax element and the interest expense. Hence the return on capital can be depicted by this formula:

$$\text{Return on Capital} = \frac{\text{Net Income} + \text{Income Taxes} + \text{Interest Expense}}{\text{Debt} + \text{Equity}}$$

Turnover Family

The turnover ratios provide an overview of the utilisation of assets and the churn of liabilities. This includes ratios such as days sales outstanding, days payable outstanding, and days inventory outstanding, which determine the cash conversion cycle discussed in Chapter 11

Debt Servicing

Debt servicing ratios enable a firm to service its debt through its cash flows.

The debt service coverage ratio (DSCR) is one of the more popular measures that provides the liquidity available to service a company's debt including principal, interest, and lease rentals. The higher the DSCR is, the better the ability of the firm to service its debt and hence its ability to assume incremental debt.

$$\text{DSCR} = \frac{\text{Net Income} + \text{Depreciation} + \text{Interest Expense}}{\text{Principal Repayments} + \text{Interest Payments} + \text{Lease payments}}$$

The debt/cash flow ratio provides a longer term perspective on the ability of the firm to service its debt.

$$\text{Debt/Cash Flow} = \frac{\text{Total Debt}}{\text{Operating Cash Flow}}$$

Valuation and Market Ratios

Valuation and market ratios have to do with finding the right value of a firm for the purposes of assessing the market or the firm's overall value.

Price/Earnings

The most common ratio for most firms is the price/earnings (P/E) ratio. It provides the market price of the firm per share as a ratio of the firm's annual EPS.

$$\text{Price/Earnings Ratio} = \frac{\text{Market Price per Share}}{\text{Earnings per Share (EPS)}}$$

This is effectively the ratio of the firm's market capitalisation to its annual earnings.

The P/E also reflects the firm's capital structure and cost of capital. Investors are more willing to buy shares of a company with a higher P/E than to buy shares of a company with a lower P/E. Hence the equity of the firm with the higher P/E is more expensive.

Price Family

The price family includes other ratios that use the price to determine value, such as:

- **PEG**. The P/E ratio divided by the growth rate, to normalise the P/E for growth (higher growth generally increases the P/E).
- **Earnings Yield**. The inverse of the P/E ratio or earnings/price. Quoted as a percentage, it is used to compare the yield across different forms of financing, especially debt. It is also an approximate measure of the cost of raising incremental equity.
- **Price/Dividend (P/D) Ratio**. An indicator of the valuation of the firm in terms of price to returns to shareholders in the form of dividends.
- **Dividend Yield**. The inverse of the P/D ratio. It denotes the effective return from a dividend perspective.

EV/EBITDA

The EV/EBITDA ratio is the ratio of the enterprise value (EV) of the firm to the EBITDA (earnings before interest, taxes, depreciation, and amortisation), which provides an alternative to the valuation of the firm.

The EV/EBITDA is agnostic to the capital structure of the firm and can be used to benchmark or compare companies across industries and to benchmark companies across a market.

We conclude this chapter with a look at a cutting-edge case study on the handling and resolution of a liquidity crisis and corresponding financial strength of a global corporation.

CASE STUDY: TYCO INTERNATIONAL: CORPORATE LIQUIDITY CRISIS AND TREASURY RESTRUCTURING

Note: This pre-release version may be used for teaching purposes but it has not yet received an official case number by the European Case Clearing House.

> [Their actions] were hidden from the board and, probably, from the accountants as well. [Kozlowski and Swartz] totally ran the financial apparatus. There were no checks and balances because the board was kept in the dark.
>
> Peter Slusser, Former Director, Tyco International

> One of the things that I liked about Tyco—and studied hard before coming in—was its ability to generate cash. The company had great businesses. They were in the right sectors. The foundation was very strong.
>
> Edward D. Breen, Chairman and Chief Executive, Tyco International

Having spent the last two years playing a key role in Lucent Technology's restructuring efforts, Martina Hund-Mejean had just started dreaming of a much-needed break when the phone rang. The caller at the other end of the line was David Fitzpatrick, Tyco's new CFO, offering her an opportunity to join his team to steer the fast-sinking industrial conglomerate through its current corporate storm.

Until six months earlier, Tyco International, led by "rock star" CEO Dennis Kozlowski, had been the darling of Wall Street. However, with Kozlowski accused of corporate fraud and the company facing an epic liquidity crisis, the industrial conglomerate with $40 billion in global sales and a presence in 90 countries worldwide faced a real threat of having to declare bankruptcy.

Already highly regarded in the industry as a turn-around specialist following stints at General Motors and Lucent, Hund-Mejean was always up for a challenge. Quickly shelving thoughts of a break, she agreed to join Tyco's new management team in fighting to save the company. At a Tyco press conference, Hund-Mejean announced, *"I believe that Tyco, with its solid operating businesses and strong market positions, has the potential to be one of the most exciting companies of the future."*

Company History and the 2002 Liquidity Crisis

Over the past decade, Tyco had grown rapidly through acquisition, snapping up more than 200 firms and creating a highly complex conglomerate in the process. By 2002, Tyco had become one of the world's largest and most diverse companies, producing a wide variety of products including burglar alarms, plastic hangers, duct tapes, automotive cabling, electronic connectors, surgical instruments, and many other necessities of daily life, justifying Tyco's marketing tagline "A vital part of your world." While most consumers were unfamiliar with the Tyco name, its brands, including ADT, Raychem and Keystone, were well known among businesses and consumers. Each day, companies under the Tyco umbrella manufactured approximately 8 million hypodermic needles, provided security (through its systems) to over 7.3 million customers worldwide and over 80% of the world's top 100 retailers. Its claim of being "vital" was no exaggeration for heart disease patients; over 240 open-heart surgeries were performed using Tyco's cardiac devices every day. In addition, Tyco Healthcare's pharmaceutical group was the world's largest producer of acetaminophen and opiate-based pain management pharmaceuticals.

As illustrated in Figure 12.3, Tyco was structured into five business segments, each of which was bigger than most of their competitors' entire companies. Tyco's Fire and Safety division alone reported $10.6 billion in sales in 2002, while its Electronic and Healthcare divisions generated staggering revenues of $10.5 billion and $7.9 billion respectively. Engineered Products and Services recorded $4.7 billion in revenue, and even its smallest division, Plastics and Adhesives, clocked up sales of $1.9 billion. Although Tyco's revenue was diversified across the globe, the majority (57%) of its $35.6 billion revenue from external customers was generated in the United States. Europe was its next largest source with $8.4 billion (24%), followed by Asia Pacific with $4.9 billion (14%), and the rest of the Americas generating $2 billion (6%).

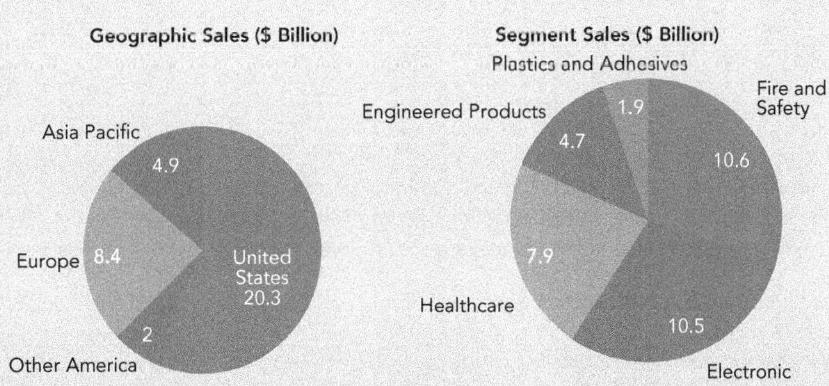

FIGURE 12.3 Tyco's Sales by Geography and Divisions (2002)

	2001 Q4	2002 Q1	2002 Q2	2002 Q3	2002 Q4
Units: Millions US$					
Cash and Short-Term Investments	2,587	3,167	6,294	2,794	6,475
Debt in Current Liabilities	18,874	16,219	20,454	5,411	7,719
Financial Leverage (Asset/Equity)	3.5	3.3	3.9	2.6	2.7
Operating Activities-Net Cash Flow	1,175	3,652	5,315	6,876	776

FIGURE 12.4 Selected Tyco Quarterly Financial Data (2001 Q4 to 2002 Q4)

Tyco's acquisition strategy had been intended to produce a "recession-proof" conglomerate through industry and geographic diversification. Instead, the acquisition spree led to a build-up of debts and resulted in expensive goodwill write-downs. Furthermore, the strategy of aggressive growth through acquisitions attracted increasing criticism amid concerns that the company's complex structure was both impossible for headquarters to manage effectively and in fact masking its true financial position. With analysts and investors unable to discern whether Tyco's reported profits came from real growth or financial manipulations, and jittered by corporate scandals including Enron, Tyco's stock had lost more than two-thirds of its value since the start of 2002.

By the time Hund-Mejean moved into her new Tyco office, the company was facing an overhang of $11.2 billion of debt maturing in 2003. More worryingly, she noted that $6.8 billion of it was due in the first quarter of 2003. With little time to settle in, Hund-Mejean rolled up her sleeves and plunged straight into resolving Tyco's liquidity crunch. Despite having approximately $6 billion of cash and short-term investments on its balance sheet, its cash was locked up in myriad subsidiaries scattered across the globe and essentially inaccessible at the corporate level where it was critically needed. In the past, Tyco had effortlessly raised funds through conventional debt refinancing routes, but various ongoing investigations arising from the fraud crisis prevented the company from raising capital in a similar fashion. In a race against time, Hund-Mejean struggled to secure financing through alternative channels.

Fighting the Fire—The Immediate Response

On 30 December 2002, the Tyco team saw its first ray of light in months. A team of accounting experts and external auditors commissioned by Tyco declared that it found "no significant or systemic fraud" in the company's financial statements. That verdict helped to nudge Tyco's bankers to commit to a new $1.5 billion credit facility just weeks before the expiration of the existing one-year agreement.

Despite the drama at headquarters, Tyco's fundamental business remained strong with its businesses generating positive net cash flows of $776.3 billion and its financial leverage (assets/equity) seemingly healthy at 2.7 at the end of 2002 (see Figure 12.4). However, bond ratings agencies, concerned about how the Tyco management was managing its debt maturity commitments, had continuously downgraded its bond rating throughout the year. For example, S&P had rated Tyco's bonds "A" in January 2002 but less than half a year later, by June 2002, its rating had plummeted to "BBB–". Moody's and Fitch went a step further and rated

Tyco's bonds "BB/Ba2," which were considered non-investment grades. Figure 12.5 shows Tyco's credit rating and default spreads over the period.

Together with her team, Hund-Mejean weighed the pros and cons of issuing new convertible bonds. Unlike previous occasions, when Tyco was in a position to issue convertible bonds on highly favourable terms, placing a convertible debt now was going to be both unfavourable and costly to the company due to its poor credit rating. The advantages of issuing the convertible debt included being able to target credit-insensitive investors, quick execution in a liquid market and the ability to put in tax-advantaged structures. However, the disadvantages were daunting—it was more expensive than straight debt, and could cause potential equity volatility which would result in Credit Default Swap (CDS) widening on issuance, and increase the financing risk of puts, as well as giving additional rights to holders.

After intense debate, the team concluded that issuing the convertible bonds was Tyco's best option under the circumstances. Following that decision, the team focused on negotiating the best possible terms with the bond underwriting banks as well as pulling out all the stops to market the bonds to potential investors. Following days and nights of tough negotiations with its six lead bond underwriters, Tyco announced on 8 January 2003 that a deal had been structured to privately place a $3 billion principal amount of 2.75% Series A Convertible Senior Debentures due in 2018, and a $1.5 billion principal amount of 3.125% Series B Convertible Senior Debentures due in 2023 through its wholly-owned subsidiary, Tyco International Group S.A. The Series A debentures were to be convertible at $22.7832 per share and the Series B debentures had a conversion price of $21.7476 per share. With the debentures fully and unconditionally guaranteed by Tyco, holders of the Series A debentures could require their repurchase at five and ten years after issuance, while holders of the Series B debentures could require their repurchase at twelve years after issuance.

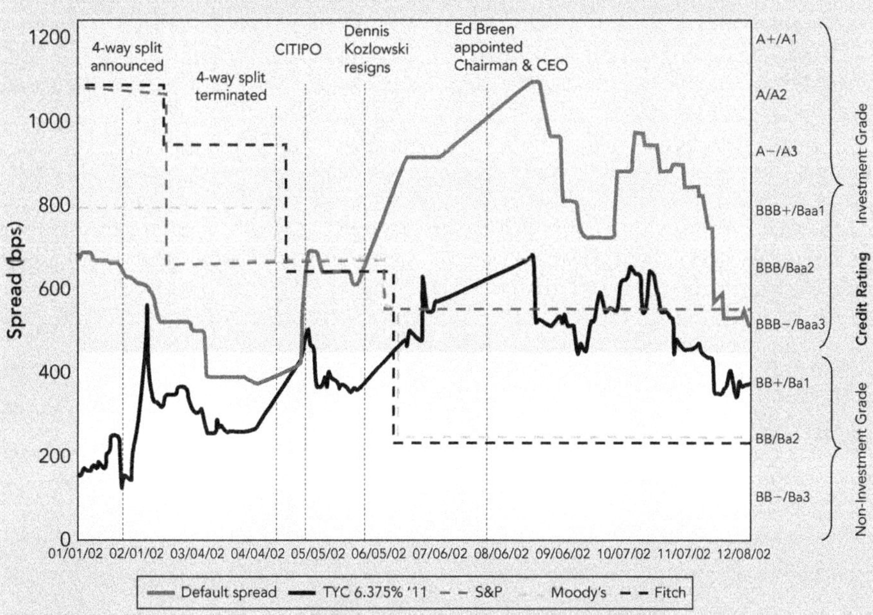

FIGURE 12.5 Tyco Credit Rating and Default Spreads (2002)

Hund-Mejean shared the team's rationale for the two issuances. Series A debentures were aimed at the market liquidity 'sweet spot' with a 5-year put and 3-year non-call which fitted nicely with hedge funds' volatility time horizons. With credit default swaps available, she estimated that the conversion premium ranged from 28–32%. In contrast, the Series B were positioned for income-oriented funds and fundamental investors who would be attracted to the higher 3⅛% to 3⅝% interest rates despite a higher equity exposure with the 12-year put option.

With a targeted strategy focused on fundamental investors, Tyco arranged a conference call with the new CEO, CFO and Treasurer, as well as follow-up one-on-one calls with either its CEO or CFO. The message to the investors was concise and consistent: leading brands, solid fundamentals, new leadership with stringent controls, and strong cash generation. In order to maximise demand for the bonds, the management also showed a willingness to indicate a relatively wide range on coupons as well as the conversion premium. Preliminary feelers out in the market reported that investors seemed eager to purchase the debentures which Tyco was planning to offer. An industry source familiar with the deal observed:

"What is interesting here is that an investment-grade company is issuing bonds paying a cash coupon. In the roaring days of zero issuance in 2001, which took off with Tyco's $3.5 billion deal for zeros in November 2000, investment-grade companies paid no interest at all. Even more interesting is that the bonds don't have a co-co."[1]

A successful sale would signal a vote of confidence in the new management team by investors and, more importantly, ensure the survival of the company. Thus the team heaved a collective sigh of relief when investors snapped up bonds worth $4.5 billion—the second-largest offering in U.S. history—exceeding by $1.25 billion the $3.25 billion that they had initially considered offering. It was also the biggest convertible bond offering in history. The announcement of the deal boosted Tyco's stock price to $17.26, up 6.2% on that day and almost 150% from a 52-week low of $6.98 on 25 July 2002 (as detailed in Figure 12.6).

The $4.5 billion debt offering marked a successful first attempt by Tyco to enlist investors' assistance in reducing the debts that had piled up during the company's multi-year acquisition binge. The bond sale also sealed the $1.5 billion credit agreement that it had earlier struck with several banks to replace an expiring loan facility. The deal had been contingent on the successful completion of the 15- and 20-year bond offering. In fact, to the surprise of some industry observers, Tyco's order books for the bonds were ten times oversubscribed which allowed them to pick their investors. Thus, six months after launching a public campaign to clean up its tarnished image, Tyco International Ltd. succeeded in closing a $6 billion bond and bank financing agreement that helped the conglomerate fend off creditors.

Strategic Reform for the Long Term—Migrating to a Centralised Treasury System

With the liquidity crisis behind her, albeit somewhat precariously, Hund-Mejean and her Treasury team were keen to ensure that Tyco would not face a repeat crisis in the future. Examining Tyco's books closely, she noted with a sigh of relief that there would be no significant scheduled debt maturities until early 2005. She

[1] The co-co that the source referred to was the contingent conversion feature, first used by Tyco in its November 2000 zeros. The debentures were much derided because the conversion premium at which a bond converts to equity kept resetting upwards, making conversion almost impossible.

	Series A		Series B	
	Indicated	Actual	Indicated	Actual
A. Transaction Details				
Annual Coupon	3% – 3.5%	2.75%	3.125% – 3.625%	3.125%
Conversion Premium	28% – 32%	32%	22% – 26%	26%
Investor Puts	5, 10	5, 10	12	12
Call Protection	NC - 3	NC - 3	NC - 5	NC - 5
Maturity	15 years	15 years	20 years	20 years
Size	$3.25 bln	$4.5 bln (A+B)		
Ratings	BBB–/Ba2			
B. Transaction Allocation				
Hedge Funds		53%		48%
Fundamental Investors		47%		52%
C. Market Reactions				

Event	Price at Event	Subsequent Stock Price Direction
New York open stock price	$16.25	UP
Investor conference call ends	$16.60	UP
Company accelerates timing to market -Accelerates establishment of short positions	$17.00	DOWN
Company announces upsizing	$16.75	UP
Heavy volume by fundamental investors, short-covering end	$17.60	DOWN
New York close stock price	$17.26	Stock rose 6.2% on the day
Total Order Book	$33 billion	

FIGURE 12.6 The Transaction—Impact on Stock Price, Allocations, Results

resolved to keep close track of future debt maturities in order to ensure that they would be better planned and distributed over financial periods. Hund-Mejean now turned her energy inward and focused on centralising Tyco's Treasury division, which until then had been completely decentralised. She explained her rationale:

> *Tyco's cash management infrastructure was very disparate, inefficient, not transparent and caused at times liquidity and control issues. Cash should be considered a corporate asset and be available when, where and in the amount needed.*

Through installing a global cash management structure and having Tyco International Group SA Luxembourg (TIGSA), the issuer of external debt, as the beneficial owner of a greater percentage of cash holdings, Treasury would have greater visibility and control over cash in the company. Restructuring to optimise liquidity would require Tyco's companies to break away from legacy structures, even if it would meet with internal resistance. Given Tyco's complexity and challenges, Hund-Mejean concluded the long-term benefits would outweigh the short-term pain of centralising the global Treasury function. In an internal meeting with Treasury staff, she outlined her objectives for the department:

- Ensure adequate liquidity
- Obtain visibility of cash balances
- Have cash available when and where we need it
- Control and protect important assets
- Improve investment performance

Having extinguished the fire of a liquidity crisis which had threatened to bankrupt the company, the first three points were straightforward and took little time to discuss. However, the last two points generated heated discussions within the Treasury team: How would the 'important assets' be controlled and protected and how could investment performance be improved? After an intense debate, the team reached a consensus that cash had evolved into a strategic asset which could be used as a hedge against market volatility and unforeseen corporate crises, and would allow Tyco to stay nimble when new business opportunities arose in the future. Furthermore, while the Treasurer's team sought to achieve the maximum investment yield from cash holdings, risk management would also be a key priority. The recent crisis had shown the importance of synchronising the credit and liquidity components with the needs and risk-tolerance of the company.

After discussing with Corporate Tax, Hund-Mejean unveiled the new corporate cash management structure. In the new structure the Treasury was divided into three distinct layers: Parent (Bermuda), Intermediate Holding Company (Europe), and the Operating Company (subsidiaries around the world). The purpose of the European holding companies was to own most of the international subsidiaries in a tax-efficient manner. Europe's strategic location from a time zone perspective allowed overlapping working hours with Asia and the Americas. Also, certain European countries provided tax incentives for managing international Treasury activities from there. Hund-Mejean wanted to leverage that structure for Treasury operations by concentrating cash from across all the global subsidiaries in various currencies at the intermediate level in Europe. (Tyco's global cash management structure is shown in Figure 12.7.)

The Treasury team also instituted a process for centralising cash, which was rolled out across its regions. With the goal of migrating banking services to key relationship banks, the team conducted a country-by-country analysis of their bank networks. Following this detailed exercise, which unearthed the fact that Tyco had almost 200 bank relationships for its 2,000 legal entities across the globe, the team selected a 'lead bank' per country, which enabled Tyco to negotiate global relationship pricing and services. In order to maintain control over the banking relationships, new standardised forms had to be filled in and proper approvals obtained prior to any establishing of new bank accounts and authorised signers. The Treasury system was also programmed to implement automated sweeps and

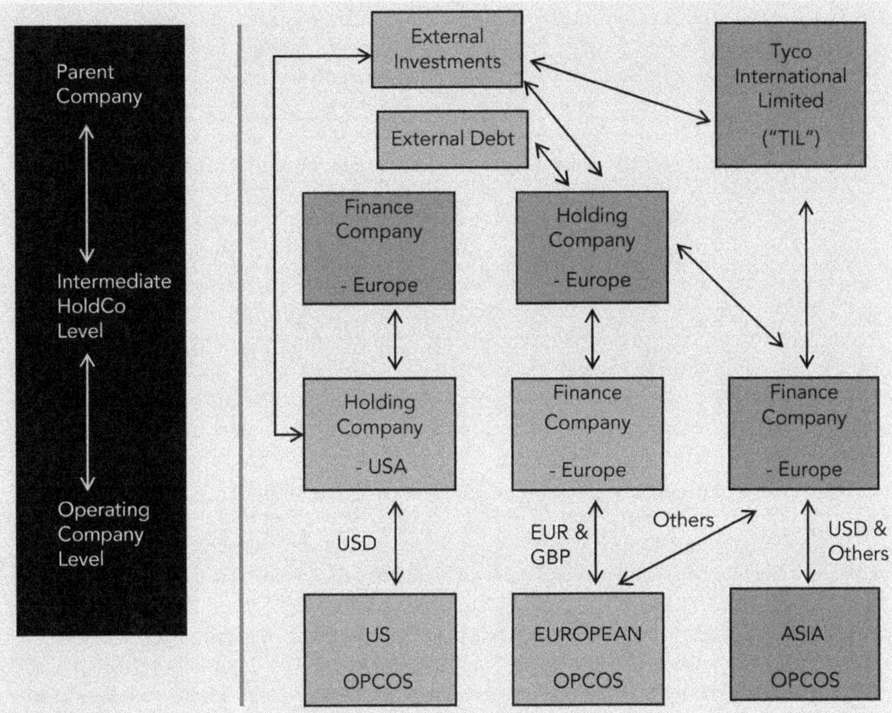

FIGURE 12.7 Global Cash Management Structure

zero balance account (ZBA) structures for in-country pools, subject to tax/legal and foreign exchange restrictions. Finally, thanks to the electronic pooling of bank account balances, Global Treasury achieved global financial visibility and the ability to monitor consolidated cash balances on a daily basis. The Global Treasury mandate was clear: centralise the subsidiary cash, obtain visibility of cash balances, and have cash available when and where it was needed.

Tyco Asia Treasury—A Centralised Treasury System Amidst a Complex Regulatory Environment

Over in Asia Pacific, the Treasury team led by Director of Asia Pacific Treasury, Gourang Shah, worked tirelessly to establish and install Tyco's new Treasury structure and processes. With $6 billion of sales in the region, a presence in 18 countries, and 225 active legal entities, the only thing in common appeared to be that they were all under the Tyco umbrella. Shah conducted a quick "as is" analysis of the existing state of Asia-Pacific Treasury. Within a couple of days the status was painfully clear—there was poor visibility and control on cash balances that spread across all the subsidiaries. To remotely manage bank accounts from Regional Treasury in Singapore, electronic banking was a necessity, but to his surprise, Shah found that in many Asia Pacific countries e-banking was a foreign concept.

Shah faced additional internal and external challenges as Tyco's organisation in Asia Pacific was particularly complex. The regulatory environments in the 18 countries where Tyco had a presence varied greatly. While Australia, Hong Kong,

Japan, New Zealand and Singapore had unrestricted markets, many others, including the large markets in China, India, Malaysia, South Korea and Taiwan, had restrictive regulatory environments. Aware that negotiating with the regulatory bodies in each of these countries would be time consuming and complex—China alone had three different government bodies overseeing capital and monetary flows—Shah faced tremendous pressure to meet the timeline set by the Global Treasury team.

Internal issues also cropped up as the Asia Pacific Treasury team hunkered down for the long and arduous task ahead. They discovered that each business unit had its own ERP system—in fact there were several instances where different ERP systems were found within individual business groups! As Shah's team continued to dig deeper, they uncovered further startling information: There were more than 150 banking relationships and 1,600 Tyco bank accounts in Asia, which resulted in widely varying pricing across its entities. Inconsistent banking services also led to sub-optimal cash utilisation and minimal cash control and visibility. Accustomed to operating independently and free from "headquarters interference," Tyco's senior managers balked at having to implement the new systems and processes. In order to convince the Asia Pacific management team as well as local financial controllers of the benefits of implementing the strategic Treasury solution, Shah personally journeyed to over 60 locations to gain their buy-in.

After gaining support from all key stakeholders, the team put together an implementation plan to generate the biggest impact in the shortest time frame while causing minimal disruption to Tyco's operations. The plan called for a phased approach based on the market size of each of its countries and its regulatory complexity. The Phase I countries were the unrestricted markets and large markets: Australia, China, Hong Kong, Japan, New Zealand, Korea and Singapore. The Phase II countries—Malaysia, Thailand and New Zealand—followed thereafter, and the final phase of the implementation consisted of India, Taiwan and the remaining Asia-Pacific countries.

Exhausted after months of travelling to all corners of the region and countless meetings, Shah still had not found solutions to overcome the regulatory challenges in China, Malaysia and Korea, the major roadblocks to the successful completion of Tyco's Asia-Pacific Treasury restructuring. With controls in place to restrict the movement of funds out of the countries, Shah faced the prospect of significant amounts of trapped cash in Asia-Pacific's emerging markets and concluded that he must personally negotiate with the government and regulatory bodies of the countries for special exemptions to be granted to Tyco. Shah started with the low-hanging fruit—Malaysia. Following the 1997 Asian crisis, Malaysia had instituted capital controls in 1998, imposing conditions on the operations and cross-border transfer of funds under capital account, i.e., loan or equity. The cross-border transfer as inter-company loans from surplus cash in Malaysia required prior approval for any amount (previously it had been freely allowed). Fortunately, Bank Negara Malaysia, the central bank responsible for monetary controls, had the authority to approve special exemptions. Keen to retain Tyco operations in Malaysia, one of the bigger multinational companies in the country, Bank Negara Malaysia officials met with Shah and granted special exemptions to Tyco's Treasury operations in Malaysia.

Korea was next on Shah's list. He approached the Bank of Korea (BOK) to apply for exemptions to Tyco's operations there. Despite language and cultural difficulties, Shah succeeded in achieving his objective of moving funds out of South Korea on a regular basis. With this experience in negotiating with central banks under his belt, he boarded a flight to Beijing, China. Expecting to negotiate with its central bank, The People's Bank of China, Shah found himself bounced back and forth between three government authorities: the Ministry of Commerce, the State Administration of Foreign Exchange, and the People Bank of China. Each maintained that they had no authority to grant exemptions and referred Shah to the "right official who could help". After months of fruitless discussions with various officials and failing to obtain meaningful concessions, Shah decided that the best strategy for China was to engage in "leading and lagging"—leading the intercompany payables out of China and lagging the intercompany receivables into China.

Tyco's Treasury Scorecard After Two Years

In January 2005, after yet another hectic day filled with meetings, Hund-Mejean reflected on her past two years at Tyco International. Tyco had quickly found its footing again after the issuance of the two convertible debts. She noted with a certain satisfaction that the liquidity structure and debt maturity profile of the company had also improved considerably since 2002. Tyco's debt maturity profile had been planned so that there was no more than $2 billion debt maturing in any one fiscal year. The Treasury team had also put in place measures to ensure that maturing debt could easily be managed with cash from Tyco's operational FCF. (Selected financial data from 2002 to 2006 are shown in Figure 12.8.)

Tyco's stock had risen steadily and had in fact outperformed the S&P Composite Average and Dow Jones Industrial Average since mid-2003. While she was proud of the way the convertible debt issuance had been pulled together in such a short time, Hund-Mejean wondered what the implicit cost of the convertible bonds might be to Tyco and made a mental note to ask an analyst on her team to make a quantitative estimate using the bond spread yields data gathered (as shown in Figure 12.9).

Over in Asia, Shah also reflected on a journey which had taken him to over 60 locations to align the stakeholders and enable the realisation of Tyco's Treasury management strategy. He pulled out his list of challenges compiled back in 2003 and was pleased to note that most of them had been successfully resolved. In the same folder, Shah also came across his "As is" status report from back when he first landed in Singapore. With a sense of satisfaction, he took out his pen and drew in the "After" status of the Asia-Pacific Treasury department (as illustrated in Figure 12.10). In addition to establishing a Regional Treasury Centre in Singapore,

Selected Financial Data ($ millions)	2002	2003	2004	2005
Cash & Equivalents	6,475	4,805	4,467	3,505
Current Debt	7,719	2,718	2,116	1,954
Total Debt	24,206	20,969	16,733	12,554
EBIT (Before Extraordinary Items & Discontinued Operations)	(1,453)	2,970	5,110	4,998
EBITDA (Before Extraordinary Items & Discontinued Operations)	11	4,442	6,588	6,445
Unlevered Cash Flow From Operations	6,591	6,517	6,349	6,952
Unlevered Free Cash Flow	(122)	6,905	5,672	6,642

FIGURE 12.8 Tyco Selected Financial Data (2002–2006)

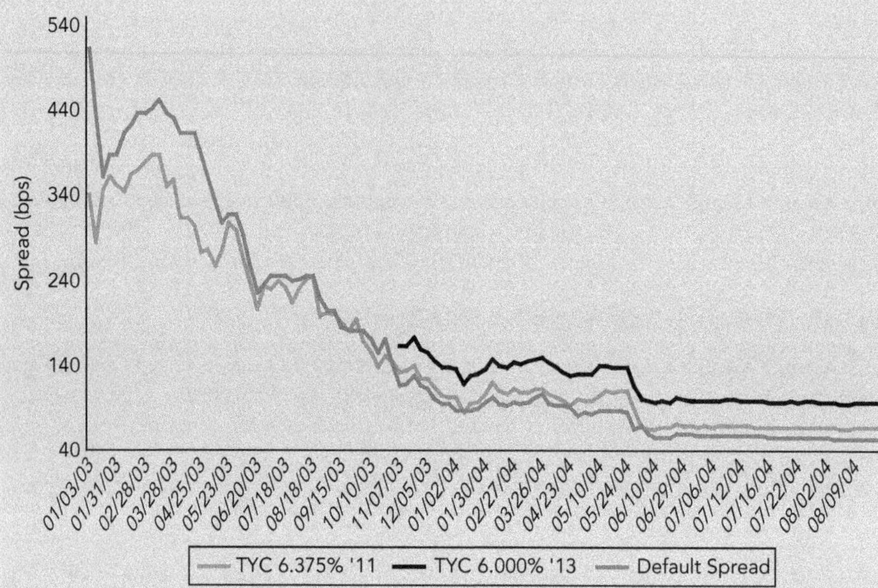

FIGURE 12.9 Tyco Bond Spread Yields (2002–2004)

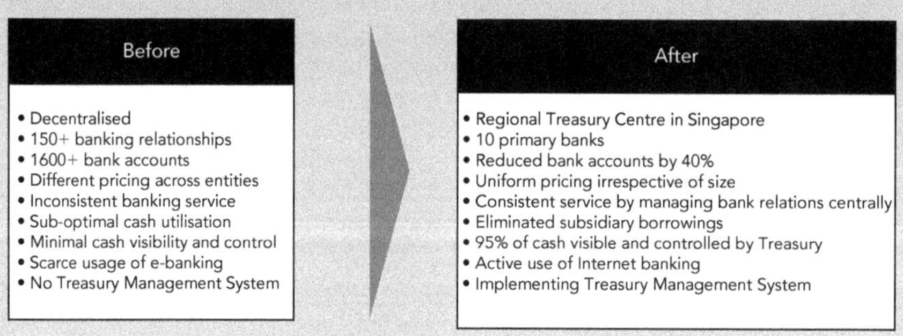

FIGURE 12.10 Asia-Pacific Treasury Before and After Status

the Asia Pacific team now had just ten primary banks and had reduced bank accounts by 40%. All its entities were entitled to uniform pricing, irrespective of size, which also ensured consistent service by the central management of bank relations. Subsidiary borrowings from external sources were replaced with internal funding and Treasury was able to maintain and control 85% of cash in the region.

Conclusion—Evolution Through Splitting

Beginning in the spring of 2005, the Tyco management team, including Hund-Mejean, began exploring whether the company should sell a unit, embark on new acquisitions or even split itself up. CEO Breen explained that these new plans had emerged in large part as Tyco had successfully reduced its once-crushing debt and "was not the No. 1 focus anymore."[2] The team argued that action was necessary to unlock Tyco's value by enabling individual units—especially its jewel-in-the-crown Healthcare division—to operate more nimbly in their respective industries.

On 13 January 2007, after almost two years of wrestling with Tyco's various strategic options, the company announced that its Board of Directors had approved a plan to separate the company's current portfolio of diverse businesses into three separate, publicly traded companies—Tyco Healthcare, one of the world's leading diversified healthcare companies; Tyco Electronics, the world's largest passive electronic components manufacturer; and the combination of Tyco Fire & Security and Engineered Products & Services (TFS/TEPS), a global business with leading positions in residential and commercial security, fire protection and industrial products and services.

Single-digit growth rates in some of its core businesses in 2006, including Tyco Electronics, had finally convinced the management team that the only way to address the growth problem was to carve Tyco up. The team believed that Tyco had reached a "crossroads" after recovering its financial health and reputation. By allowing its divisions to operate unencumbered by its corporate structure, they would be able to maximise shareholder value. In an interview with *Fortune* magazine in March 2006, Breen reiterated that the company could only evolve through a split: "It's the best way to create long-term shareholder value at the company. I really stress long term, because I'm not looking for some overnight pop here." In the press conference announcing the split, Breen elaborated on the strategic rationale behind Tyco's separation

> In the past several years, Tyco has come a long way. Our balance sheet and cash flows are strong and many legacy financial and legal issues have been resolved. We are fortunate to have a great mix of businesses with market-leading positions. After a thorough review of strategic options with our Board of Directors, we have determined that separating into three independent companies is the best approach to enable these businesses to achieve their full potential. Healthcare, Electronics and TFS/TEPS will be able to move faster and more aggressively—and ultimately create more value for our shareholders—by pursuing their own growth strategies as independent companies.

Watching the news conference from their offices, Hund-Mejean and Shah had mixed feelings as they noted the irony of coming full circle with Tyco: first to successfully keep it from breaking apart, only to subsequently help it break up successfully. While confident that Tyco's centralised Treasury structure and award-winning Treasury system would benefit its newly separated companies, they mentally sketched out how each new company would need its own centralised Treasury structures to ensure proper capital planning and cash/risk management strong enough to withstand potential macroeconomic or internal liquidity crunches.

[2]Ibid.

This case was written and contributed by Hong Zhang, Assistant Professor of Finance at INSEAD, Gourang Shah, Head of Treasury Advisory at Citi, and Anne Yang, Research Associate at INSEAD. It is intended to be used as a basis for class discussion rather than to illustrate either effective or ineffective handling of an administrative situation.

To order copies of INSEAD cases, please refer to www.insead.edu.

Tyco Case Appendix I: Tyco International Balance Sheet

Balance Sheets ($ millions)	2002	2003	2004	2005	2006
Cash & Equivalents	6,475.4	4,804.8	4,467.0	3,505.0	3,267.0
Receivables - Total (Net)	5,831.9	5,714.8	6,463.0	6,732.0	7,060.0
Inventories	5,016.4	4,679.4	4,365.0	4,197.0	4,793.0
Current Assets - Other	2,315.7	2,040.5	3,250.0	4,103.0	3,552.0
Current Assets - Total	19,639.4	17,239.5	18,545.0	18,537.0	18,672.0
Plant, Property & Equip (Net)	10,442.6	10,299.8	9,635.0	9,238.0	9,240.0
Equity and Other Investments and Advances	297.8	162.1	0.0	272.0	323.0
Intangibles	26,020.5	25,938.7	25,510.0	24,557.0	24,872.0
Other Assets	9,057.2	9,904.9	9,977.0	10,017.0	9,905.0
Total Assets	65,457.5	63,545.0	63,667.0	62,621.0	63,012.0
Accounts Payable	3,173.8	2,716.7	2,698.0	3,065.0	3,526.0
Notes Payable	0.0	0.0	0.0	0.0	0.0
Accrued Expenses	2,219.1	0.0	0.0	1,682.0	1,643.0
Debt (Long-Term) Due in One Year	7,719.0	2,718.4	2,116.0	1,954.0	800.0
Other Current Liabilities	6,578.6	5,137.2	6,338.0	5,134.0	4,615.0
Total Current Liabilities	19,690.5	10,572.3	11,152.0	11,835.0	10,584.0
Long Term Debt	16,486.8	18,250.7	14,617.0	10,600.0	9,340.0
Deferred Income Taxes	985.6	1,554.7	0.0	0.0	1,398.0
Other Liabilities	4,213.3	6,798.3	7,606.0	7,736.0	6,303.0
Total Liabilities	41,376.2	37,176.0	33,375.0	30,171.0	27,625.0
Preferred Stock	0.0	0.0	0.0	0.0	0.0
Common Stock	23,588.7	23,681.1	24,036.0	24,192.0	23,678.0
Retained Earnings (Net of Other Adjustments)	492.6	2,687.9	6,256.0	8,258.0	11,709.0
Treasury Stock	0.0	0.0	0.0	0.0	0.0
Common Equity (Total)	24,081.3	26,369.0	30,292.0	32,450.0	35,387.0
Liabilities and Shareholders' Equity	65,457.5	63,545.0	63,667.0	62,621.0	63,012.0

FIGURE 12.11 Tyco International Balance Sheet

Source: Tyco International, SEC filings

Tyco Case Appendix II: Tyco International Income Statement

Income Statement ($ millions)	2002	2003	2004	2005	2006
Sales (net)	35,589.8	36,801.3	40,153.0	39,727.0	40,938.0
Cost of Goods Sold	20,965.8	22,273.1	24,166.0	24,508.0	25,864.0
Gross Profit	14,624.0	14,528.2	15,987.0	15,219.0	15,074.0
Selling, General, & Admin Expenses	8,057.5	8,325.7	8,721.0	8,231.0	8,056.0
Depreciation, Depletion, & Amortn.	1,464.1	1,471.9	1,478.0	1,447.0	1,412.0
Operating Income	5,102.4	4,730.6	5,788.0	5,541.0	5,606.0
Interest Expense	1,177.1	1,170.8	965.0	815.0	709.0
Minority Interest on Income	1.4	3.6	14.0	9.0	8.0
Non-Operating Income (Expenses)	−6,554.0	−1,757.0	−664.0	−534.0	−21.0
Pre-Tax Income	−2,630.1	1,799.2	4,145.0	4,183.0	4,868.0
Income Taxes	208.1	764.5	1,140.0	984.0	920.0
Income Before Extraordinary Items & Discontinued Operations (EI&DO)	−2,838.2	1,034.7	3,005.0	3,199.0	3,948.0
Extraordinary Items and Discontinued Operations (net of income taxes)	−6,341.3	−55.1	−126.0	−167.0	−358.0
Net Income	−9,179.5	979.6	2,879.0	3,032.0	3,590.0
Earnings Per Share - Before Extraordinary Items and Discontinued Operations:					
Basic	−1.4	0.5	1.5	1.6	2.0
Diluted	−1.4	0.5	1.4	1.5	1.9
Earnings Per Share - After Extraordinary Items and Discontinued Operations:					
Basic	−4.6	0.5	1.4	1.5	1.8
Diluted	−4.6	0.5	1.4	1.4	1.7

FIGURE 12.12 Tyco International Income Statement

Source: Tyco International, SEC filing

Tyco Case Appendix III: Tyco International Statement of Cash Flow

Cash Flow Statement ($ millions)	2002	2003	2004	2005	2006
Income Before Extraordinary Items	−2,838.2	1,034.7	3,005.0	3,199.0	3,948.0
Depreciation and Amortisation	2,279.0	2,196.9	2,176.0	2,100.0	2,062.0
Extraordinary Items and Discontinued Operations	1,462.9	20.0	9.0	77.0	−39.0
Deferred Income Taxes	−585.2	348.9	256.0	−41.0	53.0
Sale of PPEq and Investments - Loss (Gain)	247.2	87.2	1.0	0.0	−44.0
Operating Accounts Changes and Other Adjustments	6,310.7	1,678.4	−54.0	879.0	−432.0
Operating Activities - Net Cash Flow	6,876.4	5,366.1	5,393.0	6,214.0	5,548.0
Capital Expenditures (Net of Sales and Dispositions)	2,824.8	1,282.3	1,015.0	1,272.0	1,568.0
Change in Investments and Other	5,771.3	−1,141.9	615.0	−400.0	555.0
Acquisitions	2,307.9	315.8	15.0	82.0	413.0
Investing Activities - Net Cash Flow	638.6	−2,740.0	−415.0	−1,754.0	−1,426.0
Debt - Net Change	1,951.3	−4,618.6	−4,772.0	−4,990.0	−1,235.0
Preferred Stock - Net Change					
Common Stock - Net Change	−603.5	13.6	155.0	−74.0	250.0
Financing - Other	−3,084.3	−8.0	−25.0	−104.0	−2,668.0
Dividends - Preferred	0.4	1.3	0.0	−177.0	−1.0
Dividends - Common	99.9	99.6	100.0	805.0	807.0
Financing Activities - Net Cash Flow	−1,836.8	−4,713.9	−4,742.0	−5,796.0	−4,459.0
Exchange Rate Effect	0.0	88.8	45.0	65.0	43.0
Cash and Cash Equivalents - Change	5,678.2	−1,999.0	281.0	−1,271.0	−294.0

FIGURE 12.13 Tyco International Statements of Cash Flow

Source: Tyco International, SEC filing

Tyco Case Appendix IV: Tyco Share Performance and Volume January 1999–December 2002

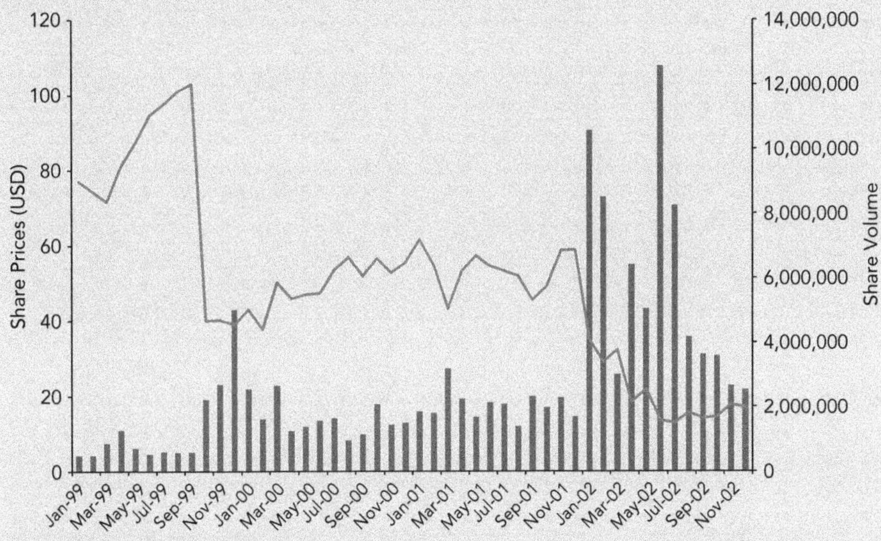

FIGURE 12.14 Tyco Share Performance

Source: http://marketwatch.com and Tyco International

Tyco Case Appendix V: Corporate Scandal of 2002

In June 2002, CEO Dennis Kozlowski and CFO Mark Swartz were asked to resign from the company largely because they had taken bonuses without proper approvals from the board and were accused of using corporate resources for their personal gain. It was in the period when Enron and MCI Worldcom had declared bankruptcy and investor faith was at an all-time low. Tyco was being talked about in the same vein as both Enron and MCI Worldcom and seen as a potential candidate for bankruptcy.

Criminal charges were subsequently brought against Kozlowski and Swartz of enterprise corruption for allegedly stealing more than $170 million from Tyco and obtaining $430 million by fraud from the sale of company shares. However, they claimed during their trial in March 2004 that the board of directors was aware of the deals and had authorised them as compensation. On 17 June 2005, Kozlowski and Swartz were convicted on all but one of the more than 30 counts against them. The verdicts carried potential terms of up to 25 years in state prison. Kozlowski was sentenced to no less than eight years and four months and no more than 25 years in prison.

Tyco Case Appendix VI: CIT Group Acquisition and Divestiture

In June 2001, under CEO Dennis Kozlowski, Tyco had acquired CIT Group, then the national's largest independent commercial finance company. Despite being unfamiliar with the industry, Kozlowski was confident that he could rev up CIT's growth, declaring "I think CIT will be one of the best deals we've ever done."

Less than a year later, CIT looked like the worst deal Tyco had ever done. Its plunging stock price, exacerbated by Tyco's corporate scandal, forced a downgrade of CIT's credit rating, and CIT was forced out of the commercial paper market, which was its bread-and-butter business. As a result, CIT and Tyco had little choice but to swap their $13 billion in commercial paper for pricier bank loans, which further heightened fears of a liquidity squeeze. It became increasingly clear to all Tyco stakeholders that Tyco would need to cut CIT loose, either through a sale or outright handover to shareholders. Barry Bannister, an analyst at Legg Mason Inc., stated, "Nearly everyone accepts that they will take a multibillion-dollar loss on a sale."

On July 8, 2002, Tyco completed the divestment of its Tyco Capital business through an initial public offering, via the sale of 100% of the common shares in CIT Group Inc.

Source: Excerpt from "Beyond Tyco's Accounting Alchemy," *Businessweek*, February 25, 2002, www.businessweek.com/magazine/content/02_08/b3771062.htm

Tyco Case Appendix VII: Timeline of the Tyco International Scandal

Key dates and events that led to the conviction of former Tyco CEO L. Dennis Kozlowski and CFO Mark Swartz are presented next.

March 13, 2001: Tyco announces $9.2 billion cash and stock deal to purchase the CIT Group, a commercial finance company. Tyco director Frank Walsh helps arrange the deal.

December 5, 2001: Tyco shares close at a high of $59.76 on the New York Stock Exchange.

January 14, 2002: *Businessweek* magazine lists Tyco CEO L. Dennis Kozlowski as one of the top 25 corporate managers of 2001.

January 22, 2002: Kozlowski announces plans to split Tyco into four independent, publicly traded companies. The announcement starts a slide in the price of Tyco shares.

January 29, 2002: Tyco shares drop sharply, one day after the company files a proxy report with the Securities and Exchange Commission disclosing that Walsh received a $10 million fee on the CIT Group deal and that another $10 million went to a charity where he was a director.

January 30, 2002: The *New York Times* reports that Kozlowski and CFO Mark Swartz sold more than $100 million of their Tyco stock the previous fiscal year despite public statements that they rarely sold their stock. Kozlowski and Swartz say they will buy 1 million shares with their own money.

June 3, 2002: Kozlowski resigns unexpectedly as the *New York Times* reports he is the subject of a sales tax evasion investigation by Manhattan District Attorney Robert Morgenthau's office.

June 4, 2002: Morgenthau announces a criminal indictment accusing Kozlowski of conspiring to evade more than $1 million in state and city sales tax on fine art purchases.

September 12, 2002: Morgenthau announces a criminal indictment accusing Kozlowski and Swartz of enterprise corruption for allegedly stealing more than $170 million from Tyco and obtaining $430 million by fraud in the sale of company shares. Former Tyco corporate counsel Mark Belnick is charged separately with falsifying records to conceal more than $14 million in company loans.

December 17, 2002: Former Tyco board member Frank Walsh pleads guilty to an alleged scheme to hide the $20 million in fees for the CIT Group deal.

October 7, 2003: The first trial of Kozlowski and Swartz begins with opening statements in which prosecutors characterise them as crime bosses who looted Tyco. Defence lawyers call them honest executives who deserved and disclosed all corporate payments and perks.

October 28, 2003: The jury is shown a video of a birthday party Kozlowski threw for his wife at a resort in Sardinia. Tyco paid roughly half the $2 million cost of the event, which featured entertainers clad in togas and an appearance by singer Jimmy Buffett.

November 25, 2003: Prosecutors show the jury a video of the $6,000 shower curtain and other lavish furnishings that decorated Kozlowski's Tyco-owned apartment in Manhattan.

April 2, 2004: A mistrial is declared after a juror says she received a letter pressuring her to convict Kozlowski and Swartz. Some observers said the juror, Ruth Jordan, had previously appeared to make an "OK" sign to defence lawyers. She subsequently denied making any gesture toward the defence team.

July 15, 2004: In a separate trial, former Tyco corporate counsel Mark Belnick is acquitted of charges that he received millions in loans from the company and failed to disclose the payments.

January 26, 2005: The second trial of Kozlowski and Swartz begins with opening statements in which prosecutors switch tactics to focus on money the two allegedly stole from Tyco. They do not mention Kozlowski's $6,000 shower curtain or the Sardinia birthday party for his wife.

April 27, 2005: Kozlowski, who did not testify at his first trial, takes the stand and testifies that the millions of dollars in Tyco payments and perks he received had been properly authorised and disclosed.

June 17, 2005: A Manhattan jury finds Kozlowski and Swartz guilty of stealing more than $150 million from Tyco. They each could face 25 years in prison.

Source: USATODAY research

SUMMARY

We looked at some of the key components of financial strength and their role and utility across the financial universe. Key ratios, determinants of strength, were reviewed, and a practical exposure to the use of financial statements in the case of a corporation was discussed. In the next chapter, we look at external sources of capital, one of the core performance areas for a global Treasurer.

CHAPTER THIRTEEN

Sources of Capital

IN THIS CHAPTER, WE COVER the various aspects of capital markets and sources of funding. The chapter continues with an overview of the capital structure decision that is one of the typical core areas of focus of the Treasurer. Debt and equity markets are explored at length, and hybrids of the two are also introduced. We also present a case study with two interesting situations—one is that the entity moves from a debt-free capital structure to one with debt, and the second is that the entity itself is an educational institution, whose capital allocation and usage is not very different in concept from that of a corporate.

CAPITAL MARKETS

We introduce the capital market discussion with an overview of the various markets and their players in Figure 13.1.

The issuers are the entities that are raising capital. The investors can come from many categories, the biggest of them being:

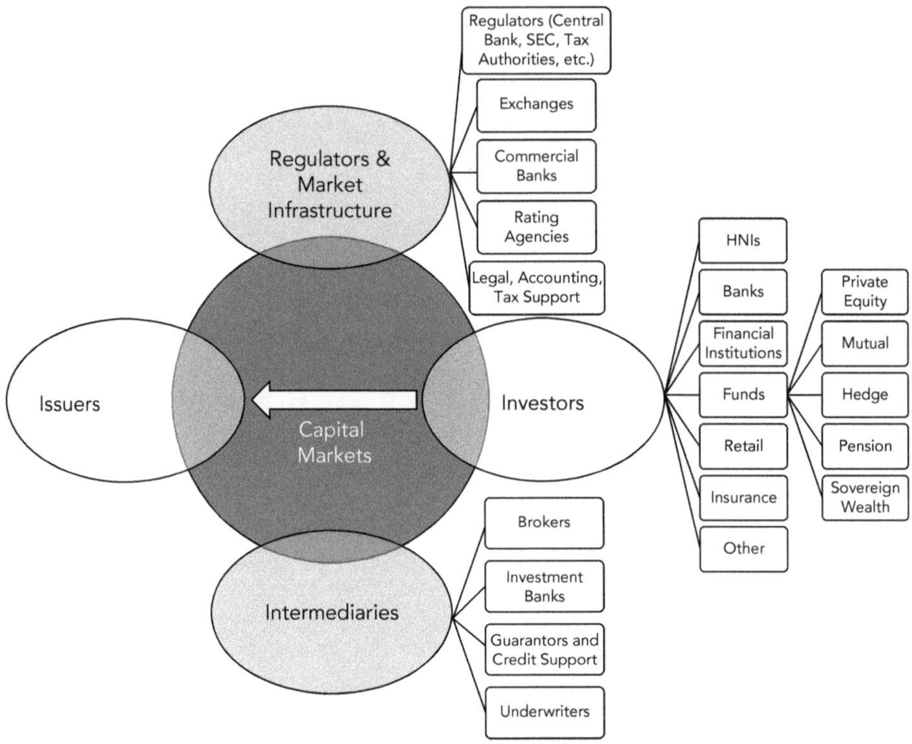

FIGURE 13.1 Players in Capital Markets

- Sovereign wealth funds
- Mutual funds
- Private equity funds
- Pension funds
- Hedge funds
- Insurance companies
- High-net-worth individuals (HNIs)
- Banks
- Financial institutions
- Retail investors

The intermediaries make the transactions happen, facilitating the entire process end to end. They are:

- **Brokers or agents**. Act as intermediaries for deal closure
- **Investment banks**. Manage and execute the deals in the market
- **Guarantors and credit support providers**. Provide their credit strength to issuers for a lower cost or more liquidity
- **Underwriters**. Commit to subscribe should an issue not go through

Capital markets activity will be possible only with the underlying infrastructure to make the transactions happen. The next entities usually facilitate or supervise the markets:

- **Regulators**. Entities such as the central bank in the country of the issuer and investor, the Stock Exchange Commission, the relevant tax authorities in the jurisdictions, and the finance ministries (which pass the relevant laws) are the key entities that create the supervisory framework for all funding transactions.
- **Exchanges**. Exchanges where transactions are listed enable the public trading of the securities once issued.
- **Commercial banks**. These provide the necessary banking infrastructure in terms of payments, collections, accounts services, securities and custodial services, and so on.
- **Securities depositories**. Securities depository institutions or central securities depositories (CSDs) are central bodies performing roles such as holding securities to enable the book entry transfer of securities, centralised comparison, and clearing and settlement. The functions of a CSD may include:
  - Safekeeping, deposit, and withdrawal of securities
  - Processing of related dividend, interest, and principal payments
  - Corporate actions such as proxy voting
  - Pledging services
- **Legal, accounting, tax support**. An army of legal firms, accountants, and tax experts support the smooth functioning of the world's capital markets and fundraising activities.

The world of capital is largely divided into three classes: debt, equity, and hybrid, which has characteristics of both debt and equity. Figure 13.2 provides an overview of these markets.

CAPITAL STRUCTURE

Capital structure is the manner in which a company is capitalised (i.e., the proportion of debt, equity, and other sources through which the company finances its investments and core assets).

The optimal capital structure is one in which the firm has least risk and least cost in order to maximise firm value and hence shareholder wealth (see Figure 13.3).

Theoretically, the cost of capital would be the one that would drive the decision of the type of capital to source. From a more practical perspective, there are other considerations including existing stakeholders, short- and medium-term management objectives, control, collateral, creditworthiness, risks, liquidity, market access, regulations, concentration, and others. We describe these risks in Part Four.

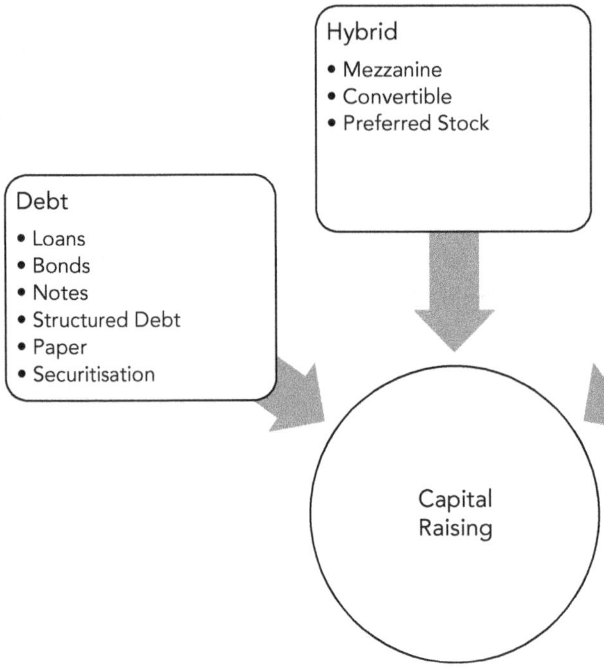

FIGURE 13.2 Classes of Raising Capital

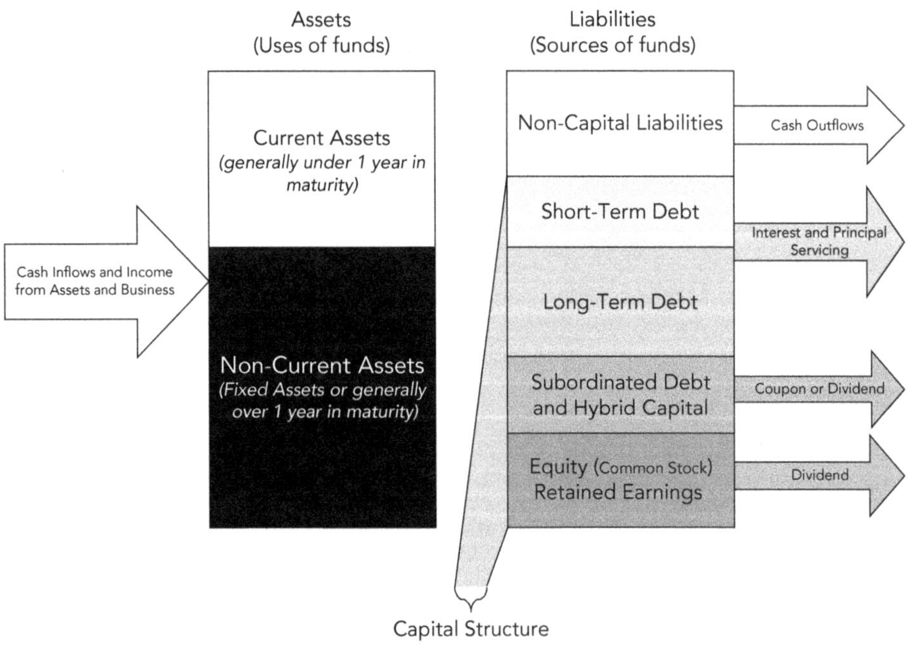

FIGURE 13.3 Capital Structure in the Context of the Balance Sheet and Cash Flows

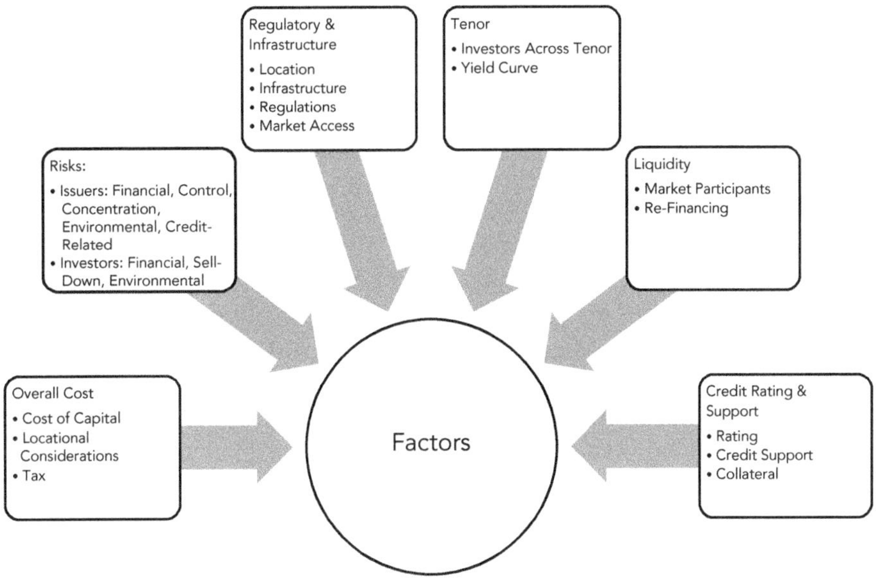

FIGURE 13.4 Factors in the Capital Decision

While more debt can enhance the return on equity in good times, it also poses a threat to cash flows, credit rating, the relative ability to raise debt, and relative cost during tight economic periods. Changing volatility and tax, regulatory, and market conditions have caused the capital structure decision itself to be a dynamic one, with companies preferring to remain flexible and tap as many sources as possible.

In this context, the key factors in the capital decision revolve around the optimal level of risk, cost, and other objective and subjective elements that, in the collective view of the management, will maximise the firm's value in the long term.

FACTORS IN THE CAPITAL DECISION

There are many decision points on the capital structure and the final decision on any incremental capital raising. These revolve around:

- Drivers or the underlying need to raise capital
- How the capital will be raised or the mode of raising capital
- Where the capital is being raised and where investors are located
- How long the capital is required for
- The investor base

To make that decision, six factors that need to be assessed (see Figure 13.4), which are described next.

Overall Cost

The cost of capital, or average cost of capital weighted to the specific components of debt and equity (WACC), remains one of the most important factors to determine capital structure. Since a lot of excellent material written by gurus of modern finance is available for readers on this subject, here I merely highlight the various aspects of these costs and their practical relevance to the Treasurer's decision making. Readers are encouraged to read further on this topic.

The WACC depends on the combination and proportion of the various components of the capital structure. A change in the proportion of different securities in the capital structure will cause a change in the WACC. Hence there can be an optimal mix of different types of capital for which WACC will be the least.

There are two issues with the WACC approach to continuously monitor and hence keep the capital structure tagged only to cost of capital.

The first is that markets, especially currency and interest rates, and the creditworthiness of an organisation are dynamic. Hence the cost component of each type of capital does vary. What seems lower priced at one point of time and would be a possible component of capital structure could change form and cost over a period of time—thus the capital structure, because it is dynamic, cannot be shifted consistently. If capital is being raised across subsidiaries and hence across locations and currencies, the relative strength of those currencies with respect to the servicing of capital repayments and cash outflows in those currencies will add to the cost of capital. For example, a company with debt in USD but revenues primarily in, say, Brazilian reals (BRL) will also have to factor in the relative appreciation of the U.S. dollar (USD) debt servicing into its cost of capital. The Treasurer must hence identify a broad capital structure, perhaps a band, and go with the plan.

The second issue with tagging capital structure only to the cost of capital concerns liquidity and refinancing—the moment a source of liquidity dries up, another alternative must be found. In turbulent times, dependence on the same kind of funding might not be possible for all firms.

Hence, while cost of capital plays a key role in determining capital structure, other fundamental factors must also be considered for a holistic structure. We discuss those factors next.

Locational Elements

Locational elements, especially taxation for investors (withholding tax, etc.) and issuers (stamp duty, registration, etc.) and infrastructural costs of setting up in that location, play an important role in the overall cost of capital. WACC includes not only the actual interest, principal, dividend, and so on being paid out but also the net outflow impact of the capital raising, including all related taxes and statutory payments and operational expenses.

Risk for Issuers and Investors

Various risk elements must be considered. For issuers, the risk element is on their own funding. To make the capital investment more attractive for investors and to trade off between pricing and other elements, issuers also consider the risk element for their investors.

Some of these elements are covered more in detail in Part Four of this book.

Issuers

Some elements for issuers to bear in mind are:

- **Concentration of lenders or funding sources.** Could pose a threat if that conduit is restricted or impacted.
- **Control.** Overdependence on equity could result in dilution of control for existing shareholders.
- **Financial.** Liquidity risk (lowering of availability of funds in the market); interest rate and credit risks (the uncertainty of interest rates and credit spreads changing and impacting overall cost of borrowing for the firm); and refinancing risk (potential issues of liquidity and rate risks when the time comes to rollover or replace the existing source) come into play.
- **Covenants.** Conditions (financial and operational) imposed by investors to ensure reasonable performance of the firm can impact incremental fundraising.
- **Cross-default.** A default on any obligation across a related party could trigger a number of events that could in turn impact the ability to raise further capital.
- **Regulatory, tax or other environmental changes.**

Investors

For investors, there are various risk elements to be considered prior to making an investment and also once the investment has been made. These are, broadly:

- **Financial.** These risks include:
  - Credit risk (of the ability of the issuer to repay or service the requisite cash flows).
  - Liquidity risk (of being unable to terminate the investment if required).
  - Cross-border risk of transferability and convertibility of the monies owed by an overseas issuer if there are clampdowns on conversion and transfer of money from that country.
- **Ability to sell down.** Any impairment to the ability to sell the investment to a third party could result in unexpected losses on costs for the investor
- **Regulatory, tax or other environmental changes**

Regulatory and Infrastructure

The regulatory environment and infrastructural elements play an important consideration in capital structure. As we mentioned, the location plays a role in the cost. In addition, the regulatory, infrastructure, and market environments play a key role in determining the sources of capital. In many cases, the location of the subsidiary or of the use of capital could determine the mode of capital owing to regulatory and market restraints that prevent access to global markets. Many global companies have the luxury of deciding the location after the capital decision.

Infrastructure, including presence of exchanges, efficient collections and disbursement mechanisms, and the accounting, tax, and legal aspects for execution, is an important aspect in the capital decision.

Regulations and the ability to raise funds with ease allow the company more and better alternatives to decide the type of capital to be raised. On the debt side, regulatory limits on exposure to single companies and groups, capital adequacy requirements for banks, and definitions of nonperforming assets, apart from restrictions on investment and overseas investors in locally issued debt, become determinants.

Market access in terms of both regulations and liquidity and the ability to tap into markets is also an important input.

Tenor

The need and the drivers for the capital must be aligned with the availability of capital for that tenor as well as the investor appetite. Different kinds of investors have different return expectations across tenors, and the presence of appropriate investors in the market will provide issuers with the choice of method of capital raising. Issuers could also evaluate the possibility of future liquidity issues and decide whether to be conservative or aggressive in the tenor of capital to be raised.

Liquidity

The available and future liquidity of the capital has to be explored in the context of the market of capital raising and the type of instrument. From the issuer's perspective, more liquidity allows more flexibility with a possible impact on cost and refinancing.

Credit Rating and Support

Credit rating, support from group or external sources, and collateral required play an important role in the capital structure decision, especially on the debt raising side.

Next we discuss the various mechanisms of accessing capital through these classes.

DEBT CAPITAL MARKETS

We begin our discussion on debt capital markets with an overview of the various elements that drive the decision to raise debt. As noted in Chapter 12, the capital structure is one of the main characteristics of firms. Once the decision has been made to raise capital, the underlying drivers of business and funding play a strong role in deciding which alternative would work.

Figure 13.5 outlines various debt financing alternatives that we discuss in this chapter.

Syndicated Loans

A syndicated loan is one created through the pooling of funds from a syndicate of financial institutions and banks, typically for the short to medium term. This method is popular, especially for leveraged buyouts and other corporate activity. Institutions that are part of the syndicate could, at a later time, sell down the obligations to other investors.

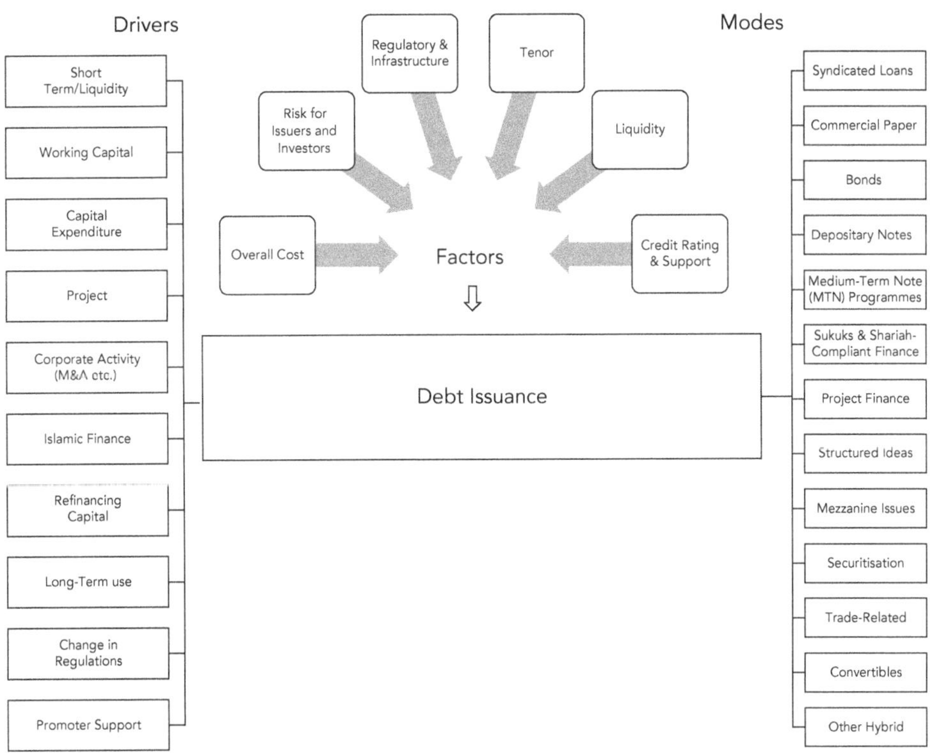

FIGURE 13.5 Debt Financing Alternatives

Syndications can be of three broad types:

1. **Underwritten.** The arrangers guarantee the entire commitment of capital to the firm (and may charge a premium for doing so).
2. **Best-efforts basis.** The arrangers make a sincere attempt without a written commitment to fulfil the entire obligation, should they not find the necessary corpus of investors and capital.
3. **Club deal.** The issuance (usually of a smaller size) is pre-marketed and agreed on within a group of banks.

Commercial Paper

Commercial paper is a short-term (usually less than 180 days with some exceptions) money market instrument issued by rated companies for working capital and immediate liquidity needs. The paper is usually in the form of an unsecured promissory note.

Bonds

A bond is a fixed income market security issued by a borrower to a lender that brings with it an obligation by the borrower to repay interest and the principal of the bond value based on certain predefined parameters. The coupon payable on the bond could be fixed or variable.

A bond usually can be sold from the holder to another party for a value that is linked to the prevalent market interest rates and the perceived creditworthiness of the issuer and the country of the issuer.

Depositary Receipts or Notes

A depositary receipt (American Depositary Receipt [ADR] in the United States or Global Depositary Receipt [GDR] elsewhere) of a firm is a negotiable financial instrument issued by a financial institution in a country to represent the firm's publicly traded securities to investors overseas. Depositary receipts usually trade on a stock exchange in the country and thus enable overseas investors to procure shares in local firms since the shares of the firms do not leave the country.

Medium-Term Note Programmes

Medium-term notes are 5- to 10-year senior unsecured debt notes issued through a programme that involves one-time documentation with flexible structuring and terms and conditions. The programme enables the issuer to draw down more flexibly and not have to negotiate terms, conditions, and documentation each time there is a need to borrow.

Structured Debt

Structured debt has many characteristics that use financial engineering, documentation and tax, legal, and accounting aspects to suit the cost, profile, and liquidity need of the issuer while matching payoff, risk, and maturity profiles of investors.

Mezzanine Issues

Mezzanine capital is a hybrid instrument in the form of subordinated debt or preferred stock, usually in the form of private placements and of higher cost than simple or vanilla debt (owing to the placement just above equity in the capital structure pecking order).

One of the differentiators of mezzanine capital is in the possibilities of return to investors. Investors can receive:

- Interest or cash payments
- Payment in kind, where the principal amount is increased to the tune of what is owed to the investor as coupon or other repayments
- Equity or increased ownership

Securitisation

Securitisation is the collective term for the pooling and sale of similar types of assets to investors as a package, which is serviced by the payment of coupons or interest and principal based on a repayment schedule of the pool of assets.

Trade-Related Financing

Various trade-related financial supply chain financing alternatives are available. They are covered in Chapter 14.

Distressed Debt

A new type of fund, a distressed debt fund, has emerged that specialises in the provision of high-yielding, high-risk debt to companies in dire need of capital.

We now direct our attention to equity capital markets.

EQUITY CAPITAL MARKETS

Some of the key drivers for raising equity capital remain long-term growth, building up the base of requisitions, adhering to regulatory conditions, or simply to provide an exit for the company's shareholders with the long-term benefit of diversifying the company's shareholding.

Figure 13.6 illustrates various equity issuances and modes. Two key deterrents to incremental equity are control and cost, but the pressure on cash flows to service the issuance is limited and at the discretion of the firm.

In public issues, the firm goes to the public, including institutional and retail investors, to request and convince them to invest in the equity of the firm. The initial public offering route is commonly taken. In this method, a firm that has been privately held thus far chooses to list itself on a stock exchange and be publicly traded. An offer for sale, as compared to a new direct issue, is a public invitation by a sponsoring

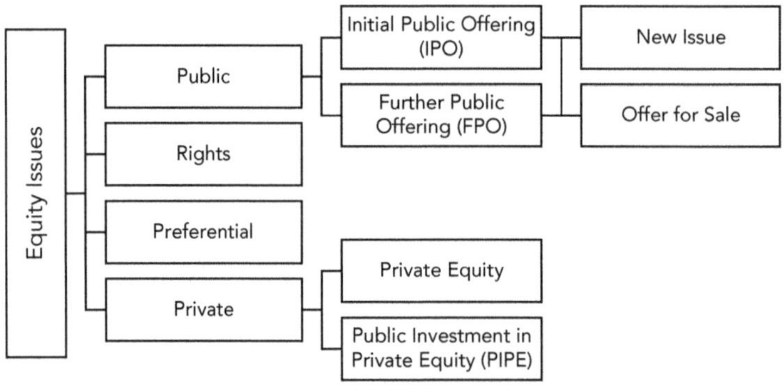

FIGURE 13.6 Equity Issuances

investment bank. Subsequent issuances, also called further public offerings (FPOs), can also go through similar routes.

A rights issue is an issue of an additional set of shares to existing shareholders (based on their interest). This is used to reduce the impact of dilution and also to try to extract more capital from existing shareholders without having to involve a new set of investors or banks for borrowing.

Private placements, of private or public firms, are agreed-on over-the-counter transactions where the investor has agreed to come on board with additional motives of control or subsequent actions and value generation.

We now explore a very interesting case—interesting not only because we are talking about a university (and not a conventional corporation), but also because this entity has taken a decision to start taking on debt.

CASE STUDY: MOVING FROM BEING A SURPLUS ORGANISATION TO A BORROWER

The Experience of Inaugural Debt Facilities at the University of Auckland

Overview

In 2010, the University of Auckland crossed the path from being a surplus organisation to becoming a net borrower. The process involved the development of stakeholder support through research, modeling and development of appropriate Treasury risk management policy and procedures, through to the arrangement of funding facilities and ongoing active Treasury management.

Background

The University of Auckland is ranked among the world's top 100 universities. To continue to achieve this standing, it needs to attract talented staff and students from throughout New Zealand and around the world, and provide them with an environment and facilities that enable and encourage them to teach, learn and research to the best of their abilities.

To support its objectives, the University has a robust programme of development and investment in student and teaching facilities, student accommodation and amenities. To facilitate such growth, within targeted timeframes, a borrowing programme had to be developed and framed.

The Path

The path to becoming a net borrower involves a number of phases. An overview of these phases is shown in Figure 13.7.

As the University had not previously borrowed funds, it was interested in the first instance to understand the level of debt likely to be considered reasonable/prudent and sustainable over the forecast period together with the funding options most suited to its requirements. This was then used to form the basis for a debt strategy or "policy."

The Assessment of Capital Structure

Establishing an appropriate capital structure, and therefore debt thresholds, involved an analysis of "capacity" to service debt and "need" to take on debt.

The capacity to borrow was assessed by analysing:

- Commercial organisations
- Peer universities

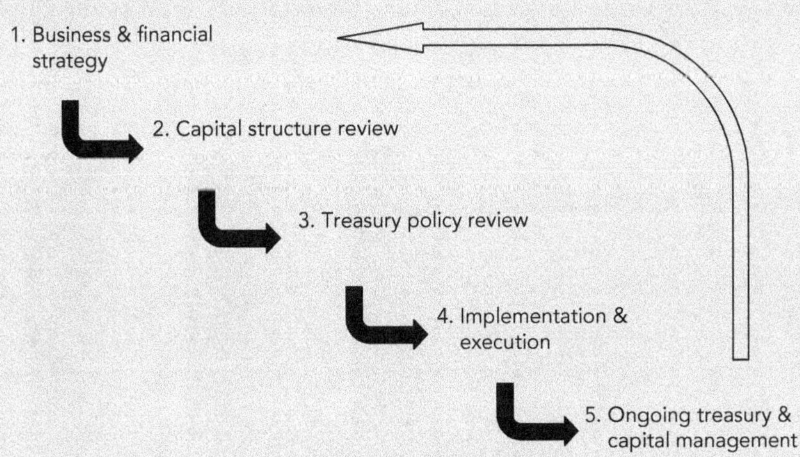

FIGURE 13.7 Bancorp's Five-Stage Path for Evolution from Lender to Borrower

(Continued)

- Indicative credit ratings
- Regulatory restrictions and benchmarks
- Indicative financial covenants

Two pieces of analysis were undertaken. The first involved assessing the relative position of the University against these benchmarks in term of whether it was projected to be in the lower, median or upper quartile; whether it was forecast to be in any 'risk' categories as defined by regulatory ratios; and what its indicative credit rating would be forecast to be and how that compared against the credit ratings of its peers (Figure 13.8).

The second piece of analysis was to apply the key benchmark ratios in reverse by stating the University's view of a reasonable debt level i.e. as being at one of the lower, median or upper quartile in relation to the benchmark group, and apply the selected ratios to determine what level of debt is consistent with that position.

As example of how this could be used is in setting policy, if it would be considered reasonable for the University to take on debt up to a level of, say, the upper quartile of the benchmark universities (assuming the benchmark ratios as set out in the Table 13.1, the corresponding policy would therefore set limits at:

- Debt to EBITDA < 3.1×; and
- Average annual Interest Cover Ratio no less than 6.1×.

This could be applied to peak or average limits and potentially with different thresholds for each, for example a peak threshold of 6.1× Interest Cover and average of 7.8×. Alternatively, this dual threshold approach might be applied against annual variation over the entire forecast period or over periods through the forecast period i.e. a threshold equal to the median but allowance to go to the peak for no more than four years during the forecast period.

This analysis illustrated what the University's projected position would be in relation to the benchmark group, but not what it should be. This raised the question of how to assess what it "should be." Two things, broadly speaking, might be

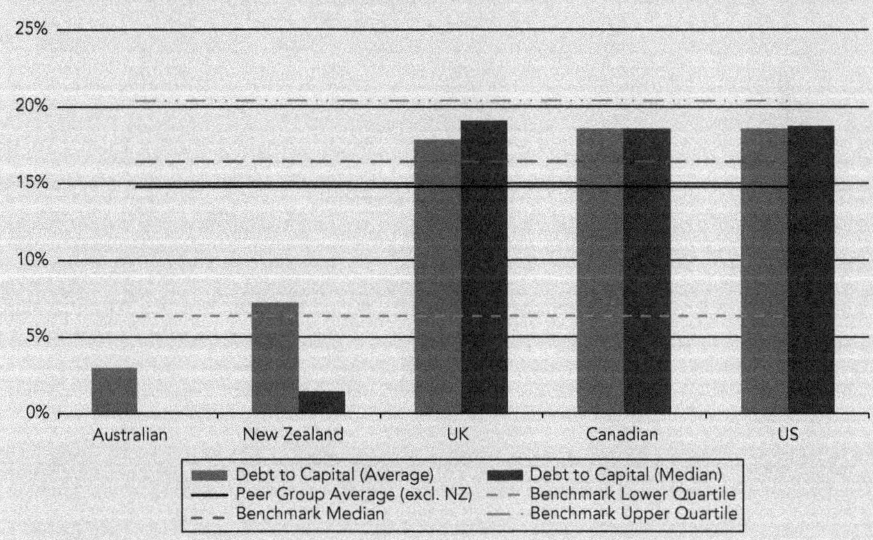

FIGURE 13.8 Historical Debt to Capital Ratio

TABLE 13.1 BENCHMARK UNIVERSITY DEBT INDICATORS

	Upper	Median	Lower	TAMU/NPD
Debt to Capital	20.4%	16.4%	6.3%	< 26%
Interest Cover[1]	6.1×	7.8×	17.9×	> 2.2×
Debt to EBITDA	3.1×	2.2×	0.8×	n/a

[1]Identified as a lower-quartile score for interest cover is an indicator of an upper-quartile level of debt, and vice versa.

considered to drive a university or organisation to choosing a position relative to debt benchmarks: capacity and need. A university or organisation might take a lower quartile position if it had little capacity to support debt, or little need to borrow. Conversely, it might look at an upper quartile position if it had significant debt capacity, or if its strategy or position demanded debt-supported investment.

The need to borrow is more difficult to quantify and measure. The evaluation for the University was completed by considering drivers that might influence the University towards a particular debt position in terms of how much it needed to borrow, as opposed to how much it could borrow. By way of example, Figure 13.9 lists a number of the drivers that might influence a university towards either a lower or upper quartile, or median, debt position in terms of how much it needs to borrow, as opposed to how much it can borrow. The two, obviously, must be reconciled and a position consistent with each adopted, but they should be recognised as separate influences on a debt policy.

In interpreting Figure 13.9, a university has more need, or a greater imperative, to borrow if:

- low or falling revenue levels reduce its ability to fund capex from cashflow, and/or
- endowments fund relatively little capex, and/or
- it faces imperatives to improve its facilities, and/or
- it seeks to protect or improve its ranking.

The University's position was then highlighted against these drivers. The view drawn was that while a number of areas indicated relatively little pressure to borrow, in the majority of instances the University's current position was consistent with a higher than average need to invest, and a higher than average need to borrow to support the necessary level of investment.

Drawing this together with the debt capacity analysis and the fact that the University had strong and embedded financial management and planning disciplines and processes, the policy parameters were proposed.

Overall, the outcome of this review was:

Having determined the "right" capital structure, the University along with its advisers then reviewed various funding options which would meet the University's objectives. This included consideration of bank debt, structured finance, project finance and capital markets funding. It had regard to elements such as funding source and diversity, maturity profile, funding characteristics (e.g. term, flexibility, security, on or off balance sheet, risk transfer etc.) and market environment including pricing and access/availability.

(Continued)

Drivers of Need for Debt			
	Position on Driver Consistent with		
Driver	Lower Quartile Debt	Median Debt	Upper Quartile Debt
Level of Government Funding	High	Average	Low
Trend in Government Funding	Rising	Stable	Falling
Level of Fees	High	Average	
Trend in Fees	Rising	Stable	
Level of Endowments	High		
Deferred Maintenance	Little		
Quantity of Space Available	Sufficient		

Notes:

Indicates current assessment

FIGURE 13.9 Drivers of Need for Debt

A further consideration in relation to funding options and implementation was whether a credit rating would be of benefit. For certain funding options it is essential and therefore the process and costs (both upfront and ongoing) were taken into account when assessing these.

The Development of a Treasury Policy

The next step involved translating the debt thresholds into a policy and establishing the governance necessary to manage debt. This required:

1. Consideration of Treasury management issues as they relate to a debt management Treasury policy including funding, liquidity, interest rate risk, and internal management/authorities as well as IFRS hedge accounting impacts.
2. Establishment and documentation of a debt management Treasury policy.
3. Liaising with regulatory bodies.

Implementation

The fourth stage of the process was the implementation of the preferred funding option. A tender approach was employed to maximise competitive tension and the prospects for optimal terms and conditions for the university. This involved, with the help of advisers, drafting of a request for proposal (RFP) and accompanying "Information Memorandum" and data pack for interested parties, the review of proposals, short-listing and selecting the preferred funding parties, and the negotiation of terms and conditions and management of external parties (e.g., legal advisers) to ensure the process was successfully completed and funding put in place.

Key Considerations for the University

Fundamental change in position. The University had been a net investor. The shift to becoming a net borrower presented not only a shift in mindset for the University and its various stakeholders, but also the need for development of the necessary policies and procedures to enable and continue to support this transition.

Aligned solution. The University had a number of key elements it [required/sought] from a funding solution. These included certainty of funding—the comfort that it had funding in place before embarking on such a significant capital programme; minimisation of cost—to recognise the capped funding environment and low operating margin; flexibility and the ability to match the university's cash flow profile and growing debt profile resulting from the seasonal nature of student enrolments and the progressive development of capital projects.

Successful outcome. Given the position of the university and the scale of the financing and projects to be undertaken with the funding it was critical that the process was successful. A major factor in this was the development and buy-in by stakeholders—government, council, staff, students, and ultimately financiers—as to the rationale, prudence and then implementation and risk management

Outcome

The university issued a request for proposal for bank debt facilities in late 2010. Following strong interest from funders, the university successfully established bilateral bank facilities with two large regional banks.

Key Learnings

- Establish a robust strategic plan and financial planning model.
- Engage with stakeholders early.

Contributed by Dean Sharrar, director, Bancorp, Treasury Services, and Derek Phillips, director, Bancorp Corporate Finance. Bancorp (a provider of Treasury, banking and corporate finance advice) developed and implemented the end-to-end strategy and execution for the University of Auckland.

SUMMARY

In this chapter, we looked at the capital structure and various modes of raising capital. We discussed why cost of capital may not be the only determinant of capital structure and other factors to be considered. Debt and equity capital markets and fundraising also were surveyed.

CHAPTER FOURTEEN

14 Financing the Supply Chain

IN THIS CHAPTER, we take on the concepts learned earlier in Chapter 11, and look at some of the solutions available for financing the supply chain today. We start by looking at financing across various legs of the supply chain, and the elements of risk associated with each. We look at creating a supply chain risk index and conclude with a case study on assessing credit risk of the suppliers, an area in which Treasury teams are now getting more involved.

PHYSICAL AND FINANCIAL SUPPLY CHAINS

Technological advancements and service sector capability growth has begun to fully integrate the physical and financial supply chains. For each leg or element of the physical supply chain (see Figure 14.1), there is a corresponding equivalent arm of the financial supply chain that provides support, liquidity, and communication to enable the physical supply chain to work more smoothly and seamlessly than in the past.

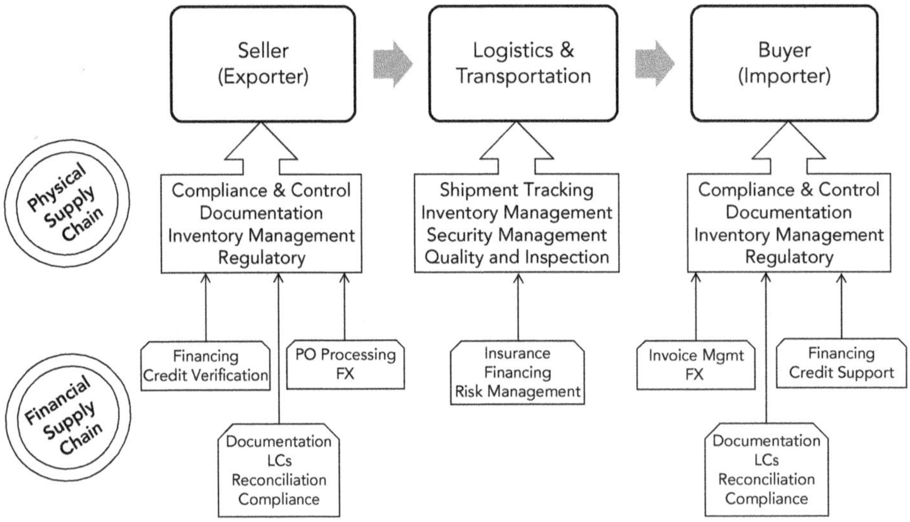

FIGURE 14.1 Integration of the Physical and Financial Supply Chains

The growth of value-added services apart from regular banking products and the long-term thinking of institutions and the trade have resulted in a number of pioneering activities and processes to reduce uncertainty and processing effort, and increase visibility and speed financial settlements for all concerned parties. These span the areas of financing, processing, regulatory, compliance, and risk management.

Some of the determinants of smooth flow in the evolution are:

- **Credit risk.** The innovation and documentation in the field of credit risk management has driven a number of solutions regarding credit risk assessment, measurement, tracking, transfer, and mitigation methods.
- **Technology.** Imaging, data transfer speeds, reliability, and integration across systems have accelerated the inclusion of technology into the supply chain. Instruments now do not have to travel physically for scrutiny or verification, and transactions can be processed without paper at the click of a few buttons. With different vendors and customers on the same platform (such as in an electronic invoice and bill payment), or with different systems being integrated, the participants in the supply chain can verify, negotiate, execute, and pay quickly and seamlessly.
- **Outsourcing and business process efficiency.** Bank and specialised institutions have made processing a core competency—handling huge volumes with amazing accuracy and cost efficiency driven by economies of scale. Many processes that were tedious to execute, expensive to staff, and provided multiple opportunities for error, owing to specialisation or scale required, have now become candidates for outsourcing or automation, or both.

DIFFERENT FINANCING SOLUTIONS

The world of banking, markets, and finance has evolved considerably over time. This evolution presents a number of alternatives for firms to consider, based on the market, need, cost, and credit.

Basic Processes and Considerations of Financing Type

Depending on the process followed and various parameters, the type of financing can be determined. Some of the processes and considerations for financing the supply chain are provided in Figure 14.2. These include:

- **Sale.** The underlying transactions themselves and the location and access of both buyer and seller as well as the source and destination of the goods or services
- **Documentation.** Which document is going to be used as the underlying for the funding, and what incremental documentation is necessary for the purpose of funding itself?
- **Funding.** Who provides the funding, whether it is partial and whether it is discounted, and in which currency it is paid?
- **Ownership (title).** Who has ownership of the goods, is there a transfer of ownership itself?

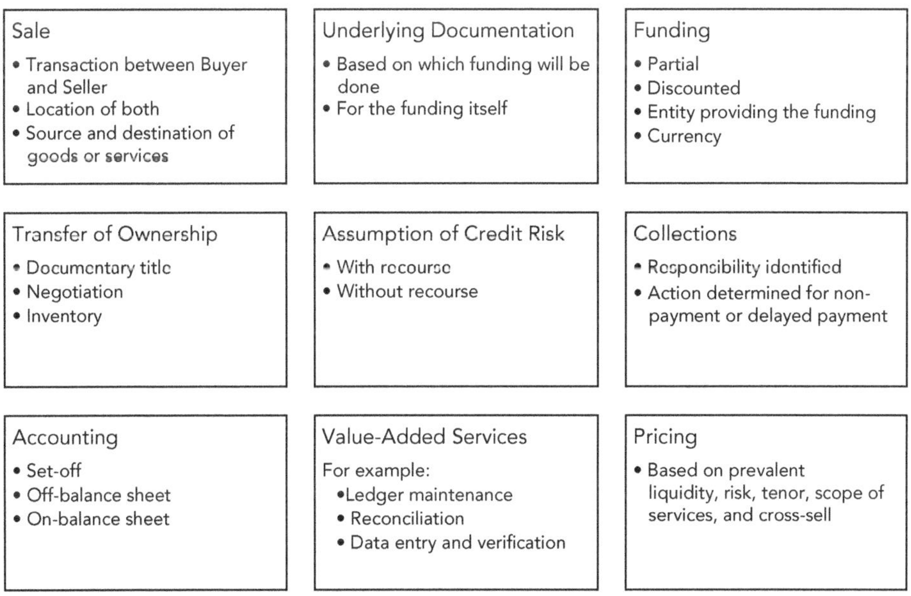

FIGURE 14.2 Processes and Considerations for Financing the Supply Chain

- **Assumption of credit risk.** Who assumes the credit risk: the funding entity, the seller, or a third party, and is the funding with recourse to the seller or without recourse?
- **Accounting treatment.** Does the funding and transfer of ownership cause the receivable to move off the seller's books, or can there be a setoff of the asset with the corresponding liability?
- **Responsibility for collections.** Does responsibility for collections of proceeds against which the funding is being done remain with the seller, or is it transferred to the funding entity or a third party?
- **Value-added services.** Are any value-added services provided by the entity—for example, reconciliation or ledger entry posting?
- **Pricing.**

We now explore the various funding alternatives.

Funding Alternatives

Figure 14.3 depicts various funding alternatives in the financial supply chain. Depending on the type of end use, the recipient of the financing, the kind of risk and underlying, regulatory environment, and techniques involved, the various alternatives are classified as shown in the figure. Financing may be in the following categories.

- **Trade based** are of different types depending on export or import, pre- or post-shipment for export.
- **Receivables based** conceptually use existing receivables or documents to raise cash prior to settlement.
- **Entity based** are specifically chalked out programmes for specific entities, such as suppliers, distributors, customers, etc. based on the recipient, companies, or banks.
- **Inventory** comprised of warehouse (bonded or non-bonded) and inventory can be financed based on requirements and types of inventory.
- **Securitisation** use a stream of similar receivables that are purchased by financial institutions with or without recourse, title, and collections responsibility.
- **Specialised transactions** can be of different types, such as factoring, forfaiting, and ECA financing, covered in detail in the section "Some Alternatives in Detail."

There are various sources to fund the supply chain. These include:

- Commercial banks
- Governments and government agencies
- Export credit agencies
- Financial institutions
- Trade associations
- Factoring houses
- Development banks
- Multilateral agencies

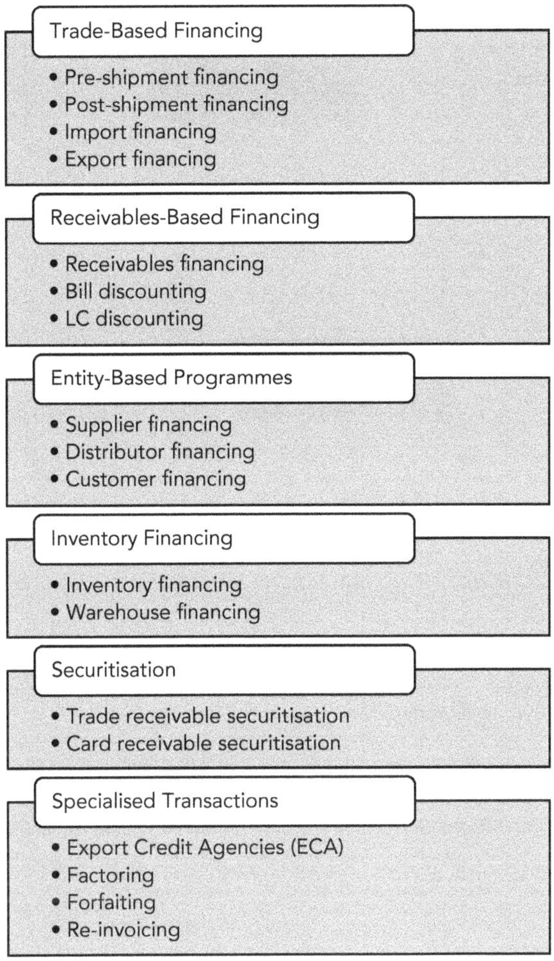

FIGURE 14.3 Funding Alternatives

Some Alternatives in Detail

Some common funding alternatives that have developed over time are discussed next.

Bill Discounting

Bill discounting is the type of financing when the legal holder of a bill (a commercial bill, such as a banker's acceptance draft or commercial acceptance draft) transfers it to a funding entity (such as a bank) to obtain cash (at a value discounted for the interest for the period) prior to its maturity date (see Figure 14.4).

Bill discounting is usually with recourse, with the drawer of the bill (the entity that is receiving the money) having the responsibility for collections. A bill may be discounted several times, but each discounting is for that bill only (i.e., each transaction involves one bill and not a group or set of bills). Discounting also does not assign ownership and keeps the asset on the balance sheet of the drawer.

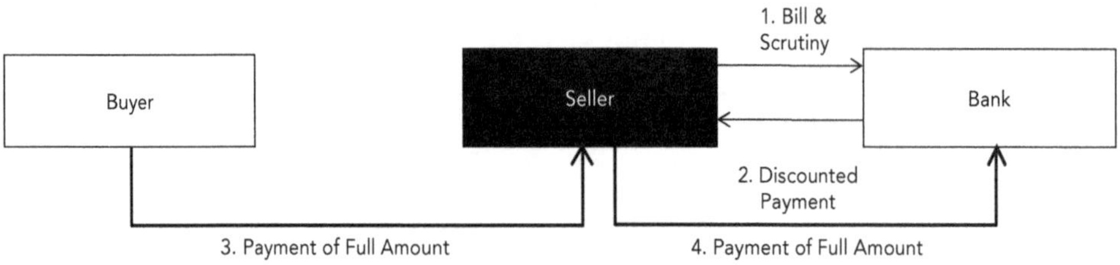

FIGURE 14.4 Bill Discounting

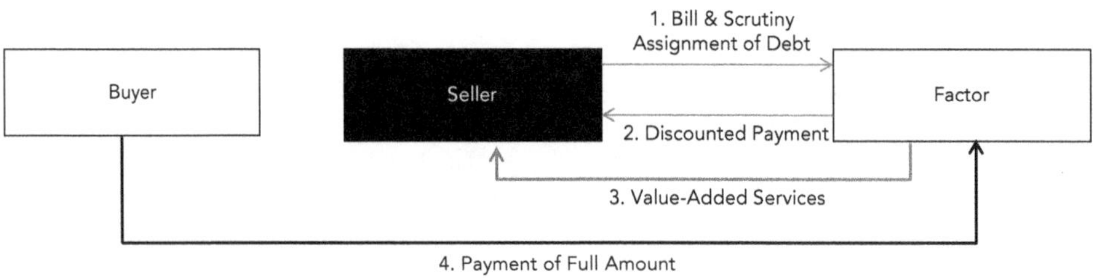

FIGURE 14.5 Factoring

TABLE 14.1 Differences Between Factoring and Bill Discounting

Aspect	Bill Discounting	Factoring
Credit Risk	With recourse	With or without recourse
Collections responsibility	Seller	Factor
Re-discounting	Possible	Not possible (refinancing may be allowed)
Accounting	On balance sheet for seller	Can be off balance sheet
Individual or portfolio	Each bill, individually	As a portfolio
Assignment of debt	None	Can be done in favour of the factor
Value-add	None	Data entry, validation, advisory, reconciliation, ledger entry posting, etc.

Factoring

Factoring of receivables is the purchase of a receivable or bill from the seller of goods or services, where the paying entity ("factor") assumes responsibility for the collection of receivables (see Figure 14.5) and in some cases the credit risk as well.

Factoring can be done on a portfolio of receivables or assets and can be both on a recourse and nonrecourse basis, where the assignment of debt happens in the name of the factor. The item then could move out from the balance sheet of the seller.

Table 14.1 shows some of the differences between bill discounting and factoring.

Factoring Centre The factoring centre is a credit management tool used by companies with intercompany sales or closely monitored sales and collection processes (see Figure 14.6).

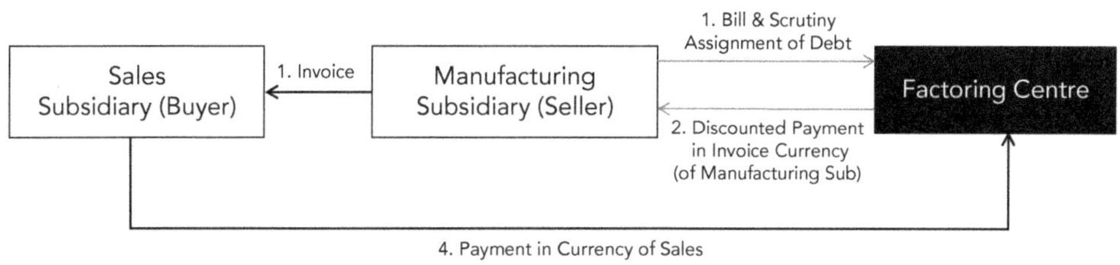

FIGURE 14.6 Factoring Centre

The process flow for the operations of the factoring centre, which is typically a subsidiary at a central location, is described next.

- The factoring centre buys the receivables from the manufacturing subsidiary after the invoice has been issued.
- The factoring centre immediately pays the manufacturing subsidiary the discounted amount in the currency of invoice (invoice of the manufacturing subsidiary); this could include the cost allocation of funding (liquidity) and risk management.
- The factoring centre collects the full payment from the sales subsidiary (buyer) in the currency of the buying entity on the due date.

Factoring centres offer several advantages. These include:

- The factoring centre allows sales and manufacturing subsidiaries to run their own manufacturing cycles and cash conversion cycles while concentrating liquidity risk centrally.
- Coupled with a Treasury centre, the foreign exchange risk management also gets addressed. Both subsidiaries in the channel are made immune to currency risk with the centre taking on all responsibility.
- Any sudden liquidity on the buyer's side can be handled with delayed payment without impacting the manufacturing subsidiary.

Forfaiting

Forfaiting, a term derived from the French word for "forfeit," is a transaction-based funding operation where a seller or exporter sells one of its trade bills or promissory notes without recourse. In a forfaiting transaction, the evidence of debt will always be endorsed to the paying party as a holder in due course, which allows the seller recourse to the payer at maturity under most laws.

The key difference between forfaiting and bill discounting is the recourse element—discounting is with recourse to the drawer. Also, the discounting usually happens for a specific period, and the seller pays the bank maturity of the bill.

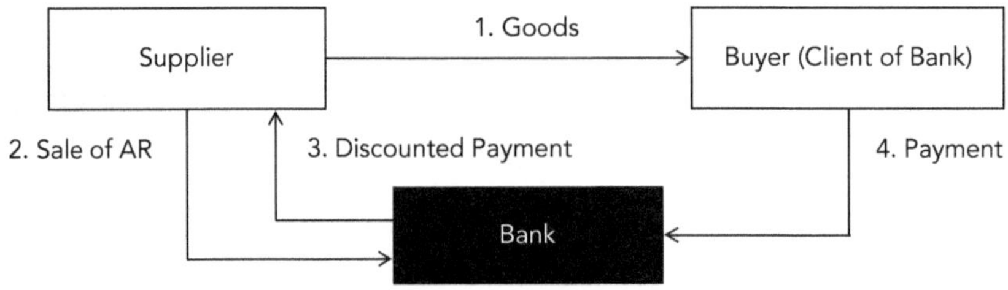

FIGURE 14.7 Supplier Financing

Supplier Financing

Supplier financing is the general term used for the early settlement to the suppliers of a large company's payables by a bank that acts as a lender by buying over the receivables of the supplier (and hence payables for the company). The company will then settle the payment on the due date directly to the bank (see Figure 14.7).

Different forms of supplier financing are available, and many banks run supplier financing programmes with pre-approved credit limits for weaker suppliers of large corporate clients. Supplier financing enables the corporate to reduce its days payables outstanding and cash conversion cycle and hence its need for working capital.

The suppliers hence get provided with more liquidity at possibly more favourable terms and cost since the bank has effectively substituted the suppliers' credit rating with the superior rating of the large corporate.

Many banks offer incremental value-added services, such as automation with suppliers, payment order processing, reconciliation, tracking, and payment services along with the regular supplier financing solutions.

Export Credit Agency Financing

Export credit agencies (ECAs) are private or quasi-governmental financial institutions set up to encourage and support exports from a country by providing financing linked to exports by entities from that country. ECAs act as intermediaries between national governments and exporters to facilitate the financial supply chain.

Depending on the agreement with the government, ECA financing can be of three different forms:

1. Credit or direct funding
2. Credit insurance
3. Guarantees

The funding is generally provided to an importer at market or better-than-market prices in order to incentivise the importer to buy from the exporter in the ECA's country.

ECA Credit ECAs employ three different funding methods:

1. Direct lending
2. Intermediary loans, where the ECA funds or guarantees an intermediary, such as a commercial bank, which funds the importer
3. Interest rate equalisation, where the ECA provides the importer's lending bank a subsidy on interest cost to be passed on to the importer for loans taken to fund imports from sellers in the ECA's country

ECA Credit Insurance ECA credit insurance covers, to an extent, commercial and political risk of nonpayment of the underlying transaction.

Commercial risks covered include:

- Buyer insolvency
- Failure to pay by due date (including a grace period)
- Importer's unwillingness to fulfil contract terms although exporter has complied

Political risks covered include:

- Changes in trade regulations and laws
- Bilateral or multilateral political issues, such as cancellations, embargoes, sanctions, and other aspects outside the control of the buyer and the exporter.

ECA Guarantees ECAs are generally meant for banks in the country that are providing financing to support exports. These guarantees encourage banks to take on additional risk for situations where they might have been reluctant to extend credit, such as for small companies (see Figure 14.8). Such guarantees are especially useful during credit or liquidity squeezes, such as during the Asian crisis in the late 1990s.

Re-Invoicing

Re-invoicing, although not technically a component of supply chain finance, is an interesting addition to the value chain. Its aim is to reduce overall group outflows and thereby increase profitability (see Figure 14.9).

The re-invoicing centre buys the product and takes ownership from the manufacturing subsidiary, which makes a small profit on the transaction. The re-invoicing centre does not take possession of the goods but pays the manufacturing subsidiary immediately and simultaneously invoices (or re-invoices) the sales subsidiary (which is selling the product to the end customer). The goods are shipped directly to the sales entity on instruction from the re-invoicing centre, the customer of the manufacturing subsidiary.

The payment to the manufacturing subsidiary is in the invoice currency (currency of the manufacturing entity). The invoice and payment from the sales subsidiary could be in the sales currency, with the residual risk being managed by the re-invoicing centre.

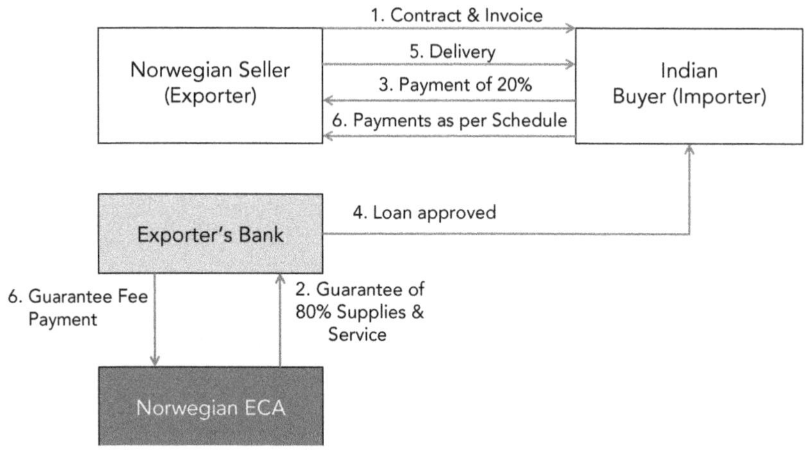

FIGURE 14.8 ECA Guarantees

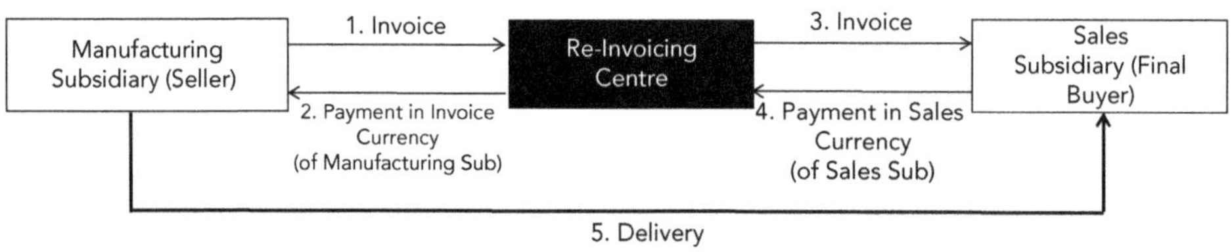

FIGURE 14.9 Re-Invoicing Centre

The re-invoicing centre uses the tax arbitrage between locations, since the re-invoicing is done from a location that is more tax efficient than the manufacturing location. This method is obviously not viewed favourably by the tax authorities in the country of manufacturing, and must be implemented with care owing to regulatory and compliance sensitivity.

CASE STUDY: SUPPLY CHAIN RISK INDEX (SUPPLIER SIDE)

This case concerns how a company can start its own supply chain risk index. Although the case discussed is on the supplier side, the same approach can be used to develop intelligence on the customer side.

The concept of risk across its four areas—business risk, financial risk, operations and technology risk, and event risk—is discussed in detail in Part Four of this book. Here we discuss the points relevant to the supply chain index in the context of identifying and monitoring risk on the supplier side (see Figure 14.10).

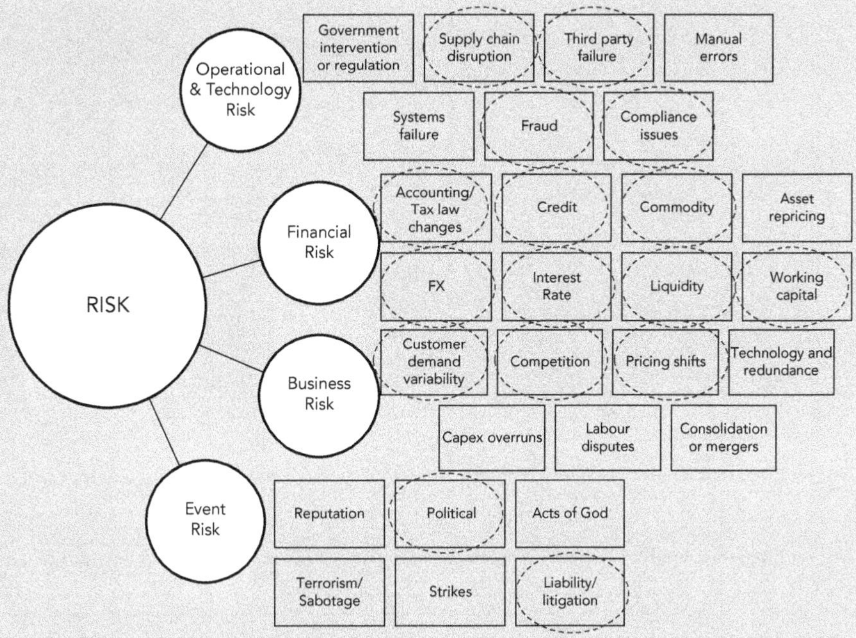

FIGURE 14.10 Risks Relevant to the Supplier Side of the Supply Chain

The risks that are circled on Figure 14.10 are those most relevant to the supplier side of the supply chain. They can be captured through four input channels (see Figure 14.11):

1. External survey of finance team and management of suppliers
2. Internal feedback of members of the procurement team
3. Market factors that are measurable inputs derived directly from market sources
4. Supplier intelligence through banks, industry sources, and market reports

The index can serve as a useful input to management by providing early-warning signals and visibility into the situation on the ground. It uses objective inputs along with behavioural and subjective inputs from the supplier, buyer, and neutral sources to obtain an optimal and balanced quantitative assessment of the situation in each market, country or environment. Typically, a segment in a country will have its individual scores.

Figure 14.12 shows the various inputs across the channels.

The inputs are fed and scored on a scale of –2 to +2 as follows. The scores for each input/question from the external survey, internal feedback, and market intelligence can be:

- Very negative (score of –2)
- Slightly negative (score of –1)
- Neutral (score of 0)
- Slightly positive (score of +1)
- Very positive (score of +2)

Inputs from market factors can be normalised to a scale based on the numbers.

(Continued)

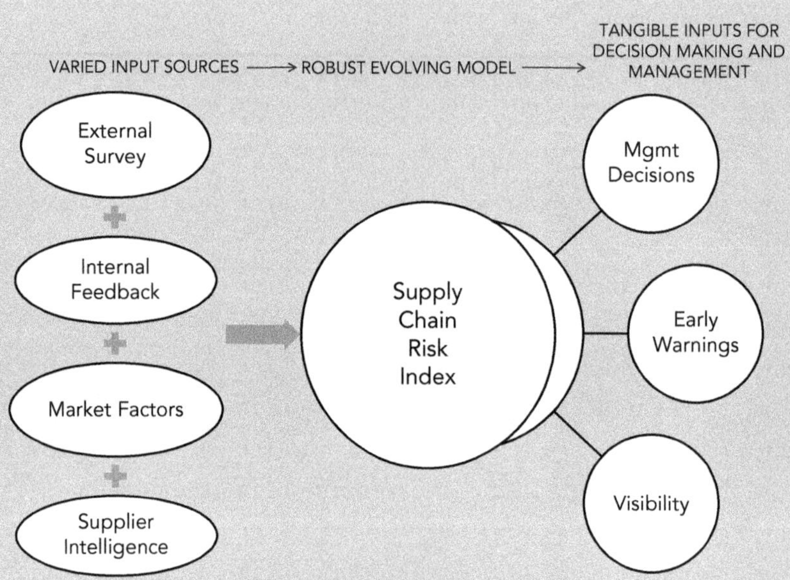

FIGURE 14.11 Input Channels and Structure of Risk Index

Each input is weighted, and a score obtained between –100 and +100. A score less than zero indicates a heightened risk level. A score close to –100 indicates an impending market disaster. A positive score indicates confidence with the environment and a low risk level.

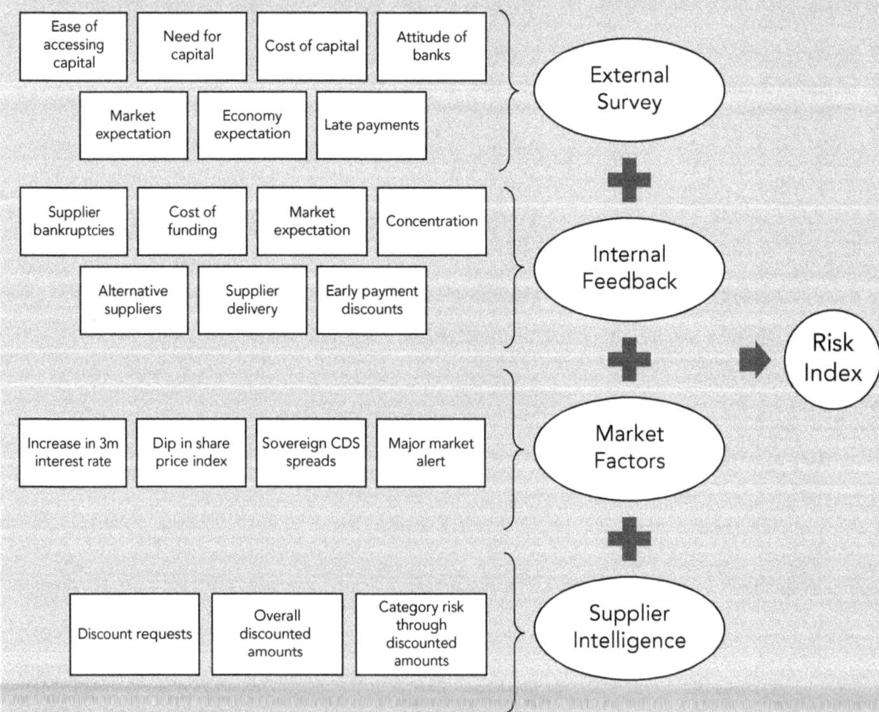

FIGURE 14.12 Inputs to Each Channel in the Index

SUMMARY

This chapter discussed the linkages between the physical and financial supply chains and their funding alternatives. We also explored the creation of a supply chain risk index and how it can be used to assess the credit risk and potential needs of the supplier.

While many alternatives exist in the supply chain financing suite, the intelligent use and the documentary elegance of the solution chosen determines the efficacy and final profitability impact of the method used.

CHAPTER FIFTEEN

Managing Operating Cash and Investments

THIS CHAPTER OUTLINES THE USES of cash available to the company. There are different cash levels, and each has its own utility and purpose, based on which investment themes can be outlined. We discuss the management of operating cash and of investments beyond the immediate horizon, highlighting key principles and practices that could be of use while formulating tactics and strategies for the same.

DIFFERENT ELEMENTS OF CASH

Cash on the balance sheet can be divided by the Treasurer, based on need and longevity of expected stay on the balance sheet. The different elements of cash on the balance sheet are delineated in Figure 15.1.

From the cash available for use to the firm, the various elements are:

- Strategic or business cash
- Restricted cash
- Reserve cash
- Operating cash

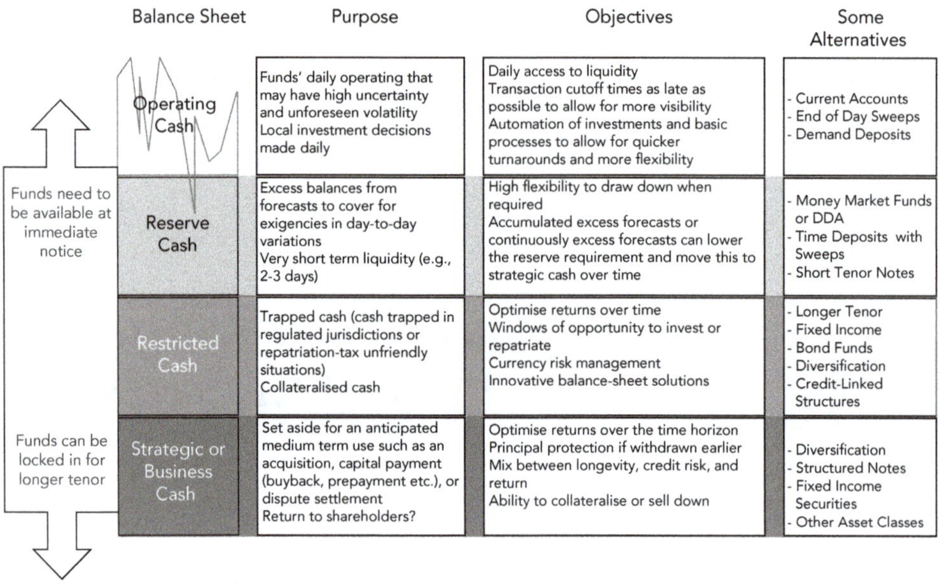

FIGURE 15.1 Different Elements of Cash

Strategic or business cash is the long-term cash that is being kept for a specific purpose, such as an acquisition or capital payment. Here we assume that the cash that is not going to be required for an identified purpose or incident will be returned to the shareholders from the strategic or business cash.

Restricted cash is the cash that is in a particular location for a reason—say to support a financial transaction for the business (such as collateral) or as a consequence of doing business in a country (trapped cash).

Reserve cash is a buffer that is held to allow for forecasting variations and to use if operating cash is fully utilised.

Operating cash is the cash required to run the operations on a day-to-day basis. Because it is the most volatile type of cash, the need for planning, forecasting, visibility, and operational efficiency is greatest here. Because decisions on operating cash are made daily, it is important that there is time flexibility to make these decisions.

First we discuss operating cash, and then we cover the other types of cash.

MANAGING OPERATING CASH

As cash flows enter the financials and become cash (see Figure 15.2), the cash gets redeployed for various uses. From a day-to-day perspective, the working of the firm is managed through cash available hence operating cash is always kept for immediate use.

Because liquidity has to be almost immediate and visibility must be maximum for a geographically dispersed group with a large presence in emerging markets that have money flow regulations, it could be useful to manage operating cash locally, with some reserve.

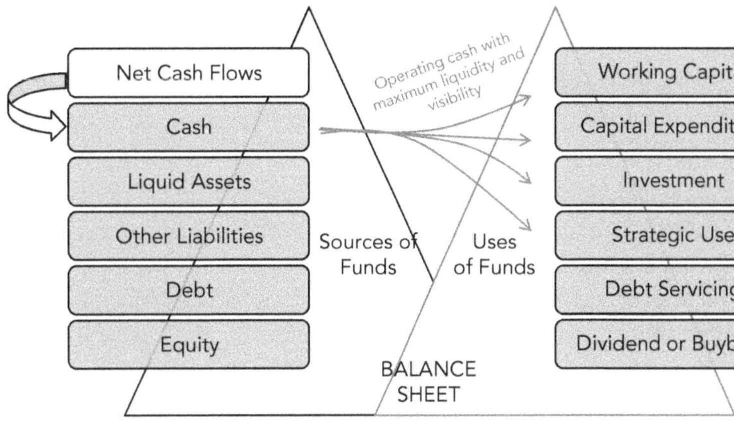

FIGURE 15.2 Operating Cash in the Context of the Balance Sheet

From a process and banking capability perspective, it is important to have in place:

- Daily access to liquidity
- Transaction cutoff times for operations as late as possible to allow for more visibility
- Automation of investments and basic processes to allow for quicker turnarounds and more flexibility

Typical banking products used with operating cash include end-of-day sweeps into overnight deposits, demand deposits, or simply leaving the money in a current account, should a country have a minimum investment period for deposits.

Since liquidity is the prime driver of operating cash, investment return or interest received should take a backseat if the Treasurer has to prioritise.

Here we highlight the importance of short-term cash flow forecasting. If forecasts show less funds than is actually the case, there is an opportunity loss of funds that are obtaining suboptimal yields. If this forecasting error has been consistent, the Treasurer will consider lowering the operating cash required and moving the excess to any other cash element. If, in contrast, the forecasts show more funds than is the actual case, the Treasurer will always be dipping into the reserve cash pool or borrowing from the local markets, as required, which may not be optimal for the firm. Thus, the Treasurer must set the levels of each cash element after examining the actual requirements, historical performance, and forecasting accuracy.

The currencies and entities with which the money is being placed or invested are also important drivers in the process. Similar processes and monitoring will have to be followed as indicated in the process for investments that we explore later in the chapter.

SURPLUS CASH AND INVESTMENTS

The three elements of cash that are not to be placed with immediate liquidity—reserve cash, restricted cash, and strategic or business cash—are grouped under the name "surplus" cash and generally are invested with both tenor and liquidity in mind.

Reserve cash is effectively the excess balance from forecasts to cover exigencies in day-to-day variations and account for investments with very short term liquidity (up to three days or a week maximum). When a large inflow does not come in or a sudden unforecasted payment has to be made or a forecasted payment advanced, reserve cash is the first source that the Treasurer turns to on falling short of operating cash. This requires high flexibility to draw down when required. Accumulated or continuously excess forecasts can lower the reserve requirement. The Treasurer can move these funds to strategic cash over time or return the money to shareholders, should the minimum amount for other elements be met.

Restricted cash can be either *trapped cash* (cash trapped in regulated jurisdictions or countries where attempts to repatriate cash face tax-unfriendly situations) and *collateralised cash*. The Treasurer looks for opportunities to use restricted cash in a net borrowing at another location and in doing so, get these funds set off from the balance sheet. Hence, while waiting for windows of opportunity to invest in the same country or repatriate back to the parent, the Treasurer will seek to optimise returns over time and also manage the currency aspect since the money is likely to be held in a local currency in that country.

Strategic or business cash is the cash that is held for an anticipated medium-term use, such as an acquisition, capital payment (buyback, prepayment, etc.), or dispute settlement. If the event does not take place, shareholders will expect the money to be paid back to them. Hence, a chief executive officer and chief financial officer will have to be very sure of the strategic cash being held when defending the strategy to the board and shareholders.

CONSIDERATIONS AND ASPECTS OF INVESTMENT DECISIONS

Figure 15.3 provides some of the aspects and considerations of investment decisions.

We discuss each of the considerations in detail. The term *issuer* is a generic term for the entity that accepts the investment or with whom the final investment is made. This could include a bank accepting a deposit.

Drivers

The key objectives and motivations behind the investment decision have to be reviewed in detail. They could be principal protection, returns, benchmarks, or tenors and end use.

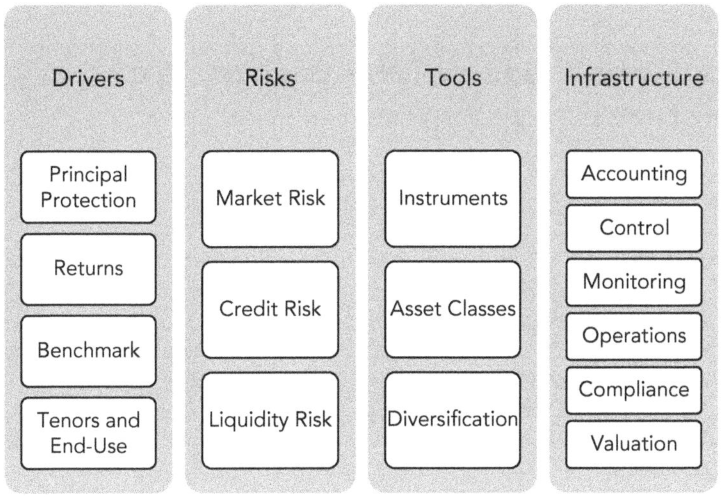

FIGURE 15.3 Investment Decision Considerations and Aspects

Principal Protection One definition of principal protection is that in any scenario, on maturity, the investor gets back, *at minimum*, the principal amount initially invested in the initial currency of investment, even if the interest or return paid is zero.

One of the underlying risks assumed is that the investee or deposit taker is solvent and can pay back the deposit or investment at maturity. However, if the deposit or investment is linked to the credit of another party (credit-linked note), and there is a possibility on paper that the investor will not get back 100% of the invested amount, the note is not principal protected.

All investments for companies with a conservative approach should be principal protected. Structured investments (outlined later in the chapter) are any nonvanilla investments that have a payoff that is variable, other than a simple floating rate.

The other important aspect of principal protection is the currency of investment. The principal returned must, at the time of maturity, be at least equal to the principal originally invested and in the same currency. Some interesting products, such as dual-currency deposits, claim to be principal protected, but in some scenarios they pay out the principal in a different currency from the invested one. When converted back to the original currency at maturity, the investor could be surprised to find that the amount could be lower.

The box below provides a peek into the mechanics of a simple principal protected structured investment.

How Does Principal Protection Work in a Structured Investment?

Principal protection as achieved by an issuer of a note or a bank with a principal-protected structured deposit can be created as shown in Figure 15.4.

In the first step, the issuer determines the current zero-coupon investment principal for that tenor. This is the principal amount. If invested with an AAA-rated issuer or the bank's own funding desk for that tenor, it returns a total value of 100. In the example given, we have assumed that the principal of USD 97 when invested for a period of one year provides a payback of USD 100 at maturity; this investment is made.

In the next step, the issuer buys options in the desired market with the rest of the amount (i.e., USD 3). (In this example we have assumed that the issuer takes no fee for the transaction; in reality, issuers do take the fee for the transaction from this amount and use the rest to buy the option.)

At the end of the period, if the option has expired worthless, the issuer returns the USD 100 from the first step to the investor. If the option has generated value, the issuer passes on the payoff generated to the investor.

In consolidation, the investor sees (a) a return of 100 (the principal invested) at the end in a worst-case scenario, or (b) a return of 100 plus the payoff, should the option have generated money.

The credit risk of the issuer still remains with the investor.

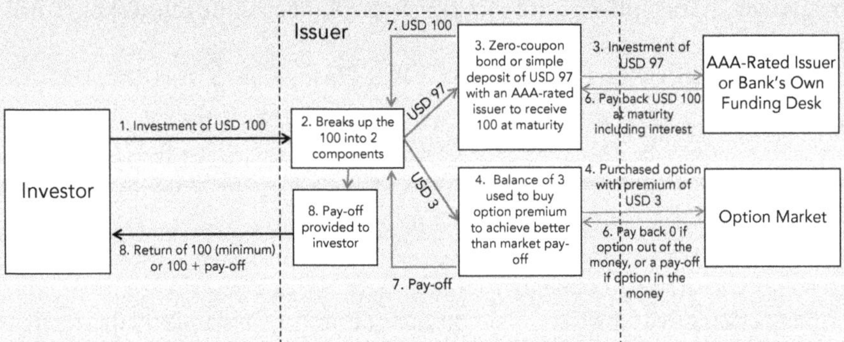

FIGURE 15.4 Sample Principal-Protected Structured Investment

It is important to evaluate principal protection in all scenarios prior to making an investment decision. Buying equities outright, for example, does not ensure principal protection; buying a simple bond and holding it through to maturity does ensure principal protection, provided the issuer does not default.

Liquidity Investment liquidity is the ability to immediately convert the investment to cash. This is an important objective for most investors, especially corporate treasuries, and is covered more in the section on liquidity risk and in Part Four.

Returns and Benchmark In conservative situations, the return objective should be lower in priority than principal protection and liquidity.

Returns have to be quantified in annualised terms and measured with respect to the original currency of investment or in terms of the base currency of the company at a consolidated level. It is critical to evaluate the payoff profile of an investment under all scenarios.

Also, if the payoff is exceptional, and much better than a simple market investment for that tenor, the investor should look at the payoff again: What is it that is being given up?

As Milton Friedman said, there is no such thing as a free lunch. In order to make a probabilistic return that is much better than the market, some risk is being taken. The only scenarios where returns can be locked in for minimal risk is arbitrage, and in today's global markets, many practitioners come in to reduce and eliminate arbitrage almost as soon as it is created.

Depending on the objectives of the investments, these returns can be measured against a benchmark, an internally fixed budget or simply from the perspectives of principal protection, availability, and liquidity.

Tenors Determined by Cash Elements Tenors are determined by the elements of cash that are being invested. For operating cash, the timelines have to be overnight or on demand, at best. For strategic or business cash, tenors can be a little longer.

Callability is a feature that has become quite popular. When an investment is callable, the bank or issuer has the ability to call the investment back and pay the cash with returns back to the investor at points before maturity. For this option, the issuer pays the investor a better return. The investor must realise that the incremental return is effectively the price of the option that the investor has sold to the issuer. What should the tenor of this investment be? To mitigate interest rate or rollover risk (discussed in Part Four), the investment must be treated as the lowest possible tenor: that is, getting the money back when rates have moved lower. From a liquidity perspective, conservative investors should take the tenor of the investment as the maximum or maturity period, since it must be assumed that the investor will hold on to funds in a period of tight liquidity, thereby locking in the amount for the full tenor.

Risks

We explore the various risks in Part Four of this book. Here we highlight some of the important points.

Market Risk Market risk is the risk that the instrument or investment payoff will change with a change in market factors (e.g., foreign exchange, interest rates, commodities, etc.). For a note linked to credit-derivative prices, the movement of the credit default swap spreads related to the note can also be defined as a market risk.

Credit Risk Credit risk is the risk that the issuer will not be able to pay back the investment principal and returns at maturity. One aspect to consider here is leverage, where an investment is taken back as collateral to fund further investments in the same note. This is not a conservative investment practice; while it increases returns substantially on theoretically the same market elements, it also introduces borrowing elements that have to be accounted for.

Liquidity Risk Liquidity risk is the ability to generate cash from the investments at any point of time. The liquidity of the market, i.e., the ability to sell or liquidate the investment in the market or with the original or different counterparty at immediate notice, is a critical determinant of the investment itself. We cover liquidity risk and its measurement in detail in Part Four.

Tools

There are various investment tools, and we classify them into type or instrument, asset classes, and diversification.

Instruments Some of the various instruments are:

- Current account balances across currencies
- Outright purchases of equities or commodities
- Bank deposits: demand or time
- Structured deposits
- Government securities (bills, bonds)
- Commercial paper
- Corporate or institutional bonds
- Notes from issuers
- Funds
- Derivatives such as options

The various payoff types include:

- Fixed rate
- Simple floating rate
- Structured

A *vanilla investment* is one that has a simple fixed rate or a simple floating rate directly linked to a regular benchmark. A *structured investment* is one that has a payoff derived from some market factor or has some feature (variability of return, currency of investment, variability of maturity, etc.) that differentiates it from the vanilla payoff.

Structured investments generally have some embedded derivative or similar transaction that provides the payoff and that is different from a normal investment. Accounting for structured investments is more complex than accounting for simple products, and the controller must be involved in determining the applicability of these products to the group.

One golden rule that has worked for many companies is not to invest in any product that they themselves cannot price or break up. The more complicated the product, the more opaque its pricing generally is, and the greater the risk if the markets move against the investor.

Asset Classes The various asset classes or investment classes available to the investor are:

- Equity
- Debt (fixed income and money market)
- Credit
- Foreign exchange
- Commodities
- Hybrid (combination of these)
- Funds (Today funds are a separate asset class by themselves, owing to different and varied products, including private equity, hedge funds, mutual funds, etc.)
- Real estate

Diversification Diversification, also covered in detail later in the book, is the spreading of risk (in this case, investments) through conscious analysis, backtesting, view taking, and planning into separate currencies, instruments, issuers, locations, asset classes, and payoff profiles, with the expectation that the mean return will provide the least loss and the most optimal return.

Diversification is employed by companies in manners ranging from the simple (holding current account balances in a few currencies) to the complex (having a very diversified portfolio across the various parameters mentioned earlier).

Infrastructure

The infrastructural aspect of investments, which must be captured across Treasury and accounting policies and operational procedures, are important to get the end-to-end process of investing correct. The infrastructure must be well equipped to handle the volumes, complexity, turnarounds, and products used in the investment. The various components of the infrastructural aspect of investments are:

- Accounting
- Control
- Monitoring
- Operations
- Compliance
- Valuation
- Evaluation

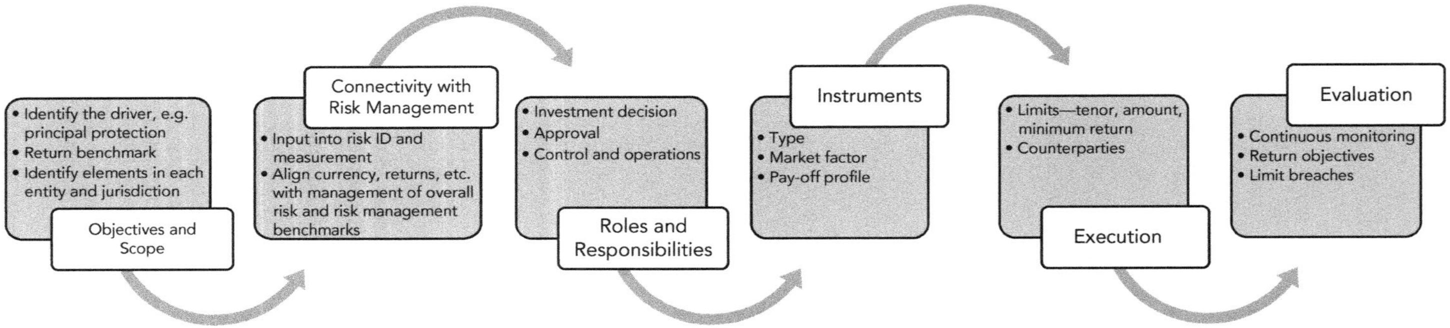

FIGURE 15.5 Investment Process Flow

INVESTMENT PROCESS

Figure 15.5 depicts a simple flowchart for the investment process.

The first step is to define the objectives and the scope of the investment process. For each subsidiary, entity, and jurisdiction, the elements of cash across operational, reserve, restricted, and strategic/business cash are identified and set, along with time horizons of each. The drivers of the investment are then decided—the primary drivers and secondary, if any.

The second step is critical: tie up the investment process with the risk management process. The two should be aligned, since the investment aspect is one part of the overall risk management of the firm, and any action taken on investments will impact the risk profile of the company.

The roles and responsibilities across all areas, including remote decision makers, have to be identified and documented. Responsibility for control, operations, and monitoring also has to be implemented, and can ride on the same infrastructure as the entire Treasury.

The instruments, with descriptions and allowable elements, have to be defined in order to meet the objectives and tenors identified earlier.

For the various elements of cash we discussed in Figure 15.1, operating cash can use the simplest of instruments. For reserve cash, we can explore some other alternatives, such as money market funds, time deposits with sweeps, or short-tenor notes including commercial paper. For restricted cash, locally available instruments or those as determined by the collateralisation agreement would restrict what can be done—hence, tenor could be one area that could add value. In some more adventurous situations, the Treasurer could look at other fixed income structured instruments or notes, bond funds, or even diversification and credit-linked structures that could provide funds to be used in another location through the use of a financial institution's balance sheet. Finally, for strategic or business cash, longer-tenor principal-protected instruments could be explored, as could be diversification or structured notes in other asset classes.

The execution parameters are also defined—limits on counterparty, type of instrument, market factor, tenor, amounts, and so on are all decided and put in place. Mechanisms to track these parameters also should to be implemented. The payoff profile of each investment should be examined and approved, in the case of structured investments.

Finally, the investments have to be monitored and evaluated done. This can be similar to the evaluation process for risk management described in Part Four.

SUMMARY

Investments and use of cash remain among the most important aspects of the treasurer's scope of operations. Geographic diversity, increasing market volatility, and business uncertainty cause the management of investments and cash, especially operating cash, to become an extremely challenging task.

In this chapter, we examined the different elements of cash and how a Treasurer can treat cash differently.

We focused on operating cash, which, because of the imminent liquidity and availability aspect, has to be dealt with differently from other elements of cash. We also looked at various aspects of investment management and concluded with a simple process of investment, which has to be aligned with the firm's overall risk management.

CHAPTER SIXTEEN

Credit Ratings and Bank Credit Assessment

A CORPORATE CREDIT RATING IS a score given to reflect qualitative and quantitative aspects that assess both business and financial risks of corporate issuers of fixed income debt and their individual debt issues. Many large banks have their own methods of assessing corporate debt from a point of view of lending to these corporates. In this chapter, we summarise both approaches and explore some of the factors that a Treasurer can incorporate during review discussions with these entities.

CREDIT RATINGS

A credit rating is generally a score that indicates an independent agency's opinion on the degree of credit risk of an issuer of debt, indicating the agency's assessment of the intention and ability of the issuer to fulfil its debt obligations over a period of time.

Ratings are typically established for short term (generally around a year or lower tenor) or long term, with various types of ratings as given in Figure 16.1.

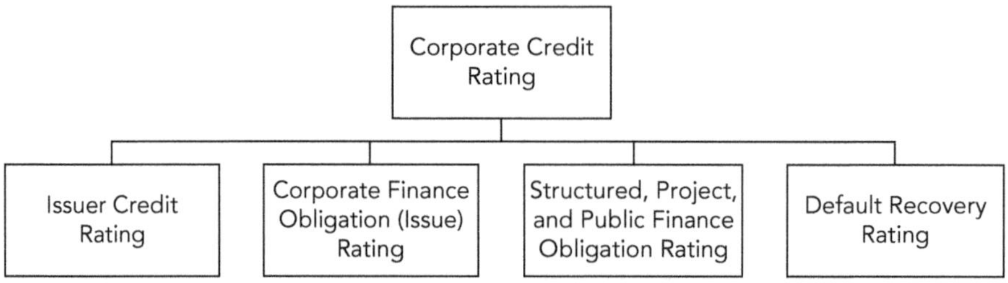

FIGURE 16.1 Different Corporate Ratings

These can be:

- **Issuer ratings.** The individual obligor is rated as an organisation.
- **Issue ratings.** The corporate finance obligation or specific issue is rated for creditworthiness.
- **Structured finance obligation ratings.** Specific issuances related to a securitised pool of assets or other derivative financing transactions are rated. This process typically is more complicated than that for a simple debt issuance, depending on various factors and market environments.
- **Recovery rating.** An indicator of the likelihood of recovery of unpaid principal in the event of a default by the issuer is provided by some agencies.

Although credit ratings are global in use, they can be misconstrued in some areas. Table 16.1 shows some of the characteristics of credit ratings and some elements of finance that credit ratings are not.

TABLE 16.1 Credit Ratings Overview

Aspect	Applicable to Credit Ratings	Not Applicable to Credit Ratings
Agency's view on the intention and ability of an issuer to fulfil obligations or a specific obligation	✓	
Probability of default of an obligation	✓	
Recommendation to buy, sell or hold or any investor activity related to the issuance		✓
Measure of value of obligation or enterprise value, or its liquidity		✓
Guarantee that issuer will fulfil obligations		✓
Forward-looking opinions on relative probability of default	✓	
Absolute or specific measures of probability of default or loss by an issuer in general or a specific issue		✓
Relative opinion of creditworthiness on a scale	✓	
Suitability and appropriateness of an issuer as a counterparty		✓
General quality of an issuer's business and its management not related directly to its relative probability of default		✓

How Credit Ratings Are Used

Credit ratings have use for investors around the world to get a better sense of the issuer's creditworthiness, as opined by an independent agency. More evolved investors use credit ratings in conjunction with their own assessment methodologies.

Market intermediaries, such as commercial and investment banks, brokers, and other institutions, use credit ratings as indications of counterparty risk while evaluating credit extension to the issuers and while marketing these issues to clients.

Corporations use credit ratings as an indication of creditworthiness of trading partners who could be important cogs in their supply chain and hence to determine the risk to their supplies and/or payments.

For issuers, the credit rating is synonymous with the appetite and the liquidity that the market has for their debt and for its pricing. Generally, the better the rating, the lower will be the cost of borrowing. Two issuers with the same rating in the same industry in the same country could have borrowing costs that could differ slightly from each other owing to differences within the same rating scale that are specific to each company. It is important for the company to determine its optimal credit rating (see the next note) in line with its long-term growth plans and not always gun for an unsustainable but better rating.

Quest for Optimal Ratings

Why is the highest rating not always the optimal one? The question that some Treasurers grapple with has been asked many times. If a higher rating is generally synonymous with more access to capital at lower rates, apart from rubbing shoulders with (relatively) financially better peers, which chief financial officer would not gun for it? The answer is relatively simple: The rating that the issuer should target is something that is sustainable in the medium term and that can be improved over time. The presence of an element of subjectivity in the rating process along with the role of projections and assumptions indicates a lack of certainty about those numbers in the future. An upgrade followed by a quick downgrade back to the original rating might not work as much in the company's favour as a consistent rating—with the Treasurer targeting a move higher when the firm has the confidence to move up and stay there for a while. The few basis points of lower cost afforded by the higher rating could be at risk should a downgrade happen, for that event might not be positive for the firm in the market. This is of course an opinion, and certain Treasurers always and aggressively target higher ratings. That is good, provided that the stay there is sustainable.

Agencies and Compensation Models

There are many credit rating agencies in the world, three of which are Standard & Poor's (S&P), Moody's Investors Services (Moody's), and Fitch. We explore the credit rating process in this book in a generic manner. Readers should refer to each rating agency for specific agency-wise rating fundamentals.

Ratings are generally done either at the behest of the issuer, who pays the agency to undertake the rating activity and issue a rating; or by the agency on its own, which then gets paid by any entity that can purchase the credit rating and report from the agency.

There are numerous pros and cons for each model, with no one school of thought finding overwhelming favour. Some agencies offer to volunteer safeguards, or mitigants, to possible conflicts of interest on either payment model.

Ratings

Each issuer is provided with long-term and short-term ratings for each time horizon. Table 16.2 depicts a sample band of long-term ratings. The ratings are alphabetical or alpha-numeric, starting with AAA (or highest grade) and moving progressively downward, to a D, or default. Relative position within a category is indicated for some categories with a plus sign (higher rating) or a minus sign (lower rating).

All the ratings agencies have a similar rating pattern, though their specific methodologies differ to some degree.

Limitations of Issuer Credit Ratings

Ratings have many uses but also quite a few limitations that were highlighted earlier in Table 16.1.

The subjective element in a rating, if present, obviously depends on the analyst's ability to assess and appreciate the benefits and caveats on the company's operations. While most agencies try to use uniform methodology through quantitative and objective analytical tools, there tends to be a subjective element that could make a quality and qualitative difference to the eventual rating provided.

TABLE 16.2 Indicative Rating Bands

	Investment Grade				**Non-Investment Grade**					
	High		**Medium**		**Speculative**	**Highly Speculative**		**High Probability of Default**		**Default**
Rating	AAA	AA	A	BBB	BB	B	CCC	CC	C	D
Relative position within category		+−	+−	+−	+−	+−	+−			
	← Higher Credit Quality					Higher Likelihood of Default →				

Note: This table is derived from Internet sources and may not be entirely accurate. It is provided for comparison purposes only. Different agencies use different ratings scales with related implications and assumptions.

CREDIT RATING METHODOLOGY

We explore a simple rating methodology, comprised of the rating process and the factors used to determine the rating in the agency's model. These ratings, through objective numbers from public sources and discussions with the company as well as estimates, are part of the analysis done by the agency along with subjective inputs. The draft rating is then discussed internally, and the agency's rating team finally puts out the rating to the public.

Rating Process

A simple rating process is provided in Figure 16.2a. Note: This is only an indicative set of steps, and each agency follows its own process. The review process is a continuous one. If events occur to alter the rating in any way, such as corporate action, business performance, change in regulatory or legal environment, and competitor actions, the agency might choose to advance the review period and issue notifications on review and any change.

Issuer Rating Factors

The components of the various rating and risk factors that could go into the model for rating issuers are provided in Figure 16.2b. The various factors on which the credit rating is based are explained next.

Business Risk

Business risk factors are those business-related aspects that impact the company's ability to service its debt and fulfil its financial obligations, such as:

- **Industry**. The rating for each company is determined in the context of its respective industry. Figure 16.3 differentiates the types of industries that could have a high risk of default from the ones that would be perceived to be low risk. Apart from these, factors such cyclicality and seasonality as well as stage in the industry's life cycle could impact the credit ratings for issuers in that industry.
- **Environment**. Environment comprises various elements of the firm's operating environment, such as regulatory, social, demographic, technological, geographical diversification, product maturity, and country related (political, economic, legal, market transparency, and stage of development).
- **Competitive landscape**. The competitive landscape includes peer group performance, the issuer's own status in the competitive landscape, and competitor capabilities.
- **Capability and business model**. The company's own performance and capability, market presence and influence, diversification, supply chain, and economies of scale are some factors to be considered.

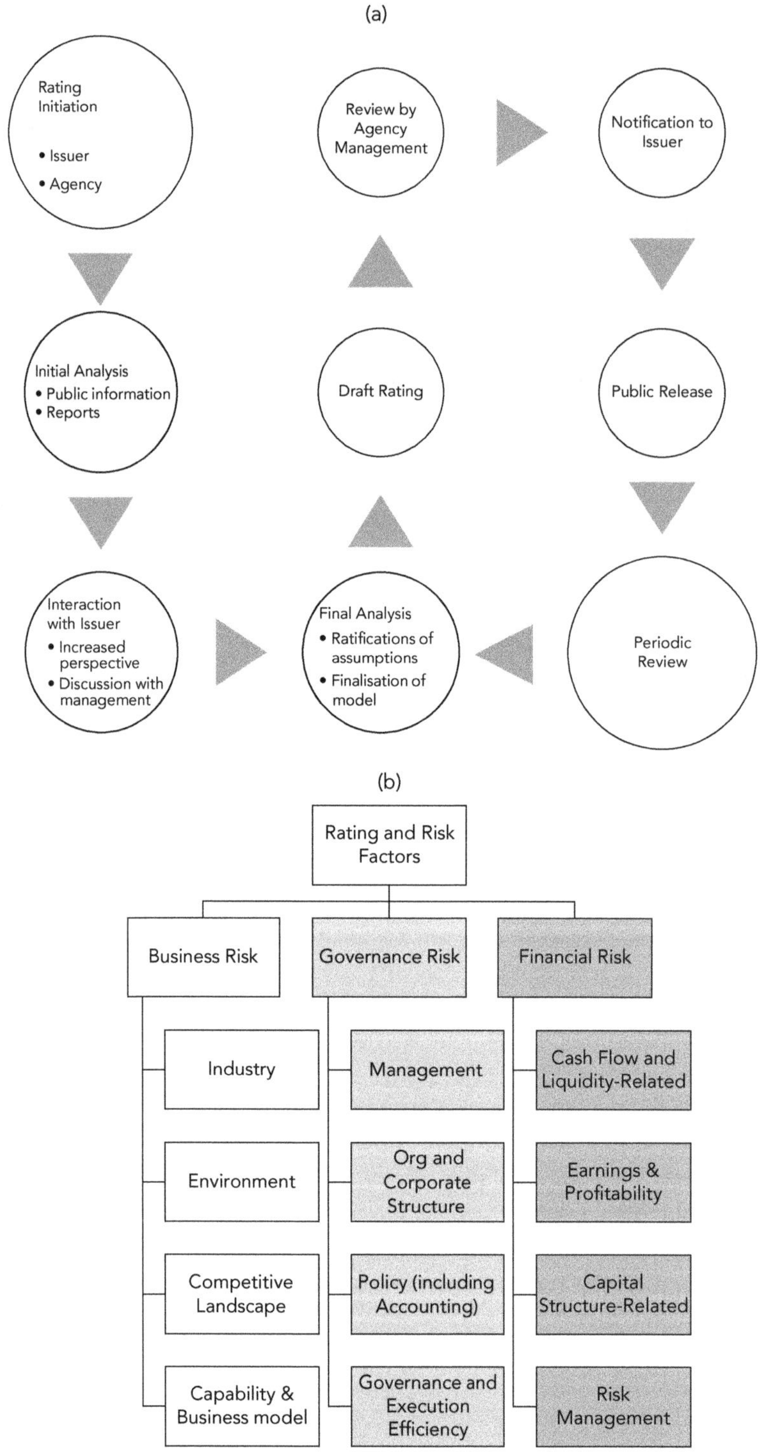

FIGURE 16.2 Credit Rating Process (a) and Factors in the Issuer Rating Methodology (b)

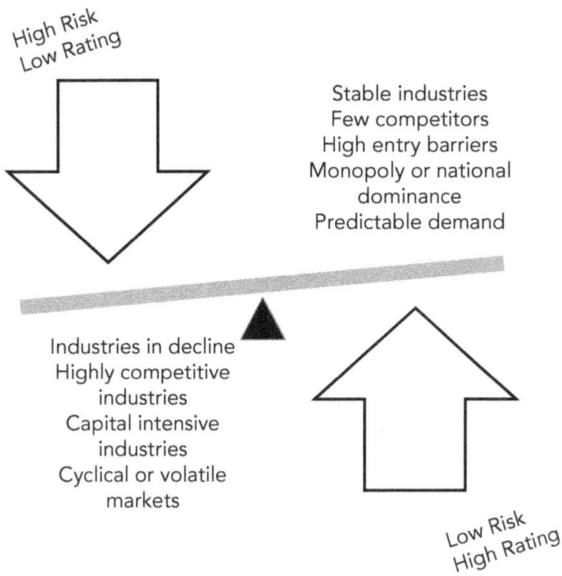

FIGURE 16.3 Dependence on Industry and Business Environment

Governance Risk

Governance risk entails the way the issuer is being managed. Components of this category of risk are:

- **Management**. The management component includes strategy and quality of management, including operating and business strategy, execution, and background and track record.
- **Organisation and corporate structure**. This component includes the legal and reporting structure of the issuer, the relationships between the parent and subsidiaries, corporate structure, documentation, associates and partner organisations, and integration.
- **Policy**. This component encompasses the various policies across the organisation and their ability and scope to cover contingencies and different business, market, operational, and organisational challenges. In many cases, the degree of transparency and clarity depends on the accounting policy adopted, especially for issuers across emerging markets that have not yet transitioned to International Financial Reporting Standards or related standards.
- **Governance and execution efficiency**. This area is concerned with how the entire governance structure is in place, including role and involvement of the board, reporting structure, and related activities.

Financial Risk

One of the most important cogs in the wheel of rating, financial risk, is considered across these parameters:

- **Cash flow and liquidity related.** This area remains one of the most critical elements of assessing an entity's creditworthiness, as it indicates overall financial health and ability to sustain and grow operations, repay debt, and withstand downturns. Liquidity-related aspects have also become critical; they denote the company's ability to manage all its payment obligations and periods of financial and market stress without a significant impact on its credit quality and dependence on external sources in times of crisis (such as the liquidity squeeze in 2008).
- **Profitability and earnings.** This area encompasses earnings stability and profitability across key businesses (adjusted for items such as certain kinds of provisions, reserves, write-downs, and one-time charges).
- **Capital structure related.** The degree of indebtedness and how the issuer funds its operations, and at what cost, become key drivers. In many cases, other key drivers include the liquidity and dependence on external sources of funding. To an extent, the industry's general capital structure (highly capitalised manufacturing concerns versus thinly capitalised service businesses) is matched with that of the issuers to determine the type of capital structure the industry needs.
- **Risk management.** This area is concerned with the manner in which the firm deals with its financial risks and how the overall risk has been reduced, including the use of derivative instruments, their treatment, tolerance to risk, and the company's understanding of their impact and tenor.

In summary, the credit rating process is an involved one. It uses both publicly available data and information provided by the company and its management. The process takes a long time, and the rating agency applies a number of qualitative inputs on top of the indications from the quantitative data. The process has been improving over time, and standards, methodologies, ratings, and efforts are converging.

Rating Changes and Their Impact

Changes to credit ratings can happen and can be caused by generic transitions in the business or by economic changes, weather, regulatory changes, by industry-specific circumstances, or by company-relevant issues.

Investors are cautioned to perform their own analysis prior to making entry, hold, or exit decisions on an investment related to a rated issuer as part of a specific company investment strategy, an industry investment strategy, or a broader strategy. Rating adjustments do play a role in the perception of an issuer or issue in the market, leading to an impact on the issuer's ability and price of raising fresh capital, and the liquidity and price of the existing debt.

Controversy

The rating process and the role of the agency have been subject to much debate, discussion and controversy in the past. Earlier in the chapter we briefly discussed the possible conflicts of interest in the compensation models. Other areas of contention are the potential "shopping" by issuers who in some cases choose to only use a favourable rating provided by any of the agencies. During the financial events of 2008, highly rated instruments derived from subprime mortgages purchased by many investors were quickly and largely devalued on concerns of default on some of their components, leading to liquidity and valuation issues. This debate is outside the scope of this book.

I recommend prudence in the process of creating ratings and that issuers, investors, and the community all use ratings diligently and as one of the decision criteria.

In Conclusion

Credit ratings as supplied by agencies should be only one of the factors used to determine an entity's creditworthiness and debt obligations. From the perspective of the corporate Treasurer, determining the optimal credit rating—something that is sustainable in the long term—should be a key priority. Paying a few cents more for debt now is a good investment to retain a similar level of creditworthiness rather than take on an incremental challenge that could prove detrimental in the medium term.

BANK CREDIT ASSESSMENT PROCESS

The bank credit assessment process varies from bank to bank. For purposes of this discussion, we take a sample illustrative bank and run through some of the elements of credit risk assessment by the bank.

Credit Assessment Cycle

The credit assessment cycle typically happens once a year. It also occurs episodically, in case of any sudden event, such as an acquisition or planned one, capital restructuring, litigation, heavy loss, unplanned capital expenditures, or any matter that would cause a shift in the business and financial aspect of the enterprise (see Figure 16.4).

The credit assessment process involves studying the corporate financial plans and historical performance, and the company's and the bank's own inputs on the needs in the coming period (needs assessment). The firm's financials are then scrutinised, and the expected performance is evaluated from both business and financial standpoints (enterprise appraisal), with a focus being on cash flows. This process provides an indicative estimate of the amount of risk that the bank would be able to take on the group and also an expectation of the documentation, covenants, security, and collateral that would make the bank comfortable with extending credit. Once these have

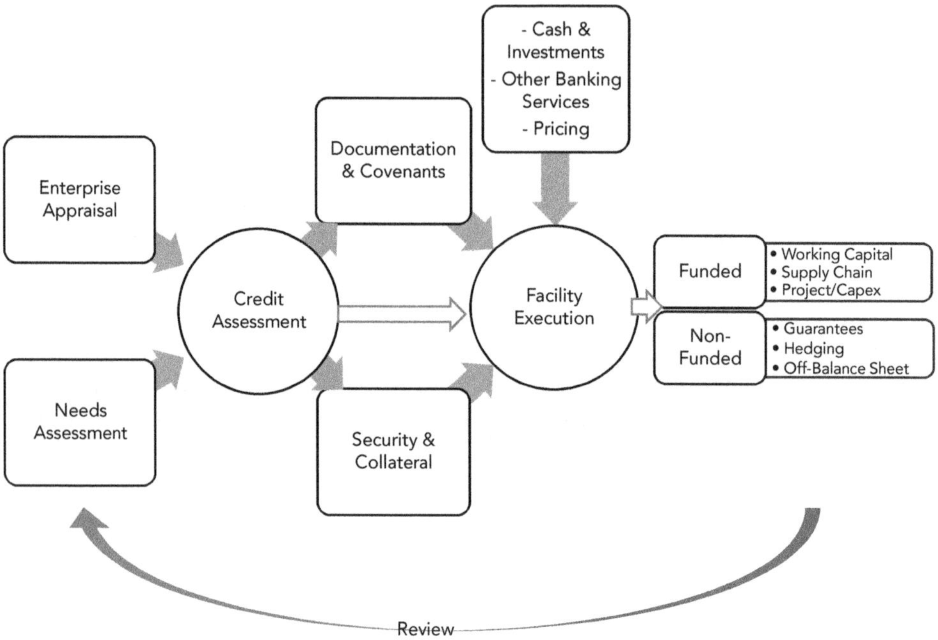

FIGURE 16.4 Credit Assessment Cycle

been agreed and executed, the facilities are provided. These can be funded (direct lending for working capital, trade, projects, and other purposes) or nonfunded (guarantees, pre-settlement risk limits for hedges, etc.).

In addition, the bank can offer a number of transactional non–credit related services that can be factored in and pricing and modalities discussed at the time of the assessment, or subsequently.

Enterprise Appraisal

The enterprise appraisal process involves a detailed study of the qualitative and quantitative aspects of a company's financials and business model. This includes physical inspection of premises, plant, and equipment; detailed discussions with management and operations personnel; independent research and verification from the industry to corroborate management's views on the company's products or services; and other activities and information gathering to allow risk managers and bank branch management to decide on the client's creditworthiness.

Figure 16.5 shows the typical enterprise appraisal components.

One of the key differences between the bank credit assessment and a rating agency's is that the bank has much deeper access to information and has a relationship with the company's management; rating agencies, in contrast, have no funding, transactional, or developmental role.

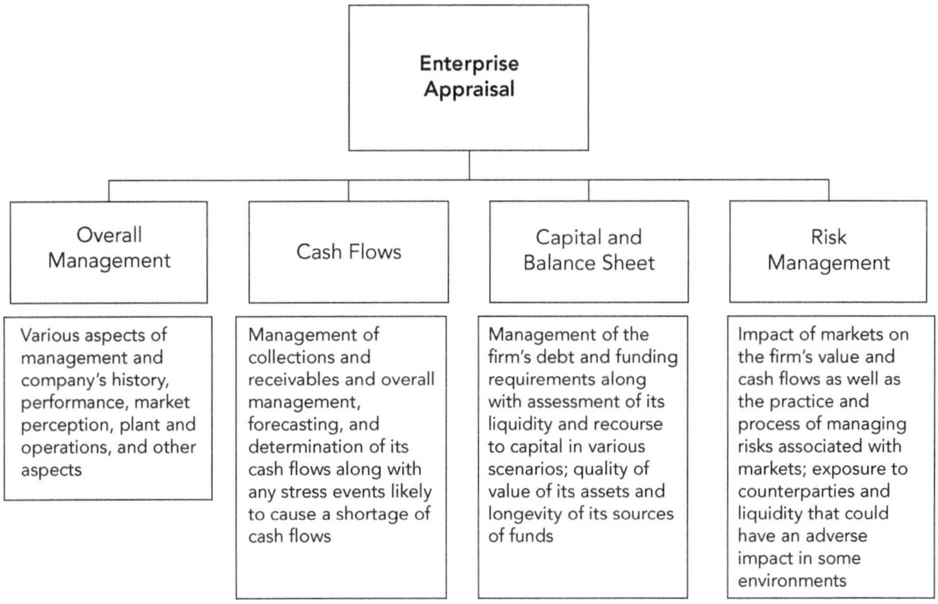

FIGURE 16.5 Enterprise Appraisal

Overall Management

The overall management assessment (see Figure 16.6) assesses the management quality and the company's business performance. The overall management appraisal of the company takes into account the company's business and industry-related performance, its standing in the industry, due diligence on its promoters, a thorough "Know-Your-Customer" (KYC) exercise, operations, historical performance, employee quality and turnover, accounting, history across markets and lenders, and overall role of the promoters and principal in management and financial support.

Cash Flows and Profitability

Cash flows form a core part of lending to a firm, and banks usually look at cash flows as the first-way out to service interest and principal on outstanding debt. The cash flow appraisal is comprised of many factors, as shown in Figure 16.7.

Assessing cash flows includes a detailed evaluation of past and future flows, seasonality and episodic impact, use of working capital, receivables and payables, promoter involvement to provide liquidity, unencumbered cash, and other aspects that could cause a drain on existing flows or future growth. Cash flows are seen as the major source for servicing debt flows (coupon and principal), and strong cash flows through the business would indicate a higher creditworthiness. The bank would be eager to lend money to the enterprise.

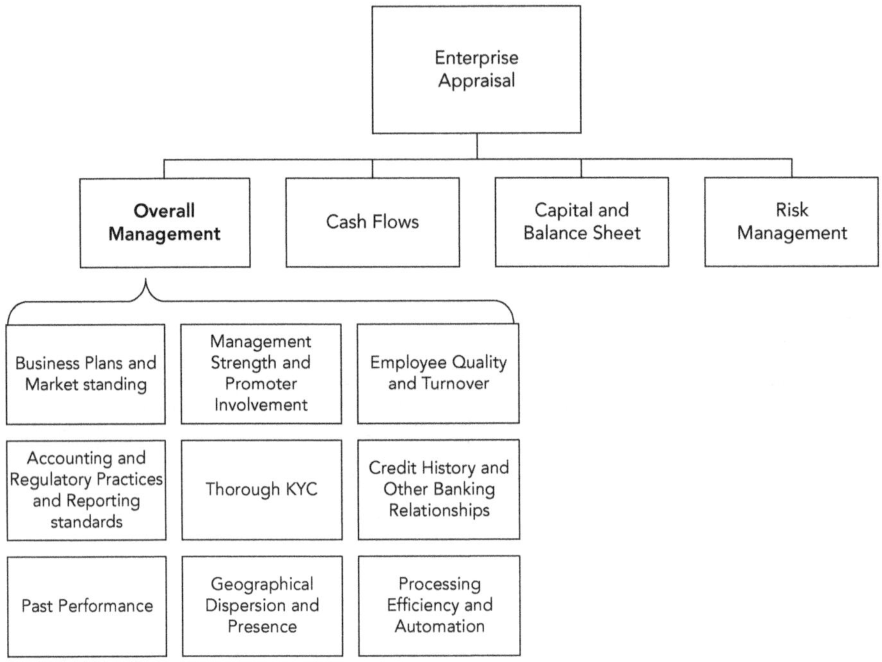

FIGURE 16.6 Overall Management Appraisals

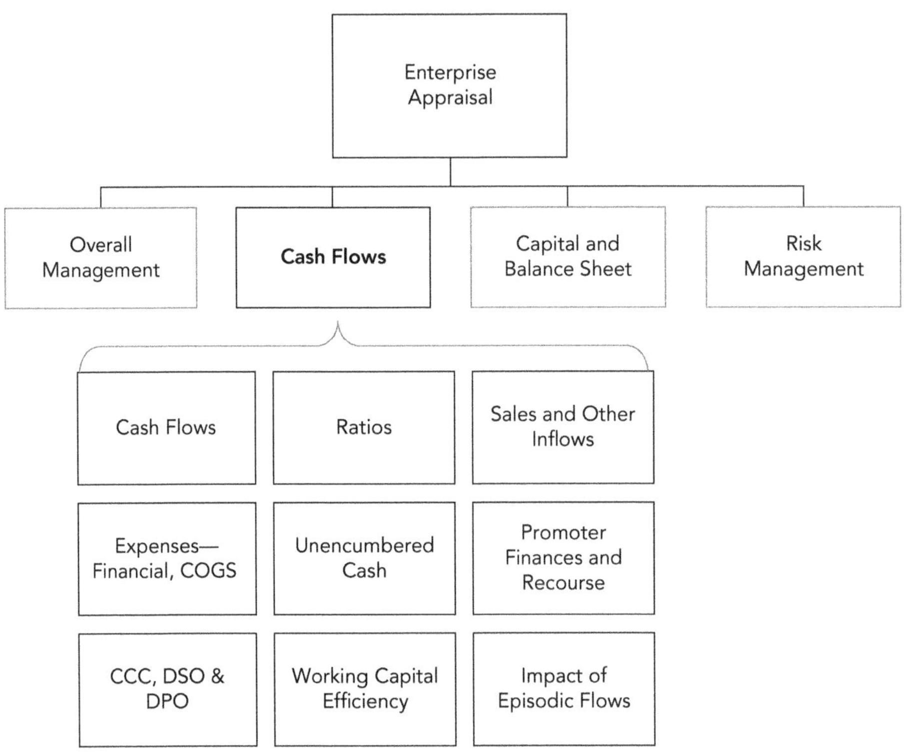

FIGURE 16.7 Cash Flows Appraisal

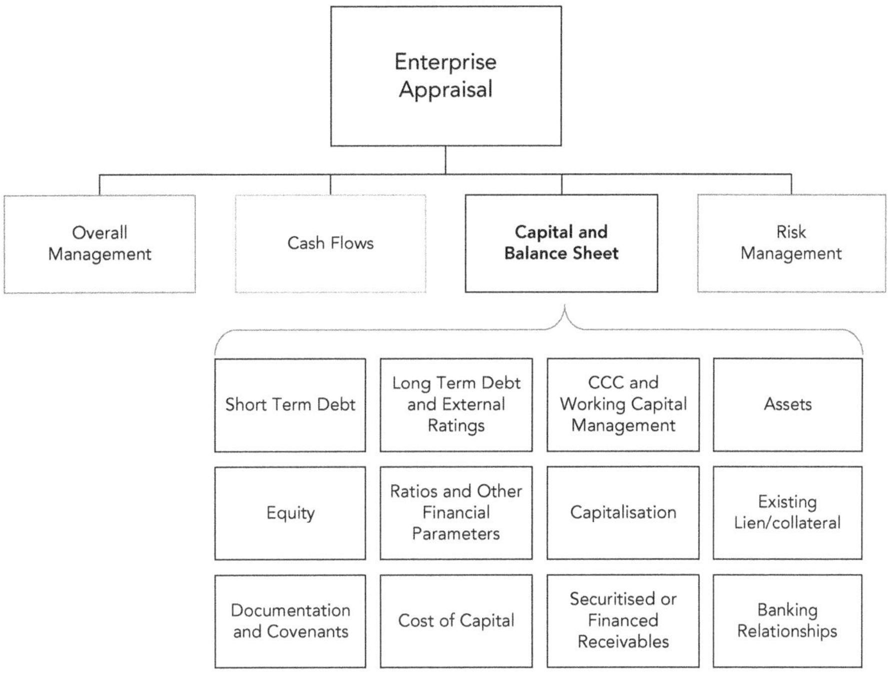

FIGURE 16.8 Capital and Balance Sheet Assessment

Capital and Balance Sheet

The assessment of capital and other elements of the balance sheet (see Figure 16.8) can provide a good window on the financial management of the firm.

While short-term liquidity aspects were covered in the cash flows assessment, this part of the assessment focuses on the capitalisation and overall sources of funds and their use, the quality of assets and liabilities, and the sufficiency of capital for short-, medium-, and long-term sustainability and profitability of the company's operations.

Risk Management

The final aspect of the appraisal, the manner in which the enterprise manages its risk, is also one of the most important aspects. It is on the radar of practically every bank (see Figure 16.9).

Different elements of financial and nonfinancial risk are evaluated, and management awareness, policy, responses, and implementation are factored in to the assessment process.

Putting It All Together

The relationship manager assists the credit risk manager to obtain information and interface with the company's finance and management teams. In turn, the credit risk manager evaluates the credit and calls on company management, if required, for further qualitative insights into the organisation's working and expectations on business, cash flow, and profitability.

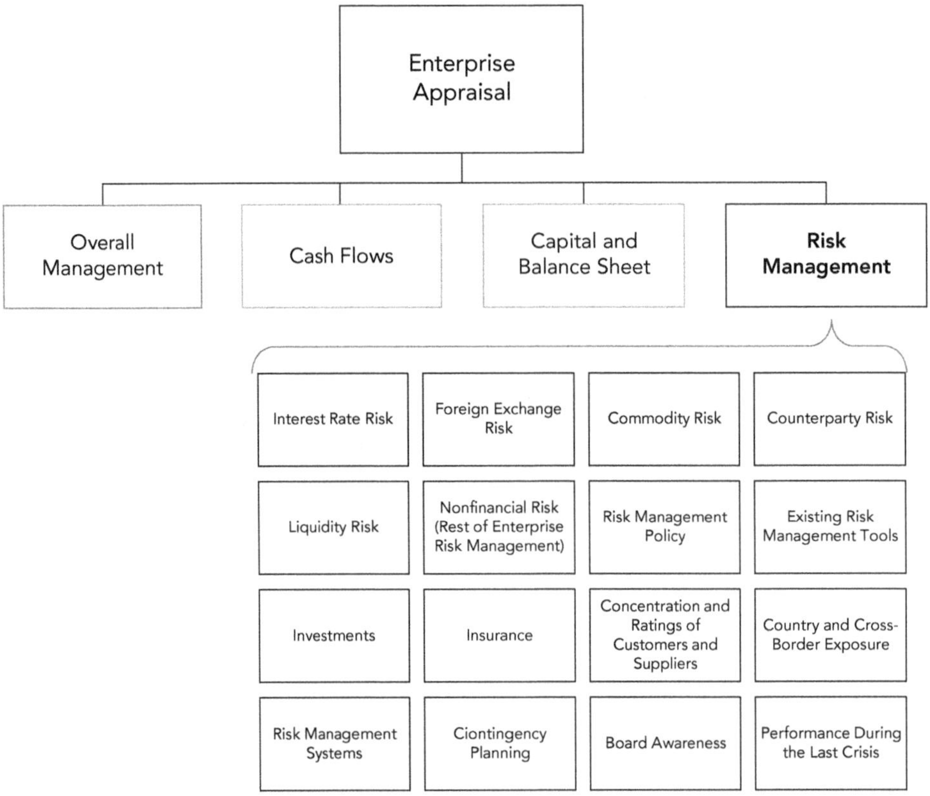

FIGURE 16.9 Risk Management Appraisal

The entire process is iterative and discussion based. Companies that are trying to get the most out of the credit relationship with banks have to find the right mix among risk, return, and relationship.

IMPORTANT FOCUS AREAS AND DISCUSSION POINTS WITH BANKS DURING CREDIT REVIEWS

During the credit review process, it is important for the Treasurer, as the main contact point with the banks, to ensure transparency and accuracy of financial data, views, expectations, and business performance. Relationships will make a difference in the nature and quality of the dialogue and also the extent to which bankers can understand the firm's needs, performance, and ability to succeed as well as the difference that credit lines will make to the company's performance.

Yet too much information can lead to an overload that could cloud the judgment of the risk reviewers or potentially highlight the company's dependence on the bank and hence allow for higher spreads.

The balanced view can be gained when the right areas are focused on. The next list highlights some good tenets to follow.

- **Balanced transparency**. Decide what level of transparency will be provided to the reviewers, what degree of detail, and so on.
- **Honesty**. There is no ambiguity about this: Numbers speak for themselves, but the qualitative responses should be the individual views of the manager and/or the collective view of the firm. They should never be what the reviewer would like to hear.
- **Level of aggression on business plans**. Often, business projections tend to be weighted to an aggressive side, depending on the chief executive and company culture. It may be prudent to provide two scenarios in case the basic projection is very aggressive.
- **Highlighting issues or potential areas of concern**. Bankers love clients who know their areas of concern and are forthright about them: It shows control and the ability and confidence to manage. If there was an issue in the past, discussion of it and the fact that the company now has a tighter, more controlled situation would do much more to supplement the bank's perception of the firm than non-disclosure and a consequent surprise discovery.
- **Optimising needs**. Some treasurers overbudget credit requirements and do not use the facilities through the year; they simply have an excess requirement for a rainy day. It is important to let the bank know how much is being used for possible contingency and how much is for projected actual use. Every bank has limited capital, and bankers will do more for companies that utilise the bank's capital wisely.
- **Let the banks make their money, but not too much**. Banks provide good service and products to most clients, but the ones who squeeze them really hard on every transaction and pinch pennies do not fall into a very high priority category. Hence, the bank's profit margins may be discussed and learned, but allowing the bank to make some money incentivises it to put more resources behind you.

SUMMARY

We have gone through the credit assessment process, including the credit rating and bank assessment practices. Also discussed were some key aspects of dealing with banks during the credit assessment period.

The principles and concepts of assessing the creditworthiness of the company are uniform between the rating agencies and the banks. The difference lies in the access to information and what weight each piece of information is given in determining the final level of credit quality. Also, the bank is the end user of its own evaluation, while agencies are only service providers to institutions and other companies, without providing financial support themselves.

This concludes Part Three. Next we turn to the third major responsibility of the Treasurer: managing risk.

PART FOUR

Markets and Risk Management

THIS PART APPROACHES THE ASPECTS of markets and risk in a unique bottom-up manner. While much literature exists on markets and risk management in particular, this part focuses on risk management purely from the standpoint of a global corporate and uses the approach that I have taken while advising firms on how to manage their market-related risk.

The tools that treasurers need to understand and work with markets are discussed in this part. I say "work with," not "protect against," because markets are not some hydra-headed monster that rises to erode profits although they sometimes seem that way.

I say "work with," not "benefit from," because treasurers of global corporates manage balance sheets of running businesses, not hedge funds, and markets for corporate treasurers are large oceans that one cannot always expect to exploit.

I say "work with," not "beat," because markets are not competing with anyone. Markets are supreme; they move with their own willpower, like winds. It would be, at best, rational to expect to sail with them as much as possible, but it is not possible to outrun them consistently or even most of the time. Not all of us have the sagacity of that master of risk and markets, Warren Buffett.

Hence, this part provides suggestions on how to work along with markets and meet risk management goals that are defined by the firm. It is important, as many authors have so correctly pointed out, to know the risks that we are trying to manage.

We cover instruments and the basics on how they are priced. Work has been done on the pricing and the instruments by some very wise men, including John Hull, and some wonderful texts cover these topics in detail. Here we do not attempt to go down the same path. What is important is to know how to use these instruments, how to identify risks, and how to strip them apart, how to get payoff profiles, and how to determine whether products meet our criteria or not.

In Part Four, you learn:

- **What risk is.** Appreciating what risk and its associated elements mean
- **Different kinds of risk.** Categorisation of the various forms of risk
- **Why manage risk.** The benefits (and risks!) of managing risk
- **Elements of risk management.** Depicted through the evolved IMAGE© methodology of risk management
- **Factors impacting risk.** Why does risk increase or decrease?
- **What risk management does to the firm.**
- **The rationale for managing risk.** Looking at the alternatives of risk management and risk reduction

We start by exploring risk management and its various components.

CHAPTER SEVENTEEN

17 Art and Science of Risk Management

THE JURY IS OUT AS to whether risk management is an art, a science, or a process. We consider it to be a way of life, and a combination of an art and a science. In this chapter we introduce risk as a concept, defining and going through various ways in which it can impact the firm by focusing on the financial risk elements that come under the treasurer's purview.

KINDS OF RISK

There are different elements of risk that you should know about. Here we discuss various categorisations of risk and some important considerations for managing risk.

The risk that we will be focusing on is the uncertainty associated with the financial performance of the company. Before we go ahead, there are some simple points to remember about financial risk.

- **Risk means uncertainty, not necessarily losses**. We usually associate risk with losses. Risk, however, is actually uncertainty. Making profits that you do not expect is also a risk. Stakeholders would be wary of profits or gains not directly linked with an increase in the business and any windfalls that would be hard to repeat by design.

The uncertainty—and not the loss—impairs the ability to predict and to ensure, assuming business was operating normally, anything that impacts the certainty or stability of the financials, such as profit and loss, cash flows, balance sheet, and finally, profitability and financial performance.

In normal use, the term *risk* is associated with losses or a negative performance.

- **What we perceive as risk is not always the actual risk that we face**. What is perceived risk and what is the risk in reality? Perceived risk is what is thought of as the risk. Actual risk causes us to be uncertain as to whether we will achieve something. Perceived risk is what we think can cause the uncertainty.

  A sad example elucidates this example. Many of us lost loved ones and acquaintances during the terrible incidents on September 11, 2001. Following the air disasters of that day, many travelers in the United States preferred to drive rather than fly. If the risk was the uncertainty of surviving the journey, the perceived risk was flying.

  Gerd Gigenzer, in his seminal paper in 2004, wrote about this (see the section on "further reading" for details on this paper). His analysis suggested that the fatalities of road accidents because people were trying to avoiding the risk of flying was more than the fatalities on the four flights of September 11, 2001. Hence, he concluded that the perception of risk was that flying was a higher risk. In actuality, driving could have been a higher risk.
- **Risk management is not necessarily about lowering risk**. Risk management is the activity of identifying risk and reaching a state of risk that is required to achieve desired objectives. For example, if greater certainty of financials is the objective, lowering risk is the solution. If possibly higher revenues or lower expenses are the objective, this could be achieved by raising or changing the degree of risk, sometimes taking on more risk than the initial scenario in order to achieve such objectives. This still remains under the purview of "risk management," but does not reduce risk and hence cannot be termed "risk reduction." This is discussed in more detail in subsequent sections.

We now study the definitions of risk, trying to unravel what the risk categories are and how they can arise. Apart from the classical definitions, we look at other ways of categorising risk: by point of origination, by cause, and by immediate consequence.

CLASSICAL DEFINITIONS

The classical definitions or classifications of risk are:

- Business
- Financial
- Operations and technology
- Event

These have been summarised in Figure 17.1

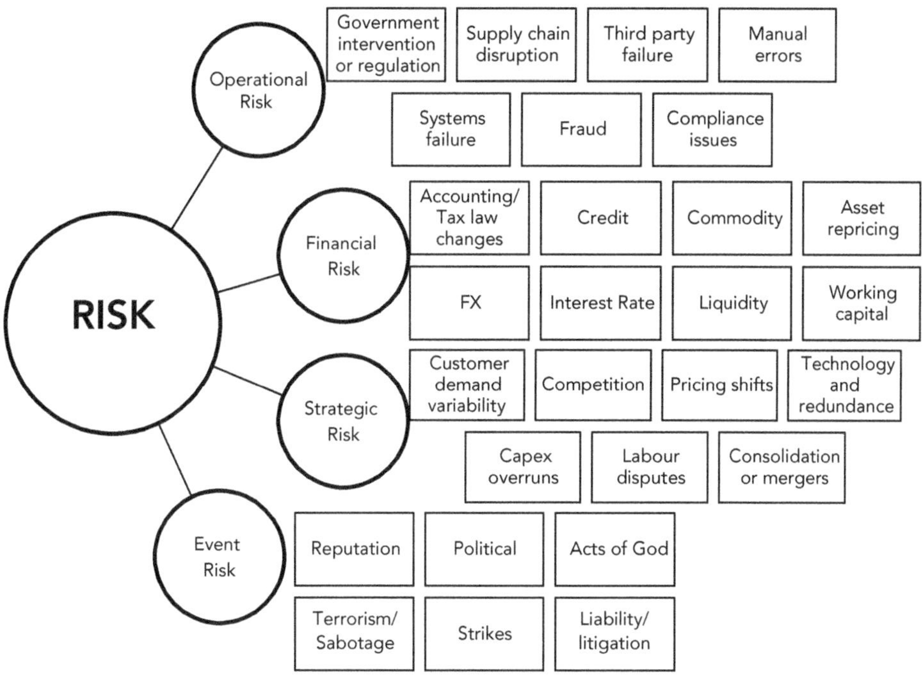

FIGURE 17.1

Business Risk

Business risk is the uncertainty associated with the actual activity of doing business for a going concern. These risks are largely determined by the business managers in a firm and on-the-ground intelligence in global companies. Some elements of business risk are:

- **Customer demand variability**. The demand of customers—wholesale or retail—who buy the products or services of a firm could vary. Need, seasonality, technology, or trends could be some reasons for this variation.
- **Competition**. Always a strong driver, competition's activities—whether they are the introduction of products, more aggressive marketing, or shifting prices—are always reasons for uncertainty of business performance.
- **Pricing shifts**. Changes in the price of raw materials, competition, customer demand, and other determinants, such as availability of capital or business reasons, could determine changes in pricing in a market. This is true in particular for price-elastic products, such as one's dependence on commodities, and less true for price-inelastic products.
- **Redundancy**. Redundancy of product and sales channels could result in risk. For example, when cathode ray tube televisions were losing market share, more astute television manufacturers quickly replaced their manufacturing assembly lines to produce more new-technology televisions.

- **Capital expenditure overruns.** Projects usually have a long implementation period, and many internal and external events can delay their progress.
- **Labor disputes.** With increasingly proactive management of labor concerns and issues, labor disputes are becoming less of a concern in today's management world. Yet, in some areas and regions, there still exists the likelihood of dispute, which in turn impacts business.
- **People issues.** Issues like employee turnover and poaching impact a business negatively.
- **Merger and acquisition activity.** Mergers, acquisitions, hive-offs, strategic sales, and other corporate finance decisions have a direct impact on the business and performance.

Financial Risk

Financial risk is possibly the toughest risk to define in a sentence. Broadly speaking, it is the uncertainty regarding the financial performance caused by creditworthiness, market movements, availability of money, accounting and tax situations, and balance sheet changes. Related yet different elements exist to create financial risk for a firm. These include credit risk, market risk, and accounting and tax risk.

Credit Risk

Credit risk is the uncertainty associated with the nonpayment of monies owed to a party by another party, for reasons of intent or financial or regulatory inability. There are various kinds of credit risk.

- **Credit default risk.** This is the most commonly used term for credit risk: It is the risk that anyone who owes the firm money does not pay it back. It usually is considered in regard to clients/customers, but recently companies are also closely looking at their exposure to credit default risk of banks. This risk could be a function of intention or ability. Management of this risk is detailed in further sections. Credit default risk is also referred to loosely as counterparty risk.

The following note highlights how a seemingly simple investment could also go wrong.

What Can Go Wrong with Investing with a Prominent Institution?

What happened to Company X, which had invested USD 10 million in a two-year Lehman Brothers structured note in 2007? Company X had not factored in credit risk, since in 2007 not many people viewed Lehman Brothers as a dangerous credit. Since then many firms have started looking at credit risk more seriously.

- **Supplier credit risk.** Usually a part of supply chain risk, supplier credit risk has increasingly entered the domain of credit risk management. While the supplier does not typically owe the firm money, a default or deterioration of credit at the supplier's end will impair its ability to raise funding, which in turn could harm operations and disrupt the supply chain. Hence the move to monitor and address supply chain issues at the corporate end.
- **Cross-border risk.** This term refers primarily to two different risks:
  - **Convertibility risk.** Assume that a customer in Borderland owes the German subsidiary of your firm 6 million euro and has every intention of paying. The customer has all its earnings in local pesos and needs to convert its pesos to euros to make the payment. Now assume that the government of Borderland, due to a national debt crisis, passes a regulation to stop all conversion of pesos to foreign currency. This is an example of convertibility risk.
  - **Transferability risk.** Now let us assume that the customer actually does have an account in euros in Borderland and was willing to remit these (without having to convert pesos to euros to comply with the new regulation). Then the government of Borderland passes another regulation that prevents any remittance of money outward from Borderland. This is an example of transferability.
- **Concentration risk.** This is the risk that exposure to a single industry or business group or set of customers would produce significant changes in the firm's financials. It is related to credit default risk in a contagious environment.
- **Settlement risk.** This is the risk that a firm's counterparty does not deliver the settlement security, commodity, or cash equivalent after the firm has delivered its end of the agreement. One of the most prominent examples is the case of the Herstatt bank, whose license was withdrawn by German regulators at the end of banking hours owing to a shortage of flows and capital to cover short-term liabilities. Other banks that had already sent through their legs of foreign exchange transactions under the assumption that Herstatt would pay back the other leg were left with open receivable positions when the license was withdrawn. Hence, this risk is also sometimes referred to as Herstatt risk.
- **Credit rating risk.** This risk is the uncertainty (usually of an increase in cost of or difficulty in procuring funds from the debt market) following an unexpected downgrade in credit rating of the firm by a credit rating agency. This risk reflects a number of aspects, including business, operations, financial and event risks, but the event itself is a credit rating downgrade, and hence it is categorised under a credit risk.

Market Risk

Market risk (also referred to as price risk) largely refers to the uncertainty caused by the changes in market factors and environment. These could be simply moves of various market factors or the availability of capital. Market risks include factor risk and volatility risk.

Factor Risk Factor risk is the direct consequence of moves in various market factors. It is usually more easily quantifiable if one knows the extent of one's exposures.

- **Foreign exchange (FX) risk.** This is the risk that the firm's value changes with changes in FX rates. This is one of the most commonly found exposures across firms and also one of the largest in terms of amount of risk for many multinational companies. Two key categories of FX risk are:
  - **Transactional**, which is caused by the need to physically convert amounts in one currency to another for a fund inflow or outflow or any activity requiring conversion to another currency.
  - **Translational**, which is caused by the need to translate an asset or a liability from a foreign currency to a local or reporting one, and has a direct accounting impact when consolidating or reporting balance sheet items across currencies.
- **Interest rate (IR) risk.** This is the uncertainty caused by shifts in interest rates. Given the linkages that most firms have with debt markets, either as surplus companies or borrowing ones, and with balance sheets and corresponding liquidity concerns, IR risk is manifested in many forms throughout a firm's financial supply chain. Some forms of interest rate risk are:
  - **Interest rate price risk.** This is the most fundamental of IR risks—which represents the impact to the firm's financials of any move in the interest rates of existing assets or liabilities—for example, a simple floating rate loan will yield a lesser cash outflow if rates move lower, or a larger outflow should the floating rate move up. Investments in bonds would get revalued when yields move, since the price of the bond is linked to the corresponding yield.
  - **Yield curve risk.** The shape of the yield curve (map of tenor-wise interest rates)—essentially the difference between short-term interest rates and long-term interest rates—changes, thereby opening up opportunities or shifting the valuation of a firm. The role of interest rates and yield curves in discounting also provides a variable element in the firm's valuation.
  - **Optionality risk.** This is the risk of any liability being recalled by the investor or any asset being placed back by the lender. When mentioned specifically (as in the case of convertible bonds or callable or put table notes), these are explicit options and can be tracked actively. In some cases, especially in customer deposits for deposit-taking companies, the ability to take back money when required is an implicit option that lies with the depositor.
  - **Repricing or rollover risk.** For liabilities or investments, the change in applicable interest rates when the time comes to renew or roll over the liabilities or investments is an uncertainty.
- **Commodity risk.** Fluctuations in a firm's value caused by changes in commodity prices are commodity risks. For companies such as oil refiners that buy raw commodities and sell processed ones, there exists a separate but related commodity exposure on both sides. Inventories are also revalued at current prices that

make the call on inventory storage closely related to the management of the corresponding risk.

- **Equity risk.** Equity risk is the change in a firm's value caused by a change in equity prices. For most firms, equity risk is restricted to equity market–related investments made by the firm, or the impact of capital instruments, such as convertible shares (whose exercise for convertibility is dependent on the underlying stock price).

Volatility Risk Volatility risk is the change in the financials of the firm owing to the change in the volatility of a given market factor. *Vega* is the term used to denote the sensitivity of the value of the firm or the portfolio to changes in volatility.

Accounting and Tax Risk

Uncertainty caused by changes in accounting rules, tax laws, and statuses of group entities is reflected in this category of risk. Usually shifts in accounting and tax regulations are developments that happen over time, but sometimes sudden and dramatic changes have financially impacted global firms. A recent example is a retrospective tax law that impacted a telecommunication service provider in an Asian country—the matter is still in litigation at the time of going to press.

Liquidity and Working Capital

Liquidity risk is the impact on the firm's financials by the inability to provide any entity within the group money required, when it is required, where it is required, and in the form that it is required. Any delay will cause a financial disruption and sometimes a very steep increase in the cost of funding if not planned well.

Why is liquidity risk different from market risk? They are related, in a way, with market liquidity being one of the primary sources of liquidity risk. Market liquidity risk is hence the risk that the firm will not be able to access money from the capital markets owing to a disruption or nonavailability of funds in the market. Funding liquidity risk arises from the firm's own inability to meet liability payments when they fall duc.

Ownership of assets that cannot be sold at a reasonable price when required is one of the key areas of concern and takeaways from the 2008 financial crisis. Instruments once thought to be highly rated and hence liquid changed characteristics (and ratings!) overnight, making a sale next to impossible and placing pressure on the firm's liquidity. Figure 17.2 provides an overview of the different liquidity risks and their interlinkages.

Operational and Technology Risk

Operational and technology risk (O&T risk or operations risk) is the uncertainty arising from the people, systems, and processes sectors of the company's Treasury and financial operations.

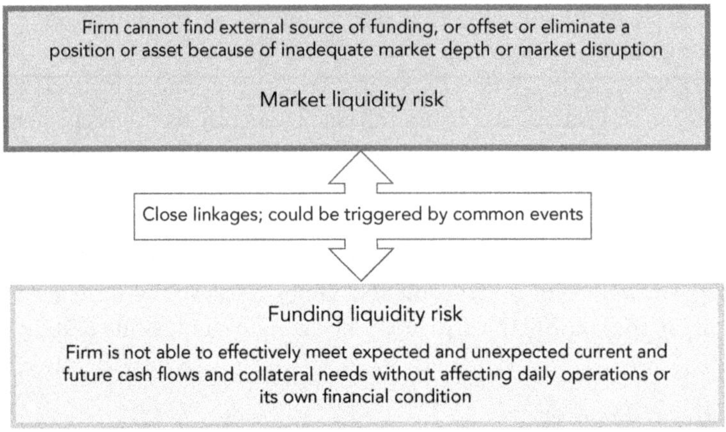

FIGURE 17.2 Liquidity Risk

Operational risk is managed differently from other types of risk, because it is not a direct variable or external aspect that can be tracked. In effect, organisations need to accept that their people, processes, and systems are not perfect and that there are chances that losses will arise from errors and nonrobust operations, technology, and controls. Determining measures and governance for operational risk is an evolving science. Some of the more common areas of operational risk are:

- Manual errors
- Systems failure
- Government intervention or regulation
- Supply chain disruption
- Third-party failure
- Fraud
- Regulatory and compliance issues

We cover the area of operations and control processes in more detail in the Toolkit in Part Five.

Event Risk

Event risk comprises these possible areas:

- Reputation
- Political
- Acts of God
- Terrorism/sabotage
- Strikes
- Liability/litigation

These risks are usually outside of the purview of a firm's Treasury. Some are insurable. The chief executive officer along with the business heads and the chief financial officer (CFO) would weigh in on the probability, costs, and hence management of these risks.

Other Classifications of Risk

Risk elements can be classified in other ways, as shown in Table 17.1. The importance of these classifications is that they help Treasurers to look for points in the system that could be potential areas or sources of risk, which would help in the first stage of the risk management process.

Risk management is a process and a philosophy as much as it is a practice. If enough thought and effort has been put in to get the process right, it reduces the chances that things will go wrong and increases the chances that the firm's financial performance is in line with the expected objectives, the variables that are more dependent on business performance and less on the markets.

TABLE 17.1 Other Classifications of Risk

Classification	Risk	Some Examples
By point of origination	Externally driven	Market risk Credit risk
	Internally driven	Operational risks Funding liquidity risk
By cause or relevance	Environmental causes	Country-specific risk Cross-border risk Market liquidity risk Systemic risk
	Process causes	Funding liquidity risk Operational risk Reputational risk Legal risk Compliance risk Technology risk
	When dealing with other entities	Supply chain disruption Credit (counterparty risk) Cross-border risk Liquidity risk Legal risk
	Event or probability of occurrence-related	Project/contingent risks Credit default risk Corporate action
	Financial Impact	Transactional Translational Economic/valuation
By immediate consequence	Reputation	Reputational risk
	Financial	Financial risks
	Legislation	Legal risk Credit risk

WHY MANAGE FINANCIAL RISK?

Some of the reasons for managing financial risk are fairly evident, yet from the perspective of the CFO and Treasurer, financial risk management provides three key elements. We go back to the key performance indicators of the Treasurer mentioned in Chapter 1 and tie them in with the objectives of risk management. This is depicted in Figure 17.3.

Increased Stability of Cash Flows and Balance Sheet

Smoother earnings and more accurate forecasts ensure that investors and lenders are more comfortable with the company's financial performance. Widely varying profits, even if they are increasing, and a very high dependence on FX rates rather than higher actual sales, for example, could result in a critical assessment of the company's financial condition. Similarly, poor management of liquidity could result in a spike in interest expense to raise money in crisis situations, which impacts the company's profitability rather severely. Similarly, stability of assets and liabilities, especially across debt and capital investments, is a good indicator of a firm's control over its financial management.

Improving predictability of earnings by determining the financial value of the expected earnings in advance also shows a high degree of management control over the firm's performance. This fosters a stable planning environment for business

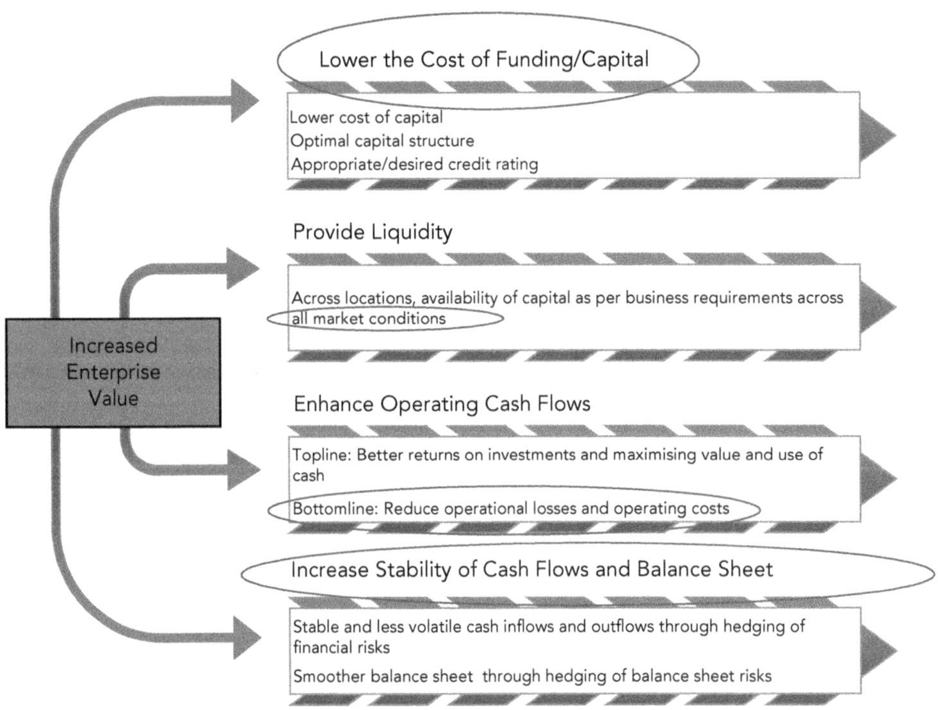

FIGURE 17.3 Key Performance Indicators of the Treasurer in the Context of Risk Management

managers, who can focus on sales and development of their client segments without having to be unduly worried about the currency, liquidity, market, or other aspects.

Lower the Cost of Capital

By managing interest rate risk and neutralising the impact of interest rates or helping to lock in long-term rates through prudent use of interest risk management devices, the Treasurer contributes directly to stable and improved capital costs.

By reducing the likelihood and potential costs of distress, a good risk management process can move the firm towards becoming neutral to performances of its key market and credit environments and hence towards a better rating. A better rating would imply increased ability to leverage and cheaper sources of funding, leading to an overall lowering of the cost of capital.

Prevent a Liquidity Problem

Managing liquidity risk is a critical part of the risk management activity. Through processes and initiatives discussed earlier we observed how the entire process of liquidity management, tracking, and preventing liquidity shortfalls through effective management of liquidity risk prevents a liquidity event from taking place.

Sometimes global events take a toll on certain markets in terms of liquidity. These events can sometimes be triggered overnight because of some financial or other event, but in most cases can be expected when there is a deterioration of market and liquidity conditions. The impact of these events on the firm's day-to-day functioning should be minimised through prudent risk management. The ability to live through any stress situations with the firm's financials intact distinguishes a great Treasurer from a good one. Some recent crises are listed in Table 17.2.

TABLE 17.2 Some Large Market Crises over the Years

Year	Crisis
1987	US market issue
1990	Collapse of junk bond market
1991	Oil price surge
1992	European Exchange Rate Mechanism (ERM) crisis
1994	US bond market crash
1995	Mexican crisis
1997	ASEAN crisis
1998	Russia
1998	Long Term Capital Management (LTCM) crisis
2000	Dot-com bubble
2001	Payment disruption post-9/11
2002	Argentina
2008	Liquidity crisis/LIBOR issue

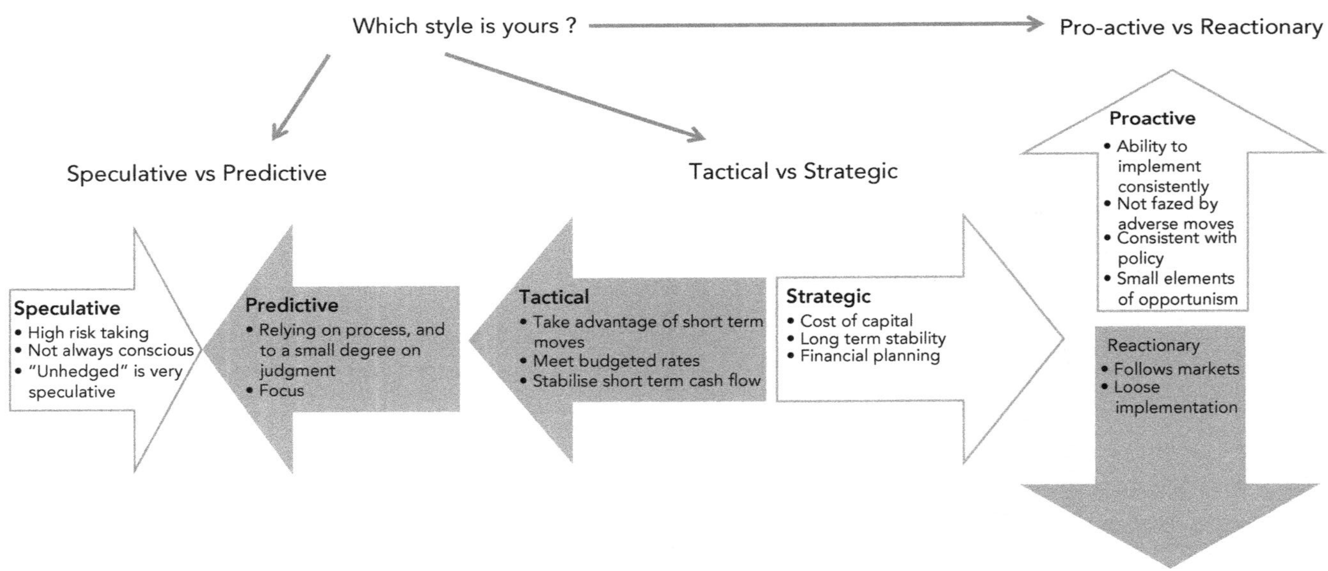

FIGURE 17.4 Styles of Risk Management

Enhance Competitive Advantage

Providing the sales team with more flexibility on pricing and hence better customer terms and conditions could help business units beat competition on pricing while retaining operational efficiency for the firm and keeping the sales margins high. Increased business is always good news.

STYLES OF RISK MANAGEMENT

Some of the various styles of risk management are indicated in Figure 17.4.

Various cases exist of each of these styles, and many treasuries have one predominant style. The risk management styles that are most effective combine various styles based on requirements. It is most important to have a defined plan based on a well-defined policy and to be consistent with that policy. A strong and flexible policy will allow for some degree of variance of styles, but most parameters should be kept within a range of operation and style.

It is important to align the style of Treasury functioning with the working style of the organisation and with management perspective. Sometimes the improvement in Treasury processes could result in improvements in the organisation process and planning itself, as we saw in the recent situation of an American firm.

Finally, many clients say: "We are very conservative. We do not hedge." As expressed in the note, this may be an example of an extremely aggressive strategy, leaving the firm's fortunes to the mercy of the market, as the following note describes.

Why is "No Hedging" not a Conservative Approach?

The objective of conservatively managing risk is usually to reduce the uncertainty around the firm's cash flows, balance sheet, and overall financials. Some firms that have an aggressive view define the objective to increase profitability, and in many of these cases, Treasury becomes a profit centre. By not hedging, a firm makes itself susceptible to changes in market forces. Not hedging is a high-risk, high-return strategy when the firm is dependent on market factors. If the factors swing in the firm's favor—for example, a steadily weakening local currency for an exporter—the firm does very well. An adverse move can completely turn the tables on financial performance. Firms generally stay put without hedging for several reasons, including:

- **Habit**. The principals and management have not really explored managing risk as a key initiative. This might not be a good approach in the long term, especially given the increasing volatility of global markets.
- **Market practice, stay put without hedging**. Potential favorable market

(Continued)

moves for competition that is not locked in could seriously undermine the position of the firm with respect to the marketplace. However, not hedging any exposure at all will make the firm's financials look poorer in the case of an adverse market move. Hence, while it may be practical not to consider hedging if no one else is doing it, being able to forecast some portion of the firm's financials, apart from narrowing the range of firm value over a period of time, would be a good enough reason to start hedging at least a small part of the portfolio at risk.

- **Past experience**. A hedge that went wrong generates a knee-jerk reaction in many companies. In one particular case, management has even given up its market information terminal and claimed a cost save. Hedges, especially ones that have the objective of lowering volatility, can never go wrong over a period of time. Losses attributable to poor policy should not mar the perceived effectiveness of a noble activity. Poor past experiences should incentivise management to put better processes, controls, policy, and risk management frameworks in place in order to derive the best results over a longer period of time.

FACTORS IMPACTING RISK

Many elements impact the formation, growth, reduction, and continuation of risk elements for a transnational firm. Some of these occur in the course of doing business and hence cannot be eliminated. The risk manager must simply assume these risks and manage them, and notify management on the extent of the unmanageable or pending risks. Management would then be able to review the continuation of the business strategy that brings these factors into the firm's risk.

Location

Locational aspects of risk are provided next. Table 17.3 illustrates these risks.

Location of the Company and Subsidiaries

The location of the parent determines the currency of the balance sheet, funding requirements, tax aspects, accounting treatment, regulations, use of cash, investment, and other critical aspects. The location of subsidiaries determines funding cost, liquidity, reparability, and cross-border and FX risk.

Location of Customers or Clients

Where the clients are located usually determines the currency of sales. Market practice on receivables and credit period impacts the balance sheet and hence funding requirements.

TABLE 17.3 Locational Aspects of Risk

Location	Aspects Impacted
Company (headquarters)	Currency of the balance sheet Funding requirements Tax aspects Accounting treatment Regulations Use of cash Investment and other critical aspects
Subsidiaries	Funding cost Liquidity Reparability Cross border FX risk
Customers	Currency of sales Market practice on receivables and credit period impacts balance sheet and hence funding requirements
Suppliers	Currency of purchases Availability of supply chain financing and credit facilities for suppliers Payment practices also determine length of credit period extended by suppliers and hence funding requirements
Invoicing	Tax Exchange Companies are increasingly selecting the location of invoicing to improve the risk and cost profile of invoicing
Inventory and Manufacturing	Translation issues Funding cost Liquidity-related matters
Treasury	Centralised treasuries or regional treasury centres have a better perspective on risk Contribute towards concentrating the risk and balance sheet elements in fewer locations

Location of Suppliers

Where the suppliers are located, similarly, could determine the currency of purchases as well as availability of supply chain financing and credit facilities for suppliers. Payment practices also determine the length of credit period extended by suppliers and hence funding requirements.

Location of Invoicing

As mentioned earlier, the location of invoicing determines tax and exchange matters. Companies are increasingly selecting invoicing location to improve the risk and cost profile of invoicing.

Location of Inventory and Manufacturing

Inventory across currencies results in translation issues as well as funding-cost and liquidity-related matters.

Location of Treasury

Centralised Treasuries or regional Treasury centres have a more holistic and hence better overall perspective of the firm's risk than the individual subsidiaries or individual entities and contribute towards concentrating the risk and balance sheet elements in fewer locations.

State of Economies and Markets

The state of the economies and markets impacts the predictability and stability of market factors and liquidity and also cost of raising or returns on invested capital. These are extraneous factors, and the CFO or Treasurer can do little to change these environments.

Processes

Internal processes and their location is a strong determinant of risk and its measure. Operational risk and control is a core element of the treasurer's responsibility, and the robustness of internal processes becomes a critical part of the firm's success.

Bargaining Power

The ability to bargain with customers and suppliers and to negotiate terms favorable to the firm is an important source or mitigate of risk.

Nature of Industry and Competition

Industry practices and competitive action impact the nature of risk that the company faces. Distribution and concentration of suppliers and clients' need to match competitor actions (e.g., entering markets with a high degree of credit risk or invoicing in a foreign currency), industry standard terms and conditions, leverage, and other factors influence the degree of risk of a firm.

What You Start Off With—Zero Base

If the firm has an existing hedging mechanism or long-term contracts that cannot be unwound or changed, they will have to be considered for risk purposes and included in the items to be managed.

WHAT DOES RISK MANAGEMENT DO?

Risk management attempts to move a firm's risk profile from an existing profile towards an intended or targeted one. In this context, it is a good idea to introduce the probability distribution as an intelligent method to describe risk in its actual and intended form.

Probability Distribution

A probability distribution curve measures the probability of where market prices can be in the future. The distribution can assume any shape, as long as the sum of all possible outcomes (area inside the curve) is 1. This distribution is similar to a set of balls falling into a bucket or a flow of grains of sand onto the floor (see Figure 17.5).

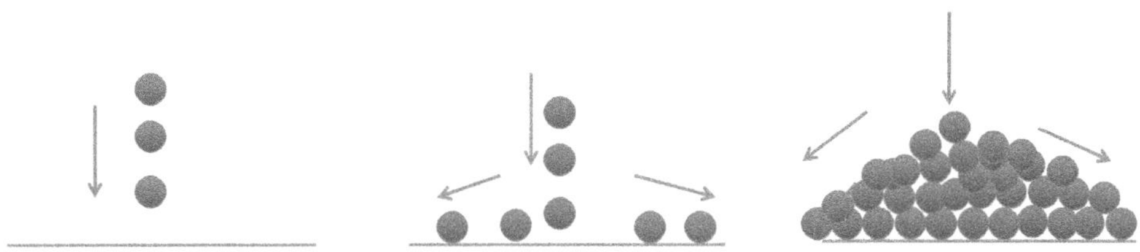

FIGURE 17.5 Probability Distribution

The balls finally take on a normal distribution, with the highest point in the same line as the halfway point on the line. This is popularly called the Bell curve. Normal distributions can be applied to many instances in our daily lives (see Figure 17.6). For example, if the average (mean) height of a class is, say, five foot six inches, the tallest person will be the most distant in the distribution on the right side and the shortest person will be the most distant on the left.

Figure 17.6 is explained in the following note.

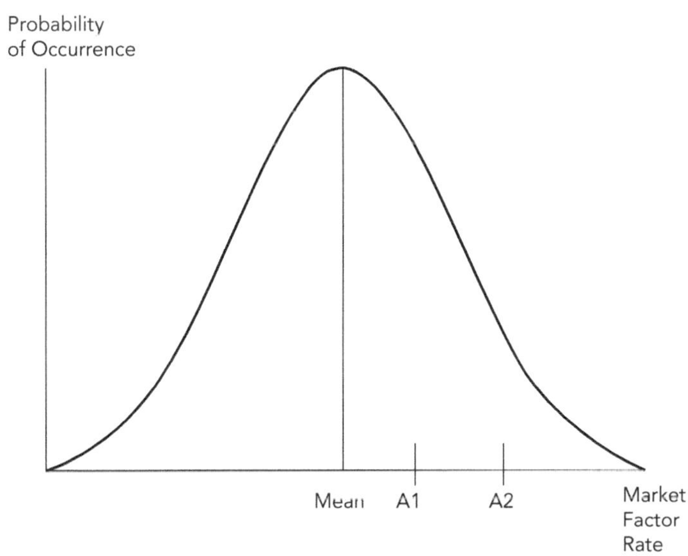

FIGURE 17.6 Mean

What Is Represented on the X-Axis and on the Y-Axis?

The *x*-axis is nothing but the market factor—the rate at which the market factor ends up after the prescribed time period: for example, the EUR USD spot rate after one year, the AUD 6-month London Interbank Offered Rate (LIBOR) after six months, and so on. The *y*-axis is the probability that that the market will end at that particular rate after the time period. Hence, as discussed earlier, it is most likely that the market will end at the rate denoted by the current forward level, for purposes of risk estimation.

So it is with markets: Statistically, we assume that the chance of the market factor rate (say EUR USD currency spot rate or USD five-year Treasury yields, or West Texas Intermediate (WTI) oil futures prices) ending on either side of the halfway point, or mean, is equal. That is, there is an equal likelihood of the market factor ending on either side of the mean rate. Let us assume that this mean rate is the forward price of today. The farther away from the mean, the less likely it is that the factor will end up at that rate. Hence, rate A2 is less likely to occur than rate A1. Or the market factor rate is less likely to end up at A2 than it is at A1.

How less likely? Figure 17.7 leads us in that direction.

The standard deviation (represented by the Greek letter sigma, σ), represents how much variation is expected from the mean value. A measure of 1σ represents a dispersion of 1 away from the mean. The reader is referred to textbooks on statistics for a detailed reading of normal distributions.

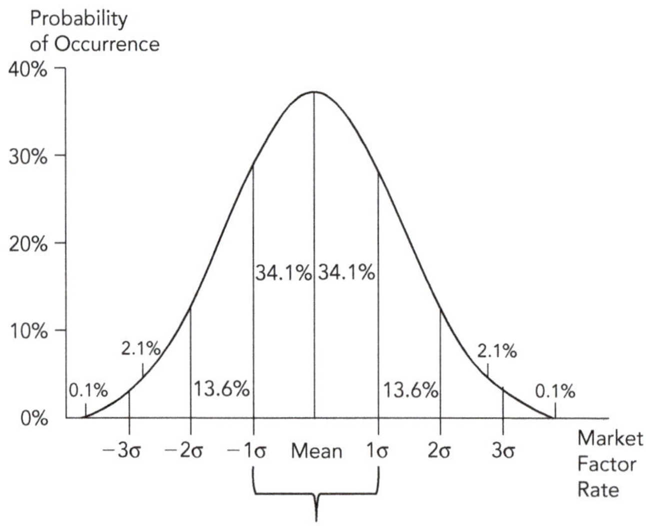

FIGURE 17.7 Probability of Occurrence and Market Factor Rate

The area inside the curve to the left of a particular point on the x-axis represents the total (cumulative) probability that the market factor will end below that rate. For example, the probability that the rate ends below a point $+2\sigma$ away from the mean is around 97.7%.

Figure 17.8 shows the mean of probability of occurrence with a market factor rate.

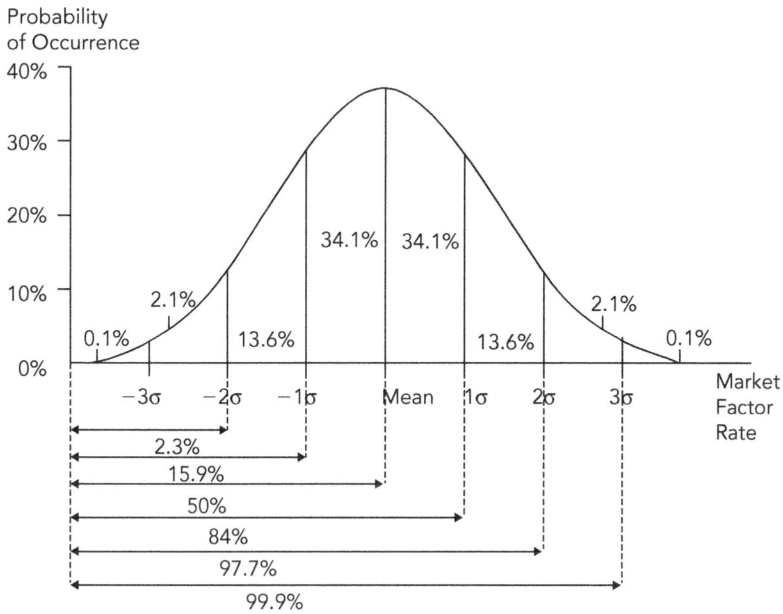

FIGURE 17.8 Mean of Probability of Occurrence and Market Factor Rate

Which do you think is the most volatile currency in Figure 17.9, A, B, or C?

The answer is C. Surprised?

A is the least volatile, because the standard deviation is fairly low. The dispersion away from the mean is least. For currency pair C, the dispersion away from the mean is the most, and hence the probability that the rate would end far away from the mean is higher, as the probability is lower that the rate will end around the mean.

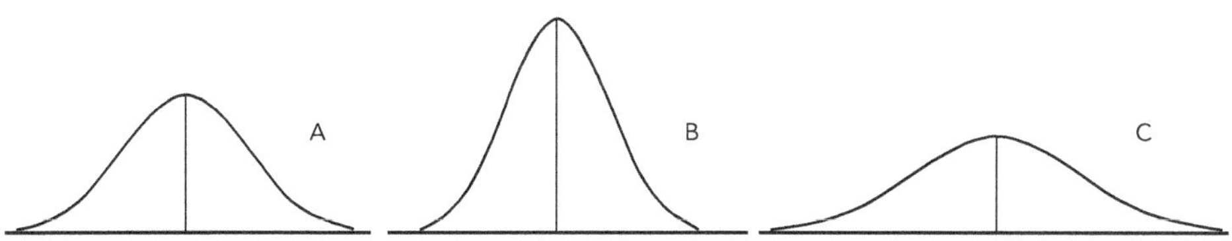

FIGURE 17.9 Which Is the Most Volatile Currency?

OBJECTIVE OF RISK MANAGEMENT

Now that we have learned the basics of a probability distribution, let us apply that to a firm's risk management. Recall that earlier we defined risk as the uncertainty that would impact the financials of a firm. Let us now draw up a distribution of the firm's expected value around the mean, with probability of achieving a particular value (Figure 17.10).

The risk to the firm is that the firm value would end up away from what is expected. An adverse performance (i.e., towards the left of the mean) would not go down well with stakeholders. Nor would an unexpectedly better performance because of market moves (i.e., towards the right of the mean), since similar market conditions would not be anticipated in following years, making an improvement over the current year's performance even more challenging.

Many CFOs prefer to keep the firm value around the expected or mean value. In such cases the firm's risk management has a risk reduction focus.

Risk reduction would hence mean being closer to the mean and less dispersion. The CFO or Treasurer seeking risk reduction would aim to achieve the curve Y as compared to curve X (see Figure 17.11). In this case, the likelihood of ending up closer to the mean is much higher, and that would be the core objective of a risk management policy and mechanism oriented towards risk reduction.

More aggressive CFOs would look towards maximising firm value. Treasurers would devise strategies to get a better rate than what the market offers. However, these kind of strategies typically entail a higher likelihood of a negative scenario. Therefore, while the chances of a higher targeted firm value than the mean increase, so do the possibilities of a worse value than the mean. The distribution of a typical targeted risk strategy is depicted in Figure 17.12.

Two terms are often used interchangeably, and this practice might not always be correct. We clarify in the following note.

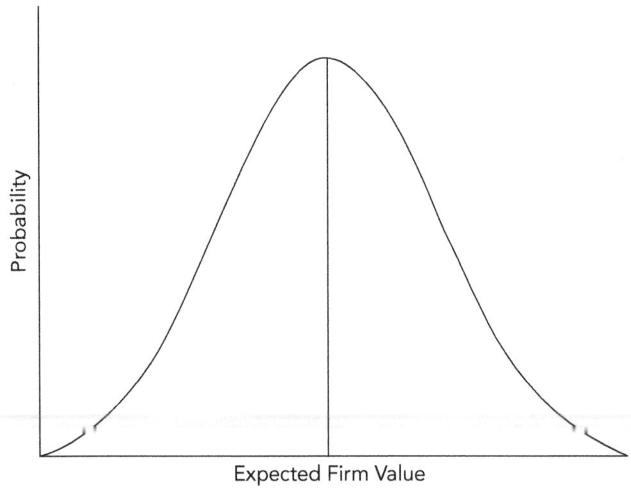

FIGURE 17.10 Expected Value of the Firm

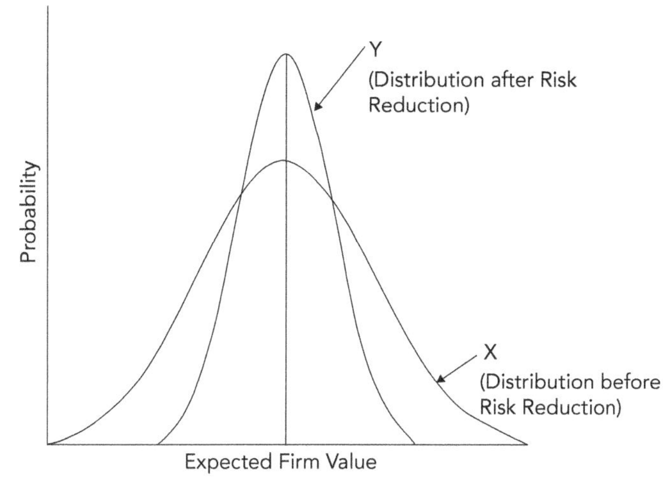

FIGURE 17.11 Risk Reduction and Risk Management

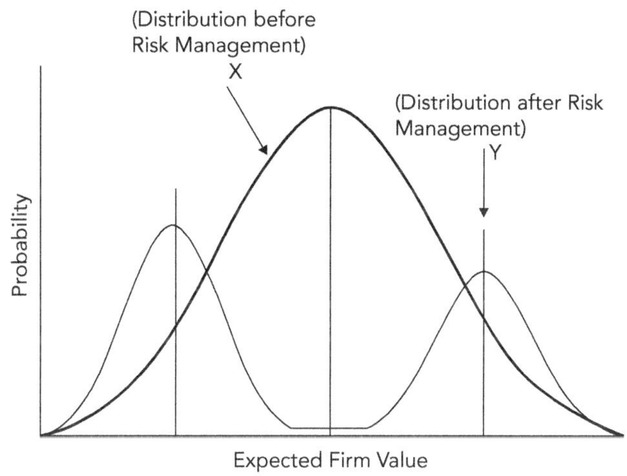

FIGURE 17.12 Sample Targeted Risk Strategy

Difference between Risk Management and Risk Reduction

Risk reduction is the process by which the activities of risk management attempt to minimise variance in market factors and hence the firm value. The objectives of the risk management exercise must be defined clearly up front. Methods of risk reduction are avoidance or hedging through fixed rate or vanilla contracts.

Risk management is the umbrella process. Risk reduction is only one of the ways to manage risk. Achieving a targeted budgeted rate, improving the rate, or keeping the portfolio balanced are different approaches to risk management. Speculative transactions, derivatives other than direct hedges, diversification, and the like are some broad tools of risk management that may not be directly linked to risk reduction.

SUMMARY

Risk can be viewed in different ways and can mean different things to different people and organisations. Also, many companies treat risk in different ways. This chapter viewed risk from different perspectives but finally quantified financial risk in regard to the impact that it has on the organisation. The rest of this part of the book is devoted to the management of various kinds of financial risk, using a best practices approach.

CHAPTER EIGHTEEN

Markets and Risk Aspects of Each Market

IN THIS CHAPTER WE COVER some of the key markets—foreign exchange (FX) markets, fixed income and money markets, equity markets and commodity markets—and the dynamics associated with each of them. We also cover some of the key economic data and indicators that emanate from governments and their broad impact on domestic markets and factors. This will set up our discussion for risk management solutions in Chapter 21.

WORLD OF MARKETS

The world of markets is divided into five main asset or risk classes, as shown in Figure 18.1.

Each market has its own characteristics and dynamics, and we explore these in the rest of the chapter.

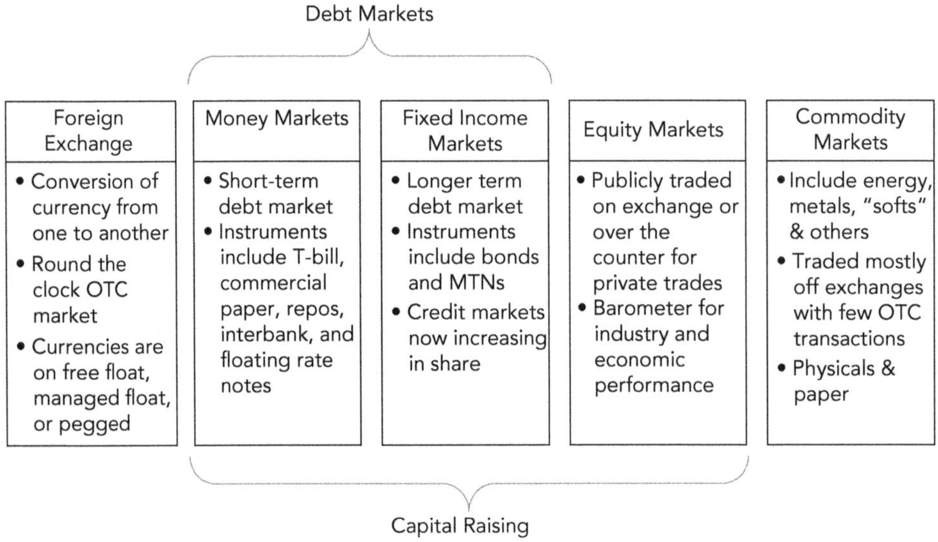

FIGURE 18.1 World of Markets

Foreign Exchange Markets

As long as international trade has been around, the need to denominate or value goods and services has been present. In ancient times, coinage and currencies were popular in different forms, but challenges arose when looking to trade across borders.

The barter system, where goods or services would be exchanged in good value for each other, became a common practice. Over time, gold came to be accepted as a universal method of exchange.

The Bretton Woods conference in the aftermath of World War II set in place the mechanics of currencies and conversion. A few hiccups later, the global foreign exchange (FX) market as we know today took shape and form, to aid the flow of money across borders and hence facilitate transactions in both the trade (or current) accounts and capital accounts.

Today's global FX market is a round-the-clock, primarily over-the-counter (OTC) market that determines the relative value of two currencies, denoted as a currency pair. The FX market is the largest in the world in terms of liquidity (estimated at around USD 4 trillion per day) and works across these types:

- **Cash.** Exchange OTC at banks, automated teller machines, exchange centers, and so on.
- **Spot.** The most extensive market in terms of volume. Spot settlement usually refers to the settlement two working days (T+2) from the date of the transaction.
- **Forward.** A combination of exchange rates and interest rates across time, the settlement rate for an exchange beyond two days, fixed today.
- **FX swaps.** A transaction to take advantage of the forward points only, where the spot is bought/sold and correspondingly sold/bought forward.

- **Currency swaps.** Exchanges of cash flows over time across two currencies.
- **Options.** One example is the right to buy/sell a currency at a particular price on a particular date.

A currency itself is denoted by a three-letter code as per the International Standards Organization (ISO) 4217 standard, made up of the two-letter ISO 3166–1 country code followed by an initial of the currency itself.

Hence, the United States (country code: US) dollar is USD, the Japanese (country code: JP) yen in JPY, and the Indian (country code: IN) rupee is INR.

Appendix B contains a list of global currencies.

A currency pair, which denotes the exchange of currency from one to the other (and hence the term *foreign exchange*), is denoted generally with a six-letter format, with the first currency being the commodity currency, one unit of which is measured in "terms" of the terms currency (the second currency of the pair).

Hence, USDJPY is the representation of 1 USD in terms of the JPY, while EURUSD is the value of 1 EUR in terms of the USD.

With the exception of EUR, GBP, AUD, and NZD, most currencies in the world trade against the United States with the U.S. dollar as the commodity currency.

Movement of Money

When money moves across borders, it changes form and has to be exchanged from one currency to another—this is the basis of FX. When money moves over time, the rate at which it gains value can be represented by interest, while the rate at which it loses value can be represented by inflation (see Figure 18.2). When money moves across borders over time, the forward market, explained more in detail later in the book, evolves.

We articulate the key differences between over-the-counter transactions and those done on an exchange in the following note.

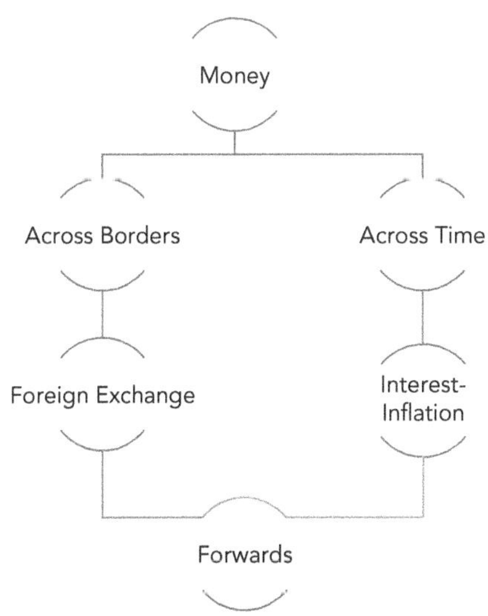

FIGURE 18.2 Linkages Between the World of Money Markets and Foreign Exchange

Difference between OTC and Exchange Trades

Over-the-counter trades are transactions between two counterparties with terms and conditions bilaterally agreed between them. The parties could be anywhere in the world. As long as the laws and regulations in either territory enable them to undertake these transactions, they are held good. Amounts, currencies, dates, and conditions are all customised to the requirements of the firms. Credit risk is managed through the use of credit facilities in case one of the parties is a bank or through the use of collateral or guarantees. Marking to market as a practice depends on the regulation, accounting practice, and transacting style of the counterparties and is not mandatory. Most FX transactions and structured derivatives fall in this category.

Exchange-traded transactions, however, occur under the aegis and on the systems of an exchange. Transaction sizes, settlement dates, and types of transactions are all standardised, and the venue of the transaction is always the exchange. Exchanges usually require placement of collateral up front by all entities that seek to perform transactions on the exchange, thereby reducing pre-settlement and settlement risk for the exchange. Transactions are marked to market on a daily basis.

When would you use exchange-traded transactions to hedge? Exchange-traded transactions work well when pricing transparency is required, where the market sizes and dates can be standardised and where the amounts are not that large. When some customisation and some structuring is required, OTC transactions work better in general.

Underlying Assets or Market Factors

Currencies can be categorised into:

- **Free float.** G7+ currencies float freely based on demand supply and expectation.
- **Managed float.** The central bank allows the market to move on its own but also sets parameters for the currency to trade within (see "Intervention"). Some countries, such as China, set upper and lower bands beyond which the currency cannot trade.
- **Fixed or pegged.** The currency is pegged to a large trading partner, such as the USD.

Currencies can also be categorised by convertibility, or the ease and flexibility with which they can be bought and sold (traded) in local or global markets

- **Fully convertible.** In this case, all transactions (on the current and capital accounts) can be executed without any prior approval from the central bank.
- **Partially convertible.** The central bank imposes restrictions on the type of transactions for which no prior approval need be taken for currency conversion and the type of transactions that need to be pre-approved. In most cases, speculative purchases or sales are not allowed and an underlying genuine trade or capital-related transaction is mandated for currency dealings.

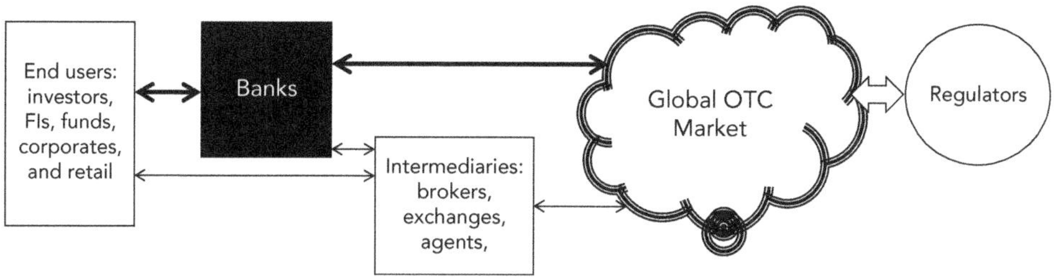

FIGURE 18.3 FX Market Participants

Intervention

When central banks are of the opinion that their currency has appreciated or depreciated beyond a point that is good for the economic, financial, or political conditions of the country, or if the market moves have been very rapid, they could choose to enter the market and buy or sell the currency to stem the flow. This is generally not a common event, but the central bank's intervention usually signals the regulator's intent and potential comfort levels to markets and traders in particular, who then understand the outer limits of immediate currency moves.

Participants

The FX market has many participants (see Figure 18.3) that are driven primarily by the OTC transactions between banks. Various exchanges and agents offer convertibility to the end-user space and themselves depend on the global market to manage and settle their own positions.

Fixed Income and Money Markets

Fixed income and money markets have been categorised together because they constitute the majority of debt or interest rate–related markets.

Money markets are shorter term (usually under one year) markets that involve liquid sources of funding, such as:

- Repurchase agreements (repos)
- Interbank lending
- Commercial paper
- Fed funds or overnight borrowing
- Bills
- Working capital borrowings

Table 18.1 shows some of the key terminologies across FX and money markets.

The term *fixed income markets* refers to any type of investment that is not equity of a tenor usually of over a year, which creates an obligation from the borrower (or

TABLE 18.1 Terminologies Across FX and Money Markets

Aspect	Foreign Exchange	Money Markets
Immediate settlement	Cash/Tom/Spot	Overnight loans Overdrafts
Future settlement	Forwards (OTC) Futures (exchange)	Forwards (OTC) Forward rate agreements (FRAs) (OTC) Rate locks (OTC) Interest rate (IR) and bond futures (exchange)
Other derivatives	FX options FX swaps	IR options Swaps Swaptions
Future fixing on future dates	Forward on forward (OTC) Forward on option (OTC) Option on option (OTC)	Same as FX (all OTC) Swaps (OTC)

"issuer") to make payments on a fixed schedule to a lender (or "investor"). The number of payments, or the amount of payments, may be variable. Examples of fixed income transactions are:

- Bonds
- Medium-term notes (MTNs)
- Structured notes and bonds
- Credit markets including credit derivatives
- Derivative markets, such as interest rate options and swaps

Participants

Figure 18.4 depicts the key participants in fixed income and money markets.

Investors can include funds, banks, individuals, corporations and institutions in a country and overseas. Each investor has a specific risk profile and would take on the tenor, rating characteristics, and profile of the investor and investment that suits its risk profile.

In the context of risk management, derivatives also form a core requirement for the investor and issuer base; issuers use them to protect against risk and investors use them to assume a specific kind of risk for improved or targeted returns.

Commodity Markets

In commodity markets, trading ownership of physical and paper transactions, usually in the future, take place. *Commodities* may be defined as uniform items of value and large volume that are in demand by users and are produced, mined, or sold by different entities.

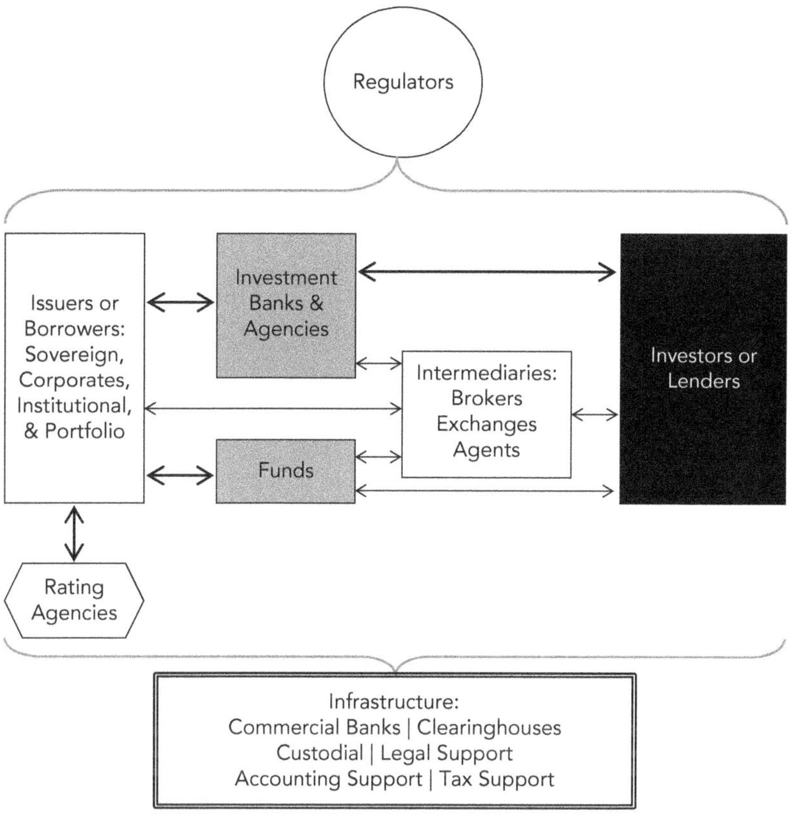

FIGURE 18.4 Key Participants in Fixed Income and Money Markets

Well-established physical commodities actively trade on exchanges or OTC. Hence, these can be physically delivered and generally stored for a reasonable period of time. Commodities can also trade as paper contracts, where settlement of physical goods does not happen at maturity; instead, a financial equivalent settlement happens at maturity.

Firms use commodity markets to hedge against exposures that they may have or as alternative investments and long-term hedges against currency depreciation and inflation. Commodity prices move similarly to the equities of commodity producers but generally do not have a steep correlation with equity or bond markets.

Futures and options are traded on many exchanges, such as the Chicago Board of Trade (CBOT), Chicago Mercantile Exchange (CME), New York Mercantile Exchange (NYMEX), London Metals Exchange (LME), and the Intercontinental Exchange (ICE), as well as OTC.

Commodities markets are largely categorised into these themes (Figure 18.5):

- **Energy**. Comprised of oil and gas (such as crude oil [WTI Intermediate, Brent, Dubai crude, etc.] and gasoil), other petrochemicals, and hard energy, such as coal
- **Metals**. Comprised of precious metals (such as gold and silver) and base metals (such as nickel and aluminum)

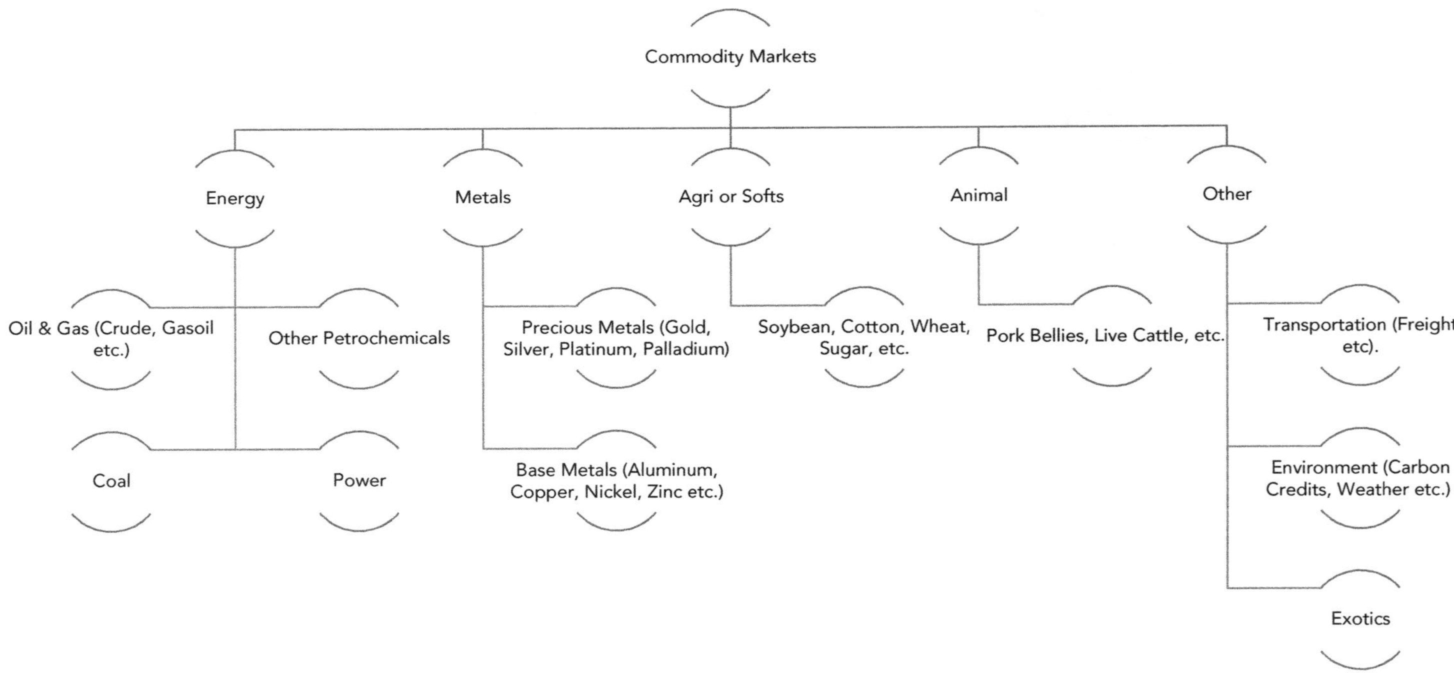

FIGURE 18.5 Commodity Markets

- **Agricultural or Softs.** Comprised of agricultural commodities, such as soybean, coffee, cocoa, sugar, wheat, and cotton
- **Animal.** Comprised of standard high-volume livestock or foods, such as pork bellies
- **Transportation.** Comprised of freight-related quotes and products
- **Environment.** Comprised of carbon-related credits and derivatives, weather-related products, and so on
- **Exotics.** Other commodities or new classes not mentioned above

Equity Markets

We have covered equity capital from an issuer's perspective earlier in Chapter 13. Equities are traded on an exchange for listed companies and OTC for private ones. From the perspective of a corporate, direct equity risk arises for three reasons:

1. Investment in equity-related products
2. Valuation of group or subsidiary companies
3. Issuance of new capital and impact on existing ones, such as action on convertible bonds

Equity markets are some of the most commonly followed markets around the world and act as a barometer for market sentiment on a country's economy as a whole.

MOVEMENT OF MARKETS

Many factors cause markets to move. The fundamental factor is the buying (and demand) or selling (and supply) of most players in a market, or the expectation of demand and supply.

Some of these factors are economic data indicators and market events.

Economic Data Indicators

Economic data indicators are measures of the strength of an economy or a region that provide insight into the actual well-being of that country or region. Governments, through their economic offices, central banks, or other authorities, usually publish some of the important indicators. Many independent agencies publish survey results of their own, and industry uses some of the credible surveys. For example, agencies such as Thomson Reuters poll economists and market experts on their own estimates of these numbers prior to the formal release of these indicators. These expectations hence get factored in along with traders' own views on the market to determine price of an asset or a group of assets.

When the number actually gets published, the variance from the expected number as well as the improvement or deterioration from earlier indicators merge with the current mood and expectation to drive markets up or down.

Figure 18.6 shows some of the drivers of markets.

Short Term Moves	Long Term Moves
Economic Indicators	Inflation Differentials
Investment Flows	Monetary Growth
Interest Rate Differentials	Trade Balance
Political Environment	Dependence on Imports (especially Crude and Energy)
Central Bank Interventions	Business Environment: Policies Affecting FDI and FII
Technical Market Factors	Political Alignment
Other Event-Based Moves	

FIGURE 18.6 Drivers of Short- and Long-Term Market Moves

Table 18.2 provides a general overview on market reactions to positive or higher economic indicator numbers.

TABLE 18.2 Movement of Markets with Data Releases

		Impact[1] with a Higher Data Point On:		
Data Point	**Description**	**Currency[2]**	**Interest Rates**	**Equities**
Gross Domestic Product	Market value of goods and services produced by a country in a given period	Positive	Positive except in the late cycle	Positive except in the late cycle
Employment	Percentage of people employed in a country. In the United States, the Non-Farm Payroll (NFP)—the number of manufacturing and service sector jobs added during the previous month—is a significant data release	Positive	Positive	Positive
Inflation	The extent to which wholesale prices (measured by a Wholesale Price Index) or consumer prices (measured by a Consumer Price Index) have changed over a period	Negative	Positive	Negative
Retail Sales and Consumer Confidence	The extent to which retail sales in a country have increased, and a measure of the general confidence and mood of the public (which could translate to further sales) that drives consumer-driver economies	Positive	Positive	Positive

TABLE 18.2 *(Continued)*

		Impact[1] with a Higher Data Point On:		
Data Point	**Description**	**Currency[2]**	**Interest Rates**	**Equities**
Industrial Production	The improvement of production in the manufacturing sector of the country	Positive	Positive	Positive
Procurement	A leading indicator that uses inputs from procurement managers (the first points of purchase in the supply chain) who make purchases based on the company's sales expectations, hence a barometer of how positive large companies are of selling products to customers in the country	Positive	Positive	Positive

[1]Generalised impact only; the situation could vary from release to release depending on the prevalent market environment and situation.
[2]Currency of that country.

Market Events

The interlinkages across global markets nowadays has increased dependence on external environments. Hence market events, such as liquidity freezes, fear, regulatory or other incidents, can have an effect on other markets and countries.

SUMMARY

We introduced debt and equity markets in Part Three. In this chapter we focused on the markets from the point of view of risk management and also some drivers of markets and their moves. Thus, we have laid the foundation to explore risk management in more detail in the coming chapters.

CHAPTER NINETEEN

19 Risk Management in Practice: Ensuring the Right IMAGE©

THERE ARE MANY APPROACHES TO risk management in practice, and each firm needs to institutionalise the practice that works for its Treasury design, culture, objectives, and management.

IMAGE© METHODOLOGY[1]

The IMAGE© methodology consists of five easy-to-implement and manage steps:

1. Identify and be aware. (What is the risk?)
2. Measure and quantify the risk. (How much is the risk?)

[1] We discuss here the IMAGE© methodology propagated and practised by independent consulting firm Aktrea Capital Pte Ltd, with whose permission the methodology has been reprinted. Although no royalty will be levied on readers who use this methodology, the company has requested that users let it know at info@aktrea.com, with a brief note on the name, address, and industry of the firm, for its own records and interest.

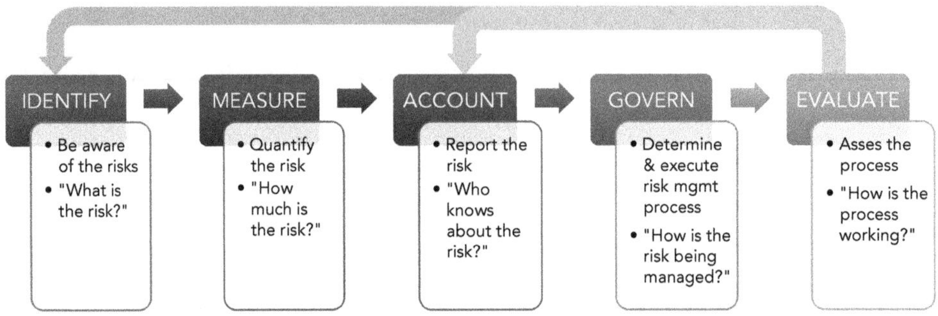

FIGURE 19.1 IMAGE© Framework for Risk Management

3. Account and report the risk. (Who knows about the risk and its management?)
4. Govern and execute the risk management process. (What is being done to manage the risk?)
5. Evaluate and assess the process. (How well is the process working?)

Figure 19.1 outlines the IMAGE© methodology.

RISK IDENTIFICATION

The objective of the risk identification stage is to identify the financial risks to which the firm is exposed. These arise because of the nature of business activity and geographical presence across markets.

How does a firm know which risk it is sitting on? Anything that moves or has variability is a risk—these include market exposures, supply chain elements, balance sheet items like accounts receivable (ARs) and inventory across currencies, dependence on liquidity, exchange control, process implementation, and so on.

Risk identification uses some simple methods to identify, bottom-up, the various risk elements, which can then be quantified so that management can decide to focus efforts on managing certain risks.

Sources of risk are easily identifiable through examining a line-by-line breakup of all elements of the balance sheet and cash flows. Any element that is impacted by need must be taken into account:

- Foreign exchange moves
- Interest rate moves
- Commodity price changes
- Liquidity of market and availability of capital
- Creditors
- Human intervention (processing)
- System impact

TABLE 19.1 Various Elements of Firm Financials and Possible Areas of Risk

Element	FX Risk	Interest Rate Risk	Commodity Risk	Equity Risk	Credit Risk	Liquidity Risk	Operational Risk
Revenue Line & Cash Inflows	✓	✓	✓	✓	✓	(indirect)	✓
Expense Line & Cash Outflows	✓	✓	✓	✓	✓	(indirect)	✓
Assets (e.g., AR, Inventory, Investments, Cash)	✓	✓	✓	✓	✓	✓	✓
Liabilities (e.g., Debt, AP, Equity)	✓	✓		✓		✓	✓
Existing Derivatives and Hedging Instruments	✓	✓	✓	✓	✓	✓	✓

- Geographic presence
- Change in regulations
- Accounting and tax changes

One of the most important aspects of risk identification is risk awareness, and all functions need to be involved in identifying potential risks in their areas. Treasury itself will manage these financial risks, but the involvement of the other functions in the identification process is critical, since the touch points to the areas of risks could arise through their interactions and domains as well. This is especially true of remote locations and interfaces, whose inputs would be the primary ones used by centralised treasury for decision making and corresponding risk management.

Table 19.1 provides an overview of the primary drivers and sources of risk. A zero-based approach to each item in the financials provides the answers to the elements of risk.

Based on the list of identified risks, each risk is quantified using the measurement tools in the next section titled "Risk Measurement." This measurement will form the basis on which the risks that need to be managed will be selected.

RISK MEASUREMENT

In this stage, financial risks for each of the risks identified in the earlier stage are measured or quantified as is their sensitivity to operations and financials of the firm.

The discussion of which methods or practice to use for measurement of risk and assessing the degree of risk is an involved one, and needs to include the Treasurer and the Treasury team along with the chief financial officer (CFO). This assessment should be incorporated into the policy and approved by the board.

Many measures can be considered. For most corporates, simple measures that are also flexible and easy to implement, when well used, yield better results than abstruse and complicated analyses using complex technical terminology and fancy graphs—these might look good on a presentation but could pose serious implementation bottlenecks on the ground.

Two aspects to bear in mind prior to starting the measurement process are highlighted in the note below.

Before the Measurement (1): Fixing the Time Horizon of Risk

The most important precursor to measuring risk is identifying the time frame for the entire risk management exercise. Usually, these time horizons are aligned with the business planning, budgeting and management focus timelines. For specific risks, such as contracts, projects and operations, the time horizon will have a specific life that could be different from the generic one being used. But for the usual measures, the time horizons need to be identified and declared up front. Sometimes a few time horizons can be used—for example, one year and five year. However, a disadvantage of using too many time horizons is the multiplicity of data points, potential complications and overload of information.

Before the Measurement (2): Deciding the Primary Financial Parameter

Knowing what to measure is either a delicate art or an exacting science, and sometimes both together. In any case, the financial parameter that is most impacted by the risks (export revenue) or the one most important to the firm (e.g., earnings before interest, taxes, depreciation, and amortisation [EBITDA]) is a good point to start. Keeping it simple might help. Firms that have their risks loaded on the top line would do well to use sales or related financials or ratios as a measure. Highly leveraged local firms could look at debt-related measures. Firms with risks distributed across various elements of their financials look at overall parameters, such as EBITDA, firm value or return on capital.

Another aspect to look at is whether to consider discounted or undiscounted numbers. Especially for companies across countries and interest rate environments, the discounting factor used (which itself can change with a change in the yield curve) can make a significant difference to the figures.

Figure 19.2 zooms in on the risk measurement process.

The risk measurement process consists of two different methods:

1. **Discrete methods**. Factor sensitivity, scenario analysis, and stress testing
2. **Statistical methods**. Value at risk (VaR), cash flow at risk (CFaR), correlation

Some methods used to measure or dimension the risk are discussed next.

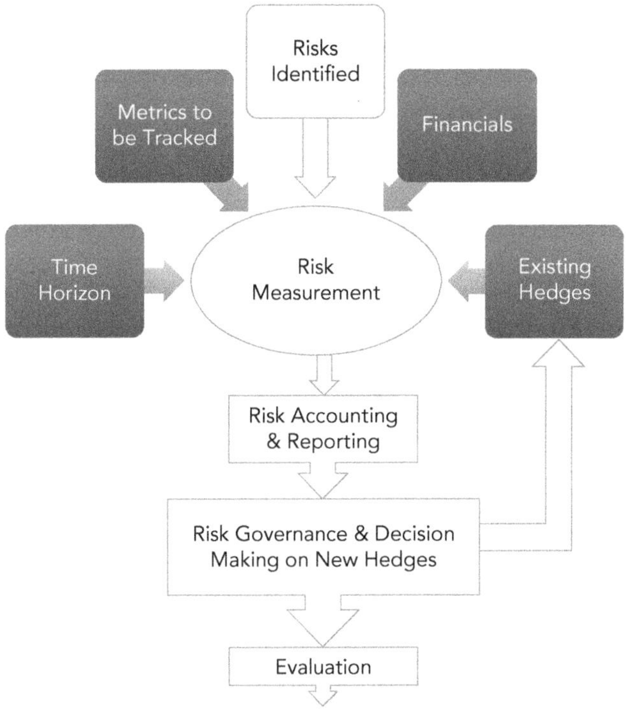

FIGURE 19.2 Risk Measurement in Context of the Entire Risk Management Process

Discrete Methods

Simple discrete methods of measuring the risk use calculable factors that depict the current status of risk at any point of time.

Factor Sensitivity Analysis

Sensitivity analysis, which is especially useful to measure items related to market risk, shows the firm how a certain change to a market factor impacts the financials (firm value).

For example, the factor sensitivity (FS) of the EUR USD on a firm's value could be USD 12.3 million for every 0.01 change to the EUR USD exchange rate.

For a leveraged company, the FS of USD interest rates could be USD 6 million for every basis point (0.01%) shift in the USD yield curve.

Factor sensitivities, when superimposed on historic moves and future scenarios, provide a strong input into deciding which risks to focus on. Materiality of the risk is a call taken as part of the decision on which risks to hedge.

The three main factor sensitivities to monitor as part of the risk management process are:

1. **Current FS**. What is the FS at current levels? For an existing hedge portfolio with a nonlinear payoff, even the FS can change dramatically at different levels. This is where the use of scenario analysis as a complementary tool becomes important.

2. **Unhedged FS.** This is important to benchmark since the effectiveness of the existing hedges need to be determined. Ideally, if the objective of risk management is to reduce risk, the FS should move closer to zero after hedging.
3. **Proposed strategy FS.** Superimposing hedges on the portfolio or specific market factors, the change in FS should a hedge be put out is captured. This is one of the parameters that management could use to make a decision.

EXAMPLE: CALCULATING FACTOR SENSITIVITY

Let us illustrate the calculation of FS with a simple example (see Table 19.2). We shall come back to our favorite example: calculating FS of the EUR USD spot on a simple portfolio.

Assume

- The metric to be used is cumulative one-year cash inflow in USD terms.
- Cash flows monthly on the last date of each month.
- Present value will not be considered.
- The portfolio is currently unhedged.
- All numbers on the table are in millions (mm).
- *Rev Ccy* stands for revenue currency.

Change in portfolio value: 415.9mm USD – 414mm USD = 1.9 mm USD
Total FS (on the metric for 0.01 increases in EUR USD rate): 1.9 mm USD

TABLE 19.2 EUR USD Factor Sensitivity

Eur USD at 1.3000													
	Month												
Rev Ccy	**Jan**	**Feb**	**Mar**	**Apr**	**May**	**Jun**	**Jul**	**Aug**	**Sep**	**Oct**	**Nov**	**Dec**	**TOTAL**
EUR	12	13	14	15	16	16	15	15	16	18	19	21	**190**
USD	10	11	12	10	11	12	13	14	15	18	20	21	**167**
In USD Terms													
EUR	15.6	16.9	18.2	19.5	20.8	20.8	19.5	19.5	20.8	23.4	24.7	27.3	**247**
USD	10	11	12	10	11	12	13	14	15	18	20	21	**167**
TOT	25.6	27.9	30.2	29.5	31.8	32.8	32.5	33.5	35.8	41.4	44.7	48.3	**414**

Eur USD at 1.3100													
	Month												
Rev Ccy	**Jan**	**Feb**	**Mar**	**Apr**	**May**	**Jun**	**Jul**	**Aug**	**Sep**	**Oct**	**Nov**	**Dec**	**TOTAL**
EUR	12	13	14	15	16	16	15	15	16	18	19	21	**190**
USD	10	11	12	10	11	12	13	14	15	18	20	21	**167**
In USD Terms													
EUR	15.72	17.03	18.34	19.65	20.96	20.96	19.65	19.65	20.96	23.58	24.89	27.51	**248.9**
USD	10	11	12	10	11	12	13	14	15	18	20	21	**167**
TOT	25.72	28.03	30.34	29.65	31.96	32.96	32.65	33.65	35.96	41.58	44.89	48.51	**415.9**

Scenario Analysis

Scenario analyses project financial performance over a period of time, across different scenarios. These analyses can be either descriptive scenarios, implying specific moves on the market factors, or numeric scenarios. Figures 19.3, 19.4, 19.5, and 19.6 depict sample scenario analyses.

Figure 19.3 shows a sample set of descriptive scenarios—it is important to remember that descriptive scenarios do have actual numeric assumptions on each market factor. The main advantage of descriptive scenarios is that it could include assumptions on more than two factors and hence can be represented in one table. Figure 19.4 provides a descriptive scenario on a specific risk (loan outflows) with more than two factors being impacted by the scenarios—for simplicity, we have depicted the top two.

Figure 19.4 shows a sample set of numeric scenarios for a generic measure. Numeric scenarios are usually across two factors and can be adjusted to include perhaps a third factor. Any more factors could impact readability. A sample numeric scenario for a specific risk is given in Figure 19.5.

The scenarios should factor in these issues:

- Historic levels (covering ranges over the past 10 years at least)
- Current expectations of levels received from banks/research desks (since these will be in a range, the elements in the range can be covered)
- Any regulator's comments
- Geopolitical situation and event probabilities
- Cyclicality
- Technical levels or big-figure levels close to current levels
- Linkages with global markets (e.g., currency depreciation in case of emerging markets pullout)

Stress Scenarios

Stress scenarios are specific scenarios that place a stress on the market in terms of:

- Extreme and sudden movement of market factors
- Cross-border events
- Liquidity problems
- Credit events and defaults
- Regulatory changes
- Supply chain disruption
- Peer or industry event
- Company-related event (such as reputational issues, operational loss, etc.)
- Regulatory or government action on the group

The aspect most critical to the functioning of a company in these situations is liquidity—the ability to provide cash or funding to group entities that need them. Mark-to-market losses, while important, are themselves not directly the most critical, for in quite a few cases, these losses can be managed or limited by restructuring the original transaction with restricted incremental losses. Liquidity, however, is usually

(LCY mm)	USD Rate Scenarios	Remains Same	Moves as per Fwd	Average Up by 1%	Avg Libor = 9.00%	Low, then Increases	Steady then Spike	YC Shift Up by 1%	YC Shift Down by 1%	YC Shift Up by 2%	Last 10 Years	Goes Up by 1% per Year	Year IRS Hedge (2.1%)
	Ccy Scenarios												
1	Remains same	7,569	8,252	8,019	10,329	7,952	7,903	8,749	7,953	9,246	8,525	9,096	8,386
2	Moves as per Fwd	9,325	10,155	9,844	12,472	9,823	9,748	10,722	9,796	11,290	10,465	11,194	10,257
3	Strengthen 1% per yr	7,153	7,802	7,586	9,817	7,511	7,467	8,281	7,518	8,761	8,067	8,600	7,942
4	Weaken 1% per yr	8,010	8,729	8,477	10,870	8,421	8,366	9,244	8,416	9,760	9,010	9,622	8,856
5	Steady, weakens 2% per yr	8,152	8,881	8,621	11,016	8,576	8,516	9,396	8,564	9,912	9,159	9,787	9,000
6	Depreciate around events	8,069	8,790	8,538	10,935	8,488	8,431	9,306	8,475	9,823	9,073	9,695	8,917
7	Average Increase of 1	7,734	8,432	8,194	10,555	8,126	8,076	8,940	8,127	9,449	8,711	9,295	8,569
8	Average price 42	8,778	9,570	9,300	11,979	9,223	9,165	10,146	9,224	10,723	9,886	10,549	9,725
9	Moves similar to 2000-2010	7,503	8,176	7,956	10,285	7,876	7,830	8,677	7,880	9,180	8,448	9,013	8,326
10	Appreciates 0.50 per yr	7,101	7,745	7,531	9,753	7,455	7,412	8,222	7,462	8,700	8,009	8,538	7,886
11	Stable, then appreciates	7,331	7,997	7,774	10,053	7,697	7,652	8,486	7,705	8,977	8,267	8,815	8,136
12	Depreciates 1.00 per yr	8,505	9,266	8,993	11,480	8,948	8,886	9,802	8,935	10,339	9,556	10,213	9,386
13	Recession followed by growth	7,811	8,529	8,282	10,690	8,202	8,155	9,048	8,216	9,568	8,815	9,400	8,664
14	Crisis in 2 years	10,334	11,295	10,905	13,767	10,877	10,803	11,913	10,882	12,532	11,613	12,426	11,350
15	Market moves up and hedge rates remain where they are	9,491	10,336	10,020	12,698	9,997	9,921	10,914	9,970	11,493	10,652	11,393	10,441
16	Market moves up and hedge levels move up	9,667	10,526	10,202	12,913	10,184	10,106	11,111	10,154	11,697	10,846	11,603	10,628
17	Market moves down and hedge rates remain where they are	9,160	9,974	9,669	12,246	9,649	9,575	10,531	9,622	11,088	10,279	10,995	10,074
18	Market moves down and hedge levels move down	8,984	9,784	9,486	12,032	9,462	9,391	10,333	9,438	10,884	10,085	10,786	9,886

FIGURE 19.3 Descriptive Scenario on Generic Measure (EBITDA)

SELECTED SAMPLE SCENARIO				FCY LOAN PORTFOLIO			
Situation: Parent Country	Situation: World	Parent Currency Move (vs USD)	USD Libor Move	Estimated Outflow on FCY Loans (LCY mm)	Difference (LCY mm)	Equivalent LCY Loan (% p.a)	OVERALL PORTFOLIO OUTFLOW (LCY mm)
Remains the same	Remains the same	Stable	Stable	45,414	(37,845)	4.46%	373,100
Country outperforms rest of world	Moves cyclically (last 10 years)	Appreciate 0.5 per year	Higher, then lower	48,054	(40,485)	6.15%	362,820
Country outperforms rest of world	Recession continues	Stable, then appreciates	Remains low, then increases	46,182	(38,613)	5.59%	367,640
Flight of capital from EM	Investment into developed economies	Depreciate 1 per year	Higher, then lower	57,336	(49,767)	9.70%	422,340
Intermittent events	Moves cyclically (last 10 years)	Depreciate around events, else stable	Higher, then lower	54,438	(46,869)	8.60%	403,830
Moves cyclically (2000 to 2010)	Moves cyclically (last 10 years)	Depreciate, then appreciate	Higher, then lower	50,688	(43,119)	7.70%	381,880
Moves into recession, then recovers	Moves cyclically (last 10 years)	Depreciate, then appreciate	Higher, then lower	52,890	(45,321)	7.90%	395,470
Moves into recession, then recovers	Recession continues	Depreciate, then appreciate	Remains low, then increases	49,212	(41,643)	6.70%	389,340

FIGURE 19.4 Descriptive Scenario on Specific Measure (FCY Loan Portfolio)

Avg USD Libor	0.26%	0.36%	0.46%	0.60%	0.80%	1.00%	1.50%	2.00%	2.50%	3.00%	4.00%	5.00%	6.00%
Avg LCY													
37	605	597	589	578	562	545	505	465	425	385	305	225	144
38	565	557	549	537	521	504	463	422	381	340	257	175	92
39	526	517	509	497	480	463	421	379	336	294	209	125	40
40	486	477	469	457	439	422	379	335	292	248	162	75	(12)
41	446	438	429	416	398	381	336	292	247	203	114	25	(64)
42	407	398	389	376	358	339	294	248	203	157	66	(25)	(116)
43	367	358	349	336	317	298	252	205	158	112	19	(75)	(168)
43.5	347	338	329	315	297	278	231	183	136	89	(5)	(100)	(194)
44	328	318	309	295	276	257	209	162	114	66	(29)	(124)	(220)
44.5	308	298	289	275	256	236	188	140	92	44	(53)	(149)	(246)
45	288	278	269	255	235	216	167	118	70	21	(77)	(174)	(272)
45.7	260	250	241	227	207	187	137	88	38	(11)	(110)	(209)	(308)
46	248	238	229	215	195	175	125	75	25	(25)	(125)	(224)	(324)
47	209	199	188	174	154	133	83	32	(19)	(70)	(172)	(274)	(376)
48	169	159	148	134	113	92	40	(12)	(64)	(116)	(220)	(324)	(428)
49	130	119	108	94	72	51	(2)	(55)	(108)	(161)	(268)	(374)	(480)
50	90	79	68	53	32	10	(44)	(99)	(153)	(207)	(315)	(424)	(532)
51	50	39	28	13	(9)	(31)	(87)	(142)	(197)	(252)	(363)	(474)	(584)
52	11	(0)	(12)	(27)	(50)	(73)	(129)	(185)	(242)	(298)	(411)	(523)	(636)
53	(29)	(40)	(52)	(68)	(91)	(114)	(171)	(229)	(286)	(344)	(458)	(573)	(688)

FIGURE 19.5 Numeric Scenario with Specific Measure (Change in Loan Outflow)

Avg LCY through First N Years	Years 38.00	40.0C	42.00	43.00	44.00	45.00	46.00	47.00	48.00	50.00	52.00	54.00	56.00
N (yrs)													
1	55.4	55.3	55.1	55.0	55.0	54.9	54.8	54.7	54.7	54.5	54.3	54.2	54.0
2	58.5	58.0	57.4	57.2	56.9	56.6	56.4	56.1	55.8	55.3	54.8	54.2	53.7
3	62.5	61.5	60.4	59.9	59.4	58.9	58.4	57.9	57.3	56.3	55.3	54.3	53.2
4	68.1	66.3	64.6	63.8	62.9	62.1	61.2	60.3	59.5	57.8	56.0	54.3	52.6
5	76.1	73.4	70.7	69.3	68.0	66.6	65.3	63.9	62.5	59.8	57.1	54.4	51.7

FIGURE 19.6 Post-Hedging Numeric Scenario with Conditional Payoffs After Each Year of Hedging

an immediate requirement, and the inability of the firm to tide itself over an absence of liquidity can be enterprise threatening. Mark-to-market losses can result in a shortfall of liquidity, as can be a credit event or a regulatory change.

Each stress level must have certain assumptions associated with it that must be ratified by the treasury management committee and approved by the board as part of the annual review.

Results are usually used to determine the focus of contingency plans, especially on liquidity. If required, the portfolio is amended or hedges are put out to reduce the stress in some cases. Trigger levels can be used to set early-warning levels that could result in action on the portfolio before such scenarios actually occur. Experiences from earlier stress events are also useful to bear in mind while evaluating scenarios and impacts of events on the financials of the firm.

Discrete Measures of Liquidity Risk

Discrete measures of liquidity risk are simple snapshots that can provide a good overview of the liquidity at any point and also targeted levels that can trigger measures in case they are exceeded.

Liquidity Gap *Liquidity gap* can be defined as the excess value of the firm's liquid assets over its volatile liabilities. A negative liquidity gap implies that a company could be underfunded in some situations and must try to build longer-term funding sources. A disadvantage of this measure is that it does not relate to the funding cost of the group.

Asset Liquidity Measures Alexandra Hachmeister has defined some asset liquidity measures: bid-offer spread, market depth, immediacy, and resilience.

The bid-offer spread is a good measure of liquidity of an asset being held by the firm. The smaller the spread, the more liquid the asset is.

Market depth is the amount of an asset that can be bought and sold at various bid-ask spreads.

Immediacy refers to the time needed to successfully trade a certain amount of an asset at a prescribed cost.

Resilience can be defined as the speed with which prices return to former levels after a large transaction.

Probability and Statistical Methods

Various probability and statistical analyses exist, implemented through formulas, models, distribution testing, and other methods. Of late, VaR has been mentioned a lot in the news.

The success of some of these methods has been debated in the corporate setting, owing to the related complexity, margin for error, and ability to work under all conditions and market environments. In my view, most corporates can measure risk prudently using simple tools, such as scenario analysis and factor sensitivities, before and after hedging.

Value at Risk

Many companies have started using VaR as a risk measure. If the complexities of the operations and assumed risks are commensurate with the use of this interesting method as a tool (see the box titled "The Art of VaR"), it can indeed be an ally.

VaR is a measure of how much the value of a firm, portfolio, or financial position can change because of movements in market factors, such as foreign exchange rates, interest rates, commodity prices, and stock prices. Hence, the Treasury or portfolio manager can state with a certain degree of confidence, in most situations, the maximum loss that the firm or portfolio can suffer over a particular period of time.

Corporates use VaR as a general measure of risk, as a limit for exposures to market factors, and to evaluate cash flows and liquidity situations (CFaR and LaR respectively, discussed in more detail later in the chapter).

There are three commonly used methods for calculating VaR: historic rate, variance/covariance, and Monte Carlo.

Back-testing the VaR result with historical performance is used in accompaniment to current VaR readings in many cases, to show how the same methodology would have fared in different times. VaR can also be used across scenario analyses and stress testing described earlier.

Many books and articles describe VaR and how to build models around it. Here we mention just the important and salient aspects here, including volatility and correlation.

Volatility

With the advent of option pricing, volatility has become one of the most studied, debated, used, and misused tools in financial management. It is essentially a mathematical measure (in percentage) of the variability of a particular market factor or instrument. Volatility is a nondirectional measure (always positive), since it measures both increases and decreases in the value of the factor or instrument. The higher the volatility, the higher the financial risk.

Volatility can be obtained using standard deviation, a popular statistical measure, usually expressed in annualised terms, such as interest rates. Standard deviation can be easily obtained from historical data using the simple formula

$$\frac{\sum_{i=1}^{n}(x_i - \bar{x})^2}{n \quad 1}$$

where:

n = number of observations
x_i = lognormal return of observation i over observation $i - 1$
x = average lognormal return of the data

Some measures of volatility are:

- **Historical volatility**. Measured by historical trends and data
- **Implied volatility**. Quoted and traded by traders in professional markets; it is commonly used in pricing options
- **Exponential weighted moving average**. More complex statistical methods that remove certain problems that creep into simpler methods

One of the commonly discussed issues with probability distributions is the fat tail—the probability of extreme values in the price being greater than estimated by a normal distribution. And when the market liquidity dries up, the fat tail tends to become fatter.

Correlation

Correlation is the extent to which the prices of two factors or instruments are linked to each other: If the correlation is close to 100% or 1, the two prices move very closely or largely in tandem. If the correlation is close to –1, the two move oppositely. If the correlation is close to zero, there has been no observable pattern or relationship between the two.

Correlation is a critical aspect when looking at diversification or optimising a portfolio. For example, if a company has payables in two highly correlated factors (e.g., EUR USD and USD CHF, as shown in Figure 19.7), the risk is more concentrated than if it had payables in two currencies that were most highly correlated (viz., the two

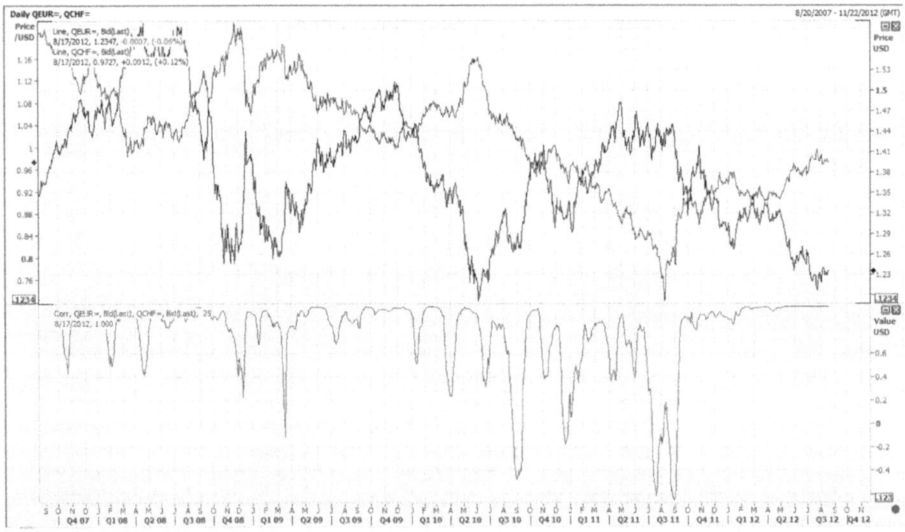

FIGURE 19.7 Correlation Between EUR and CHF

Source: Thomson Reuters Eikon

currencies have moved similarly at the same points of time over a certain time horizon). The risk of a portfolio that has two highly correlated risky assets is much greater than a portfolio of two uncorrelated risk assets.

When assessing a portfolio for VaR, the correlation aspect is generally considered since the prices of different factors move differently, and the movement of a portfolio as a whole must be factored in.

Liquidity-Adjusted VaR

A derivative of VaR is liquidity-adjusted VAR—a measure that incorporates liquidity risk into VaR. The premise here is that in some situations, the holding period for an asset could be higher than normal, and there is a corresponding cost of holding that asset prior to unwinding the position.

The Art of VaR

The evolution of VaR modelling has changed the way capital markets work today. When implemented well, it can effectively measure the relative safety of the portfolios of banks and financial institutions (FIs). Here we discuss the dangers that corporates whose primary business is not finance face while relying primarily on VaR to assess, and hence to act, on their financial risks.

The CFO of a reputed company beamed across the table, waving a piece of paper in the air. "Our VaR score has just come in," he said with the excitement of a student who has just received brilliant marks in his first exam, "and it is low. We need to do nothing on our foreign currency exposures." What did that mean—for him, for his shareholders, for all stakeholders in this company?

How Is the VaR Calculated?

VaR is defined as the potential marked-to-market loss on an open position due to adverse movement of market factors within the defeasance period. VaR is an estimate of the adverse impact on profit and loss in a conservative scenario (at a specified confidence level).

The factors that go into calculation of VaR are discussed next.

Market Factors

Market factors (MFs) are independent market variables that impact the price of an instrument or a position. A market factors group (MFG) is a group of correlated market factors, such as interest rates, foreign exchange (FX) rates, equity prices, commodity prices or implied volatilities (only in options). Positions may be sensitive to single MF (such as for FX spot) or several MFG (such as for FX forwards and options).

(Continued)

Factor Sensitivity

Factor sensitivity (FS) is the change in the value of a position due to a unit change in an independent MF with all other MFs remaining constant—for example, 0.01% in interest rates or 0.01 in the currency.

Defeasance Period/Defeasance Factor

The defeasance period/defeasance factor is the time required (normally in days) to zeroise a position by either hedging or liquidating. For small to medium positions in liquid instruments, this period is usually assumed to be one day. The defeasance period incorporates liquidity risk in risk measurement.

Volatility

Liquidity indicates the dispersion of a market variable against its mean or average. Volatile prices or rates would exhibit greater variation than less volatile prices. Measures of variation are:

Variance = average deviation of the mean for a historical sample size

Standard deviation = square root of the variance in terms of original sample prices/rates

The market expresses volatility in terms of annualised standard deviation (1 SD).

VaR revolutionised the way banks and FIs measured and viewed risk. Now various people in these firms, whether they are traders, risk managers or business managers, have a way of estimating a likely measure of the losses in their positions or portfolios. Limits could be set more easily in terms of the risk that a bank was taking, for example, to government bonds or the US dollar–Indian rupee exchange rate. If the threshold or limit was exceeded, the position had to be liquidated by the trader in order to get back within prescribed limits. Many banks and FIs were forced to adopt better systems and information flow processes to ensure accurate VaR reporting. Firms were able to take on more risk in the knowledge that they would be able to, in most cases, estimate their losses and hence were in control.

Three points need to be highlighted:

1. VaR captures a set of events with a certain degree of probability of occurrence, say, 95%. It does not cover events or market moves that constitute the other 5%. The world has seen what happened in 2008, when events unfolded that could well have been in the realm of this other unlikely, low-probability 5%.
2. If the VaR exceeds threshold or preset limits, the firm needs to liquidate its assets or exposure immediately to bring back the position to within limits. We have learned from the recent market turmoil that even markets that we take for granted sometimes lose liquidity, and we might not find a taker for our asset or position.

3. Such a sell-off or liquidation of an asset or exposure to get back within limits assumes three things:
   a. The asset or exposure can be freely traded.
   b. The firm can live without this position.
   c. The firm will have enough firepower to keep entering or exiting these positions when the VaR moves with the market.

Banks and FIs can live with these three situations in many cases. Besides, VaR is only one of the measures that they use.

Corporates embarking primarily on the VaR ship do not have the luxury of being able to live with these situations all the time. The positions that corporates usually have are generated as a result of their financial activity; for example, a receivable in US dollars for a software exporter or the purchase by an importer of an engine from Germany, denominated in euros. If there is a worst-case scenario, as with a collapse of a particular economy, the results move towards the tail end of the curve and hence are not accounted for.

For firms that move into more advanced treasury management practices, especially with diversification and portfolio optimisation or with treasury as a profit centre taking on financial positions, VaR and CFaR may be good indicators, especially with the firms' reasonable ability to liquidate positions assumed through financial products with the idea of optimising risk.

Discrete scenario-based analysis and the overall financial position in those scenarios (both without and with putting on a hedge), would be a useful tool for corporates with simple risk profiles to consider for measurement of their hedges. VaR can be used as a good indicator to support other tools but perhaps not as the primary measurement tool.

VaR is, at the end of the day, only a measure, not gospel. Like all instruments of war, it needs to be used well but wisely.

Cash Flow at Risk

CFaR borrows from the concept of firm or portfolio value and focuses it specifically on cash flows. This is more applicable to firms whose primary objective is to monitor their cash flows and their predictability since it estimates with a certain degree of confidence how the cash flows will change in most situations.

Liquidity at Risk (LaR)

LaR is a measure of liquidity—what the firm's liquidity position across most situations would be. LaR is more relevant to banks and FIs, but it can be used by companies if it adds value to their measures.

We now present a case in a parallel universe—almost literally. We go through a decision-making situation at a space agency, and will see how it is related to our world of corporate financial risk.

CASE STUDY: WHICH RISK TO HEDGE? A NASA EXPERIENCE

With constraints (such as cost or resources) to being able to manage only certain kinds of risk, it is useful to have a risk comparison structure in place to be able to make the right choice as to which risk should be the first to be hedged. We explore a parallel case here with the National Aeronautics and Space Administration (NASA) having to choose one, and their Risk Assessment process. Parallels can be drawn very easily with what the Treasurer and CFO can do in their own context.

Background: NASA's Risk Assessment Process

NASA defines risk as the uncertainty of achieving a desired outcome and has in place a detailed but simple risk architecture that covers the two key elements of risk assessment:

- Likelihood of the Risk: What is the probability that the risk will occur, or that the event that triggers the risk will happen? Various mathematical, analytical and subjective models exist for the calculation of such numbers; the final output could be a combination result of all of these.
- Consequence of the Risk: What happens once the risk is triggered? Are there consequences that could be human, financial, compliance, competitive, industrial or even political?

Risks are classified by the types and consequence of their occurrence, such as:

- **Schedule**. The risk, when it occurs, causes delays in implementation and execution. In many of these cases, there is a direct or indirect impact on cost, but when working with tight schedules, the inability to meet deadlines is a critical requirement.
- **Cost**. Most risks usually end up with a cost element. This category covers the risk elements that have a direct impact on cost, should they occur.
- **Technical/Performance**. Any risk that directly impacts the performance of a spacecraft or a programme because of technical glitches or poor performance is categorised in this heading.
- **Technical/Safety.** The most important by far of all of these, this covers the loss of human life as a result of technical malfunction. There is zero tolerance for this kind of risk in any programme under any circumstance.

The risk assessment process logically builds on the above and answers the following questions:

- What can go wrong that could lead to an undesired outcome?
- How likely is this to happen?
- If it happens, what consequences are expected?

Figure 19.8 summarises the background of NASA's risk assessment process.

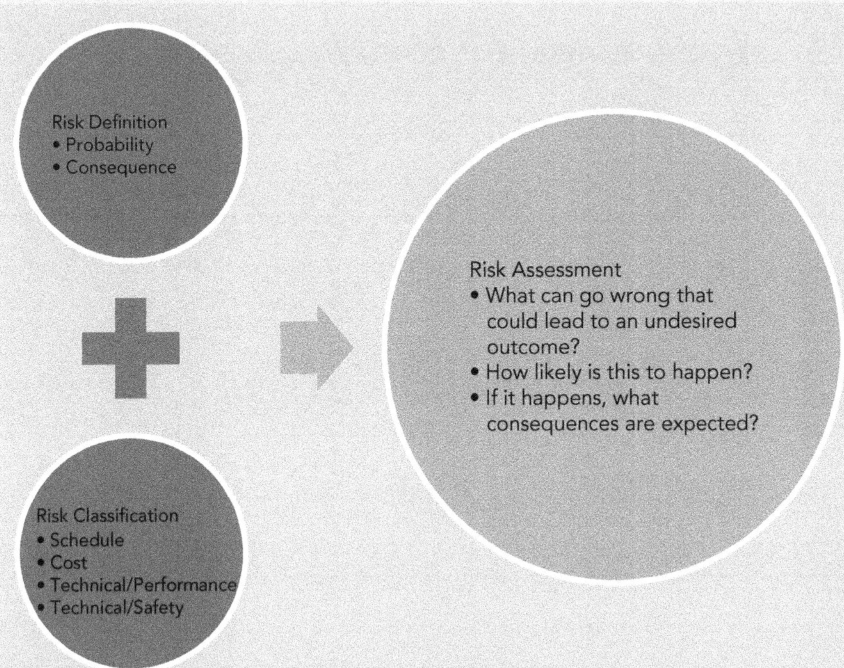

FIGURE 19.8 Background of NASA's Risk Assessment Process

Situation: Have to Pick One Risk to Mitigate—Which One to Pick?

The International Space Station (ISS) is a habitable artificial satellite in low Earth orbit (depicted in Figure 19.9). The ISS serves as a microgravity and space environment research laboratory in which crew members conduct experiments in biology, human biology, physics, astronomy, meteorology and other fields.

Because of the limited launch capabilities to bring items up to the Space Station, a risk question arose about reduce the most risk by selecting the launch vehicle manifest on two critical items to be flown. Knowing that only one risk reduction component could be flown on the next mission to the Station, either a portal window cover for the external viewing window that the crew uses for earth observation or a spare CO_2 scrubber for the environmental control system internal to the Space Station (see Figure 19.10).

Both were items that would reduce certain elements of risk, and the decision had to be taken as to which one would be flown up (limitations on spare only allowed one of these components to be flown):

- **Service Module (SM) Window Cover.** The SM window cover would reduce the damage to the SM window should it be hit by orbital debris (either space junk or natural micrometeorite debris in space).
- **Spare Vozdukh core.** Vozdukh is a permanent recycling system in the ISS that removes carbon dioxide from the air based on the use of regenerable absorbers of carbon dioxide gas.

(*Continued*)

FIGURE 19.9 International Space Station

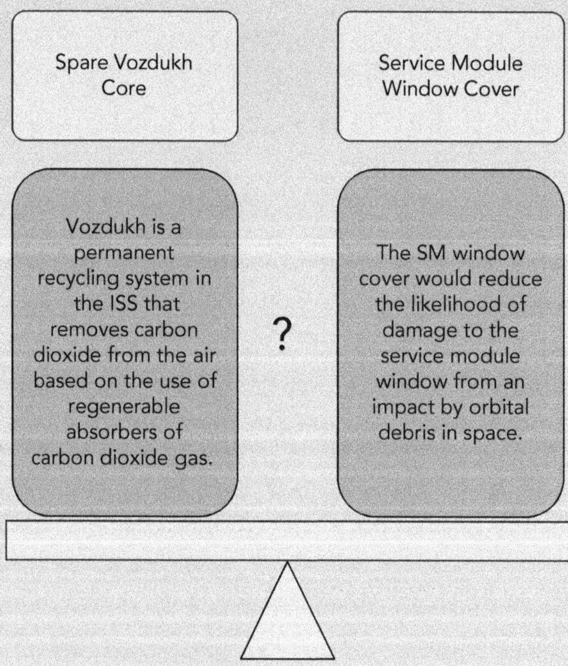

FIGURE 19.10 Which One to Pick?

Risk Assessment Process Using the Probabilistic Risk Assessment Model

This is where the risk assessment process of NASA, using the probabilistic risk assessment (PRA) model, came into play. The architecture for the PRA model is given in Figure 19.11.

Figure 19.12 articulates the process for the PRA model. As can be seen, the process follows a logical sequence of events that involve a data-gathering stage, an analysis stage, and review and decision-making stage.

The process also assumes a hard and unambiguous definition of roles and responsibilities for each activity and decision to be made. This is summarised in Figure 19.13.

Application and Decision Making

In this case, the two alternatives were compared from a risk perspective (Figure 19.14) to determine the relative reduction in the probability of defined end states (i.e., loss of crew, loss of Space Station, crew evacuation, loss of experiments/science). This analysis compared the risk reduction of supplying a SM window cover versus the Vozdukh core relative to a baseline (where neither item is flown up to the Space Station).

The evaluation and assessment of the end states was done based on different scenarios, including stress scenarios. The risk analysis demonstrated that supply the Space Station with the service module window cover reduced more risk than the Vozdukh core. The final decision was made to send through the SM window cover based on the analysis.

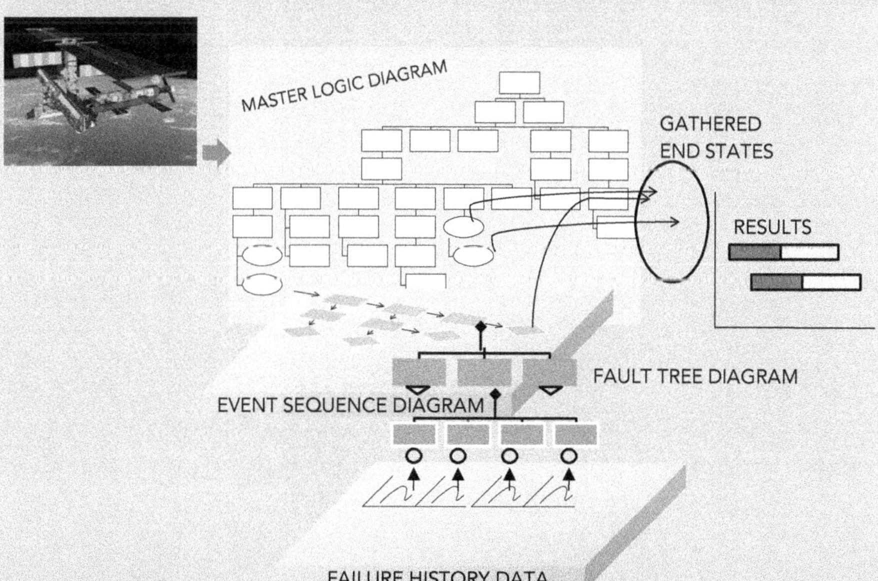

FIGURE 19.11 PRA Architecture (Futron Corporation)

Source: Futron Corporation

(Continued)

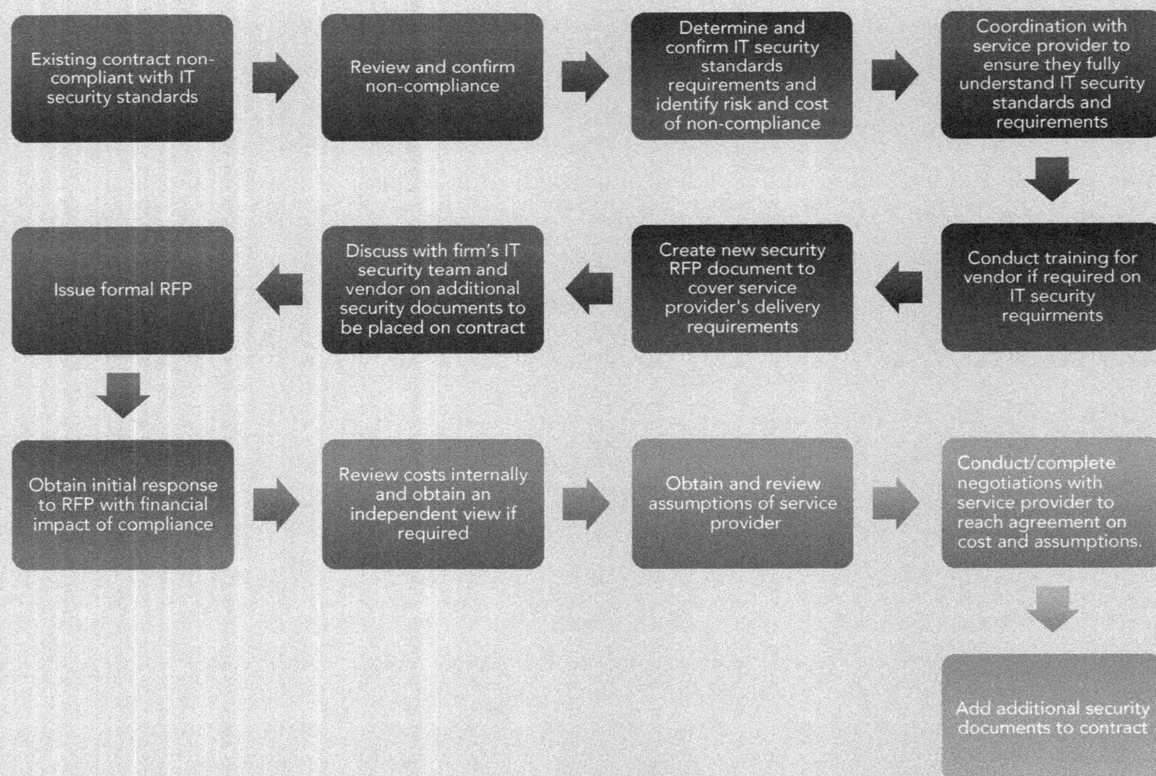

FIGURE 19.12 PRA Process

FIGURE 19.13 Clear Roles and Responsibilities

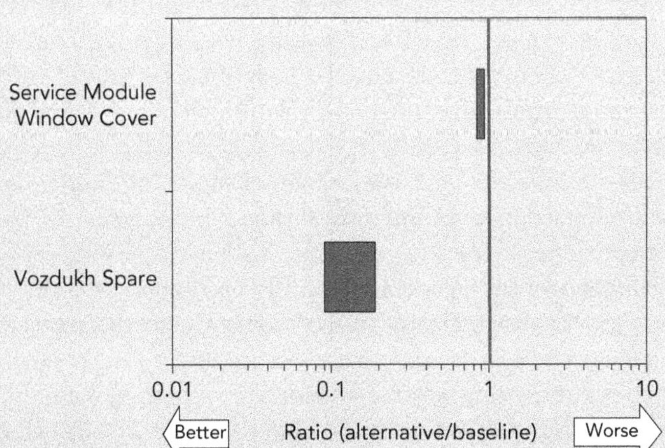

FIGURE 19.14 Results of Comparative Analysis

Contributed by Jeevan Perera, PhD, JD, Johnson Space Center, NASA

(Continued)

Learnings

In real-life treasury, we face many situations where there are constraints. These could be budgetary constraints on hedging cost or resource constraints on people managing these risks (sometimes it is more difficult to start a hedging process and to manage it if there is a shortage of resources).

NASA's approach can help us review our own decision making process for our financials, where we have limitations and can pick only one hedge to focus on. On a broader level, some of the best practices that can be derived from the case in a corporate treasury are listed next.

- Scenario analysis, historic levels, and financial impact of various outcomes are indispensable elements of the risk assessment process.
- Measurement of risk and its impact is key.
- Measurement through scenario analysis and various outcomes makes it simpler for management to make decisions on which risks to hedge and to frame the general risk governance aspect of risk management.

RISK ACCOUNTING AND REPORTING

The risk accounting and reporting stage accounts for and reports the various risks to relevant levels of management. Accounting and reporting risk have to be consistent in regard to accounting practices, rates for valuations, tallying across subsidiaries, and consolidation in parent books, regular reconciliation, independence, and regularity and format of reporting.

Clear responsibility between Treasury and financial control on ownership of data, systems, and activities is essential, as is teamwork between the two functions.

Teamwork brings us to another much-debated point: the accuracy of forecasts coming in to Treasury, based on which Treasury does its risk management activity. Inaccurate forecasts often result in adverse hedges being booked, either for short/excess amounts or for wrong time frames. In volatile markets, these could result in sufficiently negative numbers.

Since forecasts are usually the basis for many hedges, the entire exercise has to be taken with utmost seriousness and gravity by business and cost centres. Many successful firms implement processes to track forecast error, with accurate forecasting being one of the areas of evaluation for subsidiaries and country operations. Treasury can work with the businesses to provide data and trend analysis to help increase forecast accuracy.

The problem becomes more acute when accounting norms prevent losses owing to forecasting errors from being deferred and increase reporting requirements. In some cases, repeated forecasting errors could endanger long-term hedge effectiveness and hence impair the firm's ability to receive hedge accounting treatment.

Reporting is also an independent activity, and firms are moving towards automating it to reduce manual intervention and thus become more timely and accurate.

Overreporting is also a danger, and hence the treasury policy must stipulate the formats, recipients, and frequency of regular reporting.

Exception reporting must have its own separate process and escalation mechanism.

RISK GOVERNANCE

After having put in place the basic infrastructure of the risk management process, we come to the fourth stage: the "doing" of the risk management activity.

Risk governance involves stipulating the objectives, scope, risk factors, time horizons, tenors, amounts, tools, methods, timing, and personnel to execute the risk management activity. These elements are further described here.

Objectives: Why Hedge?

Different firms have different objectives for risk management—more conservative ones focus on reducing the variability on future cash flows and balance sheet and increasing the visibility of the firm's financials. Some seek to optimise the above objectives with an added flexibility of obtaining market rates and timing entry of hedges. More aggressive ones seek to create treasury as a profit centre and use the firm's balance sheet to assume specific financial risks for targeted returns.

In some situations, the firm could believe that the element of the risk is not material and that visibility and certainty of financials is at an appropriately desired level. In this case, the risk management activity becomes passive.

Scope and Risk Factors: What to Hedge?

The risks that will be managed by factor have to be stipulated. Material risks determined at the measurement stage are usually included. The basis for deciding the risks to be hedged is the impact of the risk on the organisation and the approximate factor sensitivities must be documented.

Time Horizons and Tenors: How Long to Hedge For?

The maximum allowable tenor for the hedges is determined. It usually is in sync with the time horizon as determined during the measurement stage.

Each risk class, or even each market factor, could have a different time frame, though in the absence of good systems and reporting, using different timeframes for different factors could complicate the entire process of tracking, evaluation, and reporting.

Amounts: How Much to Hedge?

The extent of the risk to be managed or hedged needs to be determined. Hedging ratios (using the M-D-U proportion) can be maintained for each of the elements. The M-D-U proportion provides for a mandatory (M%) percentage of the stated exposure

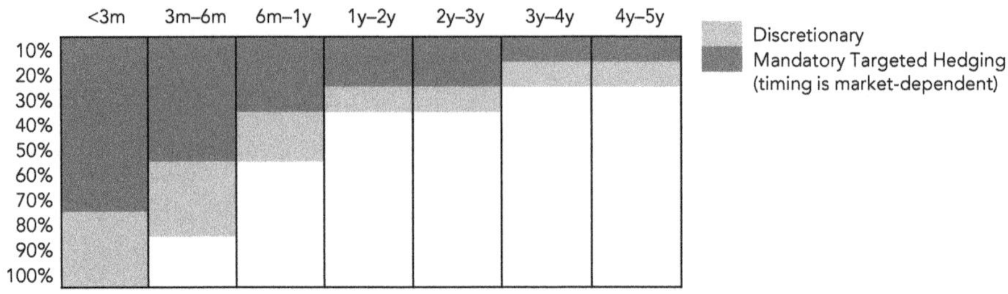

FIGURE 19.15 Layered Hedging Strategy

to be always hedged, a discretionary portion (D%) to be hedged based on the judgement of the hedger, and an unhedged portion (U%) that will always remain unhedged. Minimum and maximum ratios of the extent of hedging over the time horizon for hedging will be provided.

This can create a layered hedging strategy across tenors. Figure 19.15 depicts a typical layered hedging strategy over time, which allows for some discretionary hedging.

Tools and Methods: How to Hedge?

The tools and products that can be used are decided at this point (see the development of a hedging strategy in Chapter 22). These have to be consistent with the tenors and hedging proportions decided above.

Tools and products can be categorised into the market instruments, products related to financing and balance sheets, avoidance, and diversification or portfolio optimisation.

Market Instruments

Market instruments are available as over-the-counter or exchange-traded contracts. They require some form of credit risk limits from and with the other counterparty, collateralisation, or up-front payment of premia. Market instruments could be price insurance, price fixing, price variability, or combinations thereof.

Price insurance contracts provide protection in a worst case, while providing some extent of upside in case the interest rates move in favor of the buyer. They are like buying insurance on specific elements. There could be a premium paid up front for this insurance. Vanilla options (calls, puts, caps, floors, etc.) are examples of price insurance contracts. Figure 19.16 presents an example of a price insurance contract (USD interest rate cap); its payoff profile is shown in Figure 19.17.

Price-fixing contracts ascertain the price for the firm on any underlying market factor, with an opportunity loss being created should the markets move in their favor. Examples are forward contracts, rate locks, and interest rate swaps where the firm receives a fixed rate and pays a floating rate. An example of a price-fixing contract (FX forward) is illustrated in Figure 19.18, and its pay off profile is shown in Figure 19.19.

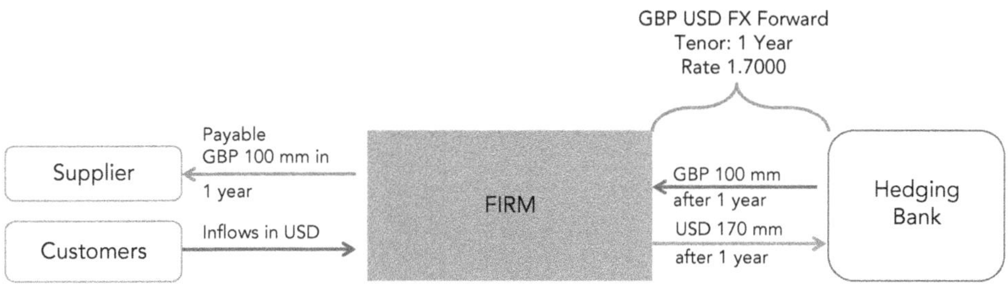

FIGURE 19.16 Example of Price Insurance Contract (USD Interest Rate Option [LIBOR Cap])

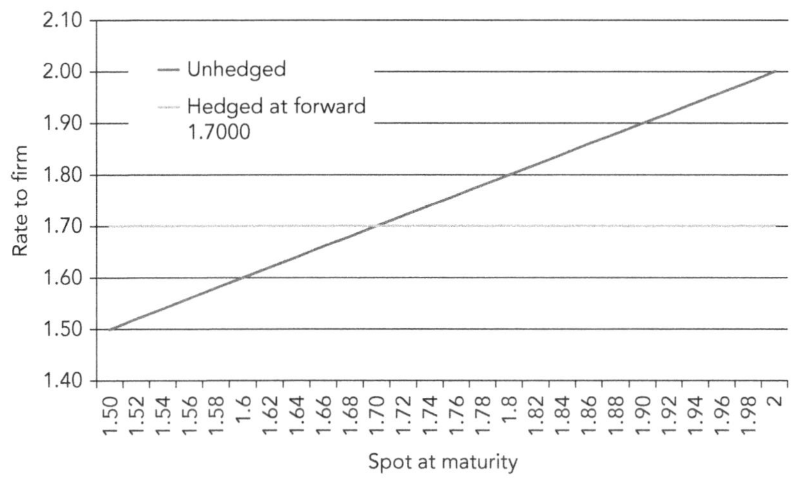

FIGURE 19.17 Payoff Profile of USD LIBOR Cap

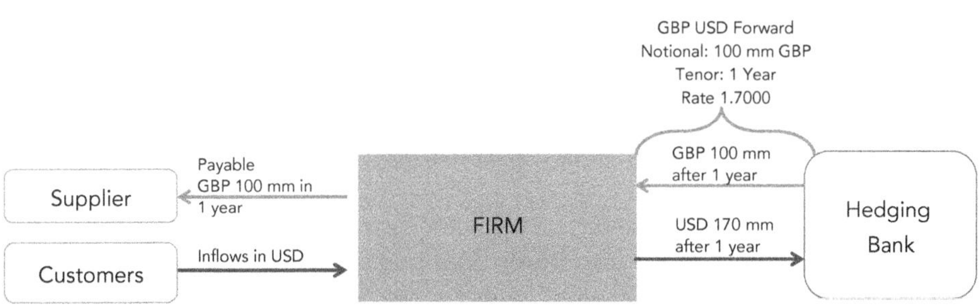

FIGURE 19.18 Example of Price-Fixing Contract (FX Forward)

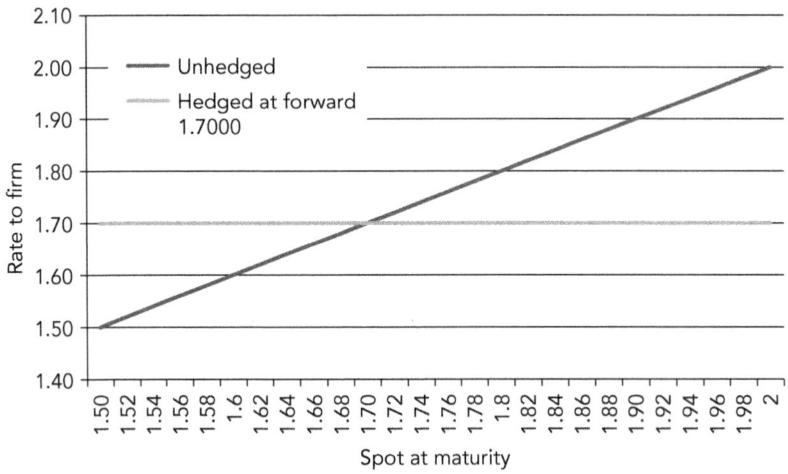

FIGURE 19.19 Payoff of Price-Fixing Contract versus Unhedged Scenario

We can illustrate the opportunity loss described above. If the corporate had remained unhedged, a move lower in the GBP USD spot rate after 1 year (say to 1.5000) would have been financially favourable, since the corporate needs to spend only USD 150mm to purchase the same number of GBP (100mm). Hence, if the corporate were to fix the transaction rate of GBP USD rate a year from now, it indicates the willingness to give up any potential benefits from a downward move in the rate. Of course, the benefit of a favourable fixed rate should the GBP USD rate move higher, and greater certainty of the USD cash outflow a year from now, remain advantages for this transaction.

In regard to price variability contracts, sometimes firms enter into contracts where they could be receiving a variable rate but could lower the risk overall. For example, a floating-to-floating EUR to USD currency swap keeps the coupons benchmarked to a floating rate but moves them to a currency of choice. This could lower the risk profile of the firm.

An example of a price insurance contract (USD interest rate cap) is illustrated in Figure 19.20.

Financing and Balance Sheet–Related Products

Using the balance sheet and the support of banking partners can provide a large set of instruments or tools to manage risk. Some of these are:

- **Supply chain finance family**. This family includes structured or off-the-shelf products and solutions on receivables financing, supplier financing, and so on that seek to reduce risk and provide more liquidity into the system.
- **Securitisation**. Removing items from the balance sheet and passing on the risk to another party while generating liquidity is common with asset-based portfolios.

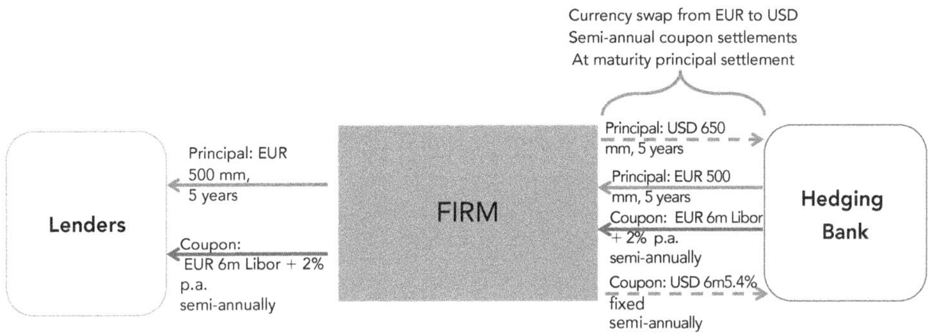

FIGURE 19.20 Example of Price Variability Contract

- **Repurchase agreements.** Short-term liquidity can be generated through the use of repurchase agreements (repos).
- **Embedded derivatives (into loans and investments).** Derivatives can be embedded into loans or investments to generate specific profiles that can either lower the firm's overall risk or make it take on a desired risk profile.
- **Risk sharing.** Especially in credit risk, agents or banking partners who share risk on a participative basis can help to mitigate portfolio exposure.

Avoidance

Avoidance of risk—not participating in a market or segment that contains risk elements which the firm is not comfortable with—remains a strategy that firms use when required. The long-term repercussions of having avoidance limits, however (i.e., putting new business or orders on hold), could create relationship issues with the other party.

Diversification or Portfolio Optimisation

Diversification involves moving the firm's portfolio of risks to a targeted and presumably optimal mix of products across market factors to achieve a targeted degree of risk–return. Diversification generally is used in line with the concept of not putting all your eggs in the same basket and the assumption that a well-diversified portfolio of risk will yield middle-of-line returns over a period of time, making the firm generally immune to large gains should the market move in its favour or large losses in case of adverse market action. Strong analytics and models, continuous revalidation, and updating and robust systems and engine support is a must-have for firms that embark on such a strategy.

Along with each of these products comes an array of requirements for processes, valuation, reporting, and control. These are important to consider, and no product or instrument should be implemented or executed without confirming the firm's ability to maintain it. The Toolkit section of the book (Part Five) elaborates on processes and controls.

Timing: When to Hedge?

A proactive style of management generally tracks markets and implements strategies on a regular basis. Online availability of the risk management portfolio, including mark-to-market values and transaction statues, will help dealers implement the strategies more effectively. If the firm uses an M-D-U proportion approach, the ratios and the layered hedges would have to refresh on a rolling basis every month. It might be a good practice to update the mandatory part of the portfolio within a few days of each month (top-up) without fixing the date for doing such transactions.

Ad hoc hedges or anticipatory hedges, with due approvals, can be done on a case-by-case basis.

Personnel: Who Will Hedge?

The quality of a cutting-edge policy and strategy will be high only if the people who implement it are capable of managing, sustaining, and developing the entire process. The human element (described earlier under Treasury Culture in Chapter 1), hence, is a very important aspect of risk management. Some aspects are especially critical:

- **Putting the right people on the job**. Recruiting good-quality talent and providing them with enough training and empowerment to be able to undertake their jobs efficiently is vital.
- **Compensating dealers for performances**. Given the criticality of the dealing function, it may be important to set unbiased parameters for evaluating dealers' performance through the year.
- **Establishing accountability, and roles and responsibilities**. This is especially important, given the many legs and handoffs involved in the risk governance process.

RISK MANAGEMENT EVALUATION

Evaluate the effectiveness of the risk management process and include the results in the reporting and accounting process is the final stage in the IMAGE© methodology. Different metrics can be used to measure the effectiveness of the risk management process. Some of these are:

- Hedge rate against budgeted rate
- Variance of profitability from budgeted profitability
- Cost of debt
- Rate against a market benchmark (or average)
- Comparison with last year's performance
- Comparison with a model portfolio (in case of diversification)

- VaR risk-adjusted rate
- Limit breaches
- Limit utilisation

Forecasting errors also have to be factored in.

SUMMARY

Risk management is not a one-time activity but an ongoing process that requires daily observation and activity. In this chapter, we went through one of the many models of managing risk through the IMAGE© methodology. The steps of risk identification, risk measurement, risk accounting and reporting, risk governance, and finally the evaluation of the risk management process form the core activities of the cycle.

We now set our sights on developing our understanding of practically managing risk.

CHAPTER TWENTY

Products for Managing Risk

WHEN WE BUY A CAR or a new appliance, we need to understand how to use it. We buy it based on what it can do and how it looks. We should know what the parts and processes are—the transmission, engineering, engine, motor, and technology that goes behind its design, assembly, and finally manufacturing—but it is not essential for us to know in detail how each part works. And so it is with financial products. We may not need to know the details of the engineering behind them, but we do need to know what the various instruments are and how we can use them.

Here we explain some of the broad mechanics behind these products. We also provide practical ways to understand the construction and pricing of some of these products.

The products are divided into four families: forwards, options, swaps, and credit. This is depicted in Figure 20.1.

Technically, credit products are a part of the broader fixed income class and use a combination of forwards, options, and swaps in some form. Since their evolution and treatment are different, they deserve, in my view, a separate family for the sake of classification.

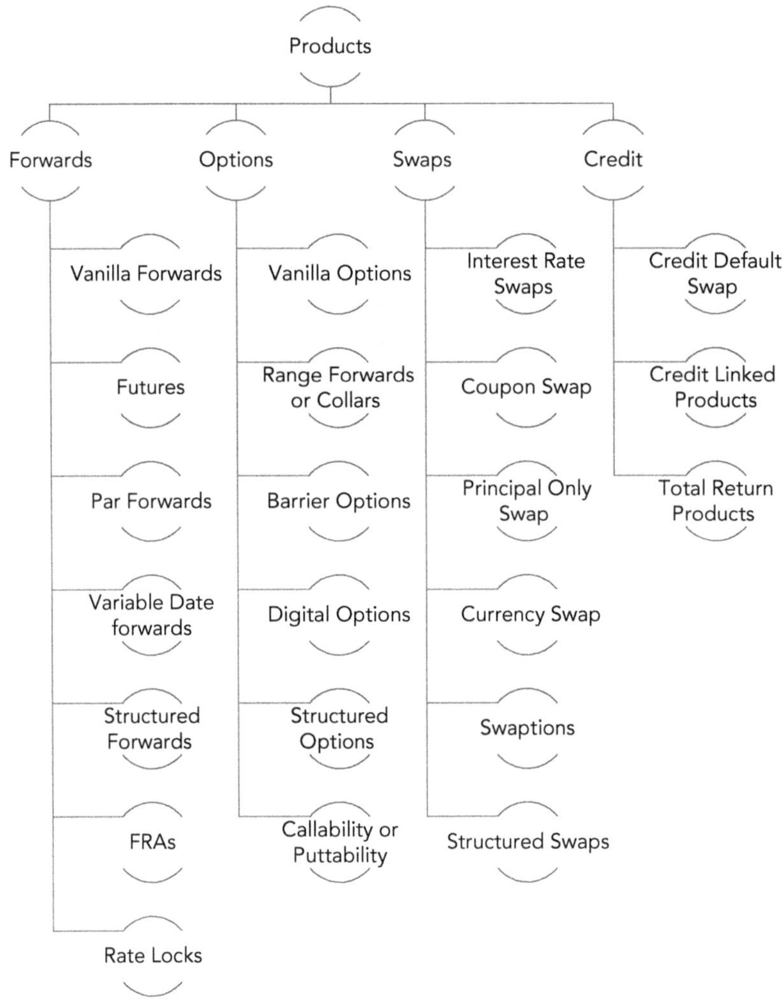

FIGURE 20.1 Family of Products

FORWARDS FAMILY

The forwards family is essentially a set of price-fixing contracts across asset classes, where two parties agree to buy and sell a particular asset or commodity at a particular price on a particular date in the future. Different date notations are provided in Table 20.1.

A simple foreign exchange (FX) forward has already been described in the previous chapter. Here we discuss different kinds of contracts in the forward family and how they can be priced.

Forward prices at any one point of time can either be lower, similar to, or higher than the current spot price. If forward prices are lower than the current spot levels, the condition is referred to as *backwardation*. If forward prices are higher, the condition is referred to as *contango*.

TABLE 20.1 Different Date Notations

Date	Description
Deal date	Date of transaction, typically the same day
Value date	Date of actual cash flow, from and to where interest and other calculations are done
Settlement date	Date at which the transaction or cash flow is settled, typically 2 working days from the value date
Maturity date	Date of final cash flow after which transaction matures/expires
Cash date	Settlement is the same as deal date
Tom date	Settlement is 1 working day after deal date
Spot date	Settlement is 2 working days after deal date
Exercise date	Date where the holder of the option decides to exercise or let the option expire

Rationale for a Forward Price Computation

The reason why forward prices are different from spot prices is that there is a cost or benefit of holding or carrying the asset for the seller of the asset; this cost could be in the form of interest and dividend (in case of equities). The current valuation of that cost is the difference between the forward price and the spot price.

We cover the conceptual example of a forward price computation for the FX asset class and follow it up with the formula.

EXAMPLE: GENERAL CONCEPT OF FORWARD PRICING

Let us generally compute the price of a EUR USD forward contract. We assume that there is no bid-offer spread on spot FX and interest rates. Hence, let EUR USD spot = 1.2000, one-year EUR interest rates are at 5% per annum (p.a.) and one-year USD interest rates are at 10% p.a.

X borrows in EUR and invests the same in USD.

1. On January 1, 2012, X borrows, say, 100 EUR at 5% p.a.
2. The amount for X to pay back after one year is105 EUR (including interest).
3. X invests the 100 EUR borrowed in step 1 in USD. To do that, she has to convert the EUR to USD. Hence, 100 EUR becomes 120 USD (@1.2000).
4. X invests the 120 USD at 10% p.a.
5. The amount that X receives after one year is132 USD (including interest).
6. X now needs to convert this money back to EUR.

(Continued)

The forward price, is the price that X fixes on January 1, 2012 itself, to convert the USD back to EUR at the end of the year. This is the rate at which there is no profit or no loss to X. In this simple case, becomes 132 USD / 105 EUR = 1.2571. This is also called the outright forward price.

The difference between the forward price and the spot price, referred to as forward points, is 0.0571. If this number is greater than the spot price, the commodity currency is said to be trading at a premium. If the outright forward price is less than the spot price, the currency is said to be at a discount.

Hence, the current forward price for the buyer of an asset is said to be the price agreed to at the current point in time, for settlement at a future date, which makes the buyer of the asset neutral to buying and holding the asset for that particular amount of time or waiting for that particular amount of time before purchasing it at a pre-fixed price.

Various formulas exist to compute forward rates. The difference between equity forward pricing and the rest is the use of dividends. FX forward pricing is different because it uses two interest rates (for the two currencies of the currency pair).

Simple equity forward pricing formula:

$$F = S_0 e^{(r-q)T} - \sum_{i=1}^{N} D_i e^{r(T-t_i)}$$

where:

F = forward price to be paid at time T
e^x = exponential function (used for calculating compounding interests)
r = risk-free interest rate
q = cost of carry
S_0 = spot price of the asset (i.e., what it would sell for at time 0)
D_i = dividend that is guaranteed to be paid at time t_i where $0 < t_i < T$. Back-of-envelope FX forward pricing formula:

$$\frac{\text{Spot} \times (I2\% - I1\%) \times \text{T}}{1 + (I2\% \times \text{T})}$$

where:

I2 and I1 = interest rates of the respective currencies 2 and 1

The FX forward for tradeable currencies is hence theoretically nothing but the interest rate differential expressed through an FX price.

Figure 20.2 below displays a typical interest rate differential between the EUR and USD on a given day and forward price. Yield curve differentials can be different for different curves—for example, the curves shown in Figure 20.2 (A) are government benchmarks and deposits.

Figure 20.2 (B) shows the EUR USD forward prices across tenors.

Hence, with the right market information tools, the Treasurer can easily determine the existing market levels for many forward family transaction types. The following note discusses the practical aspects of forward pricing.

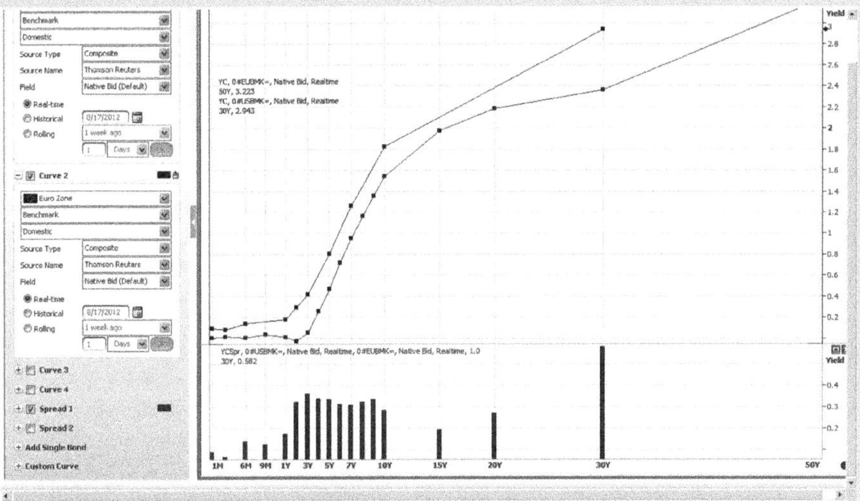

FIGURE 20.2 (A) Yield Curve Interest Rate Differential between EUR and USD

Source: Thomson Reuters Eikon

0#EUEURF= EUR/USD FORWARD ENHANCED GUIDE

EUR= 1.2344 / 49

Term	Bid	Offer	Source	Time	Start	Maturity	Outright	DayCount
EURON=	0.2800	0.3200	MSFW	10:32	17AUG12	20AUG12	1.234457/4664	3
EURTN=	0.0800	0.1100	MSFW	10:32	20AUG12	21AUG12	1.234489/4692	1
EURSN=	0.0800	0.1200	MSFW	10:32	21AUG12	22AUG12	1.234508/4712	1
EURSW=	0.67	0.79	MSFW	10:32	21AUG12	28AUG12	1.234567/4779	7
EUR2W=	1.50	1.64	MSFW	10:32	21AUG12	04SEP12	1.234650/4864	14
EUR3W=	2.29	2.41		10:26	21AUG12	11SEP12	1.234729/4941	21
EUR1M=	3.60	3.90	NDEA	10:32	21AUG12	21SEP12	1.234860/5090	31
EUR2M=	8.30	8.68	NDEA	10:32	21AUG12	22OCT12	1.235330/5568	62
EUR3M=	12.90	14.30	AIBM	10:32	21AUG12	21NOV12	1.235790/6130	92
EUR4M=	18.34	19.24		10:32	21AUG12	21DEC12	1.236344/6596	122
EUR5M=	24.57	25.33	MSFW	10:32	21AUG12	22JAN13	1.236957/7233	154
EUR6M=	29.94	30.86	MSFW	10:32	21AUG12	21FEB13	1.237494/7786	184
EUR7M=	35.62	36.78	MSFW	10:32	21AUG12	21MAR13	1.238062/8378	212
EUR8M=	41.66	43.04	MSFW	10:32	21AUG12	22APR13	1.238666/9004	244
EUR9M=	[illegible]	[illegible]	MSFW	10:32	21AUG12	21MAY13	1.239150/9720	273
EUR10M=	53.24	55.26	MSFW	10:32	21AUG12	21JUN13	1.239824/0226	304
EUR11M=	58.58	62.33		10:32	21AUG12	22JUL13	1.240358/0933	335
EUR1Y=	[illegible]	[illegible]	MSFW	10:32	21AUG12	21AUG13	1.241146/1566	365
EUR15M=	84.19	89.71	MSFW	10:32	21AUG12	21NOV13	1.242919/3671	457
EUR18M=	105.83	112.67	MSFW	10:32	21AUG12	21FEB14	1.245083/5967	549
EUR21M=	125.78	132.80	MSFW	10:32	21AUG12	21MAY14	1.247078/7980	638
EUR2Y=	146.40	153.60	MSFW	10:32	21AUG12	21AUG14	1.249140/0060	730
EUR3Y=	206.50	231.50	HSBC	10:32	21AUG12	21AUG15	1.255550/6950	1095
EUR4Y=	271.10	289.10		10:32	21AUG12	22AUG16	1.261718/5082	1462
EUR5Y=	329.44	367.56	MSFW	10:32	21AUG12	21AUG17	1.267444/1456	1826
EUR6Y=	393.30	430.50		10:29	21AUG12	21AUG18	1.273830/7750	2191
EUR7Y=	424.00	494.00	RBFW	:	21AUG12	21AUG19	1.276900/4100	2556
EUR8Y=	479.00	554.00	RBFW	:	21AUG12	21AUG20	1.282400/0100	2922
EUR9Y=	543.00	623.00	RBFW	:	21AUG12	23AUG21	1.288800/7000	3289
EUR10Y=	606.00	696.00	RBFW	:	21AUG12	22AUG22	1.295100/4300	3653
EUR12Y=	768.10	858.10		10:31	21AUG12	21AUG24	1.311310/0510	4383
EUR15Y=	943.20	1033.20		10:31	21AUG12	23AUG27	1.328820/8020	5480
EUR20Y=	1488.20	1578.20		10:31	21AUG12	23AUG32	1.383320/2520	7307

Related Data

<FWD/1>
<DEPO/1>
<FUTURES>
<SPOT/1>
<EURVIEW>
<ECBMENU>
<EURIBOR01>
<BROKER>
<EUR/HOLIDAY>

ECONOMIC INDICATORS
<ECON>
<G7TODAY>
<ECONOMY>

NEWS
[TOP/FRX]
[FRX-EU]
[INT-EU]
[ANALYSIS-M]

FIGURE 20.2 (B) EUR USD Forward Prices

Source: Thomson Reuters Eikon

Forward Markets in Practice

Why are forward prices in many currencies a little different from pure interest rate differentials?

Many emerging market currencies are usual not convertible fully on the capital account. The simplistic example we just provided assumes a free availability of borrowing and investing alternatives at global market rates as well as freedom to convert currencies from one to the other when required. Many emerging market currencies have restrictions on borrowing or lending in foreign currencies locally, different rates for doing so, and conversion guidelines with limits and situations under which automatic conversion can happen without prior regulatory approvals. Hence, demand and supply of currency in the forward markets and currency expectation play a reasonable role in the pricing of forwards; traders trade forward prices using these views and expectations.

Even for more liquid G7 currencies that are fully convertible, the equivalent LIBOR or interbank lending and borrowing rate benchmark rates published have differed from the actual rates received by a specific bank—hence the forward rates quoted by that bank will reflect the borrowing and lending rate available to that bank more than it will reflect the generally quoted benchmark rate. Hence, forward rates for G7 currencies may not always be exactly equal to the interest rate differential.

For many markets, information systems such as Thomson Reuters Eikon provide enough information on current levels. Prices that corporates transact with could be different based on the demand supply situation at the time of transacting and the spread applied by the bank, but the reference points may be easily determined through the systems.

Use of Forward Contracts versus Futures Contracts

Sometimes, during casual talk about futures and forwards, the two terms are used interchangeably. Table 20.2 differentiates between the two.

Forwards versus Actual Movements

The relationship between the forward price and the expected future spot price has been explained by many economists. From the Treasurer's viewpoint, however, two things can be inferred:

1. The forward price is not always a forecast of where the spot will end; it is the current market price that reflects the cost of holding the asset out through the time period.
2. Historical performance of the forward price versus the spot on that day can be a useful analysis for treasurers seeking to decide which forward rate might be a more appropriate rate to use in case a "better rate" was also an objective.

TABLE 20.2 Futures versus Forwards

Feature	OTC Forward Contracts	Exchange Futures Contracts
Transacting parties	Over the counter, between two parties	Party with an exchange
Nature of contract	Customised	Generalised
Notional amounts	Customised	Standardised
Maturity dates	Customised	Generally end of month
Credit aspect	Using credit facilities (nonfunded) when done with a bank, Using cash or other collateral placed by counterparties with each other	Collateral with exchange
Usage	Usually more common, when banks can customise exact amounts and delivery dates	Used for generic hedges and also where credit facilities may not be available or amounts may be too small to capture with a bank
Pricing	Easily available in market information systems for liquid markets Opaque for nonliquid markets	Transparent—available with the exchange at any point of time
Spread to seller of contract	Banks build in the spread for the firm and can vary from entity to entity depending on relationship and credit standing	Transparent and standardised

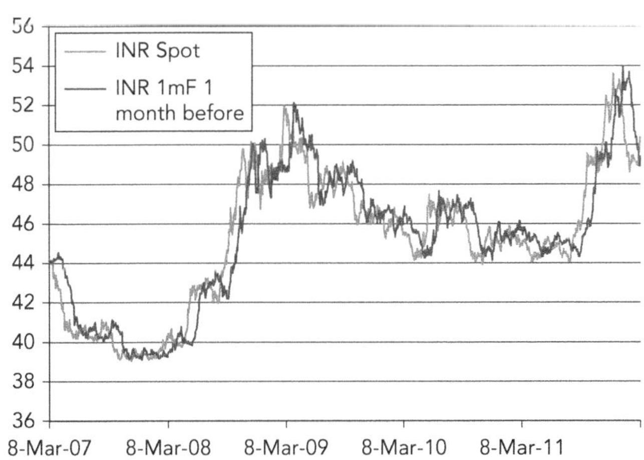

FIGURE 20.3 Historical Performance

Data Source: Thomson Reuters Eikon

Figure 20.3 depicts a sample historical performance. It also shows whether the forward hedging strategy would yield a better rate or lesser opportunity loss than the spot price when seeking lower variability.

Forward Variants

The different variants of the typical forward contract are representative of the differentiators in customisation of the over-the-counter (OTC) family of products.

Par Forwards

A par forward is a single rate for an exchange over a series of forward dates and possibly different notional amounts, with the same forward delivery price. How can a single rate be achieved if the interest rate differentials are different across tenors? The par forward rate is effectively an average rate of all forward dates in the contract, weighted by the notional amount for each date.

Variable Date Forwards

Some banks offer variable date forwards. In these, the forward price is fixed while the date for settlement is left at the discretion of the customer (within a range). Here, the price of the forward could be worse than a regular forward, taking into account the bank's charge for the optionality provided to the customer.

Nondeliverable Forwards

Nondeliverable forwards (NDFs) are forward contracts where cash flows in each currency are not exchanged at maturity. Instead, the amounts are converted back to one currency and net settled. Figure 20.4 gives the example of an NDF.

NDFs are popular with emerging market currencies that have currency convertibility restrictions or exchange control. Hence, NDF markets operate in large financial centres, such as Singapore, London, and New York, for trading forwards across many emerging markets currencies. NDF transactions of a country's currency are usually

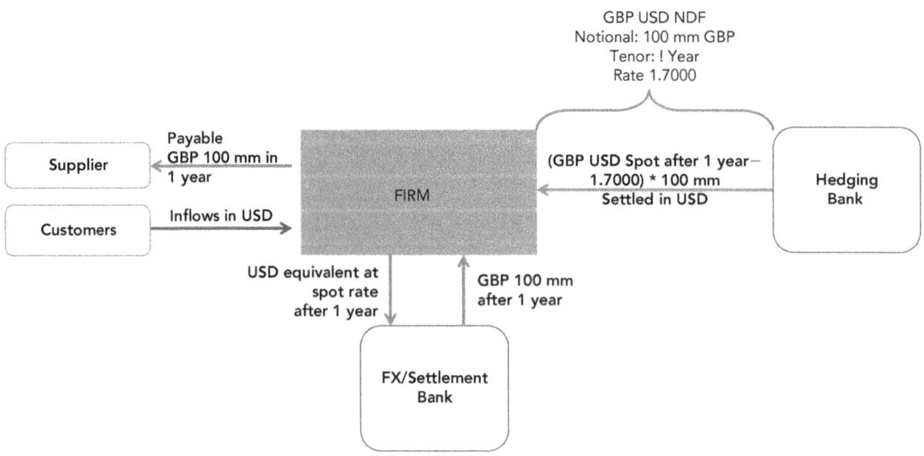

FIGURE 20.4 Example Nondeliverable Forward Contract Settled in USD

not legal in that country (with exceptions) and are also an item of regulatory sensitivity in many countries, owing to central bank views on overseas trading on a currency under its control.

Forward Rate Agreements

Forward rate agreements (FRAs) are forward interest rates, for different benchmarks such as the London Interbank Offered Rate (LIBOR). While the rates may be easily determined through some quick back-of-the-envelope computations, the rates are readily available from market information systems (see Figure 20.5).

The notation for a FRA is Start Period × End Period, usually in months. Hence, a 3 × 9 implies a 6-month rate, set 3 months from today (start period = 3 months and end period = 9 months). Figure 20.6 shows the forward curve for the EUR and USD. As can be seen, the shape of the forward curve is generally upward sloping, implying current market views of an increase in short-term interest rates into the future.

Rate Locks

Rate lock is a general term indicating the holding of a particular rate linked to debt. Rate locks can be for a loan (a rate lock fixed by the banker for the client to borrow a committed amount on a committed date for a committed period) or on instruments, such as U.S. Treasury bonds. These rate locks are customised to specific dates that indicate the proposed risk to be managed.

USDFRA   USD FRA FOCUS   LINKED DISPLAYS   MONEY

<USDVIEW> <USDIRS> <USDOIS> <USDFRA> <0#ED:> <USD/1>

	USD		DEALING		
1X4	0.394	0.434	BROKER	GFX	09:35
2X5	0.400	0.440	BROKER	GFX	10:10
3X6	0.393	0.433	BROKER	GFX	10:10
4X7	0.388	0.428	BROKER	GFX	10:10
5X8	0.386	0.426	BROKER	GFX	10:10
6X9	0.397	0.437	BROKER	GFX	10:10
7X10	0.416	0.436	BROKER	GFX	09:35
8X11	0.415	0.455	BROKER	GFX	08:30
9X12	0.4250	0.4650	BROKER	GFX	10:20
1X7	0.671	0.711	BROKER	GFX	10:10
2X8	0.663	0.703	BROKER	GFX	10:10
3X9	0.655	0.695	BROKER	GFX	10:10
4X10	0.648	0.688	BROKER	GFX	10:10
5X11	0.641	0.681	BROKER	GFX	10:10
6X12	0.645	0.685	BROKER	GFX	08:30
9X15	0.632	0.672	BROKER	GFX	10:20
12X18	0.656	0.696	BROKER	GFX	10:20
1X10	0.771	0.811	BROKER	GFX	04:35
2X11	0.770	0.810	BROKER	GFX	04:35
3X12	0.764	0.804	BROKER	GFX	04:35
6X18	0.894	0.934	BROKER	GFX	10:20
12X24	0.926	0.966	BROKER	GFX	10:25

FIGURE 20.5 USD FRAs

Source: Thomson Reuters Eikon

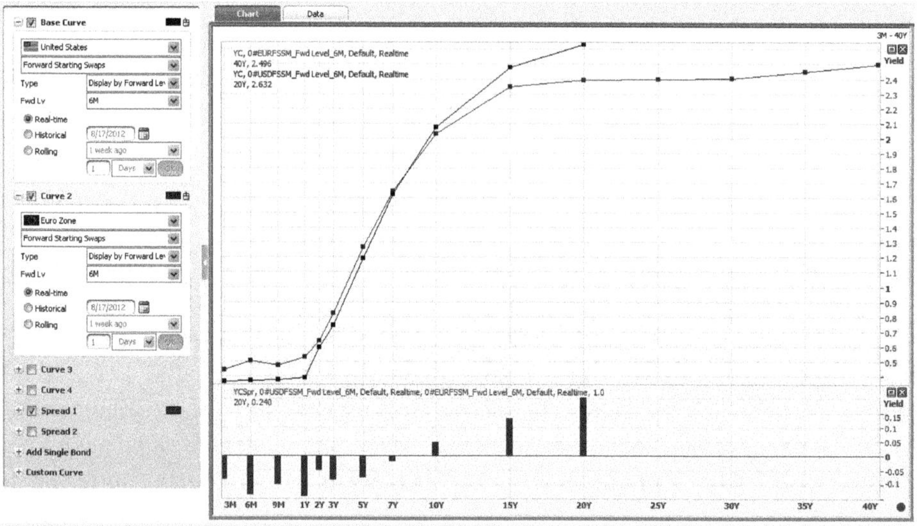

FIGURE 20.6 Forward Curves for EUR and USD

Source: Thomson Reuters Eikon

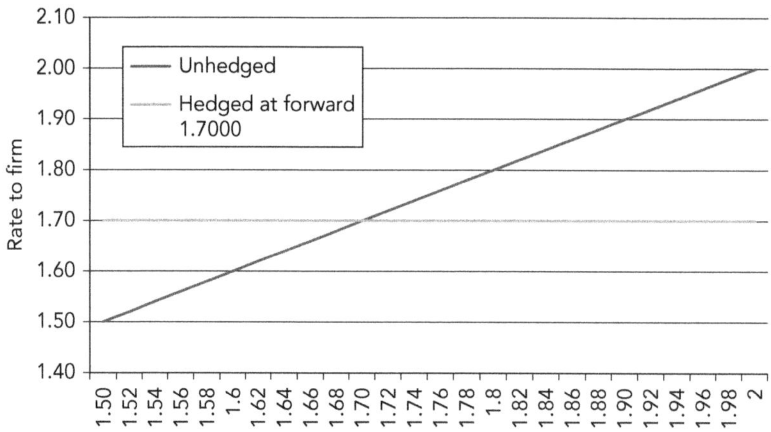

FIGURE 20.7 Opportunity Loss and Fixed Rates for Forward Contracts

A rate lock with a Treasury bond benchmark, however, is generally linked to a basis risk—the borrowing for the corporate may be linked to the Treasury rate with a spread, but the spread itself may be uncertain.

Benefits and Disadvantages of Using Forward Family Products

Forwards and related transactions are some of the most commonly used products owing to the certainty that they provide on cash flows or items being hedged. The sample payoff profile described earlier in Figure 19.19 is depicted again in Figure 20.7.

Should the rate move adversely, the buyer of the forward contract would get a better than expected price than an unhedged scenario.

The chief disadvantage of a forward contract is the opportunity loss that it provides by locking in the rate. If the rate moves in favor of the hedger (as shown in the example), having fixed the rate forward, the firm is unable to make use of these moves in its favor.

When using a proxy to hedge forward, such as Treasury bond prices for borrowing or liquid commodity benchmarks (say using WTI Brent to hedge Dubai crude oil), the basis risk of the price differential between the proxy and the actual underlying could still add to variability.

OPTIONS FAMILY

The advent of options and the ability to price options have been key developments that have made financial engineering the wizardry that it is today.

An option is essentially a financial agreement giving the buyer the right, but not the obligation, to buy or sell specified amounts or quantities of an asset or instrument at a specified rate on a specified date.

The vanilla option contract is very similar to insurance. Just as we buy insurance for our car and pay a premium to be compensated in case there is any damage to the vehicle, so too do buyers of options get "insurance" against any specific financial event happening. If there is no car accident (which we hope), the insurance contract expires and is worthless at the end of the period. So too does an option contract for which a premium has been paid: If the financial event (e.g., the stock price moving over 100 or the FX rate moving under 1.20) does not happen, the buyer of the insurance is free to go and procure the same asset or instrument at the prevalent market price since the hazardous event has not happened. In case the financial event has occurred, the buyer of the option has the right to approach the seller (e.g., a bank) and claim back the compensation—in this case, it could be the delivery of the asset or instrument at a predefined better-than-current market rate.

The following note articulates the difference between the right of the buyer of an option and the obligation of the counterparty of a forward.

Options versus Forwards: Rights versus Obligations

The buyer of a vanilla option contract (simple calls or puts, simple caps or floors) has the right to exercise or use the option at expiry, while for the seller, the contract remains an obligation should the buyer choose to exercise the option. In the case of a forward contract, in comparison, both counterparties have an obligation to exchange the respective cash flows or assets on the maturity date at the forward price fixed on the date of the contract.

TABLE 20.3 Option Terminology

Term	Description
Call option	Right to buy a commodity or asset.
Put option	Right to sell a commodity or asset.
FX-specific terminology	FX options: The call in one currency becomes the put in the other (when we buy one currency, we sell the other currency in the pair). Hence, the notation for FX options cites both currencies: USD call EUR put, or AUD call JPY put.
Premium	The cost (usually paid up front) for purchasing the option, expressed as a percentage of the notional amount or as a value.
Strike price	Rate above or below which the option right can be exercised.
Expiry date	Date on which the right to exercise is determined.
European-style option	The right to buy (for a call) or sell (for a put) occurs on expiry; most options are European style for settlement.
American-style option	The right to exercise is available any time up to and before expiry.

Options Terminology

Various option terminology are presented in Table 20.3. In essence, options are described using these characteristics:

- Type
- Strike price
- Expiry
- Notional amount
- Currency

A simple call option payoff is shown in Figure 20.8. The difference between the unhedged position and the hedged position is the option premium; hence, for a spot at expiry below the strike price, the call option payoff is always worse than the unhedged position. Table 20.4 shows the payoff table that explains the respective rate under each scenario.

In this example, the buyer of the option chooses to exercise the option only above 1.70; otherwise, he can get the market rate, which is more beneficial. The worst-case rate is hence quantified, and the buyer knows that the GBP does not have to be purchased at a rate more than 1.73 (including the premium paid up front).

Figure 20.9 shows the put option payoff for a GBP put USD call. Table 20.5 is the corresponding payoff table.

Similarly, the buyer of the right to sell GBP against the USD (i.e., the buyer of the GBP put USD call) knows that, in any scenario, she will not receive less than 1.48 GBP per USD.

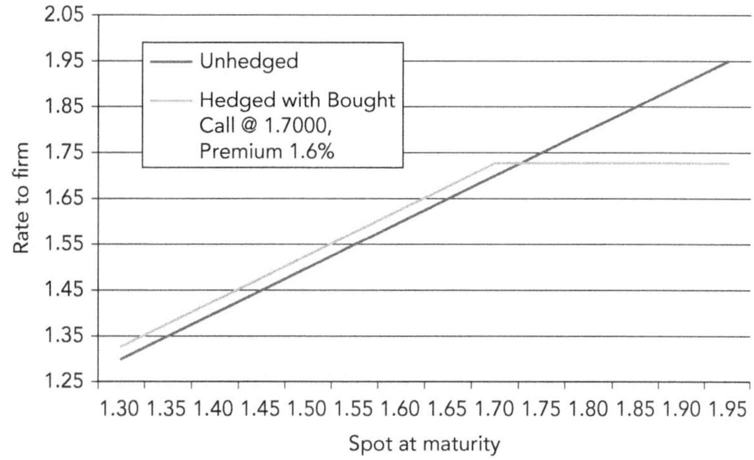

FIGURE 20.8 Option Payoff Diagram

TABLE 20.4 Payoff Table for GBP Call USD Put

GBP USD at Maturity	Unhedged	Hedged with Bought Call @ 1.7000, Premium 1.6%	Whether Option Is Exercised or Not
1.30	1.30	1.33	No
1.35	1.35	1.38	No
1.40	1.40	1.43	No
1.45	1.45	1.48	No
1.50	1.50	1.53	No
1.55	1.55	1.58	No
1.60	1.60	1.63	No
1.65	1.65	1.68	No
1.70	1.70	1.73	Yes
1.75	1.75	1.73	Yes
1.80	1.80	1.73	Yes
1.85	1.85	1.73	Yes
1.90	1.90	1.73	Yes
1.95	1.95	1.73	Yes

Options Mechanics

How are options priced? Their pricing is based on the famous Black-Scholes formula, which used a then relatively unknown component: volatility. Here we discuss the basic concepts without getting too deeply involved in the mathematics of option pricing. Many great books exist that discuss, model, and debate option pricing, and readers are advised to review them.

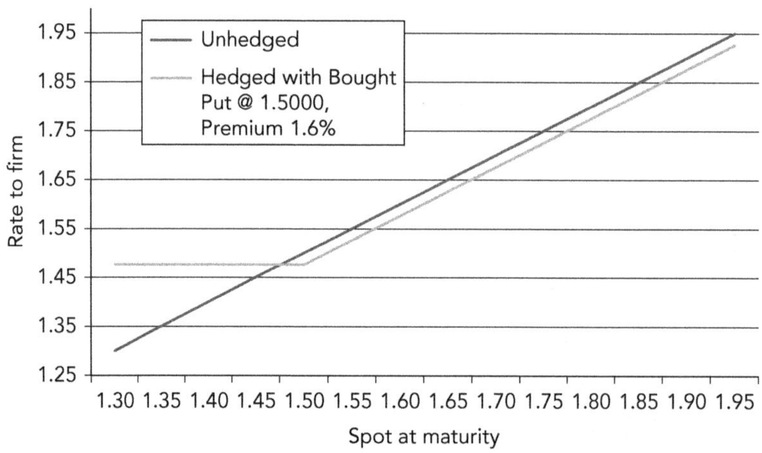

FIGURE 20.9 Put Option Payoff (GBP Put USD Call)

TABLE 20.5 Put Option Payoff Table

GBP USD at Maturity	Unhedged	Hedged with Bought Put @ 1.5000, Premium 1.6%	Whether Option Is Exercised or Not
1.30	1.30	1.48	Yes
1.35	1.35	1.48	Yes
1.40	1.40	1.48	Yes
1.45	1.45	1.48	Yes
1.50	1.50	1.48	No
1.55	1.55	1.53	No
1.60	1.60	1.58	No
1.65	1.65	1.63	No
1.70	1.70	1.68	No
1.75	1.75	1.73	No
1.80	1.80	1.78	No
1.85	1.85	1.83	No
1.90	1.90	1.88	No
1.95	1.95	1.93	No

There are two things to note about option prices: They are based on forward prices for the tenor, and there are two essential elements of an option price: how far the strike price is from the current forward rate for the same expiry (intrinsic value), and how likely the price is to move in the time left for maturity (time value).

Inputs into option pricing are diagrammatically represented in Figure 20.10.

The intrinsic value is easily discernible from prevalent forward prices and the current spot. Table 20.6 shows how we can determine whether an option is in the money or out of the money for intrinsic value.

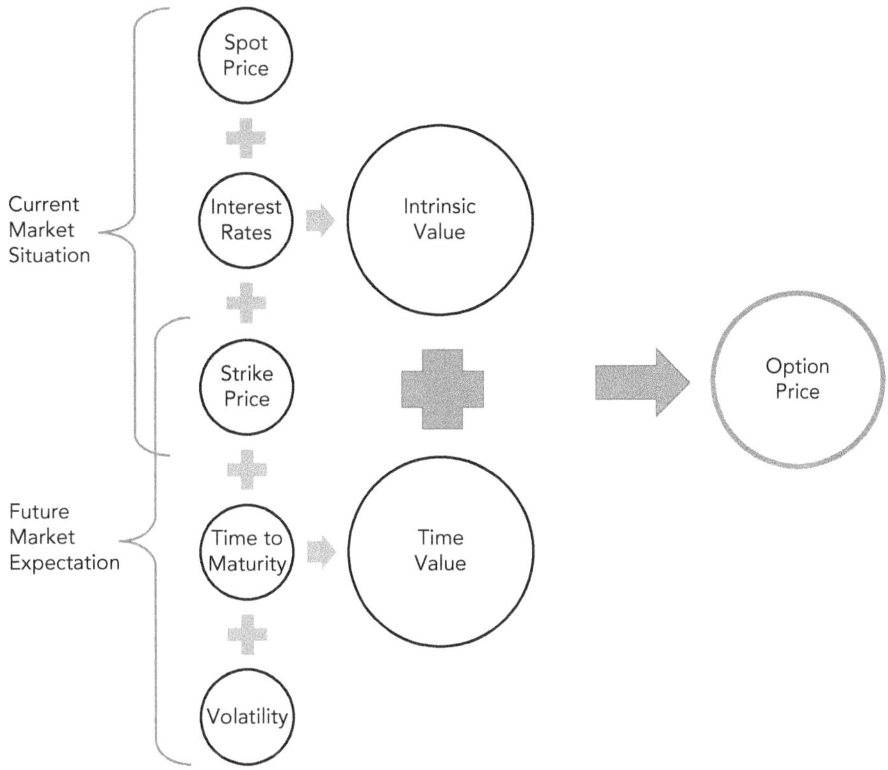

FIGURE 20.10 Inputs into Option Pricing

TABLE 20.6 Intrinsic Value and Time Value

GBP Put USD Call Strike	Outright Forward for Same Expiry	Intrinsic Value	Status
1.50	1.35	0.15	In the money
1.50	1.40	0.10	In the money
1.50	1.50	0.00	At the money
1.50	1.60	−0.10	Out of the money
1.50	1.70	−0.20	Out of the money

At the money (ATM) is the status when the strike is at the current forward level.

The time value, however, depends on the volatility. For a more volatile asset, there is an increased probability that the price will change. Hence the premium is higher for a higher-volatility option.

The volatility used here is implied volatility, usually a market-traded number that the market estimates will be the volatility in the period.

With the advent of the Option Pricer (see Figure 20.11), it has become relatively easy to obtain indicative levels of OTC option pricing. While the final trade will be

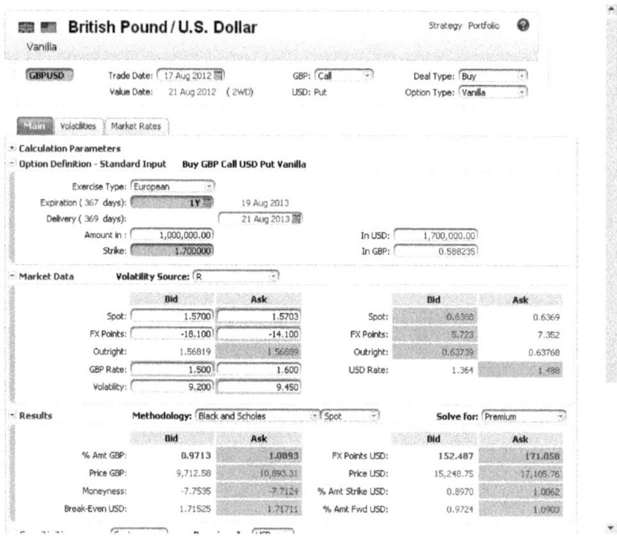

FIGURE 20.11 Currency Option Pricing Calculator

Source: Thomson Reuters Eikon

executed with a bank, for many corporate needs, indicative pricing allows the Treasurer to be aware of where market levels are and to understand different pricing levels across different market conditions.

The Black-Scholes model remains a very popular pricing basis for many options. The Garman Kohlagen model has been derived to price currency options, incorporating the use of two interest rates (since each currency has an interest rate).

Caps and floors are the interest rate equivalent—a cap on an interest rate benchmark (e.g., LIBOR) is used to put a ceiling on the movement of the interest rate benchmark. A buyer of a cap thus takes the view that interest rates could rise beyond a point and seeks to be compensated through the option should that happen. Caps typically are bought by borrowers to protect against any rises in interest rates beyond the strike price. A sample pricing screen of a USD cap is given in Figure 20.12.

A floor is used to put a lower level below which the buyer of the option is willing to pay an up-front premium and will be compensated should the interest rates fall below the strike price. Investors who seek a higher interest rate level typically buy floors.

Relationship of Option Prices with Changes in Different Parameters

Table 20.7 summarises some of the changes of an option price (premium) for the buyer of the option with the change in various parameters (all other aspects being the same). The table also introduces the Greeks letters used to denote the change of option price with a respective change in each parameter.

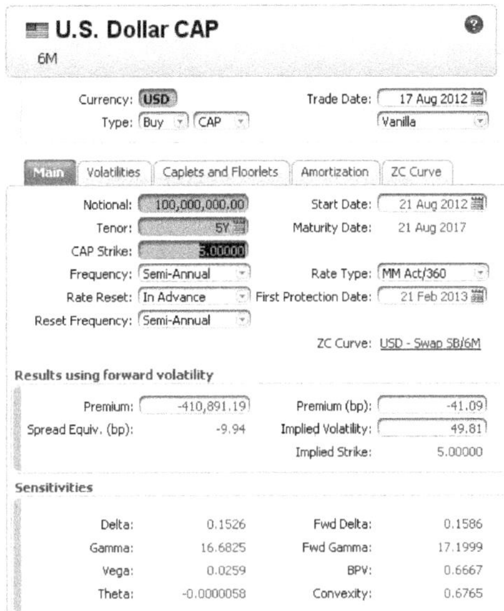

FIGURE 20.12 USD Cap Pricer with All Numbers Sourced from Market

Source: Thomson Reuters Eikon

TABLE 20.7 Relationship of Option Prices with a Change in Each Parameter

Parameter	Greek Letter Symbol	Change	Price of ATM Call Option	Price of ATM Put Option
Spot price	Delta	Higher	Falls	Rises
		Lower	Rises	Falls
Time to maturity	Theta	Becomes shorter	Falls	Falls
		Becomes longer	Rises	Rises
Volatility	Vega	Higher	Rises	Rises
		Lower	Falls	Falls

Constructing Zero-Premium Options

A zero-premium option (often inappropriately called a zero-cost option) combines at least one bought option and one sold option, where the total premia of all the bought options is equal to the total premia of all the sold options.

The buyer of the zero-premium option (who has bought and sold options under the structure) pays or receives no premium for the transactions. Similarly, the seller of the zero-premium option receives or pays no premium.

We can use the same example of the call and put options on the GBP USD discussed earlier to construct a popular zero-premium structure called Range Forward (in FX), Collar (in interest rates), and Risk Reversal (generic).

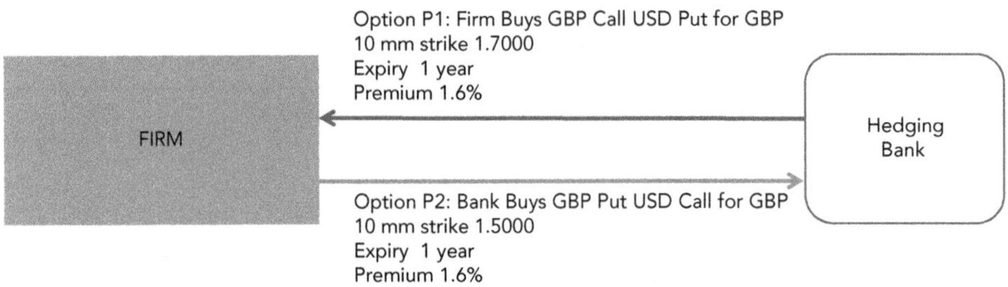

FIGURE 20.13 Zero Premium Option (Range forward)

Let the firm, which has to buy GBP (for some payments to be made) against USD, enter a structure for one year, with two components P1 and P2.

Notionals for both P1 and P2 = GBP 10,000,000
Expiry for both P1 and P2 = 1 year
Spot reference = 1.588, 1-year ATM forward = 1.584
Option P1: Firm buys GBP call USD put, premium 1.6%
Option P2: Firm sells GBP put USD call, premium 1.6%
Net premium paid/received: 0

Figure 20.13 shows a zero-premium option constructed based on Table 20.8.

As can be seen in the table, above 1.7000, it becomes the right of the firm to buy GBP from the bank at 1.7000 against the USD and thus the option hedges the firm at this level. However, below 1.5000, it becomes the right of the bank to sell GBP to the firm at 1.5000 against the USD (and hence becomes the obligation of the firm to buy GBP against USD). The firm has given up any upside that it would have got (lower GBP USD rate) below 1.5000.

Figure 20.14 presents the payoff diagram.

Various zero-premium structures can be priced—with different payoffs. The same concept of sold options can be used to lower the option premium payable up front. For example, if the structure just discussed were to be repriced and the put option strike was higher, say around 1.2, the premium of the put option will be lower than 1.6%, and the firm will have to pay a net premium of the difference between the two options as an up-front payment.

Exotic Options

A vanilla option may be defined as one that has a simple or direct relationship between the difference between the spot and strike at maturity. In contrast, an exotic option is one that has a different kind of payoff profile.

TABLE 20.8 Constructing a Zero-Premium Option (Range Forward)

Spot at Expiry	Action under Option P1: GBP Call USD Put with Strike of 1.7000 — *Buyer: Firm*	Action under Option P2: GBP Put USD Call with Strike of 1.5000 — *Buyer: Hedging Bank*	Right of	Obligation of	Effective Rate to Firm to Buy GBP
1.3000	—	Exercise (Bank sells GBP at 1.5000)	Bank	Firm	1.5000
1.3500	—	Exercise (Bank sells GBP at 1.5000)	Bank	Firm	1.5000
1.4000	—	Exercise (Bank sells GBP at 1.5000)	Bank	Firm	1.5000
1.4500	—	Exercise (Bank sells GBP at 1.5000)	Bank	Firm	1.5000
1.5000	—	—	—	—	1.5000
1.5500	—	—	—	—	1.5500
1.6000	—	—	—	—	1.6000
1.6500	—	—	—	—	1.6500
1.7000	—	—	—	—	1.7000
1.7500	Exercise (Firm buys GBP at 1.7000)	—	Firm	Bank	1.7000
1.8000	Exercise (buy GBP at 1.7000)	—	Firm	Bank	1.7000
1.8500	Exercise (buy GBP at 1.7000)	—	Firm	Bank	1.7000
1.9000	Exercise (buy GBP at 1.7000)	—	Firm	Bank	1.7000

There are two commonly used building blocks for exotic option structures: barrier options and digital options.

Figure 20.15 shows the building blocks of exotic options.

Digital options, as the name suggests, have a digital payout. If an event occurs, the option pays out a predefined amount of money, for which an up-front premium is

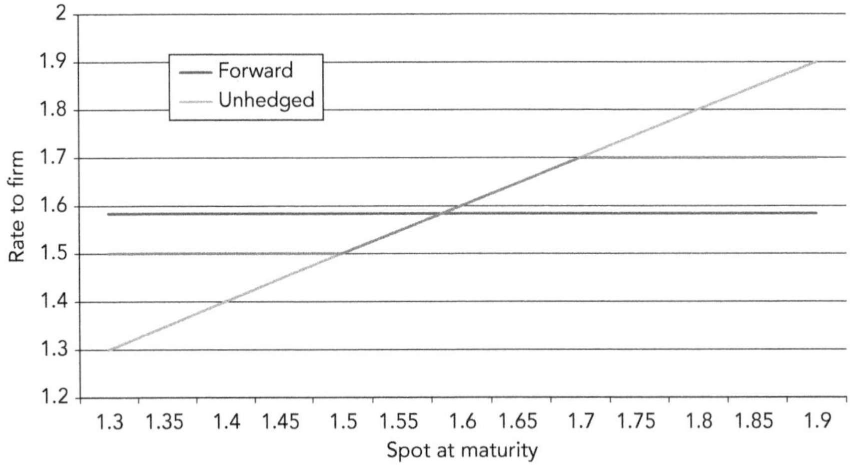

FIGURE 20.14 Payoff Profile for a Zero-Premium Structure (Range Forward)

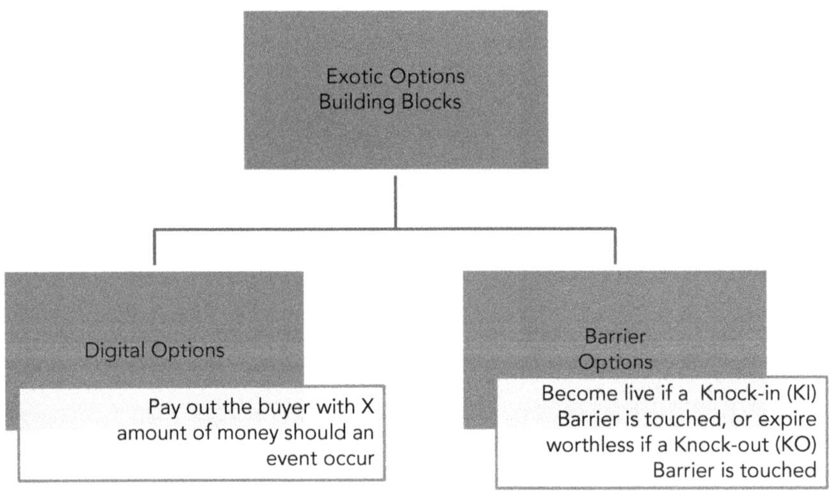

FIGURE 20.15 Building Blocks of Exotic Options

paid. Digital options are rarely used as stand-alone structures; instead, they are used to add further value to an existing option structure (see Table 20.9).

Barrier options are those that get triggered, or become invalid, if an event occurs. Like digital options, they are generally used to add further value in existing option structure. Table 20.10 shows barrier option conditions.

Hence, an up and in call is a call option that gets triggered (KI) when the spot price hits an upper barrier. A down and out put is a put option that gets extinguished (KO) when the spot price hits a lower barrier.

The next example shows how a simple structure can be created using barrier options.

TABLE 20.9 Digital Option Conditions

Condition	Action
Single touch	Buyer gets paid if a single level is touched (a level either higher or lower than current spot).
Double touch	Buyer gets paid if either one of two levels is touched (one level is higher and one level is lower). Option premium generally is higher than a single touch with a common barrier since the probability of hitting either level is higher than the probability of hitting only one level.
Single no touch	Buyer gets paid if the spot remains lower or higher than a single prespecified level (so the buyer starts being in the money).
Double no touch	Buyer gets paid if the spot remains within a prespecified range. Option premium generally is lower than a single no touch with a common barrier since the probability of hitting either level and hence getting knocked out is higher than the probability of hitting only one level.

TABLE 20.10 Barrier Option Conditions

Condition	Action
Knock in (KI)	The option is not live until a particular barrier is hit. Once the barrier is reached, the option becomes live. The premium of this kind of option is lower than the premium of an equivalent vanilla option. For a KI option, the closer the barrier is, the higher the price will be. Conversely, the farther the barrier is, the lower the price will be, assuming that the probability of knocking in will be less.
Knock out (KO)	The option is live until a particular barrier is hit. Once the barrier is reached, the option expires worthless. The premium of this kind of option is lower than the premium of an equivalent vanilla option. For a KO option, the closer the barrier is, the lower the price will be. Conversely, the farther the barrier is, the lower the price will be, assuming that the probability of knocking out will be less.
American barrier	This kind of barrier can occur at any time on or before the expiry date of the option. Once the barrier has been touched, the KI or KO conditions get triggered.
European barrier	This kind of barrier is an observation at the time of expiry. Irrespective of whether the barrier level was touched during the life of the option, if the barrier level has not been touched when the option expires, the KI or KO conditions do not get triggered.
Up or down	The direction that the spot has to move in order for the barrier to get triggered is denoted by up if the barrier is higher than the spot and down if the barrier is lower than the spot.

EXAMPLE OF STRUCTURING AN OPTION USING BARRIERS

This example uses the same GBP USD option as was used earlier. Let us say that the same firm that needs to buy GBP in a year wants a worst-case scenario hedged at 1.7000 but some participation in case the GBP weakens. The chief financial officer (CFO) does not want to pay an up-front premium for the structure. How can we structure this transaction using options?

1. If the firm wants a worst-case hedge at 1.7000, it purchases a vanilla GBP call USD put (Option P1), with strike of 1.7000 and expiry one year hence. The premium for this is 1.6%.
2. The firm sells another option (GBP put USD call) whose strike is 1.7000 but with a premium of 1.6%, which knocks in only if a particular lower barrier is touched. Hence the option needs to be a 'down and in' GBP put USD call (Option P3), with a strike of 1.7000 and a barrier of B. Using the Option Pricer, we solve for B, which is 1.3300.

The payoff of the structure looks as shown in Table 20.11. This structure is also referred to as a participating forward, since it acts as a forward if a barrier is touched, while allowing the buyer of the structure some participation in a favourable currency move (GBP depreciation).

TABLE 20.11 Structuring a Zero-Premium Option (Participating Forward)

	Action Under Option P1: GBP Call USD Put with Strike of 1.7000	Action Under Option P3: GBP Put USD Call with Strike of 1.7000 and KI at 1.3300 *If Barrier of* 1.3300 *Is Not Touched*		Action Under Option P3: GBP Put USD Call with Strike of 1.7000 and KI at 1.3300 *If Barrier of* 1.3300 *Is Not Touched*	
Spot At Expiry	**Buyer: Firm**	**Buyer: Hedging Bank**	**Effective Rate to Firm to Buy GBP**	***Buyer: Hedging Bank***	**Effective Rate to Firm to Buy GBP**
1.2000	—	—	N.a.	Exercise (Bank sells GBP at 1.7000)	1.7000
1.2500	—	—	N.a.	Exercise (Bank sells GBP at 1.7000)	1.7000
1.3000	—	—	N.a.	Exercise (Bank sells GBP at 1.7000)	1.7000

TABLE 20.11 *(Continued)*

	Action Under Option P1: GBP Call USD Put with Strike of 1.7000	Action Under Option P3: GBP Put USD Call with Strike of 1.7000 and KI at 1.3300 *If Barrier of* 1.3300 *Is Not Touched*		Action under Option P3: GBP Put USD Call with Strike of 1.7000 and KI at 1.3300 *If Barrier of* 1.3300 *Is Not Touched*	
Spot At Expiry	**Buyer: Firm**	**Buyer: Hedging Bank**	**Effective Rate to Firm to Buy GBP**	***Buyer: Hedging Bank***	**Effective Rate to Firm to Buy GBP**
1.3300	—	—	N.a.	Exercise (Bank sells GBP at 1.7000)	1.7000
1.4500	—	—	1.4500	Exercise (Bank sells GBP at 1.7000)	1.7000
1.5000	—	—	1.5000	Exercise (Bank sells GBP at 1.7000)	1.7000
1.5500	—	—	1.5500	Exercise (Bank sells GBP at 1.7000)	1.7000
1.6000	—	—	1.6000	Exercise (Bank sells GBP at 1.7000)	1.7000
1.6500	—	—	1.6500	Exercise (Bank sells GBP at 1.7000)	1.7000
1.7000	Exercise (Firm buys GBP at 1.7000)	—	1.7000	—	1.7000
1.7500	Exercise (buy GBP at 1.7000)	—	1.7000	—	1.7000
1.8000	Exercise (buy GBP at 1.7000)	—	1.7000	—	1.7000
1.8500	Exercise (buy GBP at 1.7000)	—	1.7000	—	1.7000

Hence, the firm gets a forward at 1.7000 should the barrier be hit; if the barrier is not hit, it gets spot with a maximum rate of 1.7000.

Firms generally use exotic options in an attempt to decrease the cost of hedging or risk management, achieve a desired rate that is not a forward rate, or obtain a risk profile, return, or structure customised to their view.

Note that the payoffs of exotic options do not guarantee any of the results discussed, and adverse results could cause losses much larger than possible gains from beneficial market conditions. We discuss exotic options further in the case study on derivatives in emerging markets in Chapter 21.

SWAPS FAMILY

A swap is an exchange of cash flows over time, with prespecified methods of deriving the amount and currency of each cash flow. The basic characteristics of a swap transaction between two parties, A and B, are the descriptions of the two legs—what Party A pays B and receives from B respectively. These are:

- Notional amount
- Currency
- Fixed/floating rate
- Principal or coupon
- Day count fraction (i.e., A/360, 30/360, etc.), to calculate the interest or coupon
- Rate calculation for floating rate
- Benchmark for floating rates
- Spread over benchmark
- Any conditionalities (i.e., embedded options)
- Callability (i.e., whether any entity can call the swap or terminate unilaterally)
- Dates of each payment
- Dates and period for each calculation and benchmark observation
- Whether the benchmark is observed in advance (at the beginning of the calculation period) or in arrears (at the end of the calculation period)
- Amortisation schedule of principal
- Spot reference
- Any other legal or documentation requirements
- Underlying asset or liability (where such exchange control requirements exist)

In calculating any swap, the forward curve is used to compute the floating rate values of all the applicable legs and to obtain the present value (PV). The rates (spreads in the case of floating rates) at which the PV of both legs is identical is the break-even level of the swap.

Interest Rate Swap

The interest rate swap (IRS) is the simplest type of swap and typically is used to move from floating rate to fixed rate or vice versa within the same currency. The

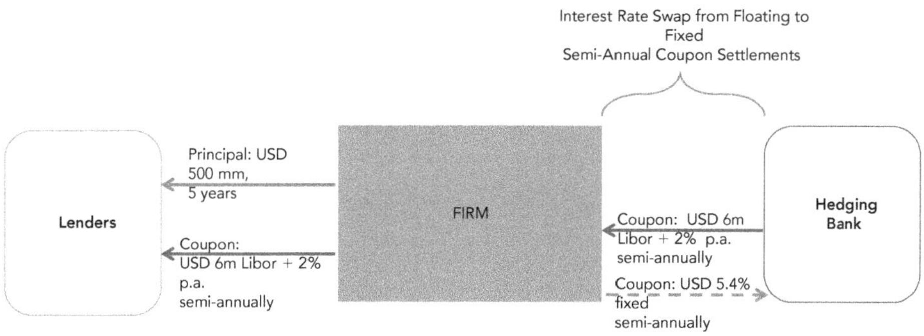

FIGURE 20.16 Interest Rate Swap

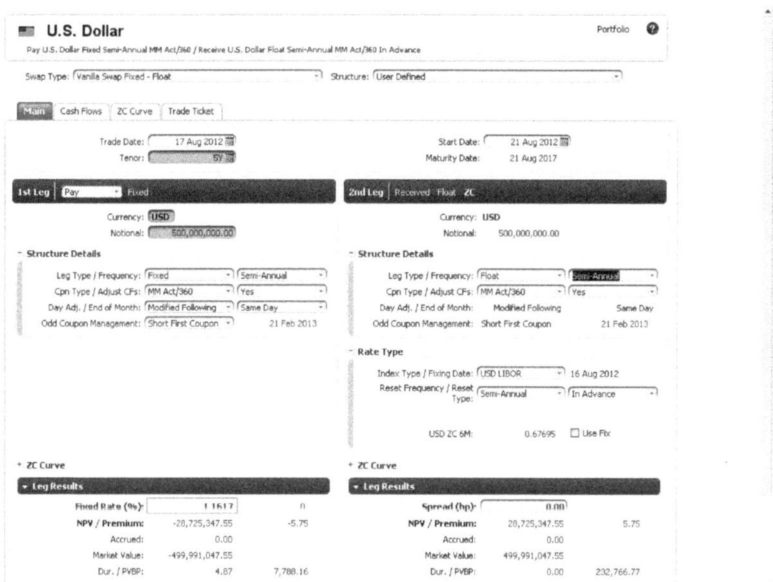

FIGURE 20.17 Pricing Screen for USD IRS Pricing

Source: Thomson Reuters Eikon

corporate payer of the IRS (who pays a fixed rate while receiving a floating rate) typically has a floating rate liability that is to be hedged as a fixed rate or believes that long-term interest rates are going to rise. Figure 20.16 shows a typical IRS. The corporate receiver of a floating rate chooses to diversify borrowings or achieve a targeted hedge ratio or believes that rates (especially the benchmark, such as LIBOR) will move down.

Pricing an IRS with customised dates and requirements, especially in the G7 currencies, is very simple if one has access to a market pricer (see Figure 20.17).

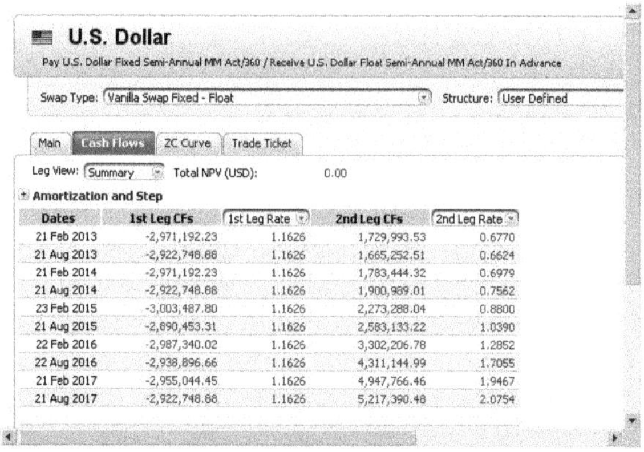

U.S. Dollar

Pay U.S. Dollar Fixed Semi-Annual MM Act/360 / Receive U.S. Dollar Float Semi-Annual MM Act/360 In Advance

Swap Type: Vanilla Swap Fixed - Float   Structure: User Defined

Main | Cash Flows | ZC Curve | Trade Ticket

Leg View: Summary   Total NPV (USD): 0.00

+ Amortization and Step

Dates	1st Leg CFs	1st Leg Rate	2nd Leg CFs	2nd Leg Rate
21 Feb 2013	-2,971,192.23	1.1626	1,729,993.53	0.6770
21 Aug 2013	-2,922,748.88	1.1626	1,665,252.51	0.6624
21 Feb 2014	-2,971,192.23	1.1626	1,783,444.32	0.6979
21 Aug 2014	-2,922,748.88	1.1626	1,900,989.01	0.7562
23 Feb 2015	-3,003,487.80	1.1626	2,273,288.04	0.8800
21 Aug 2015	-2,890,453.31	1.1626	2,583,133.22	1.0390
22 Feb 2016	-2,987,340.02	1.1626	3,302,206.78	1.2852
22 Aug 2016	-2,938,896.66	1.1626	4,311,144.99	1.7055
21 Feb 2017	-2,955,044.45	1.1626	4,947,766.46	1.9467
21 Aug 2017	-2,922,748.88	1.1626	5,217,390.48	2.0754

FIGURE 20.18 Use of Cash Flows and Computation of the Break-Even Rate

Source: Thomson Reuters Eikon

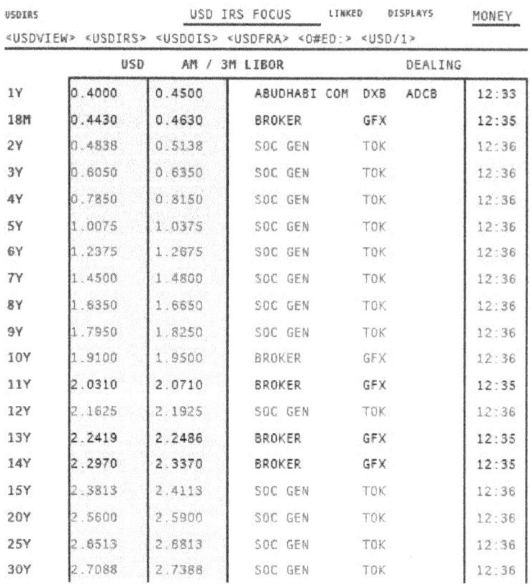

USDIRS   USD IRS FOCUS   LINKED DISPLAYS   MONEY

<USDVIEW> <USDIRS> <USDOIS> <USDFRA> <0#EO:> <USD/1>

USD   AM / 3M LIBOR   DEALING

1Y	0.4000	0.4500	ABUDHABI COM	DXB	ADCB	12:33
18M	0.4430	0.4630	BROKER	GFX		12:35
2Y	0.4838	0.5138	SOC GEN	TOK		12:36
3Y	0.6050	0.6350	SOC GEN	TOK		12:36
4Y	0.7850	0.8150	SOC GEN	TOK		12:36
5Y	1.0075	1.0375	SOC GEN	TOK		12:36
6Y	1.2375	1.2675	SOC GEN	TOK		12:36
7Y	1.4500	1.4800	SOC GEN	TOK		12:36
8Y	1.6350	1.6650	SOC GEN	TOK		12:36
9Y	1.7950	1.8250	SOC GEN	TOK		12:36
10Y	1.9100	1.9500	BROKER	GFX		12:36
11Y	2.0310	2.0710	BROKER	GFX		12:35
12Y	2.1625	2.1925	SOC GEN	TOK		12:36
13Y	2.2419	2.2486	BROKER	GFX		12:35
14Y	2.2970	2.3370	BROKER	GFX		12:35
15Y	2.3813	2.4113	SOC GEN	TOK		12:36
20Y	2.5600	2.5900	SOC GEN	TOK		12:36
25Y	2.6513	2.6813	SOC GEN	TOK		12:36
30Y	2.7088	2.7388	SOC GEN	TOK		12:36

FIGURE 20.19 USD IRS Market Levels Page

Source: Thomson Reuters Eikon

In Figure 20.17, USD 500 million floating to fixed IRS has been priced, and the pricing window and the curve used to arrive at that price is displayed here.

Figure 20.18 shows how the fixed rate is iteratively changed to arrive at the PV of the floating rate. The fixed rate thus arrived at becomes the break-even rate.

Market information systems, such as Thomson Reuters Eikon, apart from specific pricers shown in the three earlier figures, have pages that display indicative market prices of IRS. An example is shown in Figure 20.19.

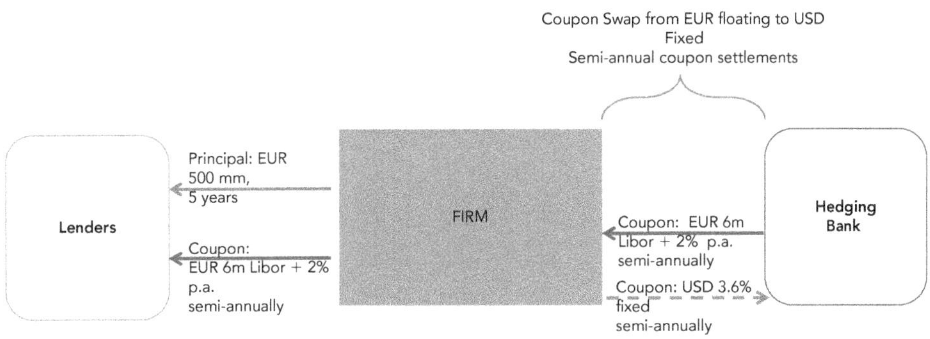

FIGURE 20.20 Coupon Swap

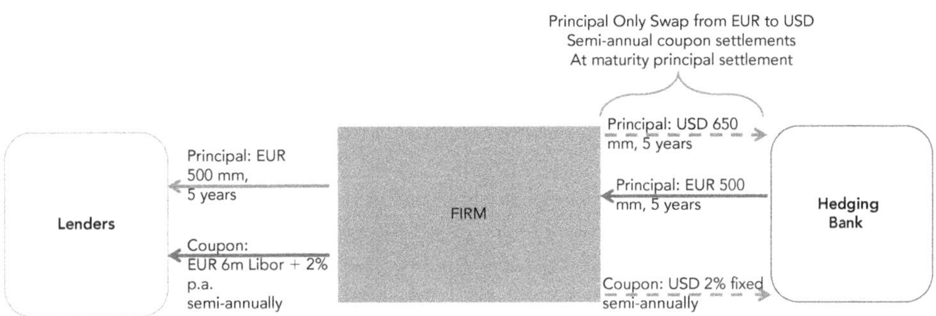

FIGURE 20.21 Principal-Only Swap

One of the main disadvantages of the payer of the IRS is the opportunity loss if rates stay down or the consequent marked to market () or cash outflow, should the payer be taking on a view or a position.

Coupon Swaps

The coupon swap (see Figure 20.20) is a variant of the simple IRS, where one of the legs is in a different currency. In the example, the firm has a liability in EUR but wishes to convert the interest servicing of the EUR floating coupon into a USD fixed, in order to have more visibility on interest outflow and move it into a currency of choice. The opportunity loss of EUR LIBOR remaining low or moving lower or of possible EUR depreciation (which means fewer USD have to be converted to pay off the same amount of EUR coupon) are two disadvantages of this locking in.

Principal-Only Swaps

Principal-only swaps (POSs; see Figure 20.21) are used to hedge the currency element of the principal of an asset or liability. In the example, the principal amount

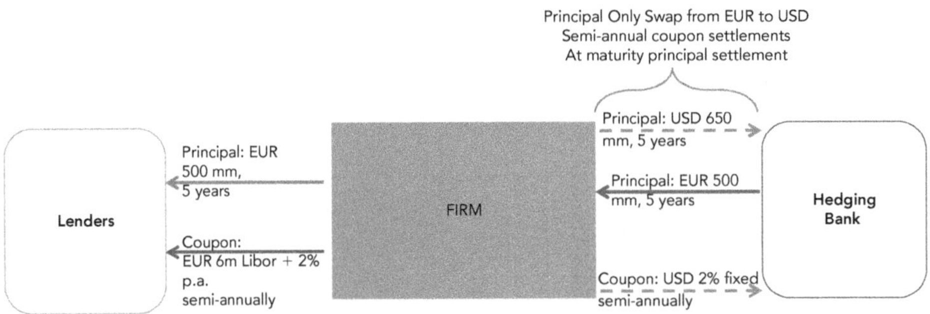

FIGURE 20.22 Cross-Currency Swap

of a EUR liability is being hedged through the use of a POS. In effect, the POS is a forward contract with the settlement or exchange of principals happening at today's spot price; the forward premium or discount takes the shape of coupon cash flows payable periodically through the life of the transaction. Unlike most forwards that have one back-ended exchange at maturity, the POS encourages premium payments over the course of the transaction, thereby making it easier for the hedger POS to time and integrate the coupon payments of the hedge with interest payments on the loan. It also is easier for the hedger to quantify the overall debt burden and get certainty around the principal FX risk—which could be a very large one if the hedger does not have significant EUR inflows, especially back-ended in the final year, as in this case.

Cross-Currency Swaps

If the hedger with a EUR liability wishes to hedge both principal and coupon, we combine the coupon swap with the POS, thereby locking in both coupon and principal payments in USD and fixed amounts. This would provide the hedger with maximum visibility on debt servicing and also eliminate currency risk on the debt payments, given that they do not have large EUR inflows. Figure 20.22 depicts a typical cross-currency swap.

Exotic and Structured Swaps

The swaps just described are building blocks for more exotic and structured transactions. Various elements, such as optionality, commodities, equity, and credit, can be built into these swaps to create more exotic and structured payoffs.

The types of swaps discussed earlier should give most treasurers the requisite arsenal on the swap side to solve a large part of their risk management problems that require swaps. Seasoned practitioners with very specific risk views and appetites may use more structured transactions, after having assessed and understood the risk profile and payoffs in detail.

CREDIT FAMILY

Credit derivatives are one of the largest growing and evolving fields of financial management. Credit markets, as they are now called, are based on finding the price for, and trading, the underlying credit risk in specific instruments or obligors. These markets are closely tied in with fixed income markets, since the underlying tradeable fixed income instruments or assets form the core of credit trading.

When an investor buys a tradeable bond, for example, he or she takes on credit risk. An investor who is long a bond (i.e., owns a bond) is also now the owner of the credit risk associated with the bond (or long the credit risk of the bond); hence, the investor is exposed to the risk (however remote) that the bond issuer will fail to make interest or payments as and when they fall due.

In Chapter 13 the cost of debt for a firm was shown to be a function of:

- Benchmark
- Credit rating spread (generic to all equally rated firms in that market)
- Obligor-specific rating spread
- Liquidity spread (specific to that market at that time)

For purposes of this discussion, we assume that the liquidity spread is zero and that the coupon of a newly issued bond, or the current borrowing rate for the issuer, is benchmark + credit spread.

Figure 20.23 shows us the relationship between the bond and credit risk.

This figure sets us up to delve into the pricing and defeasance of the credit risk.

Credit Default Swap

A credit default swap (CDS) is an exchange of cash flows (swap) on an underlying instrument, asset, or enterprise (reference asset) that gets triggered when there is a default on that asset (credit default), for which a premium is payable (CDS spread).

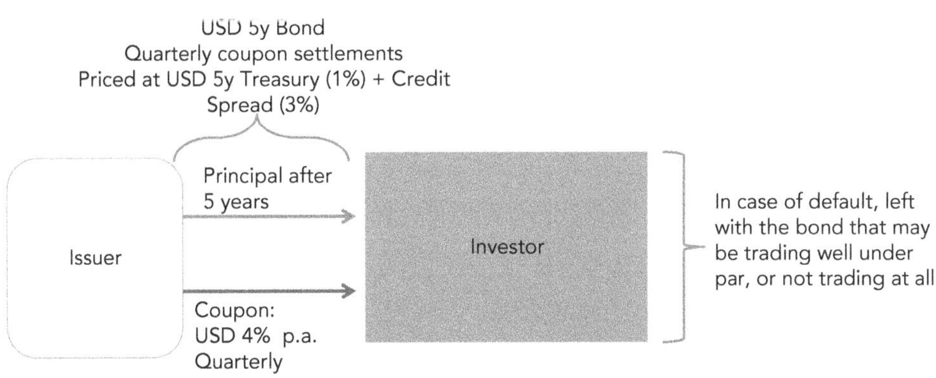

FIGURE 20.23 Long a Bond, Long Credit Risk

In effect, a CDS is a derivative contract between two counterparties, whereby the party seeking credit protection (buyer) makes periodic payments to another party providing credit protection (seller) and receives the promise of a predefined amount if a specific issuer (reference entity) defaults. It is akin to an insurance contract on an event happening. In this case, the event is the default of the reference entity or obligor for that asset. In case of default, the buyer of the insurance or the payer of the CDS receives full compensation for the bond or reference asset, while paying back to the seller of the insurance (or CDS) the bond itself a similar bond or the cash equivalent of the bond.

Figure 20.24 depicts how the credit risk of the bond can be synthetically taken out through the CDS.

Effectively, the bank or market maker that is taking on the credit risk of the issuer is getting a return of 3% (equivalent to the credit spread of the issuer) for taking on the risk. This is a simplistic example, and in practice the actual numbers may vary a little, but it puts into context the role and operations of a CDS.

How Can a CDS Be Used?

A CDS can be used to hedge existing credit risk or exposure on an entity (provided markets can be made on the credit of that entity). For example, let us say that Firm F has a large exposure to Client C on whose debt CDS trading occurs. If C goes through financial distress, the probability that C will default on its existing debt and its obligations to F are high. F can hedge its credit exposure to C through a CDS if it believes that the risk of default is high. The more in distress the market perceives C to be, the higher the CDS spread or risk premium for insurance the market will charge.

There are multiple ways to embed credit protection into transactions or balance sheets through creative credit structuring. The CDS is the building block for many of these methods. Many books explain the construction, pricing, and workings of the CDS. Readers may want to look into the topic in more depth.

Using Credit Derivatives to Solve Financial Situations

Credit derivatives can be used across different areas:

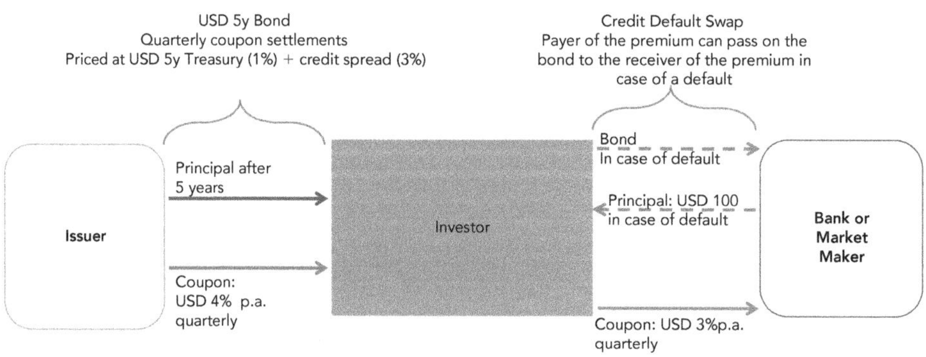

FIGURE 20.24 Stripping Out the Credit Risk of the Bond Through the CDS

- Risk reduction (through the use of simple or structured CDSs)
- Investments on specific credits or a basket (through the use of embedded credit derivatives into notes)
- Utilising items in one balance sheet into another—with full disclosure, of course
- Other specific objectives that require the use of balance sheet, debt, and liquidity

The important thing to note is that credit transactions tend to require fairly comprehensive documentation and legal checks. A lot of time is required to understand the various elements involved in most structuring activities. Many credit structures also do not qualify for conventional hedge accounting, and treasurers must be well aware of disclosure, valuation, and liquidity aspects and downsides of these transactions prior to entering into them.

SUMMARY

The world of products and instruments is large and involved; this book discusses some of the basic building blocks that treasurers and CFOs can use to achieve most financial objectives. To solve complex situations or problems, it is important to keep the solution simple and manageable.

CHAPTER TWENTY ONE

21

Combining the Products to Manage Risk: Risk Governance

WE HAVE DISCUSSED VARIOUS PRODUCTS to manage risk in Chapter 20. How do we combine these products to manage risk? What are the various things we can do to manage our risk? We explore the answers to these questions and other themes of risk governance in this chapter.

We see how different kinds of risks can be managed in different situations. These risks include:

- Foreign exchange (FX) risk using spot, forward, options, and swaps
- Rate risk using the yield curve instruments such as swaps and options and longer tenor funding
- Funding and liquidity risk using long-term credit facilities and raising capital when possible
- Credit risk using credit default swaps (CDSs) and other tools
- Legal and compliance reporting using simple tools
- Operational risk, which is covered in detail in Chapter 23 and in the "Operations" section of the Toolkit in Part Five

We also introduce some basic recommended tenets and put together the pieces from the arsenal to formulate strategies in Chapter 22.

DEVISING RISK STRATEGY USING PRODUCTS

The starting point of devising a strategy for risk governance, after the risks have been identified and measured, is to frame the objectives. Once that has been done and the metrics have been finalised (see Figure 21.1), the time horizon is frozen. As has been mentioned earlier, this horizon needs to be aligned with management time horizons. Then comes the task of short-listing the possible instruments and proportions to be hedged. Two to three alternatives to the mix may be determined, since more alternatives can complicate the decision-making process.

Each of these alternatives, with the mix across tenors and products, should then be tested through scenarios. This simulation, such as the ones provided by Aktrea's ARTEMIS, can be a useful tool—something that lets the company experience what could happen under various situations. The alternatives that most match the objectives across these scenarios could be the ones that are finally chosen for consideration.

The process of deciding the final mix is a comprehensive one and a full-time activity. The simulation must be kept simple, though rigorous, with the reports conducive to decision making. Overload of information might end up hindering the decision-making process. In this chapter, we cover the use of alternatives of instruments and some of the analyses that go with prudent risk management. In Chapter 22, we evaluate a few sample strategies and weigh their benefits and potential issues.

It must be noted that no strategy or process is foolproof—some are more effective than others in certain environments and circumstances, while some great strategies can fall apart with poor implementation.

There are four basic tenets that I follow when deciding strategies and approaches to risk governance.

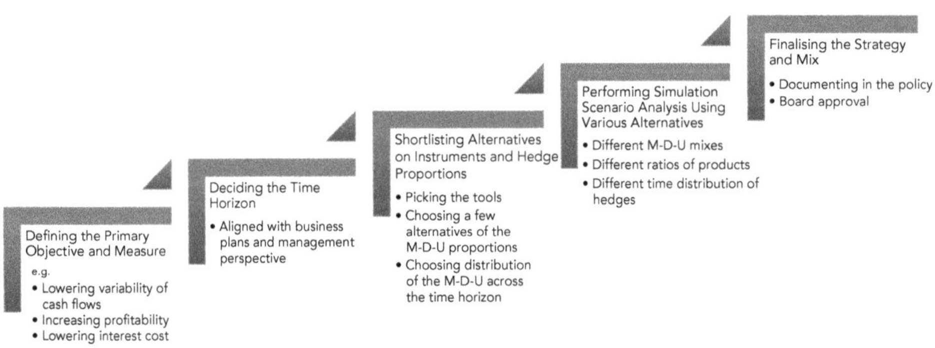

FIGURE 21.1 Devising a Risk Management Governance Strategy

Tenet 1: Never Choose Products or Structures Whose Payoff You Cannot Understand

Payoff profiles are some of the most important decision criteria for any transaction. In all scenarios, the payoff has to be within the framework, loss norms or return ranges as per the policy and need. While it may not always be possible for the Treasurer to understand how the product has been structured, he or she must know what it does. I used the example of the car earlier: We may not know the details of the engineering and technology that goes into the car, but we need to know how to drive it and how it responds at various speeds, on various track and road conditions, and if it gives us the mix of fuel efficiency, comfort, appearance, and ease of driving and maintenance that fits our requirements.

Tenet 2: Choose Products That You Can Price (at Least Approximately)

Pricing for most products and market levels, with information systems such as Thomson Reuters Eikon, is generally available. For simple products, especially forwards and simple options, data are now available for many currencies. Hence, most simple products can be priced easily with the right tools. The ability to determine the price of a structure on one's own cannot be the exclusive domain of a structuring specialist on a banking markets desk. A structure that is very complicated is priced using models or complex pricers. The complexity of the model is generally commensurate with the complexity of the product. Not knowing how to determine the basic price of the product usually indicates that it is more complex, with possibly more opacity and less liquidity,

Tenet 3: Decide Up Front Who Bears Cost of Hedging

The allocation of the market rates to various units has to follow a set of guidelines to prevent disputes at a later time on possible preferential treatment by Treasury to certain units. Especially on days of high volatility, two transactions done minutes away from each other could have very different rates. Prior agreement on the distribution of rates to each unit—a good transfer pricing method—will remove any ambiguities and uncertainty around the rates.

Tenet 4: Use Simulation, but Wisely

Simulation is a very strong method to decide the best strategy to use and also to revalidate strategies midway and prior to review dates. Two caveats come to mind:

1. Decisions based on simulation are only as good as the firm's assessment on which scenarios in the simulation are more likely. Hence, simulation does not take away the subjective element in the decision process.
2. Overuse of simulation or over-information is a risk in itself. Having too much information, many data points, and lots of tables are a common result of excitement

and enthusiasm. Scenarios and solutions need to be optimised to allow the decision makers to properly evaluate all alternatives as efficiently as possible.

USING PRODUCTS TO MANAGE RISK

In Chapter 20, we examined various products and tools and discussed briefly how they could be employed. Here we run through, risk by risk, possible exposures and how products and instruments can be used to manage each kind of risk. Table 21.1 provides an overview of the arsenal of products available to global treasurers to manage market risks. Not all products are available in all markets, and many require counterparty risk limits with banks. Similarly, we look at tools to manage credit risks and liquidity risks later in the chapter. The darker shading implies more frequent use, while the lightly shaded cells depict possible but less frequent use of tools for each situation or risk.

In order to judge tools and strategies as successes or failures, they have to be tested over time and implementation. Well-thought-out conservative policies and strategies with well-defined objectives and unambiguous structures, consistently applied over time, are more likely to see positive results. Successes or failures of well-thought-out strategies cannot be declared after one or two beneficial or adverse results; their efficacy over a longer time frame is a better yardstick to judge them by.

Foreign Exchange Risk

The FX arsenal has possibly the most weapons, which range from the simple to extremely complicated. Cash flows such as sales and expenses, and translation items can be generally hedged using FX forwards or options.

To manage the FX risk of debt, especially principal, principal-only swaps (POSs; effectively forwards with premium payments in intervals) can be appropriate tools. FX risk of interest payments can be handled through coupon swaps.

Diversification of portfolio across currencies can also be a useful tool—subject to the selection of a conservative portfolio, regular reassessment, and consistency.

Interest Rate Risk

The tools to manage interest rate risk are also quite varied and can handle the many interest rate risks that fall into the treasurer's ambit. These include:

- **Price (rate or benchmark movement).** Interest rate swaps, quantos, or options (caps, floors, and combinations) can be used to handle specific benchmarks or price risks.
- **Yield curve risk.** Swaps or products to handle yield curve shapes can be structured to enable the Treasurer either to reduce variability or to benefit by taking a view on the yield curve steepening or flattening.
- **Reinvestment/rollover.** Rate locks, forward rate agreements, or options can be used to lock in rates either forward or for longer terms. There could be some residual risk, especially on credit spreads, that can also be hedged using CDSs of peer groups.

TABLE 21.1 Arsenal for Market Risk

Market Factors	Arsenal	Common Hedgable Items—Market Risk							
		Sales	Expenses	Principal Repayments	Interest Repayments	Other Flows	Investments	Other Sources of Funds	Balance Sheet Items
FX	FX Forwards								
FX	Par Forwards								
FX	Variable Date Forwards								
FX	Vanilla FX Options								
FX	FX Range Forwards								
FX	Variable Rate Forwards								
FX, Other	FX Structured Options								
FX	Principal Only Swap								
IR	Interest Rate Swap								
FX, IR	Coupon Swap								
IR	Quantos								
FX, IR	Cross Currency Swaps								
Any	Structured Swaps								

(Continued)

TABLE 21.1 Continued

Market Factors	Arsenal	Common Hedgable Items - Market Risk							
		Sales	Expenses	Principal Repayments	Interest Repayments	Other Flows	Investments	Other Sources of Funds	Balance Sheet Items
IR	Vanilla IR Options								
IR	Collars								
IR	Forward Rate Agreements								
IR	Rate Locks								
IR	Duration Swaps								
Cmdty	Commodity Futures								
Cmdty	OTC Commodity Options								
Cmdty	Commodity Swaps								
Cmdty	Fixed Price Contracts								
Eqty	Equity Options								
Eqty	Structured Equity Derivatives								
Any	Diversification								

- **Residual basis risks and other risks.** These also can be addressed through specific tailored over-the-counter (OTC) swaps. Diversification can be used to find optimal or lower pricing depending on objectives and focus.

Table 21.2 shows some of the cases where products could be used for cash flow hedging.

Other Risks

Commodity and equity risks are managed through OTC or index futures and derivative contracts. They can also be embedded into swaps, loans, or other contracts. Especially for commodities, fixed price purchasing contracts may be a good alternative

TABLE 21.2 Cash Flow Hedging

Possible Objective	Up-front Cash Flow Constraint	View	Possible Strategy	Possible Issues
Maximum possible visibility and certainty on economic basis	High	—	100% forward	Opportunity loss Marked to market (MTM) changes
	High	Want some benefit in case of favourable market move but want worst-case protection	Range forward or collar Other structured options	Opportunity loss MTM changes
Worst case guaranteed	Low	Want upside on favourable moves with protection on worst case	Range forward or bought option with sold option at a high level to reduce premium	Up-front cost
Using existing recently good market levels or opportunities	High	Market could move adversely or not move as beneficially as forward	100% forward	Opportunity loss MTM changes
	High	INR could weaken beyond the forward but want a worst-case hedge	Zero premium Range forward	Opportunity loss MTM changes: balance sheet and profit and loss volatility
	Medium	Level could depreciate further but want a worst-case hedge	Mix of forwards and options	Opportunity loss MTM changes: up-front cash outflow
	Low	Unclear, would like to benefit from INR depreciation with a worst-case rate	100% options at targeted level	Opportunity loss High cash outflow up front

CASE STUDY: TRYING TO KILL TWO BIRDS WITH ONE STONE

Figure 21.2 shows a possible variation to an interest rate swap where the firm also has underlying commodity price risk that has been built into the swap payoff. The firm has an underlying bond that has a fixed coupon. With the possibility of commodity prices increasing, the firm wants to link the interest outflow on the loan with commodity prices. If prices fall, the firm has the ability to service a higher interest cost, but if commodity prices shoot up, the firm would like to lower its outflow on interest expense.

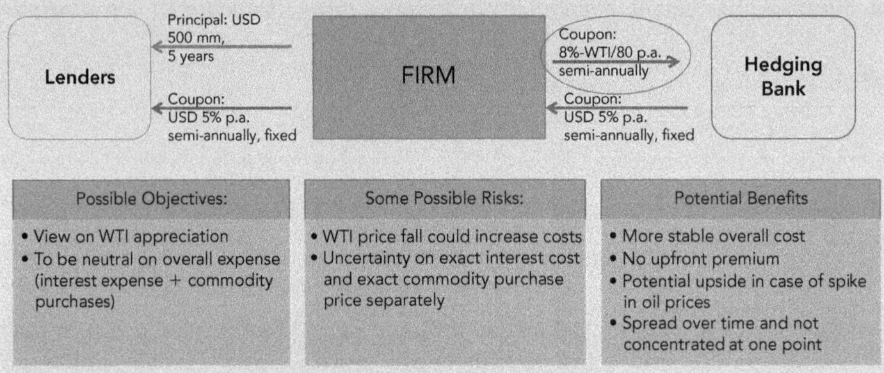

FIGURE 21.2 Structured Interest Rate Swap

for long-term visibility—where the supplier takes on the risk (and passes on the cost in some cases) to the company.

A case of structured interest rate swap that provides management of two factors in one transaction, is given in the next case study.

Equity or commodity-price linked derivatives transactions can also be embedded into loans.

A disadvantage of embedded derivatives in a conservative accounting environment is the massive increase in accounting work (to potentially strip the derivatives and the underlying asset or liability, get different MTM levels and possible inability to get hedge accounting treatment on such structures).

CREDIT RISK

An overview of tools used to manage credit risk is given in Figure 21.3 The darker shading implies more frequent use, while the lightly shaded cells depict possible but less frequent, use of tools for each situation or risk.

The CDSs described earlier remain the most common tools for hedging credit risk. However, liquid CDS pricing is generally available only for large entities that have issued bonds. For countries that do not have a developed CDS market, nondeliverable forwards (NDFs) can could be used as proxy hedges if the related risks on the proxy

Arsenal	Common Hedgable Items - Credit Risk				
	Receivables (Counterparty)	Long Term Client dependency	Country and Cross-Border Risk	Supply Chain Disruption	Concentration
FX Forwards					
Non-Deliverable Forwards					
CDS					
Credit Linked Notes					
Total Return Deposits					
Other Credit Derivatives					
Forfaiting					
Credit Insurance					
Factoring					
Receivables Financing					
Other Supply Chain Financing					
Securitisation					
Collateralisation					
Avoidance Over Limits		(negative)			
Diversification					

FIGURE 21.3 Tools to Manage Credit Risk

hedge itself are borne in mind (i.e., a credit event may not trigger a sale on the currency, the currency itself could strengthen with no credit event, thereby increasing the cost of the hedge, etc.).

Other related methods, such as credit insurance and factoring, can be used to manage credit risk. Increasingly, the use of supply chain finance tools has taken on more and more importance with the increasing role of banks as service partners across the supply chain.

Cash collateralisation is one method that could work, especially if the customer is much smaller and is willing to help reduce risk to an extent.

Avoidance comes with related long-term issues since it usually means staying away from a market or customer for a period.

Diversification has historically been a prudent exercise, provided it is done consistently and the diversification aspects are thought out and analysed.

LIQUIDITY RISK: BALANCE SHEET AND ASSET-LIABILITY MANAGEMENT

Figure 21.4 provides a snapshot of the tools to manage liquidity risk. As with the tools for other risks provided earlier, the darker shading implies more frequent use, while the lightly shaded cells depict possible but less frequent use of tools for each situation or risk.

We have already mentioned that the key to a good liquidity risk management strategy is to have:

- Cash
- Reliable access to bank credit lines
- Assets that can be repurchased (or "repo"-ed or liquidated under most circumstances)

Arsenal	Common Hedgable Items—Liquidity Risk		
	Funding	Gapping	Trapped Cash
Buffer			
Credit Lines/Facilities			
Total Return Deposit			
Credit-Linked Structures			
Early Warning Borrowing			
Structured Swaps			
Repurchase Agreements			
Asset Liquidation			
Barrier Options			
Diversification			

FIGURE 21.4 Tools to Manage Liquidity Risk

The figure matrix elucidates some of these strategies in detail.

When there is a systemic liquidity problem, treasurers must decide whether it is better to utilise some of the credit lines or facilities for long-term borrowing when a crisis looms. The related costs and changes to balance sheet, should there be no crisis, can prove to be a problem.

USE OF ANALYSIS

Many tools are available to the Treasurer to analyse and make decisions on market levels, next steps, and future situations. We discuss a few of them here.

Fundamental and technical analysis seek to determine values of market factors or firm performance through different means. Scenario analyses help to rationalise thoughts on the risk management strategy, while payoff profiles help to ascertain the applicability of a set of tools to manage particular risks.

Fundamental Analysis

Fundamental analysis assesses the health an economy, market, industry, or company through detailed study of its various constituents, environments, dependencies, competencies, and markets with the objective of making financial and market-related decisions. Fundamental analysis can be of three types:

1. **Analysis of an economy or a market or market factor**. Here, the research and conclusions can be drawn on a specific country or market, or even a market factor, such as WTI crude oil.
2. **Analysis of an industry**. The focus of the analysis is a specific industry, usually used for business and/or credit reasons.

FIGURE 21.5 Technical Analysis (A)

Source: Thomson Reuters Eikon

3. **Analysis of a company or a group of companies.** Specifically focused for purposes of procurement, sales, or investment, this is a micro study with more details on the specific group.

Technical Analysis

Technical analysis is a technique to forecast the direction of market prices by studying historic data on movement and volume of prices. Technical analysts believe that information required to forecast future price movements has already been reflected in historical movements of the factor. The underlying assumption is that the collective behavioral response of market participants to price movements results in patterns that are recognisable—this makes changes in trends or any other move follow a sentiment change that is predictable.

Hence, technical analysis is more concerned with extrapolating information from existing price patterns and less concerned with the actual price of a market factor.

Figures 21.5 and 21.6 show typical series of technical analyses using available tools from Thomson Reuters Eikon.

Simulation

As described, simulation uses take a set of exposures through various scenarios and considers the impact of those scenarios over time. At various points, the simulator system also allows the risk manager to make decisions that would lead to further possibilities that can be captured.

FIGURE 21.6 Technical Analysis (B)

Source: Thomson Reuters Eikon

Simulation provides a real-life feel to actual data and simulated situations: What if this event happened? What if this client went under? What if cost of borrowing shot up? What happens to my balance sheet and financials—what is the cost of borrowing and cost of capital, and how do they affect my ratios?

Simulation is an invaluable tool as long as the subjective elements are thought through and there is no data overload. The more complex the simulation becomes, the more decision points there will be and the more decisions there are to make.

Simulation also allows the Treasurer to superimpose hedges on a portfolio, watch the performance of the hedging strategy over time, make changes midway, and reassess what might have happened had the changes not been made. This method gives the Treasurer a good feel of what the strategy might evolve into in the company's financials.

More details on simulation may be found on the book's Website www.wiley.com/go/treasuryhandbook or at www.aktrea.com.

Payoff Profiles

Payoff profiles are, in my view, a must-have for deciding any product, especially when comparing two products. The payoff profile can be in chart or graphical form. A graphical payoff profile from an ARTEMIS simulation for a EUR USD decision is provided as a sample in Figure 21.7. The firm, after having started hedging through vanilla options, debated various scenarios, including leaving the rest of the portfolio unhedged or covering fully through forward. Finally, based on the firm's objectives and

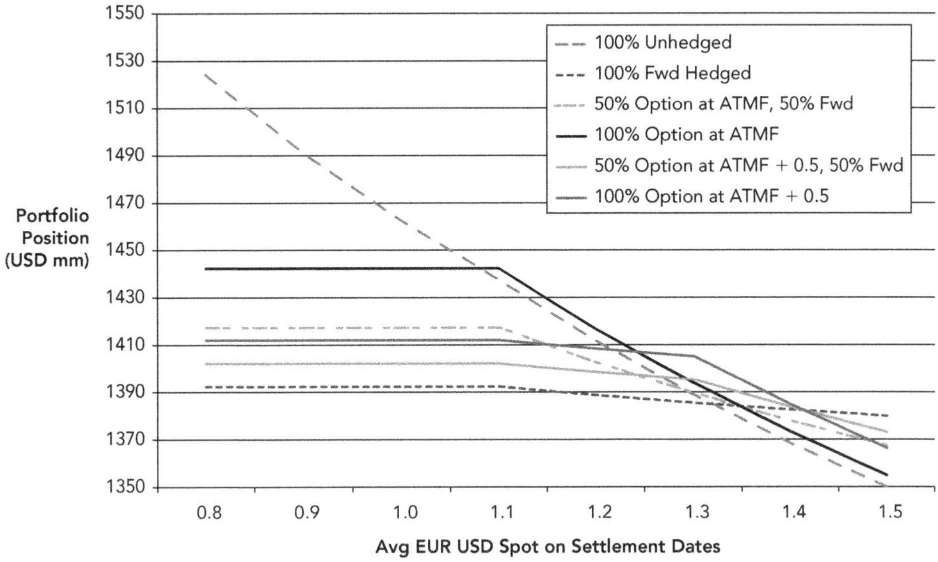

FIGURE 21.7 Sample Payoff Profile

a corresponding possible trade-off between certainty and opportunity loss, a decision can be made.

OPERATIONS AND TECHNOLOGY RISK

The aspect of operations management and its risk are detailed in Chapter 24 in Part Five. Avoidance is the primary method for managing operations risk, and all efforts on operations and technology risk management is geared towards preventing any outage or error. Increasing control and rigor of process backed up by automation and integration reduces the probability of occurrence of this type of risk.

LEGAL AND COMPLIANCE RISK

Managing legal and compliance risk on the balance sheet and capital side of things is a critical activity for the Treasurer. While every company has different processes to manage these risks, a sample set of processes and checklists could be the best way to address these. A more holistic compliance management methodology through automation is provided in the next case study.

CASE STUDY: COMPLIANCE MANAGEMENT SYSTEM (CMS): FROM ADMINISTRATIVE HEADACHE TO BUSINESS IMPROVEMENT

The Background

The chief financial officer (CFO) noticed a new unread mail icon on his laptop. The mail was from the financial controller, and the subject, "*List of Non-Compliances,*" made him brace himself as email opened up. The list of all the different compliance requirements not fulfilled in the last quarter was long, and the same story—that the auditors were always bringing this issue up during the review meetings—was being retold. The enormity of the problem and the potential disaster that was around the corner hit hard, and the CFO called the CIO to look into any possible market application that could solve the problem easily.

A few days of research threw up some alternatives, but many presentations and proposals later the CFO was not convinced about the available solutions: They were not able to handle his requirement in a comprehensive manner, and despite looking at expanding his tight budget (it was 2009, and cost cuts had taken over the world), the products and applications did not provide the desired level of functionality.

The CFO decided to invest his biggest commodity—time—into doing a zero-based exercise on what the system should actually contain. Brainstorming with his team and a few peers, the CFO put together a user specification document with key functionalities. Some of these are provided in Figure 21.8.

Discussions with the CIO followed, and after examining and analysing different approaches, the team concluded that using the company's existing IT team for developing a product in-house to meet all the requirements would be the best alternative. The company had IT enterprises and resources in the United States, Taiwan, and India, and the three areas were compared from the perspectives of efficiency, cost effectiveness, and turnaround. The IT team in India was a mature and dedicated team that had won the Best Department award just a month back. They had already developed a Visitor Management System (VMS) successfully for the company's use and had received a good response from visitors and employees alike after implementation.

The IT enterprise team in India was the one finally selected.

The Execution

The selection of the platform (SQL server in the background and Visual Basic and .NET in the front end or client side) was done, and the CFO and CIO, as end users, were actively involved in the development.

The project team dedicated to the development of the application included members from the finance, accounts, Treasury and IT departments. Further brainstorming addressed core issues brought out by different areas, and solutions and functional specifications debated and agreed (Figure 21.9).

Responsibility

- Ensuring that subsidiaries and overseas operations are completing their compliance requirements on time
- Assigning responsibility for different levels of compliance, with back-ups
- Automatic escalation matrix for responsibility

Integration

- Direct uploading of the compliance requirements specific to a firm from a source rather than manual entry into the application
- Ability to upload supporting documents and workflow
- Integration with inhouse mail, workflow and reporting systems

Functionality and Coverage

- Database of compliance requirements
- Different compliance requirements for different countries, legal entities, and organisation structures
- Different compliance requirements for different functions
- Calendar for recurrence and bring-ups (reminders) before due date
- Automated system alerts for reminders and reporting for breaches
- Risk matrix to assess severity of the compliance and cost of-noncompliance
- Cost effectiveness
- Flexibility to add new regulations and aspects as and when they come up
- Customisation of documentation requirements

Reporting

- Reporting dashboards for senior management and country management in subsidiaries
- Availability of customised reporting, especially to the board
- Assurance to regulators, auditors, exchanges, and bankers on compliance levels

FIGURE 21.8 Zero-Based Functionality Specifications for a Compliance Management System

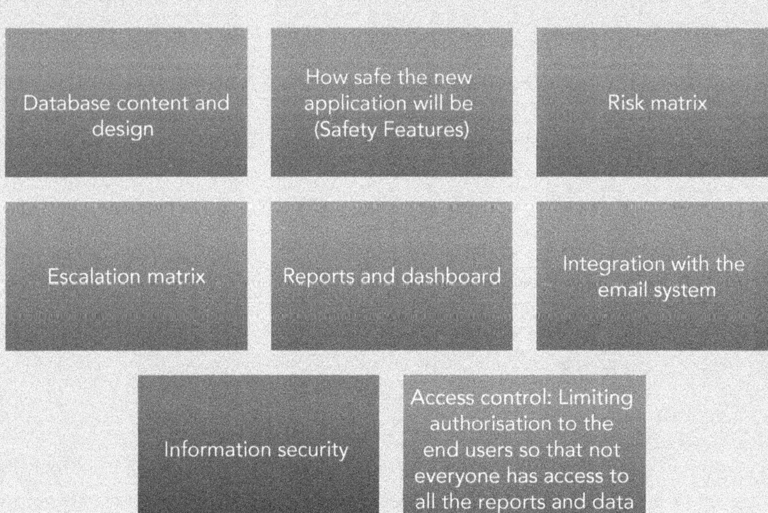

FIGURE 21.9 Functional Specifications

(Continued)

After critical review, the project scope document was created. The team began working on the defined scope and released the first version. The functionalities were repeatedly tested in a rigorous User Acceptance Testing (UAT) environment.

Cost/Benefit

A detailed cost/benefit analysis was done for the entire project, as depicted in Table 21.3, with benefits shown in Table 21.4.

TABLE 21.3 Some of the tangible cost elements were:

No.	Item	Cost
1	Platform (existing MS SQL 2008,.Net framework platform and Crystal Report Writer 2008)	
2	Cost of developers' effort (4 man-months)	Rs. 400,000
3	Cost of design and development relating to additional features	(Rs. 40,000)
4	Training	(Rs. 50,000)
5	Testing and piloting	(Rs. 100,000)
6	Master data compilation	(Rs. 200,000)
7	Total cost of ownership	Rs. 790,000

TABLE 21.4 Tangible Benefits

No.	Item	Cost
1	5% saving through productivity increase of work force using tool per month = 20 × 50,000 × 5% = Rs. 50,000 × 12 =	Rs. 600,000
2	5 man-days saved on account of compiling information per month: Rs. 2,280 × 5 = Rs. 11,400 × 12 =	Rs. 136,800
3	Difference in penalties paid in previous year—penalties paid in first year of operations =	Rs. 400,000
	Total savings =	Rs. 1,136,800

Intangible Benefits

- Cost Effective
  - Automating the system saves a lot of man-hours for follow-up
  - Lesser penalties due to real-time monitoring
  - Zero tolerance against noncompliance
  - Real-time clarity in the compliances relating to the organisation
  - Responsibilities are clearly defined and monitored accordingly
  - Employee profile management
  - Easy-to-manage change
  - The organisation is connected with respect to compliances
- Controlled Legal Exposure
  - Not all documents are accessible to everyone and hence risk is controlled

- Increased Productivity and Confidence
  - More time spent in doing value-added work rather than follow-ups and reminders
  - Senior management confident of one-time compliance and has full visibility
  - The implementation period: around five months

End-to-end and the ROI period (actual): 8.33 months.

Piloting

Post the product development, a pilot run was carried out in the Finance and Accounts department. The compliance items were uploaded into the system (directly from MS Excel) and were checked for proper functioning of the application. With the success of the pilot run, the product was implemented throughout the organisation.

The End Product

After three months of extensive detailing and efforts, the IT team came out with the first version of the CMS. After the first version was available, extensive user testing was done with dummy data with the roll-out of the first version. Once the system stabilised, the product was rolled out throughout the organisation. Some screenshots of the systems are provided in Figures 21.10 to 21.14.

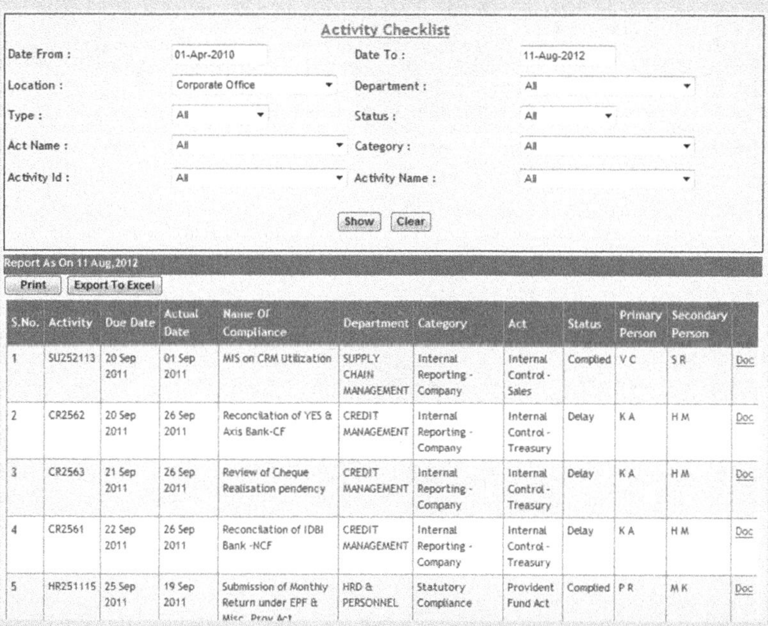

S.No.	Activity	Due Date	Actual Date	Name Of Compliance	Department	Category	Act	Status	Primary Person	Secondary Person	
1	SU252113	20 Sep 2011	01 Sep 2011	MIS on CRM Utilization	SUPPLY CHAIN MANAGEMENT	Internal Reporting - Company	Internal Control - Sales	Complied	V C	S R	Doc
2	CR2562	20 Sep 2011	26 Sep 2011	Reconcilation of YES & Axis Bank-CF	CREDIT MANAGEMENT	Internal Reporting - Company	Internal Control - Treasury	Delay	K A	H M	Doc
3	CR2563	21 Sep 2011	26 Sep 2011	Review of Cheque Realisation pendency	CREDIT MANAGEMENT	Internal Reporting - Company	Internal Control - Treasury	Delay	K A	H M	Doc
4	CR2561	22 Sep 2011	26 Sep 2011	Reconcilation of IDBI Bank -NCF	CREDIT MANAGEMENT	Internal Reporting - Company	Internal Control - Treasury	Delay	K A	H M	Doc
5	HR251115	25 Sep 2011	19 Sep 2011	Submission of Monthly Return under EPF & Misc. Prov Act	HRD & PERSONNEL	Statutory Compliance	Provident Fund Act	Complied	P R	M K	Doc

FIGURE 21.10 Department-wise Checklist, Functional Head-wise Checklist

(Continued)

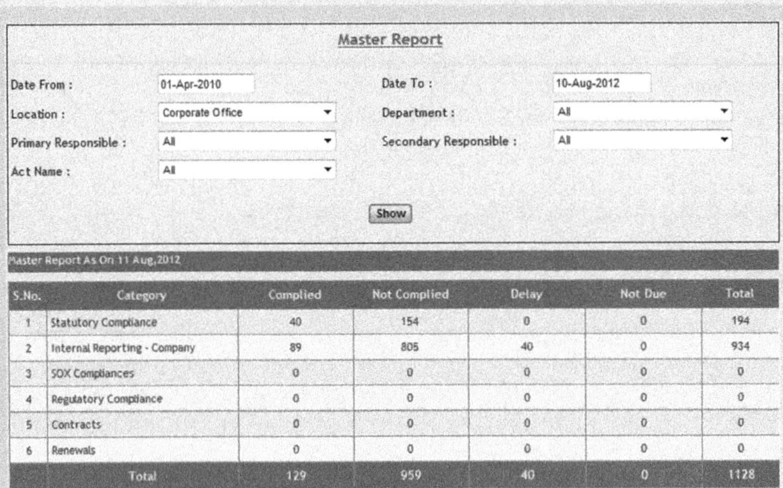
Master Report

Date From : 01-Apr-2010 Date To : 10-Aug-2012

Location : Corporate Office Department : All

Primary Responsible : All Secondary Responsible : All

Act Name : All

Show

Master Report As On 11 Aug,2012

S.No.	Category	Complied	Not Complied	Delay	Not Due	Total
1	Statutory Compliance	40	154	0	0	194
2	Internal Reporting - Company	89	805	40	0	934
3	SOX Compliances	0	0	0	0	0
4	Regulatory Compliance	0	0	0	0	0
5	Contracts	0	0	0	0	0
6	Renewals	0	0	0	0	0
	Total	129	959	40	0	1128

FIGURE 21.11 Compliance Index

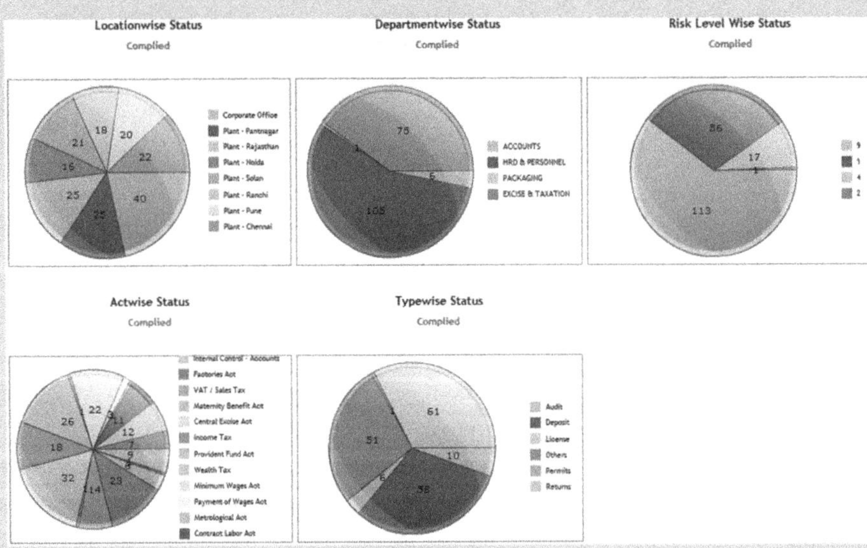

FIGURE 21.12 Monthly Compliance Report

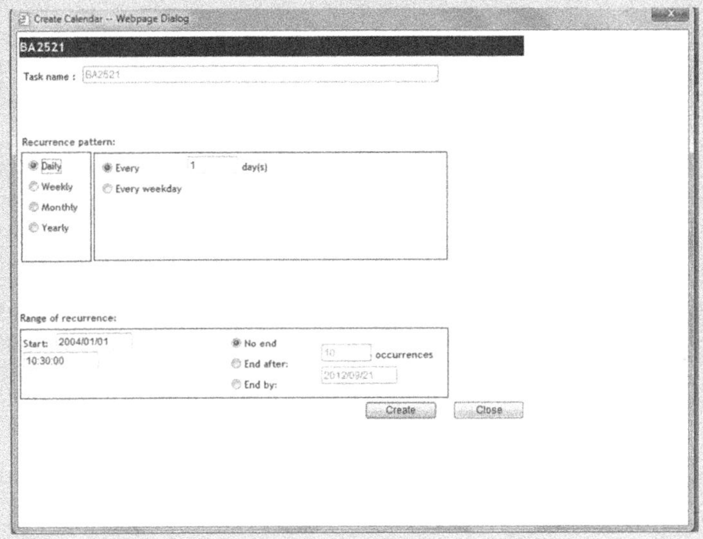

FIGURE 21.13 Recurrence Calendar

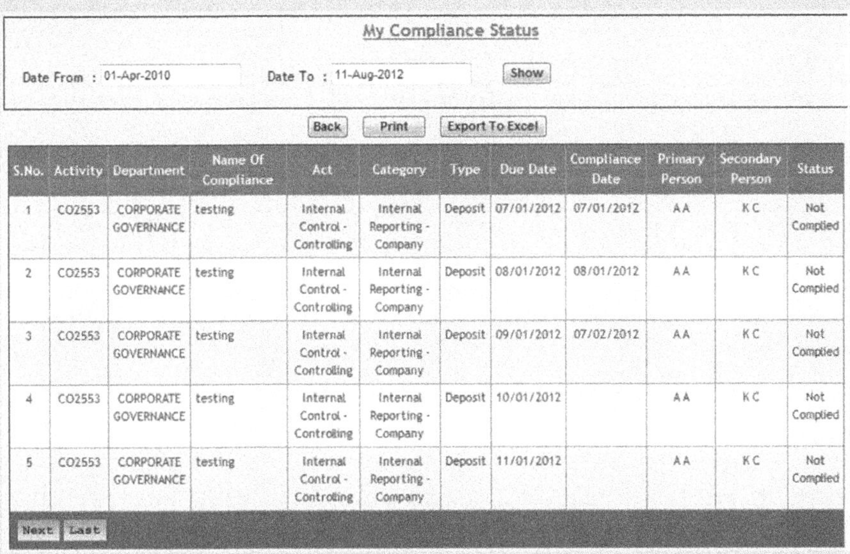

My Compliance Status

Date From : 01-Apr-2010 Date To : 11-Aug-2012 Show

Back Print Export To Excel

S.No.	Activity	Department	Name Of Compliance	Act	Category	Type	Due Date	Compliance Date	Primary Person	Secondary Person	Status
1	CO2553	CORPORATE GOVERNANCE	testing	Internal Control - Controlling	Internal Reporting - Company	Deposit	07/01/2012	07/01/2012	A A	K C	Not Complied
2	CO2553	CORPORATE GOVERNANCE	testing	Internal Control - Controlling	Internal Reporting - Company	Deposit	08/01/2012	08/01/2012	A A	K C	Not Complied
3	CO2553	CORPORATE GOVERNANCE	testing	Internal Control - Controlling	Internal Reporting - Company	Deposit	09/01/2012	07/02/2012	A A	K C	Not Complied
4	CO2553	CORPORATE GOVERNANCE	testing	Internal Control - Controlling	Internal Reporting - Company	Deposit	10/01/2012		A A	K C	Not Complied
5	CO2553	CORPORATE GOVERNANCE	testing	Internal Control - Controlling	Internal Reporting - Company	Deposit	11/01/2012		A A	K C	Not Complied

Next Last

FIGURE 21.14 Compliance Dashboard

In conclusion, the automation of a typically manual set of activities gave the CFO the ability to browse through the status of different compliance items straight from his dashboard, in effect transforming an administrative headache into a valuable area for cost savings and efficiency while minimising operational and compliance risk.

Contributed by Rakesh Dhamani, Times Internet Ltd.

SUMMARY

Management and governance of risk is a set of deeply involved, effort-intensive, and time-based activities that requires rigor, discipline, and maturity to implement and sustain over a long term. Unfortunately, there is no one right answer, no one ideal solution. Each company, with its own individual DNA, management views, risk appetite, and market dependence, has to identify and sort out its own governance structure. The company's risk strategy will evolve over time and grow with the company's needs performance and risk profile. This chapter summarised some of the tools and resources to manage risk, with a case study on managing compliance risk, which tends to be an understated and under-covered element of a company's risk profile.

22

CHAPTER TWENTY TWO

Risk Management Governance Strategies

A RISK MANAGEMENT GOVERNANCE strategy—which covers the governance aspect in the company—consists of many elements. In this chapter, we discuss some of the strategies, with illustrative examples. In our discussion, we use the M-D-U (mandatory-discretionary-unhedged) proportion across each and provide a summary of each strategy with descriptions of the layering in practice.

KEY ELEMENTS OF THE GOVERNANCE STRATEGY

Some of the key elements of the governance strategy have been described in Chapter 19. To recap, these are:

- Objectives
- Scope and risk factors
- Time horizons and tenors
- Amounts

- Tools and methods
- Timing
- Personnel

Objective

The objective of the risk management activity has to be defined up front. This is important since the selection of the entire mechanism for the governance will be based on this definition.

Scope and Risk Factors

The focus for each class of risk is the specific market factors and measures that will be managed for that asset class. The focus determines what to hedge—the scope and the risk factors to hedge.

Time Horizon and Tenor

The scope of the risk being measured in terms of time sets the tone for the focus, measurement, and management of the various risk elements. Sometimes these risks could be different for different asset classes. Some treasurers may also choose to look at different time horizons for different types of hedging—for example, focus on stability and visibility of cash flows in the one-year horizon while looking at lower cost of capital in the five-year horizon. The more dispersed the time horizon and objectives, though, the more complicated the entire risk management process becomes. The attempt to do too much can backfire, and sometimes it is better to start with small objectives and then increase complexity.

To aid the proportion and to make it more implementable, the tenor limits by year put in a maximum ratio for each particular year's exposure that can be covered at any point of time.

Amounts

The proportion for hedging or risk management should be identified. It generally can be a combination of mandatory (M), discretionary (D) and unhedged (U) portions of the portfolio over the time period being discussed. The percentage of M and U stipulates the minimum percentage of the portfolio that must be covered and left open respectively. A 100% discretionary proportion is the most flexible, since it assumes a portfolio that can be even 0% covered or fully covered at any point. Limits are also put in place to ensure that the amounts covered are commensurate with the policy and view of the firm.

Tools and Methods

The tools for risk management specify the specific instruments or products that are used to manage the risk.

Prior to deciding which strategy to recommend for approval, the Treasurer would do well to run simulations using various scenarios with some short-listed strategies. In the sample Treasury policy in the appendix of the *Handbook*, these elements are depicted.

Timing and personnel will also play important parts of the governance structure.

Next we briefly discuss three sample strategies. Note that none is recommended by the author. They are provided only for the purposes of illustration, to show some thought processes and approaches that can be put into practice.

SAMPLE STRATEGY A

Strategy A (summarised in Table 22.1) is a simple strategy that focuses on short-term visibility. On the foreign exchange (FX) side, it deals with receivables and payables in one currency pair each (USD JPY and EUR USD respectively) and seeks to mandatorily hedge any identified on-the-book exposure forward. There is no unhedged booked exposure. This method might be very effective if the time horizon for such cash flows is reasonably long. If the items are booked a few months before they become due, the effective time horizon for hedging becomes those few months, since any unbooked exposure up to a year is still left uncovered.

TABLE 22.1 Sample Risk Management Strategy: Strategy A (Simple "On-Book")

Strategy		A (simple "on-book")
Objective		Lowering variability of profit and loss in USD
Time Horizon		1 year
FX Risk	**Focus**	EUR payables and JPY receivables on books (variability of cash flows) Translation exposure not material
	Proportion (%)	100% mandatory
	Tenor limits by year	100% year 1
	Instruments	FX forwards
IR Risk	**Focus**	Short-term borrowings (net cost of capital)
	Proportion (%)	100% hedged
	Tenor limits by year	100% year 1
	Instruments	IRS (floating 3m USD LIBOR to fixed)
Credit Risk	**Focus**	Top 3 creditors Deposits and FX pre-settlement risk with Banks (not hedged)
	Proportion (%)	30% of exposure
	Tenor limits by year	None
	Instruments	Tracking concentration and diversifying to ensure top 3 do not exceed 30% Avoidance in case the limit exceeds 30%

(Continued)

TABLE 22.1 Continued

Liquidity Risk	**Focus**	Short-term borrowings
	Proportion (%)	Liquidity: 40% mandatory; 60% discretionary
	Tenor limits by year	100% year 1
	Instruments	Liquidity buffer of 20% liquid assets Unutilised but committed facility of 20%
Strategy Positives		Well managed in the short term Easy to implement and manage
Possible Issues		Longer-term exposures and unbooked exposures still open to variability

On the interest rate risk side, the company hedges its exposures for the year through an interest rate swap (IRS), where it receives a floating rate (which it ultimately pays out on its working capital) and pays a fixed rate. The company is comfortable to live with a basis risk and a timing risk (since it will not be borrowing or setting the London Interbank Offered Rate [LIBOR] for its working capital loans on the date of the IRS floating rate fixing, and sometimes it will not use the 3m USD LIBOR as the benchmark for the interest of some of its working capital loans).

The company does not have significant commodity or equity risks.

On the credit risk side, the firm prefers to manage its credit risk by diversifying its customer base. Hence, it tracks its top three customers to not be more than 30% of its overall revenue. The firm goes as far as using avoidance—by not quoting to its top customer should the total exposure to the top three exceed 30%. The firm does not measure or track its pre-settlement exposure of derivatives and hedges or even its deposits with its banks as a source of credit risk, since the firm does not have large cash surpluses and the short-term nature of its hedges, in management's view, does not create material mark-to-market (MTM) variances to include in its risk management. Also, the firm is happy with its two banks and does not seek to maintain banking relationships beyond those, which have provided it with support through its existence.

Finally, the company provides for liquidity situations by targeting at least 20% of its funding need in liquid assets that can be sold to generate liquidity and 20% of its needs through committed but unutilised funding facilities from its two banks. This provides the firm the comfort of having 40% of its funding needs met should there be a liquidity crisis. The success of the strategy will be determined by the ratification of the firm's assumptions on the continued ability to sell its 20% liquid assets if required, along with the valuation of those assets at that point, and on the assumption that the two banks will be able to provide the liquidity committed in times of crisis.

SAMPLE STRATEGY B

This strategy (summarised in Table 22.2) uses a slightly longer time frame and correspondingly more tools to manage risk. Typically the strategy would be used by a larger group of companies with more exposures than the one in Strategy A.

TABLE 22.2 Strategy B (Long-Term Layered)

Strategy		B (long-term layered)
Objective		Lowering variability of financials (in EUR)
Time Horizon		3 years
FX Risk	**Focus**	Transaction risk: G7 and emerging markets currency receivables and USD payables Translation risk > EUR 50 million in value
	Proportion (%)	40% mandatory; 30% discretionary; 30% unhedged
	Tenor limits by year	Transaction risk: 100% year 1; 70% year 2; 40% year 3 Translation risk: 3-year hedge—lower tenor if market is not liquid
	Instruments	FX forwards (nondeliverable forwards [NDFs] for translation) Vanilla options Qualify for hedge accounting
IR Risk	**Focus**	Lower variability of interest expense in EUR terms
	Proportion (%)	50% mandatory (fixed) 50% unhedged (floating)
	Tenor limits by year	None
	Instruments	IRS (floating 6m EUR LIBOR to fixed) Principal-only swaps (other currencies to EUR fixed)
Commodity Risk	**Focus**	Crude palm oil (CPO) purchases
	Proportion (%)	75% mandatory; 25% discretionary
	Tenor limits by year	100% all years
	Instruments	Fixed price contracts OTC options OTC variable-date forwards
Credit Risk	**Focus**	Top 25 customers Any customer over 5% individually Any country with over 10% exposure banks (with deposits or investments) and risk management transactions
	Proportion (%)	Discretionary 100%
	Tenor limits by year	None
	Instruments	Where customer is over 5%, use CDS or receivables financing For countries over 10%, hedge the portion over 10% with CDSs or NDF for banks, not more than 25% of cash with each bank Pre-settlement risk not being managed

(Continued)

TABLE 22.2 Continued

Liquidity Risk	**Focus**	Short-term borrowings Trapped cash
	Proportion (%)	Liquidity: 50% mandatory; 50% discretionary Trapped cash: 100% discretionary
	Tenor limits by year	100% up to 3 months
	Instruments	Liquidity buffer of 15% cash in EUR terms and 20% liquid assets or those that can be repurchased ("repo"-ed) Unutilised but committed facility of 15% each from two banks
Strategy Positives		More layered and balanced over a longer period
Possible Issues		Requires very good processing, systems and reporting for good implementation Likely to work only in a centralised Treasury

The group is headquartered in Europe and hence denominates its consolidated financials in EUR. The group has described its hedging objective as lowering the variability of its financials and has designed its strategy over a three-year horizon.

On FX, the strategy seeks to focus on transaction risk in its revenues around the world, denominated in different currencies, as well as its purchases that are largely USD based. Translation risks for all individual items over 50 million EUR in notional value have also been included. The group seeks to follow a 40–30–30 M-D-U strategy of layered hedging, with a cap of 100% for year 1, 70% for year 2, and 40% for year 3. Hence, in a maximum allowable hedge scenario (40% mandatory + 30% discretionary), the firm would have hedged a maximum of 70% of its exposure across the three years (depicted in Figure 22.1).

The instruments used in this strategy are a combination of FX forwards and vanilla options; the caveat is that the group designates all its transactions as cash flow or balance sheet hedges as per accounting policy, and hence each transaction would need to be an effective hedge. This necessitates huge teamwork between the Treasury and the control teams and also good systems to track and account for these transactions.

On the interest rate side, the group seeks to average out the potential moves across rates (and currencies in case of non-EUR debt) by fixing half of its debt cost (including the effect of currency changes on net principal repayment in EUR). The group effectively manages this through swaps back into EUR and into fixed rates where possible.

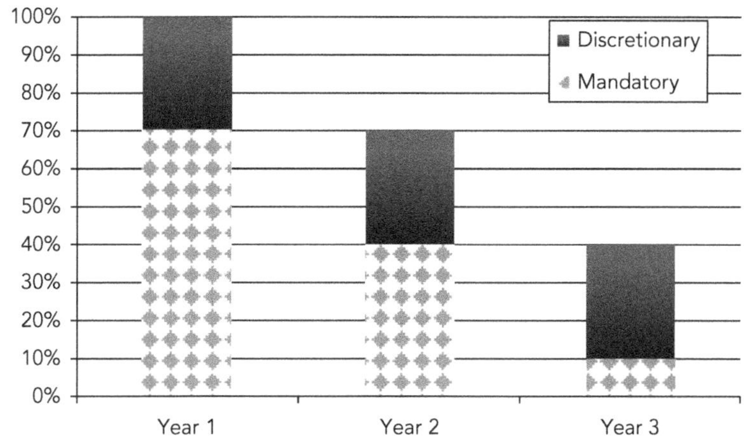

FIGURE 22.1 Layered Hedging Proportions for Strategy B

Commodity exposure (on CPO) is managed through combinations of OTC transactions customised to the notionals and dates of the underlying exposure in order to derive maximum accounting effectiveness on the hedge.

Credit exposure is tracked actively for customers and banks (for deposits). Where customer exposure is over 5% of total sales, tools such as CDSs or receivables financing is used to manage the exposure, where possible. Similarly, CDS or NDF (as a proxy hedge) is used to hedge potential cross-border risk for countries with exposure over 10% (from a sales perspective). For bank deposits, the limit method is used where not more than 25% of overall available cash is placed with any banking group on a consolidated basis. The group prefers to use banks exclusively for risk management owing to their specific capabilities and service levels in this area. Hence, operating accounts, cash management, etc., could be done through other banks. Pre-settlement risk, though, is not managed actively. MTM exposure by the banking group is provided to management on a regular basis to enable any ad hoc decisions on risk concentration to be taken.

Liquidity risk is managed and mitigated through the use of a liquidity buffer of 15% cash in EUR terms and 20% liquid or repo-able assets, with unutilised but committed facility of 15% each from two banks being used.

This strategy is layered and balanced but not comprehensive. It does assume some element of system automation and integration.

SAMPLE STRATEGY C

Strategy C, depicted in Table 22.3, is a more aggressive and revenue focused one where Treasury acts as a profit centre. Here the objective is for Treasury to contribute to an increased profitability of the firm, where financial risk is taken within parameters authorised in order to generate profit.

TABLE 22.3 Strategy C

Strategy		C (aggressive profit centre)
Objective		Increasing profitability in GBP terms
Time Horizon		5 years
FX Risk	**Focus**	All currencies—limit on each non-GBP currency capped at 75% of overall exposure Consolidated exposure to not exceed 150% of overall exposure
	Proportion (%)	150% discretionary
	Tenor limits by year	150% year 1–5
	Instruments	FX forwards Vanilla and structured options that can be priced by Treasury independently Notional on sold options capped at 30% of overall exposure
IR Risk	**Focus**	Using balance sheet to lower overall cost of borrowing If moving liability to currency with no receivables, total notional will not exceed 10% of overall exposure
	Proportion (%)	150% discretionary
	Tenor limits by year	150% year 1–5
	Instruments	IRS, CCS, structured and vanilla options, rate locks, forward rate agreements, swaptions, duration swaps
Commodity Risk	**Focus**	All energy, base metals, and precious metals
	Proportion (%)	USD 500 million of notional
	Tenor limits by year	3 years (no year-wise limit)
	Instruments	Index futures and derivatives OTC forwards and derivatives Fixed and variable price contracts
Equity Risk	**Focus**	Investments
	Proportion (%)	USD 500 million of notional
	Tenor limits by year	3 years (no year-wise limit)
	Instruments	Principal protected equity-linked notes subject to overall institutional limits
Credit Risk	**Focus**	Any customer with over GBP 10 million of sales Banks and institutions for investments and risk management transactions
	Proportion (%)	Customers: discretionary 100% Banks and institutions: mandatory 100%
	Tenor limits by year	3 years (no year-wise limit)
	Instruments	CDSs and receivables financing for customers over GBP 10 million Limit of GBP 50 million with each financial group (covers all investments and deposits and negative MTM of risk management contracts)

TABLE 22.3 Continued

Liquidity Risk	**Focus**	Short-term borrowings
	Proportion (%)	Liquidity: 30% mandatory; 70% discretionary
	Tenor limits by year	6 months
	Instruments	Liquidity buffer of 5% cash each in GBP, EUR, USD and JPY terms and 10% liquid or repo-able assets Unutilised but committed facility of 10% each from three banks
Strategy Positives		Very thorough and high-return strategy Can be well run with a strong team and analytics
Possible Issues		High-risk strategy with possibility of extreme losses in case of rapidly deteriorating market position

In this case, all the business risks are managed by Treasury and transfer prices are passed on to business as per a pre-agreed plan; for example, prevalent forward rates at the beginning of the planning period (say one year) can be used. All further risks thereon (and returns) are to the account of Treasury.

Hence, the scope of the risks as would be detailed in the policy, including limits on each market factor, concentration, and other items would be detailed, even if that item is not directly linked with the market risks specifically linked to the business (i.e., either specific risks assumed by Treasury or residual risks managed by Treasury). For example, if the company is net long EUR (e.g., it has more euro receivables), the Treasury could take a call to move, within approved parameters and limits, to an overall short position in EUR should it have a negative view on that currency.

On the interest rate risk side, the group looks to use the balance sheet to lower overall cost of borrowing. This could include moving debt to a third currency different from the original currency or the base currency (GBP). This is a high-risk, high-return strategy, with the group retaining the ability to use embedded options to manage or mitigate risk.

Commodity and equity risks are managed actively using available products. Credit risk is also managed actively, with the evolution being the use of credit limits for pre-settlement risk, and hence including negative MTM values along with the deposit or investment amounts to compute net exposure with a bank. Regarding liquidity risk management, the group has moved towards diversification of the buffer across currencies.

We now look at a case of a company owned by a private equity firm, whose risk management strategy went through some transition.

STORYBOARD: WHOSE PERSPECTIVE?

And so it happened that the private equity firm PEX, which had turned around the operations of investee company ICX, had reached that time in its relationship with ICX when it was looking for sellers or, better still, the gold mine of the initial public offering (IPO). Over the past five years, PEX had invested time, money, talent and resources to ensure that ICX, a manufacturing firm, had gotten its act together. Costs were slashed, economies of scale were achieved and the firm had grown from a small player to a serious contender in the markets in which it operated. The one area that ICX had not focused on was the management of its foreign currency risk. Given that most of its manufacturing was in emerging markets with locally procured components (which meant that 60% of the firm's expenses were in emerging market currencies), the dollarised enterprise was facing its toughest call yet—whether it should continue with its generally laissez-faire risk strategy or not (see Figure 22.2).

The management of ICX, largely recruited and placed by PEX (the 100% shareholder), had hired a full-time Treasurer to relieve the CFO. After much brainstorming and analysis, a layered hedging strategy of 30–30–40 (M-D-U) was decided on, and the risk policy was about to be rewritten. Other industry players usually managed their short-term risks aggressively, but a few had gone out longer term. The time horizon that ICX had planned to hedge was around two years, which was generally the period around which the firm had reasonable visibility and perspective (see Figure 22.3).

Then came the thunderbolt. Emerging market currencies had weakened considerably (see Figure 22.4), and the principals at PEX, with a potential IPO looming large, wanted to lock in the exposure to emerging markets currencies at these levels—and out to three years!

From the perspective of PEX, the idea of locking in the rate at historically good levels carried strong favour; if the plan was to exit in the next few quarters, FX risk would be taken out of the equation. The proposed strategy is depicted in Figure 22.5.

The CFO was in a bind: The opportunity loss of locking in cash flows up to three years looked quite enormous, as did potential MTM volatility since the firm was not set up to implement hedge accounting. The economic rationale of PEX's proposal

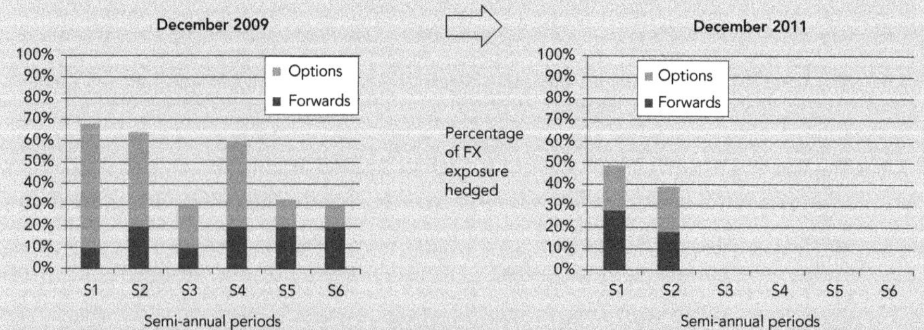

FIGURE 22.2 Laissez-Faire Approach to Risk Until Now

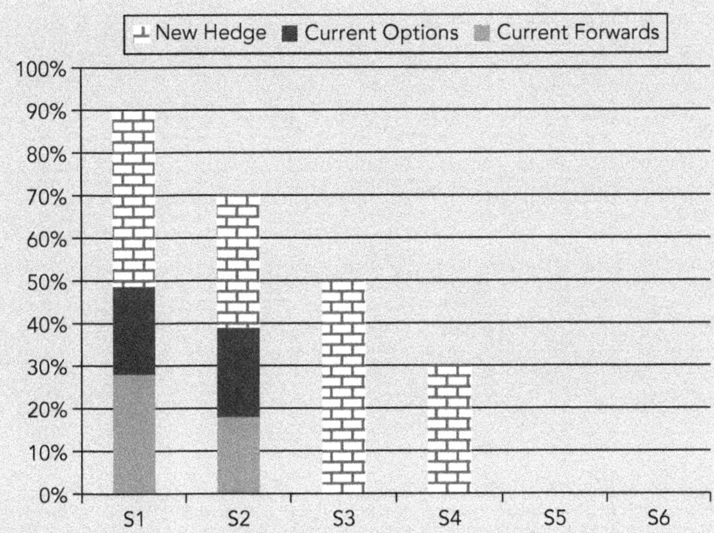

FIGURE 22.3 ICX's Proposed Strategy

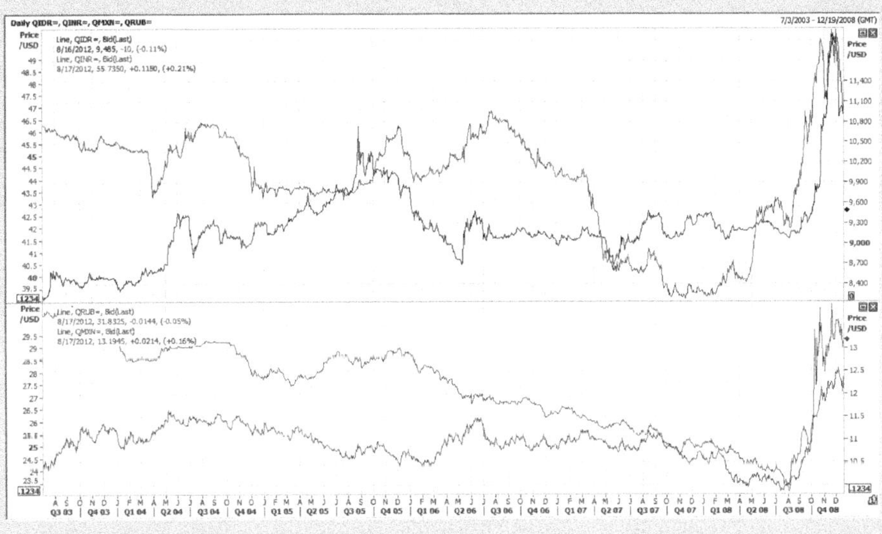

FIGURE 22.4 Emerging Market Currency Moves

Source: Thomson Reuters Eikon

was reasonably sound, as was the overall impact and visibility of cash flows on an economic basis.

Which view would prevail? Was the company being put at risk since no peer firms were fully hedged? Or were shareholder interests being best preserved by locking in a historically good price with the objective of good valuation?

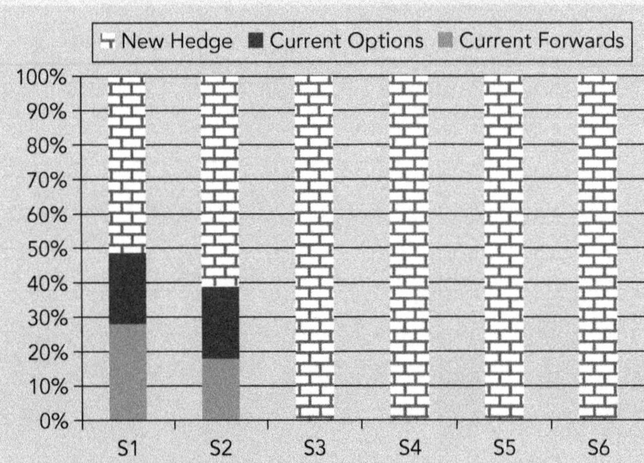

FIGURE 22.5 PEX's Proposed Strategy

SUMMARY

In conclusion, different strategies can be formulated based on the inputs. In this chapter, we covered three sample strategies in detail. These strategies use the tools provided in Chapter 21 with the DNA of the firms and the market environments in which they operate.

CHAPTER TWENTY THREE

Operational Aspects

Documentation and Execution

IN THIS CHAPTER, WE COVER some of the operational aspects of risk management: documentation and execution. Other aspects will be covered under the general control and operations in Chapter 29 of the Toolkit in Part Five.

DOCUMENTATION

Risk management is a documentation-intensive exercise, but it can be implemented easily—if appropriate efforts are put into establishing or writing out the one-time documentation, the rest of the processes can work strongly and seamlessly. Table 23.1 provides documentation generally in place for purposes of robust risk management.

Of these, we will focus on the International Swap Dealers Association (ISDA) agreement that is the gold standard for markets and risk management related documentation.

TABLE 23.1 Some Documents for Risk Management Execution

Documentation	Internal	External (as Required)
One time	Treasury policy Board approvals Authorisations Limits Incorporation document ISDA approvals	Abbreviated policy (for shareholders, auditors, banks, etc.) Board resolutions Signature cards Incorporation document Legal opinion (if required) Any regulatory norms or approvals Executed ISDA master and schedules Credit support (where required) Credit facilities from banks Financial reports (for credit facilities and ISDA)
Transaction wise	Deal ticket Model validations Tax clearance (if required) Hedge effectiveness Accounting opinion (if required)	Indicative term sheet with payoff profiles and risks documented (bank) Desk confirmation (dealer) Transaction confirmation under ISDA (operations) Documentation related to funds transfer and settlements Valuations and statements Underlying documentation (if required by regulators or banks)

ISDA FRAMEWORK OF DOCUMENTS

The ISDA framework of agreements has become a market standard for comprehensive coverage of over-the-counter (OTC) types of derivative and market-related transactions.

The framework comprises:

- Master agreement
- Schedules
- Transaction confirmations
- Definitions
- Credit support annex (CSA)

ISDA: Background

Major company and bank defaults have, over time, led to increasing awareness of credit risk. The need to standardise market terms and documentation and have simpler and more common forms of settlement, standardisation, and definitions as OTC global transaction levels increased led to the formation of the ISDA in 1985, and the subsequent drafting of the ISDA framework and set of documents. Adoption by banks and the largest institutions around the world have since led to more extensive use of the ISDA framework and set of documents.

The ISDA agreements are simply agreements between two counterparties to a transaction or a set of transactions related to capital markets and credit, usually derivatives. These transactions are usually executed as OTC trades. The counterparties can be both professional counterparties (i.e., banks, market makers, and financial institutions) and nonprofessional (e.g., corporate). The ISDA framework provides guidelines on the transactions and on its terms, calculation, settlement, jurisdiction, payments, and credit treatment. It also provides the way forward in case of default, dispute, or termination.

In many cases nowadays, a default under the ISDA master agreement could trigger default clauses of funding facilities (or vice versa), with severe consequences. Hence, many transactions under ISDA have now reached par status with other liability transactions.

The overall advantages that such standardisation provides are immense. The ISDA framework contains provisions to govern multiple transactions, provides for exchange of separate confirmations on each transaction, and includes provisions for determining market values in case of early termination. Overdependence on the master agreement, however, has tended to put undue pressure on the wording of the agreement itself and its execution. Also, the legal risk of no documentation before dealing and the suitability of the counterparties to enter into nonstandard transactions are cause for some concern.

ISDA Master Agreement

The ISDA master agreement is the basic agreement between two counterparties that governs the fundamental obligation and contractual provisions for transactions executed between them. This is usually a one-time agreement that is updated only in case of any major changes or renegotiation. As parties to a master agreement, participants do not need to redraft and execute new general terms and conditions every time they enter into a transaction.

The master agreement is the core around which the rest of the document structure is created. In usual practice, the preprinted master agreement is altered only to insert the names of the parties. Customisation happens through the schedule that contains elections, additions, and amendments to the master agreement.

Read in conjunction with the schedule, the master agreement puts out all general terms and conditions necessary to allocate the risks of the transactions between the parties.

Neither the master agreement nor the schedules generally include the commercial terms of each transaction. Once the master agreement and schedules have been executed, the parties can enter into numerous transactions by agreeing to the material commercial terms through separate confirmations under the ISDA framework, without having to revisit or redraft the underlying terms contained in the master agreement.

There are two versions of the ISDA master agreement:

1. A single-currency local version (for transactions between parties located in the same jurisdiction)
2. A multicurrency version (for transactions between parties located in different jurisdictions; these would include issues such as taxes, currency of payment, use of multiple offices or branches, designation of agents, etc.)

Figure 23.1 provides some of the key themes in the master agreement and in the schedules.

Events of default as defined in the ISDA are critical to the smooth running of the transactions. When defined up front, any breach could trigger termination of the transactions under the ISDA. Corporates would do well to go through these events and clauses as defined in the draft and negotiate them with thought-out numbers. Some events of default could be:

- Failure to pay on time
- Breach of the agreement
- Defaults relating to documentation (especially the CSA)
- Defaults under specified transactions
- Covenant breaches
- Bankruptcy
- Insolvency
- Liquidation

Master

- Transaction dynamics: payment obligations and methods, rate and valuation determination methods and process
- Credit aspects: netting and settlement, warranties, guarantees, undertakings, credit support provisions, events of default, cross-default, termination mechanics
- General agreement or contractual provisions: representations, governing law, notices, dispute resolution

Schedules

- Works with the master agreement
- Incorporates local regulatory and legal aspects
- Can be tailored to suit any counterparty
- Factors in policy, credit, market and other requirements
- Common provisions that are areas of focus: termination provisions, events of default, payment provisions, other provisions

FIGURE 23.1 ISDA Master and Schedules

- Merger without assumption
- Cross-default events

The concept of a single agreement—wherein the ISDA master agreement, schedules, and transaction confirmations are considered part of the same agreement—is integral to the framework and forms part of the netting-based protection offered by the master agreement. The fact that all transactions are one contract allows for them to be closed out with a single net amount payable, should a default occur.

ISDA Schedules

The ISDA schedule customises the general terms of the ISDA framework to relationships between the parties, including local jurisdiction legal and regulatory provisions. The schedule supplements the master agreement and allows the parties to tailor terms to suit. It also includes common provisions that are areas of focus, such as termination provisions, payment provisions (such as payment measures and methods), material threshold amounts over which certain events are categorised officially as a default, offices or branches through which parties can act, setoff clauses, and others.

Setoff provisions provide a party a certain degree of relief from the other party's bankruptcy by allowing obligations due and from the other party to be set off (viz., to be able to net off receivables with payables and consolidate the net amount receivable/payable). However, they do not provide relief from exposure to future positions that have not yet become due. Hence, the ISDA framework allows for termination provisions, which permit a creditor to terminate and liquidate transactions in the event of the other party's bankruptcy or default under the agreement.

The agreement and all transactions under it may be terminated upon the occurrence of specified events:

- An event of default (which, when it occurs for a party, allows the other party to terminate the master agreement and liquidate all transactions with the first party)
- Termination events (the result of the actions of a third party that could provide the affected party with a grace period to cure the termination event before the other party can terminate and liquidate the master agreement)

It is important to highlight the underrated concept of cross-default here. A party's failure to fulfil unrelated financial or operational payment on a relevant due date could automatically lead to an event of default under the ISDA agreement if such an event is covered under the cross-default clause. The occurrence of a cross-default gives the nondefaulting party the right to designate an early termination date.

Threshold amounts—material amounts (whether specific amounts or percentages) over which defaults are triggered—and grace periods provide some relief to affected parties and gives them an opportunity to regularise the credit conditions under the ISDA. These usually vary depending on the credit rating of each party.

Credit Support Annex

The annex is an optional document that is gaining increasing use. It is included in cases where collateral or a third-party support is required to fulfil the credit requirements of the ISDA agreement or if the threshold amounts of the exposure under the ISDA agreement have been exceeded.

An annex contains provisions on the collateral, including posting, return, types, and treatment.

Transaction Confirmation

While a large percentage of transactions, especially deals booked between professional counterparties or between banks and corporates, are entered into over the phone (on recorded lines, at least at the banks' side) or on secure messaging systems, such as Thomson Reuters, the transactions are deemed complete only once the physical confirmation is signed and agreed to between the two parties. This physical confirmation is a legal document and included as part of the ISDA agreement where applicable.

Depending on the legality and information security requirements of each counterparty, these transaction confirmations can be in the form of printed documents, faxes, or emails. The form of the confirmation is set out in the master agreement. In some cases, a little time is allowed for objections or amendments to be raised and made. Dates, amounts, rates, payment mechanics, and settlement details are included in confirmations, and these are usually exchanged at the time of entering into the transaction to minimise the possibility of a dispute.

It is strongly recommended that all entities that undertake these transactions thoroughly understand the ISDA document and get trained on it. The ISDA requires understanding of market practices and legal language; hence, companies work closely with their legal teams in formulating and negotiating this documentation.

EXECUTION

A few elements of the execution aspects of risk management transactions are discussed here.

Transfer Pricing

If the objective of the firm's risk management is to reduce the volatility of factors to the overall business numbers, it becomes important to pass on the benefits to the business. If Treasury is a profit centre, a prudent practice would be to guarantee a specific rate based on which business results are reported, with the residual gain (or loss) of the market and risk management activities residual with Treasury. If Treasury is a cost centre, the dynamic becomes more relevant, since Treasury itself will not see the hedging impact on any of the lines that are all finally allocated to the businesses or countries.

In this case, it becomes important to earmark the effective rate that is being passed on to the business. Since practically in many cases it is cumbersome to book individual hedges for each entity, especially if there are a lot of transactions, usual practice at a centralised Treasury is to book the transactions with the bank once and to allocate the rates internally for the same legal entity with different businesses, or with the bank in case of multiple entities.

In the former case, the transfer price at which the rates are allocated to the businesses could become a sensitive issue, especially if rates have moved significantly. Which rates do you pass on to which business unit? How do you allocate the rates to ensure a fair allocation?

There are many approaches to this. The first, and perhaps the most fair, would be to use the weighted average rate for each set of transactions on a monthly basis. At the end of each month, that transfer-priced rate will be provided to the planning department to use as an actual rate for conversion.

One disadvantage of this method is that if the transactions are of shorter maturity—perhaps even cash transactions for same-day value—then the rates have to be booked on a first-come, first-served basis. Another concern would be if one of the transactions comes up for early delivery and has to be settled at the prevalent market rate. The difference between the cancellation or early pickup rate and the transfer-priced rate would then have to be passed on to the relevant business as well.

What is required for the success of these processes and mechanisms is a good system backed by a strong process that can accommodate this degree of complexity.

Controls

Controls are essential for the Treasury policy, especially the risk management side, to be implemented efficiently. Independence of front-, middle-, and back-office roles from the perspectives of responsibility, handoff, and organisational reporting is essential. The booking process is especially susceptible to error, given the complexity of the operation and the many access channels between the counterparties. Proper control processes can also capture operational errors on the side of the bank. A more detailed discussion on control is done in the Toolkit in Part Five.

Booking

The booking process also is an area of focus.

Typically, the dealer in Treasury has access to the indicative term sheets that are used for decision making and closure on structure and approximate pricing. When the dealer has discussed and gotten internal approvals, and with appropriate authorisation in place, he or she closes the transaction on the phone or on the dealing systems. Ideally, the phone lines are recorded at the corporate Treasury, subject to legal conditions and relevant procedures. On the initiation of the deal, the dealer books the transaction in the system or originates a deal ticket. This is used for the basis of booking the deal in the back end and verified with the actual transaction confirmation under the ISDA, which should always be sent to independent operations. For a stronger process, even the operations team of the corporate can create a confirmation and send it to independent operations at the bank's end. The deal is then verified and recorded in the system.

Delivery

The delivery process, like the booking process, is also independent of the front office or dealer. The operations teams from both ends liaise with each other to close the process. In case of a complicated transaction, the dealer may provide inputs but in no way should be allowed to handle the settlements or provide or influence reports based on which settlements are due to occur.

SUMMARY

We have covered some key practical aspects of control, operations, and execution in this chapter. A more detailed overview on controls and processes is given in the Toolkit in Part Five of the book.

PART FIVE

The Toolkit

THE TOOLKIT IS A LOGICAL conclusion to the material in this book. It contains actual practical and implementation tools that readers can put in use on the job. Here we provide the bases for some of the infrastructural and executional aspects of treasury management including templates, design elements, checklists, and aspects to be considered. The various themes are treasury policy, treasury systems, treasury centralisation, key performance metrics, banks and service relationships, operations and control, outsourcing, and treasury culture. We also explore some real-life examples and case studies.

The various components of the Toolkit are not a one-stop solution to a treasurer's problems; they are only some of the parts that go into the mix of efficient treasury management. Readers are welcome to adapt any of these to suit their needs, picking and choosing what works for their firm and superimposing firm policies, management approaches, and organisational DNA into the frameworks provided.

We wish the readers all success in their implementations. We would be grateful if you could drop us a line at toolkit@treasuryhandbook.com to let us know which part of the Toolkit you have used in your company and, if possible, share with us a copy of what you have used so we can apply what you have learned to later editions of the book.

CHAPTER TWENTY FOUR

Treasury Policy

IN THIS CHAPTER, WE RUN through the key elements of a Treasury policy. The template in Appendix A is available for download. Please refer to the "About the Website" page at the end of the book for more information.

FRAMEWORK

The Treasury policy typically is divided into the body, which contains the overall thought process and approach to Treasury management, and the annexes, which contain the specific execution aspects.

In principle, the board can approve the body of the policy and annexes, providing the Treasury management team with the flexibility to conduct Treasury activities on a regular basis with oversight by the chief financial officer.

The annexes may be reviewed every quarter to ensure synchronisation with market and business developments, and the entire policy and performance under the policy itself may be reviewed annually.

The body of the policy itself can largely be divided into these sections:

- **Foundation.** Contains the rationale, background and philosophy, scope, operations and control, objectives, policy approval and review, non-compliance and exception resolution, conformance with accounting policy, and code of conduct
- **Roles and responsibilities.** Contains the organisation structure, role or function-wise responsibilities, committees, and groups
- **Transactions Management.**
- **Balance Sheet and Liquidity Management.**
- **Risk Management.**
- **Annexes.** Risks to be managed, tenors, amounts and time horizon for risk management and investment, authorised products and arrangements, authorised signatories and limits, risk management tools such as budgeted rates, and scenarios

A sample policy can be found in Appendix A. This pro forma document can be taken and amended by readers to suit their needs.

ASPECTS OF POLICY IMPLEMENTATION THAT NEED CLOSER SCRUTINY

Some aspects of Treasury policy require a closer look.

Exception Handling

Exceptions occur as a way of life, the larger the Treasury is. The policy must contain, elements of exception handling with resolution and escalation methodology, levels, and tracking. Every exception must be reviewed, and confirmation that this type of exception has already been included in the policy must be obtained. To start with, a policy cannot include every kind of exception. Hence, the Treasurer must ensure that, apart from correcting the root cause of the problem, the policy itself includes the new exception or issue type and its resolution during the next review.

Being Close to the Market

It is not very easy to run risk management or a balance sheet by doing periodic market monitoring. It is the job of a Treasurer to be close to the market, to understand dynamics and market moves, and also to be prepared to take immediate action should there be suitable market opportunities or adverse market moves. Hence, access to market information systems, such as Reuters Eikon, that provide market dynamics and regular news updates through various media, is an almost indispensable weapon in a Treasurer's arsenal.

Competition Strategy

What competition does in their Treasuries is an important parameter in framing policy and approaches. The Treasurer can choose to follow a contra-industry strategy if the firm or Treasury has a leadership position. Many Treasurers, especially in growing firms, choose to look at market best practices and industry dynamics prior to confirming the approach.

Choosing the Right Products

The right products to hedge are critical. Sometimes the company chooses to utilise hedging products that may not be the most appropriate in the context of the firm.

REVIEW

The review element is extremely important to the successful implementation of a Treasury.

Review of Limits and Utilisation

Review of limits and the utilisation of these limits are important. Limits are maximum (or minimum) levels of exposure for market factors. These may include, for example, not more than USD 100 million of investment in money market funds, not less than 10% of spare cash to be retained in EUR, not more than 70% of JPY exposure to be hedged, and not more than USD 25 million of WTI crude oil exposure for the first year to remain unhedged. While a limit excess is not good and has to be corrected immediately, regular limit breaches have to reviewed in the context of both operational or trader discipline as well as from the point of view of limit adequacy. Similarly, having large unutilised limits has to bring about a review of the need for having high limits in that particular market factor. Limits can also be for counterparties (investments or deposits) and for authorised personnel.

Success and Failure of the Policy

Often, boards and chief executive officers assume that Treasury decisions or policies that have generated profits soon after implementation are great ones, while losses incurred shortly after policy implementation cast a poor shadow on the same policy. The thought process has to be reinforced.

Linkages with Company's Business Plan

The Treasury policy, from all aspects of growth, cash flow, funding, investment, and risk management, has to be closely aligned with the business plan of the firm. Well-managed firms have more visibility on their business plans and prospects.

They involve the Treasurer at the outset for his or her views on the plans and to be prepared for balance sheet, risk, or other implementational requirements for implementation of business decisions and strategies. A simple case in point is a large U.S. industrial corporation looking to enter southern Africa as a market. The Treasurer has to start working closely with the business leaders to put in place the financial infrastructure for payments, collections, funding, and currency by the time the business hits the ground.

IMPLEMENTATIONAL ASPECTS

This section discusses some of the implementational aspects of the policy that tend to be overlooked and underestimated during policy creation.

Dealer-wise Limits

Assigning appropriate dealer-wise transaction limits for market-related transactions is a heuristic process and an aspect in which the firm will find equilibrium over time. Aspects of these limits come from frequency of dealer usage, situations expected where such limits may be required without delaying the decision making, increased empowerment, and frequent breach of dealer-wise limits.

Time Taken Between Finding the Right Price and Decision Making

Sometimes large levels of transactions require senior approvals, and seniors may not be immediately available, due to frequent travel and meetings or conferences. In these cases, and with large pending transactions, it may be more appropriate to have preapprovals of target levels or ranges where authorisation may be provided on a case-to-case basis. Markets are unlikely to wait for chief financial officers to return from meetings.

Maker-Checker

Especially for entries in the back end, it is important to have a maker and authoriser for each entry. Irrespective of the size of the entry, unless automated, entries have to be passed and approved by separate officers. Instruments, disbursements, account transfers, and the like should also be done by two people to ensure a level of control. In some cases, on materiality, thresholds may be set below which such approvals may not be required.

Independent Back Office

Independence of the back office, especially when the Treasurer is an active transactor, is critical from a control perspective. Also, the middle-office reporting has to be independent from both front and back offices.

Confirmations with Banks

Confirmations with banks have to made by employees independent of transaction booking.

Transfer Pricing Mechanism

Treasury must agree with business as to the price at which funds and market transactions get transferred to the business.

SUMMARY

The Treasury policy, while being an overarching document, must find the balance between a comprehensive document and a practical one. In many cases, large corporations tend to oversimplify their processes and policy and emerge with a document that is light but inadequate. Conversely, smaller companies sometimes get saddled with onerous amounts of documentation that are very unwieldy and hence difficult to implement. As a result, processes begin to lapse over time.

CHAPTER TWENTY FIVE

Treasury Systems

TREASURY SYSTEMS TOOK their baby steps with the advent of computing, and banks, for which Treasury is a core and critical function, led the way with automation and management of balance sheet and liquidity. The emergence of markets, asset classes, and market risk increased the rate of automation of processes and bookkeeping, leading to today's world of interconnected system environments that span a multitude of purposes, environments, and budgets.

This chapter provides an overview of what Treasury systems are, how the entire system universe is connected, and how the benefits accruing from a system implementation can be assessed. We end with a process and checklist that you can adapt to suit your needs while doing your own system assessment and implementation.

TREASURY MANAGEMENT SYSTEM BACKGROUND

Treasury systems have evolved over time, use, and the corresponding growth of global markets and their complexity. While there is a cost and maintenance resource impact (as is the case for every system), more often than not, a good system

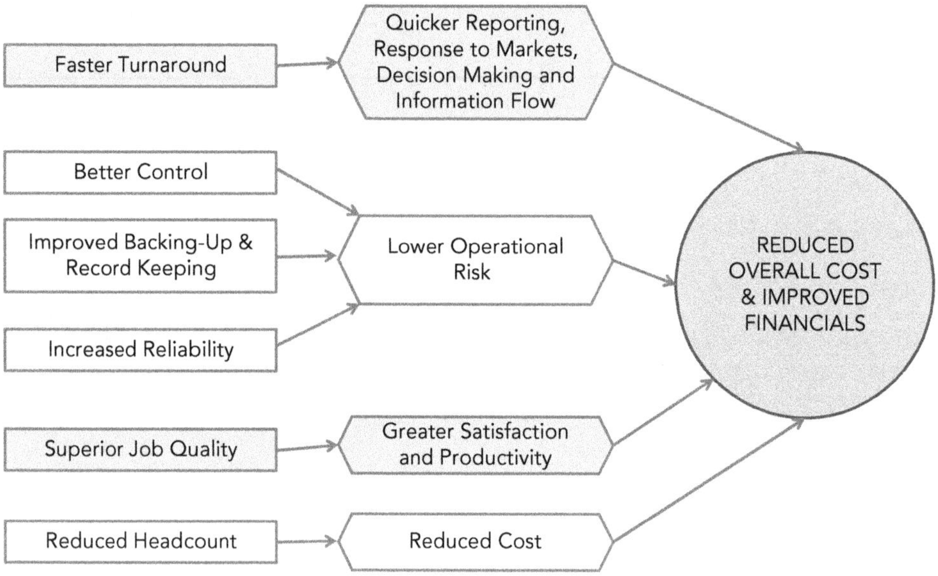

FIGURE 25.1 Financial Impact of Good System Establishment

implementation has far-reaching efficiency effects for Treasury and hence the corporation as a whole.

Why Do We Need a System?

The topic of why we need a system may sound generic and clichéd, but we would like to discuss this important aspect at the outset. It is important because it feeds into the final impact: better financials. The success of any project, including system implementations, is to achieve efficiency and hence financial benefits for the firm. A system implementation (or nonimplementation) decision is successful only if it results directly and indirectly in the firm's improved financial performance.

Hence, we present some of the key process wins of a good system implementation that result in tangible improvements in the firm's financial performance. Figure 25.1 depicts some benefits of establishing a good system.

What Is a Treasury System, and How Does It Fit into the System Universe?

The world of the Treasurer is becoming increasingly dependent on technology and the processes and information flows that are based on technology. Figure 25.2 provides an idea of the firm's systems universe, which works off a centralised Treasury and distributed centres at the country and subsidiary level that also have their own systems and linkages. The elements may exist under one single Treasury management system (TMS) or may be distributed by their systems functionality expertise.

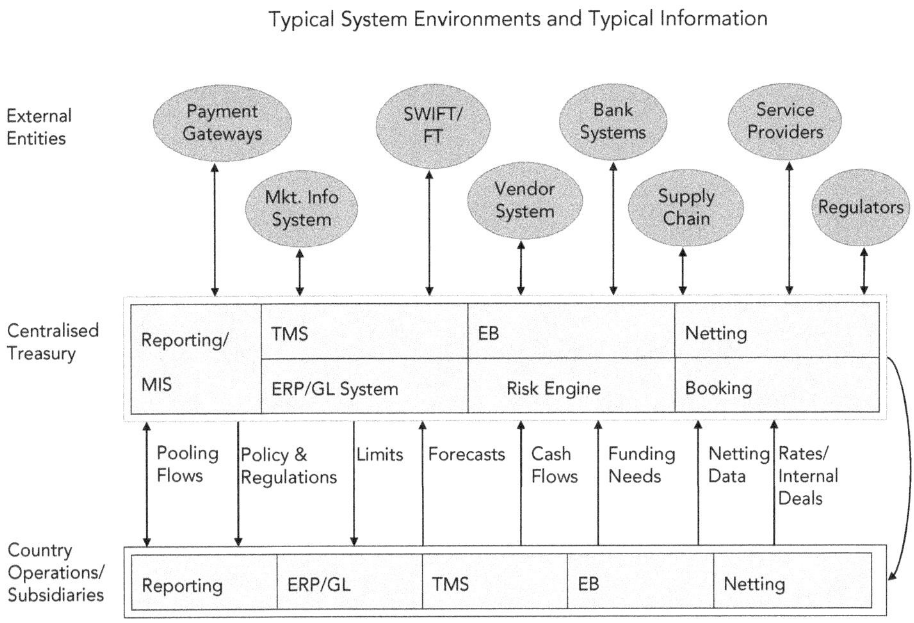

FIGURE 25.2 System Environment and Interfaces

The TMS helps the Treasury function in processing and supporting processes with some or all of these broad functionalities:

- Banking
- Balance sheet and capital
- Markets and risk
- Cash flow
- Deal entry
- Back office (operations)
- Middle office (process and control)
- Cash flow and forecasting
- Analytics

The TMS is usually linked with the general ledger (GL) system or enterprise resource planning (ERP) of the organisation and also has linkages with other systems in the firm's universe. Figure 25.3 is a pictorial summary of some of the TMS-related information flows and linkages. The three key themes of risk management, accounts and cash, and value-add are only one way to represent or classify the various roles and processes.

What Important Characteristics of a System Do We Need to Know?

Some of the key characteristics of a TMS, and hence considerations for selecting the most appropriate one for a firm, are depicted in Figure 25.4 and outlined next.

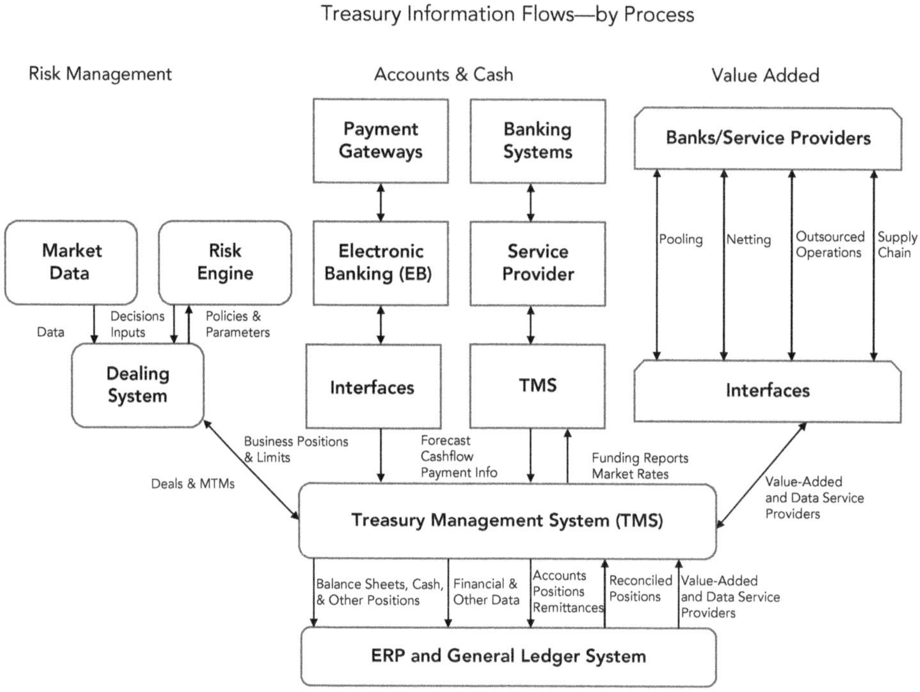

FIGURE 25.3 TMS Linkages and Information Flows

Functionality

The functionality of the TMS denotes the various capabilities of the system and would be a direct relationship to the actual processes and activities of the Treasury. Broadly, these would be:

- **Balance sheet and capital.** Debt and capital management, inter-company cost of capital, working capital (WC), accounts receivable (AR) and accounts payable (AP) management, debt and capital-related payments, investments tracking and monitoring

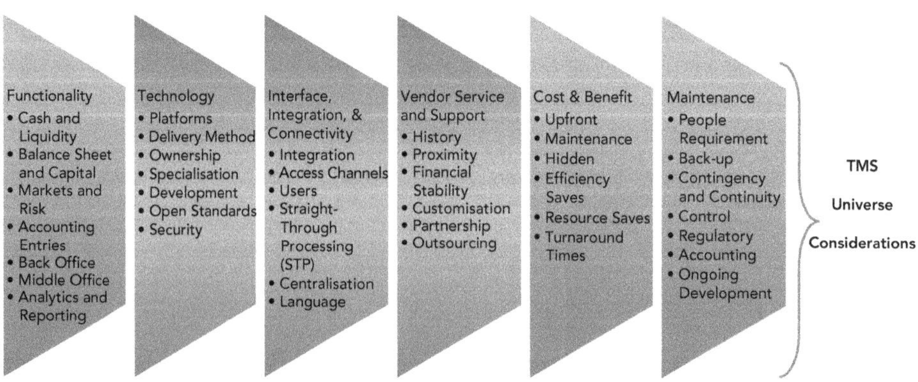

FIGURE 25.4 Characteristics of a TMS

- **Markets and risk.** Risk limits, measurement, tracking and booking, maturities
- **Cash and liquidity.** Cash flow analysis, forecasting, collections and payments management, reconciliation, in-house banking, funds transfers, and bank interfaces
- **Accounting entries.** Transaction entries, data entry and interface, accounting entries
- **Back office.** Transaction processing, tracking, and settlement
- **Middle office.** Control, monitoring, model validation, limit and position verification, mark-to-market data, reconciliation
- **Analytics and reporting.** Supporting each business unit for its analytics and reporting, providing automated and objective evaluation and benchmarking results

Technology

The infrastructure and use of technology is the second key characteristic of the TMS. The good thing about technology is that one can be a great user of technology without being a technical expert. Here we attempt to simplify and translate some of the concepts and terms to enable readers to make well-informed and rational decisions on their own on which technology solutions to implement.

- **Platform.** The platform is a combination of the hardware architecture and the software framework used to run the applications on the hardware. It also includes decisions around the kind of databases used, the front end and the choice of client (what you see and access the system through, the front end) and server (the back end that is the backbone of the system). The vendor should provide you with a detailed list of advantages and disadvantages of each. One important aspect to bear in mind is the ability to upgrade or sustain a particular platform—will this last for the next few years?
- **Delivery method (hosting and ownership).** The delivery method indicates how the system reaches the user—where it is physically located (hosting) and who owns it (ownership). Depending on the number of locations, complexity of data, and locational bandwidth availability and cost, the reader can determine which method would work best for them. Vendors typically have a preferred delivery method and, depending on requirements and budgets, will be able to offer a suitable solution to match user needs. Some alternatives are given next.
  - **Software as a service (SaaS).** Software and data are resident at the vendor's servers and accessed by users through a browser or simple application at their end. SaaS uses the application services provider (ASP) model.
  - **Cloud computing.** The software and data are stored on servers on the Internet, with the users being agnostic to exactly where the data are located. This method provides the vendor with more flexibility on computing power and storage, which could result in continuous improvement to user response times and cost structure.
  - **On premises.** The system resides on hardware and servers at users' sites.

   - **Software-plus services (S+S).** This method combines on-premises solutions with cloud computing to intelligently enhance the user experience and provide cost and performance efficiency.
- **Specialisation.** Many service providers, such as banks, brokers, information service providers (such as Thomson Reuters), accounting firms, and consultants, offer some components of a TMS to their clients. In many cases, these can be integrated with existing systems to provide a good experience, depending on the specialisation. Some ERP systems also have Treasury modules that have good capabilities. Many technology firms also offer specialised stand-alone TMS solutions. Users can make appropriate decisions depending on their existing system establishment and needs.
- **Development and customisation.** The decision on whether to customise systen development or use an existing system is a critical decision with long term impact. For many needs, using an available system might prove to be a more effective method. Customisation involves effort, time, cost, and the chances of error owing to the tinkering around with a tried-and-tested system.
- **Open standards.** If the TMS uses open source development software, the costs could be significantly lower. Many TMS systems, however, work off proprietary technology.
- **Security.** Information security is a critical aspect, usually closely tied in with the hosting solution and the firm's existing information security standards. Firewalls, virus protection, data integrity, and security form some of the components of this characteristic.

Interface, Integration, and Connectivity

How the TMS connects with the outside world, how it merges with existing systems, and how users can access it form some of the strongest differentiators among different systems.

- **Interface.** The interface of the TMS with various systems, such as payment gateways, electronic banking (EB), and ERP is a critical aspect. Some considerations here involve whether this interface is online or with delays, batch processed or real time, or encrypted.
- **Integration.** Integration involves connecting with some of the critical internal and external systems that are part of the environment, such as the ERP and EB platforms. For example, it can involve:
   - ERP integration
   - Payments
   - Collections
   - Inter-company account booking
   - Reconciliation
   - Bank account management
   - Payables and AP
   - Receivables and AR

    - Supply chain management
    - Entry automation
    - Accruals and cash movements
    - Data flow
    - Reporting
    - Bank reconciliation, cheques, deposits, cash balances
    - Registers of vendors, customers, and transactions
    - Processing
    - Posting transactions to the general ledger
    - Automatic reconciliation
- **Connectivity**. Access to the system, through specific applications or even the mobile phone, is an important determinant. Also, reporting and control elements become critical.

Vendor Service and Support

The technology partner or systems vendor plays one of the most critical roles in a system implementation, and the selection process must be well thought out and with the long term in mind. Some of the points for consideration are:

- **Background**. The vendor's past performance, success record, and level of expertise are good measures, especially when comparing across vendors. The vendor's own financial stability becomes critical to determine its staying power and longevity.
- **Geographical spread**. Geographical spread and availability of the vendor in the areas of implementation becomes more important, the more complex the requirements.
- **Customisation**. The lesser the need for customisation required in the system to meet client requirements, the greater the chances of system stability.
- **Partnership**. The degree of the vendor's participation in meeting requirements and long-term vision as envisioned by the pricing and contracting must be considered.
- **Outsourcing**. The ability of the vendor to take on activities either immediately or over a period of time (to allow for opportunities and flexibility to outsource should the time come) also must be considered.

Costs and Benefits

Some of the cost and benefit aspects to be considered in the system decision are:

- **Up-front costs.**
- **Maintenance costs**. These include running costs and maintenance costs on an ongoing basis; includes hardware support, bandwidth, software licence, and per-user fees.

- **Hidden costs.** Incremental storage and bandwidth expenses, licence fee for non-TMS support (e.g., database, etc.).
- **Efficiency saves.**
- **Resource saves.** Reduction in the number of full-time employees.
- **Turnaround times.**

Maintenance

Once the system has been implemented, life begins. The day-to-day as well as long term running of the system will require resources and will have an impact on the functioning of the company. Some of the aspects to be considered for the maintenance of the system include:

- People requirement
- Backup
- Contingency and continuity
- Control
- Regulatory
- Accounting
- Ongoing development

SOME SYSTEM-RELATED QUESTIONS

Some questions always arise when talking about systems and their implementation. The next two questions are critical ones to ask, and answers are subjective, depending on the user's experience levels. The views given here are mine only and might not fit readers' specific situations:

- Should we change processes to use the new system or amend/customise the new system to fit existing processes?

  The objective of new system establishment is usually to improve existing processes. Any system change or customisation usually involves significantly higher cost, apart from time and the need for thorough functionality, integrity, and connectivity testing. Existing systems, taken off the shelf with minimal customisation to integrate data and systems, usually meets many requirements—a tested and well-used system generally turns out more robust than something stitched together.

  With these aspects in mind, a new system establishment provides Treasury with an opportunity to revisit, explore, amend, and improve existing processes to extract maximum value from the new system.
- Should we aim for fantastic utilisation of normal systems or normal utilisation of fantastic systems?

  Making the most of existing systems is usually the place to start. An existing system needs to be changed only once it has been utilised to the fullest possible extent, and its technology, including functionality and design, is redundant or obsolete. If processes, activities, and geographies have evolved significantly to require fresh automation (e.g., centralisation or outsourcing implementation), investment in a new cutting-edge system is warranted.

TMS ESTABLISHMENT PROCESS

A simple 10-step process for TMS establishment is discussed next and depicted in Figure 25.5. Note that the process will vary in actual implementation from company to company.

Project Team and Tool Creation

The project team that will decide on the system and assist in taking the project through to closure should be comprised of key players who would be direct or indirect beneficiaries of the systems. A simple team structure is presented in Figure 25.6.

It is important to have members across functions, led by the project manager, who should be a Treasury team member with a good end-to-end understanding of the working of Treasury. Inclusion of members from other functions are optional, depending on the complexity of the operation. Some Treasurers insist on representation of all functions in the team—the need to be on the team will also drive contribution and enthusiasm from the team members, and prudence is advised in deciding the representation.

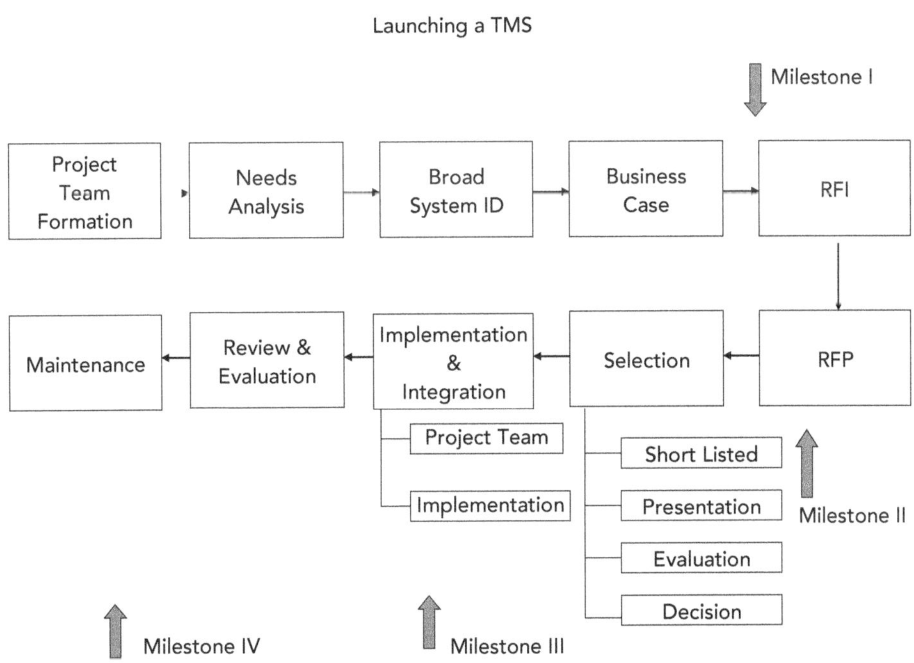

FIGURE 25.5 TMS Establishment Process

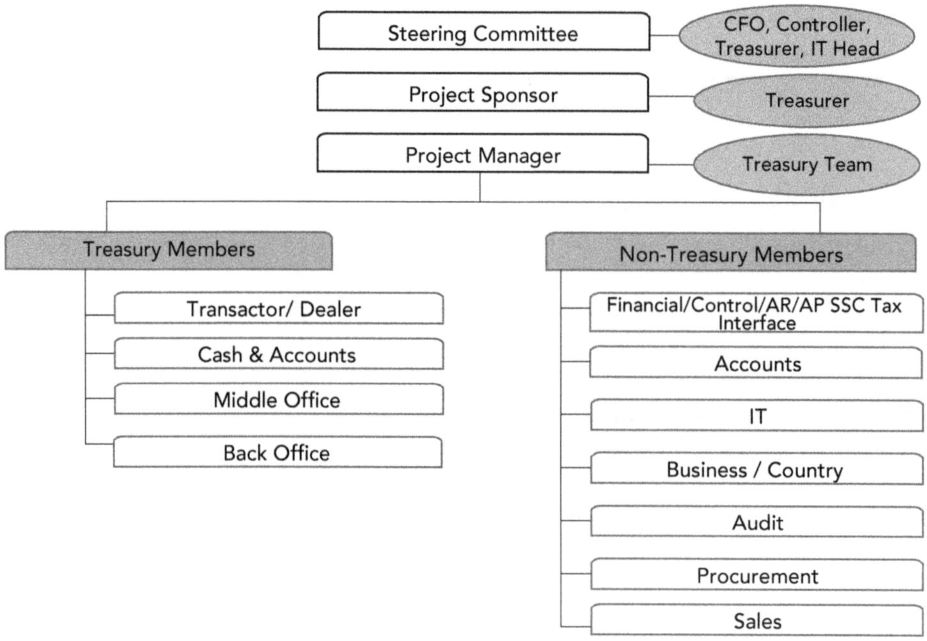

FIGURE 25.6 TMS Project Team Composition

The responsibility of this team officially ends with the selection of the TMS, with the team composition changing slightly when the implementation team takes over. For reasons of continuity, it is preferable to have the same members on both teams.

Needs Analysis

The needs analysis part of the process seeks to establish the key requirements going into the request for information (RFI) stage. The checklist provided could be one of the reference elements to consider, using the key characteristics of a TMS. Some of the critical aspects that need to be focused on include:

- The current system environment and automation levels, including ERP/GL system and other entities.
- Which processes to automate. Is the system replacing an existing one, or is it a completely new automation? Which processes and activities are being replaced or made more efficient by the proposed implementation?

Broad System ID

A scan of systems available as well as decisions on implementation and approximate budgets for implementation with available systems is obtained at this stage, which enables smooth preparation of the business case. A long list of vendors should be created based on the information gathered.

Business Case—Milestone I

The first milestone is reached while preparing the business case and obtaining management approval for the project. This stage quantifies some of the gains established on potential saves and efficiency increases, along with reduction in opportunities for operational losses and control lapses. Both initial and annualised estimates of saves need to be dimensioned. The parameters provided in Figure 25.1 could be a good starting point. The dimensioning of the costs would also provide an approximate indication of the maximum or break-even cost for system implementation.

The business case typically should be approved by the management team comprised of the chief executive officer, the chief financial officer, and perhaps a business head.

Management approval, apart from obtaining the official sanction and budget for going ahead, is a good test of the understanding and comprehensiveness of the team's work thus far. Queries from management provide perspectives and depth that increase the robustness of the requirements and capabilities that the system is expected to provide.

Request for Information—Milestone II

The RFI is the first milestone in the process of implementation. The objective of the RFI is to identify the various vendors and get information from them to create a short list for the request for proposal (RFP), apart from ensuring that the list of capabilities that you are seeking from the TMS covers everything relevant.

The vendors from the long list should be contacted and briefed with further details that would help short-list them for the RFP. Some aspects to be remembered here are:

- Provide enough information to help vendors show their broad understanding of a solution, but not so much that you give the vendor little opportunity to display its own intelligence and creativity.
- Encourage vendors to provide their own value and points that they think would be applicable for your firm. Remember, this practice will help you enhance your own requirements list and perhaps trigger some aspect that might be important for your setup that you had missed.

Request for Proposal

Once the inputs from the RFI stage have been incorporated, the list of requirements and the final RFP template can be frozen. The vendors to be short-listed are decided on, and the selected vendors are approached for the final stage of selection.

The short-listed vendors should preferably deliver a presentation at the client's office, with a demonstration of the system and its capabilities. If possible, guest IDs on a dummy or trial system should also be provided so that team members can access the system on their own time and explore its capabilities. Vendors should be encouraged to provide as much relevant information as possible for you to make the decision but not to overload you with too much information.

The following note highlights the importance of the much used "references," which could degenerate into a routine form-filling exercise.

What References to Ask for? A Different Approach

It is sometimes useful to ask vendors to provide a list of clients who have faced implementation issues. There is no such thing as a 100% seamless integration and implementation. You can gauge the attitude of the vendor, along with its approach and effectiveness, while talking through the various problems faced and the vendor's experience of handling these problems.

Selection—Milestone III

The selection process and the decision of the vendor mark the third milestone, and the most critical one. One approach would be to weight the criteria and then score each vendor across all the weights. If all team members are providing scoring inputs, the top and the bottom score for each criterion could be removed prior to computing the average.

The checklist only provides a numerical number. You must also factor in the overall approach, tenor, and subjective aspect of the firm's own experiences and relationship with the vendor and attempt to quantify and make transparent and auditable as much of the process as possible.

If more than one vendor finishes in the top position or close to the top score, all vendors near that score deserve a second look. The cost element is important but should not be the only basis on which a vendor is chosen.

Implementation and Integration

Once the vendor has been decided on, it is time to implement the TMS. We categorise integration along with implementation, since the system needs to be integrated into the firm's processes and existing systems and environment.

A team, which could be a derivative of the selection team, must be formed. The addition of members from the vendor side who have fixed responsibilities enables the transition process to proceed smoothly.

Representatives from some of the functions need to be involved primarily at the testing phase. Figure 25.7 shows the sample composition of an implementation and integration team.

The implementation and integration process is to be managed with rigor using project management tools and tracking methodologies. A typical stage-wise and time-wise plan is given in Figure 25.8.

The planning stage lays out the timetable and responsibilities.

The second stage (Specifications [Spec] and Data ID) outlines the specifications and identifies the data elements that need to be captured. This sounds like a simple activity, but adequate attention paid to this stage would reduce the rework and further

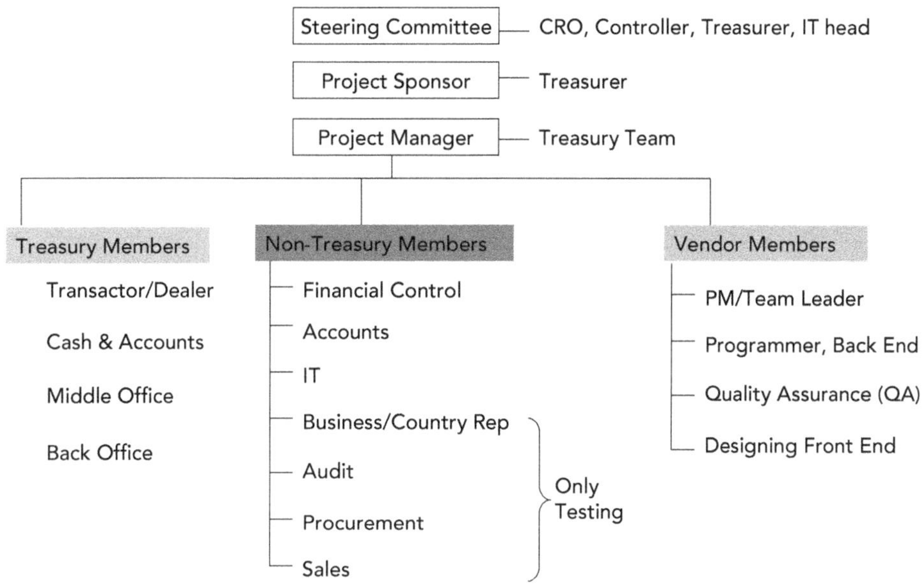

FIGURE 25.7 Implementation and Integration Team Composition

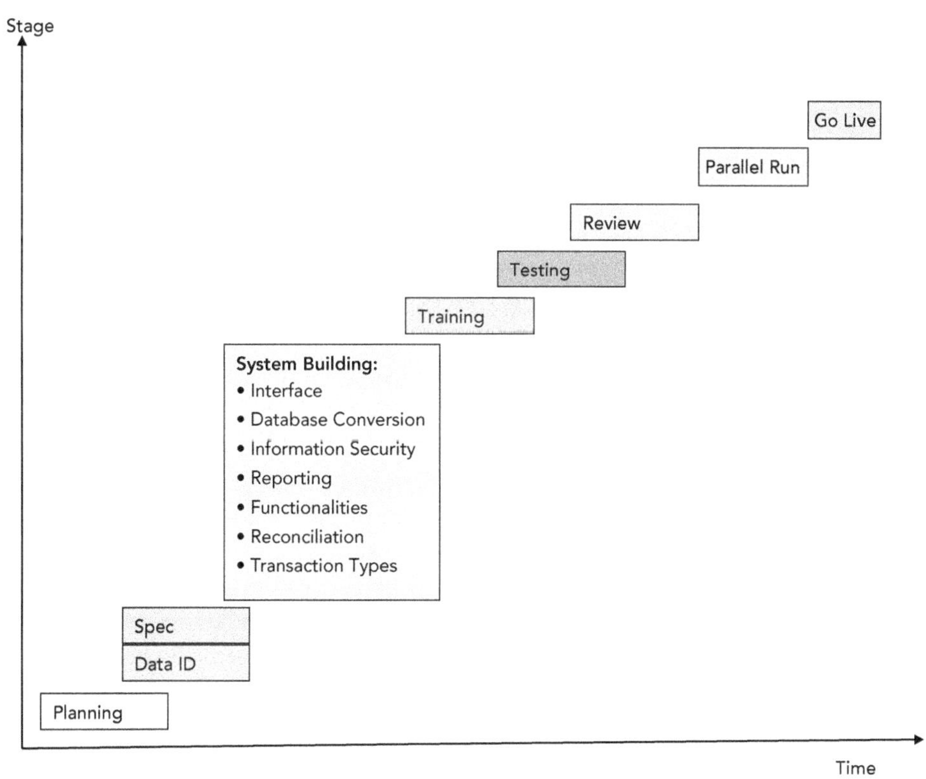

FIGURE 25.8 Project Stages for Implementation and Integration

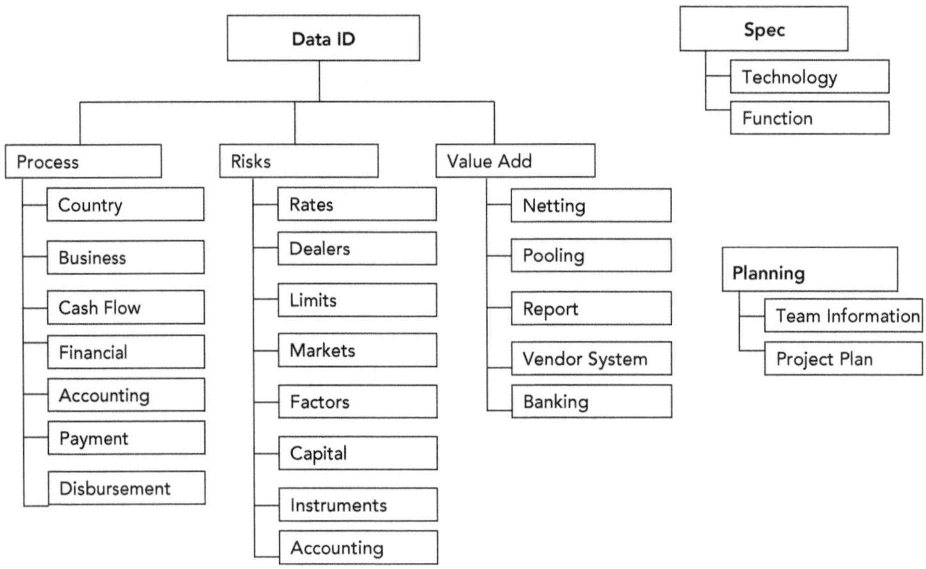

FIGURE 25.9 Data ID Types, Spec and Planning Stages

development that sometimes accompany a system implementation. Figure 25.9 lists some of the data points that can be captured during this stage.

The specifications are primarily divided into:

- User specifications, derived from the contents of the RFP document
- Functional specifications, consisting of the vendor's understanding and articulation of the functionalities
- System specifications, which are the architecture and environment of the proposed system

Once the specification and data ID stage is completed, the vendor provides a more specific cost estimate with deadlines, which you might have to negotiate on.

The next stage is the system building stage, which is the core activity. It includes adapting an existing system or creating code for a new system and integrating with existing systems.

The training stage follows. It distinguishes the various roles that each team member will play and customises the training to their needs. For example, training for information technology (IT) and technology team members could focus more on the technology, maintenance, and information security administrator aspects; training for the financial control team could focus on the AR/AP aspects; and training for dealers could focus on the market aspects.

The testing stage involves drawing out detailed plans and expected results for user acceptance testing (UAT). Possible functionality-based beta testing could be done prior to the system being delivered for the UAT. Once the system has been handed over for UAT, it moves into the control environment, where every change, every version, or every release is controlled and recorded. The members of the team doing the UAT must have a list of expected results and compare the expected results with the actual ones. They must document the variances and agree with the vendor on the variances. If a particular functionality is found to be missing and has not been documented as part of user functionality, it can be classified as a new requirement and can have billing and cost implications. The cost and time estimates of the reworked aspects have to be reviewed and criticality established. Good practice is to consolidate the errors on a daily basis and evaluate criticality. Critical elements missing or not working would lead to immediate action to rectify.

The review process can start once testing is under way and continues once the sign-off has happened on the system. After the sign-off, the system, under a controlled environment, is handed over to the vendor for implementation and integration on actual systems.

Based on our experience, we believe that doing a parallel run before going live can help sort out some of the teething issues that typically occur during a launch. The parallel run helps to slowly integrate the processes and systems into the mainstream, with the ability to pull back should some large issue occur.

Review and Evaluation—KPI/Milestone IV

It is important to evaluate and measure the success of the system implementation. Key performance indicators (KPIs) should be established (usually early in the process) and used to test system effectiveness and utility. The KPIs should be measurable and quantifiable. This review and evaluation is the final project milestone.

Maintenance

Ongoing management of the system, periodic reviews, and managing the vendor is an ongoing process. It can be adequately managed by the Treasury function with the support of the IT function.

DEVELOPMENTS AND STANDARDS

Many changes are happening in the world of financial technology, and much of it is based on dramatic improvements in communication, connectivity, and messaging. One of these improvements, very pertinent to the Treasury professional, is the International Standards Organization (ISO) 20022 financial messaging standard and the Common Global Implementation (CGI). We present a short note on the CGI in the book and provide a summary of Industrial Products and Service Category standards in online Appendix D of this book (www.wiley.com/go/treasuryhandbook).

CGI: ISO 20022 on the Mainline

Synopsis

As corporates seek to reduce costs and mitigate risk, they are struggling to manage their relationships with multiple banking partners. As such, they are increasingly looking for multi-bank, multi-payment types and multi-country solutions. SWIFT's creation of a universal financial messaging system is a key element supporting this trend and together with the ISO 20022 financial messaging standard and the Common Global Implementation or CGI are driving the underlying global market practice.

What exactly is CGI? The first thoughts of those involved in the financial sector might be towards a well-known provider of IT outsourcing services. Others may think of computer-generated imagery or common gateway interface, or perhaps even the Clinton Global Initiative. It is time now to brace ourselves for a new and innovative interpretation of a popular acronym in the world of financial messaging. The Common Global Implementation embodies the notion that, "A corporate can use the same message structure (for each message type) to interact with all of their transaction banks across the globe for payments initiation (credit transfer and direct debit), account and status reporting."

Multi-Bank Factor

CGI is being driven by bank customer demand for multi-bank coordination of implementations where the projects are often characterised by:

- Commitment of a global corporate, multi-banked, multi-payment types, multi-country implementations (mixed payables)
- Direct involvement of multiple participating banks that may wish to individually offer additional value-added services
- Active engagement as a corporate-bank partnership; and
- Global or regional roll-out that may involve customer's consolidation of internal payment infrastructures, for example through a payment factory platform.

Large corporates, more often than not, have multiple bank relationships, a trend that has grown in the wake of the global financial crisis as companies seek to mitigate risk, to reduce cost, and to obviate the need to "put too many eggs in one basket." Managing multiple bank interfaces can be quite a challenge, particularly if different channels, different protocols, different formats, and different data requirements need to be factored into the implementation process. In some cases, management and maintenance overheads are costly and onerous and become amplified when they are proprietary.

CGI seeks to redress the multiplier effect inherent in managing the interfaces for multi-bank implementations (see Figure 25.10), through the use of the universal financial industry message scheme ISO 20022 as the base message standard and a corresponding message implementation template as the single harmonised format.

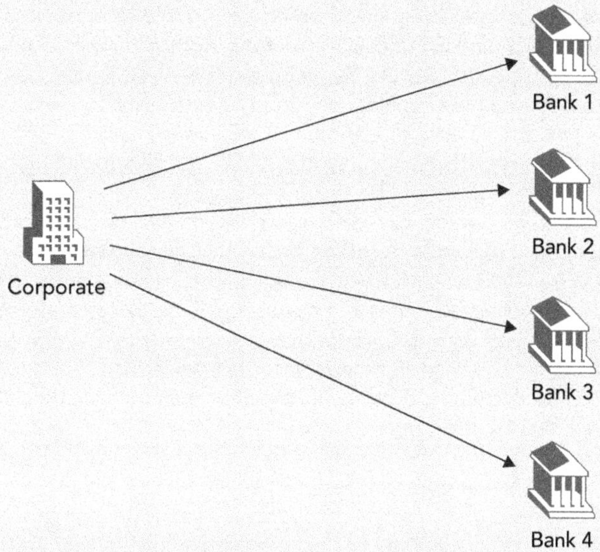

FIGURE 25.10 Multi-Bank Communication

ISO 20022

The International Organization for Standardization (ISO) is the world's largest developer and publisher of international standards, formed through a network of national standards organisations from 162 countries. ISO 20022 is one such standard promulgated by ISO. It is a free and open standard.

ISO 20022 has been aptly described as a recipe for making financial messaging standards. The ISO 20022 methodology provides a systematic means to define and describe financial business interactions and a discipline to create the underlying messages that support the exchange of information in a structured format among the players involved in those processes. However, such exchanges will only work when both the sender and recipient can fully interpret and understand the message contents. Furthermore, the concept of straight-through processing (STP) depends on the automated exchange of precise and unambiguous information. The ISO 20022 standards go a long way towards making all of this possible
and practical.

ISO 20022 in itself grew out of the need to attain convergence across numerous overlapping standardisation initiatives that were looking at XML financial messages. It was built on the work of an earlier standard, ISO 15022, a syntax used for the developing securities messages. In the payments world, it brought together four organisations involved in the development of messages for the financial industry: IFX, SWIFT, TWIST, and OAGI. Known as the ISTH, it sought to use ISO 20022 and the XML syntax as the new messaging approach.

XML has firmly established itself as a ubiquitous means of formatting data and has gained wide acceptance as the basis for data storage and data exchange in all areas of data processing.

(Continued)

ISO 20022 has progressively gained momentum and its impact on the financial messaging landscape is increasing—in total, some 300 messages at various stages of use. Since 2006, ISO 20022 messages have been published for the entire end-to-end payments chain, covering the corporate-to-bank payment initiation, bank-to-bank payment clearing and settlement, and bank-to-corporate account and status reporting. For payments, ISO 20022 adoption gained impetus from it being the format of choice for the Single Euro Payments Area (SEPA) in seeking to replace domestic retail credit transfers and direct debits with standardised European payments based on ISO 20022 messages. Real-time gross settlement (RTGS) systems and low-value payments systems around the world have also shown increasing interest in adopting ISO 20022 (for example, the Zengin System in Japan and the International Payments Framework), while others are focusing on building alignment with the standard.

The ISO 20022 payments messages have, for example, enabled the ability to capture remittance information and pertinent commercial data along with payment information, the use of multi-byte characters, enhanced references, and reporting of interest and charges.

It should be noted that in many respects the real business value of ISO 20022 lies in the support it gives to collaboration, allowing the financial industry and adjoined stakeholders to openly agree and align global business requirements in a uniform and standardised way. This has certainly been the case in the payments arena through the ISO 20022 Standards Evaluation Group (SEG), the Payments Market Practice Group (PMPG) and, more recently, the CGI.

ISO 20022 represents the next generation messaging standard for SWIFT.

CGI

While the ISO 20022 payments message definitions in themselves provide a comprehensive basis for data exchange, they have also led to mapping variations and differences in how the messages are implemented. The design of the payment messages caters for a range of payment initiation (credit transfer and direct debit) instrument types, methods, and reporting requirements. There are hundreds of elements (for example, over 1,300 in the Credit Transfer—pain.001.001.03), most elements are optional and external code sets often shared across different message types. Consequently, implementation inconsistencies were encountered across different financial institutions, in particular highlighted by large corporates embarking on multi-bank implementations.

The CGI was designed specifically to address these inconsistencies. Created in October 2009, CGI currently includes 50 registered members, of which 36 are contributing members. It is an ad hoc, voluntary forum that is open (without membership fees) to organisations that have a common interest in collaboration, promotion, and adoption of the ISO 20022 XML financial message set.

The goal of CGI is to provide this forum for both financial (banks and bank associations) and non-financial institutions (corporates, corporate associations, vendors, and market infrastructures) to progress various corporate-to-bank implementation topics on the use of ISO 20022 messages and to other related activities in the payments domain. In particular, it is to simplify implementation for corporate users and thereby promote wider acceptance of ISO 20022 as the common XML standard used between corporates and banks.

The CGI goal is being achieved through consultation, collaboration, and agreement amongst all players on a series of common implementation templates for relevant ISO 20022 financial messages, leading to their subsequent publication and promotion in order to attain widespread recognition and adoption. The high level of collaboration that has been attained among the major banks is significant to achieving global coherence with their respective implementations.

To date, six implementation templates have been released:

Customer Credit Transfer Initiation (pain.001.001.03)
Customer Direct Debit (pain.008.001.02)
Customer Payment Status Report (pain.002.001.03)
Bank To Customer Account Report (camt.052.001.02)
Bank To Customer Statement (camt.053.001.02)
Bank To Customer Debit Credit Notification (camt.054.001.02)

Figure 25.11 depicts these message flows.

These CGI templates detail specific implementation guidance (or market practice) on the use of the respective ISO 20022 XML schema, element by element. Each element is designated a usage status, for example, "R"—Required,

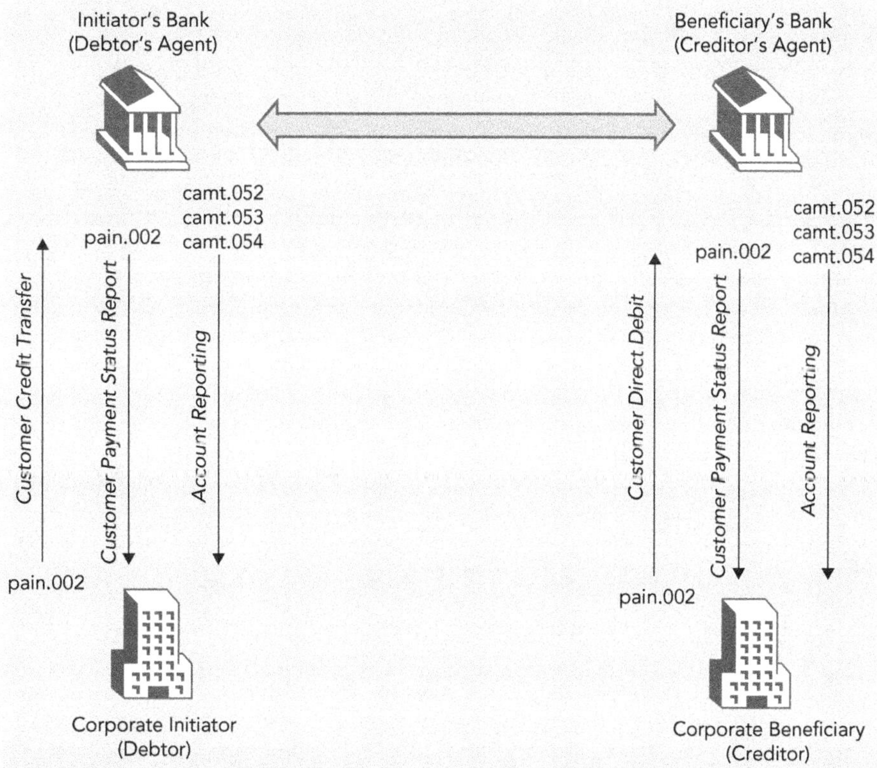

FIGURE 25.11 CGI Message Flows

(Continued)

"C"—Conditional, "BD"—Bilaterally Determined, "NU"—Not Used. For the credit transfer, this detailed guidance is further segmented by:

Automated clearinghouse—domestic and international. General usage is equivalent to low-value or nonurgent transactions. It typically is associated with a batch process and/or low-priority transactions.
Wires—domestic and international. General usage is equivalent to high-value or urgent transactions with high priority.
Cheques/drafts. Typically, paper-based transactions.

Users of these templates can benefit from a common and unambiguous approach to market practice that is designed to work across multiple financial institutions. In practice, this means that bank customers can take their payments initiation processing to a more consistent level based on a single global common implementation template for each of their outbound payments initiation message types (credit transfer and direct debit) and for their various inbound account and status reporting message types. From a competition and risk management perspective, it should simplify the process for a corporate to expand or switch to a new bank.

The CGI templates incorporate a concept of 'data overpopulation' that allows corporates to effectively provide not only the same information, but also all of their information to each of their target financial institutions. This information is then filtered by each receiving institution based on the requested payment method, clearing channel, and any institution-specific requirements. The use of a single common template in this manner will reduce cost and complexity.

Another dimension to the CGI implementation templates is the use of appendices to provide further elaboration and specific guidance. For example, a list of individual payment system service level codes, country/region specific requirements, and implementation use cases. Appendices support a more frequent maintenance cycle and are created, based on the business requirements of a specific message. These appendices recognise that certain markets may be subject to slightly different regulations, and each may have its own local market practices that change over time with the emergence of new regulations and business requirements. For example, where a bank branch identification is required, or where local language is required, or where country specific regulatory and/or tax reporting is required.

Significantly, the CGI implementation templates are also serving as a blueprint for enterprise resource planning (ERP) and Treasury management system (TMS) vendors to incorporate these as part of their solution offerings. SAP made product announcements to this end in December 2011.

MyStandards

An ongoing development by SWIFT is MyStandards. It encompasses standards definitions, usage guidelines, bilateral agreements, and analysis tools. MyStandards is positioned as a collaborative web-based tool to efficiently manage new releases and better understand market practice. MyStandards is currently moving from pilot to production, with the first official release expected in May 2012.

It is anticipated that the implementation templates from CGI have been incorporated in MyStandards and will be an important reference point for the formulation and analysis of this and related market practice.

Conclusions

The potential for CGI to streamline the broad community adoption of ISO 20022 for payments is large and illustrates that effective collaboration in defining market practice can be a win-win situation for all players involved, notably the financial institutions and their corporate customers. Achieving true multi-bank integration depends on a common template for information exchange that not only caters to the core data elements but also extends to providing support for those banks that may wish to offer value added solutions that are over and above the core CGI message implementation template. Here the concept of 'data overpopulation' plays a key role, and should not be overlooked in implementation.

A challenge for CGI will be how it provides implementation guidance for the migration from one version of the base ISO 20022 standard to the next. Later in 2012, version 4 of the pain.001.001 will be published, the current template is based on version 3.

Finally, promotion of CGI needs strengthening. Consistent with ISO 20022, the open and free availability of the CGI collateral should be a given, but a dedicated and more visible home for CGI is something that should be brought to the fore.

Contributed by David Dobbing, business manager banking and payments standards, SWIFT

SUMMARY

Good system selection, implementation, and maintenance are far more than mere concepts. Many hurdles can crop up that can impede any of these stages, but with adequate and simple but intelligent thought and execution, Treasury systems can emerge as true winners in adding to a company's profitability.

CHAPTER TWENTY SIX

26 Centralisation

EARLIER IN THE BOOK WE introduced the concept and features of centralisation in Part One. We now look at the rationale, framework, and broad executional elements of centralisation.

RATIONALE FOR CENTRALISATION

In Part One, we mentioned that the key objectives for centralisation are to increase efficiency, increase control, and reduce cost related to Treasury activities. All three elements directly impact treasury's performance. Elements of centralisation and various models were discussed in Chapter 2 (centralisation) and Chapter 5 (account structure). Here we provide the context for the centralisation decision, the process for decision making, and the criteria for evaluation.

Figure 26.1 presents various models of centralisation, which also were covered in Part One. Figure 26.2 shows some of the determinants of the centralisation decision. These determinants are discussed in more detail next.

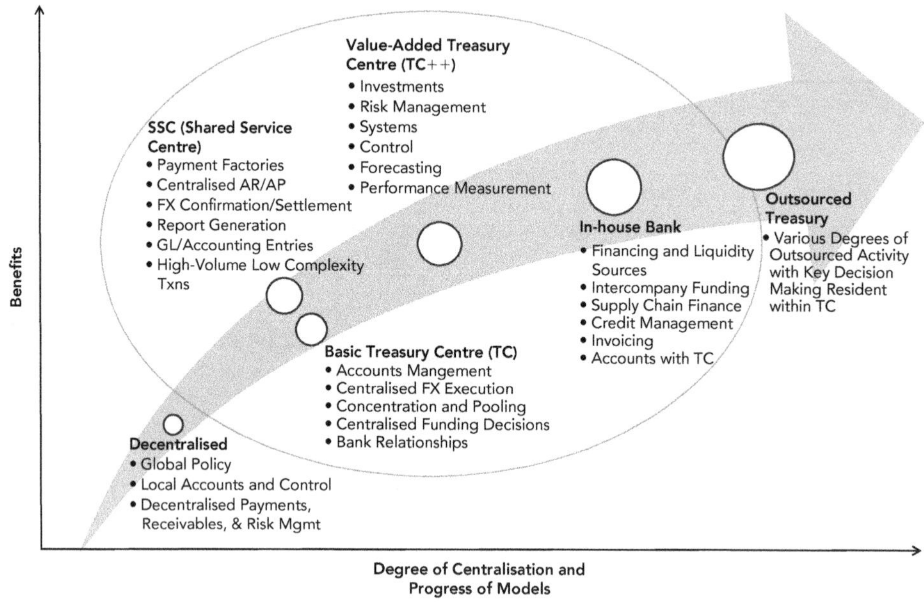

FIGURE 26.1 Different Models of Centralisation

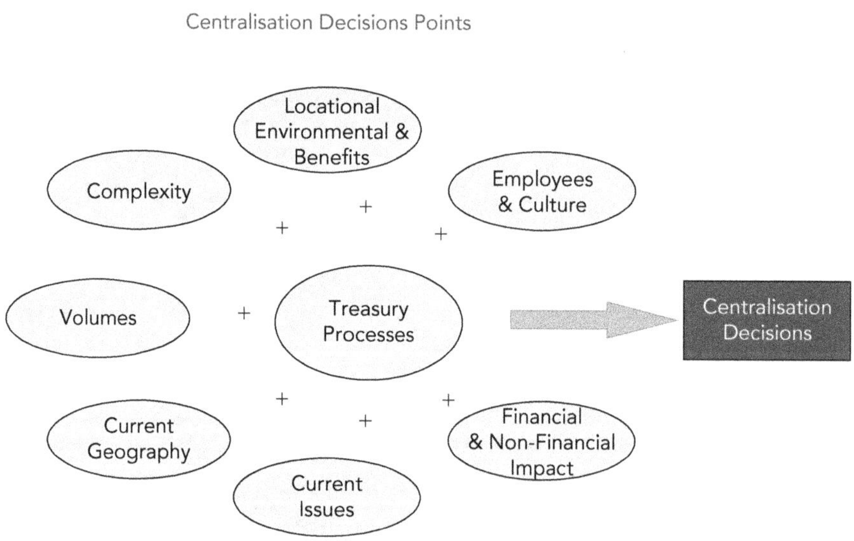

FIGURE 26.2 Determinants of the Centralisation Decision

- **Treasury processes.** Change or process improvement and implementation of new systems can be one of the drivers of the decision to centralise Treasury processes and controls. As cash visibility, process efficiency, and control systems become critical to the functioning of Treasury, centralisation will become increasingly important.

- **Volume of transactions.** Scales of operations and increasing transaction volume will drive the need for achieving economies of scale and uniformity of processes.
- **Current geography.** Operations across many countries, time zones and markets might create the need for central coordination and consistent support.
- **Complexity of transactions.** As the complexity of businesses and models grow, the need to have more involved support from the Treasury side will increase. Along with this will come the need to develop more expertise and standardisation in order to transfer successful solutions across areas.
- **Financial and nonfinancial impact.** Cost/benefit over time and turnaround times and quality of service internally and from external service providers will be large determinants of centralising Treasury functions.
- **Location environment and benefits.** Relative attractiveness of a location (discussed in detail under "Basic Design Model" later in the chapter) can be another driver for moving operations there.
- **Employee impact and cultural background.** The success of a centralisation exercise is determined by one of the most sensitive areas and impacts of centralisation: employee acceptance, resistance, redeployment ability, involvement, and empowerment, in addition to company culture centralisation. Some company cultures enable such process improvements; others are not conducive to centralisation. For the latter, it is important to institute the process of change slowly and build processes of change and transition well before the actual project commences. In some cases, if the culture does not change, leaving operations distributed and the way they are might be less detrimental than forcing centralisation. In others, the centralisation itself might force a cultural change. This is an area in which the chief executive officer (CEO), senior management, and human resources must be actively involved.

Figure 26.3 shows a possible structural framework of the centralisation decision.

BASIC MODEL DESIGN

The initial inputs that go into the basic model design involve process inputs, location inputs, and infrastructure inputs.

Process inputs involve process changes, current issues with process, human resource capabilities and skill inventory, complexity of envisioned inputs, and volumes.

Location inputs involve deciding the attractiveness of a location and the current geographical spread and location of operations. Table 26.1 and online Appendix E provide some of the themes of deciding on a location along with some indicative weights.

Infrastructure inputs involve system inputs, resource inputs, and inputs and review of the accounting, tax, and legal environment.

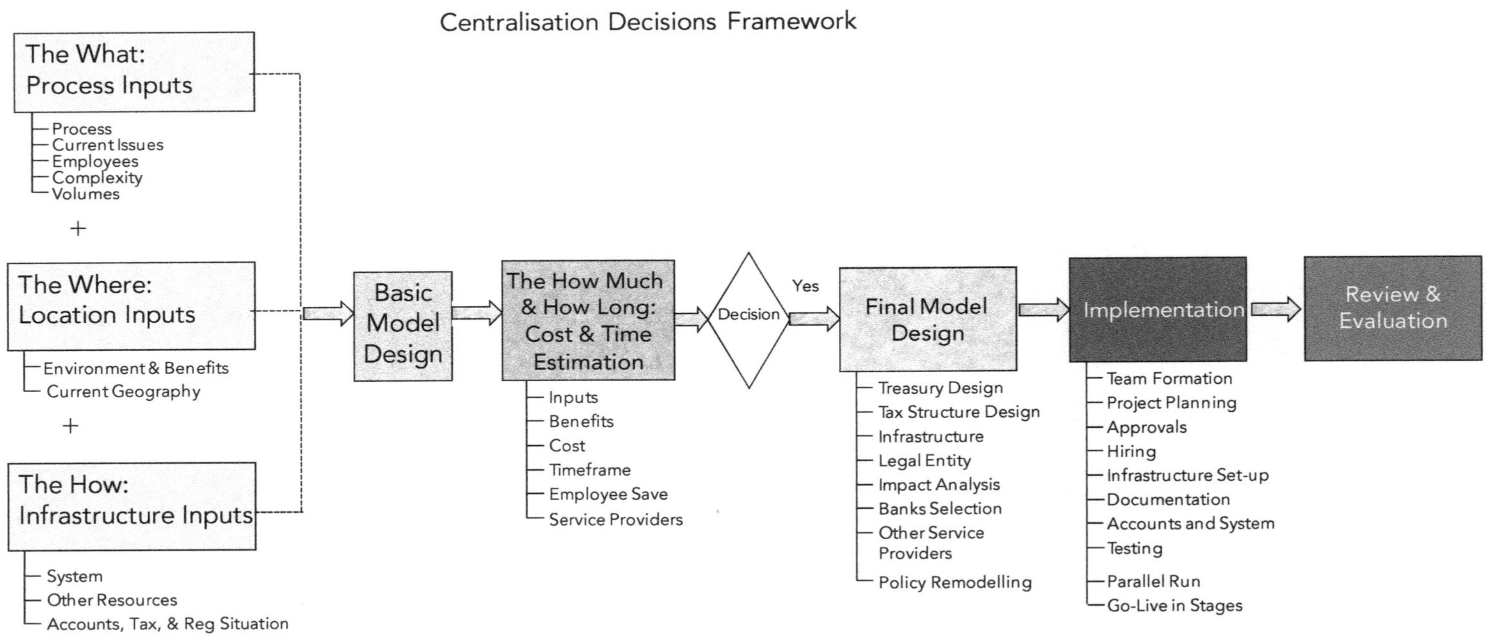

FIGURE 26.3 Structural Framework of the Centralisation Decision

TABLE 26.1 Broad Themes of Location Identification

Theme	Factor	Weight
Environment	Legal framework and history	10
	Tax environment	18
	Political environment	5
	Regulatory environment	10
Infrastructure	Infrastructure	5
	Cost	5
	Accessibility	3
Human Resources	Language	3
	Resource pool	10
	Standard of living	7
Sector and Markets	Banking sector	7
	Capital availability	7
	Special status	3
	Market development	7

POST-MODEL DESIGN STAGE

Once the basic model has been designed, the cost and time estimate of the project is complete. Synergies and saves are quantified, and benefits and turnaround aspects are estimated. Potential service providers are identified, and approximate cost estimates are obtained from them.

Once the decision to go ahead has been made, the final model is worked on. This is followed by implementation and then review.

Implementation is best done in stages and in a few countries at a time, a few processes at a time. The company may also choose to implement pieces of the model at every stage—for example, a shared service centre can be implemented first, followed by basic Treasury centre activities. It is best not to move everything at the same time.

Senior management involvement, support, and assistance is important at every stage, given the various sensitivities.

BARRIERS TO CENTRALISATION

The guest note on centralisation by Damien Glendinning, Regional Treasurer, Lenovo, in Chapter 2 covers some of the implementation issues. Some of the barriers to centralisation are summarised below.

Technology Integration

Different systems and the lack of connectivity can be an impediment to achieving a centralised process and Treasury management. A starting point for centralisation can include a one-time investment in integration and creating uniformity at least in the Treasury system.

Culture

The compelling business and financial case and goal congruence will help overcome organisational barriers to centralisation. Tying the goals of decentralised centres of power and influence to success of the centralisation aspect and empowering country operations with more managerial time to focus on the business by moving a support function would be a logical next step, but one that would have to be articulated by senior management, including the CEO.

Merger Activity

An agglomeration of various companies will have a large mix of legacy systems, processes, and business practices. Technology will be a starting point for overcoming these hurdles, and the process changes that follow based on central systems will be a logical precursor to centralisation.

SUMMARY

The need for centralisation is a debate that brings with it heated debates about control, cost, efficiency, human resources, technology, and governance. The underlying emphasis is that of change. Change is for the better when it has a long-term goal and is aligned with the objectives and plans of the firm and when the relevant issues that it causes, especially for the people involved, are addressed appropriately.

Successful centralisation depends on teamwork and goal congruence. And therein lies the solution.

CHAPTER TWENTY SEVEN

27

Key Performance Metrics for a Treasury

A SCORECARD FOR TREASURY PERFORMANCE needs a balanced combination of objective and subjective elements. Various firms use different methods to evaluate the performance of their Treasury. Some firms use just one method. Some firms do not find the need to have an objective evaluation of the performance of the Treasury function; we do hope that the reading of this book will encourage them to develop metrics for their Treasury.

INTRODUCING PERFORMANCE METRICS

For a global Treasury that works as a cost centre, Figure 27.1 provides a simple summary of the key organisation and financial goals.

How these are achieved and how the many elements that contribute to the success of a global Treasury are captured form the core of this chapter. All activities involve people, and without extensive interaction and teamwork among people of the Treasury function and the rest of the organisation, no success would be possible.

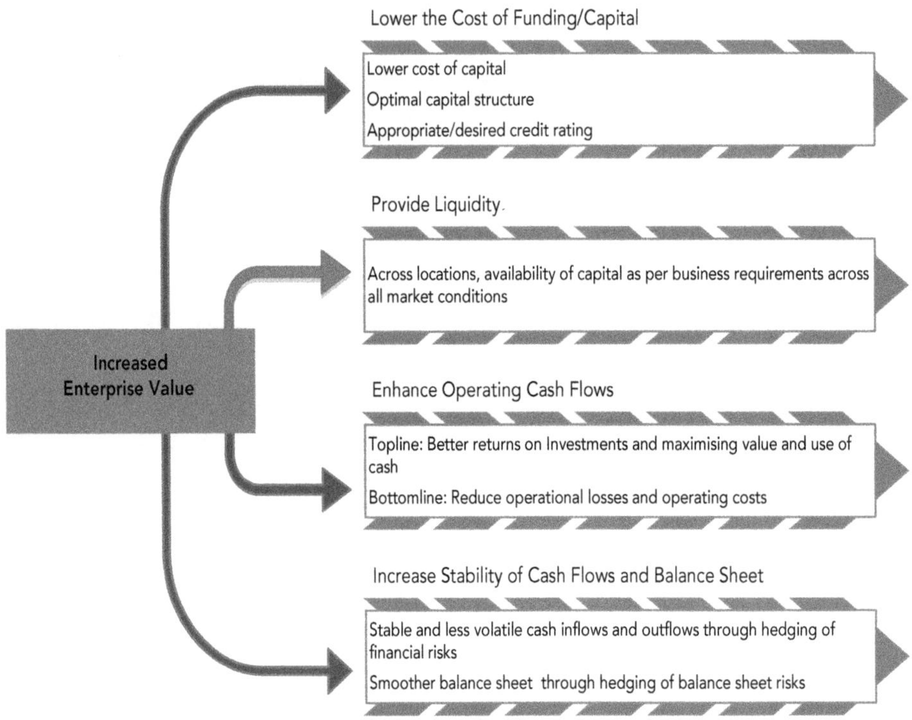

FIGURE 27.1 Key Metrics

Some of these subjective performance elements should be captured in metric form. Performance metrics and benchmarks have to be comprehensive in coverage and simple in design and execution.

In this chapter, we provide just one of the many scorecards that can be used. The performance evaluation for a Treasury can be divided into three steps:

1. Decide the metrics to be evaluated.
2. Compare these with identified performance benchmarks.
3. Evaluate the performance objectively based on steps 1 and 2.

A sample performance evaluation process is depicted in Figure 27.2.

SOME CRITERIA FOR DECIDING PERFORMANCE METRICS

Next we turn to some of the criteria for deciding which performance metrics to use.

- **Profit centre versus cost centre.** If the Treasury is a profit centre, the metrics would be more oriented towards financial profits and less on volatility and

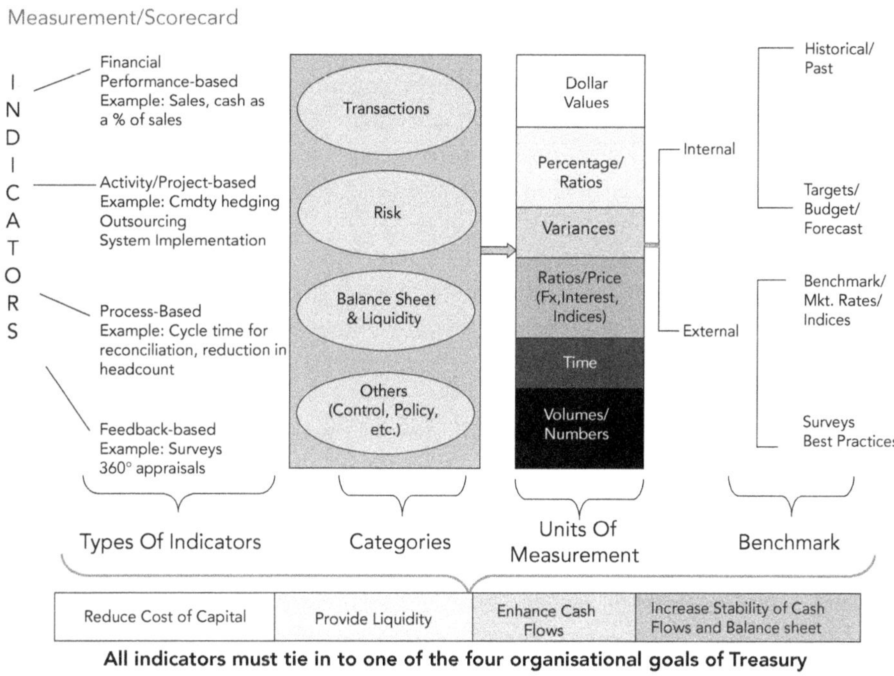

FIGURE 27.2 Scope of Metrics and Measurement

visibility of cash flows. For purposes of the sample metrics in this book, we have assumed the more conservative approach of Treasury as a support function and cost centre focused on reducing volatility.

- **Geographic spread of operations.** As the locations in which the group is present grows in number, there is an increase in complexity of operations and management. Metrics should reflect that fact, with different countries having appropriate benchmarks depending on their development and stage in the life cycle.
- **Nature of markets where the group is present.** Different markets have different regulations on the movement of money and market factors. For example, Singapore-based operations would be different from Kenya markets in terms of liquidity, market forces, benchmarks, capital movement, and regulations. Hence, the two country operations would have different benchmarks to reflect the nature of their respective markets.
- **Outsourced activities.** The degree of outsourcing could have an impact on the metrics—the outsourced operations might have a different (usually tighter) metric and benchmark depending on the terms of the service agreement.
- **Degree of centralisation.** Presence of centralised activities, such as centralised treasuries, in-house banks, shared service centres, and the like could change the benchmarks as compared to those of firms with more distributed and on-site activities.

- **Competition and industry practices.** What competition and industry peers practices could impact the setting of benchmarks for evaluation?
- **Organisational culture.** Many cultures encourage predominantly objective management, and the metrics for Treasury would help in delivering such measures. However, there are a number of subjective evaluation aspects to be factored in, and attempts must be made to make these as quantifiable as possible (through formal interviews, surveys, etc.).
- **Direct dependence on Treasury function.** Some of the metrics would be a combination of the performance of other functions. Hence, importance and thus weight for Treasury's contribution towards those metrics should be adjusted accordingly. Care should be taken to highlight those aspects that Treasury is directly responsible for.
- **Availability of data, frequency of measurement, and ease of the performance measurement process.** It is important to have good measures of Treasury performance. However, the collation of data should not be so onerous as to make performance measurement itself a full-time activity. Increasing automation and recording of data makes it easier to retrieve numbers and report them in the required formats, but the reporting frequency and intensity has to be a meaningful exercise that the Treasury management committee must review thoroughly before making recommendations to the chief executive officer and to the board. The use of each metric must also be reviewed during the annual review process of the Treasury policy.

PERFORMANCE METRICS

We now discuss the metrics themselves.

Themes of Performance Metrics

Performance metrics can be divided into these themes:

- **Financial performance based.** These metrics have a direct impact on the financials of the group. They include operating cash flow (increase is better), cost of capital, and cash position.
- **Activity or project based.** These metrics are based on a certain activity or project, such as stability of cash flows because of hedging, cost of hedging, and cost save because of outsourcing.
- **Process based.** These metrics are tracked at an individual process level and are the most micro-level of all metrics. Examples are: turnaround time for data entry, invoice float, and employees directly involved in foreign exchange settlements.
- **Human feedback based.** These metrics are direct responses to the overall impact of the Treasury team on the organisation. Part of the Treasury team's responsibility is internal customer service and supporting the businesses and

country operations; hence, internal customer and employee satisfaction surveys are important metrics to consider.

The importance of the themes is to ensure that the material universe of Treasury performance is captured. To do this, the Treasurer must go through financials impacted by Treasury, activities, and projects in which Treasury plays a key role or is the owner, and processes that Treasury runs or plays a key role in. This bottoms-up approach ensures a comprehensive scope of metrics used.

Measurement Units of Performance Metrics

The use of various metrics entails the use of various measures. We group these measures by units of measurement, which would enable users to ascertain the benchmarks and a score for each metric.

Dollars or Value

The value, usually the currency value of any metric, provides an absolute numeric measure of performance. Many measures, such as cash flows, costs, and gains, are measured as values. Some items, such as bank credit limits, are dependent on external entities.

Since most other measures finally show up in some form on the enterprise value (a form of discounted value of future cash flows), it is important to consider the various forms of dollars of value depicted. Table 27.1 shows some measurement units.

TABLE 27.1 Measurement Units

Dollar/Value	Description
Vanilla	Simple nominal numbers (e.g., sales or expenses or balance sheet values) taken without any discounting or adjustments. This is useful for very short term numbers or for simple back-of-the-envelope calculations
Discounted	Discounted over time, these are the most commonly used adjustments, especially for cash flows over time. The discount rate used is critical to determine the efficacy of these numbers, since the longer the tenor being examined, the more critical the impact of the discount rate. Also, different currencies have different discount rates, and these must be factored in.
Tax adjusted	Tax plays an important role in determining the financial position; hence, usually tax-adjusted numbers are considered for profitability and cross-border transactions.
Risk adjusted	Risk-adjusted assets and portfolios, especially where capital is concerned, are used in many firms.
Accounting adjusted	From an accounting standpoint, the numbers that are reported are those compliant with generally accepted accounting principles or International Financial Reporting Standards. These could be different from an economic value standpoint, and care must be taken to determine the economic value of financials and longer-tenor transactions such as hedges.

It is important to remember to compare like numbers with similar ones—for example, a discounted cash flow adjusted from tax but not risk must be compared with an equivalent cash flow and benchmark.

Market Rates

Market rates could be percentages for cost of capital, targeted share price for buybacks, budgeted or meaningful target rates for foreign exchange and commodities, and so on. Selection of the benchmark is especially important for evaluation, especially because market rates seldom remain static, and the benchmark market rate at the end of the financial year could be very different from that at the beginning.

Time

The time taken for a cycle, processing, cash realisation, or any other activity is a good indication of process efficiency or liquidity. In many cases, such as the cash conversion cycle, an equivalent dollar value (working capital requirement) could be used as well.

Numbers or Volume

Numbers, such as number of employees for an activity or a full-time employee headcount reduction, are useful big-picture metrics. As a process, these typically get converted to value and reflect as a benefit or concern in the financial statements.

Volumes, such as the throughput of hedging transactions or cash collections by cheque, indicate scale of operations and sometimes help in redirecting focus to high-sensitivity, low-spotlight areas. Also, volumes provide a good estimate of the impact of automation and scalability of Treasury operations.

Statistical Measures (Percentages, Ratios, Variances)

Financial ratios form a core component of any Treasury performance measurement. Other measures, such as percentages (which show process improvements or loads, or balance sheet strengths and areas of concern) and variances, are brought in as required to supplement more standard measures and to delve deeper into some numbers or to throw more light on policy/practices. Risk limit utilisation, for example, is a good indication of how stretched the limits are and provide feedback to the Treasury management committee for the next review.

Rating or Survey Results (Ratings/Rankings)

Credit rating exercises, industry surveys, employee surveys, and other exercises provide different elements that indicate performance on various grounds.

Benchmarks

The role of benchmarks in the evaluation process is critical. Once the metrics have been collated, it is important to determine what to evaluate them against since inappropriately chosen benchmarks or levels tend to distort the performance. Each organisation would have to do its own assessment of the benchmarks and values to use.

Internal Benchmarks

Historical Numbers Historical numbers, past performance, or metrics are some internal benchmarks. These are useful to look at performance relative to previous years or quarters and good indications of performance over time. Growth numbers and process improvement are well measured with historical numbers. Remember to compare similar values with the same basis.

Targets/Budgets/Forecasts Targets are set internally, and most firms have a well-managed process to set them. Budgeted rates, especially for market factors that are beyond the firm's control, are trickier to handle, especially when the firm's risk management policy does not lay down a long-term perspective for carrying out such transactions. The importance of forecasts, especially for near-term ones, is highlighted when they are used for performance evaluation.

External Benchmarks

Market Benchmarks/Indices Benchmark rates or index values from market sources are an independent verifiable parameter to use. However, many of these are variable. For that reason, the equivalent current level at any point of time must be considered.

Market Surveys/Industry Best Practices Market surveys and peer reviews could provide good feedback on the benchmark to be used with respect to the outside world. This method can be reliable, especially for process times and operations and control environments, where firms are more willing to disclose their own numbers to obtain a market benchmark. It is important also to select the right candidates for benchmarking—select peers and industries that have similar elements to yours. For a conglomerate with diversified interests, each company within the group should be benchmarked, and groups with similar interests should be picked for a consolidated comparison.

SOME CAVEATS ON METRICS AND EVALUATION

There is never a perfect method for performance evaluation, especially for a unit such as Treasury, which has multiple interfaces with other entities.

Many Metrics Are Not Directly Governed by Treasury

Treasury is only partially responsible for some of the metrics—for example, increased base currency value of sales. Hence, the metric should be weighted adequately to accommodate this aspect. Also, subjectivity or choice regarding metrics to be used is required if the accuracy of the inputs is not consistent.

An example is the hedging of sales or revenue cash flows in the longer term. Based on forecast inputs from sales and business lines, Treasury undertakes some hedges. These forecasts will change over time, and Treasury will keep making adjustments to the hedges. For a specific evaluation metric, both the final financial result and the efficacy of the original hedge must be considered for fair evaluation.

Many Factors Are Market Based

While Treasury may be the only entity in the firm that is managing market-related risk, some moves may be beyond envisioned levels. In these situations, care must be taken to value the restorative action that Treasury would have done in adverse situations. If the market has gone through a crisis of liquidity or volatile moves, how well Treasury has managed the situations should be considered.

Information Availability

Treasury's performance is only as good as the information it works with. Hence, the quality of inputs coming in from business and countries on which Treasury relies for accurate information and meaningful forecasts should be considered.

Accounting versus Economic Value

It can be tempting and sometimes simpler to use accounting value of transactions and activities, especially risk management products. However, especially for longer-tenor transactions, economic value of the transaction over the life of the deal should be considered as a fair measure of performance. Similarly, while up-front carry or profits could be recognised from a swap or option, the entire life of the transaction and possible reversals should be kept in mind. An alternative in these cases is to create a virtual escrow into which the large gains from these transactions are deposited, with the money used to provide for any adverse payouts, should market situations reverse. The performance evaluation for Treasury in this case should be over a reasonable time period, with the credit or points for benefits accruing over time.

SAMPLE TREASURY PERFORMANCE METRICS

Table 27.2 shows a sample set of performance metrics for an organisation. Each firm must determine its own set of metrics and assign and evaluate them accordingly.

TABLE 27.2 Performance Metrics

Primary Main Metric	Ref No	Metric	Area (t/R/B)	Sub-Area
Cash Flows	T01	Average number of bank accounts/unit as well as unit high and low	Transactions	Cash & Accounts
Cash Flows	T02	Numbers of collections vs. disbursements vs. operating accounts	Transactions	Cash & Accounts
Cash Flows	T03	Total cost of bank accounts; out-of-pocket bank maintenance fees; cost of transfers out to other accounts; reconciliation costs	Transactions	Cash & Accounts
Cash Flows	T04	Number of wire transfer requests after 2 or 3 pm	Transactions	Cash & Accounts
Cash Flows	T05	Number of lost transaction instructions	Transactions	Cash & Accounts
Liquidity	T06	Average end of day available balance	Transactions	Cash & Accounts
Cost of Capital	T07	Average daily/weekly net cash flows from forecast	Transactions	Cash & Accounts
Liquidity	T08	Cash position	Transactions	Cash & Accounts
Liquidity	T09	Trapped cash as a percentage of cash	Transactions	Cash & Accounts
Cost of Capital	T10	Available cash vs. target	Transactions	Cash & Accounts
Cost of Capital	T11	Cash position as a percentage if sales	Transactions	Cash & Accounts
Cash Flows	T12	Total banking collections costs (worldwide); soft dollar cost of availability	Transactions	Cash & Accounts
Cash Flows	T13	Total banking disbursements costs; soft dollar cost of backwards value plus float benefit	Transactions	Cash & Accounts
Cash Flows	T14	Ratio/percentage of electronic vs. paper instruments for collections and disbursements	Transactions	Cash & Accounts
Cash Flows	T15	Cycle time for finalising cash position	Transactions	Cash & Accounts
Cash Flows	T16	Cycle time for cash journal entries	Transactions	Cash & Accounts
Liquidity	T17	Collections float (bank deposit to good value)	Transactions	Cash & Accounts
Liquidity	T18	Disbursements float	Transactions	Cash & Accounts
Cost of Capital	R01	Actual weighted average interest rate	Risk	IR Risk

(Continued)

TABLE 27.2 *Continued*

Primary Main Metric	Ref No	Metric	Area (t/R/B)	Sub-Area
Stability	R02	Future value of interest expense assuming all floating rates fixed with FRA's	Risk	IR Risk
Stability	R03	Earnings-at-risk (book return basis)	Risk	IR Risk
Stability	R04	Value-at-risk (total return basis)	Risk	IR Risk
Stability	R05	Floating rate and fixed rate debt as % of total debt	Risk	IR Risk
Stability	R06	Weighted average maturity	Risk	IR Risk
Stability	R07	Duration	Risk	IR Risk
Stability	R08	Convexity	Risk	IR Risk
Cost of Capital	R09	Company's spread above T's for specific maturities	Risk	IR Risk
Stability	R10	DV01	Risk	IR Risk
Stability	R12	Counterparty exposure or position limits	Risk	FX Risk
Cash Flows	R13	Average transaction size	Risk	FX Risk
Cash Flows	R14	% of trades <$500,000 equivalent	Risk	FX Risk
Cash Flows	R15	Bank winning bid percentage	Risk	FX Risk
Cash Flows	R16	Average pips between the high and low bids	Risk	FX Risk
Stability	R17	Bank settlement failures	Risk	FX Risk
Stability	R18	Company's settlement failures	Risk	FX Risk
Cash Flows	R19	All-in cost of foreign currency payments by payment instrument	Risk	FX Risk
Cash Flows	R20	Opportunities for error	Risk	FX Risk
Cash Flows	R21	Sigma	Risk	FX Risk
Cash Flows	R22	Actual errors	Risk	FX Risk
Stability	R24	Derivative mark-to-market	Risk	FX Risk
Stability	R25	Future value of existing hedges against	Risk	FX Risk
Stability	R26	Hedged positions (i.e., not full expected position)	Risk	FX Risk
Stability	R27	Full forecast position	Risk	FX Risk
Stability	R28	Hedge gain/loss only	Risk	FX Risk
Stability	R29	Hedge plus underlying gain/loss	Risk	FX Risk
Stability	R30	Average transaction rate	Risk	FX Risk
Stability	R31	FAS 133 ineffectiveness	Risk	FX Risk
Stability	R32	P&L FX related to balance sheet FX exposures	Risk	FX Risk
Stability	R33	Calculation of forward premium/ discount	Risk	FX Risk
Stability	R34	Forecast to actual variance analysis	Risk	FX Risk

TABLE 27.2 *Continued*

Primary Main Metric	Ref No	Metric	Area (t/R/B)	Sub-Area
Cost of Capital	B01	Ratios	BS & Liquidity	Balance Sheet
Cost of Capital	B02	Credit rating	BS & Liquidity	Balance Sheet
Cost of Capital	B03	Cost of capital	BS & Liquidity	Balance Sheet
Cost of Capital	B04	Cost of debt	BS & Liquidity	Balance Sheet
Cost of Capital	B05	Cost of equity	BS & Liquidity	Balance Sheet

Disclaimer: These metrics are indicative for teaching purposes only. You need to ascertain the use of each for your organisation.

TREASURY FITNESS

Treasury Fitness, introduced in Chapter 1, is a concept developed by the author and Aktrea Capital Pte Ltd, that serves as a diagnostic tool for a Treasury much in the same way that a fitness test indicates any potential points of stress or problem for a human body. The mobile App that is being developed for this book will allow first-time buyers of the book limited access to a free diagnostic fitness test for their Treasury. This feature is expected to be available from April 2013.

SUMMARY

Designing a scorecard that objectivises the entire performance gamut of an operation with the width and depth of a global corporate Treasury is a challenge for chief executive officers and chief financial officers. As in all true appraisals, having a set of balanced measures and reviewing the measures themselves periodically over time will help the firm arrive at a steady-state set of performance metrics.

28

CHAPTER TWENTY EIGHT

Banks and Service Relationships

MANY OF THE DISCUSSIONS ON transactions, balance sheet and liquidity, and risk involve the use of banking products and relationships. It can be said that the bank and the product and service capability and offerings differentiate two identically staffed and structured treasuries. Indeed, the same bank and service team can provide diametrically opposite service levels to different corporate clients. In this context, a discussion around managing the banking and service relationship, evaluating the bank's performance, and picking the right banks with a long-term relationship in mind is important and the aim of this chapter.

SAMPLE BANK ORGANISATION STRUCTURE

Banks have evolved over time to streamline their organisation to maximise customer impact. A typical commercial bank is comprised of various functions, as shown in Figure 28.1.

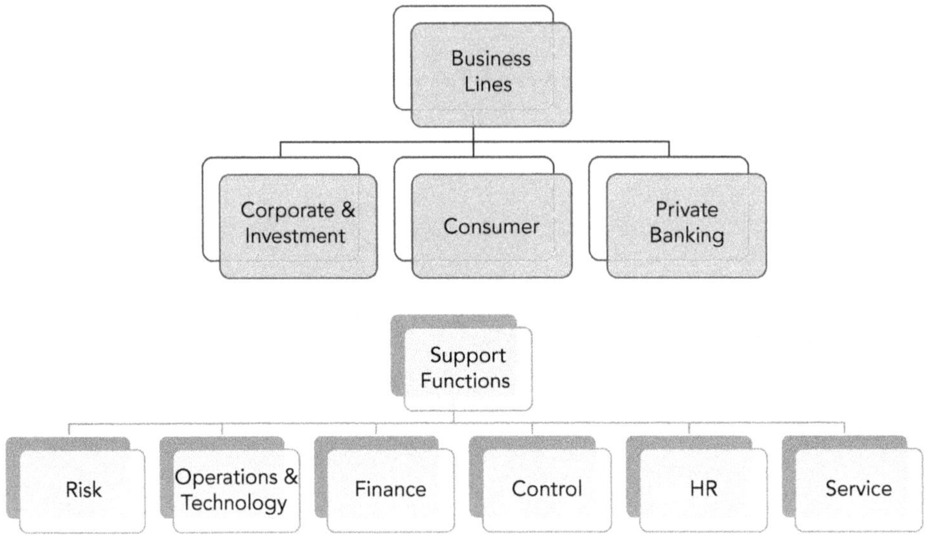

FIGURE 28.1 Typical Bank Functions

Business-wise, commercial banks have a corporate and investment (or wholesale) arm, a consumer division that caters to individual banking needs, and a private banking division that caters to high-net-worth individuals.

The key support functions are:

- Risk management, which has oversight of the credit, market, and liquidity risks of the organisation
- Operations and technology, which runs the bank operations; these may be unified across the three businesses or separate, depending on scales and technologies
- Finance
- Control, which includes the middle-office function and audit/review teams
- Human resources
- Service (sometimes reports in to operations)
- Other functions, including tax and legal

Multinational banks that are listed as banking corporations in their home country can have their entities overseas in different structures, such as subsidiary (locally incorporated and hence treated as a local firm), branch (using the same legal vehicle of the parent bank), or representative or liaison office (only for purposes of liaison and business building, but not offering any banking products or services to onshore entities).

Offshore banks or branches are legally present in tax-friendly countries or financial hubs, where simple and efficient banking and tax rules or availability of capital and investment products and opportunities and liquidity make it convenient for firms to have their accounts and transactions resident with these banks or branches.

If we zoom into the corporate and investment bank structure (as shown in Figure 28.2), we find the businesses split into relationship management and products. The relationship manager (or RM) for each client has the final responsibility for the account and covers all aspects of products, services, structuring, solutions, and issues for that client.

Since specific specialist expertise is required for many of the banking products and services in a complicated and turbulent environment, the product teams were created with responsibilities for their respective products and to work with the RM to deliver solutions for the client. The key product groups are:

- Transaction services, covering account and cash management, trade and supply chain services, and custodial services.
- Capital markets and Treasury, covering sales, trading, and origination of capital market deals. The asset liability (Treasury) function of a bank should ideally report to the chief financial officer but can be housed in the capital markets room in smaller banks or branches.
- Investment banking and corporate finance, which does the advisory, mergers and acquisitions, and other capital-related deals.

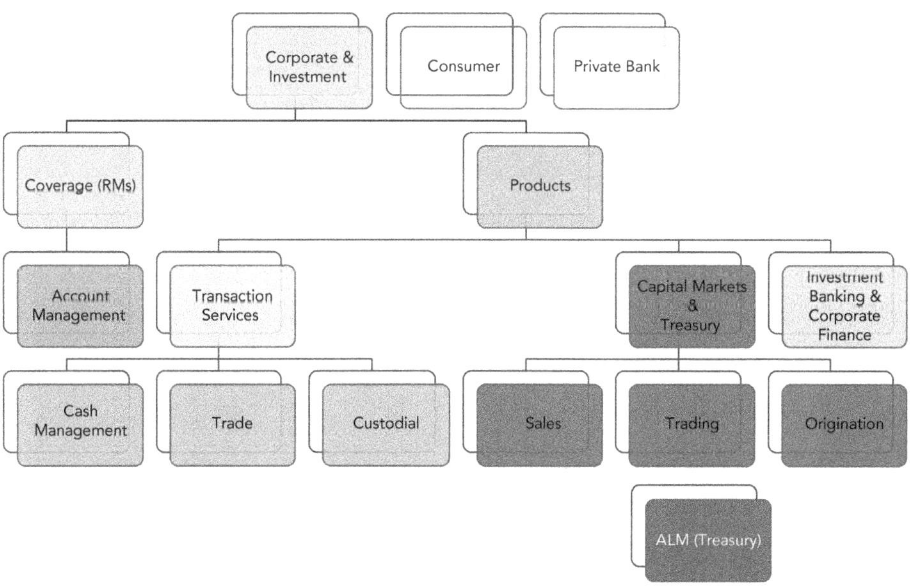

FIGURE 28.2 Corporate and Investment Banking

We delve into the touch points for a corporate in the next part of this chapter. For interested readers, we also provide a figure depicting the sample organisation of a consumer bank business in Figure 28.3.

BANKING SERVICES AND PRODUCTS FOR A CORPORATE TREASURY

Table 28.1 lists some of the key banking services and products for a corporate Treasury and their likely touch points for both the firm and the bank. For reasons of consistency, we have assumed a reasonably centralised Treasury (including shared service centre activities) and a global bank with multicountry presence.

Many of the products and services have been covered earlier in the book.

The interface with banks for banking solutions and services for transaction services is further articulated in Figure 28.4. The emphasis is on the transactions management function of corporate Treasury with some areas of balance sheet and liquidity management (such as supply chain finance and cash concentration and pooling).

The interface with banks for banking solutions and services for capital markets and investment banking and corporate finance is provided in Figure 28.5. The emphasis is on the balance sheet and liquidity management and risk management functions of corporate Treasury.

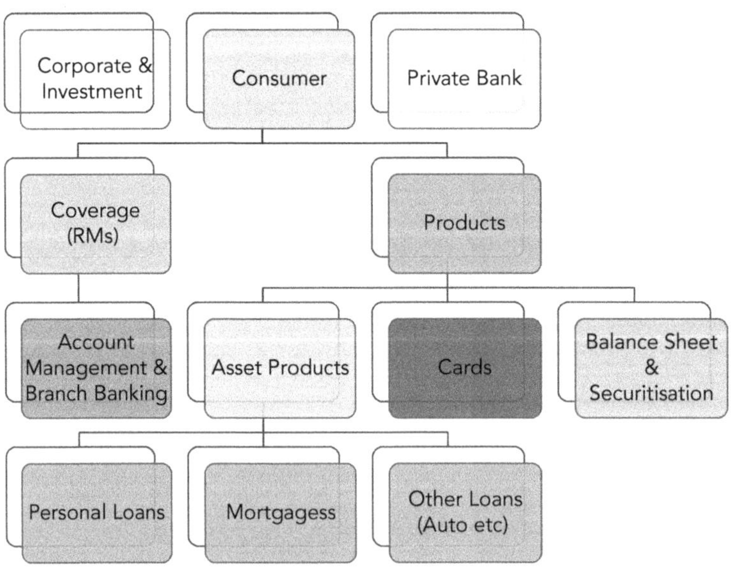

FIGURE 28.3 Consumer Banking

TABLE 28.1 Services and Products and Their Touch Points

Service or Product	Treasury Function	Company Touch Points	Bank Touch Points for
Syndicated loans	Balance sheet and liquidity	Centralised treasury	Origination, RM
Arranging debt or equity	Balance sheet and liquidity	Centralised treasury	Origination, RM
Project finance	Balance sheet and liquidity	Centralised treasury	Origination, RM
Trade and supply chain finance	Balance sheet and liquidity	Centralised treasury, supply chain, sales, procurement, subsidiaries	RM, transaction services sales, product
Working capital	Balance sheet and liquidity	Centralised treasury, subsidiaries	Global and local RM
Account management	Transactions	Centralised treasury, subsidiaries	Global and local RM, service, operations
Electronic banking	Transactions	Centralised treasury, subsidiaries	Transaction services implementation
Cash management—collections	Transactions	Centralised treasury, subsidiaries	Transaction services sales, operations
Concentration and pooling structures	Balance sheet and liquidity/transactions	Centralised treasury, subsidiaries	RM, transaction services sales and product, operations
Cash management—payments	Transactions	Centralised treasury, subsidiaries	Transaction services sales, operations
netting	Transactions	Centralised treasury, subsidiaries	RM, transaction services sales and product, operations
Value-Added services	Transactions	Centralised treasury	Global and local RM, service, operations, transaction services sales and product
Custodial services	Transactions	Centralised treasury	RM, sales, service, operations
Investment banking and corporate finance	Balance sheet and liquidity	Centralised treasury	RM, investment banker, service
Trade processing	Transactions	Centralised treasury, supply chain, sales, procurement, collections, subsidiaries	Transaction services sales and product, operations, service
Investments	Balance sheet and liquidity	Centralised treasury	RM, markets sales
Risk management execution	Risk management	Centralised treasury	Markets sales, service, operations
Structuring	Risk management	Centralised treasury	RM, markets sales and structuring

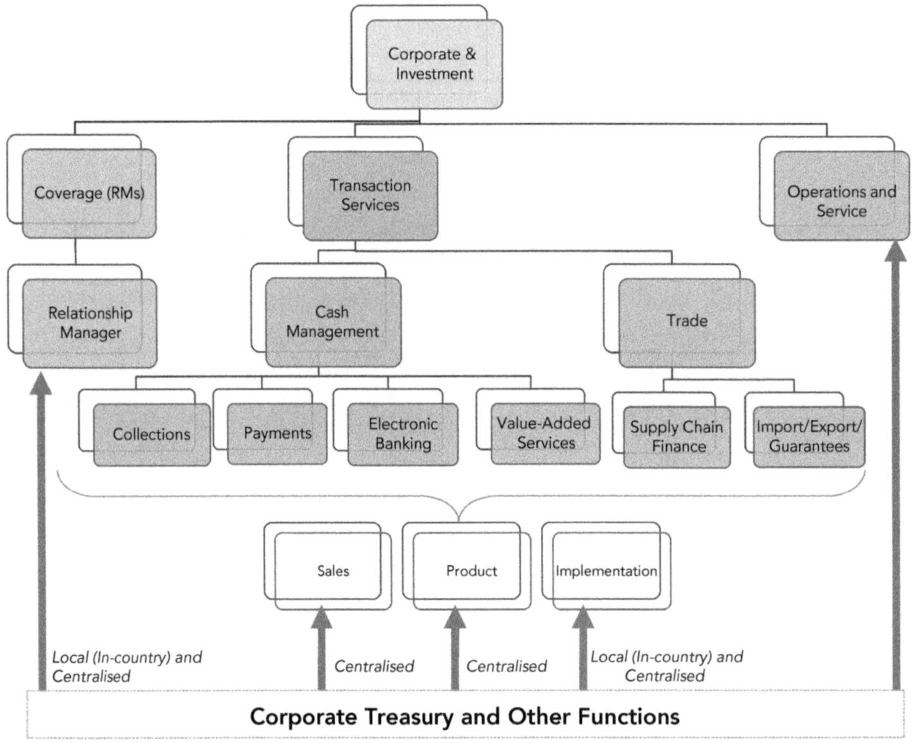

FIGURE 28.4 Transaction Services—Interface with Corporate

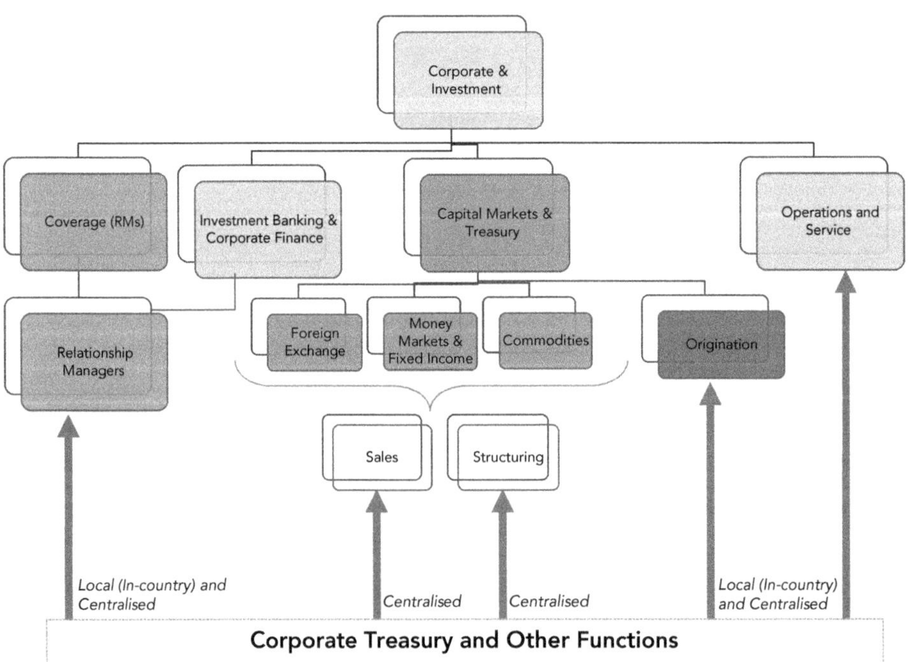

FIGURE 28.5 Capital Markets and Investment Banking and Corporate

BANK SELECTION AND RFP PROCESS

We went through the request for proposal (RFP) process for a system service provider when moving to a new system. Why do we need to do the same with banks? There could be different reasons for doing so.

- **Treasury design**. The Treasury could be reengineering its design elements, such as systems, processes, and centralisation, based on process reviews or project implementation proposals.
- **Pricing**. A bank review or significant pressure on the bottom line could trigger a review of banking services pricing and hence the opportunity to look at the banking service provider itself. I usually prefer to have this as a more proactive measure during regular review—doing so eliminates the need to be reactive about a pricing decision and the need to change banking partners based on that decision. Some of the pricing elements to bear in mind are:
  - Transactional cost. Throughput-based pricing versus volumes-based pricing
  - Value-added services
  - Commissions
  - Benchmark-linked pricing and the liquidity of such a benchmark
  - Hidden interest and costs
  - Payment costs and float
  - Foreign collections
  - Foreign exchange and risk management spreads
  - Electronic banking charges
- **Organisational changes**. A new acquisition or takeover can trigger the need for larger operations, and a banking solution might precede a more important Treasury design review and solution.
- **Nonperformance or large operational or service issue with existing bank**. Usually, banking relationships are strong and unlikely candidates for serious misunderstanding. However, I have seen cases where a large operational issue, or the withdrawal of certain credit facilities (without going into whether the withdrawal was justified) have caused companies to issue RFPs and change banks in a short span of time.

REVIEW PROCESS

Figure 28.6 shows a self-explanatory figure of a typical bank review process.

The selection team here is more Treasury focussed, with representatives from the supply chain side (if supply chain finance is a criterion), technology (for linkages and information security), and financial control (for linkages with accounts payable/accounts receivable and bank accounting entries) usually participating. Also, a business manager and the chief operating officer could be a part of the committee.

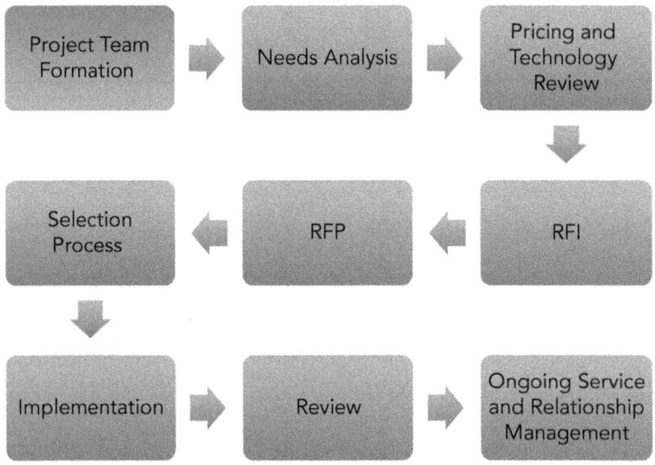

FIGURE 28.6 Bank Review Process

The needs analysis is important since it also puts into perspective the revised requirements in terms of the market and banking sector developments. Criteria are ranked or rated in terms of importance and weightage. Table 28.2 shows a typical set of criteria with weights for bank selection. Weights can vary depending on the requirements of the firm. The Excel sheet provided on the accompanying website (www.wiley.com/go/treasuryhandbook) gives a template that the reader can amend to suit company requirements.

Current relationship banks and market leaders are factored in for the request for information (RFI) part of the process, with strengths and weaknesses of each being an input into short-listing for the RFI itself.

The inputs from the banks on the RFI serve two purposes: They help to hone the final RFP document and provide enough information to short-list the banks for the RFP process. It is usually a good practice to call all existing banks unless there has been a serious issue with one.

Some of the decision points and degree of relevance across multi-country and single-country operations are given in Table 28.3.

The RFP stage comes next. Preparation of the RFP document is a challenging but interesting project. The RFP contents should include:

- Products and services
- Pricing and execution
- Bank performance and relationship management
- Technology
- Banking implementation
- Outsourcing
- Value-added products
- Geographical coverage

TABLE 28.2 Bank Selection Criteria

Factor	Weightage
Technology	
Depth and breadth of platform	2
Connectivity and coverage	2
Information security	2
Contingency planning	2
Total Weightage	**8**
Integration & Implementation	
Experience level and ownership	2
Degree of documentation	2
History on similar implementations	2
Total Weightage	**6**
Outsourcing	
Turnaround	1
Cost	1
Flexibility	1
Total Weightage	**3**
Supply Chain Finance	
Continuity of platform	1
Understanding of supply chain	1
Criteria for supplier/customer financing	1
Total Weightage	**3**
Coverage	
Regulations and laws	2
Regulator relationships	2
Track record of approvals	2
Depth of country presence	2
Cross-country coordination	2
Central point of contact	2
Branch network	2
Corr bank & vendor network	2
World-wide presence	2
Total Weightage	**18**
Products & Services	
Account structure	2
EB: Information, access, infosec	2
Payments	2
Collections	2
Cheque facilities: PAP, FCY	2
Capital markets services	2
Credit facility	2
Trade services	2
Others	2
Total Weightage	**18**

(Continued)

TABLE 28.2 *Continued*

Factor	Weightage
Pricing and Execution	
Pricing	3
Value	3
Timings and cut-off	3
Availability schedules	2
Service quality	3
Back ups arrangement	2
Services disaster recovery	2
Innovation	1
Total Weightage	**19**
Bank Performance & Relationship Management	
Relationship team	4
Contacts & escalation matrix	2
Documentation requirements	2
Process requirements	4
Systems requirements	2
Implementation schedules	2
Awards	2
References	2
Profitability	1
Language capability	2
Ownership	2
Total Weightage	**25**
TOTAL SCORE:	**100**

TABLE 28.3 Some Decision Points Between Multi-Country and Single-Country operations

Criterion	Multi-Country Operation	Localised Operation
Coverage—international	High	Low
Coverage—in-country (includes correspondents)	High	High
Clearing centres	Medium	High
Access channels	High	Low
Technology and integration (including EB)	High	Medium
Turnarounds and cutoff times	Medium	High
Value-added service	High	Low

The coverage must be the scope of products and services required by the firm. Potential areas (those envisioned in the future) must also be covered, and functionalities in support, such as technology and information security, must be addressed. Next we list sample product/service inclusions in an RFP:

- Account structure
- Electronic banking: information, access, information security
- Payments
- Collections
- Cheque facilities: payable at par, Foreign Currency (FCY)
- Capital markets services
- Credit facilities
- Trade services
- Foreign exchange execution
- Investments coverage and product availability

Table 28.1 shows a typical suite of products and services.

The evaluation or selection process then comes into play, when each bank parades its wares and presents to the committee on its capabilities. Some of the aspects to remember are:

- **Compare apples and apples**. Not all banking offerings are standardised. A strong RFP document will articulate the requirements unambiguously, so banks' responses will be standardised.
- **Pricing is not the only aspect**. Attractive pricing may not always be a differentiating criterion; it is easy to run with the cheapest bank, but coverage is critical—service quality, reliability, and credit are some of the factors for which payment of a premium is worth every penny.
- **References make a difference**. Talking to references, including ones who have had issues, is always good to do.
- **Look at the failures and information learned**. No bank has a 100% track record. Banks that are honest up front about areas in which they have failed in the past could be more transparent and honest with their approach, and sometimes this reflects the desire to work harder.
- **Access to bankers**. Irrespective of how good a bank is, the banker makes the difference between service and great service. Likewise, for a pan-country or global solution, it is important to have round-the-clock access to someone in the bank who can address issues and solve problems—in a global firm, issues do not tend to time themselves to occur during daylight hours at central Treasury. Hence, access to empowered bankers is a must-have.
- **Benchmarking and comparison**. It is important to be fair and unbiased and to look at all aspects as a team.
- **Consider the total cost including time**. Time for implementation and turnaround has a cost element and is a critical component for comparison.

- **Credit ratings**. The banks' credit ratings are very important. Longevity of the banking partner is a given, and sometimes the more attractively priced banks, especially for investments, are not always the most attractive from a credit point of view.

SERVICE AND RELATIONSHIP MANAGEMENT

Once the banking implementation has been done, it is important to benchmark and continuously review the bank's performance. Service reviews every quarter and senior management reviews annually are important. For this, feedback must be taken across every point of contact, and feedback has to be honest, with the aim of ensuring seamless delivery that the banking partner has to promise and deliver.

We next go through a case study of a corporate that was evaluating banking partners for an RFP.

CASE STUDY: WHICH BANK WOULD YOU PICK?

Three banks—What Bank, Which Bank, and How Bank—have been short-listed from a set of 10 banks. All of them have the same scores. Which one would you pick for your organisation? Table 28.4 has the scores across the parameters.

TABLE 28.4 Selecting the Right Banking Partner

		Vendors		
Factor	**Weightage**	**What Bank**	**How Bank**	**Which Bank**
Technology				
Depth and breadth of platform	2	2	1	1
Connectivity and coverage	2	2	1	2
Information security	2	2	1	2
Contingency planning	2	2	1	1
Total Weightage	**8**	**8**	**4**	**6**
Integration & Implementation				
Experience level and ownership	2	2	1	1
Degree of documentation	2	1	1	1
History on similar implementations	2	1	1	1
Total Weightage	**6**	**4**	**3**	**3**
Outsourcing				
Turnaround	1	1	1	0
Cost	1	1	1	0
Flexibility	1	1	1	0
Total Weightage	**3**	**3**	**3**	**0**

TABLE 28.4 *Continued*

		Vendors		
Factor	**Weightage**	**What Bank**	**How Bank**	**Which Bank**
Supply Chain Finance				
Continuity of platform	1	0	1	0
Understanding of supply chain	1	0	1	0
Criteria for supplier/customer financing	1	0	1	0
Total Weightage	**3**	**0**	**3**	**0**
Coverage				
Regulations and laws	2	2	1	2
Regulator relationships	2	2	2	2
Track record of approvals	2	2	1	2
Depth of country presence	2	2	2	2
Cross-country coordination	2	2	1	2
Central point of contact	2	2	2	1
Branch network	2	2	1	1
Corr bank & vendor network	2	2	1	2
World-wide presence	2	2	2	2
Total Weightage	**18**	**18**	**13**	**16**
Products & Services				
Account structure	2	1	2	2
EB: information, access, infosec	2	1	2	1
Payments	2	1	2	2
Collections	2	1	2	2
Cheque Facilities: PAP, FCY	2	1	2	2
Capital markets services	2	1	2	1
Credit facility	2	1	2	2
Trade services	2	1	2	1
Others	2	0	2	0
Total Weightage	**18**	**8**	**18**	**13**
Pricing and Execution				
Pricing	3	1	3	3
Value	3	2	1	3
Timings and cut-off	3	1	3	3
Availability schedules	2	1	1	2
Service quality	3	2	1	3
Back ups arrangement	2	1	1	2
Services disaster recovery	2	1	1	2
Innovation	1	0	1	1
Total Weightage	**19**	**9**	**12**	**19**

(Continued)

TABLE 28.4 *Continued*

		Vendors		
Factor	**Weightage**	**What Bank**	**How Bank**	**Which Bank**
Bank Performance & Relationship Management				
Relationship team	4	3	3	1
Contacts & escalation matrix	2	2	2	1
Documentation requirements	2	2	2	2
Process requirements	4	3	2	4
Systems requirements	2	2	1	2
Implementation schedules	2	2	1	2
Awards	2	2	1	0
References	2	2	1	1
Profitability	1	0	1	0
Language capability	2	2	1	1
Ownership	2	2	1	1
Total Weightage	**25**	**22**	**16**	**15**
TOTAL SCORE:	**100**	**72**	**72**	**72**

SUMMARY

The banking partner remains the most critical of the external agencies with which Treasury interfaces. The banking industry, even as it transforms itself, is aligning itself more and more to be a solution-centric, advisory, long-term service partner to the multinational organisation, which makes the selection of banks even more important to the financial success of the firm around the world.

CHAPTER TWENTY NINE

29

Operations and Control Checklist

THE IMPORTANT ASPECTS OF OPERATIONS and control have been covered earlier. In this chapter, we discuss some of the key processes consolidated across all aspects of the Treasury function and provide an important checklist of items that need to be factored in as a step towards a more efficient, tighter, smoother operations process. A checklist for some of the key controls in the Treasury process is also provided online in the accompanying website.

Organisations may use this checklist as a basic core to build their checks, processes, and balances.

LIST OF PROCESSES

The processes of Treasury across various functions are classified in Figure 29.1.

A detailed list of Treasury processes is provided in Appendix F. This is a generic list of processes and can vary from firm to firm. An attempt has been made to distinguish

FIGURE 29.1 Treasury Processes

by activity, and each of these processes will have inputs from some other process and can hand off to another process. It is important to draw out process maps for each of these processes and to document and ensure that the handoffs are appropriately controlled and fed.

RIGHT CONTROL AT TREASURY

The objective of a control is to ensure that the processes, procedures, systems, and policies that have been designed and implemented are being followed in letter and spirit and to determine if there are any chinks in the Treasury world that could cause potential damage, financial or otherwise, to the firm.

The control process, for example, is not expected to cover what happens when there is a breach of process, or an excess of a risk limit, or a liquidity shortfall, or a systems failure. The control review does not look at the corrective action to be done in these situations. Those should already be documented under the Treasury policy and the various process notes approved by management. The control process should look for instances where these are not being detected and whether the right procedures have been followed in the normal course of business or in the event of detection of exceptions.

Controls define the robustness of the process, which in turn determines the reduction in the chances of anything going wrong. In a way, control processes are risk reviews of the dependence of the entire organisation on Treasury processes.

Control processes work across various themes and can be classified as shown in Figure 29.2.

The infrastructure themes focus on the backbone of the Treasury function including technology, middle office, and information security.

The operations theme dwells on the various non-risk processes, including cash and accounts, investments, borrowing and lending, intercompany, reporting, reconciliation, and back-office activities.

Policy and organisation compliance includes front-office activities, roles, responsibilities, and regulatory aspects.

Risk occupies a separate section since it involves many complicated aspects, and auditing and reviewing of risk is a specialised activity in itself.

CONTROL CHECKS AND REVIEWS

Checks and reviews are designed to reduce disruptions to processes and functions or leakages in money flow owing to intentional or unintentional reasons. In some cases, the checks are post facto and management needs to be aware of the potential issues should any lapse be detected after it has occurred.

Periodicity

The periodicity and frequency of control reviews and checks must be designated by senior management and documented in the Treasury policy.

FIGURE 29.2 Classification of Treasury Control Themes

Self-Review and Independence of Main Review

Each unit must do its own quarterly review—a person independent of an activity must be designated to review the activity of another person. Each person or process must have its own checklist for control. Annual process and control reviews must be done by persons independent of the activities. Ideally the audit department or an independent control unit should be responsible for the process and control review.

Independence of Data Sources

The data for review should be obtained from independent sources as much as possible. Where physical records have to be assessed, the reviewer must determine the dates for the samples.

Sampling

In case of physical verification where system data cannot be used (e.g., manual deal tickets, invoices, etc.), the reviewer must decide on the samples and use a statistically verifiable measure. Also, it is important not to have dates close to each other in date-wise samples.

Reporting

Reporting of the results of the review should be directly to the Treasurer and the chief financial officer (CFO). Before the results are circulated to the board, the Treasurer must be allowed an opportunity to respond to the issues raised. An appropriate assessment of the responses must be made prior to the finalisation and circulation to the audit committee and other senior management. Each process can be assigned a rating with a corresponding degree of criticality. Table 29.1 shows example ratings.

Corrective Action

The reviewer must agree with the Treasurer on the corrective action steps to be taken along with the timeline for each. These steps must be tracked and a post-corrective verification done for each element that has been corrected.

TABLE 29.1 Recommended Rating of Each Process

Rating	Description
1	Low risk and high efficiency and control
2	Robust, but some long-term issues need to be addressed
3	Needs attention
4	Potential hazard—needs attention on priority
5	Emergency—critical issue

SOME COMMON CAUSES FOR ERROR AND CONTROL LAPSES

Some common causes for lapses in control and possible errors are:

- No maker-checker in the process, or not followed
- Password sharing
- No independence of processing and transacting or review
- Data sources inadequate or not independent
- Handoffs process weak, especially manual ones or through e-mail
- System rights for front and back offices for the same employee
- Review process not rigorous
- Ageing of exception items not adequate
- Invalidated and unsecure worksheets used for reporting and tracking
- Lack of awareness of one function of the roles and responsibilities of other functions

Appendix G (online at www.wiley.com/go/treasuryhandbook) provides some of the control elements that can be used as a basis for a checklist.

The next case study highlights the importance of controllership in growth markets and practical and experiential learning from an industry veteran.

CASE STUDY: AN EXPERIENTIAL LOOK AT CONTROLLERSHIP AND GOVERNANCE OF TREASURY IN EMERGING MARKETS

This may be the case study that saves your career. Once, an old manufacturing controller gave me the greatest advice for a financial person: "If you want to get ahead, exceed your budgets; if you want to keep your job, make your forecasts, and if you want to lose your job, fail an audit." While we are naturally inclined to the glamour part of our responsibilities, like strategy, portfolio management, or capital structure, we should only tend to those after the foundations are met.

Every business requires that management insure its fiduciary responsibility with controls. "Failing an audit" might not sound like a career-ending move, but it certainly will be a major detractor should there be theft or gross negligence. First, you must ensure that governance fundamentals are achieved for proper reporting and asset control. Thereafter, focus on understanding the business dynamics, which allows you to make your forecasts and, eventually, to add value through strategy and creativity to exceed your budgets.

Having been with multiple global Fortune 50 companies (IBM, Tyco International, Cisco Systems) and had the privilege to live and work on three continents (America, Europe, Latin America) over the past 30 years, I could share all

(Continued)

sorts of wonderful stories of international capital, financing, and pricing relevant to Treasury, but the subject of this piece is an essential part of operations that all treasurers must first attend to.

Structure: Think Global, Transact Local

The emerging markets of the world have much higher multiples of growth than developed markets. Corporations that seek growth will establish business operations in the high-growth markets that are expanding their populations and gross domestic product per capita. However, these emerging markets pose a high-risk, high-reward environment. For every opportunity of outstanding growth, there are multiple other traps to be considered, such as local business customs, terms, regulations, and competition. For Treasurers, the allure of high yields on investments is surrounded with complicated currency risks: cash export regulations, tax implications, and financing requirements.

At first, basic Treasury activities to establish working capital will suffice with cash management from headquarters coupled with local banking relationships. Eventually, the local business will demand greater Treasury participation in accounts receivable, collections, payables, hedging transactions, credit management, financing major projects, reciprocal banking transactions, and government import/export relations. While it is alluring to maintain a centralised Treasury operation that supports basic activities, eventually the emerging markets will demand higher managerial attention owing to the complexity of working environments and growth rates and opportunities of businesses.

Having one centralised global Treasury team in a major financial centre is certainly beneficial for controllership purposes, but there is no substitute for local knowledge and participation. Hence, most major companies establish a central Treasury function for uniform strategy and policy setting but have local Treasurer presence in major emerging markets to gain competitive advantage. There are various structural models to consider based on the international importance of your business versus the local involvement required. A very high degree of international business will dictate that a company has a global perspective in its Treasury function; else, it will just have a national parochial view. On the other hand, it is important to establish the degree of local involvement of the Treasury function. For some companies, it is very low, particularly for exporters of capital goods. For other companies, it may be very high as local operations demand significant investment, significant headcount, and complex transactions.

Which one is best for your company?

The answer depends on the level of global business in your company versus the level of local Treasury involvement. The following Global Treasury Structure Matrix (Figure 29.3) should assist with the options.

On one end of the spectrum, one would have a "national" Treasury team if business was mostly local. As the business becomes more global but does not require local involvement in transactions, then a central "global" function can be established. This is the case for Cisco Systems, which exports its networking products, priced in US dollars, around the world. They make all major decisions in their California headquarters, with some assistance from a small team in Switzerland. The "local" model is more appropriate for a company that is expanding into one or two new emerging markets in a significant way. For example, some large US agricultural companies establish secondary operations in the rich terrain of Brazil or

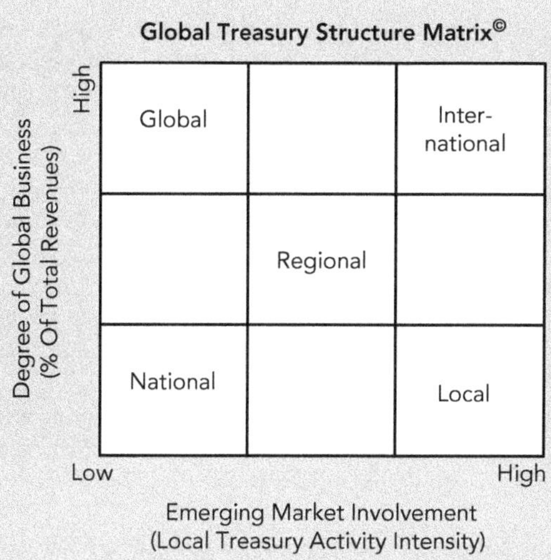

FIGURE 29.3 Global Treasury Structure Matrix

Source and Copyright: Mick Lopez, Lopez L.L.C.

major global energy companies explore Russian oil fields. They will need to have to have a local Treasurer team to supervise the large amount of investment and activity in those two countries. This Treasurer will usually report to headquarters but have a large amount of local freedom. As some firms grow into more of emerging markets, it makes sense to have a "regional" approach with several Treasury teams (e.g., Asia-Pacific, East Europe/Middle East/Africa, South America) that cover a larger geography with some local knowledge. Finally, large companies with most of their revenues from global customers that demand local involvement will require an "international" approach. This entails having a strong central Treasury team at headquarters but with delegation of local activities to some key regional Treasury offices. The main difference between a regional and an international approach is the level of centralisation of strategies and policies. The regional model is usually a stepping-stone for the international model as companies mature because a coordinated global strategy is required for effective Treasury governance.

Regardless of the model used, it is important that the global leader effectively set the Treasury strategy and effectively monitors its implementation. If every region or business unit has their own strategy, you run a high risk of ineffective Treasury operations and effectiveness. One group may be paying to hedge against one currency, while another is paying to hedge in its favor. Yet another group may be saving cash at low rates, at the expense of another that is borrowing at high interest rates.

The most basic controllership consideration for organisational design in emerging markets is to strive for segregation of duties. Given the relative small size of revenues in new emerging markets, affordability of large teams is rarely justified on an expense-to-revenue basis. Instead, the basis of affordability should be the high risk of loss if all Treasury activities are in the hands of one or few individuals. Certainly, a basic control is to have all major transactions reviewed and approved, in writing, by more than two people, but that is not always feasible with a high number of transactions.

(*Continued*)

To avoid opportunities for fraud, a small Treasury team in an emerging market should be complemented with assistance from other finance or operation groups. For example, the confirmation of Treasury transactions from the banks should be sent to another individual than the person doing the transaction. In this day, with all the digital imaging software, bank records can be easily manipulated by an individual. A currency trader could properly report all the losses, but keep half of the profits from trades as he moves them into his own account. The auditors could be fooled by documentation that has been expertly forged electronically; only an unusual confirmation from the bank would lead to suspicion. A simple request for the bank to send all confirmations to the accounting department, for quarterly reconciliation by the accountants, would provide a basic segregation of duty aspect. There are many more processes that require this perspective.

In summary, keep a very high level of strategic overview for your global organisational design but, at the local level, maintain a very high degree of checks and balances to thwart any person from opportunities to collude against the company's financial well-being.

Structured Governance: Rules and Tools

Organisational culture drives the ethics of a company. The task of developing a strong ethical culture is the main responsibility of any corporate executive, for it is known in audit committees that the tone from the top is the single biggest indicator of corporate compliance. If a climate of integrity and honesty is repeatedly exalted by all levels of management, it will become part of the corporate ethos.

In emerging markets, the concepts of ethics may be entirely different. You must be wary of ingrained corruption in some countries, where it is acceptable in daily life to bribe a local politician for any kind of favor. The World Bank estimates that corruption accounts for losses amounting to 0.5 percent of the global GNP each year, and certainly, a higher percentage for emerging markets. If you are astray of the law, such as United States' FCPA (Foreign Corrupt Practices Act) and United Kingdom Bribery Act, you could face criminal charges.

For Treasury, where there are large amounts of cash transactions, having ethics is essential. Ensure that the company's corporate values clearly demand honesty, transparency, and accountability. These values should be visible to all and repeatedly mentioned. It is great governance practice to have dedicated channels of communication to the audit committee, especially to protect the identities of whistle-blowers—individuals who risk their careers to highlight corporate issues. Ethical training and annual certification are great concepts easily done through the Web. Sometimes businesspeople get caught up in a vortex for profit maximisation and must be reminded of the ethical parameters. Furthermore, every time corporate values and morals are tested, executives must be brutally consistent to get the message across. I have seen multiple cases before audit committees where high performers in the company have a small ethical misstep. Regardless of their importance to the profits of the company, the individuals should be reprimanded or terminated, because ethics are more important than profits. In any organisation. In any context.

All Treasury operations must have clear and established strategies, policies, and procedures. If they are not written down, they simply do not exist. Policies are the best insurance that a Treasurer can have. If a key employee leaves the company, you will find policies to be invaluable. If there are unusual circumstances, the policies will guide the team to do as expected. Employees are naturally hesitant to write down their daily process and procedures, for it is tedious work that constantly needs change. In a large organisation that had neglected its policies for years, we threw a "Saturday Policy Party," where we invited the employees to come in exclusively to write their procedures and have some pizza, with fun games in the afternoon. In another company, we had a $100 bounty for every desk procedure. Finally, I insist that all transactional employees have updated procedures and checklists signed by their managers at their annual performance evaluation.

Documentation of segregation of duties in a Treasury function is fundamental. Ensure that you have clear delegation matrices and adequate supervision for basic control features. Even if you must leverage other finance or operations people, strive for key segregation of duties for basic controls. Even if you do, be wary of collusion. There is a famous case of collusion of a complete Treasury team of about a dozen individuals in a major tech company in Brazil in the 1980s. During this hyperinflationary era, the whole Treasury team conspired over years to sweep the funds on Friday afternoon into their own personal accounts, gain significant interest, and re-deposit back on Monday morning. The team was audited multiple times by headquarters, but they had covered the tracks well. They were only caught because of their own greed, as is often the case. The team cut off a former employee, who blew the whistle on them to corporate auditors.

The greatest advent for governance has been the emergence of integrated Treasury modules into enterprise resource planning (ERP) systems. However, the ease, flexibility, and economies of spreadsheet programs make them the most prevalent Treasury management systems today. The overuse of spreadsheets by management is a controllership nightmare. They are inherently unreliable, not integrated, and prone to calculation mistakes over time. Since minor errors in cash management can lead to huge expenses, integrated Treasury modules provide a greater degree of reliability. They are worth the investment for global reporting, even if parallel spreadsheet systems for analysis are maintained.

All of this is relatively easy to implement. You can hire the global accounting and auditing firms to consult for you to ensure that you have a proper set of desk procedures, controls, and segregation of duties. You can also leverage banking relationships for prevalent Treasury strategies and policies. All the large ERP firms and IT consultants can implement integrated systems. Finally, there are multiple consultants that specialise in Treasury matters, such as Aktrea Capital, that can assist, implement, or fine-tune basic governance.

Testing: Inspect to Get Respect

Good controllership entails establishing, measuring, and controlling processes. Once the processes and systems are established, the real work of controls starts. You should create a corporate culture where testing is expected and welcomed. In many societies, asking many questions and asking for documentation may seem intrusive or distrustful, so management must ensure that it is seen in a positive light and reward good behavior.

The usual test mechanism is to have corporate audits descend into emerging market Treasury teams for a couple of weeks. They will pore over policies and procedures to insure that they are being followed. That is why it is important that they be well established and written down. The audit team will also test for major transactions and cash balances. They will look at good COSO and SOX 404 practices. It

(Continued)

is important to have these audits done on a random and consistent basis, to keep everyone alert. However, one cannot rely exclusively on them because they are not meant to detect fraud and, especially, because most corporate auditors are not Treasury experts.

The best-controlled environments have a large degree of continuous self-assessment. Each Treasury team should report against established control metrics (e.g., bank accounts reconciled, daily investments updated, accounts receivable collected) to compare various historical trends, forecasts, and benchmarks. It is a great idea to have individual checklists for daily activities, based on an annual calendar.

There is no substitute for the global Treasurer to come visit the Treasury desks at emerging markets. It creates great teamwork, and serves to educate both teams about the nuances of their different roles. I have found that more is learned from one dinner conversation than days of telephone conferences. Treasurers usually have a broader strategic perspective, but it is prudent to always inquire about the controls, postures, and self-audits.

Peer reviews are an excellent way to have a friendly approach to testing. Treasury teams from another region or headquarters will visit an emerging markets operation for a week or two. This is a great chance for teamwork, but also for cross-pollination of ideas. It is important to have the visiting teams perform basic audit tests to prepare for the real audits later in the year.

A very important safeguard is to have background checks on all your employees in Treasury. This is a very inexpensive cost in most countries and can save you from the embarrassment of hiring a professional thief. In one major company I worked for in the United States, I noticed that we had a contractual employee performing state sales tax returns and payments for over three years. I asked that she be made a full employee to recognise her "outstanding work over the years." The employee came up with all sorts of excuses why she did not want to be a full-time employee, which required a background check. It turned out that she had a false identity and was a convicted felon who had been falsifying records and signatures to defraud our company. Last time I heard of her, Interpol had found her in Spain doing something similar. Had we had a background check, we would have avoided the losses.

If you suspect anything, it is better to have a deep forensic test performed by an outside expert. Consultants will dig deep into all the cash flow transactions and have a higher degree of finding fraud. In some countries, it may be prudent to have routine credit checks on key employees to see if they are financially secure. If warranted under special circumstances, you may have private detectives determine whether the lifestyle of your local team is justified by their salaries. We had a case in Southeast Asia where a new collections leader was performing extraordinarily, collecting very old accounts, but at a small discount that was justified based on the cost of money. Tipped off by an extravagant lifestyle, an investigation led us to a kickback mechanism where a part of the discount of the settlement was transferred to the employee.

From an operational perspective, you should also test your team to be ready for different situations. In emerging markets, it will just be a matter of time before there is a dramatic change in the environment. During the annual planning cycle, the Treasury team should have various scenarios for currencies, interest rates, hedge prices, and local regulations. It is almost guaranteed that there will never be an exact plan as one started with, but it is the process itself that creates the right thinking. Having played out policies under different scenarios is much better than having to do it when the situation changes.

Finally, prepare your team for the unexpected. One way to make it fun is to actually run random stress tests on the emerging markets Treasury teams. You can unexpectedly call the teams with a particular situation, such as a currency devaluation, major bank system failures, closure of repatriation of funds, or credit crisis. For a couple of days, you ask the team to work on the project after hours. You can actually make it a positive learning experience, and make sure you reward them.

Train to Retain—The Value of Great People

The mark of all high-performance organisations is great leadership and outstanding personnel. This is even more important in emerging markets because of the usual lack of qualified personnel. As markets grow, the demand for talent is much higher than the supply of the local pool.

There are some markets that are growing so fast that the local Treasury talent pool is just a revolving door of people from one major international organisation to another. CFOs quickly find that there is only a small set of individuals with fluent multicultural, multilinguistic, and international accounting knowledge. The local talent knows that every time they switch companies, they will gain a salary premium, so there are escalating payroll costs. However, of greater impact to the organisation is the perpetual loss of institutional knowledge every time the local Treasurer leaves for another opportunity. If companies just offer monetary compensation, employees are much more likely to leave for the next best offer.

Talent retention is probably the single biggest concern for continuity of Treasury operations in developing markets. In my experience, the best tool for establishing longevity of emerging market teams is to develop a very high degree of trust and respect. Management must be engaged with the local Treasurer.

For international teams, having clear and constant communication is essential for these teams can be thousands of miles away from headquarters. People who feel part of a global team are more likely to stay longer. Having personal contact also helps to establish bonds. These should actually be regularly scheduled in-person meetings in emerging markets and also at global headquarters. Consider a lengthy visitation period at executive housing for one or two quarters so that new employees from emerging markets get acclimated to corporate values and feel like part of the global team.

It is very common for new Treasury operations in developing markets to bring in expatriate leaders to set up the operations and establish the firm's values and beliefs. While this certainly serves to get a qualified individual with great trust, it certainly comes at very high expenditure. When you add international assignment bonus, living expenses, family relocation, tax equalisation, and travel to an individual's base salary, you may pay two to three times more than if they remain in their home country. The goal for expatriates would be to establish operations but quickly in two or three years, and establish a local leadership team in Treasury that can effectively take over at substantial savings. The local leadership will provide benefits of local relationships with government, customers, and banks that an expatriate will take years to gain. If local team members do not see a career path to the local Treasurer's office, they may not be motivated to stay.

(Continued)

Career paths are never clear in this ever-changing world. However, they are a great motivational tool for young talent to stay with the firm. Having a Treasury role as part of a job rotation strategy for emerging market finance organisations is highly recommended. You will get a fresh set of talent every one to two years that will develop into great general finance managers later on. Give your local treasurers the chance to get closer to the business with an interim planning or business support role; they will be much more valuable when they return to Treasury operations. Allow local talent to apply for regional and global roles so that they feel that there is a career path with the company.

The world's top talent knows the value of education, and they value companies that invest in it. If you can, establish training programs for the finance teams. For specialised Treasury skills, it would make sense to have your key personnel attend outside conferences and training forums to learn about the latest trends and, especially, to allow networking with other firms. Sponsoring high-potential talent to an international assignment or to a global MBA program would be a great investment on an individual that will always be remembered.

Moving Markets

Managing working capital globally is challenging, but especially in developing markets, where the opportunities are large but the perils are too. Global treasurers are wise to establish clear governance and controllership principles. Losing some basis points in a transaction will pale in comparison to a major ethical breach that can bring the whole company down. Saving some pennies in travel will be meaningless when the local Treasury teams leave due to neglect.

The lifeblood of a company is entirely based on the financial liquidity of its operations. Treasurers in developing markets can safeguard financial assets through sound governance. Corporate controllership requires establishing process, measurements, and controls. At the design stage, provide clear organisational structure, detailed policies, automated tools, investment in personnel and, especially, a consistent ethical corporate culture.

These could be the soundest investments you could hope to make.

Contributed by Mick Lopez, chief financial officer, Aricent Group, a growth company in technology and innovation services, with over 11,000 employees in multiple countries.

SUMMARY

Investing in operations and control and ensuring that there is adequate infrastructure for both remains one of the key priorities for CFOs and treasurers. Some of these functions may not report directly to the Treasurer but they remain the key responsibility of the Treasurer. Ensuring continuity and smooth functioning of the Treasury and correspondingly the flow of money through the organisation, as well as ensuring that there is no slippage, will increase the chances that company will function in an incident-free and efficient manner.

CHAPTER THIRTY

30

Outsourcing

WE HAVE DISCUSSED THE BENEFITS of, and potential issues with, outsourcing Treasury and its operations. In this chapter, we examine the key elements of any outsourcing programme and discuss, item by item, items (see Figure 30.1) that need to be present when outsourcing Treasury activities. Outsourcing can be divided into four stages: selection, pre-implementation, implementation, and post-implementation.

SELECTION STAGE

The process starts from the idea origination through to the selection of the vendor.

- **Needs analysis**. A list of processes to be outsourced is determined through discussions and identification of areas that could be done more efficiently with higher control and lower cost by experts in those areas. Decision-making activities

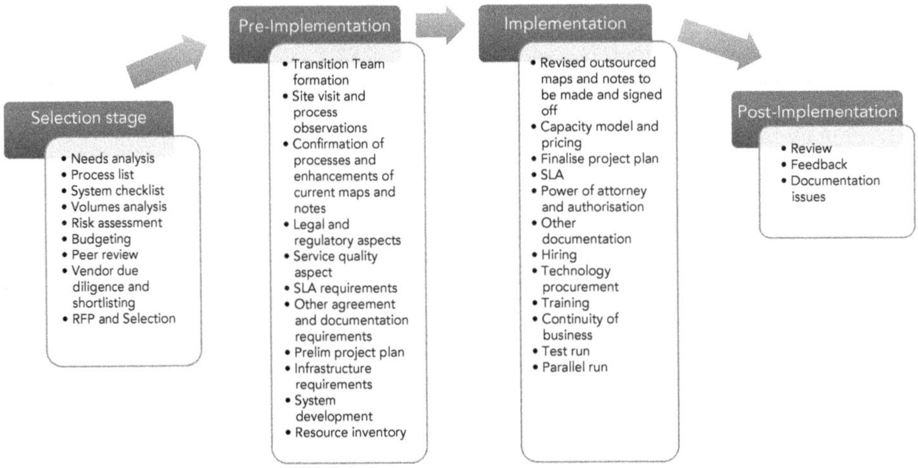

FIGURE 30.1 Outsourcing Checklist

typically rest within the firm. The existing process maps and notes provide a good indication of the activities/processes to be considered for outsourcing.

- **Process list.** The list of processes to be outsourced is prepared.
- **System checklist.** The list of system activities and systems to be outsourced is prepared, along with a list of potential system access points for each outsourcing activity.
- **Volumes analysis.** A list of transaction volumes in the future is projected for all process and system activities to be outsourced.
- **Risk assessment.** A risk assessment across various risks is made for the outsourcing project. Hedgeable or insurable risks are highlighted, and potential financial loss owing to any of the risks being manifested is also made as part of the risk assessment process.
- **Budgeting.** Approximate budgets are made, as is the break-even point where outsourcing would make financial sense.
- **Peer review.** If possible, a visit to peers who have successfully implemented outsourcing for Treasury should be made, and key elements discussed with them.
- **Vendor due diligence and short-listing.** A list of outsourcing partners/vendors is made, and due diligence is performed on the likely candidates. The request for information process (similar to the banks/system selection process) may be followed in this case.
- **Request for proposal and selection.** The final request for proposal is sent out, and the partner is selected. If possible, prior to selection, a visit should be made to the top three vendors' outsourcing sites to get a better feel of the processing on the ground. A recommended practice is to have informal discussions with processing officers to get a firsthand feel of the levels of motivation, control, and process ownership.

PRE-IMPLEMENTATION

A high degree of preparedness for the implementation stage is essential, and a few detailed but simple initiatives set the stage for a smooth execution when the time comes.

- **Transition team formation**. The project or transition team is formed; this team will run the entire migration and launch process, and should be a cross-functional team with members from both the vendor and the firm.
- **Site visit and process observations**. The vendor team starts visiting the site of operations. It performs process observations and data gathering and gains a better understanding of the systems available.
- **Confirmation of processes and enhancements of current maps and notes**. The transition team confirms that the processes are as per existing process maps and notes, and makes any amendments or enhancements to the process maps and notes to reflect current status.
- **Legal and regulatory aspects**. The legal and regulatory aspects of outsourcing must be assessed and discussed. If required, external opinion should be obtained.
- **Service quality aspect**. Preliminary discussions around service quality and turnarounds can occur. Internal clients of Treasury must be involved to determine what they expect overall Treasury service levels to be.
- **SLA requirements**. The service-level agreement (SLA) is one of the most critical elements in the outsourcing chain. The SLA requirements are drafted and discussed at this time.
- **Other agreement and documentation requirements**. A list of other documents and agreements required is prepared and drafting work begins.
- **Preliminary project plan**. A ballpark project plan is prepared with effort and timeline estimates.
- **Infrastructure requirements**. A list and estimate of infrastructure requirements, especially telecom and system, is made. The requirements on the ground at the vendor location and availability of such infrastructure are determined.
- **System development**. Any changes to the systems, either through functionality or interface, are estimated, and discussions with the system vendor are organised.
- **Resource inventory**. A talent and skill inventory of resources at the vendor's end is prepared, and a few senior people interviewed for their views, in order to be able to incorporate their perspectives and experiences into the plan.

IMPLEMENTATION

The implementation phase begins once the preparations are complete. It has to be meticulous and seamless. Solid grounding, thinking through, and anticipation of issues prior to the start of the implementation will ensure that the resources, time, and effort are utilised in smooth execution during this phase.

- **Revised outsourced maps and notes to be made and signed off.** The process maps and notes need to be amended to reflect the revised outsourced process. Handoffs have to be accurately documented, and processes must be redesigned to reduce handoffs between the firm and the vendor. Control processes are documented, control elements are designed, and responsibilities are identified.
- **Capacity model and pricing.** Based on the volume estimates and revised process, the vendor prepares a capacity model of resourcing with prices.
- **Finalise project plan.** The project plan is finalised once the go-ahead on pricing is obtained. Milestones and critical paths are established.
- **SLA.** The SLA is finalised. Its contents cover:
  - Scope
  - Cutoff times
  - Turnaround standards
  - Exceptions (turnaround, documentation)
  - Records
  - Reporting
  - Billing
  - Exit costs
  - Contact points
  - Contingency plan
  - Review process
  - Changes
  - Liability
- **Power of attorney and authorisation.** The mandate to execute transactions on behalf of the firm is created and reviewed with legal.
- **Other documentation.** Other agreements, such as management agreements, information security, system and system access, people, and fiduciary are finalised.
- **Hiring.** The hiring process based on job profiles begins. The firm may be involved for hiring into key/supervisory roles. Existing firm employees are redeployed into other roles.
- **Technology procurement.** Systems and infrastructure items are procured and set up for operations at the vendor site.
- **Training.** The hired employees are trained on company practices and new operations. The firm is involved in this process as well, led by the transition team.
- **Continuity of business.** Contingency planning must be developed and tested. Backups could be back with the firm or another vendor site.
- **Test run.** A test run is performed, including system entries and the like in the controlled environment. Existing processes continue, and any teething issues that materialise are ironed out.
- **Parallel run.** Finally, a parallel run is conducted, where both sides perform their tasks. Once the Treasurer is satisfied of the efficacy of the new processes, the cutover is formalised.

POST-IMPLEMENTATION

- **Review.** The review process is ongoing but should be extremely detailed and diligent in the first few quarters to set a strong and robust precedent for the long term.
- **Feedback.** Feedback must be provided to the vendor on performance levels and improvements. Remember to include all that the vendor is doing well too.
- **Documentation issues.** Pending or incomplete documentation is completed and reviewed, followed by corrective action where required.

Next we present a case study of the practicalities of outsourcing a Treasury function by Kelvin Hayes, who has had much experience in outsourcing the Treasury of his firm.

CASE STUDY: OUTSOURCING TREASURY: A HANDS-ON EXPERIENCE NOTE

In an environment where the role of the corporate Treasurer is under greater scrutiny than ever, the decisions made in the treasury department need to be of the highest standard possible. One way for Treasurers to improve the quality of their decision making is to allow themselves dedicated time to think about, and act upon, the strategic aspects of their business.

It is in delivering this precious resource of time that the outsourcing of core Treasury functions can improve the quality of a corporate Treasury and the decisions made within it. This is not the only reason of course, the advantages of outsourcing non-core functions that can also be realised include: increased scalability of operations, cost savings, the reduction of operational risk, and the transfer (or adoption) of best practices.

Many Treasurers may be reluctant to give up control of what they feel are their bread-and-butter transactions. However, it is in realising that control can still be maintained while freeing up the Treasurer to perform higher-value tasks that the outsourcing proposition truly delivers value to an organisation. This is especially important as many small and midsise corporations may have a relatively small or resource-challenged Treasury department. As the business grows, the demands on Treasury grow, and outsourcing low-value transactions can greatly aid the Treasury department with these challenges. Indeed it is often the growing Treasury department where outsourcing will have the greatest impact as outsourcing can lead to efficiencies of scale and cost savings from the specialisation provided by the outsourcing partner. This is because the addition of labour resources to the Treasury department is usually "lumpy" and may require considerable training and adaptation, while growth may continue unabated on a linear growth path. An outsourced treasury function is less constrained under these circumstances.

When contemplating the decision to outsource, the Treasurer needs to consider which functions, actions, and responsibilities will be delegated to the outsourcing

(Continued)

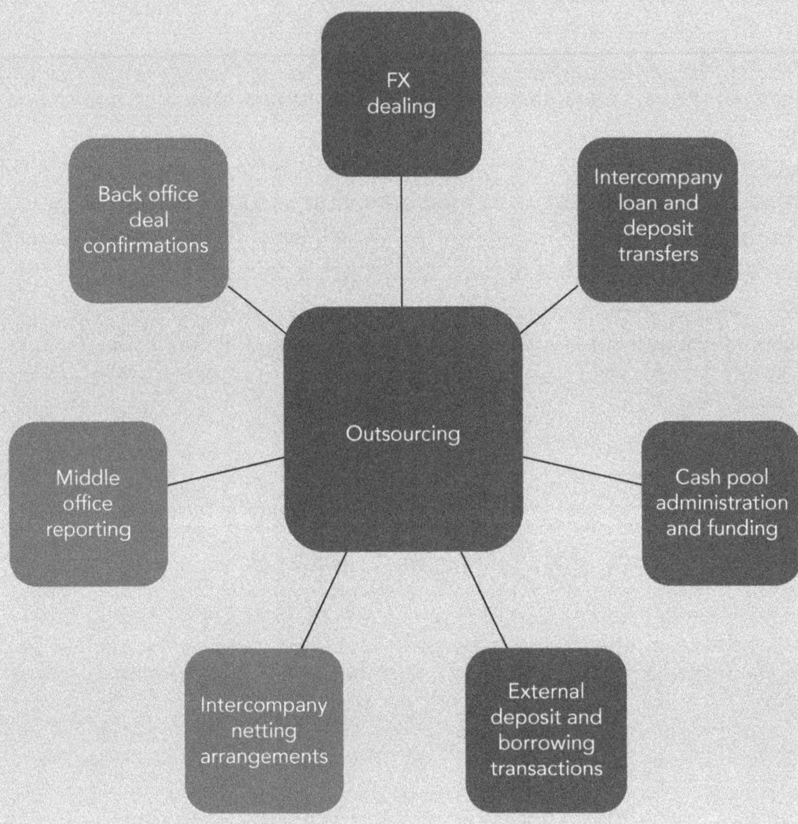

FIGURE 30.2 Candidates for Outsourcing

provider. Treasury should seek to farm out low-value add, repetitive transactions that are time consuming. The classic candidates here are foreign exchange dealing, intercompany loan and deposit transfers, cash pool administration and funding, external deposit and borrowing transactions, intercompany netting arrangements, middle office reporting, and back-office deal confirmations (see Figure 30.2). All of these tasks are recurring and, while important, are a product of Treasury department decisions rather than the reason to be of the Treasury department. Additionally, all of these tasks can be governed by written guidelines such as to amounts, counterparty facility limits and credit ratings, so as to eliminate any subjectivity that could otherwise concern a Treasurer.

It is important for the Treasurer to retain control over the outsourcing partner's actions and to carefully define the relationship between the partners. For this reason, the treasury department should retain full control over the setting of the Treasury policy and guidelines, control over the banking relationships and as prudence would dictate, financial control over the results of the treasury department and outsourcing actions.

Presently there are three main outsourcing models in common use, as shown in Figure 30.3.

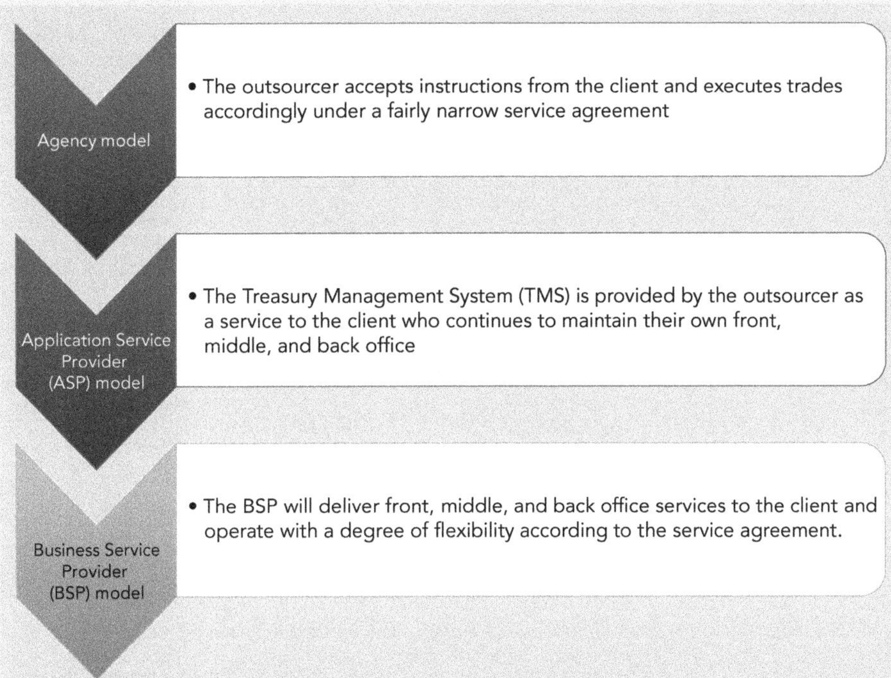

FIGURE 30.3 Different Treasury Outsourcing Models

Which model a Treasurer will choose is an individual corporate decision that will take into account the business needs and costs as well as the relative merits and disadvantages of each. Obviously cost and complexity are crucial factors in the choice of the model. In general the Agency and Application Service Provider (ASP) models will provide their services at a lower external cost; however, there will be higher costs retained within the Treasury department. A full Business Service Provider (BSP) model will have higher contractual costs but has the advantage of freeing up the scarce resources within the Treasury department. The Treasurer should familiarise themselves with the pros and cons of all the models in order to determine which will make the most appropriate fit with their business needs.

Within the author's experience of outsourced Treasury, the "Full Service" Business Service Provider model has proven to be a robust solution to expanding demands on the Treasury department. This model fully leverages the scalability advantage.

Once the decision has been made to implement an outsourced treasury function the Treasurer must begin the process of analysing and selecting a business partner. It may be that the available choice of model will change or evolve depending on the business partner offerings within the company's region or location. While the functionalities of the various proposed Treasury Management Systems (TMS) may appeal to the Treasurer and indeed are often the "selling points" of the business partners it should be recognised that systems will do the job they are

(Continued)

built for. Bells and whistles are nice to have but the most important variable in the decision equation is the choice of business partner itself.

The business partner decision is critical and should not be made hastily. Analysis of the track record and more importantly the commitment of the business partner to the outsourcing model must be undertaken. Future changes in the market, or a change in business conditions could result in the undesirable situation of the business partner exiting the outsourcing business—this could happen even if the underlying model is profitable, say, in the case where an outsourcing partner is a smaller part of a larger group which wishes to restructure in order to focus on their core competencies.

Partner Management—Learning the Hard Way

What happens when the outsourcing partner decides that they do not want to focus on outsourcing as a business model anymore? In this case, ask what would be the contingency plan should the partner vanish and who will own the TMS software for example or even ownership of the data itself? Indeed, this point is raised deliberately as the first business partner, a large commercial bank, which our company used as the primary outsourcer, decided to exit this "niche" operation. While not the end of the world, there was certainly a great deal of angst knowing that a new partner and solution would need to be found and implemented within a fixed time frame. And since this change was inevitable, there was no point in trying to waste time, but to just move on with trying to make the change as seamless and smooth as possible. It was also a sign of the maturity of the company's management that the partner's decision and the possible aftermath did not cloud their decision on the need for outsourcing itself. Instead, the identification of a new partner became the focus of the discussions and way forward. This support from management helped Treasury focus on the transition, since the business case had anyway been made at the time of the outsourcing, and nothing had changed on that front.

Considerable thought should be given to the service agreement when engaging the business partner. The agreement should clearly define the relationship and responsibilities of the parties in order to meet the expectations of the Treasurer. Corporate policies, guidelines, and limits will need to be integrated into the agreement and so it is an opportune time to either review, (or define if the case requires it) all corporate treasury policies, authority levels, and position limits.

In any event, once the treasurer has determined the most appropriate model and chosen a business partner for the future, the process of planning and executing the transfer of operations to the outsourcer will begin. Usually the integration and onboarding capabilities of the business partner will have been explained in or during the request for proposal process. However, a treasurer should not underestimate the time and difficulty involved even with an experienced outsourcing partner. The model and partner choice obviously have a large influence on the amount of work that will need to be done and who will have the expertise to execute that work. However, a realistic and solid planning process will help guide the implementation and ensure that the necessary responsibilities are clear and that the project is a success from the go-live.

In practice, the Treasurer and chosen service provider need to draft and review operating procedures, arrange signatory and dealing authorities, hard-code settlement instructions, arrange external and internal counterparty confirmation procedures, and work out the reporting requirements and how these will be met. Some of this work is simply rote—the information must be collected, provided, and input; however, some will require critical thinking about the structure of the organisation or the reporting entities as this will determine system functionality.

Planning needs will vary from operation to operation but some of the basic considerations will remain the same. In a large scale case one of the major challenges will be to define and implement the various interfaces that will be required. Consideration here needs to be given to which direction data will flow to or from the treasury system. This raises a whole host of challenges for the Treasurer and for their IT support. The Treasurer must liaise closely with the IT department and it is important that the IT resources assigned to the project understand the multitude of interfacing requirements.

IT Integration: Core of the Treasury Outsourcing Model

Integrating the TMS with electronic bank statements, e-payment systems, and the accounting or Enterprise Resource Planning (ERP) system will also need to be addressed. Here the treasurer may have considerable work to perform in terms of arranging the necessary electronic or MT940/941 reporting authorisations or testing electronic payment systems, for example via SWIFT MT 101 instructions. Additionally, any existing deals or data will need to be transferred to the new system and then checked and reconciled. The old adage: "garbage in, garbage out" holds true!

Practical consideration will need to be given to the hardware requirements of the new operation as well as communications lines, email addresses, and contact details. If remote access to the treasury system is to be available then this will need to be tested and backup procedures will need to be put in place.

If the Treasurer plans to interface the Treasury related dealing transactions with the accounting system then this should not be underestimated and dedicated project resources should be applied to ensure that the data generated is correct and thoroughly tested before any live data is input into the accounting results. The Treasurer will not make any friends in the accounting control department by causing delays or errors to the monthly or annual reports.

Ideally there would be a perfect cut-off time to make the switch to the new provider, but the reality of many corporates is that the constant cycle of month end reporting means that there is no perfect changeover time. Instead it is strongly recommended to engage in a parallel run in order to identify any problems or issues with the new TMS or associated processes.

Once the processes and systems are proven to be robust and effective the Treasurer can go live with some confidence that the outsourcing solution will perform to their satisfaction. This does not negate the need for subsequent periodic reviews of the performance of the TMS and the business partner however. It is important to review, improve, refine, and correct the processes and systems. Additionally it is essential to regularly review the interaction of the Treasury department with the business provider and the provider's performance against expectations, in order to smooth out operations and adjust for any problems which will arise.

(Continued)

When the hard work has been completed and the Treasurer has an outsourced model performing to expectations the benefits will begin to accrue. One should expect that, whatever the model, there should be improved reporting and more timely analysis of positions and exposures. Outsourced execution of deals should result in time savings, lower error rates, and potentially better pricing arising from scale and the specialisation (or division) of labor. Improved compliance and a solid audit trail should also be expected. A well-built Straight Through Processing (STP) system and integrated interfaces add to the robustness of the solution.

The key, though, comes from the release of the Treasurer's time—wherein having released oneself from the repetitive, low value tasks, focus can be given to the higher level strategic and risk management roles within the job.

Contributed by Kelvin Hayes, deputy group treasurer, SGS. SGS is the world's leading inspection, verification, testing, and certification company. SGS is recognised as the global benchmark for quality and integrity.

SUMMARY

Outsourcing, unlike centralisation, requires a strong will on the part of company management to implement. Only the brave take this on, for the entire concept of allowing a third party to run a critical function (even if it is an implementation role) is difficult for many to digest. Yet as the race for hyperefficiency and focus on core competence continues, outsourcing is an alternative that many more firms are now considering, and at the right price, control, and resource point, the migration would take place.

CHAPTER THIRTY ONE

31

Building and Sustaining a Treasury Culture

IN PART ONE WE DISCUSSED how building and sustaining a Treasury Culture is a part of building Treasury Leadership (see Figure 31.1).

In this chapter, we examine how to integrate Treasury Culture into the company's human resources (HR) cycle and some parameters for the critical aspects of development and evaluation (Figure 31.2).

The Treasury Culture can be a key criterion when looking for potential Treasury recruits. Young raw talent with the right approach need to be screened for essential Treasury Culture qualities, while experienced personnel need to be evaluated in addition for basic and technical skills of Treasury Culture, apart from job skills.

Training and development is a crucial element in the HR cycle. Companies often focus their training and development dollars on specific job requirements. Simulation-based training (see note) has become an increasingly popular method to impart and test job-related knowledge.

In addition, managerial time and effort should be invested in mentoring and planning job rotations, and training budgets should focus on general and technical skill-based training apart from simulation-based job skill-related trainings.

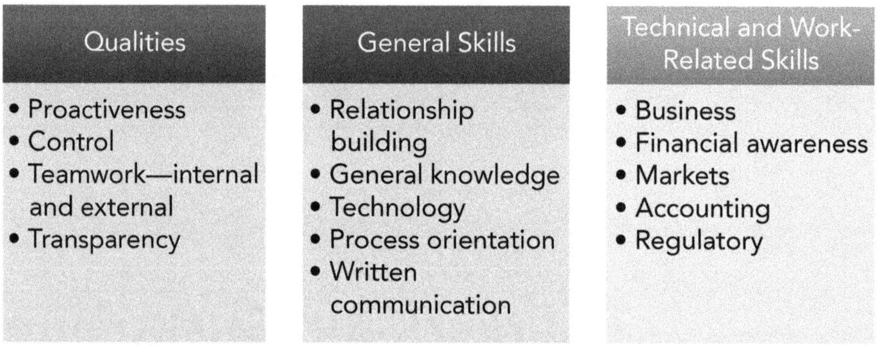

FIGURE 31.1 Treasury Culture

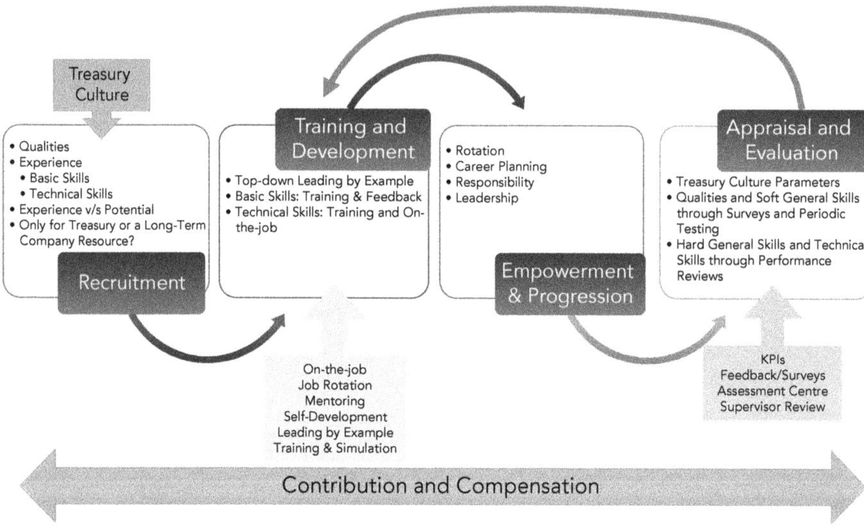

FIGURE 31.2 Integration of Treasury Culture into a Firm's HR Cycle

Advantage of Simulation-Based Training

Oftentimes, despite the best intentions of the trainers, trainees, and companies, learning from traditional training programmes ends when the course certificates are handed out. Little follow through is done. If an employee performs better in the coming year, the training is deemed to have been successful. Recently, more and more companies are using simulation or game play modes of training—where participants undergo real-life simulations on a system or by playing a game and applying theoretical learning in situations similar to what they might face at work. These methods give participants an opportunity to try out different solutions, varied approaches and, most important, see if these approaches can work. It is a

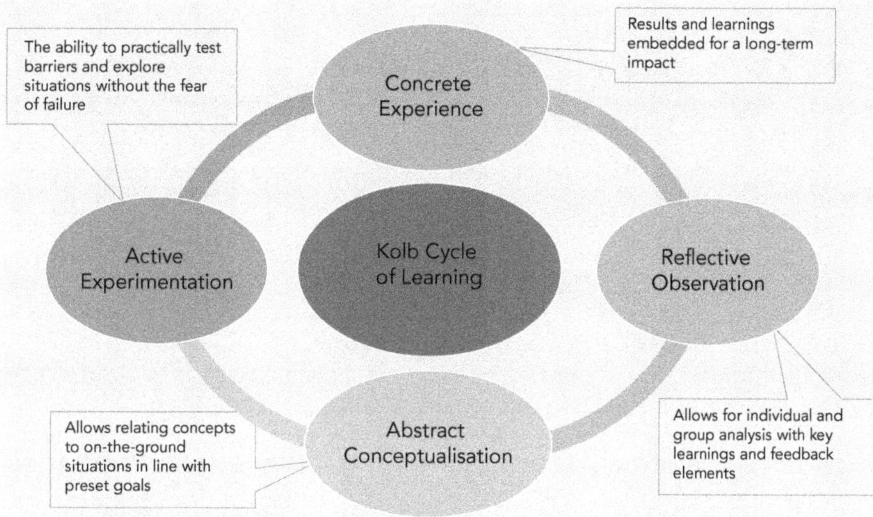

FIGURE 31.3 Kolb Cycle of Learning

Source: Created by David A. Kolb

rehearsal before the real event, where there are no penalties for being wrong but only upsides because the learning has actually been tested. There is no substitute for doing a task; it does not compare with merely listening to someone talking about doing the task. With simulation and game play, more value can be extracted from the same training dollars, and travel time and infrastructure setup time are reduced dramatically. Some simulation training firms, such as Aktrea, provide Internet-based simulations that participants can use on their own time, thus reducing continuous time away from their desks. On-site simulations have their own value, inculcating concepts in environments away from work that can promote lateral thinking and problem solving and also build teamwork as participants interact with each other outside of work and create long-lasting professional relationships.

The concept of game play and learning through simulation can be traced back to the Kolb cycle of learning (see Figure 31.3), propagated by American educational theorist David A. Kolb, whose interests and publications focus on experiential learning. The concept shows how active experimentation and testing barriers to explore situations allows relating concepts to actual work situations, enabling individuals and groups to analyse and reflect on information and paving the way to permanently imprint the learning that can be used practically at work.

The way in which this method can reinforce learning is shown in Figure 31.4.

Treasury can use simulation-based training in different ways and through different themes (see Figure 31.5).

How does game play actually work? What does a typical simulation contain? Figure 31.6 provides a snapshot.

Simulation and game play are here to stay, and smarter firms are already adopting them as a way of life in their training calendars.

(*Continued*)

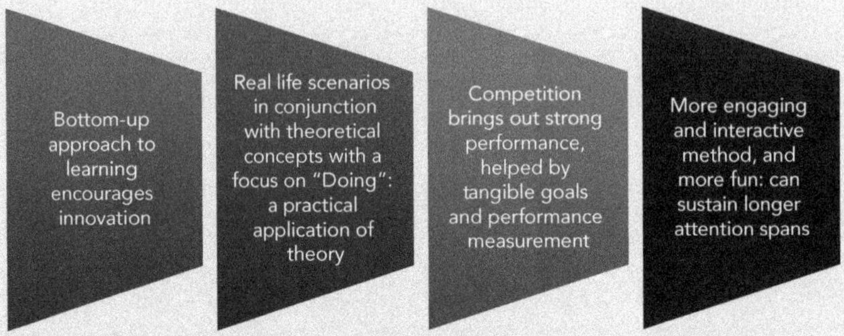

FIGURE 31.4 Reinforcing Learning Through Simulation

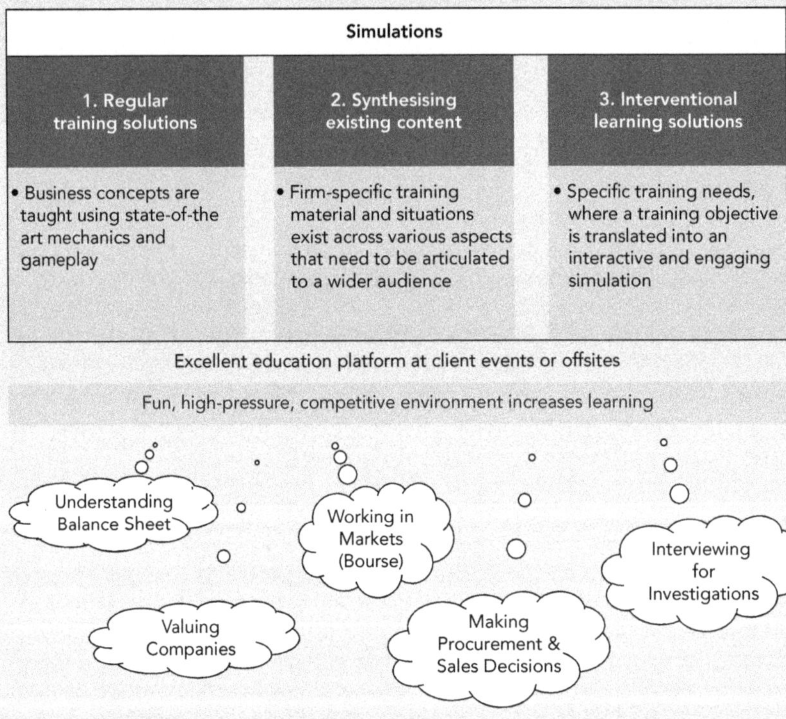

FIGURE 31.5 Simulation-Based Training Related to Corporate Treasury

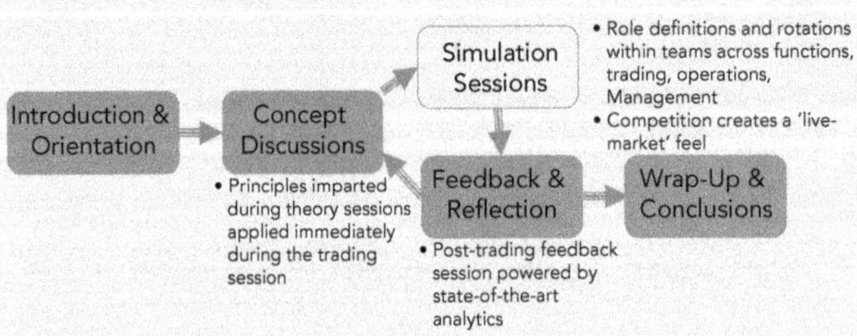

FIGURE 31.6 Typical Simulation (Markets Simulation or Bourse)

Empowerment and progression is the next stage in the process, and this is worked on by the Treasurer and chief financial officer along with the HR function in line with the organisation's processes and practices. Also, the Treasurer needs to start involving the next level of management in the parallel support and consultative work that is part of the treasurer's responsibility (see the next note), as an enabler of empowerment.

Importance of Hats

In the larger context of treasury, the various hats that a treasurer wears (see Figure 31.7) are exceedingly important. The treasurer needs to start making the next level of management aware and ready to take on some of these roles, preparing them to move up the responsibility ladder.

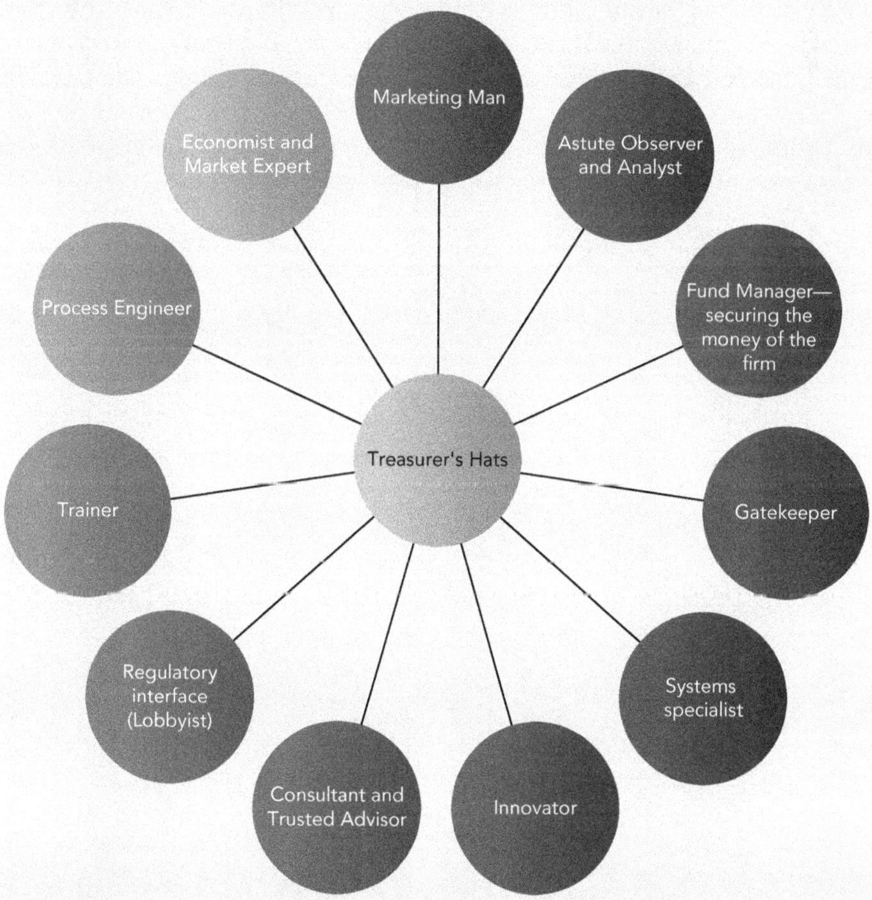

FIGURE 31.7 Many Hats of a Treasurer

EVALUATION

The area of evaluation of employee performance and their absorbing and practicing of Treasury Culture is perhaps the most challenging part of putting in place a Treasury Culture, especially when some of the aspects of culture are not tangible or measurable by conventional methods or key performance indicators (KPIs). Specific job-related aspects, such as control mind set; process orientation; regulatory, accounting, and technological skills; business skills; and job-specific performance are measurable by KPIs (see Figure 31.8).

Some of the measurement tools that can be used apart from the performance metrics are assessment centres, surveys, and supervisor reviews.

Assessment Centres

Assessment centres are used for the qualities that cannot be measured by conventional KPIs. An assessment centre is typically a programme that makes the assessee participate in a number of tests across a period of time and finally arrives at a consolidated and consistent score across the aspects that are being evaluated. Many of the situations are subjective and decision based, and good assessment centres try to objectivise the performance on some of these situations and generate scores and assessments after removing potential bias and measurement error (since the

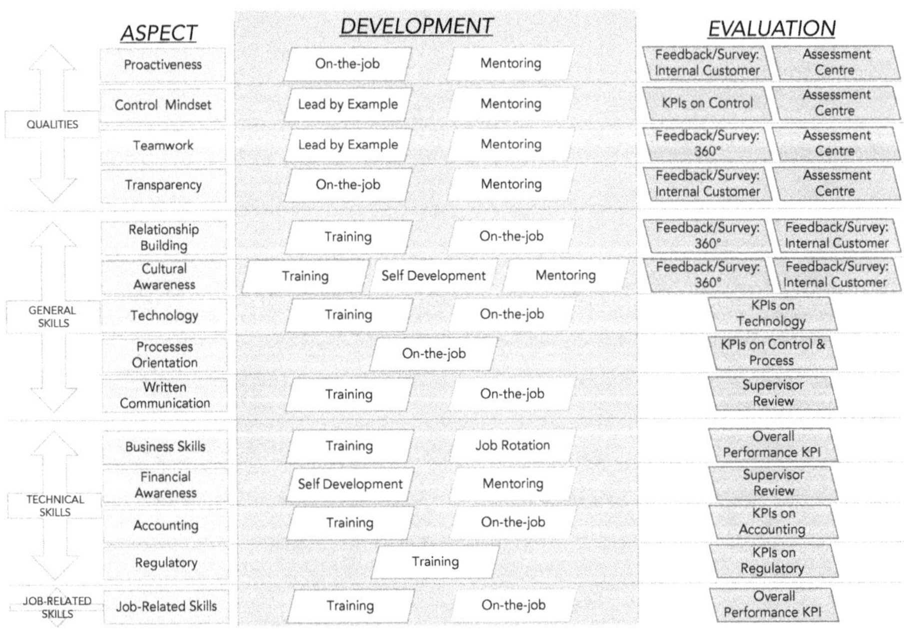

FIGURE 31.8 Development and Evaluation of Treasury Personnel in the Context of Treasury Culture

assessment is over a period and range of tests instead of a single questionnaire). The author's preference is to use assessment centres rather than single questionnaires or surveys.

Surveys

Internal customers, such as business and country operations, are the direct end users of Treasury activities and services. Hence, treasury's output and approach from an internal client's perspective is best observed through surveying the direct beneficiaries of Treasury performance. For some of the softer aspects, such as cultural awareness for global teams, 360-degree reviews are useful if implemented well.

Supervisor Reviews

Since supervisors have direct responsibility for employee development and performance, it is imperative for some of these aspects of Treasury Culture to be factored in to supervisors' assessments of their subordinates.

SUMMARY

The role of the Treasurer as people manager is generally underrated. Unlike all true team leaders, the treasurer's role becomes even more complicated with the need to build a very diverse yet deep set of skills and to ensure that the team remains motivated—the degree of interface and the pace of work at Treasury has seen some churn in organisations. With Treasury roles, continuity is a core asset. That is where a strong Treasury Culture, which necessitates reinvention while playing in a larger organisational team, plays a key role in the development of the Treasury organisation.

CHAPTER THIRTY TWO

Managing Treasury in Uncertain Times

THIS CHAPTER, A LATER ADDITION to the *Handbook*, comes in response to requests from readers who visited the book's website (www.wiley.com/go/treasuryhandbook) as the book progressed and from participants in my training programmes and clients whom I advised during the periods of uncertainty following the events of 2008. No comprehensive checklist can cover every single element that needs to be looked at and no prescription solves all uncertainties.

Rather, this chapter, and the checklist in the Toolkit on the Web site, contains simple guidelines based on common sense and experience that will guide Treasury teams through various bouts of uncertainty.

UNCERTAINTY AND ITS IMPACT ON TREASURY MANAGEMENT

Uncertainties in the Treasurer's world can exist in many forms, can be created by various factors, and can have varying consequences—and sometimes none at all. A typical sequence of events is given in Figure 32.1.

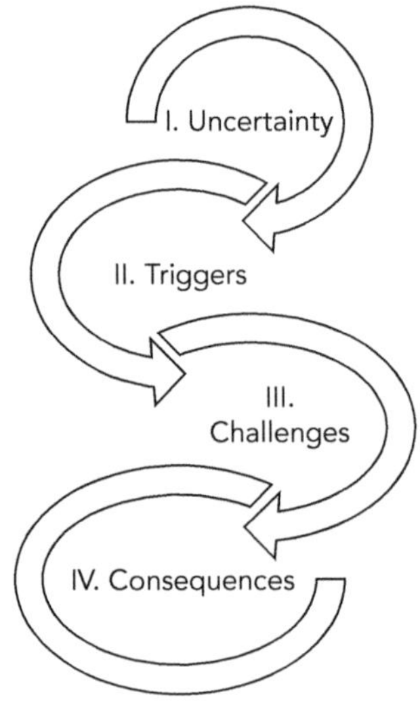

FIGURE 32.1 Uncertainty and Sequence of Events

An uncertainty can be defined loosely as a condition in the market or environment that increases the unpredictability of market and environment behavior, usually based around a series of events that could be political, economic, financial, or natural. Specifically for the firm, a trigger event or set of events cause a certain change in the market and environment that could have a direct impact on the functioning of the company, its access to resources and the continuity of its supply chain. These are what we term *challenges*, uncertainties that directly impact the organisation. Finally, these challenges, if not addressed, could lead to undesirable consequences for the firm that could be reputational and finally financial.

While many of these aspects are covered in Part Four on risk management, and indeed the solutions discussed in the Toolkit checklist do overlap largely with the solutions in Part Four, managing a contingency or uncertainty requires a specialist project approach, not a business-as-usual way to manage the Treasury function.

Various uncertainties are depicted in Figure 32.2. For simplicity, we classify them in two stages, the first of which usually occurs before the second. At some point, based on triggers, the uncertainties could morph into a challenge that impacts the firm directly. As long as it has not happened, the particular event or environment remains as an uncertainty. Its occurrence and subsequent change to the company makes it a challenge to manage.

The various uncertainties are briefly described next.

Stage 1 Uncertainties

The first type of uncertainties, called *stage 1 uncertainties*, could be legal, regulatory, or market-related in nature. These are expanded below.

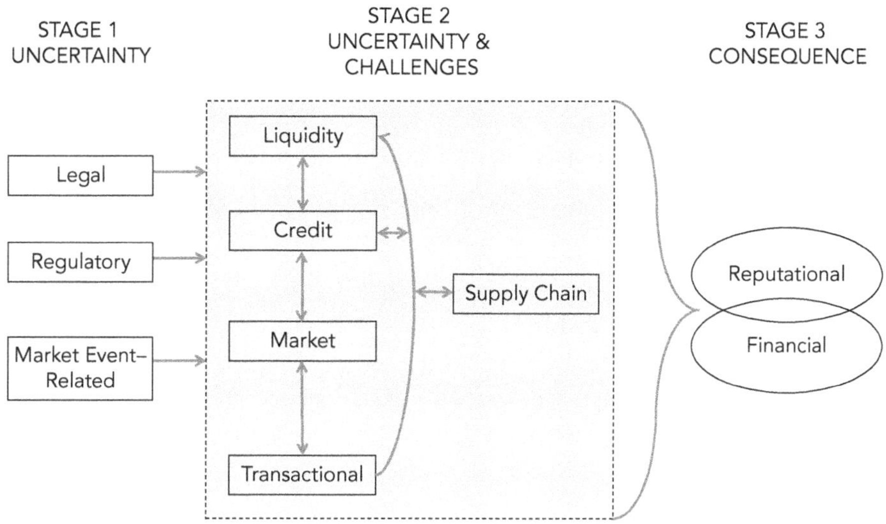

FIGURE 32.2 Various Uncertainties

- **Legal uncertainty.** Caused by a change in law or a legal event. These are usually triggered politically, such as the legality of euro transactions with a country should that country exit the European Union.
- **Regulatory uncertainty.** A result of change in regulations undertaken by a government, central bank, or other regulator, typically as a defense mechanism against some economic harm expected to the country or as a reaction to some event.
- **Market event–related uncertainty.** Caused by a one-off or concentrated set of events, such as the collapse of a fund, a credit default, or a spike in commodity prices, that could have a more long-term impact or cause other related events in other markets and environments.

Stage 2 Uncertainties

The next stage of uncertainties are given below.

- **Liquidity uncertainty.** The nonavailability of liquidity in the immediate term, either through the banking channel, public and private markets, or internally. A liquidity challenge is one of the most critical challenges for a Treasurer to face. It creates liquidity risk for the enterprise.
- **Credit uncertainty.** Events could cause counterparties that the firm is linked to either directly or indirectly to face a crunch and hence not be able to make payments necessary—this could include banks with whom deposits have been placed, entities and partners in the supply chain, and so on. Managing this would mean managing the credit risk for the enterprise.
- **Market uncertainty.** Market factors across relevant asset classes move unpredictably causing market-related risk for the enterprise.

- **Transaction uncertainty**. Events in the financial system and political system occur that create potential blocks in the flow of money and transactions in the normal course of business.
- **Supply chain uncertainty**. More a consequence of the other stage 2 uncertainties, players along the financial supply chain are impacted because of an inability to fund or run their business normally, thereby increasing chances of a disruption in the supply chain of the organisation.

TRIGGERS AND EVENTS

Various kinds of triggers can happen across each area of uncertainty (see Table 32.1). Some of these triggers can be used as early warnings (see Figure 32.3), and some can be used as triggers to take contingency action.

TABLE 32.1 Triggers and Events

Uncertainty	Triggers	Challenges/ Consequences	Key Management Objective
Legal	Change of law Cross-border events	Inability to execute contracts with counterparties Inability to conduct business in jurisdictions	Ensure continuity of business and dealings Preempt any potential legal issues
Regulatory	Exchange control Queries by central bank Market misconduct	Inability to continue existing business or dealings Reduced ability to manage funding, risk, and other financial dealings	Minimise market and regulatory impact of existing transactions Ensure new transactions and dealings are within the ambit of possible regulations
Market related	Default by any entity Supply shortage for commodities Fraud or crisis (localised)	Contagion to other markets Dependence on company's counterparties on the events Market, credit, liquidity related risks	Preempt any resultant market and credit events Reduce impact of external market infrastructure disruptions by reverting to manual processes if required
Liquidity	Liquidity shortfall Sudden spike in rates Act of God Fraud or irregular market activity	Reduced ability to fund business and day-to-day functioning Supply chain challenges Credit challenges	Ensure that enough funding and cash is available at locations where it is needed Ensure forecasting process factors in the uncertain environment

TABLE 32.1 *(Continued)*

Uncertainty	Triggers	Challenges/ Consequences	Key Management Objective
Credit	Act of default Credit downgrade Sovereign event	Reduced ability to recover receivables Reduced ability to get funding if entity directly related Liquidity challenges Supply chain challenges	Reduce instances of losses and credit events
Market	Sudden moves in market factors Correlated factors also move adversely	Change in market value Exposure to market factors Liquidity challenges	Minimise variability on financials Changes to regulations to reflect in transactions and policies
Transactional	Inability to move money Accounts blocked Systems failure	Liquidity challenges Credit challenges Supply chain challenges	Minimise disruption to funds flow and dependence on company's liquidity on transactional elements Ensure staffing plans are revised to reduce surprises Ensure that the team is motivated and has clear direction on external and internal aspects Reduce impact of external systems nonperformance
Supply chain	Supplier default Client default Logistics vendor default	Reputational Credit challenges	Ensure flow of money and goods

SIMPLE METHOD TO MANAGE TREASURY DURING TIMES OF UNCERTAINTY

Figure 32.3 provides a simple step-by-step process for managing Treasury in uncertain times. Responsibility for managing Treasury typically lies with the Treasurer him- or herself—and the Treasurer appoints a set of people to work with. The various entities also need to support the Treasurer and provide inputs.

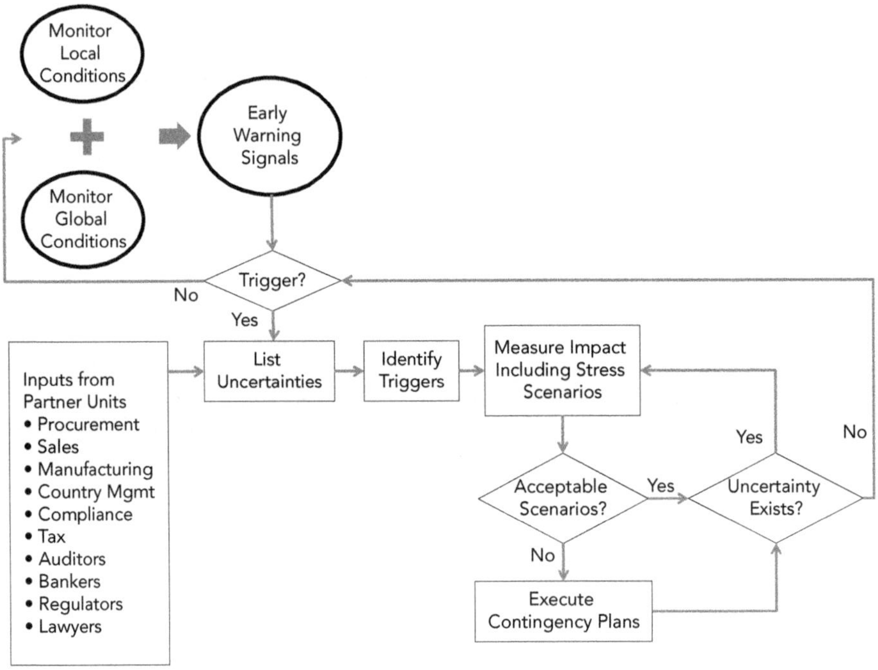

FIGURE 32.3 Simple Method of Managing Treasury During Times of Uncertainty

Internal Entities

- Procurement
- Sales
- Manufacturing
- Country Management
- Compliance
- Tax

External Entities

- Auditors
- Bankers
- Regulators
- Lawyers

The first step is to have local and global triggers that would set the ball rolling for any action to be taken. These triggers can be set with the help of country management and the chief financial officer. These triggers can be set off by any employee on the business or Treasury function in consultation with the country chief executive or management.

The triggering would result in the assessment of the situation (identifying the situation using IMAGE© methodology). A list of potential triggers based on the situation would be arrived at, and the impact of potential market moves and other events based on these triggers would be assessed. If the stress testing does not produce a satisfactory end result, the contingency plans would have to be invoked for each aspect.

It is better to have generically defined contingency plans for each risk element in the chain; this makes the job of planning before any specific market contingency even easier.

SUMMARY

Managing during prolonged periods of uncertainty requires dexterity, patience, and a huge amount of positivity. While different companies have different approaches to managing their contingencies, the approach and aspects mentioned here and the checklist provided in the Toolkit section of the Web site can serve as a reminder that the company can add to the process of honing and getting its planning to a steady state.

No test of a contingency plan is better than an actual situation. If markets and fate conspire to have you face a dire situation, what you learn from an actual case would be very strong inputs when revisiting the plan and subsequently incorporating the real-life learnings to augment the existing plan and make it more robust.

And of course our wishes are with you. We hope you never need to execute your contingency plans in real life.

Happy Treasurying!

Glossary

Account Structure The organisation of accounts within the group, in terms of type of accounts, currencies, ownership, and location.

ACH (Automated Clearinghouse) Electronic network for financial transactions, generally riding on the real-time gross settlement (RTGS) network and coordinated by the central bank, that process large volumes of credit and debit transactions in batches.

ACH Credit Transaction An automated clearinghouse transaction that sends funds from a payer's (originator's) account to a beneficiary account.

ACH Debit Transaction An automated clearinghouse transaction that pulls funds to the beneficiary (originator)'s account from the payer's account.

Acquirer or Card Acquiring Bank The bank that buys credit card transactions with recourse from a merchant and will pay the merchant and settle the transaction with the card issuing bank (the merchant's bank).

Advising Bank The bank that advises the beneficiary (exporter or seller) of a letter of credit (LC) opened in its favour.

Alpha Measure of performance on a risk-adjusted risk.

ANI (Adjusted Net Income) Method Method of cash budgeting in which cash flow is determined indirectly by adjusting the net income on cash.

AP (Accounts Payable) The amount that a company owes its trade creditors.

AR (Accounts Receivable) Assets resulting from the extension of trade credit to a company's customers.

Arbitrage The process of purchasing an asset or security and simultaneously selling it in another market through direct or indirect means, which leads to profit without market risk.

ARM (Accrual Reversal) Method Method of medium- to long-term indirect cash forecasting that uses reversal of accruals to forecast cash flows.

At-the-Money Forward An option strike price that is the same as the at-the-money forward price.

Back Office The unit, independent of dealers, that executes treasury and financial transactions that could include administration, record keeping, settlements, and accounting.

Back-Testing A process of testing of a risk management strategy through testing with historic numbers and performance.

Back Value Date A process where a bank reflects an accounting entry to a customer's account or an internal account on a date prior to the actual fund flow.

Bank Draft A negotiable instrument drawn by a bank on itself that is purchased by the payee's bank and sent back to the paying bank for reimbursement.

Base Currency The domestic or reporting currency of a company; also the first currency (commodity) in a currency pair.

Base Rate A generally accepted and published interest rate or benchmark over which a credit spread is applied, such as the Fed funds rate, the prime rate, or the London Interbank Offered Rate (LIBOR) on which a rate of interest is based.

Basis Point One-hundredth of a percentage point (.0001 or 0.01%).

Basis Risk The risk associated with hedging or assuming a position in a benchmark or terms that is not directly the exposure that is being hedged.

Basket Option A financial option where the underlying asset is a group of commodities, securities, or currencies.

Benchmark A published rate or index that is used to fix prices of financial transactions or measure performance and risk.

Benchmark Yield Curve The yield curve for a set of benchmarks, such as government securities.

Beta A measure of volatility of a security to the market, used in the capital asset pricing method (CAPM), which calculates the expected return of an asset and market return.

Bid Rate The price at which the quoting bank or market maker will buy or borrow the asset, commodity or market factor for which the price is being quoted.

Bid–Offer Spread The difference (spread) between the bid rate and the offer rate quoted by a market maker.

Bill of Exchange A written order from a drawer of the bill to a drawee, to pay a specified sum on demand or at particular point in time, used to finance trade transactions and to obtain credit when discounted by a bank.

Black-Scholes Model The pathbreaking model used as the basis for option pricing.

Buy Backs Repurchases of outstanding shares by a company to reduce the number of shares in a market.

Call Option The right to buy a specific amount of a commodity at a specific price at a specific time.

Callability The ability of a borrower to pay back the monies owed and reduce its indebtedness prior to a maturity date.

Calling Bank The bank that calls or asks for a price from the quoting bank or market maker.

Capital Asset Pricing Model (CAPM) A model for valuation that describes the relationship between risk and expected return and is used in the pricing of securities.

Capital Structure The proportion or structure of debt, equity, and a hybrid of the two in a firm's capital base.

Cash Concentration The movement of funds from outside locations to a central account for efficient utilisation.

Cash Forecasting The activity of estimating cash inflows and outflows and hence liquidity in the short and long term.

Cash Flow Hedge Hedging activity that is targeted at reducing the variability of cash flows across various currencies.

Cash Flows at Risk A measure with a certain degree of certainty of a company's potential inability to meet payments or obligations.

Cash Pooling The process to combine the liquidity across a group to lower volatility and increase efficiency of cash utilisation with potential cost savings and lower borrowing.

Cash Terms Credit terms in a trade transaction in which the buyer has a short period (a few days) to make the payment.

CCC (Cash Conversion Cycle) A measure in number of days that provides an indication of how soon the company churns its cash and the general measure of the period for which it requires external sources to fund its daily operations. It can be computed by the formula CCC = Days Inventory Outstanding + Days Sales Outstanding – Days Payables Outstanding.

Centralisation The relocation of activities and oversight to one location from different geographic and subsidiary locations. Centralisation can be of many aspects, including people, processes, systems, activities, and accounts.

Cheque Truncation The process by which key information on a paper cheque is captured electronically for further distribution and processing.

Clearing Float The time delay between the deposit of a cheque and the debit in the payer's account.

Clearing The transmission, reconciliation, and confirmation of payments or securities before settlement. This could include netting of instructions and determination of final settlement amounts.

Clearinghouse An association or institution that facilitates the exchange of payments and settlements of funds and/or securities in a geographic area. In many cases, it also takes on counterparty risk for the transactions.

Collecting Bank The remitting bank's correspondent bank in a documentary collection transaction. The collecting bank collects the amount from the buyer and releases the relevant documents.

Collection Float The time gap between the dispatch of the cheque and the credit to the payee's account.

Commercial Paper (CP) Unsecured short-term corporate debt in the form of promissory notes, generally used to fund working capital or other short-term needs.

Commodity Risk Uncertainty of firm value and financials caused by changes in the prices of commodities.

Confirmation Written acknowledgement exchanged between two counterparties to a transaction with all terms and conditions.

Confirming Bank The bank that adds its confirmation to a letter of credit transaction, increasing its creditworthiness by committing to the beneficiary (and its bank) that payment will be made irrespective of the issuing bank's ability to pay, provided all other conditions are met.

Controlled Disbursement A bank-provided payment service that provides almost immediate notification of cheque amounts cleared that day.

Convertibility The ability to convert money from one form (currency) to another; usually regulated by the regulator of that country (see *Exchange Control*).

Correlation The high degree of relationship in the moves of two market factors. A correlation of 100%, or 1, means that the two move completely in tandem, while a correlation of –100%, or –1, means that they have an inverse relationship.

Correspondent Bank A bank that provides its client banks (those that hold accounts with it) in different locations with payment and other services.

Counterparty Risk The uncertainty that a counterparty that needs to deliver assets or money will fail to fulfil its financial obligations through a lack of either ability or intention to pay.

Coupon Swap An exchange of interest cash flows on a prespecified notional amount where the two legs are in different currencies.

Credit Default Swap (CDS) An agreement between two parties where one party agrees to assume ownership for an underlying debt asset and pay the other party the original value of the asset in the event that the obligor of the debt asset defaults, in exchange for a premium (called CDS spread).

Credit Exposure The total amount of credit or obligation extended to a borrower.

Credit Rating An assessment of creditworthiness of individuals, companies, or countries.

Credit Rating Agency An entity that assigns credit ratings for issuers of debt obligations and debt instruments themselves.

Credit Spreads The difference between a benchmark (such as a treasury security) and the rate at which an obligor can borrow.

Cross-Currency Swap An agreement between two parties to exchange the interest payments and principal amounts on prespecified notional amounts in different currencies.

Cross-Border Risk The uncertainty of payments owed from an entity in another country to be made because of changes in exchange regulations in that country.

Daylight Overdraft (DLOD) or Intraday Credit A credit limit extended by a bank to a counterparty for regularisation or payback before the end of that business day; usually used for payment and settlement purposes.

Debt/Equity Ratio The ratio of a company's debt to its equity capital, which provides an absolute and relative measure of the degree of a firm's indebtedness.

Defeasance The ability to reduce or liquidate assumed risk.

Delta The change in the price of an option caused by the change in the price of the underlying market factor spot price.

Demand Deposit Accounts (DDAs) A bank account that gives the owner the ability to transfer funds to a third party via a cheque.

Direct Debit A preauthorised debit through the clearing system initiated by the payee.

Disbursement Float The time between the dispatch of a cheque and the debit to the payer's account.

Distribution Method A forecasting technique used in cash scheduling wherein the distribution of cash flow over a given period is estimated.

Documentary Collection An international payment method involving the collection of a draft and accompanying documents through correspondent banks across countries.

Derivatives A transaction between two parties where the exchange of cash flows or payments is derived from the price movement of one or more market factors.

DIO (Days Inventory Outstanding) A measure of the longevity of the inventory on the balance sheet, expressed by the value of inventory as a percentage of the cost of goods sold projected as a number of days.

Diversification A risk management technique that distributes the risk across a set of market factors.

DPO (Daily Payables Outstanding) A measure of the longevity of the payables on the balance sheet, expressed by the value of accounts payable as a percentage of the cost of goods sold projected as a number of days.

Draft A written order to pay a party (payee or bearer), from a drawer to a drawee bearer, a specified sum either on demand (sight draft) or at a specified point in time (usance).

DSO (Days Sales Outstanding) A measure of the average number of days that a company takes to collect revenue after a sale has been made, expressed by the value of accounts receivable as a percentage of sales projected as a number of days.

Economic Capital The amount of capital that a firm should have to support any risks that it assumes.

Economic Exposure An exposure that changes the economic returns and financials of a company over a period of time. It is different from accounting exposure, which is the accounting impact at any point of time of the risk elements.

Electronic Data Interchange (EDI) The electronic exchange of business data between or within commercial entities (including their agents or intermediaries, in some cases also public administrations) in a standard format, for transactions such as orders, invoices, remittance advices, and payments.

Electronic Lockbox A service provided by a vendor that includes recording receipt, compilation, processing and electronic transmission of incoming payments across different payment methods.

End-of-Day Gross Settlement System A system for funds transfer where payment orders are received throughout the business day but the final aggregated settlement takes place at the end of the day on a gross basis.

Equity Risk Uncertainty to the financials of the firm caused by a change in equity prices, usually related to investments or capital.

Exchange Control Regulatory restrictions on the conversion of currency in that country to a foreign one, typically for the current account (trade and related transactions) or the capital account (debt, equity, and related transactions); usually administered by the central bank of each country.

eXtensible Markup Language (XML) A standard data format used for efficient exchange of data between different applications.

Factoring A financing transaction where receivables are sold to a third party at a discount in return for assumption of risk.

Fixed or Pegged Currency A currency whose exchange rate is established in terms of another currency and does not change when traded in the interbank market.

Float Nonavailability of funds for use owing to internal or external inefficiencies.

Floating Currency A currency whose exchange rate is determined by the foreign exchange market through demand and supply and trading.

Foreign Exchange Settlement Risk The risk that one party to a foreign exchange transaction will pay the currency it sold but not receive the currency it bought owing to regulatory or credit events related to the defaulting party.

Forfaiting Purchasing of a specific receivable from a seller by an agency called a forfeiter.

Forwards An over-the-counter (OTC) transaction for a prespecified amount at a specified price on a specified date more than two working days from the current date.

Front Office The part of treasury that initiates transactions with other counterparties.

Funding Liquidity Risks The inability of a company to meet its funding requirements.

Futures Generally a standardised exchange-traded transaction for the sale and purchase of a standard amount of a market factor or asset at a predetermined future date and price.

FX Risk Change in the value of a firm owing to a change in foreign exchange (FX) rates.

Garman-Kohlagen Model An extension or derivation of the Black-Scholes model that helps to price foreign exchange options.

Hedge Accounting The accounting treatment adopted by companies that allows them to enter into genuine hedge transactions and reduce volatility on the profit and loss statement.

IMAGE© Methodology An advanced but simple five-step risk management methodology (copyright of Aktrea Capital); the steps are risk identification, measurement, accounting, governance, and evaluation of the risk management process.

Implied Volatility Traded volatility as a percentage used to price options.

Interest Rate Risk Uncertainty to a company's financials caused by changes in interest rates.

Interest Rate Swap An exchange of interest cash flows in the same currency.

ISDA (International Swap Dealers Association) A trade organisation of market participants that provides governance guidelines for market-related transactions.

Letter of Credit (L/C) A trade-related document issued by a bank to a seller as a commitment to make a trade payment on behalf of a buyer (its customer) as long as specified conditions are met.

Lockbox A collection system in which a vendor collects or receives, processes, and deposits a company's cheque receipts.

Long Position Buying an asset or creating a positive position in a market factor.

Market Factor A particular asset, such as a specific equity, bond, or commodity, or item of an asset class, such as a currency pair or interest rate benchmark.

Market Factor Risk The change in the financials of a company caused by a shift in a specific market factor.

Market Liquidity Risks The risk of not being able to sell off a position or an asset owing to an absence of buyers.

Mark-to-Market (MTM) The current fair value of an asset, liability, portfolio, transaction, or position based on the current market price of all market factors that comprise the fair value.

Mark-to-Market (MTM) Accounting Refers to the accounting practice where changes to the fair value of an asset or liability directly impact the profits and losses based on the current market price of the asset or liability.

Mark-to-Market (MTM) Value The current market value of a contact, derivative, position, or portfolio.

Master Agreement The flagship agreement issued by the International Swap Dealers Association that serves as the bulwark of over-the-counter transactions between two counterparties.

Mezzanine Financing Hybrid capital that has qualities of both debt and equity, which provides the lender with the rights to convert an ownership or equity interest in the company if a loan is not paid back in time.

Middle Office A department that is independent of, and sits in between, the front and back offices, and is responsible for control, valuation, and review activities.

Multi-Currency Notional Pooling A pooling process that involves multiple currencies, but the money does not physically get pooled. Instead, the pooling agent (bank) provides the net effective interest payable or receivable centrally.

Multilateral Netting A netting payment arrangement among three or more parties.

Net Settlement The settlement of obligations between counterparties on a net basis.

Netting The process of settling outstanding payments between a set of parties through a single consolidated net payment from a central entity called a netting centre.

Nostro Account An account (usually in a foreign currency) of a bank with another (usually foreign) bank in the country of the currency.

Notional Amount A predetermined amount on which payments for swaps or other derivative transactions are based.

Offer Rate The price at which the quoting bank or market maker will sell or lend the asset, commodity, or market factor for which the price is being quoted.

Open Account A trade transaction in which the seller issues an invoice that is formal evidence of an obligation and dispatches the goods to the buyer.

Operational Risk Uncertainty regarding the company's performance owing to lapses in processes, control, and execution.

Option A contract that gives the buyer the right to sell or buy a commodity, asset, or market factor at a future date at a future price.

Payment Float The time between the receipt of an invoice and the debit to the payer's account.

PBS Method (Pro Forma Balance Sheet Method) A cash forecasting method used for medium- to long-term forecasts.

Pooling See *Cash Pooling.*

Positive Pay A cash management service provided by banks where only those cheques with numbers, beneficiary details, and amounts (as provided by the customer) are honoured, to try to reduce the instances of cheque fraud.

Principal-Only Swap An exchange of cash flows (principal on capital or debt transactions) in which principal amounts in different currencies are exchanged.

Processing Float The time between the receipt of the cheque by the payee and the deposit.

Put Option An option contract giving the owner the right but not the obligation to sell an asset at a specified price within a specified time.

Puttability The ability of a lender to force the borrower to repay before scheduled maturity.

Quanto Swap An exchange of interest cash flows in which one leg is denominated in one currency but settled with the benchmark of another currency.

Quoting Bank The market maker or the bank in an over-the-counter transaction that receives the request for a price.

Real-Time Gross Settlement (RTGS) System A settlement system in which processing and settlement take place in real time and on a gross basis without netting off the payments.

Receipts and Disbursements (R&D) Method A simple method for very short-term cash forecasting that uses schedules of cash receipts and cash disbursements.

Receivables Financing Asset-financing arrangements in which a company sells its receivables from customers to receive discounted cash payments up front, with or without recourse to itself in case the customer eventually does not pay.

Re-invoicing A process by which a group company acts as an intermediary between a manufacturing subsidiary in one country and the sales subsidiary in another country, in order to make use of tax and other regulations and create a positive financial impact for the company.

Repricing or Rollover Risks The uncertainty associated with the renewal of a debt or an investment on maturity and the possible prevalent interest rates at the time of the maturity of the existing item.

RFI (Request for Information) A business process whose purpose is to collect written information about the capabilities of various suppliers or service providers.

RFP (Request for Proposal) A business process where the customer issues an invitation to vendors or service providers to bid or send a proposal for an activity, service, or product.

Risk Engine A computer-based model, such as Aktrea's ARTEMIS, that provides various risk scenarios and simulations to assist in intelligent decision making regarding risk management.

Scenario Analysis An assessment of the financials of the company across various scenarios that impact markets and the business environment.

Securitisation A financing transaction in which assets are pooled and securities representing different interests and risks in the pool are issued to investors in exchange for cash up front.

Sensitivity Analysis The analysis of the degree of dependence of the company's financials on market factors.

Settlement A business process where funds, securities, or interest in securities are delivered to fulfill obligations.

Short Position A position where a party has a net negative or sold position in an asset or market factor.

Smart Cards Cards with inbuilt technology or intelligence through chips that can store monetary value and can be electronically replenished.

Spot Transaction A price for settlement typically two business days from the date of the transaction.

SSC (Shared Service Centre) A common entity of many or all functions of a global company or companies of a global group responsible for the execution and handling of specific operational tasks of payments and collections of the company or group. These are typically high-volume, repetitive, and relatively low-value-added tasks.

STP (Straight-Through Processing) Payment transactions that move end to end without manual intervention.

Stress Testing Scenario analysis in extreme conditions; used to determine the ability of a given entity to withstand dramatic deterioration of a market or environment.

Strike Price The price at which a holder can buy or sell an option.

Swaption An option that gives the owner the right to enter into an underlying swap.

Target Balance A balance that is 'targeted' to be maintained at the end of each day.

TMS (Treasury Management System) A system that helps in managing the Treasury function and interfaces with the general ledger (GL) or enterprise resource planning (ERP) system of the company and banking systems.

Transactional Exposure The risk that a company is exposed to (usually foreign exchange) owing to specific transactions, such as purchases or sales in different currencies or investments or obligations in another currency.

Transferability The regulatory ability for a buyer in a country to remit the payable money to the seller in another country.

Translational Exposure The uncertainty to a group's balance sheet (investments, debt, other assets and liabilities) owing to change in (usually foreign exchange) rates.

Trapped Cash Cash in a subsidiary in another country that can be brought back only with severe tax and other negative financial implications, or cannot be brought back at all owing to exchange control regulations; this is typically liquidity that is trapped and cannot be used elsewhere in the group.

Treasury Culture A work and participation ethic and environment within Treasury that enables an atmosphere of knowledge and positive teamwork to ensure the highest work and motivational standards.

Treasury Design The activity of creating the right processes, structures, and approaches at the right place with the right infrastructure and the right people.

Treasury Fitness The degree of efficient functioning of a corporate treasury, akin to a fitness test for the human body, determined by assessing the treasury to identify potential pain points with the end objective of addressing these pain points and preventing any potential significant breakdown.

Treasury Leadership The ability of Treasury to positively influence the performance of the firm and drive the organisation towards industry and segment leadership; creates an environment that fosters excellence of capital building, execution, and support across all aspects of Treasury, and works with the business to produce outstanding performance.

Underlying The basic asset, liability, cash flow, or other component of a firm's financials whose risk or variance is being managed.

Unwinding Positions Exiting or liquidating a position, transaction, derivative, or asset at a profit or loss.

Value-at-Risk (VaR) An estimate with some degree of confidence on the losses to a portfolio or financials based on statistical analysis and assumptions.

Vanilla Option A simple stand-alone put or call option.

Volatility The variability of a market factor measured as a percentage; usually denoted as historic (based on past prices) or implied (traders' or market estimate over a tenor).

WACC (Weighted Average Cost of Capital) Calculation of a firm's cost of capital as a proportion of its capital structure (percentage of different kinds of debt and equity); the lower the WACC, the more efficient the company's capitalisation.

Working Capital Effectively the amount of external capital that a company needs to run its operations on a day-to-day basis.

Yield The percentage gain (usually annualised) that an investor derives from a financial asset.

Yield Curve A graph of current interest rates (government bond yields, AAA benchmarks, swap or forward rates) on the y-axis with the corresponding tenor of investment on the x-axis, depicts the current position of the market on the interest rates over time horizons.

Yield Curve Risk Uncertainty to the financials of a company owing to shifts or changes to the shape of the prevalent yield curve to which the company is exposed.

Zero-Balance Account (ZBA) A bank account whose debits or credits are swept at the end of each day to a zero balance; part of a physical pooling arrangement.

Zero-Premium Option An option structure that is a combination of bought and sold options to achieve a particular payoff, where the sum of premiums payable by one leg of options (sold by the first party to the second) is the same as the sum of the premiums payable by the other leg (bought by the first party from the second).

Further Reading

Aktrea Capital. www.aktrea.com.

Association of Finance Professionals. www.afponline.com.

Greenwich Treasury Advisors. www.greenwichtreasury.com.

GTNews. www.gtnews.com.

Blanchard, David. *Supply Chain Management Best Practices*. Hoboken, NJ: John Wiley & Sons, 2010.

Bragg, Steven M. *Treasury Management*. Hoboken, NJ: John Wiley & Sons, 2010.

Chorafas, Dimitiri N. *Liabilities, Liquidity, and Cash Management*. New York: John Wiley & Sons, 2001.

Cooper, Robert. *Corporate Treasury and Cash Management*. Palgrave Macmillan, 2004.

Damodaran, Aswath. *Investment Valuation: Tools and Techniques for Determining the Value of Any Asset*. Hoboken, NJ: John Wiley & Sons, 2012.

Dermine, J., and Y. F. Bissada. *Asset and Liability Management*. Upper Saddle River, NJ: Prentice-Hall, 2002.

Dodd, Randall. *Exotic Derivatives Losses in Emerging Markets: Questions of Suitability, Concerns for Stability*. International Monetary Fund, 2009.

Frazelle, Edward H. *Supply Chain Strategy*. New York: McGraw-Hill Professional, 2001.

Geman, Helyette. *Commodities and Commodity Derivatives*.

Gigerenzer, Gerd. "Dread Risk, September 11, and Fatal Traffic Accidents." *Psychological Science* 15 (2004).

Hachmeister, Alexandra. *Informed Traders*. Hoboken, NJ: John Wiley & Sons, 2007.

Horcher, Karen A. *Essentials of Managing Treasury*. Hoboken, NJ: John Wiley & Sons, 2005.

Hull, John C. *Fundamentals of Futures and Option Markets*. Upper Saddle River, NJ: Prentice-Hall, 2010.

International Trade Centre. *How to Access Trade Finance*. Author, 2009.

Jackson, Mary, and Mike Staunton. *Advanced Modelling in Finance Using Excel and VBA*. New York: John Wiley & Sons, 2001.

Lind, Magnus, Peter Bergstrom, and Kenneth Andersson. "The Role of Key Performance Indicators for Corporate Treasury." *Journal of Corporate Treasury Management* (July 2007).

Penman, Stephen H., and Theodore Sougiannis. "A Comparison of Dividend, Cash Flow, and Earnings Approaches to Equity Valuation." January 1995. Available at SSRN: http://ssrn.com/abstract=15043 or http://dx.doi.org/10.2139/ssrn.15043.

Saunders, Anthony, and Linda Allen. *Credit Risk Measurement*. Hoboken, NJ: John Wiley & Sons, 2010.

U.S. Department of Commerce. *Trade Finance Guide: A Quick Reference for U.S. Exporters International Trade Administration*. Author, April 2008.

Wallace, Jeffrey B. "The Group of 31 Report: Core Principles for Managing Multinational FX Risk." Greenwich Treasury Advisors LLC, 1999.

About the Author

Rajiv Rajendra has spent many years across different aspects of corporate and institutional banking, from capital markets to transaction services, mostly with a global bank. He has advised customers on managing their risk, conceived and executed client solutions to increase efficiency and lower cost, managed and grown balance sheets and sales and trading businesses, been a part of exciting new business launches across continents, and migrated and managed outsourced critical business and financial processes.

Rajiv leads Singapore-based Aktrea Capital, a firm focused on delivering high-quality, cutting-edge training, consulting, and process solutions to financial institutions, corporates, and funds across the world in the areas of capital markets, Treasury, risk, and financial supply chain management.

Rajiv has built course content and been an active trainer in the areas of capital markets and process management for external and internal customers, including a state-of-the-art Bourse game, covering more than 2,000 participants to date. He has presented and delivered sessions at many leading business schools and has been a speaker at various forums, including corporate Treasury seminars and industry association meetings.

Rajiv believes that the learning process is complete only with relevant practical exposure and a fun environment, and many participants in his training sessions would testify that both elements are significant reasons for his popularity as a consultant and trainer.

By education, Rajiv is a computer engineer with a master's degree in finance and marketing. He is a published novelist, and has written and directed plays across a number of countries.

Rajiv has recently founded Blu Lotus, an international not-for-profit organisation focused on the promotion of arts and culture, and on development of cultural, ethical, and moral values and standards.

About the Website

Please visit this book's companion Website at www.wiley.com/go/treasuryhandbook. The Website includes these documents to supplement the information in the book:

- Appendix A: Draft Treasury Policy Document
- Appendix B: List of Currencies with Currency Codes
- Appendix C: Clearing and Settlement Systems
- Appendix D: Industrial Products and Service Category Standards Summary
- Appendix E: Detailed Aspects of Locational Decision with Some Indicative Scores
- Appendix F: List of Treasury Processes
- Appendix G: Typical Controls

Aside from these downloadable materials, readers can find:

- Various elements of the Toolkit that can be used as templates to develop and customise to their own needs
- A blog where views, solutions, and other aspects of treasury management will be posted—this will be a useful forum to interact with other readers, the author, and business experts on cutting-edge aspects of the treasury and financial supply chain functions
- A glossary of important treasury-related terms.

A login with initial password is supplied along with the print edition of *The Handbook*. Buyers who wish to access the "Readers" content of the book, including the appendices, will need to first login (in the "Readers" section of the Website) and register themselves by filling in the form. Please note that only one user will have access to the content for every book purchased. Thanks for your understanding.

ABOUT THE APP

First-time buyers of the book will have access to an accompanying mobile application ("app") available on Android and iOS (iPad/iPhone/iPod) platforms, available at the Google Play store and iOS App store respectively. These will be made available after June 2013.

The accompanying app will have the same login and password for access to the app-specific content.

The app includes features to supplement the information in the book:

- An "Ask" section where first-time buyers can ask three topical questions to the author
- A glossary
- A "Treasury Fitness" section (from December 2013) where first time buyers can determine their treasury's fitness level and store and monitor the same over time
- Other exciting features that may be added from time to time

Index

Account structure, 58
account operation and approaches, 62
consideration for multiple current accounts, 60
consideration for non-resident accounts, 60
decisions, 58
design and implementation, 59
drivers of, 64
location and bank alternatives for design, 61
pooling capability, 65
rationalising of, 65
Asset liquidity measures, 302
Automated clearing house (ACH), 77
Avoidance, 319

Back office, 48
Balance sheet, 12
principal protection, 232
Bank credit assessment process, 247
Bank organisation structure, 443
Bank review process, 449
Bank selection and RFP process, 449
Bill discounting, 217
Bonds, 204

Capital markets, 195
Capital structure, 197
Cards, 74
Cash:
elements of, 227
management, 228
operating, 228
cash concentration, 123
cash conversion cycle, 149
impact on financials, 157
Cash flows:
enhancing operating cash flow, 17
increasing stability of cash flow, 17
at risk, 307
Centralisation, 24
model design, 427
rationale, 425
Cheques and drafts, 72
Commercial paper, 204
Commodity markets 284
Common global implementation (CGI), 418
Contango, 324
Continuous link system, 93
Control checks and reviews, 459
Correlation, 304
Credit assessment cycle, 247
Credit default swap, 351
Credit family, 351
Credit rating, 239
methodology, 243
rating changes, 246
Credit support annex, 392
Currencies:
fixed or pegged, 282
free float, 282
fully convertible, 282
managed float, 282
partially convertible, 282

Cycles:
netting, 103
operating cycle, 148
order to cash, 153
procurement to payment cycle, 150
working capital, 148

Date notations, 325
Days payable outstanding (DPO), 151
calculation of, 153
Days sales outstanding (DSO), 154
calculation of, 155
Debt capital markets, 203
Decentralisation, 25
Depository receipts or notes, 204
Direct debit mechanism (ACH model), 78
Distressed debt, 205
Diversification, 319

Electronic fund transfer, 75
Enterprise appraisal, 248
Equity capital markets, 205
Evaluation of Treasury personnel, 484
Exotic and structured swaps, 350
Exotic options, 340
Export credit agency (ECA) financing, 220
credit, 221
credit insurance, 221
guarantees, 221

Factor sensitivity analysis, 295
Factoring, 218
centre, 218
Float, 111
kinds of, 111
Forecasting, 139–143
Forfaiting, 219
Forwards, 324
forward rate agreements, 331
non-deliverable forwards, 330
par forwards, 330
rate locks, 331
variable date forwards, 330
Front office, 48
Fundamental analysis, 364

Intermediaries, 196
International Swap Dealers Association (ISDA):
credit support annex, 392
master agreement, 389
schedules, 391
Intervention, 283
Investment Process, 237
Investors, 195
risk, 201
Issuers, 195
risk, 201
In-house bank, 29

Liquidity:
providing to firm, 16
management, 109–110
gap, 302
Liquidity at Risk (LaR), 307
Local FX clearing, 92

Markets:
capital, 195
debt capital, 203
equity capital, 205
fixed income and money markets, 283
foreign exchange market, 280
movement of, 287
world of, 279
Market instruments, 316
Mechanism of money transfer, 72
Medium term note programs, 204
Method:
accrual reversal, 142
adjusted net income, 142
distribution, 141
pro forma balance sheet, 142
receipts and disbursement, 140
Mezzanine issues, 205
Middle office, 48

Netting, 95
 implementation, 101

Operating cash:
 managing, 228
Operations and control, 457
 treasury control themes, 459
Options, 333
 mechanics,335
 pricing, 337
 zero premium, 339
Outsourcing, 469–478
 checklist, 470
 model, 30

Payments:
 cross-border, 82
 high value, 76
 ordinary low value, 77
 procurement to, 150
Performance metrics, 431
 measurement units, 435
 themes, 434
Pooling, 111
 structure, 127
Portfolio optimisation, 319

Ratios:
 balance sheet, 172
 cash flow statement, 173
 hybrid, 174
 profit and loss, 171
 valuation and market, 175
Real-time gross settlement (RTGS), 76
Reinvoicing, 221
Risk:
 classification, 258
 credit, 234
 financial, 246
 governance, 245
 kinds, 257
 liquidity, 234
 market, 233
Risk measurement, 293
 discrete method, 295
 probability and statistical method, 302

Scenario analysis, 297
Securitisation, 205
Settlement, 75
Simulation, 365
 based training, 480
Society for Worldwide Interbank Funds Transfer (SWIFT), 83
 standardised gateway, 89
Stress analysis, 297
Structured debt, 204
Supply chain:
 pain points, 158
 physical and financing, 213
 risk index (SCRI), 222
Supplier financing, 220
Surplus cash and investments, 230
Syndicated loans, 203
System:
 environment, 405
 interfaces, 405
Swaps family, 346
 coupon swap, 349
 cross currencies, 350
 interest rate swap, 346
 principal-only swaps, 349

Technical analysis, 365
Trade relating financing, 205
Transactions confirmation, 392
Transfer pricing, 392
Treasury:
 Design, 4, 21–36
 Fitness, 5
 Functions, 10
 Leadership, 4
 infrastructure, 13
Treasury Culture, 27
 basic Treasury Culture (TC), 27
 hats, 43

Treasury Culture (*Continued*)
  integration into a firm's
    HR cycle, 480
  shared service centre (SSC), 26
  value-added Treasury
    Culture (TC++), 28
Treasury models, 25
Treasury policy, 397
  framework, 397
Treasury processes, 458
Treasury systems, 403–423
  characteristics, 405
  development and standards, 417
  establishment process, 411
  Treasury management
    systems (TMS), 403
Treasury management systems
    linkages, 406
Triggers and events, 490

Uncertainties:
  stage 1, 488
  stage 2, 489
  risk as, 257

Value at risk (VaR), 303
  liquidity-adjusted VaR, 305
Volatility, 303